SECURITIES TECHNOLOGY HANDBOOK

SECURITIES TECHNOLOGY HANDBOOK

Edited by

Jessica Keyes

CRC Press
Boca Raton London New York Washington, D.C.

Library of Congress Cataloging-in-Publication Data

Securities technology handbook / Jessica Keyes, editor.
p. cm.
Includes bibliographical references and index.
ISBN 0-8493-9991-2 (alk. paper)
1. Financial services industry—Technological innovations—United States. 2. Stock exchanges—Technological innovations—United States. I. Keyes, Jessica, 1950–
HG181-S37 1998
332.6′-285—dc21 98-40860
CIP

This book contains information obtained from authentic and highly regarded sources. Reprinted material is quoted with permission, and sources are indicated. A wide variety of references are listed. Reasonable efforts have been made to publish reliable data and information, but the author and the publisher cannot assume responsibility for the validity of all materials or for the consequences of their use.

Direct all inquiries to CRC Press LLC, 2000 Corporate Blvd., N.W., Boca Raton, Florida 33431.

International Standard Book Number 0-8493-9991-2
Library of Congress Card Number 98-40860
Printed in the United States of America 1 2 3 4 5 6 7 8 9 0
Printed on acid-free paper

Contributors

DAN ADLER, *Chief Technology Officer, Inventure America, New York, NY*
CHARLES BASSIGNANI, *Market Segment Manager, Financial Products Group, The Mathworks, Natick, MA*
PAT BITTON, *Market Development Manager, Trend Micro, Inc., Cupertino, CA*
TIM BROCK, *Creative Director, Sealund & Associates Corporation, Clearwater, FL*
JOHN BUCKNER, *President and Chief Executive Officer, IMIS Inc., San Francisco, CA*
DONALD F. COOKE, *Founder and Chief Executive Officer, Medici Technology, Inc., Hanover, NH*
GREG CRANDELL, *Vice President, Marketing, Corillian Corporation, Beaverton, OR*
RHONDA R. DELMATER, *Program Manager, Computer Science Innovations, Melbourne, FL*
GREGORY DOBBIN, *Technical Writer, Comprehensive Software Systems, Ltd., Golden, CO*
JIM DOUTHITT, *Director of Product Marketing, SS&C Technologies, Inc., Windsor, CT*
CHRIS HAMILTON, *Marketing Director, GlobeSet, Austin, TX*
MARGARET HAMILTON, *Founder and Chief Executive Officer, Hamilton Technologies, Inc., Cambridge, MA*
MONTE F. HANCOCK, *Chief Scientist, Computer Science Innovations, Melbourne, FL*
KNOX HENDERSON, *Communications Specialist, NICE Systems, Richmond, British Columbia, Canada*
INFORMATION TECHNOLOGY ASSOCIATION OF AMERICAN, *Arlington, VA*
EVAN KAPLAN, *Founder, Aventail Corporation, Seattle, WA*
JESSICA KEYES, *President, New Art Technologies, Inc., New York, NY*
JODY LYON, *Marketing and Product Line Manager, i.d.Centric Products, Firstlogic i.d. Centric, La Crosse, WI*
GARY MANGUS, *Product Marketing Group Manager, Litton Network Access Systems, Roanoke, VA*
CHRIS MARINO, *Founder, Resonate, Inc., Mountain View, CA*
MICHAEL A. MCNEAL, *President and Chief Executive Officer, Absoft, Boca Raton, FL*

C. KENNETH MILLER, *Founder, Chairman, and Chief Technology Officer, StarBurst Communications, Concord, MA*

DAVID PETERSON, *Founder, Goldleaf Technologies, Inc., Lake Mary, FL*

TIMOTHY PETERSON, *Associate Director, Performance Measurement, Portfolio Management Consultants, Inc., Denver, CO*

JERRY RACKLEY, *Director, Teubner & Associates, Inc., Stillwater, OK*

MARY ROSE, *Vice President, Business Development, ARKSYS, Little Rock, AR*

TIM SCATLIFF, *Senior Vice President of Technology, Rescom Ventures, Winnipeg, Ontario, Canada*

BARBARA SEALUND, *President and Founder, Sealund & Associates Corporation, Clearwater, FL*

HENRY SEILER, *Founder and President, Rule Machines Corporation, Indialantic, FL*

STEVEN SEMELSBERGER, *Strategic Alliances and Market Development Manager, Acuity Corporation, Austin, TX*

FREDERIC M. WILF, *Special Counsel, Saul, Ewing, Remick & Saul, LLP, Berwyn, PA*

DAVID WILLIAMS, *Member, Board of Directors, Corillian Corporation, Beaverton, OR*

DAVE YEWMAN, *Principal, Insync Communications, Portland, OR*

Contents

Preface

FINANCIAL SERVICES IS AN INTERESTING AMALGAM NOWADAYS. Where there used to be nice, neat boundaries between the subindustries of banking, securities, and insurance, today's financial services industry has become a chameleon. Bankers are dabbling in securities, securities are dabbling in banking, and everyone is dabbling in insurance.

Merger mania has a lot to do with it. Traveler's Group has megamerged with Citicorp and now call themselves Citigroup. Morgan Stanley is now sleeping with both Dean Witter and Discover. It's a wonder these new post-merger names will ever fit on a business card. But it's more than just the names that are being changed: these are not just vertical mergers where companies take over competitors in their own industries, these are horizontal mergers where companies merge to take advantage of the opportunities in multiple industries.

As changeable as the financial services industry is, the high-tech industry is more so. Just a few short years ago the Internet was merely the plaything of academics and tech heads. From the corporate intranet, which is used for everything from job postings to enhanced team communications, to whole new departments being created for the purposes of e-commerce, today the Internet/intranet/extranet triple-whammy is probably the most critical component of most Information Technology (IT) shops.

But there's a lot more new technology out there than just the Internet. There's a whole information explosion just ready to be tamed by the new intelligent agents ready to take on such diverse functions as customer profiling and data mining. And not a moment too soon. A workplace study conducted by the Gallup Organization and the Menlo Park, California-based Institute for the Future found that workers are bombarded by an avalanche of information from an ever-expanding array of computerized devices. The study found that the 1035 employees, who were surveyed and observed at work, received an average of 190 messages (via fax, e-mail, and phone) each day. Obviously, the computer revolution has created somewhat of a problem; however, what the computer broke it can fix.

There's a lot of technology out there and a lot of change in the financial services industry. And the pace of change keeps accelerating. So what's a financial services IT manager to do?

That's the purpose of this book — to provide a guide to the tools and techniques of technology geared specifically for the securities IT manager. A place where he or she can go to get the lowdown on not only the up-and-coming "hot" technologies of tomorrow, but also on the tried and true technologies of today. The Handbook does this from a technological perspective and — most importantly — from a business perspective (finally, an end-user's take on the subject).

In Section I, we discuss some of the fundamental technologies within the securities industry such as *A Portfolio Management System for the Twenty-First Century* and *Straight Through Processing*. We'll discuss the fine aspects of *Logging Monitoring in the Financial Services Industry* and delve into the proper way of *Designing and Evaluating Investment Performance Systems*. We also touch base on the *Converganece of Trust and Brokerage*.

The Handbook then provides a rather lengthy section on general financial services technologies. Here we'll find interesting discussions on everything from *Applications of GIS Technology*, to *Designing a High-Performance, High-Availability Network*, to *n-Tier Design* — all from a financial services perspective. Interspersed throughout the section are topics such as *Business Rule Systems*, *A Guide to Total Quality for the Financial Services Technology Manager*, and *Multicast Applications*. I also took the liberty of including quite a few sections on the Internet; topics ranging from *e-Commerce* to *Internet Banking*.

In this section, I also decided to let you in on a secret. There's a methodology out there called *Development Before the Fact* that's not only going to knock your socks off — it's going to radically alter the way you develop financial services applications — to the tune of fewer programmers, lower costs, and more correct systems.

Finally, the Appendix contains a brief state-of-the-art product guide.

All in all, the Handbook is a tailor-made guide for the securities IT manager who wants to stay on top of technology in the financial services industry.

Jessica Keyes

Section I
Securities Trends in Technology

WHEN I FIRST STARTED AT THE NEW YORK STOCK EXCHANGE my first project was to build a system that monitored registered representatives. Called REGIS, it used the then state-of-the-art Dialog Management System from IBM to deliver an online interface to end users. Later, REGIS was expanded into EAGLE (yes, there were jokes about bird droppings) which encompassed the breadth of the Exchange's regulatory functions such as complaint processing and enforcement actions.

If only today's technology had been available yesterday! What was painstaking yesterday is fairly easy today. The EAGLE developers even built their own e-mail system. Everything, and I mean everything, had to be jury-rigged because the technology just wasn't there. Today's technology consists of visual development systems, program generators, groupware, and Internet-based technologies — replete with add-ins and Java applets.

Just two decades ago the pace of technological change was very slow indeed. Today it's so rapid that those on the vendor side of the community consider 3 months to be equivalent to a full year! Once again, we can go to the trade articles to prove this point.

> The CDPD wireless digital data network is currently installed in over 75% of the U.S. metro areas. Reuters is the largest financial service provider porting data over this type of technology to palmtops.
>
> Designed by financial software firm Spectra Securities Software Inc. in New York and Toronto, the real-time trading system Spectra Bonds delivers a wide-ranging inventory of between 7,000 and 10,000 bonds live to PCI broker desktops, with buy or sell order confirmations taking place in about three to five seconds.

By the time you read this book:

> The Chicago Board Brokerage (CBB), a joint venture of the Chicago Board of Trade and inter-dealer broker Prebon Yemane, will have launched MarketPower, an anonymous interactive trading system covering U.S. government securities, overnight repos and Treasury bond and note basis contracts.

> New York City-based brokerage, Wall Street Discount Corp., embarked on a pilot program to provide its customers with wireless Internet access to online trading in the Spring of 1998.
>
> A proliferation of consumer-level investment sites has sprung up on the Web. The most popular, with more than 1.6 million visitors checking in regularly, Microsoft Investor features a highly detailed portfolio manager, a "Strategy Lab" feature where experts go over their investment strategies with readers, mutual fund information, and advisor alerts.

In this section we discuss some of the fundamental technologies within the securities industry such as a portfolio management system for the twenty-first century in Chapter 2 and straight through processing in Chapter 4. We'll discuss the fine aspects of logging and monitoring in Chapter 3 and delve into the proper way to design investment performance systems in Chapter 5.

Like banking and insurance, the securities industry has been forever altered by the advent of the Internet. We can expect more Internet-based investment services, touching the areas of risk management and performance monitoring. The profits of many of the brokerage firms will rise astronomically as attendant costs decrease due to the proliferation of individual investors rushing to the Internet to do online trading — of course, a large and sustained downturn in the current bull market could very well do away with that.

But even if there is a downturn in the market, the technological boom is here to stay.

J. Keyes

Chapter 1

The Future of the Securities Industry: Convergence of Trust and Brokerage

John Buckner

THE CONTINUED RELAXATION OF *GLASS-STEAGALL,* the reduction in January 1997 of the ineligible revenue rule for the securities subsidiaries of banks, and a 7-year bull market have fueled unprecedented M&A activity in financial services over the last several years. In 1997 we saw a number of banks acquire broker/dealers. Bank of America acquired Robertson Stephens, NationsBank bought Montgomery Securities, and Fleet Financial bought Quick & Reilly.

At the same time, driven primarily by the relaxation of *Glass-Steagall,* banks and insurance companies have formed their own brokerage units, some from scratch, others engendered from traditional bank capital markets operations which have often become Section 20 companies. Moreover, the consolidation trend, with a possible year 2000 hiatus, appears likely to continue well into the future.

John Wimsatt, an analyst at Friedman Billings Ramsey who follows the financial services industry, agrees. "When compared to the international financial services paradigm, such as the European community, financial services consolidation in the United States has much further to go." The Year 2000 problem may delay some merger activities due to the inability of IT departments to integrate systems while undergoing Year 2000 development efforts, but financial services consolidations are likely to resume in earnest well into the first decade of the next millennium.

During this same period, brokerage firms have been quietly establishing broker-affiliated trust companies for their high-net-worth customers and to

0-8493-9991-2/99/$0.00+$.50

support pension plans. Just a few of the major brokerage firms with trust company subsidiaries include: Alex Brown, Merrill Lynch, Charles Schwab, Legg Mason, Raymond James, Hilliard Lyons, American Express Financial Advisors, Southwest Securities, and Piper Jaffrey.

THE OPPORTUNITY

The new environment therefore results in trust and brokerage entities operating within the same holding company — be it a broker, a bank, or an insurance company. Indeed, mergers and acquisitions at some of the larger banks have resulted in the accumulation of a variety of similar securities processing operations. Operational consolidation efforts notwithstanding, it would not be unusual for a money center bank today to have separate platforms for the following businesses:

- Retail brokerage
- Institutional brokerage
- Bank capital markets
- Private banking
- Personal trust
- Institutional trust
- Retirement services
- Corporate trust
- Custody/global custody
- Other (derivatives, risk management, foreign exchange, investment portfolio)

With redundant securities processing technology and operations expertise at work across these units, executives at many firms are wondering if there may be opportunities to further collapse securities processing operations. Others are focusing on what may be more significant — opportunities to attract and retain customers by offering a wider range of products and services at substantially lower costs by leveraging the strengths of the technology across the different industry segments.

Regulations, in many cases, limit the extent to which these businesses can be integrated. But regulations continue to change and continue to be relaxed, so let's explore not the regulatory possibilities but rather the technological and operational implications these opportunities present.

FORCES OF CHANGE

While the M&A activities represent one force of change, there are several other catalysts for seeking out operational and technological synergy across these industries. Below is a list of some of these factors and how they might influence both industries separately and financial services generally.

Customer Awareness

The popularity of mutual funds, 401(k) and IRA plans, the explosive growth of the Internet in general and Internet trading specifically, and the longest bull market in history have resulted in a population of Americans who are much more aware of the securities industry than ever before. It is not surprising then, that according to a Tower Group research report, mutual fund investments in this country have grown from approximately $500 million in 1985 to more than $2.5 trillion in 1996.

These new investors are generally unaware of the regulatory or traditional boundaries which have always separated brokerage and trust. A young trust beneficiary who 20 years ago might have left her trust assets in the trust department without question, may now demand Internet account access and discount brokerage commission rates from her trust bank. The same investor, however, accustomed to highly automated tax reporting, might also demand tax-lot accounting from her discount broker. To this new class of investor, the distinctions between trust and brokerage are irrelevant. What is relevant is service, product, convenience, and price.

In tacit acknowledgment that their customers fail to discern these traditional distinctions and are demanding more meaningful and comprehensive products and services, the private banking groups of some major money center banks (e.g., Banker's Trust, Bank of America, and Chase) now offer customers consolidated accounts. While each of these products differ, all of them attempt to combine customer data on statements from as many areas of the institution as possible, regardless of industry segment, including traditional banking (DDA, CD, credit, etc.), trust, and retail brokerage. Some even permit customers to trade securities within trust or brokerage through a link to the DDA system. Today's savvy investor will continue to pressure players in both industries to offer more valuable services and products regardless of industry segmentation. This trend will force financial services firms to develop the same features repeatedly across industry platforms, link platforms together, or integrate the businesses entirely.

Pricing Pressure

Price consciousness among today's investors accompanies this newfound awareness of service and product opportunity. According to many trust company managers who declined to be interviewed for this analysis, personal trust departments are witnessing a runoff in trust accounts to discount brokers due to improved custodial and execution services and lower or nonexistent custodial fees.

At the Private Asset Management department of Montgomery Asset Management L.L.C., Manager Karyn Rozenoff recalls how "just last year we witnessed a significant runoff of high-net-worth personal trust customers to discount brokers offering essentially identical services at substantially lower fees." Trust accounts are legally permitted to choose their custodian, and, after considering their options, many are unwilling to pay a trust company its custodial fees in addition to pass-through brokerage commissions. Choosing a discount broker over a trust company can eliminate an unnecessary layer and additional costs.

On the institutional side, the capture by brokerage firms of a portion of the custodial services offered by banks and global custodians through the introduction of "prime brokerage" clearly underscores the importance that price has already had on that industry segment. At the same time, customers are demanding higher quality service and a wider range of products from their prime broker, sometimes demanding services and products that brokerage systems are unaccustomed to providing. This pressure on price as well as functionality will likely lead to more creative technological solutions to the data processing paradigm in both industries, possibly resulting in a hybrid solution. Moreover, pressure on prices will lead to pressure on cost reduction within operations, which may lead firms to further reconstruct the technical paradigm.

Entry of New Players

Regulations overseas are of course different. While Asian markets tend to more clearly differentiate trust and brokerage services, the recent collapse of these markets has already resulted in relaxation of cross-industry ownership and operation of securities businesses there. In Europe, however, there is little distinction between trust, brokerage, and insurance, with the same firm seamlessly offering all types of services. Doug Dannemiller of the Tower group notes that "these full-service foreign financial services companies tend to view the securities industry less myopically and have entered the U.S. markets with a different perspective toward the business and the customer." In fact, with the availability of 128-bit encryption in the last year, both UBS and Credit Suisse now "lead the way with integrated trust and brokerage services," continues Doug, "by offering U.S. customers Web-based securities trading for private banking customers."

While foreign firms making U.S. acquisitions must adhere to the same regulatory restrictions as U.S.-based firms, they may be more likely to challenge them. Moreover, the large insurance company, a dominant player in Europe, has been until recently a sleeping giant here in the U.S. Already, Travelers has made a significant play to fully integrate financial services and stretch the limits of the regulations by leaping into brokerage with the acquisitions of Smith Barney and Salomon and then merging with Citibank to form the largest domestic financial services company offering an unprecedented array of products and services. Other insurance companies, many of whom possess a large capital base, have made or are planning to make brokerage acquisitions or are in the process of building their own brokerage subsidiaries. These firms come into the securities industry with no preconceived notions regarding boundaries between trust and brokerage systems and services and are likely to lead the challenges to these ideological boundaries.

Over time, the entry of these new players — insurance companies, foreign financial services firms, and mutual fund companies — will force the entire financial services industry to look at securities processing less ideologically and may lead the way to fundamental change in the technical paradigm.

Shear Size

Currently, the largest packaged-software applications for the trust industry can support somewhere in the vicinity of 150,000 to 250,000 accounts. Packaged software for brokerage can support more than a million accounts and tens of thousands of trades per day. The account base of the largest trust banks is approximately 100,000 accounts. One more mega-merger among the largest banks or a series of smaller acquisitions by one of the larger trust banks will encumber system and operations integration efforts on these platforms.

As a result, CIOs of some large firms are already exploring alternatives, including brokerage applications. Undoubtedly, trust industry executives pleased by the capacity of brokerage systems may be disappointed by the lack of certain trust functionality. Could these searches, however, lead to some sort of hybrid solution whereby generic, high-volume processes are handled by the brokerage systems, leaving the trust systems to perform trust-specific functions? Continued consolidation coupled with trust system volume constraints may push some of the largest money center banks to look at cross-industry alternatives to securities processing.

SIMILARITIES AND DIFFERENCES

While an exhaustive list of the similarities of the brokerage and trust industries from a functionality standpoint would be prohibitively long, there are several key areas of similarity that are worth noting:

- Street-side interfaces
- Trade execution and clearance
- Order routing and execution
- Security master information
- "Stock record" processing (dividends, interest, maturity, corporate actions)

The similarities tend to be in the most generic functions of the business and in those functions which are closest to the "street." As we move away from the street and toward the customer or the legal entity of the business, we begin to see differences:

- Regulatory reporting/compliance
- Accounting for the firm
- Accounting for the customer
- Customer reporting

DIFFERENCES NARROWING

Traditionally, not only did customers consider trust and brokerage services as ideologically distinct, but the types of features and functions offered were substantially different and priced accordingly. Trust systems traditionally offered more robust functionality, such as tax-lot accounting, accrual accounting, and common trust fund processing, and charged more for these services in addition to charging for the fiduciary responsibility for the account. Over time, however, these differences have narrowed as rules have changed, systems have been enhanced, and services have been unbundled.

The conversion of common trust funds to mutual funds beginning in August of 1996, for example, meant that a host of investment management expertise previously only accessible to trust customers was suddenly available to trust and brokerage customers alike. Since the broker/dealers had developed more efficient processing engines and industry links (NSCC networking and fund/serve, for example), they could, ironically, deliver these trust products (the converted common trust funds) more cheaply than could the trust companies from which they originated.

Nor have the brokers been sitting by idly from a technology standpoint. Both vendor-supplied and in-house brokerage applications over the last several years have begun to unveil a host of traditional trust system features. Below is a list of just some of these new enhancements to brokerage applications:

- Average cost accounting (for customers in addition to inventory)
- Tax-lot accounting (for customers)
- Portfolio modeling (asset allocation/wrap fee)
- Cash and accrual basis reporting
- Multicurrency accounting (not just dual currency)
- Systematic (periodic) purchases and redemptions
- Customer performance measurement

Meanwhile, trust companies have borrowed some brokerage system efficiencies. Below is a list of just some of the functionality trust systems they have either recently developed or are in the process of developing which have been part of most brokerage application for years:

- ACATS
- Fund/Serve
- Networking
- Margins

CUSTOMER FOCUS

David Pottruck, president and CEO of Charles Schwab & Co. noted at a recent San Francisco Operations Association meeting that one of the key factors for the success of Schwab over the years has to do with the company's focus on the customer:

> All the movement at our company ... all the innovation and change ... is driven by the customer's experience. It is the premier benchmark against which we evaluate every service we provide, every change in pricing, every internal realignment. We look for the product and the delivery system the customer will think is best.

Successful financial services firms of the future will focus on the customer's needs rather than industry tradition and deliver products and services the customer demands in the manner the customer demands them.

One example of this in the brokerage industry is the proliferation of numerous delivery channels for securities products in order to allow the customer the convenience of choice. At many firms, customers can conduct securities transactions through any number of the following delivery channels:

- Touch-tone
- Internet
- Branch-office
- Call center
- Registered representative

UNBUNDLING THE COMPONENTS

Regulatory boundaries aside, brokers might add "trust administration" or "private banker" to the list of available delivery channels. What would stop a brokerage firm from adding trust industry functionality to its brokerage system and running its "trust department" from the same platform? Could the brokerage firm simply provide "fiduciary" services for an additional fee through its trust department?

> According to H. David Johnson, COO of BancAmerica Robertson Stephens Inc., ... if we unbundle trust services, we find four basic functions: custody, transaction execution, asset management, and fiduciary administration. Brokerage firms already perform custodial and transaction execution services in competition with banks and custodians; registered investment advisors as part of any financial services company

> can perform the asset management function; and broker affiliated trust companies can (and do) clearly provide fiduciary administration. The real question is how to best deliver these services to customers in the most cost-effective manner.

PUSHING THE LIMITS

Customer focus will force brokerage firms to determine how to leverage trust system features and functions without increasing costs, while it will force trust companies to figure out how to provide traditional trust features at brokerage prices. Over the last several years, Will Derby, senior vice president and CIO of the Asset Management group for NationsBank in Dallas, has evaluated proposals to develop a common securities processing platform.

> In the future, a single base processing platform for all securities subsidiaries will not only provide financial services companies additional processing efficiency but will enable these firms to better serve their customers through consolidated reporting, data warehousing, and client credit risk management.

From a technological and operational standpoint, personal trust and retail brokerage may have more in common than retail and institutional brokerage. If we can get past this paradox and look beyond our ideological tendency toward viewing the industries as inherently different, then we are left with the problem of building the most cost-effective solution. What might this efficient, high-capacity and generic securities processing platform of the future look like?

SINGLE STREET-SIDE PLATFORM

At both Charles Schwab & Co. and Raymond James, some mutual fund trades for the trust company are executed through the brokerage systems to take advantage of more efficient brokerage system processing of mutual fund transactions. The 1998 plans at several money center banks also call for the brokerage units to clear mutual fund trades for the trust department in order to leverage brokerage system capacity and fully operable NSCC fund/serve and networking features which might take months to develop and test in the trust system. SEI Investments now offers its customer a "no transaction fee" or NTF arrangement for processing mutual funds on its Trust3000 system through an omnibus account at the brokerage firm of Jack White & Co.

In essence, these companies are leveraging the strength of the brokerage platform on the back end (high volume capacity, better efficiency) without compromising the uniqueness of the customer requirements best served by the trust platform on the front-end. By linking different front-end systems to a common, generic securities processing platform or back-end system, the differences across industry segments in terms of customer needs and "firm" needs can be addressed without having to tax the more volume-sensitive systems with the overhead of street-side processing.

This model is not very unusual. Many brokerage firms have different front-office systems feeding a common back-office system. The needs of trading and sales staff who are very customer or firm focused are often best served by state-of-the-art front-office systems, while generic clearing and stock record functions are best performed by large-scale back-office legacy applications. The trust industry also supports this model, with workstations for investment management, trade/order entry, custody, and cash management feeding traditional back-office trust accounting systems. According to the Tower Group, 50% of the large account-based assets under management that changed custodians in 1996 went to the 10% of the service providers that have a full suite of workstation-based applications.

If implemented properly, the customer benefits from access to the functionality of all the systems across all industry groups and legal entities while the firm benefits from the cost savings associated with less redundancy in operations and more fully leveraging efficient technology. "The convergence of advanced technology and the evolving diversified financial services industry will dramatically alter our systems and support architectures," explains Hank Alexander, president and COO of BA Investment Services, Inc., a BankAmerica company. "Facing the customer, we will look across products and legal entities; support organizations will consist of a blend of product specific factories and generic shared utilities." While building a single system capable of supporting both industry lines is not unimaginable and would clearly offer the most efficient solution, the front-end/back-end system configuration is much more readily implementable and more fully appreciates the differences which do exist in the businesses.

MODULAR SOLUTIONS

With the proliferation of front-office technology for investment management, trading, and trust administration, the trend toward modular, component-based technology solutions continues in the securities industry. As the technology continues to be based on more and more "open" standards, deployment of "best-of-breed" applications becomes more and more readily achievable. The future may find financial services companies meeting securities industry operations requirements by patching together software applications in a best-of-breed solution which spans industries. For example, it seems conceivable today that a trust company could connect a fund/serve application sold by a brokerage system vendor to its trust system.

Ten years ago few predicted the significant relaxation of *Glass-Steagall* that has occurred over the last several years and the subsequent entry of banks into brokerage and investment banking and insurance companies into brokerage and banking. Ten years from now how far will those boundaries have fallen and what will the technology that supports these new financial services conglomerates look like? If the customer matters, they may be one and the same.

Chapter 2
A Portfolio Management System for the Twenty-First Century

Tim Scatliff

MANY FIRMS HAVE FAILED TO INSTALL AN ENTERPRISE-WIDE PORTFOLIO MANAGEMENT SYSTEM because of the flaws in the plan, not flaws in the product. Attempting to exceed the capabilities of the installation team, trying to build a product that will be all things to all clients, and failing to understand the data model have all been major contributors to extended and failed plans. But the single most important obstacle has been in the delivery. Poorly constructed plans, vendors inexperienced in enterprise-wide solutions, and most importantly, product platforms that are insufficient to support the firms' current and future needs all contribute to a disappointing result.

Investment advisors and clients are consistently demanding contact and portfolio management features as a part of the services offered by their clearing organization. National firms have implemented proprietary portfolio systems at immense expense and resources, while balancing priorities within their organizations. They have had to develop the initial design for these products, build platforms compatible with their technological foundation, and implement this service across a diverse set of investment advisors and clients. The solutions have taken assorted forms, but the key element to success has always been a smooth, timely implementation.

The ability to construct and execute a proven implementation methodology will quickly increase the credibility of the Information Systems (IS) department and the installation team. The product will gain wide acceptance within the firm with a successful plan completion.

0-8493-9991-2/99/$0.00+$.50

This chapter will define a blueprint for a successful enterprise-wide portfolio management solution. The chapter begins with the evolution and rationale behind these systems over the past 10 years. Then follows the functionality that customers have begun to expect in these systems. Finally, this chapter discusses the single, most effective differentiator in this market: an architecture that encompasses all portfolio management functionality and enables easy additions to these services. The architecture must allow a flexible, generic approach to building portfolio systems within an enterprise. This will allow new applications to be built, leveraging the database and overall architecture.

EVOLUTION AND RATIONALE

- Institutional firms have used professional portfolio management systems for decades.
- Managed money has gained wide acceptance and with it the need for professional portfolio reporting.
- Private label funds spring up almost daily, again requiring accurate, automated reporting.
- A bull market increases the acceptance of performance measurement as investment advisors have positive results for their clients.
- Hundreds of financial planning firms are started by professional investment advisors to provide a new niche with more personal investment strategies. Their investment results are now expected to be presented professionally.
- Client statements showing only positions, balances, and check and credit card transactions are no longer sufficient. Clients are demanding current portfolio returns, comparable indices performances, risk analyses, and future life-style needs. They must be easy to use and integrate with other systems.
- Today's investment advisors demand applications that operate seamlessly with other applications on their desktop. Keystrokes to re-enter customer names, account numbers, cusips, etc. are no longer acceptable. The desktop is increasingly required to run the investment advisor's day. These requirements demand a portable, reliable solution that will meet the industry's needs into the next millennium.
- Internal solutions are too difficult to maintain to remain competitive. Professional firms specializing in this niche industry continually "raise the bar" in features, service, support, and technology.

An enterprise-wide object-oriented portfolio solution has now become the industry standard. All wire houses have built or purchased solutions. Correspondent clearing firms have solutions, in-house and "bolt-ons." Many regionals have built solutions with outside vendors that appear seamless. Some discounters and smaller boutiques are offering portfolio solutions. All private money managers have portfolio and performance solutions, although not always automated.

Recruiting clients and investment advisors has become difficult without a proven portfolio solution. Investment advisors cannot merely promise these features; they must be immediately deliverable. Delivery must be automated, seamless, scalable, reliable, and vendor neutral. The technology teams in the firm cannot be required to support another database, a new platform, or additional TP monitors.

Contact management and client information systems also have become the norm. Most high producers use manual contact management systems, not linked to the back office. This increases the duplication of data, adds problems of data integrity, "many people touching data," and multiple sources of data. Clients receive multiple mailings for the same product. Address changes take months as old databases with nonreplicated data continue to mail information to the client, causing the aggravation level to rise.

Solutions exist, but few offer an automated, technically sound, integrated answer. An effective portfolio solution requires an innovative, well-planned architecture. An effective architecture permits a successful implementation. An effective solution requires a flexible, scalable architecture.

There are many contact management, time management, and prospect management products on the market today. They are designed to automate an investment advisor's schedule, keep track of client's call-back objectives, various accounts, and even assets not held in the investment account. Competitive pressures have created a proliferation of portfolio management tools for the retail broker.

The financial services industry has escalated the baseline for services to include portfolio management services and reporting. Real-time market data was once a luxury. Debit and credit card services linked to the brokerage account were once only for the large investor. These and many other services have become part of the basic package required to attract clients and new investment advisors. Now clients expect portfolio management services as a part of the financial services offering.

The challenge is to differentiate the solutions that are appropriate for single investment advisors, small independents, and large, enterprise-wide portfolios.

WHAT A GOOD PORTFOLIO MANAGEMENT SYSTEM MUST HAVE

- Integrated contact/client management — investment advisors must be able to use client and portfolio information interactively. There can be only a single source for customer data.

- Automated back-office download — back-office trade and client data must be integrated with the books and records of the firm. This process must be stable, well tested, and relatively seamless.
- Strong reconciliation processes — keeping the back-office data, positions, and balances synchronized with the portfolio product is imperative to building the confidence of the sales force.
- Portfolio management and reporting — clients' view of the product is in the reporting. Strong basic online inquiries and hard-copy reporting are important to the investment advisor and is the primary view of the product from the clients' perspective.
- Market data interface — real-time market data, quotes, research, and news add to the investment advisor's interactive use of the system.
- Capital adjustments (corporate actions, splits, etc.) — corporate actions and reorganizations happen on a daily basis. The sales force must have an automated process to insure that positions are maintained correctly. Particular attention must be paid to the maintenance of a cost basis for each lot.
- Graphics interface — color graphs, charts, and reports are expected in today's environment.
- Word processing interface — lead-generating letters, prospecting letters, seminar invitations, and client follow-ups are also expected in today's automated office environment.

A few of the leading-edge systems offer a wider range of features. More robust features include:

- Financial risk analyses — how does a client's risk profile match the current portfolio?
- Financial planning model — clients today want to know "What if ... ?" in their financial planning strategies. New products present new opportunities and clients can receive assurance that their investments are meeting their goals or can simulate the results of various investment strategies.
- Automated account rebalancing — how would the assets be changed to meet the client's profile?
- Straight through trading — an investment advisor and/or client (based on the firm's practices) must have the ability to electronically facilitate the order entry, processing, and management processes. This should be applicable to order entry through to the affirm and confirmation process.
- Flexible report writer — many systems have robust reporting capabilities, but the appetite for new reports and inquiries is infinite. An easy-to-use report writer also needs advanced database interfaces.
- Multicurrency capabilities — an international capability is in most firms' business plan.

- Multilingual — an international language capability will allow future growth and acquisition opportunities.
- Lot management — the ability to define separate lots for each transaction will provide unlimited future flexibility in client reporting and accounting.
- Outside assets — asset gathering is facilitated by offering portfolio reporting to the client on assets not held in the firm. Products integrating these asset types provide a more complete view of the client's risk, return, and future strategies.
- Interactive computer-based training — the geographic diversity of most firms today requires alternatives to on-site sessions and train-the-trainer methodologies.
- Internet capabilities — this facility must be a part of the design and architecture of the product from its inception. A character or Windows-based product requires extensive redesign and re-engineering to operate effectively on the WWW.
- Intranet capabilities — similar to Internet services, the product must be engineered to run on the firm's intranet, not simply moved to the investment advisor's workstation.
- Remote access support — investment advisors and clients are demanding portable systems, accessible from clients' homes, home offices, and travel locations.
- Client/server compatible — again, systems must be engineered to take advantage of client/server technologies. Choices of objects, database elements, and network variables can all have dramatic effects on the performance and reliability of the product. Products engineered for client/server usage are far more effective than retrofitted products.
- Real-time updates — the proliferation of instant market data access for quotes, prices, research, and news has caused investment advisors to expect similar service levels from their portfolio systems. Most single-user systems require daily manual input of all changes. Some enterprise-wide solutions have built daily "download" solutions, but these are always yesterday's news. Today's systems are building dynamic interfaces to keep the client's assets synchronized with instantaneous changes in positions, balances, and prices.
- Strong service and support organization — customer service, quality assurance, experienced implementation teams, and strong senior management commitment to customer service are key to a successful implementation of these products. Smaller, more marketing-oriented firms will often cut corners in these areas when pursuing new sales.

THE SELECTION PROCESS

The product must be flexible, portable, and scalable. The architecture should support the capability to add new applications without changing the database structure or access, the network qualities, and the message layer. A technologically advanced structure supports:

- Object-Oriented Design.
- Layered Application Design.
- Three-Tier Client/Server with Transaction Processing.
- Platform Adaptable/Portable.
- Database Adaptable/Portable.
- Thin Client.

There are a variety of products that can provide investment advisors with basic features and services. A few can support some of the myriad advanced needs of the market place. Fewer still can complete this on an architectural platform that meets the needs of clients, investment advisors, and operational and technical personnel. Add to this the requirement of protecting the firm from massive future redesigns, and there are few solutions indeed.

That selection process must start with a review of the features listed on preceding pages, rated in accordance with the specific firm's immediate and anticipated requirements. Implementation of a single-user product is simplistic. Implementation of an enterprise-wide solution requires all and more of the listed features, as well as a clearly defined plan.

An experienced vendor will have a process that is adaptable to each client's environment. The resulting process should identify all requirements necessary to guide the client from contract commitment to a complete rollout of an enterprise solution. Teams will be assembled, responsibilities assigned, milestones set, and communication established to all levels of the overall plan.

The implementation process will include several phases. In the Exploratory Phase the vendor and client review the general applicability of the product and architecture within the client's environment. The client will learn the advantages of the product and architecture. The significant issues will be discovered and mapped into the project plan.

Points covered are

- Review architecture of the system (technical and application).
- Review the functionality of the product for the client.
- Verify the technology in the client's current environment.
- Discussions on the relational database, use of a transaction processor monitor, etc.
- Review the logical data model.
- Estimate the time and costs for the Detailed Design and Specification Phase.

- Estimate the implementation time frame, strategy, and training requirements.
- Estimate initial and ongoing costs.

After the Exploratory Phase, the plan will evolve into a detailed plan fitting the client's specific needs. The blueprint is completed with details of file definitions, milestones, teams, etc.

Steps included are

- Defines customer and vendor teams.
- Details design, testing, implementation plan.
- Defines hardware and communications requirements.
- Details file descriptions.
- Approximates project schedule.
- Defines key milestones.
- Defines testing and rollout phases.
- Integrates spiral model techniques.
- Defines training needs.
- Defines subsequent release schedules, testing methodologies, implementation.
- Defines travel schedule, support requirements.
- Initiates and trains on project planning tools.
- Initiates issue management systems.
- Defines data conversion requirements.
- Defines testing methodologies.
- Sets performance and scalability requirements.
- Obtains sign-offs from both client and vendor.
- Review and define implementation and conversion strategies.

An effective development methodology is the Spiral Model, detailed later in this chapter. The vendor should have a development life cycle that encompasses the following:

- Proof of concept experience.
- Design specifications processes.
- Benchmarking, simulating, and modeling procedures.
- Strong quality assurance team.
- Strong system and user documentation.
- Proven pilot-testing program methodology.
- Reliable rollout program.
- Experienced training team.

Portfolio systems require effective integration with back- and front-office providers, including:

- Back-office data.

- Front-office systems data.
- Trust systems data.
- Market data input.
- Research input.

A vendor that can bring wide experience in these installations, with the depth of features as defined above, is required in order to meet the needs of an enterprise solution. This type of methodology combined with an expandable and adaptable architecture is mandatory.

TECHNICAL ARCHITECTURE

The technical architecture is the foundation on which any application can be built. Whether it be a financial system, a manufacturing application, or a healthcare system, it is the infrastructure that can really make the difference.

Similar to a vast highway system and intercontinental transportation network, it is the infrastructure that ties all the business logic together with all of the various technologies and resources, wherever they may be deployed. It allows users anywhere in the enterprise to connect to application logic on local or remote servers. It allows centralized administrative staff to manage this process, along with the data and information it transports to serve the end user. In its purest form, it is the infrastructure that glues the application logic together with the various operating systems (e.g., Windows NT™, Unix, etc.) and resource managers (e.g., database managers, etc.).

The following is a prime example of this type of architecture. A system should be built with a three-tiered client/server infrastructure designed to support a variety of enterprise solutions. It must be scalable, flexible, and vendor neutral; an object-oriented approach that integrates the power of products like BEA's Tuxedo, and traditional relational database managers such as Sybase and Oracle. The end result is a fully three-tiered client/server infrastructure that makes it possible to be vendor neutral in the ever-changing world of technology.

This same infrastructure can be scaled down to achieve the implementation of the application on a single PC or notebook. The architecture of the infrastructure allows for disconnected computing, where the end-user may occasionally use the application off-site, disconnected from their regular server.

Add-ons can be designed that allow sophisticated developers to leverage a very comprehensive data model designed for the financial industry. These models support global markets, multicurrency, multilingual, performance reporting, accruals, contact management, and client reporting. An application framework or "cookie cutter" can be leveraged by large organizations to integrate new applications into their mission-critical systems.

The system should be based on an object-oriented, three-tiered client/server infrastructure developed entirely in C++ and designed to give the client the best of all worlds. The architecture can include a fully complied C++ thin client, minimizing its use of PC and Windows™ resources.

With a large number of workstations, as is characteristic of an enterprise-wide system, organizations must minimize the maintenance requirements on a per user basis. This is one of many reasons why it is important to keep the business code of the application on one or more distributed servers and not on the workstation itself. In this framework, only the user interface has to reside on the client's computer — all of the business logic is designed to be implemented on branch, regional, and/or central servers. These servers can be managed centrally by the organization's network management and administrative teams.

An open systems environment means you have a choice in the technology you use internally and the systems you interoperate with. It means being vendor neutral and highly portable. It means investing in software that is adaptable and maintainable. It means a living infrastructure that can constantly evolve to take advantage of new technologies or business opportunities.

Reliability and integrity are fundamental to the transaction processing model. Transactions can be defined at a logical level, involving several sequential or nested procedures, instead of being limited to the scope of a single, stored procedure. They can be implemented as real-time and/or batch systems. This is the same technology used by the largest banks and the largest airline reservation systems to handle hundreds of thousands of mission-critical transactions per day across wide geographic regions.

Performance and scalability are inherent to the infrastructure, yet the developer is insulated from the complexities of the environment. Each developer uses a "cookie cutter" to add new transactions. The result is a transaction that inherits all of these features through the application framework.

All objects should be standard C++ objects. They can be transported across the network and be recreated on virtually any server. The industrial strength of C++ and its acceptance as the language of choice for the creation of operating systems and large-scale applications give it the durability and performance that a true enterprise system requires.

The server waits for client-initiated requests. It must be capable of handling a large number of requests simultaneously. It must prioritize its work, handling the most important requests first. It must alert the caretakers when exceptions occur or high-water marks are reached. To be effective, it must initiate and run background task activities. It must always keep running. As the load increases, it needs to be able to scale up and spawn new processes on either the same or alternate servers — it needs to be able to load-balance.

The server cannot be limited to a family of processors that top out early. This is where the portability of the business code is so important. To provide a wide range of server capacities, it should run on both Windows NT™ and Unix operating systems.

The server and its network should support a single login, a standard clock for network time, network monitoring, systems management, a database, transaction services, and object-oriented services.

In summary, the technical architecture is the infrastructure that will support current and future applications. It must be portable, scalable, flexible, and compatible with a variety of operating platforms that it will meet.

FIVE-LAYER DESIGN

The architecture is based on a five-layer design that isolates the various areas of concerns with respect to portability and interoperability. The business code resides within the middle layer and is separated from the user interface via a messaging layer. The database layer is where the physical data model is implemented using either Sybase or Oracle. The database access layer separates the physical data model from the logical view that all application code shares. It is in this layer that the native database drivers are implemented for maximum throughput.

The layers give the architecture the flexibility that enterprise software needs. For example, the message layer that connects the thin client user interface to the business code could be implemented as a WAN or as an Internet connection. The business code can remain virtually unaltered.

The database access layer can use native drivers for Oracle in one implementation and native drivers for Sybase in another.

An object-oriented framework is provided to allow entire applications to be built as a collection of logical units of work — objects that encapsulate the work to be done (e.g., inquiry or update). By using this framework, the developer focuses on the business logic and the resulting code automatically inherits and encapsulates the three-tiered client/server features.

The framework includes a referential integrity engine, a replication engine, an exception-handling engine, and a reporting engine and all the features of a sophisticated TP monitor and relational database manager. To implement the resulting application on a single stand-alone notebook, for example, the message layer is flattened out at the infrastructure level. A new build is done, and all the business code inherits the new environment.

THE SPIRAL MODEL THEORY

Another key to a successful project is the project development techniques used. An object-oriented design should be built on the Spiral Model Theory of system development as described by Boehm. System development goes through the life cycle of requirement specifications, analysis, design, implementation and unit testing, integration, and implementation. This allows a product to develop incrementally over time, and incorporates maintenance into the normal development life of a product. Using this methodology in the design enables more complete functionality, but more importantly it allows a smoother, more predictable implementation plan. It enables products to grow without major redesign, incorporates new database and TP processes more easily, and concentrates the firm's resources on the business logic and rules.

We are living in a world where there are new technologies evolving on a continuous basis. Often, they represent opportunities that influence the area. For a system to last for years and decades, it must be designed to evolve.

An enterprise system has to adapt to many platforms and to varied technological requirements. The business code has to be portable to other systems that are designed to handle different loads. The number of online users may be measured in the thousands or more. Because of the large number of users utilizing a common integrated system at the same time, reliability, integrity, and scalability must be inherent in the infrastructure. Central management tools must exist to manage and report on the system and on its performance. A single system password should be supported.

To maintain the performance, the servers must be able to spawn additional processes or level the load between a number of servers. Because of the potentially vast number of users, the state of the user has to be carried primarily in the client PC and passed to the server only when required. Servers cannot possibly maintain the state of each user in the system and still have resources left to process the work. It must act as a funnel to seriously reduce the number of communications sessions, memory allocations, file allocations, database connections, and other resources.

It cannot use "chatty" protocols to connect the thin client with the server and the server with the database or other resource managers. Ideally, it has to support mainstream technologies from multiple vendors and yet be vendor neutral, allowing a choice for the user when establishing new systems and permitting integration and interoperability with existing systems.

It must be positioned to handle new requirements, many of which are unknown at the time of the initial implementation. It must evolve naturally as the opportunities arise. It must be designed for modularity and change. For example, there may be a future requirement to address disconnected computing (e.g., an end-user working at home, without a network) and interoperability with the Internet and the WWW. It has to support many user interfaces or views, including issues concerning the presentation, availability, and security of the data.

Not all firms have the time or skill sets required to customize or integrate new systems in the timeframes required by the market. But all firms require office, front office, product mix, investment advisor needs, database, client/server environment, etc. A product with the above design criteria allows these differences to become opportunities to improve the firm's processing capabilities and introduce efficiencies, rather than becoming obstacles. Customization becomes focused on the business rules and investment advisor's needs rather than on the technology platform.

The decision to add contact and portfolio management capabilities to an enterprise's suite of products has progressed beyond the point of "should we?" to the point of "which one?" Firms cannot remain competitive without these services being offered to their investment advisors and clients. Top-producing investment advisors have long since offered portfolio summary information to their best clients as a value-added service. They have accomplished this at great personal and operational expense without the benefit of extensive automation.

New products proliferate; back-office operations areas strive to maintain reporting methods that are discrepant. This has resulted in an inconsistent offering to their client base and a geometric increase in problems. For compliance, legal, and purely professional reasons, firms today need to present a consistent, reliable image to their clients. Investment decisions should be presented professionally with a minimal level of manual intervention. Investment advisors and their support staff need to have a confidence level in these products that mirrors the quality of the data from their back office.

To achieve this, three main decisions must be reached. What level of functionality do I need now and for the future? What architecture will support my current and future Information Systems needs? And which firm has the implementation plan that can be executed confidently within my organization?

This chapter outlined many of the decisions that need to be made to achieve these answers. It can be used as a blueprint to evaluate the market alternatives and to examine the available competitors. No single product fulfills all needs for all firms. No single product can be implemented without some degree of modification, adaptation, and customization. The goal is to select a vendor that can deliver an architecture that supplies the greatest level of flexibility in design, implementation, and future versatility. Limited platforms, limited database structures, limited interface capabilities, and limited experience in completing enterprise solutions will all inhibit the opportunity for a successful installation.

Chapter 3
Logging Monitoring in the Financial Services Industry

Knox Henderson

This can — and does — really happen:

Broker: "Buy fifty thousand shares of XYX Corp. (fictitious name) at fifteen and one half."
Trader: (verifying the request): "OK, buy fifteen thousand shares of XYZ at fifteen and one half."
Broker: "Right."
Trader: (later, after the stock's price has moved up) "Bought fifteen thousand shares of XYZ at fifteen and one half."
Broker: "I said buy fifty thousand shares."
Trader: "You confirmed fifteen thousand at fifteen and one half."

Anyone involved in the securities industry knows these kinds of discrepancies do occur and thousands of dollars can end up going in the wrong direction. Sometimes it works in the trader's or broker's favor, more often it does not. If the customer, through his broker, ordered 50,000 shares at fifteen and one half and the trader purchases only 15,000 — when the stock price moves up, the broker must purchase the additional 35,000 at the higher price and guarantee the customer the fifteen and one half price.

Here is solid justification for recording transactions in the securities industry. In this case, the trader is probably off the hook, because the onus is on the broker to confirm the order when the trader repeats it. But the only way to confirm who said what to whom is to go back to the original transaction.

There are a variety of reasons for recording telephone conversations or capturing computer screen activity in a bank, a securities firm, or an insurance agency. Some reasons are obvious, while others are not. Generally, re-

0-8493-9991-2/99/$0.00+$.50

quirements for logging and monitoring can be placed into three categories: Compliance, Performance measurement, and Risk management — or CPR.

COMPLIANCE

In many cases there are legislative requirements for recording certain securities or financial transactions. For the most part, financial organizations and insurance companies use recordings to settle disputes or to protect themselves against liability.

In 1996 the SEC issued its 21A Report on the improper activities of numerous NASDAQ market makers involving their colluding to fix price spreads. The tactic: ensure that price spreads were quoted only in $^1/_4$-point segments rather than $^1/_8$-point spreads. Twenty-four market-making firms were named in a Department of Justice (DOJ) antitrust case, each of whom was requested to comply to new guidelines set by the DOJ. These guidelines outline recording and monitoring procedures, including how many and how often traders would be monitored, and that the recordings would be monitored without their knowledge. All recordings are to be kept available for 30 days in the firms' compliance departments. The DOJ can come into an office at any time, without notice, and check recordings for antitrust violations.

In addition to voice transactions, the securities industry also relies heavily on written documents such as transaction instructions, recommendations, company prospectuses, etc. These are often sent by fax because of the timeliness of fax transmissions. Here, rules set by the National Association of Securities Dealers (NASD) require supervision and review of the communications between a firm's registered representatives and the public. For outgoing communications, compliance officers must create review procedures and demonstrate reasonable sampling techniques. Member firms must also retain all incoming and outgoing communications for at least 3 years. Proper disclaimers must also accompany any written information regarding securities and other financial instruments.

Fax transmissions can also be stored and archived using advanced fax logging and management technologies. By integrating all of an enterprise's fax machines and fax servers, all incoming and outgoing faxes can be tracked, routed, and permanently stored on a hard drive or DAT (digital audio tape) cassettes to meet a variety of compliance issues. Fax logging also provides a record of fax traffic: where it was sent from and to whom, when it was sent or rerouted and who it was reviewed by. With this new fax logging technology, the chance of losing or misplacing critical and compliant-sensitive fax transmissions is virtually eliminated.

Because banks and insurance companies are heavily involved in investment, they are subject to many of the same compliance issues as the securities industry. In banking, there are requirements for recording wire service transactions, where large sums of money are often transferred between two parties at distant points through verbal instructions. Similar regulations apply to trust account management and well as money market and foreign exchange transactions. Financial institution must maintain archives of voice transactions for at least six months. They also must be able to provide a mechanism for disaster recovery, which requires off-site redundant data.

Insurance companies which provide variable or self-directed policies for their client's assets must also comply with SEC regulations.

PERFORMANCE

The fastest-growing market segment for voice and data monitoring technologies is the call center. Bank-by-phone and insure-by-phone services are becoming the mainstay for financial organizations looking to provide faster and more convenient services. Computer telephony integrated (CTI) technologies have automated many of the telephone functions that have in the past required human intervention. These include call routing, call-holding procedures, and providing screen pops for agents. A screen pop uses the calling-line ID to access data associated with the caller and automatically "pops" the account or customer information in front of the agent while the call is being received.

While banks, investment service providers, and insurance companies are tripping over each other in order to obtain these "have to have" technologies, there will always remain a need for human, voice-to-voice contact in these industries. In fact, the deciding factor for gaining and retaining customers is not the technology, it is still — and always will be — quality of customer service.

Enter the age of performance monitoring. "Your call may be recorded for quality purposes" is becoming a phrase more and more commonplace over the phone. Right off the top, most financial and insurance organizations considering call-monitoring technologies want to explore the legalities around it. Without going into a lot of legalese, the requirements are as follows.

Currently, all but nine states require what is known as one-party consent. That means that at least one person — and this can include the agent — must be aware that the conversation is being recorded. Call centers comply to this requirement by having their agents sign a waiver, stating that they understand and approve of their conversations being recorded. The remaining states require two-party consent, where both parties agree prior to recording the conversation. In these states, callers may hear a message at the beginning of the call: "If you do not wish this call to be recorded, press one," or the system may offer some other method of opting out of the recording. The two-party-consent states include: California, Delaware, Florida, Illinois, Maryland, Massachusetts, Michigan, Pennsylvania, and Washington.

So what is the justification for call monitoring and performance measurement? First you must consider that the most significant cost in your call center is the cost of human resources. This typically accounts for about 70% of your investment in the call center. As a rule of thumb, only 15% goes towards technology and another 15% goes towards paying the phone bill. Quality monitoring ensures that you are getting the best return on investment for the human resources in the call center.

In the 1980s, as call centers began to emerge, agents were monitored using a "silent observation" method, where the reviewer sits side-by-side with the agent and listens in on the conversation. Another method was to record the conversation on reel-to-reel tape recorders. The drawbacks of these methods soon became apparent: supervisors had to spend peak call-center time reviewing agent calls and locating calls on a endless stream of reel-to-reel tape was cumbersome and time-consuming. Besides, there was typically no streamlined process of evaluation providing feedback to the agents. Further, reel-to-reel devices allow only one individual to listen to the calls at a given time.

Today, computer telephony integrated (CTI) quality measurement solutions provide an effective means of gathering a relative sample of calls and provide an arsenal of applications for efficiently and objectively evaluating agent performance levels. These systems interface directly with the PBX/ACD, convert calls into digital format, and store them in a centralized database for easy retrieval. Any number of agents, even in a free-seating environment, can be recorded on a specified schedule (e.g., all agents recorded three times per month). During convenient times, the supervisor can search the database, retrieve calls, and score them using online grading templates. These templates provide data reports that are generated to compare the agent's performance vs. his peers, compare reviewer scores to ensure consistency, and to provide overall call-center productivity reports. Details of the technology are provided later in this chapter. This translates into superior customer service, higher customer retention, lower turnover, a decrease in training time, and a more knowledgeable staff who, in turn, sell more securities and insurance policies, etc.

It doesn't stop there! The latest rave in the industry is a new technology known as screen capture. Call centers can not only capture the original conversation, but can also recreate the computer screen activity that the agent sees during the conversations. This provides insight into how the agent is using the technology available to him or her, or whether the customer interaction system (CIS) itself is effective. Screen capture technology is available for both IBM mainframe systems as well as the PC.

Integrated screen capture and voice monitoring products allow both the voice and the screen activity to be played back simultaneously, exactly as the agent would have seen and heard it.

RISK MANAGEMENT

Imagine you are a registered nurse offering over-the-phone insurance services. A few months ago you had underwritten a health insurance policy for a client. Along with the policy you provided written documentation which included detailed information regarding the scope of the policy. Because this information may have been too technical and complex for your client to fully understand, you describe for the client in full detail what is covered and what is not. Now you receive a call from a physician who is about to perform a procedure on the client. After discussion, you determine that the procedure falls outside the scope of the policy. Later, you receive another call from the irate client who was convinced he had the appropriate coverage, and that you had assured him that he did.

Whether the end result falls into your favor or not, recreating the original transaction brings immediate resolution as to what transpired between the two parties. Bitter arguments that cost valued customers, lengthy legal disputes, and conflicts that negatively affect employee relations and morale, can all be avoided. As one mortgage provider puts put it: "[Call recording] is saving us over a million dollars a year in just settling rate disputes."

This mortgage company and other financial industry executives are finding that recording calls leaves no room for misinterpretation, and that logging and monitoring technologies today can be considered absolutely reliable and fail-safe.

Outside of compliance issues, recording is a must for brokers and dealers who want to address risk management issues such as:

- Transaction verification.
- Prevention against liability posed by lost or misinterpreted voice communications.
- Reconfirmation of major orders.
- Dispute resolution in the event of client complaints.
- Reduced liability insurance costs.

METHODS OF LOGGING AND MONITORING

Now that we have explored some of the whys of logging and monitoring let's look at the hows. As mentioned before, there are a variety of recording requirements — all which fall under the general heading of compliance, performance measurement, and risk management. As we look closer at the actual technology, meeting these requirements is achieved through the following methods of recording:

1. Full-time logging (total recording) — this is required for validating transactions or legal notifications over the telephone typically are required by health, financial, insurance, and investment institutions or by law and government offices to meet legal or legislative requirements.
2. Scheduled recording — the most basic of recording solutions for call centers. Call recordings are automated by time, by agent, or by groups of agents.
3. Selective recording — here is where CTI applications are particularly valuable. Recordings can be initiated via IVR, DNIS, ANI, and CLID and can be organized in databases for ease of analysis for marketing and quality assurance purposes.
4. Event-driven recording — a term often used in the same context as selective recording. However, "selective" recording typically refers to "telephony" occurrences, while event-driven can be seen as computer application-driven. For example, when an agent types in any amount more than $1000 in a particular field, a recording is initiated. Later, those recording can be easily retrieved using the same criteria.
5. Record-on-demand (controlled by the agent) — the agent can press a "Start Record" button on his/her workstation. This is valuable where third-party verification is required or when a call is transferred to a supervisor, who is typically not being monitored.
6. Quality measurement — any of the above recording methods can be used to gather calls to evaluate quality. However, the most effective way to gather a consistent and relevant sample of agent calls is to use a scheduler to collect a percentage of agent calls (e.g., one call per agent per week between 8:00 a.m. and 11:00 a.m.).

TYPES OF RECORDING SOLUTIONS AVAILABLE

Here is an overview of the configurations and interfaces used for computer telephony integrated logging and monitoring technologies.

Trading Turrets

On floors of the world's stock exchange, and in the trading rooms of stock brokers, banks, institutional investors, and other financial organizations, stocks, commodities, money market funds, and debt issues are primarily traded on turrets. The major difference between a turret and a PBX is that a PBX switches a fixed number of lines to a telephone at a given time. A turret switches all of the lines to all of the extensions (turrets). Everyone has access to everyone and several people or locations can be on many lines at the same time. This allows the broker or trader to listen in or talk to groups, obtain prices, and conduct trades.

On the trader's desk, the turret is referred to as the "dealer board" which includes phone lines, speaker lines, and line indicators telling the trader who is on the line. The "back-office" component of the turret, where the switching takes place, takes incoming lines that may or may not be connected to the central PBX/ACD. This is because there can also be lines that run directly to branch locations or other key offices.

The voice logger is directly connected to the turret and records all calls that come through it, inbound, outbound, and internal. Therefore, private lines that the company does not want recorded bypass the turret and are channeled directly to the PBX.

Turrets come with two handsets and typically one or more speakers. The speakers are used to monitor other exchanges, news or wire services in real time, or other exchanges. It is not uncommon for a foreign exchange trader to have up to 30 speakers. For monitoring purposes, each handset and speaker requires its own channel for recording. Sometimes, however, these two handset channels are "summed" together for economy. The drawback of summing is that when the call is played back, the company may not want the conversation with the other party heard by any party reviewing the call. Exhibit 1 shows a generic configuration of a trading turret.

Switches — PBX/ACD

A typical telecommunications environment uses a PBX (private branch exchange) and an ACD (automatic call distributor). Some switches such as

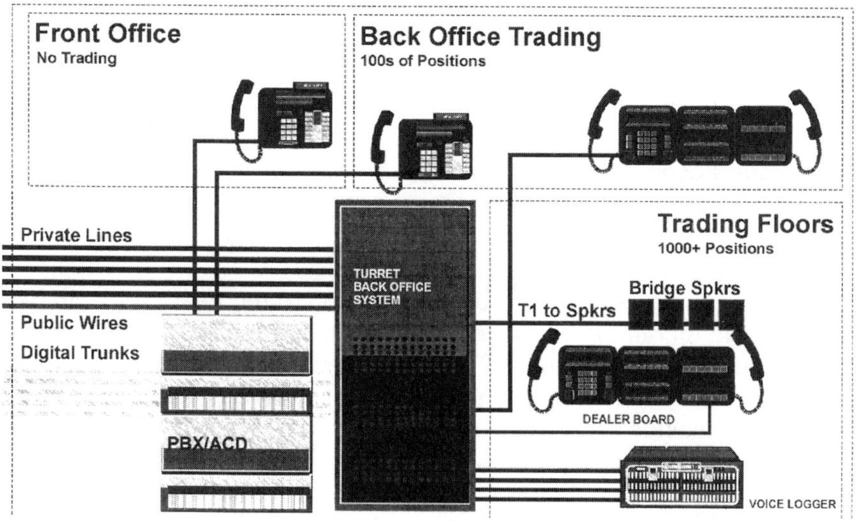

Exhibit 1. Telephone anatomy of a trading firm.

Lucent's Definity have the ACD capabilities built in. Other vendors, such as Aspect, manufacture ACDs that interface with other PBXs.

There are two key interfaces to a computer telephony integrated recording. First, there is the audio interface, where the actual conversation is recorded. Secondly, there is the call detail interface where call details are sent from the switch, via the CDR (call detail report) port or CTI link. This provides information as to time, date, trunk, extension, and duration of call.

The CTI link, which is the integration between the telephone switch and the computer network, adds further intelligence to the call traffic in the financial or insurance call center. CTI logging means that other call center applications and telephony events can help to tag and identify specific calls, trigger recordings, and narrow search criteria.

For example, a common CTI identifier is DNIS (dialed number identification service). DNIS tells you what number the customer dialed (typically a 1-800 number) The DNIS number is provided in a number of ways — in-band or out of band, through a ISDN line, or by a separate data channel. The DNIS number can be used by the CTI monitoring system to trigger a call recording. For example, this means that all banking customers who call 1-800-OUR-RRSP will have their calls recorded to verify transactions in a self-directed RRSP.

Similarly, ANI (automatic number identification) or CLID (calling line identification) can also recognize the caller ID and, through the CTI interface, trigger calls "from" a specified area code or a direct line from suppliers, clients, service providers, etc.

Recording technologies today provide a variety of options as to exactly where the recording takes place, as shown in Exhibit 2. There are advantages and disadvantages to each configuration. The three key recording interfaces are as follows.

Trunk-Side Recording

Here the logger is directly connected to the incoming trunks (24 channels per trunk) before they are terminated at the switch (PBX/ACD).

Advantages. Trunk-side recording allows you to record all segments. Everything the incoming caller hears and says is recorded, including the touch tones entered into the IVR, the voice recordings from the messaging system, or conversation held with other outside parties conferenced in on the call. Trunk-side recording supports selective recording, used with a call detail logging system, and provides the best audio quality.

Disadvantages. With trunk-side recording, all channels need to be recorded to ensure no calls are missed. You need to use a call detail logging

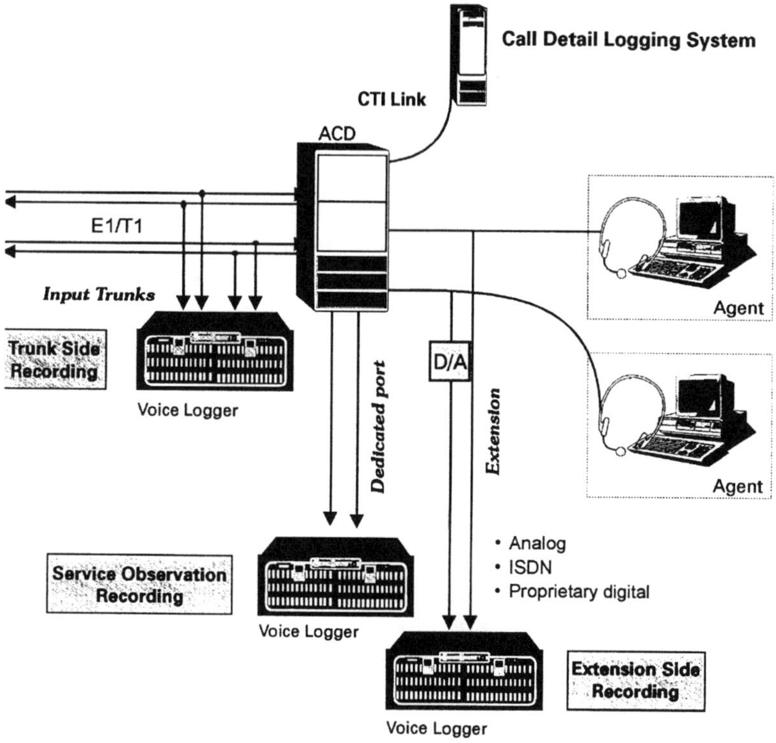

Exhibit 2. Where can voice loggers record?

system to map the appropriate channels and extensions for retrieving the call and it does not record internal calls.

Uses. Consequently, trunk-side recording is best used for full-time recording to meet compliance requirements and provides the safest solution for risk management. It is not a cost-effective solution for measuring quality.

Station-Side Recording

This takes place after the switch, on the line leading to the agents' extensions. These extensions can either be digital or analog. Because digital lines use a proprietary protocol, the voice must be converted to analog to allow the logger to accept the audio and then converted back to digital in the logger's proprietary format.

Advantages. Station-side recording requires fewer channels to record because no matter which trunk channel is used, the calls are routed to a set number of predetermined extensions. A call detail logging system is not required to locate the extension/agent to retrieve the call.

Disadvantages. Station-side recording requires more cabling because an independent line is needed for each extension. Proprietary digital protocols require D/A (digital to analog) conversion, and the agents themselves can void the recording.

Uses. It is an economical means of recording full-time in smaller call centers and permits record-on-demand where seating is assigned.

Dedicated Port

Today's PBX/ACDs are built with a "service observation" port that allow supervisor to conference in on another call between two parties and monitor the call as it occurs. Typically, this permits the supervisor to listen only, although some systems also provide access for the supervisor to join in on the conversation.

Manufacturers of recording and logging products have designed interfaces that allow their technology to utilize the service observation feature of the switch for recording calls.

Advantages. Dedicated port recording, or service observation, requires limited cabling, and is the best solution for selective recording and quality monitoring.

Disadvantages. Service observation is not the best solution for full-time recording because it is dependent on the limitations of the service observation port on the PBX/ACD.

Uses. Service observation is used for "selective recording" where you only want to record specific extensions/agents or groups of agents such as money market traders, wire transfer services, self-directed RRSP services, etc. Service observation is also the best means for obtaining quality monitoring where call recordings are initiated on a predetermined schedule. For example, if an insurance call center wants to record each agent three times per month, the logger continues to record those agents until the schedule is satisfied.

FINAL NOTE

Methods of recording and storage for voice logging systems vary, but digital recording technology ensures reliable, high-quality recording with high storage capacity. Systems today can provide thousands of hours of online storage and unlimited storage on DAT tape (and other media). CTI capabilities in today's digital loggers allow the user to quickly search and retrieve calls from yesterday, last month, or last year using a variety of criteria. It is these capabilities that permit end users to address all of their compliance, performance, and risk management needs.

Chapter 4
Straight Through Processing

Jim Douthitt

ASK FIVE PEOPLE WHAT STRAIGHT THROUGH PROCESSING (STP) MEANS and you're likely to receive five different answers. More and more, STP is coming to represent a continually evolving set of aspirations rather than an existing reality. The early use of the term referred to automation of all processes involved in the purchase and sale of securities. More recently, STP has been taken to mean complete automation of all aspects of investment operations. As more goals of STP are realized, additional goals are introduced. The scope and aspirations of STP will probably continue to expand for quite some time.

Achieving STP can have vastly different requirements for different entities. For example, the processes to be automated will be different for a brokerage firm than for a stock exchange, which has different requirements than a buy-side financial institution. And, while the focus of STP is frequently on the buy side, the term still applies to virtually all parties involved in executing, clearing, and settling securities transactions.

Analyses of the state of STP often focus on the various entities which contribute to the automation of securities trading, such as FIX, SWIFT, DTC, ISITC, and others. However, the roles that these standards and entities play is constantly changing; generally toward expanding their scope of work in advancing STP. This trend has led to competition among standards and may ultimately lead to the emergence of a single set of standards and clearly defined roles for the remaining players.

History is yet another variable complicating the analysis of STP. The infrastructure which manages investment operations today is a result of evolution, not engineering. For instance, the SEC has long advocated the concept of a single national stock exchange. Yet regulation continues to support a multiple exchange system. Regulation itself has been a result of evolution. With the advent of financial futures, the SEC and the CFTC (Commodity Futures Trading Commission) have, at times, been in conflict. They divide, between them, regulation of financial instruments, each of

0-8493-9991-2/99/$0.00+$.50

which can impact the value of those regulated by the other. Furthermore, these entities have had to work out disagreements as to their regulatory jurisdictions.

It is easy to see that the scope of what is commonly referred to as STP is very broad; encompassing the universe of investment operations topics. In this analysis, we will focus more on the end objectives of STP and less on the current players and their near-term approaches to the issue. We will focus on the buy-side financial institutions using the broader definition of STP which has more recently become accepted. STP, therefore, is taken to mean complete automation of all aspects of investment operations. Against this backdrop, the analysis of STP will focus on the following:

1. The elements required for buy-side financial institutions to achieve STP.
2. Required elements in the flow of a securities transaction.
3. How various entities add value to securities transactions.
4. How investment systems achieve automation of securities operations in areas other than trading.

ACHIEVING STP ON THE BUY SIDE

Nothing puts the objectives of STP in better perspective than simply stepping back and examining what it is that a financial institution is attempting to accomplish. A buy-side institution is attempting to meet or exceed established investment objectives as efficiently as possible with the best possible customer service. If the institution has achieved STP, trade modeling would be comprehensive enough to automatically adjust the portfolio to better meet objectives within compliance limits and seamlessly result in trade orders. The trade order management system would easily leverage all available venues for execution. Finally, executed orders would automatically result in accounting, performance, analytical and historical data facilitating investment monitoring, analysis, and reporting to management, regulators, and clients.

An STP environment should see a higher portion of labor devoted to portfolio management, analysis, and trade modeling. Less labor would go toward trade affirmation, settlement, custodial reconciliation, front- to back-office system reconciliation, report production, and trade entry. The use of real-time information for flexible trade modeling and trade management would also result in more efficient use of cash. In short, STP would result in reduced overhead and better execution of portfolio management strategies.

Steps in Buy-Side Operations

1. **Perform analysis to determine how best to meet investment objectives** — This includes economic, industry sector, and security-specific

analysis. Such analysis is performed to achieve established investment objectives which may be dictated simply by the liabilities offsetting the assets or by an investment policy. These functions lead to a dynamic model portfolio which may require additional adjustments for specific client criteria. The more efficiently this process is achieved, the more effective the firm will be in meeting client objectives.

2. **Model trades** — Trade modeling includes all the functions involved in determining how to adjust portfolio holdings to better meet the objectives. This can be the purchase of a stock identified, through analysis as cheap, or simply adjusting the duration and/or convexity of the portfolio to better match the attributes of offsetting liabilities. This process is frequently stymied by a variety of factors which may include:

- *Inability to identify favorable trade opportunities.* This is as much a function of investment analysis as it is a function of trade modeling. If data cannot be sorted and analyzed on a timely basis against existing holdings, opportunities will be missed.
- *Inadequate trade modeling facilities.* Oftentimes, the rebalancing criteria can be complicated by special requirements for specific portfolios or by requirements for maintaining sector weights across portfolios with vastly different total holdings. These complications can delay or possibly prevent the timely rebalancing of portfolios and again result in missed opportunities.
- *Inadequate ability to manage the effects of trading.* Purchasing securities requires either the use of idle cash, borrowing, or the selling of another security. Active managers historically have required additional cash balances, and this is at least in part attributable to the shortcomings of their systems. Trade modeling is often not reflective of real-time positions and, frequently, is entirely separate from trade order management. Comprehensive trade modeling needs to consider, and model for, the effects of trading on the remaining portfolio on a real-time basis.

Overcoming system shortcomings often means adopting a simpler, but perhaps less effective, portfolio management strategy.

3. **Manage the trade orders** — Since trades cannot always be executed at one time and, instead, must be executed in separate fills, adequate trade order facilities must be available. Step-outs are sometimes required and additional rebalancing may dictate new trades before a given order is completely filled. Allocations of trades may need to follow different scenarios under different circumstances. Trade order management was once considered the point of initial entry. Now, some systems can take the results of trade modeling and create orders automatically. Automated links for electronically executing trades with counterpartys also improves the trade order management process. The ability to manage all these functions

efficiently has a tremendous bearing on the effectiveness of the firm in meeting its investment objectives.

4. **Monitor and analyze holdings against market conditions, liabilities, investment objectives, and restrictions** — For each of Steps 4 and 5, a tight integration of front-office trade management, modeling, and analysis systems with the back-office is critical to achieving STP. Timely review of current positions requires a reliable portfolio accounting system. Such a system must have facilities for timely, automated reconciliation of holdings, trade affirmation, and settlement. Tight integration of front- and back-office systems improves execution of investment strategies and reduces overhead. It is with Steps 3 and 4 that we see the traditional focus of STP on automating trades. Trade automation reduces trade risk and also reduces middle- and back-office overhead. Trade automation will be examined in detail in the next two sections.

5. **Provide reporting to management, regulators, and clients** — To effectively provide all the reporting and analysis, the portfolio accounting system must take minimal transactional data from the trading system, automatically pull data from external sources, and compute accounting, performance, compliance, and other data as well as automatically generate custom reports using either electronic or paper form. The last section of this chapter will explore the elements of automation necessary to accomplish this aspect of straight through processing.

Having established the objectives of the buy side, it is now appropriate to take a closer look at the minimum required elements of a trade. Automating these elements help to achieve Steps 3 and 4 which, in turn, reduces risk and overhead.

MINIMUM ELEMENTS OF A TRADE

Trading of securities is a regulated process. The process can be different depending on the type of security being traded. The vast majority of SEC-regulated securities are traded on one of the major exchanges and clear through the DTC and the NSCC. For purposes of simplifying this discussion, we will focus on transactions of stocks and bonds clearing through the DTC.

Parties Involved

- Buy-Side Institution: places order with a broker-dealer to execute the transaction; the institution is the initiator of the process.
- Broker-Dealers: brings buyers and sellers together.
- Stock Exchange/NASDAQ/Order Crossing Systems: all of these different entities represent venues for finding an appropriate market price.

- Depository Trust Company (DTC): functions as the clearing house and repository where stock and bond certificates are exchanged. It is a member of the Federal Reserve and is owned by most of the brokerage houses on Wall Street and the NYSE.
- National Securities Clearing Corporation (NSCC): nets the securities and cash transacted by the major counterparties on a daily basis.
- Safekeeping Agent: holds securities on behalf of the owner (i.e., either the buy-side institution or its client). A safekeeping agent can be a custodian bank or a broker-dealer.

Steps in the Process

1. The institution indicates interest in a securities transaction with one or more broker-dealers.
2. The broker-dealers provide offers.
3. The institution places the order with a given broker-dealer.
4. The broker-dealer must then provide a confirmation (a legal requirement) of the trade to the institution.
5. The institution acknowledges the confirmation and submits to the DTC.
6. The DTC affirms the trade upon receipt of acknowledged confirmation from the institution. Affirmation binds the parties to the trade. The affirmation notice must go to the institution, the broker-dealer, and the custodian.
7. Custodians can receive notice either from the institution or from the DTC, depending on the arrangement.
8. Upon the settlement date, securities and cash change hands between the safekeeping agent and broker-dealer, as facilitated by the DTC.

While this basic process can be complicated by block allocations and step-out broker arrangements, the above represents the minimum required steps to complete a simple securities transaction. Each required element adds to the administrative burden and can create delays which would be unacceptable should settlements move from the current T+3 to T+1, as expected sometime in the next few years.

Value for the Buy Side is in Automation

1. Means of signaling intent and agreeing on terms.
2. Trade confirmation.
3. Trade affirmation.
4. Notification of the safekeeping agent.

The next section will cover some of the entities working to make the process more efficient and discuss the products and services they offer.

ENTITIES AND PROTOCOLS AUTOMATING THE SECURITIES TRADING PROCESS

In addition to acting as the repository for most SEC-regulated securities transactions, the DTC offers a number of products which facilitate various aspects of the trading process:

- Institutional Delivery (ID) System is used to coordinate the confirmation, affirmation, and settlement processes for the institutions, broker-dealers, and custodians. Until a recent SEC ruling, it was the only system for accomplishing the affirmation function. ID is capable of accepting SWIFT messages and is expected to soon incorporate FIX message formats as well.
- Institutional Instructions (II) allows an institution to electronically communicate allocations to an executing broker-dealer. It also provides facilities for managing step-outs. II messages can also include matching instructions read by the ID system.
- Notice of Order Execution (NOE) System allows brokers to send order fill details to institutions.
- Standing Instructions Database (SID), like ALERT, is a data warehouse of settlement instructions.

Financial Information Exchange (FIX) Protocol is a standard for sending and receiving messages regarding indications of interest, orders and order acknowledgments, fills, account allocations, news and other administrative messages. It was started by some of the largest buy-side and sell-side institutions in the U.S.

Industry Standardization for Institutional Trade Communication (ISITC) started as an effort to improve trade notification to custodians. The scope of its work has expanded and the organization now has messages for many aspects of the trade process. There are several affiliate ISITC organizations around the globe.

Society for Worldwide Interbank Financial Telecommunications (SWIFT) is a bank-owned consortium which was founded to create settlement messages. It too has expanded its role to include messages to facilitate other aspects of trading. SWIFT creates protocols and manages a telecommunications network.

In one way or another, all these formats and systems (and many others not mentioned here) represent different ways of accomplishing trades electronically. Different providers specialize in different aspects of the transaction sequence. It is unknown which standards, if any, will ever emerge as dominant. In fact, it is more likely that no standard will emerge anytime soon. Complicating the issue is the fact that standards vary from country to country. The long-run objective, however, is to have an environment where the buy side and sell side can use a single set of standards, one for each message type or step in the trade process, regardless of the security type or country in which it's traded. Therefore, the next trend for STP will likely be in the areas of communications protocol conversion and message format translation services. The DTC, for one, already sees itself fulfilling this role.

Automating the Front and Back Office

As stated before, the benefits of STP come from:

- Improving the execution of investment strategies.
- Reducing risk.
- Reducing overhead.

While this can be realized through automation of trade communications, of equal importance is the automation of the front and back office. Below, some of the key points of front- to back-office automation are outlined. Automating these areas of investment operations can have at least as much impact on achieving STP as efforts to improve the efficiency of trade execution.

Portfolio Modeling. Modeling includes all of the processes traders use to determine what positions to open and close. Most front-office trading systems include rebalancing, trade allocation, and trade order management functions. Unfortunately, such systems do not always incorporate the modeling facilities that actually result in trades. To the extent that some modeling capabilities are included in trade order management systems, they tend to be inflexible in their methods. Conversely, traders tend to develop their own modeling techniques. As a result, much modeling takes place outside the trading system on spreadsheets and elsewhere. Historically, custom-tailored modeling techniques have not been easy to incorporate in trading systems in ways that allowed data to flow directly from models to trade orders.

Trade Order Management. Trading systems often present users with interesting compromises. Complex systems can handle a wider variety of trading scenarios but generally carry with them greater overhead in the form of additional required labor. That overhead can carry through even to simple trading scenarios. If a system does not have the ability to handle complex trades involving many steps, manual processes must be used to work around the system limitations. Conversely, if the trade is simple but the trading system is complex, there can be additional overhead associated with one-step trades. A trading system that allows traders to go through only those steps that are necessary to enter the trade is ideal. For instance, if the trade order will be filled over several executions with several broker step-outs, the system should account for each step of the process and allocate across accounts at any point. If, however, the trade is executed all at once through a single broker, the trade system should act as a simple trade capture system, requiring minimal data entry to record all levels of trade information.

Custodial Reconciliation. Reconciliation to custodian records is facilitated by a strong portfolio accounting engine. Many systems can only reconcile holdings, purchases, and sales because the accounting facilities are inadequate to do more. Without greater depth of accounting facilities, income and MBS principal payments must be reconciled manually at greater labor expense and, practically speaking, at the cost of longer delay in identifying custodian error. Ideally, a system would be used that gives complete and accurate cash projections across all security types, thus accomplishing complete and accurate custodian reconciliation automatically across all major custodian banks and many smaller ones.

Securities Accounting. Required depth of accounting functionality is a function of the security types managed, transactions performed, and client needs. Even if broad requirements are not currently present, having the extra accounting capability can provide comfort that new strategic directions will not require significant operational and systems overhauls. Furthermore, securities accounting facilities and extensive relational data storage are critical to automating custodial reconciliation and back-end reporting. In ensuring that the capability currently needed, or possibly needed in the future, is present, some key attributes must be evaluated. These requirements include:

1. Does the system have a verifiable ability to add new security types drawing on a comprehensive set of security attributes? This ability should extend to all types of instruments including derivatives, asset-backed securities, and various foreign instruments.
2. Does the system have all functionality to properly account for multiple currencies? This is not always an easy question to answer. Not only must the system account for a base and local currency, it must also account for the settlement schedules of each country. The system vendor must also have demonstrated a commitment to developing Euro functionality once the rules for this new currency become fixed. Finally, the multicurrency functions must extend to every other aspect of the system, from custodial reconciliation to general ledger entries.
3. Does the system include comprehensive accounting alternatives? These would include a full complement of yield, amortization, and tax lot/average cost accounting methods. Also of value are the abilities to maintain multiple accounting methods for the same holdings and track tax information, such as original issue discounts.
4. Can the system manage corporate actions?

5. Does the system provide enough additional data elements so securities data can be segmented to meet a variety of back-end reporting requirements?

A system meeting all of these requirements is critical to automating custodial reconciliation and producing management and client reports.

Management Reporting and Ad Hoc Query. Management reporting serves a variety of functions. It supports the process of generating client reports. It supports the portfolio and trade modeling functions. And it supports audit and verification processes. Ad hoc queries also support these functions but in a less formalized way. Management inquiries can often generate long cycles of report generation followed by additional queries. Ending such cycles depends on the ability of analysts to provide insightful analysis that gets at the issues management may currently be pursuing. However, such analysis can only be provided if the data needed are both within the scope of system functions and accessible by the analyst.

If reporting facilities are inadequate, the back-office staff can, at times, become entirely consumed attempting to meet new reporting requirements. This type of inefficiency is typically caused by:

1. Inadequate reporting tools. Reporting applications do not have adequate depth to access and manipulate the needed data.
2. Inadequate data. The back-office system does not store the data required.
3. A lack of distributed systems. Management staff does not have adequate desktop tools to query the data on the fly. For such tools to truly save labor, they must be easy to use for non-users.

A portfolio accounting system overcomes all these problems and allows users to realize enormous labor savings if it stores the majority of calculated data. Modern report writing applications are so versatile, they allow reports to be formatted in any way that a spreadsheet can. The calculation and logic functions allow unlimited data analysis. Special custom queries need only be written once. Thereafter, the same query or report can be used again and again. All this is possible if the accounting system stores the majority of data and is ODBC compliant.

Client Reporting. Investment systems often limit the extent of client reporting. Even in this age of considerable computerized modernization, client report packages from sophisticated asset managers are printed and mailed out today with limited, text-based reports of transactions, holdings, and other investment data. Such reports, while providing information, generally do not become an integral part of client operations. Most asset management firms supplement these reports with additional reports providing greater depth of analysis, which are created manually using spreadsheet software. Custom reporting is a service of considerable value which can help to retain clients, especially when clients rely on such reports as integral parts of their own operations. When such services are provided, clients value investment managers, not only for their investment performance and adherence to style, but also for the support they provide to client operations. Custom client reporting is an important means for asset managers to provide additional value-added services and improve client retention.

Managers agree there is tremendous value in providing custom reporting for clients. However, custom reports are not always done to a great extent because they must be generated manually each reporting period. The cost becomes excessive and the process is impractical. If, however, an ODBC-compliant database which stores the majority of calculated data is used, reports, once designed, can be queued to run at appropriate intervals and be sorted and collated with the appropriate number of copies. And with a modern reporting application, the process can go one step further. Reports can be e-mailed to clients or placed on a secure web page in HTML format for them to pick up. Because customization is a one-time labor effort and reports can be batched to run in a production environment, a high level of client customization is economically feasible.

Compliance. Compliance is unusual in that it fits into two parts of the investment operation continuum. At the front end, trades are (ideally) tested for compliance in advance of execution. Since many trade operations are modeling in separate systems, placing orders by phone and *then* entering trades in the trading system, automation can do little to prevent a compliance violation. In the absence of automated compliance testing, traders may rely on lists generated by the back office, showing positions near the limits of compliance rules. Obviously, such methods are less reliable when the array of rules is complex.

Whereas front-end compliance is a preventive function, back-end compliance is a function of verification. Regardless of the degree of automation achieved, both front- and back-end compliance functions must be maintained. In attempting to automate compliance, the most difficult issue is that the same rules must be applied to both the front-office and back-office systems. This either requires the maintenance of rules in two systems or using a single module that is mapped to both systems.

Performance Measurement. The requirements of a quality performance measurement system are often overlooked. Data should be stored to the security identifier level. Without this detailed level of storage, the ability to segment performance results will run into limitations that may be material in some circumstances. Aggregated performance should also be stored at appropriate levels to facilitate ease of reporting. The ability to build composites and run performance from and to any user-defined points in time is also important to automating performance. Finally, the performance system should have adequate facilities to account for late adjustments and complex cash flow and prepayment patterns.

CONCLUSION

STP now represents a set of continually increasing standards to which the investment community aspires. Efforts to improve trade execution are moving faster and will likely focus on the need for translation facilities to accommodate the multitude of disparate message protocols. This focus is likely to remain until T+1 is finally realized. From the operational perspective, efforts to improve STP will continue to focus on the integration of the front and back office and the automation and distribution of reporting and query functions.

Chapter 5
Designing and Evaluating Investment Performance Systems

Timothy Peterson

PERFORMANCE MEASUREMENT HAS GAINED GROWING ATTENTION in the investment industry. Industry's *de facto* adoption of the Association of Investment Management and Research Performance Presentation Standards™ has raised as many questions as it has attempted to answer, as firms struggle to understand and comply with the rules. Expansion of institutional investing into overseas markets and derivative securities is dating existing investment systems and forcing systems vendors to accommodate new industry needs with respect to performance measurement calculations and international presentation standards.[1] Technological advances, too, are having their effect. Lower data storage costs and greater interconnectivity are fostering the expectation of timely yet detailed investment performance information. Yet the technological aspects of system development are probably simple when compared to the functional requirements in such a dynamic and demanding industry.

Therefore, the focus of this chapter is on identifying the most important issues in the development of software that measures investment portfolio performance. Current and anticipated trends in the financial services and technology industries are also considered. Technical design is not emphasized, though some techniques for implementing functional features are presented. Firms wishing to assess the adequacy of a performance measurement system can readily look for the design characteristics outlined

0-8493-9991-2/99/$0.00+$.50

herein to assist in their evaluation. Unfortunately, the practice of performance measurement is too broad a topic to discuss in detail. To simultaneously relate these practices to the specific development issues described would be a tremendous task, so this chapter assumes much about the reader's knowledge of accounting, investment management, and performance measurement. However, some background information will provide perspective for those unfamiliar with performance measurement practices.[2]

PERFORMANCE MEASUREMENT AND THE PORTFOLIO MANAGEMENT PROCESS

Though some perceive performance measurement at "the end" of the investment management process, it is really just one step in a cycle, as shown in Exhibit 1. But its position in the cycle is unique. Not only does performance measurement relate information about past investment strategies, it provides guidance for future strategies. Understanding this link between past and future actions can have considerable implications for performance systems design. This is especially true in integrated investment systems: in many cases the performance system functions as a "data bridge" between back-office accounting and analysis and front-office trading operations.

Performance measurement has three primary functions: to evaluate the ability of a portfolio manager to meet quantifiable objectives, to determine

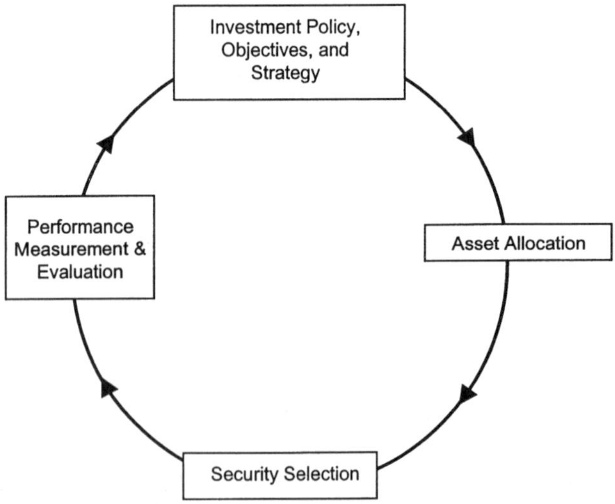

Exhibit 1. The portfolio management process.

the effectiveness of an investment strategy, and to measure wealth creation through investing. Institutions will use the former while individual investors are more concerned with the latter. In practice, the statistical techniques used in performance measurement can identify whether returns were earned through skill vs. luck, and even identify specific aspects of an investment strategy that contributed to the overall rate of return earned.

Nevertheless, performance measurement remains a dark horse, even within the financial services industry itself. Information is used internally for management and externally for marketing and client service. Its functions are sometimes located in the accounting department, sometimes in the analysis department, and sometimes absent altogether. Everyone knows what the performance department does, but few outside the process can articulate the work required to produce performance reports. This is because, in part, performance is a relatively new profession. As such, it is growing in complexity year by year. With this in mind, it is not surprising that performance measurement is often overlooked in the software development process. More frequently, performance functionality is typically designed as an "add-on" to the core investment and accounting system, once demand justifies the development (or marketing needs a new product to tout). Such approaches often result in inadequate performance systems, not because of a lack of domain knowledge, but because of the development constraints imposed by the core accounting or investment system.

Performance analysis is typically performed at four major levels, referred to as "performance levels." In order of decreasing data granularity they are

- Security lot (transaction): the lot or transaction level specifies performance for an individual security in a portfolio.
- Asset class: a group of like securities, such as stocks, bonds, and cash. It is a mutually exclusive aggregate of securities.
- Portfolio: sometimes called an account, the portfolio level is usually specified based on investment objective.
- Composite: used primarily for reporting purposes, the composite level is an aggregate of asset classes, portfolios, or both.

In addition, performance measurement has three general areas:

Absolute performance comparison — Comparative performance involves calculating rates of returns for each lot, asset class, portfolio, and composite. The rates of return are then evaluating against a predetermined benchmark. It is a first approximation of whether investment objectives are being met.

Risk-adjusted or relative performance evaluation — Risk-adjusted performance involves evaluating a historical return against the volatility (variance or standard deviations) of those returns. This is a measure of performance stability and consistency. Benchmarks are also used in this process. This is the most valuable type of performance measurement and analysis to the client or prospect of an investment manager.

Performance attribution analysis — Performance attribution involves using statistical techniques to allocate a historical return to specific, predefined security characteristics such as duration, convexity, yield curve, credit risk, and market capitalization. It is also used to determine if rates of return were gained via security selection, market timing, or foreign currency return. With this information, managers can more precisely evaluate their investment strategies and decisions.

When implementing a large-scope performance system, it makes sense to do so in phases. However, design considerations for each area specified above must be addressed at the outset, even if certain functionality will be deferred to a later development effort. However, prior to designing system architecture, the data elements, business rules, and functional requirements must first be specified.

FUNCTIONALITY REQUIRED IN A COMPREHENSIVE SYSTEM

Ultimately, good performance software design is about flexible design and building high user confidence. While the information needs and requirements for firms within the financial services industry may be similar, the way firms acquire, process, and distribute that information can vary widely. Stated differently, user-specific requirements can be addressed either during the design of the product or when the package is integrated into the firm's operations. Selecting the latter approach is akin to asserting that the product's design and technical implementation are well suited to such a migration. For mass-produced software packages, this is a bit unrealistic. And when money is involved, users must be able to trust the systems on which their firm or its clients depend.

In truth, the purpose of investing is to earn a rate of return. From this admittedly simple perspective, performance takes on added importance, and ideally should not be worked in on top of existing systems. Integrating performance measurement functionality with the rest of the development process will at least identify, if not alleviate, the constraints imposed by the core investment accounting system. When this approach is not practical, there are features which can increase the versatility of the performance system without risking data integrity and disrupting process flow. With this in mind, the following list proposes several key functional requirements, in descending order of importance:

User-defined reporting — In particular, the ability to create reports that will assist in the reconciliation of a calculated and reported value to its components is paramount. Typically, "canned" reports are sufficient to provide commonly used information. However, report writer capability at the user's fingertips serves to integrate an otherwise "off-the-shelf" package into the operating procedures of the company using the software. Ideally, the firm should be able to report from an ODBC-compliant database.

Adequate validation tools — The ability to quickly identify accounts with abnormal values is essential. This can be done by setting variance tolerances at the system or account level, and by reporting portfolios, asset classes, or securities with returns that lie outside a specified standard deviation from the mean. Robust systems will identify when and which individual components of the return formula exceed user-specified parameters.

Ability to monitor changes to the components of current and historical performance values via an audit trail — This requirement is an acknowledgment that systems break, people make mistakes, and incorrect information finds its way into an otherwise clean process. Changes to historical information will occur and will affect performance. The volume of data and reporting time pressures necessitate an automated mechanism to detect such corrections *at the time of occurrence.* If the performance system cannot automatically post updates resulting from such corrections, then the appropriate level of maintenance is a record of the change that was made along with affected values and processes. This is necessary not only for changes to the accounting data, but for changes to the performance data if direct edits to those data are permissible.

Performance comparison, risk-adjusted analysis, and attribution at the security lot, asset class, portfolio, and composite level, for any time period — Regardless of the performance formula used, the user should be able to get the return for any given measurement period and granularity. The implication is that the components to calculate returns exist in the performance database, and that the user may choose the desired processing and reporting frequency without being limited by the database architecture.

User-defined performance classifications — Asset class categories in portfolio management are primarily based on common security characteristics. The degree of detail for each classification or subclassification is a function of the portfolio manager's judgment, strategy, and style. Consequently, proper evaluation of portfolio performance requires that the end user define the individual categories within the asset class level of performance. Lack of flexibility in this respect provides only marginally beneficial information for the end user. Another related requirement involves the ability to blend individual market indices into a benchmark that will match the portfolio's investment objective.

Flexible data delivery — Paper presentation is becoming archaic. The Internet is becoming the Gutenberg printing press of the twentieth century, and the trend for "information at your fingertips" will find its way into the realm of performance measurement. In addition to the traditional paper and direct connect data delivery methods, database architecture should accommodate FTP, web server, and e-mail delivery. Web-based delivery will likely dominate the market. Initially, firms will post performance results for distribution via the Internet or intranet for consumption by their clients or investment management departments. This method, as with other online presentations, should permit "drill down" capability through the performance levels, and temporal drill-down evaluation within each performance level.

Though the technology industry is quick to implement these methods of information transfer, their acceptance by the financial services industry will be slow. Conversions, upgrades, and systems migrations are lengthy processes in large firms. Smaller firms face budget constraints that typically result in acquiring new software only when technology or growth demands it. Even so, firms need only an e-mail connection and a simple, customized, browser package to take advantage of a hypertext file sent via e-mail to simulate push technology. The most sophisticated vendors of performance data will utilize true push and pull technology, with the latter being used for firms with highly specialized data acquisition and performance reporting needs.

Technological advances in information storage and delivery will place the practice of performance measurement into a conflict between sound investment policy and client expectations. Modern Portfolio Theory asserts that performance measurement is a long-term process.[3] Despite that, the combined effect of reduced processing time, cheap data storage, and information-on-demand will be that investors will be able to view returns at will, evaluate their performance, and then examine several different proposed investment scenarios in reaction to their current position and prespecified market assumptions. Though such actions are regarded as inappropriate in many academic circles, performance software vendors should prepare to face this demand, particularly in the individual investor market.

Import/export utility — Few accounting, performance, and investment systems are able to seamlessly interface with other software packages. Yet data will inevitably need to be ported from place to place when an integrated system is not employed, or when stand-alone systems lack interoperability. The ability for the user (with technical assistance) to define single and multiline record formats for data import and export alleviates this persistent problem. Also, such a utility facilitates the conversion from one performance system to another. The ability to easily transfer historically reported data from a legacy system can be a major selling point for newer systems.

Likewise, universe comparison data (such as benchmark indices) are often provided by numerous vendors. These data must be stored uniformly within the performance system database architecture, and a customized field mapping import facility makes this routine function less burdensome for the user.

A third application is the importing of return data for asset classes that are absent from the security models used by the accounting application. In the process of portfolio management, it is important to evaluate the performance of *all* assets under management, not just the traditional securities in your investment accounting systems. Direct population of performance tables through the import of such data ensures that performance reporting is comprehensive.

Customized calculations using stored component information — Each firm's techniques for financial management will vary, and certain additional calculations may be required to accommodate their operations. This is particularly important when internal performance metrics are dependent on the choice of accounting basis (calculation of "book yield" for example).

DATA CONSIDERATIONS

To begin, the basic components of the return formula must be identified. There are numerous formulas for calculating and analyzing rates of return. However, they all use the same components:

- Realized and unrealized capital gains and losses.
- Income accrued and received.
- Buy and sell transactions.
- Transfers, contributions, and withdrawals.
- Market index values or rates of return.
- The associated dates for each data element.

Porting these data to the performance system will largely be a function of the accounting database architecture, or the data file supplied by an external accounting system. Beginning and ending period balances are often used, though this is primarily a function of the return formula chosen. Also, classification of each security's reporting asset class through the security master table is necessary in order to construct meaningful performance reports. The basic performance flows typically come from three sources: the security master file, the accounting transaction database, and the market price history database.

There are several additional reporting requirements: portfolio returns may be reported without a cash component or with a cash component. This is not as simple as it sounds, because the industry definition of "with cash returns" is counterintuitive: cash returns are not reported separately, but are allocated to those of other existing asset classes. AIMR's Performance Presentation Standards identify at least two algorithms for allocating cash returns to those of other asset classes.[4]

There are at least four other additional variations to standard rate of return calculation and reporting:

- Inclusion or exclusion of management fees.
- Inclusion or exclusion of tax effects.
- Inclusion of derivatives and leverage on a hedged and cash basis.
- Inclusion or exclusion of the effects of foreign exchange.

Once the lot performance table has been generated, additional functionality is relatively simple. The lot data can be summarized in asset class and portfolio tables, and these in turn can be summarized into a composite table. Risk-adjusted and attribution performance functionality can be implemented relatively easily with only minor modifications to the existing data tables to create the necessary additional links and associations, though the complexity of the attribution model may necessitate a few additional tables.

In packaged software products, it's important to keep the product functionally scaleable. Not all users will require attribution. Some may require tax performance analysis but not foreign currency performance analysis. "Add-in" functionality, commonly found in spreadsheet programs, is an effective means of marketing a single, modular product to firms with varying degrees of sophistication.

Database Structure and Required Data Tables

Performance database structure is fundamentally a function of the accounting system design. Typical tables include the Security Master, Lot Holdings Master, Accounting Basis Master (if tax information is required), Transaction History, Market History, and Foreign Currency Table, as shown in Exhibit 2.

The data from these tables are used to create the "performance flows" and populate the performance tables at each level of granularity. Separately, index and universe comparison data are stored. In some designs it will be possible to store the index data with the market price history data. The four performance data tables, in conjunction with the index and benchmark tables, represent the source for the creation of a data dictionary from which nearly all necessary reports can be generated.

Return Formula Selection

There are several formulas used by industry to calculate a rate of return.[4] When performance measurement systems began to be developed in earnest in the early 1990s, many designers chose to implement the Modified

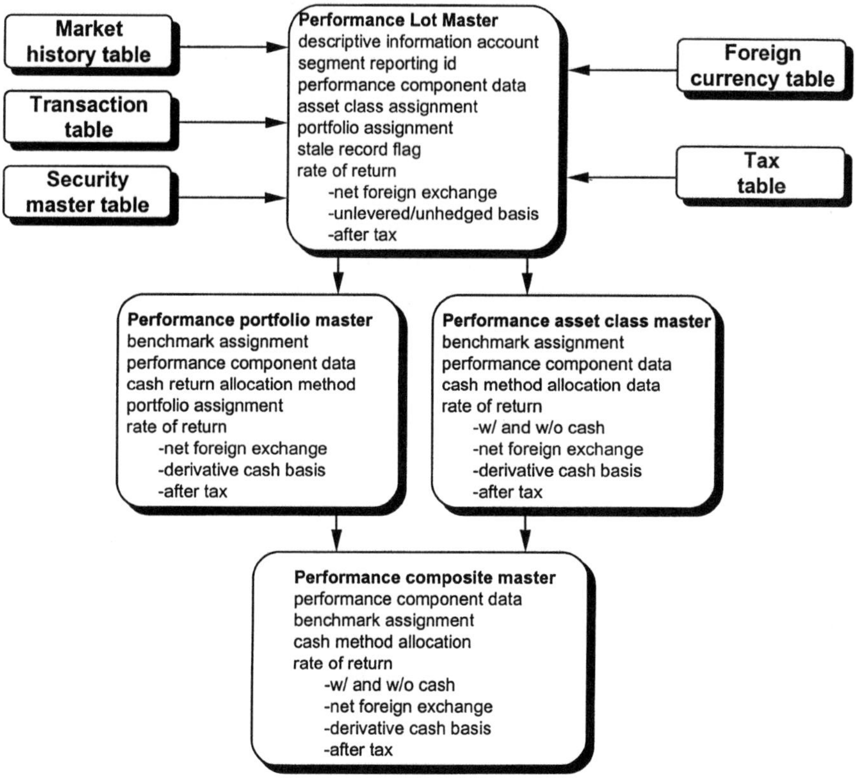

Exhibit 2. A typical accounting system design.

Dietze method and formula for "total time-weighted estimates of return" calculations. The rationale, presumably, was that this formula was the most suitable to the nature of software and database design. The formula required predefined measurement periods and so was suited to monthly or quarterly returns generation. The Modified BAI method is similar in its component requirements, but requires an iterative solution, making it unattractive from a hardware performance standpoint, especially when transactions volume is large. The Modified Dietze method, however, offered reduced computation time and data storage requirements because it meant that there was only one record per security per measurement period.

Unfortunately, the Modified Dietze and Modified BAI methods both have certain mathematical limitations that can complicate processing requirements,[5] and neither formula is simple to reconcile or explain to clients. Recently, the industry has begun to move to a daily pricing standard, making the Modified Dietze and Modified BAI formulas obsolete. Yet there is little reason to fear that newer systems will have difficulty adhering to this standard. The components of return for the daily valuation formula are essentially the same for each of the time-weighted estimate formulas, making a database conversion more manageable. Additionally, faster processing speeds and cheaper data storage will mitigate the technological constraints that drove earlier designs.

Storing Return Data: Bane or Blessing?

Unlike most other aspects of the financial management process, performance measurement requires an ever-growing store of historical data. As stated earlier, when the investment accounting data change, performance reports are affected. Many systems will not store rates of return for this reason. The argument is that by calculating returns "on the fly" any performance return reported will always be up-to-date, and that storage space can be reduced. This is predominant in large systems that handle volume transactions. The trade-off is that reporting becomes a more time-consuming process.

There are several reasons why rate of return data should be stored:

1. Reporting a return is done far more frequently than calculating it (theoretically, the return is calculated only once). Thus it would make sense to store the calculated value, increasing processing time up front but reducing it for the more commonly used retrieval procedures.
2. The rate of return is a summary of the underlying transaction information, which admittedly is subject to change. But storing performance returns along with the associated performance components facilitates external reconciliation and validation of the formulas and methodologies used by the system. This, in turn, serves to bolster user confidence in the system's internal calculation and processing methods.
3. Data storage is cheap and storage processes can be batch-processed in time of low-volume data traffic.
4. Data delivery options cannot be limited to paper output. Warehousing return data expands data delivery options to numerous online and web-based applications. Over time, it also provides an in-house data mine for analytic investment research.

There is of course a drawback to comprehensive data warehousing, since performance data are as much a function of time as are the underlying accounting and performance flows. If returns are stored, then changes to historical flow data must trigger recalculation of all subsequent return information, as shown in Exhibit 3.

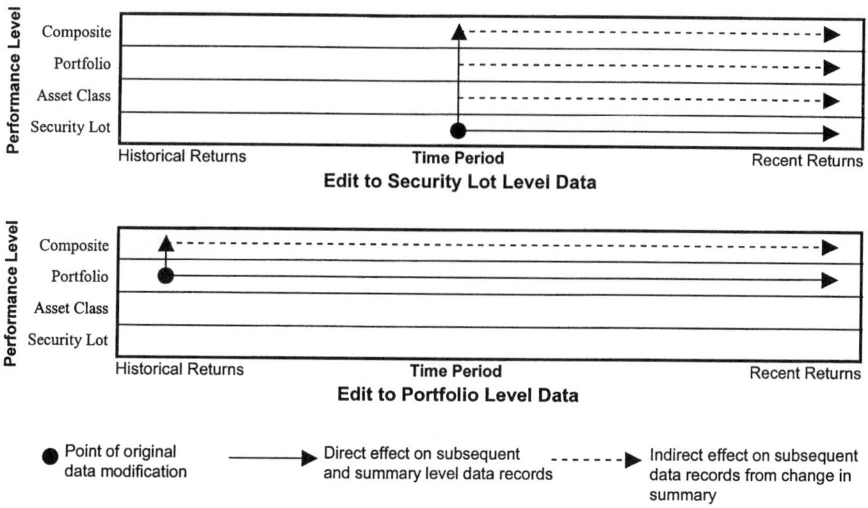

Edits to detail data records will affect higher level summary records. All edits will affect return records subsequent to the effective date of the edit.

Exhibit 3. Effect of historical changes on existing data records.

There are at least two possible methods for handling this difficulty. The first is to identify a materiality threshold. An example is by comparing the dollar amount of the change of the flow to its beginning value. User-specified *de minimus* exceptions will filter out trivial but common corrections to account transactions.

An additional approach is to build a "performance wall," behind which data cannot be modified, as shown in Exhibit 4. The term "wall" is a misnomer. In fact, historical data are deleted because they are included in the summary-level calculations and records. Records at the lot level are short lived. But in some cases, corrections to transactions may occur up to a year later, so these records will persist for some time. A satisfactory lot-level performance wall is 6 to 24 months. Performance walls for summary-level data are longer. Composite records, and arguably portfolio and asset class records, can be kept indefinitely, since these records will represent a small fraction of the entire database.

Similar data management techniques can and should be used for market price history and index data. However, the summation level is temporal: after the data has aged for a period of 6 months, daily records are discarded and only monthly records are retained.

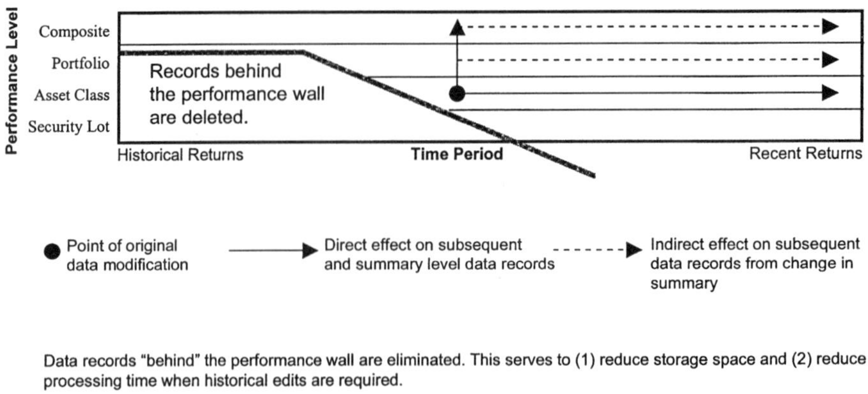

Exhibit 4. Managing database changes with a performance wall.

COMPLIANCE ISSUES

The financial services industry is heavily regulated. In addition to the Securities and Exchange Commission and state regulatory agencies, the industry is rife with self-regulating organizations such as AIMR, the National Association of Securities Dealers, and the Investment Management Consultants' Association. And there are myriad regulations from foreign jurisdictions that are probably unknown to most U.S. software developers. As investing practices continue to expand globally, firms will find themselves subject to even more constraints, particularly when it comes to reporting achieved investment results in overseas markets.

Determining the appropriate level of rule validation is a dilemma for any software package intended for use in a regulated industry. The assumption by developers is that regulation within an industry is uniform. In fact, it is not, particularly when a firm falls under a regulator's remedial action plan. Regulatory considerations that are "hard coded" into software can cause more headaches than benefits. Inevitably there are always a handful of users who, for whatever reason, require the system's functionality but do not need to comply with the regulatory rules, or have had additional rules imposed upon them by enforcement agencies.

It is important to emphasize that software does not and can not comply with such regulations. Performance rules, in particular, set standards for firms and individuals, not software. But complete understanding of these relatively new rules is not yet widespread, and the tendency for firms to market their performance software as "in compliance" with a set of standards (particularly the AIMR Performance Presentation Standards™) is great.

There are several risks when aligning a system with a set of industry regulations or the standards of a rule-making body:

1. The rules may be interpreted or enforced differently by different firms or agencies (as is the case in the insurance industry).
2. The validations implemented to enforce the rules may be inadequate or incorrect.
3. The functionality implemented to enforce the rules may be a hindrance to those users not subject to the rules, or to those who wish to obtain performance metrics for internal purposes.
4. Rules change, and developers are committed to accommodating these changes in the software.
5. Embedded regulatory functionality requires added education and support for users who are unfamiliar with such compliance standards.

For these reasons, firms acquiring performance software should be wary of claims of software compliance with specific industry standards. Typically, the database structure at initial implementation was not designed around multiple compliance issues, and thus the required data simply have not been recorded. Again, design limitations of the associated investment accounting system make it unlikely that any performance package is the perfect regulatory solution. Software is a tool, and as such, the emphasis and evaluation of a system should be made as to its *ability to assist* the firm in meeting its compliance obligations.

CONCLUSION

Designing an investment performance application involves much more than calculating rates of return. It is about understanding information flow and use in a dynamic process. Performance measurement data are consumed internally and externally: as a quantitative measure in the investment analysis and policy setting process, as a product to clients, as marketing material to prospects, and in some cases as a remuneration tool where performance-based compensation is used.

Identifying how the information will be applied will guide users and developers in prioritizing the functional requirements suggested above, with the result being a system that will be adaptable to the most common business and technological needs.

In the financial services industry, there is a well-known saying, "Some people work for their money, others have their money work for them." If you replace the word "money" with the word "technology," the goal of competitive and efficient performance systems design becomes clear.

Notes

1. Simpson, J. D., European economic and monetary union, its impact on portfolio management and performance measurement systems, *J. Perform. Meas.,* 2(1), 5, 1997.
2. For an overview of the performance measurement process and calculations, see Spalding, D., *Measuring Investment Performance,* McGraw-Hill, New York, 1997.
3. Ellis, C. D., *Investment Policy,* 2nd ed., Irwin, Chicago, 1993, pp. 64–70.
4. See *AIMR Performance Presentation Standards Handbook,* 2nd ed., Association for Investment Management and Research, Charlottesville, VA. 1007; *Performance Reporting for Investment Managers.*
5. Revaluation at a performance period mid-point and subsequent recalculations is one such consideration.

Section II
Technology Trends in Financial Services

IN SPITE OF THE RAPID PACE OF CHANGE, there are some things that must stay the same. One of these is the stringent standards of developing systems within the financial services community.

It might be because it's so heavily regulated, or maybe it's because the technologists that are attracted to it are so darn good, but the systems developed by financial services companies are some of the best in the world. Although quite complex (just try to figure out how to program a hedge fund), accountability and auditability are routinely programmed into financial services systems.

When I began working at the New York Stock Exchange in the early 1980s it was not uncommon to find extensive R&D technology departments up and down Wall Street. Here, the best and the brightest were experimenting with the tools that are routinely being used today. Using Dragon's Naturally Speaking on your PC? Well back in the very early 1980s the Exchange was already experimenting with voice recognition on the Floor. Using Natural Language to structure a query to a database? Back in the early 1980s RAMIS, a 4GL, had a Natural Language interface that was routinely being used by regulators at the Exchange.

But these were primitive first implementations of technologies that have since grown up. As Henry Seiler explains in Chapter 12, business rules represent the codified policies and decision-making practices of an organization. Historically, business rules have been coded directly in the program logic of an application. Today, the terms *business rules* and *knowledge management* are used to describe the isolation of business policies and decisions from application logic. That the financial services community has endorsed the concept of codifying business rules is very much in evidence in Chapter 14. Here you'll find out how the *avant-garde* of the industry created systems, known as expert systems, that were the precursors of most of the intelligent systems used on the Street today.

These systems permit those in banking, insurance, and securities to access such things as customer profiling, geographic information systems, personal financial appliances, and even computer systems that can build themselves. All of these topics are covered in this section.

Even though we're moving squarely into the realm of Web-based interfaces to corporate information systems, these systems need to exhibit the same high standard of quality as conventionally developed systems. That's something that most folks forget in this era of visual and easy-to-use development tools. Towards that end I've included a rather lengthy chapter on total quality (Chapter 6) that covers everything from the meaning of quality, to Deming's 14 quality points, to a ton of techniques and formulas that you can use to improve both quality and productivity in your own shop.

Jody Lyon in Chapter 13 asserts that in order to stay ahead financial services companies are turning to decision support solutions to help identify and manage their customer relationships. Solutions such as data warehouses or data marts provide a solid foundation of accurate information upon which they can base their decisions. Accuracy is one of the biggest obstacles blocking the success of many data warehousing projects, hence Chapters 6 and 13 are "must-reads."

Even if you're using a Total Quality approach to system development it doesn't mean that your systems are error free or even functioning properly. In this section I take the opportunity to promote one of the most novel methodologies to come along in a long time. "Development Before the Fact," discussed at length in Chapter 24, is a radical departure from any of the techniques that have come before it. Born of the Apollo and Skylab missions where software is man-rated (meaning that its failure can cause human harm or even death), the "Development Before the Fact" methodology, in this era of distributed integration of systems, is something that financial services managers will be intrigued with.

Finally, given the preponderance of financial services companies that have moved onto the Web it's wise to find out what's legal and what's not. Frederic M. Wilf, Esq., has graciously provided us with thousands of dollars worth of free legal advice (Chapter 26) — advice that every manager needs to take before embarking on a Web development project.

J. Keyes

Chapter 6

The "Must-Have" Guide to Total Quality for the Financial Services Manager

Jessica Keyes

IN TRACY KIDDER'S LANDMARK BOOK *SOUL OF A NEW MACHINE,* he details the riveting story of a project conducted at breakneck speed, and under incredible pressure. Driven by pure adrenaline, the team members soon became obsessed with trying to achieve the impossible. For more than a year, they gave up their nights and weekends — in the end logging nearly 100 hours a week each! Somewhere buried in the midst of Kidder's prose we find that at the end of this project the entire staff quit. Not just one or two of them, but every single one!

The Financial Services field is rife with stories such as this one. Software development projects are usually complex and often mission-critical. As a result the pressure on staff to produce is great. And sometimes, as in the Kidder example, even with success comes failure.

Successful software development projects (i.e., get the product done on time — and *not* lose staff members) have something in common. Each of these projects, in some way, shape, or form, followed one or more principles of quality and productivity. Some of these principles are clearly intuitive. But most are learned or culled from vast experience over a number of years and projects.

In today's competitive environment, Information Technology (IT) is a major partner with the business units. And because of this the push is on

0-8493-9991-2/99/$0.00+$.50

for enhanced software productivity and quality. In addition, the Y2K, Dow 1000, and Eurodollar crises has put a renewed emphasis on quality and productivity — often with the legal department looking over IT's shoulder. Let's face it, intuition just won't cut the mustard any longer. Nor can an organization wait until software developers learn their quality lessons over so many projects in as many years.

This chapter has condensed several decades worth of quality studies into a few brief pages. Here you'll find everything from formulas to measure productivity to measures to take to enforce stringent quality goals. Putting some of these guidelines and techniques into your bag of tricks will improve not only the quality of your software, the productivity of your staff, but the company's bottom well too.

THE MEANING OF QUALITY

Although quality and productivity are foremost on the minds of management, few truly understand how to correlate the tenets of quality to the process of information technology.

Total Quality Management, or TQM as it has come to be known, was actually born as a result of a loss of competitive edge to countries such as Japan. In fact, the father of TQM, W. E. Deming, finding no forum for his radical new ideas on quality in the U.S., found eager listeners in Japan. Today, Deming's 14 points on quality, listed in the next section, are considered the basis for all work on quality in this country as well as Japan.

But Deming's studies were only the start of a flood of research in the field. For example, Y. K. Shetty, a professor of management at Utah State University's College of Business and the co-editor of *The Quest for Competitiveness* (Quorum Books, 1991), suggests that even though most corporate executives believe that quality and productivity are the most critical issues facing American business, many do not know how to achieve it. Shetty lists 16 organizations that have vigorously attacked this challenge: Catepillar, Dana Corp., Delta, Dow Chemical, General Electric, Hewlett-Packard, IBM, Intel, Johnson & Johnson, Marriott, Maytag, McDonald's, Procter and Gamble, Texas Instruments, 3M, and Xerox.

What Shetty found was that these organizations shared some characteristics in common. He refers to these as the Seven Principles of Quality.[1]

Principle 1 — Quality improvement requires the firm commitment of top management. All top management, including the CEO, must be personally committed to quality. The keyword here is personally. Many CEOs pay only lip service to this particular edit. Therefore, top management must be consistent and reflect its commitment through the company's philosophy, goals, policies, priorities, and executive behavior. Steps management can take to accomplish this end include: establish and communicate a clear vision of corporate philosophy, principles, and objectives relevant to product and service quality; channel resources toward these objectives and define roles and responsibilities in this endeavor; invest time to learn about quality issues and monitor the progress of any initiatives; encourage communication between management and employees, among departments, and among various units of the firm and customers; and be a good role model in communication and action.

Principle 2 — Quality is a strategic issue. It must be a part of a company's goals and strategies and be consistent with and reinforce a company's other strategic objectives. It must also be integrated into budgets and plans and be a corporate mission with planned goals and strategies. Finally, quality should be at the heart of every action.

Principle 3 — Employees are the key to consistent quality. The organization must have a people-oriented philosophy. Poorly managed people convey their disdain for quality and service when they work. It is important to pay special attention to employee recruitment, selection, and socialization and to reinforce the socialization and quality process with continuous training and education. It is also a good idea to incorporate quality into performance appraisal and reward systems and to encourage employee participation and involvement. Effective communication throughout the department, between department, and throughout the organization is required to reinforce the deep commitment of management and creates an awareness and understanding of the role of quality and customer service.

Principle 4 — Quality standards and measurements must be customer driven. It can be measured by:

- Formal customer surveys
- Focus groups
- Customer complaints
- Quality audits
- Testing panels
- Statistical quality controls
- Interaction with customers

Principle 5 — Many programs and techniques can be used to improve quality, such as:

- Statistical quality control
- Quality circles
- Suggestion systems
- Quality-of-work-life projects
- Competitive benchmarking

Principle 6 — All company activities have potential for improving product quality; therefore teamwork is vital. Quality improvement requires close cooperation between managers and employees and among departments. Total quality management involves preventing errors at the point where work is performed, and ultimately every employee and department is responsible for quality.

Principle 7 — Quality is a never-ending process.

- Quality must be planned
- Quality must be organized
- Quality must be monitored
- Quality must be continuously revitalized

TQM METHODOLOGIES

Since early TQM programs were largely manufacturing oriented, IT researchers, academicians, and consulting firms were required to interpret and extrapolate TQM tenets and create quality paradigms that could be used to significant advantage. As a result, there is no single TQM methodology in use today that has garnered wholesale industry acceptance. All of these methodologies, however, are based on TQM tenets and all, if used properly, will provide organizations with a clear path towards better quality in their systems.

Be warned though, one size does not fit all. In a report by the New York City think tank, American Quality Foundation, the notion was challenged that quality programs were universally beneficial for all organizations. Based on a study of 584 firms in North America, Japan, and Germany, the report noted that TQM practices are not generic. What works for some organizations may well turn out to be detrimental to the performance of others.

The Problem with Quality

Information technologists have long realized that there was something askew. Deadlines were often stretched, more and more money was being poured into never-ending development projects, and an ever-larger percentage of the budget was being allocated to maintenance to fix problems that should never have occurred in the first place. According to oft-published statistics of all software projects with over 64,000 lines of code, 25% failed to deliver anything, 60% were significantly over budget and behind schedule, and only 1% finished on time, on budget, and met user requirements. In the fall of 1997, I personally surveyed over 500 managers in charge of large, complex systems. Only 10% of those surveyed indicated that they had delivered their project on time, within budget, and with less than a 5% error rate. This is particularly true in financial services systems where the pace of change is rapid and the complexity of systems is increasing.

The Systems Engineering Institute (SEI) at Carnegie-Mellon University has developed a five-level framework — shown in the next section — that can be used to assess the quality of the software development process in an organization. It is disheartening to note that SEI has determined that over 86% of the companies assessed fall in Stage 1, while only 1% of firms achieve Stage 5.

It comes as no surprise, therefore, that the majority of software development projects are late, over budget, and out of specification. Project managers point to a number of technical problems, most of which are related to technical tasks specific to software development.

Understanding the symptoms of the quality problem is the first step in recovery. The most common reasons given by project managers for failure to meet budget, time scale, and specifications are these:

Incomplete and ambiguous requirements
Incomplete and imprecise specifications
Difficulties in modeling systems
Uncertainties in cost and resource estimation
General lack of visibility
Difficulties with progress monitoring
Complicated error and change control
Lack of agreed metrics
Difficulties in controlling maintenance
Lack of common terminology
Uncertainties in software/hardware apportionment
Rapid changes in technology
Determining suitability of languages
Measuring and predicting reliability
Problems with interfacing
Problems with integration

Organizations auditing their systems development departments as a result of these problems find several shortcomings in how their projects are structured and managed, including:

Lack of standards
Failure to comply with existing standards
Nonadherence to model in use
No sign-off at end of states
Lack of project plans
No project control statistics recorded or stored
No quality assurance (QA) procedures
No change control procedures
No configuration control procedures
Records of test data and results not kept

Software Quality Management in Today's Environment

While total quality management and software quality management (TQM/SQM) are laudable goals, most organizations realize that these are truly long-term goals. What processes, then, can be instituted on a short-term basis to provide the organization with a short-cut to quality improvement? Redmill[2] offers us a series of quick-hit tactics:

1. *Training.* Project manager and team must be trained in TQM concepts and facilities.
2. *Management Commitment.* Must always be seen to be 100%.
3. *Standards.* A comprehensive set of standards for all aspects of work should be instituted and used. The project life cycle must be covered as well as other pertinent issues.
4. *Guidelines, Procedures and Checklists.* Assist workers to meet the standards and QA agents to check the products.
5. *Quality Assurance.* Should be carried out at all stages of the life cycle and for all end-products. The QA team should be independent of the development team and audits should be carried out during the project to ensure that management and QA procedures are being adhered to. The project manager should always initiate a review of the auditors' recommendations and of all resulting corrective actions.
6. *Planning.* The project manager should be fastidious in drawing up plans and ensuring their use for control. Plans should include the project plan, stage plans, and a quality plan, which details the quality requirements of the project.
7. *Reporting.* A reporting system, to ensure that problems are quickly escalated to the management level appropriate to the action needed, should be instituted.
8. *Feedback.* Statistics that assist in project control and the improvement of quality should be collected, analyzed, and used.
9. *Continuous Review.* The whole quality system (components, mode of operation, and quality of results) should be reviewed and improved continuously.
10. *Project Manager.* Must not be too technically involved. Technical duties should be delegated to a development team manager who reports to the project manager.
11. *Nontechnical Support Team.* Should be appointed to assist in nondevelopmental matters, including coordination and interpretation of resource and time statistics, recording all expenditures, and tracking against the budget (tracking milestone). This team should report to the project manager.

The rest of this chapter is a synopsis of what I consider to be the very best of techniques and/or ideas that financial services IT managers can use for boosting quality in their development efforts. The ideas are something to mull over.

SEI'S SOFTWARE PROCESS MATURITY FRAMEWORK

The Software Engineering Institute at Carnegie-Mellon University is the bulwark of engineering productivity research. In their studies of thousands of firms they've discovered some common characteristics that can be used to pinpoint how progressive a firm is in terms of its maturity in the quest for productivity and quality.

The five levels of process maturity are outlined below.

Stage 1: Initial
  Ad hoc
  Little formalization
  Tools informally applied to the process

Key Actions to Get to Next Step:
  Initiate rigorous project management, management review, and quality assurance

Stage 2: Repeatable
  Achieved a stable process with a repeatable level of statistical control

Key Actions to Get to Next Step:
  Establish a process group
  Establish a software development process architecture
  Introduce software engineering methods and technologies

Stage 3: Defined
  Achieved foundation for major and continuing progress

Key Actions to Get to Next Step:
  Establish a basic set of process managements to identify quality and cost parameters
  Establish a process database; gather and maintain process data
  Assess relative quality of each product and inform management

Stage 4: Managed
  Substantial quality improvements
  Comprehensive process measurement

Key Actions to Get to Next Step:
  Support automatic gathering of process data
  Use data to analyze and modify the process

Stage 5: Optimized
  Major quality and quantity improvements

Key Actions to Get to Next Step:
Continue improvement and optimization of the process

Productivity/Quality Metrics Checklist

There are as many metric systems as there are firms using them. I've compiled a list of those most frequently used.

- Lines of code
- Pages of documentation
- Number and size of tests
- Function count
- Variable count
- Number of modules
- Depth of nesting
- Count of changes required
- Count of discovered defects
- Count of changed lines of code
- Time to design, code, test
- Defect discovery rate by phase of development
- Cost to develop
- Number of external interfaces
- Number of tools used and why
- Reusability percentage
- Variance of schedule
- Staff years experience with team
- Staff years experience with language
- Software years experience with software tools
- MIPs per person
- Support to development personnel ratio
- Nonproject to project time ratio

Quality Factors Checklist

Quality is eminently quantifiable. In this section, I provide a ratings checklist on a 1 to 5 scale that can be used to assess the perceived quality of any delivered system.

How easy is it to use?	1	2	3	4	5
How secure is it?	1	2	3	4	5
Level of confidence in it?	1	2	3	4	5
How well does it conform to requirements?	1	2	3	4	5
How easy is it to upgrade?	1	2	3	4	5
How easy is it to change?	1	2	3	4	5
How portable is it?	1	2	3	4	5
How easy is it to locate a problem and fix?	1	2	3	4	5
Is the response time fast enough?	1	2	3	4	5
How easy is it to train staff?	1	2	3	4	5
Ease of testing?	1	2	3	4	5
Is the software efficient in terms of computing resources?	1	2	3	4	5
Ease of coupling this system to another?	1	2	3	4	5
Does the system utilize the minimum storage possible?	1	2	3	4	5
Is the system self-descriptive?	1	2	3	4	5
Does the system exhibit modularity?	1	2	3	4	5

Is there a program for ongoing quality awareness for all employees?	1 2 3 4 5
Do you check supplier quality?	1 2 3 4 5
Is there a quality department?	1 2 3 4 5
Is this the "right" system to be developed?	1 2 3 4 5

Rubin[3] Measurement Assessment Questions

Howard Rubin, a professor of Computer Science at Hunter College and a principal of Rubin Associates of Pound Ridge, NY uses the following questionnaire to assess an organization's ability to manifest change. Responses are based on a sliding scale of 1 to 5.

1. How intense is the organization's desire to improve its performance?
   (0) No Desire (5) Intense
2. How much is the organization willing to invest to improve its performance?
   (0) $0 (5) Up to $100,000 per professional
3. What is the current level of the systems skills inventory in regard to software engineering?
   (0) Abstractions and models not used at all (5) Formalization and models used by all
4. To what extent are basic software engineering concepts known and understood by the systems staff?
   (0) No staff has been exposed (5) 100% trained
5. Is the systems culture adverse to using new tools, techniques, or innovations?
   (0) 100% against (5) Anxious to implement
6. To what extent is a support structure in place to foster measurement software engineering technology transfer?
   (0) None (5) In-place team of critical mass exists
7. What is the current software engineering platform?
   (0) Dumb terminals (5) Client-server workstations

Rubin's[3] Questions About Management Practices

It is necessary to take a long, hard look at the organization's infrastructure in terms of management practices.

1. How are planning and prioritizing done?
2. How does the organization translate requests into systems?
3. How defined is the systems development life cycle?
4. What is in the organization's tool inventory and what is actually used? (Tool penetration.)
5. What is organization's current software process maturity level? (Perform a formal or informal SEI assessment.)

MALCOLM BALDRIDGE QUALITY AWARD RATINGS

The Malcolm Baldridge Quality Award looks at quality from a total firm perspective — IT makes up only one component. However, since IT is but a microcosm of the whole organization, the Baldridge criteria are equally applicable to IT as to the whole organization.

Rate your organization in the space provided. The maximum points you are allowed to allocate is listed to the left of the space in which you mark your award. The section level displays the maximum number of points for the entire section. For example in Section 1.0, Leadership, the maximum is 100 points distributed across its sublevels (i.e., 1.1, 1.2, etc.).

1.0 **Leadership**	100	___
1.1 Senior Executive Leadership	40	___
1.2 Quality Values	15	___
1.3 Management for Quality	25	___
1.4 Public Responsibility	20	___
2.0 **Information and Analysis**	70	___
2.1 Scope and Management of Quality Data and Information	20	___
2.2 Competitive Comparisons and Benchmarks	30	___
2.3 Analysis of Quality Data and Information	20	___
3.0 **Strategic Quality Planning**	60	___
3.1 Strategic Quality Planning Process	35	___
3.2 Quality Goals and Plans	25	___
4.0 **Human Resource Utilization**	150	___
4.1 Human Resource Management	20	___
4.2 Employee Involvement	40	___
4.3 Quality Education and Training	40	___
4.4 Employee Recognition and Performance Measurement	25	___
4.5 Employee Well-Being and Morale	25	___
5.0 **Quality Assurance of Product and Services**	140	___
5.1 Design and Introduction of Quality Products and Services	35	___
5.2 Process Quality Control	20	___
5.3 Continuous Improvement of Processes	20	___
5.4 Quality Assessment	15	___
5.5 Documentation	10	___
5.6 Business Process and Support Service Quality	20	___
5.7 Supplier Quality	20	___
6.0 **Quality Results**	180	___
6.1 Product and Service Quality Results	90	___

6.2 Business Process, Operational and Support Service Quality Results	50	___
6.3 Supplier Quality Results	40	___
7.0 Customer Satisfaction	300	___
7.1 Determining Customer Requirements and Expectations	30	___
7.2 Customer Relationship Management	50	___
7.3 Customer Service Standards	20	___
7.4 Commitment to Customers	15	___
7.5 Complaint Resolution for Quality Improvement	25	___
7.6 Determining Customer Satisfaction	20	___
7.7 Customer Satisfaction Results	70	___
7.8 Customer Satisfaction Comparison	70	___

QUICK-HIT PRODUCTIVITY RATIOS

Productivity is never easy to measure. Use the following three metrics to give you an overall feeling for productivity in your organization.

1. Raw productivity = system size/work hours
2. Delivery rate = system size/elapsed weeks
3. Defect density = number of defects/system size

Deloitte & Touche Misuses of Methodology

It probably comes as no surprise, but you can misuse as well as use any technology. The following list reflects the collected wisdom of one of the largest consulting firms.

1. "Religious Fanaticism" — This is the situation where an organization holds to the theory that there can be nothing else but the methodology. A "methodology-centric" view of the world if you'll permit the use. Such rigidity is seldom useful or productive. It also may be a symptom of other poor management practices.
2. "Bureaucracy" — Here the methodology gets wrapped up in a less-than-effective organization which adds yet another layer of protection and excuse as to why no products are produced. Using a methodology in an organization which may already have top-down communications problems and seven or more management layers between the programmers and the management will not help. It will just cause people to push more paper.
3. "The end in itself" — Very similar to (2) is the failure resulting from the total focus on the process of developing systems and not on the end results. Personnel are indoctrinated into the process and become wedded to the idea that Step "16" must come after "15" and before "17," and that every last step must be completed and documented, even when it is obvious that performing the activities

in a step will add no value to the result, or that what they are doing has no real business benefit.

4. "Using the wrong one" — This is rare but is sometimes seen. The few cases I have seen personally seem to arise because a methodology in place has failed to keep up with the times. For example, having no methods that focus on JAD or on structured testing or, trivially, a customer's methodology which still requires the use of a paper screen layout form when screen painters and prototyping provide far faster and more effective user interaction. A methodology incorporating no guidance in data modeling would be of little help in implementing a system using a modern relational database system.
5. "Lack of organizational penetration" — The most common problem is still lack of consistent use, starting with lack of commitment by management. Project leaders who get trained and start off by trying to conform will tend to fall by the wayside if not encouraged and coached to do better. In *Strategies for Software Engineering,* Martyn Ould identified "14 dilemmas of software engineering" that he concluded impeded the introduction of new techniques into organizations. Among the more notable examples of these "Catch 22s" are
   - We can't use a new method on a project until we have seen it work on other projects.
   - We could justify the use of a new method if we could quantify the costs of using it. But we use traditional methods even though we are unable to quantify the costs of using them, resulting in a continuation of the status quo and generally unreliable estimates.
   - Tools that are generally applicable are generally weak. Strong tools are very specific and therefore generally inapplicable.
   - An important feature of new methods is that they tend to be powerful in particular areas. This makes them generally inapplicable. The traditional methods are weak in all areas. This makes them generally inapplicable as well.

PRESSMAN'S[4] COMMON MANAGEMENT QUESTIONS

Roger Pressman is one of the luminaries in the field of IT. Here Roger poses some pertinent questions about the relationship between change and management.

1. *We are very set in our ways; is change really possible?* The *modus operandi* of every software development organization appears to be cast in concrete. The fact is that organizations change regularly; new tools, new people, new policies new products and applications, and even new organizational structures are commonplace in the software development community. Even if your organization is "set in its ways," a move toward a software engineering culture (and the changes it portends) is often essential for the continued production

of high-quality systems. Change is certainly possible, but only if both managers and technical staff take a systematic approach to it.

2. *We're going a million miles an hour, how can we make the time?* This question is often asked by managers of young, high-technology companies that are growing at a precipitous rate, or in large, well-established companies that are experiencing a significant growth in software demand. It is true that rapid growth stretches resources to their limit. But it is also true that rapid growth exacerbates any underlying software development problems that do exist. The need for change becomes more important.
3. *OK, we have to change, what do we do first?* If this question is asked, the first thing has already been done — the speaker has recognized that change is required. Once the decision to change has been made, many managers and most technical people feel that immediate action is necessary. Although a "bias for action" is commendable, the road to a new software engineering culture must be viewed as a journey with many steps. Before beginning the journey, you must understand where you are now. Understanding your current "location" is the first thing that you should do.
4. *We've worked hard to develop internal standards and procedures, isn't that enough?* Although standards and procedures can help to guide technological change, they are not enough. Many software development organizations have fallen into an "S & P trap." That is, they have expended time and resources developing voluminous standards and procedures documents that few staff members understand or use. Just because an approach to software development has been codified does not guarantee that it will be followed.
5. *Should technological change be driven from the top down or from the bottom up?* When successful technological change occurs, it usually occurs in a way that might best be called a "sandwich." Senior management establishes goals and provides resources, driving the process from the top down. At the same time, technical staff obtain education and apply methods and tools driving the process from the bottom up. Both meet in the middle.
6. *Software engineering requires a new approach and a substantial learning curve, won't this cause upheaval?* It is true that cultural change can cause upheaval if it is not managed properly. Therefore, our primary goal in implementing change is to do it in a manner that does not negatively impact the progress of ongoing projects. In a later section we discuss a strategy for implementing change that will minimize upheaval while at the same time having a reasonable likelihood of success.
7. *What about project managers, won't they resist?* If software engineering is viewed as a destabilizing influence, project managers will resist it. To gain the support of project managers, we must look at

software engineering from their point of view and ask the question: "What's in it for me?" The answer is simple — control. Software engineering procedures, methods, and tools will improve the manager's ability to control a project, something that every manager desires. Once the project manager recognizes this benefit, resistance will disappear.

8. *Money is always tight, how do I get resource commitment from management?* Too many requests for resources (to be allocated to software engineering transition) continue to use the "trust me" school of justification. That is, a request for resources attempts to sell middle and senior management on the overall qualitative benefits of new software engineering technology without translating these benefits to the bottom line. Although this approach sometimes works, it is being viewed with increasing skepticism by many senior managers. For this reason, it is necessary to develop concrete measures of the software development process and establish an historical baseline that will enable quantitative justification to be made.
9. *Why can't we just buy some good CASE (computer-aided software engineering) tools and leave the rest alone?* Any power tool can be a wonderful thing. Whether you are cutting wood, washing dishes, or building computer software, a power tool can improve the quality of your work and the productivity with which you do it. But this is true only if you understand the methods and procedures that must be applied to properly use the tool. If a power tool is used without an understanding of underlying procedures and methods, it can be both unproductive and even dangerous. Most of us wouldn't use a large chain-saw without first understanding the procedures and methods that guide its use. Few people would attempt to wash socks in a dishwasher. Yet, many software developers attempt to use sophisticated CASE tools with little more than a passing understanding of software engineering methods and procedures. Then, they wonder why "these tools don't work for us."

BOULDIN'S[5] QUESTIONS TO ASCERTAIN READINESS FOR TECHNOLOGICAL CHANGE

In *Agents of Change*, Bouldin lists the following criteria as benchmarks for readiness for technological change.

1. Is your organization newly formed?
2. Are the functions your organization performs new to your organization?
3. Is your organization growing at a reasonably rapid rate?
4. Is your organization responsible for the development of new systems?
5. Is there a general attitude of optimism, and is morale high?

6. Are your technical staff utilizing tools or methods that improve productivity?
7. Does your management support the concept of productivity in any way?
8. Is staff experiencing motivation problems?
9. Is your staff responsible for mature systems that are primarily in the maintenance mode?
10. Does your organization have a backlog of user (or customer) requests?

COOPERS & LYBRAND QUANTITATIVE MEASUREMENT SYSTEM

Coopers & Lybrand uses the following measurement system to gauge the predictability, business impact, appropriateness, reliability, and adaptability of any system.

Issue: Predictability
- Attribute: Schedule
  - Metric: Deviation from estimated number of elapsed weeks
- Attribute: Effort
  - Metric: Deviation from estimated number of hours per phase
  - Metric: Deviation from estimated number of rework hours per phase
- Attribute: Cost
  - Metric: Deviation from estimated number of hours × cost per phase
  - Metric: Deviation from estimated number of rework hours × cost per phase

Issue: Business Impact
- Attribute: Time to market
  - Metric: Number of elapsed weeks
  - Metric: Deviation from schedule
- Attribute: Cost savings
  - Metric: Personnel cost savings
  - Metric: Hardware, software, and facility cost savings
  - Metric: Cost of quality savings
  - Metric: Turnaround time
- Attribute: Customer satisfaction
  - Metric: Turnaround time
  - Metric: Number of support hours
  - Metric: Number of problem reports
  - Metric: User satisfaction rating

Issue: Appropriateness
- Attribute: Satisfaction of system requirements
  - Metric: User satisfaction rating

Metric: Percentage of requirements that can be traced to code
Metric: Number of design changes
Metric: Number of perceived goals met
Metric: Number of hours spent in requirements collection
Attribute: Fitness for use
Metric: Number of prototype iterations
Attribute: Conformance to business objectives
Metric: Percentage of business objectives that can be traced to requirements
Metric: Number of design changes

Issue: Reliability
Attribute: Correctness
Metric: Number of defects
Metric: Number of rework hours × cost
Metric: Number of rework hours per process product
Attribute: Availability
Metric: Percentage of time system is up

Issue: Adaptability
Attribute: Responsiveness to changes
Metric: Number of rework hours
Metric: Problem request completion date
Attribute: User support
Metric: Number of problem reports
Metric: Percentage of problem reports completed

DEMING'S 14 QUALITY POINTS

W. E. Deming is considered the expert who got away. Ignored in the U.S., he took his ideas and headed for Japan where he was responsible for their meteoric rise in productivity, quality and competitiveness.

1. Create constancy of purpose toward improvement of product and service, with the aim to become competitive, to stay in business, and to provide jobs.
2. Adopt a new philosophy. We are in a new economic age. Western management must awaken to the challenge, must learn its responsibilities and take on leadership for change.
3. Cease dependence on inspection to achieve quality. Eliminate the need for inspection on a mass basis by building quality into the product in the first place.
4. End the practice of awarding business on the basis of the price tag. Instead, minimize total cost. Move toward a single supplier for any one item, on a long-term relationship of loyalty and trust.

5. Improve constantly and forever the system of production and service to improve quality and productivity, and thus constantly decrease costs.
6. Institute training on the job.
7. Institute leadership (see Point 12). The aim of leadership should be to help people and machines and gadgets do a better job. Leadership of management is in need of overhaul, as well as leadership of production workers.
8. Drive out fear, so that everyone may work effectively for the company,
9. Break down barriers between departments. People in research, design, sales, and production must work as a team, to foresee problems of production and use that may be encountered with the product or service.
10. Eliminate slogans, exhortations, and targets for the work force, asking for zero defects and new levels of productivity.
11. (a) Eliminate work standard (quotas) on the factory floor. Substitute leadership. (b) Eliminate management by objective. Eliminate management by numbers, numerical goals. Substitute leadership.
12. (a) Remove barriers that rob the hourly worker of his or her right to pride of workmanship. The responsibility of supervisors must be changed from sheer numbers to quality. (b) Remove barriers that rob people in management and in engineering of their right to pride of workmanship.
13. Institute a vigorous program of education and self-improvement.
14. Put everyone in the company to work to accomplish the transformation. The transformation is everybody's job.

HUMPRHEY'S[6] PRINCIPLES OF SOFTWARE PROCESS MANAGEMENT

Watts Humphrey is the father of the concept of the "software factory." Here he elucidates on the major principles of the management of the software process.

People Management

1. The professionals are the key to the programming process, and they must be intimately involved in its development and improvement.
2. Management must focus on programming defects not as personal issues but as opportunities for process improvement.

Process Support

1. Special process groups need to be established.
2. Necessary management and professional education is provided.
3. The best tools and methods are obtained and used.

Process Methodology
1. The process is formally defined.
2. Goals and measurements are established.
3. Statistical data are analyzed to identify problems and determine causes.

Process Control
1. Management practices are established to control change.
2. Periodic process assessments are conducted to monitor effectiveness and identify necessary improvements.
3. Procedures are established to certify process quality and implement corrective actions.

MOTOROLA'S SIX SIGMA DEFECT REDUCTION EFFORT[7]

In 1987, Motorola set in motion a five-year quality improvement program. The term Six Sigma is one used by statisticians and engineers to describe a state of zero defects. The result of this program has produced productivity gains of 40% as well as winning the Malcolm Baldridge National Quality Award in 1988. Benefits include:

- Increased productivity by 40%
- Reduced backlog from years to months
- Increased customer service levels
- Shifted IS time from correcting mistakes to value-added work
- More motivated staff
- Saved $1.5 billion in reduced cost

Listed below is Motorola's quality improvement program.

1. Identify your product. Determine what is the service or product you are producing. IS must align what they do with what the customers want.
2. Identify customer requirements. Information Systems (IS) must determine what the customer perceives as a defect-free product or service. The unit of work that the user is dealing with must be considered. For example, in a general ledger system in which the user worries about defects per journal voucher and not defects per thousand lines of code.
3. Diagnose the frequency and source of errors. Four categories of metrics were established to target defect reduction:
   - New software development
   - Service delivery
   - Cycle time
   - Customer satisfaction, which is composed of a detailed service with the intent of validating the first three metrics
4. Define a process for doing the task. Motorola refers to this process as mapping but it closely aligned to the reengineering process. The

process involves using personal computer-based tools to determine flow-through of processes and answering the following questions:
   - Which processes can be eliminated?
   - Which processes can be simplified?
5. Mistake-proof the process. By streamlining a process and eliminating any unnecessary steps, it is possible to make the process mistake-proof. By using metrics, a process control mechanism is put into place so that problems can be addressed before they affect output.
6. Put permanent control measures in place. Once Six Sigma is reached, this level must be maintained. At this step, the Six Sigma metrics are set up to be used to continuously monitor the process: monthly quality review meetings are held where each person gets up and discusses their metric, its trend, diagnosis of source cause of errors, action plan to correct.

ERNST & YOUNG CENTER FOR INFORMATION TECHNOLOGY AND STRATEGY TQM SOLUTION

The basic tenet behind Ernst & Young's TQM consultancy is to get organizations to understand a single principle — that change is painful and lengthy. In order to effectuate any kind of change you need a 10-year plan, and management's patience is short. So, how do you motivate change over that time period? The secret is to make management extremely dissatisfied with the status quo. And to do that you need to look at the cost of the status quo. One way of accomplishing this is to examine the cost of poor quality.

By answering questions such as, "What are we spending on detecting defects?" the IT organization can begin to accumulate the statistics it needs to make the push for change. The data need not be hard to track; in most cases, they are already available through project management systems that track walkthroughs, reviews, defect rates, etc.

The following nine steps constitute Ernst & Young's quick-hit approach to tackling TQM in IT departments:

1. Create a massive discomfort with the status quo. This can be accomplished in any one of a number of ways, including using numerical data or using a customer survey.
2. Use what was found in Step 1 to get management sponsorship of the TQM process.
3. Develop a commitment to quality. Top management needs to make a visible and personal commitment to any quality program.
4. Involve others. Customers/suppliers must be involved in the TQM process.
5. Define the processes.

6. Determine value measurements. Have customers of the processes outputs determine value measurements.
7. Form teams. Form process (quality) improvement teams that use these measures.
8. Innovate/improve the process. Come up with ways to innovate or improve the process.
9. Continue to improve. Create an environment where the processes continually improve.

COOPERS & LYBRAND TQM METHODOLOGY[8]

Coopers & Lybrand have taken appropriate elements of TQM and successfully applied them to software delivery organizations. It has developed a specific four-phase methodology, dubbed Software Quality Management (SQM) which provides a framework for managing continuous improvement for software delivery.

Assessment

The purpose of the Assessment phase is to evaluate the organization's current environment and determine how well the organization meets or is likely to meet its customers' software quality requirements. In any Assessment phase, a measurement system must first be designed as a tool and to establish a quality baseline. The Goal/Question/Metric approach described below can be used to produce this measurement system.

During Assessment, it is important to understand the activities involved in the software development process as well as the organizational roles and responsibilities. The measurements currently being used by the organization must also be identified and assessed. Whenever possible, existing measures should be used as part of the quality assessment to promote familiarity and acceptance.

Nevertheless, the overall approach is to develop questions and metrics that have the greatest importance to the organization. This is achieved by focusing on the three dimensions of the goals of the Assessment: the phase under scrutiny, the relevant quality issue, and the role from which the phase and quality issue are viewed.

When conducting an Assessment, it may also be necessary to hold briefing sessions with respondents to clarify the meaning of some of the metrics. Moreover, respondents who feel that they are being imposed upon or are fearful of the measurement effort are likely to provide questionable data. It is especially important to make clear that the metrics are not being used as a mechanism for punitive actions. Since many sensitive and perhaps embarrassing issues may arise during the Assessment, it is often easier for an outside third party to manage the process and gather data.

It is also desirable to collect the data during a fixed period of time with a specific deadline. During the Assessment period, the collection team should be available to answer questions and clarify procedures. After the data are collected, they are compiled, analyzed, and translated into graphic depiction's of the major findings. The key outcome of the Assessment is the identification of opportunities for improvement by studying the consolidated findings. This resulting list of opportunities is essential for the planning and implementation of pilot improvement projects.

Getting consensus from management as to the validity of the analysis and the opportunities for improvement is also essential. Specifically, the Assessment team must be sensitive to the possible misinterpretation of the findings and conclusions which may result in assessing blame. Prior to moving on to Planning, the management sponsor must help the team identify potential trouble spots and devise methods for defusing them.

Planning

The analysis of the data collected during the Assessment provides the foundation for the quality improvement plan. The Assessment defines the organization's quality profile and identifies opportunities for improvement. The objectives of the Planning phase are to establish strategic and tactical direction, as well as consensus and commitment for improvements identified in the Assessment. A Process Improvement Plan is the final outcome of this strategic planning effort.

Typically, two different types of problems surface as a result of the Assessment: some with relatively simple, quick solutions and some more deeply rooted in organizational practices, requiring a longer period to solve. To address the first type of problem, the organization must devise short-term, measurable projects with a consistent sequence encompassing the Plan/Do/Check/Act process.[7] The second type of problem requires an effort aimed at longer-term organizational and behavioral changes. The focus of the Planning effort will be on these long-term projects.

Nevertheless, a critical success factor for any SQM project is the perception that quality improvement is attainable. The quality improvement team's ability to achieve successes on the short-term projects will help to pave the way for the entire process. Furthermore, quick management decisions on short-term projects will show the development staff that their improvement ideas have been taken seriously and that management is willing to take actions based on staff input.

Because participation and consensus of management is essential to the Planning effort, there is always considerable risk of delay. The Planning team must, therefore, conduct an intensive quality planning session with managers early in the process. Ideally, all of the planning work could be accomplished at such a session. At a minimum, the result of the meeting will be to define the "quality vision" and to establish the roles and responsibilities of the groups to be charged with the organization's quality program.

The organization's vision of what quality software means and where it expects to be must be agreed upon early in the Planning effort. Most organizations find that there are several areas where improvement efforts can be focused; however, trying to do too much at once is not a good idea. Priorities should be assigned to targets based on the following criteria:

- Criticality
- Cost
- Resources
- Timing
- Risks
- Opportunity for near-term success

The projects that are selected as top priorities will require further discussion and decisions regarding the manner in which the improvements are to be implemented. The result will be a prioritized statement of quality objectives, the process improvements to be achieved, and the measurements that will demonstrate success. In addition, each quality improvement project should have:

- A mission statement that includes improvement goals
- Schedules and resource and cost estimates for each project
- An organization structure responsible for quality management
- Measurement procedures to validate the meeting of goals

In addition to establishing procedures, it is essential that top management realize the implications of committing to SQM. It must be understood that SQM is not a pilot program but an ongoing process to enhance the way the software organization conducts business. SQM requires changing procedures, cooperating with other departments, emphasizing the process, and changing management philosophies that are ineffective yet pervasive. If senior management is not willing to commit themselves, their organization, and their people to the process, an SQM program is probably not worth starting.

Planning for software quality improvement requires more than just top management commitment and sponsorship. It also calls for attention to cultural and behavioral issues. For example, the initial reaction of staff to a measurement program may be apprehension, fear, and resistance. It must be shown that the program and data collected will be used for improvement purposes and not punishment. One or more short-term successes will demonstrate the real value of the measurement system. Also, a measurement system should indicate process and product strengths that need encouragement as well as weaknesses that need improvement.

The primary goals of the Planning phase of SQM are to define quality objectives and strategies for instituting improvement solutions. It is also important for the plan to establish the roles and responsibilities for the individuals and teams whose mission is to promote and oversee continuous quality improvements. The final product is a plan that prioritizes the quality objectives, details the means for achieving improvements in the short term, identifies and analyzes quality-related risks, and creates an agreed-upon framework to achieve long-term quality improvement objectives.

Implementation

Introducing measurement systems and the concept of continuous improvement will require far-reaching changes to an organization. During the Implementation phase, these changes begin to occur. Implementing the quality improvement plan means incorporating the measurement and improvement efforts into the organizational culture and discovering which behavioral changes need to occur. This effort, therefore, requires a corresponding change in the reward structure. A reward system should motivate the staff to change development procedures in a way that is consistent with the goals of the improvements efforts.

Once a new reward system is in place, Implementation should turn to those short-term projects that were identified in the Planning phase. These may include:

- Project tracking techniques and tools
- Formalizing reviews and walk-throughs
- Implementing Joint Application Design (JAD) sessions
- Applying new approaches to testing

Most of the efforts at improvement will require training of staff and project management in the relevant techniques and tools. These training efforts must be undertaken with the same commitment and level of support given to the entire SQM effort. If staff is not supported in its effort to change, all of the assessments and strategic planning sessions in the world will not effect change. For an SQM program to be successful, staff and management must be encouraged to experiment, take risks, and take charge of improving the process.

Once the framework of rewards, training, and empowerment is established, the long-term process improvements can be attempted. These may include:

- Implementing risk management techniques
- Introducing a structured development methodology
- Instituting Rapid Prototyping techniques
- Evaluating and implementing new CASE tools

Institutionalization

Institutionalization requires that the lessons learned during Implementation be captured and transformed into organizational assets to form the basis of a continuous improvement culture. As a first step, the experiences gained in near-term improvement projects should be analyzed, packaged, and communicated to everyone in the organization. Successes must be validated and publicized. The experience is packaged into self-contained units including approach, results, techniques, tools, manuals, and training to transform the knowledge gained into the organization's culture.

The basic techniques for institutionalizing continuous quality improvement include:

- Analyzing the results of short-term projects and comparing the results with the targets defined in Planning
- Synthesizing the experience into lessons learned, domain expertise, rules and models
- Packaging the experience as products that can be delivered to the organization

Institutionalizing SQM requires comprehensive reuse of the experience from several projects or several phases of a project. Much of the work done at this stage of the program involves educating the individuals who develop and maintain software. This education involves not only formalized training on specific process improvements, but also formal and informal quality awareness education via the promotion of quality improvement successes.

CORBIN'S METHODOLOGY FOR ESTABLISHING A SOFTWARE DEVELOPMENT ENVIRONMENT[9]

The Software Development Environment (SDE) is actually the integration of a number of processes, tools, standards, methodologies, and related elements whose purpose is to provide a framework for building quality software. This section discusses the elements of SDE and shows how to develop one.

The Elements of SDE

Project management
Business plan
Architecture
Methodologies
Techniques
Tools
Metrics
Policies and procedures

Technology platform
Support
Standards
Education and training

The Benefits of SDE

Improved problem definition
Selection of the "right" problem according to the customer
Joint customer/IS responsibility and accountability
Acknowledgment of customer ownership of system
Reduced costs of systems development and maintenance
Reusability of software, models, and data definitions
Acceptance of the disciplined approach to software engineering using a consistent methodology
Productivity improvements through team efforts and tools such as CASE

Sample Goals of SDE

Reduce systems development costs
Reduce maintenance costs
Reduce MIS turnover rate

These goals should be quantifiable wherever possible.

For example, the first goal could be stated as "reduce systems development costs by 50% over the next 5 years."

Architecture

Many organizations do not have a formal, documented architecture. There are three types:

- Business Architecture is a model of the business and identifies such things as processes and entities in the form of models.
- Computing Architecture, which at a minimum identifies hardware, software, and data communications. This breaks out into components such as operating systems, data resource management, network protocols, and user interface.
- Enterprise Architecture is a combination of the Business and Computing Architectures.

Business Plan

- Create a Steering Committee that provides direction to the MIS function.
- Translate the organization's business plan into an actionable MIS plan that supports the business' goals and objectives.

- The Steering Committee should be responsible for funding projects, setting priorities, resolving business issues, and reviewing MIS policies and procedures.

Education and Training

Make sure that analysts, programmers, and users are all trained and ready to start the development project. Training might include the following:

- Software engineering concepts
- Prototyping
- System development life cycle
- Joint application development
- Software quality assurance and testing
- Project management
- Data and process modeling
- CASE/application development toolsets

Methodologies

Whether the methodology chosen by the MIS department is a standard one, from a vendor, or developed internally, the MIS group must follow one to ensure consistency from project to project. This will enable staff to be able to move from project to project without retraining, while at the same time ensuring consistent deliverables. Questions to ask when selecting a methodology are

- Does your methodology support the entire systems development life cycle?
- Does it include maintenance?
- Is it clearly documented?
- Does it focus on deliverables instead of activities?
- Is it Application Development tool independent?
- Can you use your metrics and techniques with it?

Project Management

Questions to ask include:

- Do you have a formal project management discipline in place?
- Do you have a training program to support this?
- Is a software tool used?
- Do you have program planning and control to help manage the project?
- Do you get routine reports showing the project work breakdown structure, status reports, resource loading, and cost projections?
- Is there a formal reporting mechanism done on a timely basis to resolve problems?

Standards

Some of the areas in which standards are required are

- Systems analysis and design
- Data administration
- Database administration
- Systems testing
- Prototyping
- Documentation
- Data entry
- Systems production
- Change/configuration management

Questions to ask: "Have you identified all of the standards that are required to support your SDE? Do you have someone responsible for developing and maintaining standards?"

Support Options

- External consulting
- A sharing arrangement where you can provide services in exchange for those needed
- User groups
- Special interest groups

Automated Tool Questions

- Have you identified the tools you need in the SDE?
- Have they been approved, acquired, and installed?
- Do they support the methodologies?
- Do they support the technology platform?
- Do they support the standards?
- Is technical support available to support the tools?
- Do you have templates for use in systems development?
- Do you have a data dictionary, or repository for your data?
- Do you have tools to support each phase of the life cycle?

SIMMONS STATISTICS CONCERNING THE EFFECT THAT COMMUNICATIONS HAS ON GROUP PRODUCTIVITY[10]

This section details the many factors that dominate software group productivity. Simmons defines dominator as a single factor that causes productivity to decline tenfold. The two dominators that are discussed are communications and design partition.

What follows is a set of rules and statistics that the reader can use as a comparison in his or her own efforts to increase productivity.

1. Factors that developers must cope with in developing large systems:
   - Personnel turnover
   - Hardware/software turnover
   - Major ideas incorporate late
   - Latent bugs
2. A Delphi survey performed by Scott and Simmons to uncover factors that affect productivity found that the main factors are
   - External documentation
   - Programming language
   - Programming tools
   - Programmer experience
   - Communications
   - Independent modules for task assignment (design partition)
   - Well-defined programming practices
3. Improvement statistics:
   - Any step towards the use of structured techniques, interactive development, inspections, etc. can improve productivity by up to 25%.
   - Use of these techniques in combination could yield improvements of between 25% and 50%.
   - Change in programming language can, by itself, yield a productivity improvement of more than 50%.
   - Gains of between 50% and 75% can be achieved by single high achievers or teams of high achievers.
   - Gains of 100% can be achieved by database user languages, application generators and software reuse.
4. Dominators are factors that can suppress the effects of other factors and can reduce software group productivity by an order of magnitude.
5. Poor design partition can dominate group productivity. To obtain high productivity in the development of large software systems, the designer must break down the system into chunks that can be developed in parallel. The difference between great and average designers is an order of magnitude.
6. Communications can dominate productivity. Most project problems arise as the result of poor communications between workers. If there are n workers on the team, then there are $n(n-1)/2$ interfaces across which there may be communications problems.
7. Productivity of individual programmers varies as much as 26 to 1.
8. An individual working alone has no interruptions from fellow group members and, therefore, the productivity can be quite high for a motivated individual. It is estimated that one programmer working 60 hours a week can complete a project in the same calendar time as two others working normal hours, but at three-quarters of the cost.

9. Small groups of experienced and productive software developers can create large systems. An example is given of a company, Pyburn Systems. They scour the country for the best analytical thinkers. Its senior programmers typically earn $125,000 a year and can be paid bonuses of two to three times that amount. They work in small teams, never more than five, to produce large, complex systems. In comparison, most MIS departments produce large systems using normal development teams with developers of average ability.
10. In general, the difference between the cost to produce an individual program to be run by the program author and the cost to produce a programming system product developed by software group is at least nine times more expensive.
11. There is a point where coordination overheads outweigh any benefits that can be obtained by the addition of further staff. Statistics that support this were pioneered during the nineteenth century in work on military organization. It was noted that as the number of workers who had to communicate increased arithmetically, from 2 to 3 to 4 to 5 ..., the number of communication channels among them increased geometrically, from 1 to 3 to 6 to 10 .... From this study, it was concluded that the upper limit of effective staff size for cooperative projects is about 8.
12. In studies, it has been shown that when the number of staff increased to 12 or more, the efficiency of the group decreased to less than 30%.
13. The productive time of a typical software developer during a working day can vary from 51 to 79%. It was found that the average duration of work interruption was 5 minutes for a typical programmer. The average time to regain a train of thought after an interruption was 2 minutes. Thus, the average total time spent on an interruption was 7 minutes. It we assume five productive hours each day, then each interruption takes 2.33% of the working day, 10 interruptions would take up 23.3% of the day, and 20 interruptions would take up approximately 50%.
14. The optimum group size for a software development team is between five to eight members. The overall design should be partitioned into successively smaller chunks, until the development group has a chunk of software to develop that minimizes intragroup and intergroup communications.

BURNS' FRAMEWORK FOR BUILDING DEPENDABLE SYSTEMS[11]

The role and importance of nonfunctional requirements in the development of complex critical applications have, until now, been inadequately appreciated. It has been shown through experience that this approach fails to produce dependable systems.

Nonfunctional requirements include dependability (e.g., reliability, availability, safety, and security), timeliness (e.g., responsiveness, orderliness, freshness, temporal predictability, and temporal controllability), and dynamic change management (i.e., incorporating evolutionary changes into a nonstop system).

The purpose of the framework described in this section is to:

- Impose a design discipline that ensures that appropriate abstractions are used at each level of the design.
- Allow assertions to be developed that the nonfunctional requirements can be met by the design if implemented in a particular environment.
- Allow interactions between these nonfunctional requirements to be analyzed so that dependencies can be identified.
- Allow the nonfunctional and functional requirements to be traded off against each other.

Notes pertaining to the framework are listed below.

1. A constructive way of describing the process of system design is a progression of increasingly specific commitments which define properties of the system design which designers operating at a more detailed level are not at liberty to change. For example, early in the design there may already be commitments to the structure of a system, in terms of module definitions and relationships.
2. Those aspects of a design to which no commitment is made at some particular level in the design hierarchy are the subject of obligations that lower levels of design must address. For example, the behavior of the defined aspects committed to modules is the subject of obligations which must be met during further design and implementation.
3. The process of refining a design — transforming obligations into commitments — is often subject to constraints which are imposed primarily by the execution environment.
4. The execution environment is the set of hardware and software components on top of which a system is built. It may impose both resource constraints (e.g., processor speed) and constraints of mechanism (e.g., data locking).
5. The framework controls the introduction of necessary implementation details into the design process by distinguishing two phases in the construction of an architectural design of any application:
   - Logical architecture — embodies commitments which can be made independently of the constraints imposed by the execution environment and is aimed at satisfying the functional requirements.
   - Physical architecture — takes constraints into account and embraces the nonfunctional requirements.

6. The nonfunctional requirements of an application can be considered as projections onto the physical architecture. Distinct projects apply to timeliness, safety, and so on. The physical architecture makes it explicit where projections interact and enables criteria to be developed that cater for these interactions.
7. The framework is grounded in the object-oriented approach to system design. The object-oriented approach is widely regarded as offering a conceptual framework for mastering the complexities of the design process:
   - Objects are an adequate modeling tool for the functional requirements of the system.
   - They can be used to provide traceability through all stages of the design process.
   - They are an adequate basis for expressing nonfunctional requirements.
   - They provide an appropriate granularity for replication, checkpointing, dynamic change management, configuration, and dynamic reconfiguration.
   - They assist error containment through encapsulation.
   - They can support dynamic security by access right mechanisms on operations.
   - They can represent schedulable entities.
   - Commonly encountered standard architectures can be implemented by means of redefined classes and methods.
8. The logical architecture is concerned with defining a set of object classes, their interfaces, and relationships, which together meet all the functional requirements. In the logical architecture, communication between the classes is represented by invocation of methods.
9. The physical architecture is concerned with objects, that is, instances of the classes defined in the logical architecture. If refines the logical architecture in two ways:
   - It instantiates objects from the classes defined in the logical architecture and maps them onto the target execution environment.
   - It annotates the objects and their methods with attributes (such as deadlines) derived from the nonfunctional requirements.

FARBEY'S CONSIDERATIONS ON SOFTWARE QUALITY METRICS DURING THE REQUIREMENTS PHASE [12]

In this section Farbey expands on the general view of quality as the difference between what is expected and what is experienced:

$$\text{Quality} = \text{expectations} - \text{experience}$$

Four questions are addressed:

- Effectiveness — does the specification, considered as a solution, solve the right problem?
- Serviceability — does the specification, considered as a starting point, provide a firm basis on which to proceed?
- Prediction — does the requirement specification (together with the system test specification) provide useful measures for predicting the final quality outcome?
- Process — does the process by which the specification is produced encourage effectiveness, serviceability, and quality prediction?

1. Effectiveness. The first question concerns the quality of the specification as a solution — how well does the specification capture the problem? The ultimate effectiveness of a system depends not on the quality of software or specification, but on the degree to which the problem is correctly perceived. Focus on the specification as a product by asking questions like those that follow:
   - Is the process by which it has been produced conducive to bringing out and clarifying objectives?
   - Is it complete in that it exhausts the objectives and needs that are known?
   - Is the specification maintainable?
   - Is it readable?

   Quality attributes covered here include:
   - Functionality — does the specification capture all of the required functions.
   - Performance — does the specification meet the users' demands.
   - Usability — ease of use, learning, and relearning.
2. Serviceability. The second question concerns the quality of its content and implications for later system development. The following is a list of questions of efficiency, in this context meaning "doing things right."
   - Are the requirements consistent?
   - Are the requirements unambiguous?
   - Are the requirements compatible with the methods of later development stages?
   - Are the requirements readable?
   - Are the requirements modifiable?
   - Are the requirements traceable?
   - Are the requirements usable after implementation?
   - Are the requirements maintainable?
   - Are the requirements in compliance with documentation standards?
3. Prediction. The third question concerns the value of measures of quality that will act as predictor measurements for the eventual quality of the finished software. A predictor metric is used to predict

the value of a property of a system that will only become directly observable during a later stage of system development.

4. Process. Three processes of development are worth considering:
   - Life-cycle process such as SSADM (Structured Systems Analysis and Design), which is based on a waterfall model. In this model requirements specification occurs at an early stage and is then fixed as would be any associated metrics.
   - Prototyping approach offers an early normalization but also offers a more flexible model of system development that recognizes the problem of changing requirements.
   - Approaches that recognize specifically the social setting in which requirements specifications takes place. Control of quality during any process will probably be one of instituting checklists together with a program for completing them and acting on the results. Questions to ask at this point include (1) Is the system easy to learn? (2) Is the system easy to relearn? (3) Is there stability and maturity in the system?

HEWLETT-PACKARD'S TQC (TOTAL QUALITY CONTROL) GUIDELINES FOR SOFTWARE ENGINEERING PRODUCTIVITY[13]

Engineering productivity is extremely important to HP because they rely on new product development to maintain their competitive strength. HP introduces an average of one new product every business day; 70% of HP's engineers are involved in software development. Half of all R&D projects are exclusively devoted to software development.

It was this significant investment in software development that prompted HP's president to issue a challenge to achieve a tenfold improvement in software quality within 5 years. He also asked that new product development time be reduced by 50%.

This section points out the techniques HP utilized to meet this vast quality and productivity challenge. It's worthwhile reading for those who are responsible for spitting out new financial services products on a daily basis.

1. HP's productivity equation:

$$\text{Productivity} = \text{function of doing the right things} \times \text{function of doing things right}$$

2. Cultural and organizational issues addressed to be able to motivate and support positive changes:
   - Productivity managers are used in each division to understand productivity and quality issues; evaluate, select, install CASE tools; communicate best software engineering practices; training; and establish productivity and quality metrics.

- A group productivity council is created to share the best R&D practices across divisions, metrics definition, metrics tracking, productivity councils, software quality and productivity assessment, and communication of best practices.

3. The Software Metrics Council is composed of both R&D and QA managers and engineers, whose objective is to identify key software metrics and promote their use.
4. Project/Product quality metrics used are
   - Break-even time measures return on investment, defined as time until development costs are offset by profits. The three numbers plotted are R&D investment in dollars, operating profit in dollars and time, and sales revenue in dollars and time.
   - Time-to-market measures responsiveness and competitiveness. It is defined as time from project go-ahead until release to market.
   - Kiviat diagram measures variables that affect software quality and productivity. It is a bull's-eye chart which graphs results of quality and productivity assessment.
5. Process quality metrics used are
   - Progress rate measures accuracy of schedule. It is defined as the ratio of planned to actual development time.
   - Open critical and serious KPRs measures effectiveness of support processes. It is defined as the number of service requests classified as known problems (of severity level critical or serious) that are not signed off.
   - Post-release defect density measures effectiveness of design and test processes. It is defined as the total number of defects reported during the first 12 months after product shipment.
6. People quality metrics used are
   - Turnover rate measures morale. It measures that percent of engineers leaving the company.
   - Training measures investment in career development. It is defined as the number of hours per engineer per year.
7. Basic software quality metrics used are
   - Code size (KNCSS, which is thousands of lines of noncomment source statements).
   - Number of prerelease defects requiring fix.
   - Prerelease defect density (defects/KNCSS).
   - Calendar months for prerelease QA.
   - Total prerelease QA test hours.
   - Number of postrelease defects reported after one year.
   - Postrelease defect density (defects/KNCSS).
   - Calendar months from investigation checkpoint to release.
8. Strategy for code reuse:
   - Share code (use exactly as is) whenever possible.
   - If sharing is not possible, try to leverage (minimal modifications).

- If neither sharing nor leveraging is possible, look for similar algorithms (design reuse).
- As a last resort, invent something new.

9. The Systems Software Certifications program was established to ensure measurable, consistent, high-quality software. the four metrics chosen were
   - Breadth — measures the testing coverage of user-accessible and internal functionality of the product.
   - Depth — measures the proportion of instructions or blocks of instructions executed during the testing process.
   - Reliability — measures the stability and robustness of a product and its ability to recover gracefully from error conditions.
   - Defect density — measures the quantity and severity of reported defects found and a product's readiness for use.

SPECIFICATION THOROUGHNESS SURVEY

Circle the appropriate number for each item below as it applies to your current project. For many companies surveyed, the bulk of the responses are either 1 or 2.

	Often				Seldom
1. Program specifications contain (hidden) errors and omissions	1	2	3	4	5
2. Design decisions are made on personal preferences	1	2	3	4	5
3. Program design process is informal	1	2	3	4	5
4. Programmers begin to code before design is complete	1	2	3	4	5
5. Inadequately defined software objectives	1	2	3	4	5
6. Programmers spend too much time correcting errors that are the result of poor specifications	1	2	3	4	5
7. Poor and inadequately enforced standards contribute to poor quality programs	1	2	3	4	5
8. Far too many omissions and errors are discovered after implementation	1	2	3	4	5
9. Inadequate commitment to quality software by management	1	2	3	4	5
10. Inadequate commitment to quality software by end users	1	2	3	4	5

CRITERIA DEFINITIONS FOR SOFTWARE QUALITY

Traceability — Those attributes of the software that provide a thread from the requirements to the implementation with respect to the specific and operational environment.

Completeness — Those attributes that provide full implementation of the functions required.

Consistency — Those attributes that provide uniform design and implementation techniques and notation.

Accuracy — Those attributes that provide the required precision in calculation and notation.

Error Tolerance — Those attributes that provide continuity of operation under nonnominal conditions.

Simplicity — Those attributes that provide implementation of functions in the most understandable manner. (Usually, avoidance of practices which increase complexity.)

Modularity — Those attributes that provide a structure of highly independent modules.

Generality — Those attributes that provide breadth to the functions performed.

Expandability — Those attributes that provide for expansion of data storage requirements or computational functions.

Instrumentation — Those attributes that provide for the measurement of usage or identification of errors.

Self-descriptiveness — Those attributes that provide explanation of a function.

Execution efficiency — Those attributes that provide for minimum processing time.

Storage efficiency — Those attributes that provide for minimum storage requirements.

Access control — Those attributes that provide for control of the access of software and data.

Access audit — Those attributes that provide for and audit the access of software and data.

Operability — Those attributes that determine operation and procedures concerned with the operation of software.

Training — Those attributes that provide transition from the current operation to initial familiarization.

Communicativeness — Those attributes that provide useful inputs and outputs that can be assimilated.

Software system independence — Those attributes that determine the software's dependency on the software environment (operating systems, utilities, input/output routines, etc.).

Machine independence — Those attributes that determine the software's dependency on the hardware system.

Communications commonality — Those attributes that provide the use of standard protocols and interface routines.

Data commonality — Those attributes that provide the use of standard data representations.

Conciseness — Those attributes that provide for implementation of a function with a minimum amount of code.

TYPICAL QUALITY FACTOR TRADE-OFFS

Integrity vs. efficiency — The additional code and processing required to control the access of the software or data usually lengthens run-time and requires additional storage.

Useability vs. efficiency — The additional code and processing required to ease an operator's tasks or provide more usable output usually lengthens run-time and increases storage.

Maintainability vs. efficiency — Optimized code increases maintainer's efforts. Using modules, instrumentation, etc.; however, increases overhead.

Testability vs. efficiency — The above applies to testing.

Portability vs. efficiency — The use of direct, optimized, or utilities decreases the portability of the system.

Flexibility vs. efficiency — Generality for a flexible system increases overhead.

Reusability vs. efficiency — The above applies to reuse.

Interoperability vs. efficiency — The added overhead for data conversion and interface routines decreases operating efficiency.

Flexibility vs. integrity — Flexibility requires very general structures. Security may be harder to insure.

Reusability vs. integrity — As above, reusable software provides severe security problems.

Interoperability vs. integrity — Coupled systems allow for more paths; that can allow either accidental or purposeful access to data.

Reusability vs. reliability — The generality required by reusable software makes providing for error tolerance and accuracy difficult.

STEPS TO REFOCUSING IT ACTIVITY

The process of squeezing extra resources from systems can be broken down into three steps, each with several components.

Step 1: Streamline the Current Systems Environment

Objectives — 15 to 20% of real cost reduction with payback in 6 to 12 months.

Activities —

1. Choose relevant organization units for analysis.
2. Allocate and costs to end products.
3. Generate ideas for streamlining costs.
4. Plan implementation.

Step 2: Focus on High-Value Priorities

Objectives — 30 to 40% reduction in current development projects, with resources reallocated to highest impact investments.

Activities —

1. Identify cost drivers and leverage points.
2. Group planned projects around leverage points.
3. Identify new opportunities and possible cutbacks.
4. Restate priorities.

Step 3: Build Ongoing Organizational Capabilities

Objectives — (1) Consolidation of gains on ongoing basis, and (2) maintenance of major improvements in organizational effectiveness.

Activities —

1. Evaluate planning and decision-making procedures.
2. Interview users and participants regarding the effectiveness of those procedures.
3. Identify weaknesses and opportunities for improvement.
4. Design procedural changes.

Notes

1. Shetty, Y. K., A point of view: seven principles of quality leaders, *Natl. Prod. Rev.*, Winter, 1991–1992, pp. 3–7.

2. Redmill, F. J., Considering quality in the management of software-based development projects, *Information and Software Technology,* Vol. 32(1), January/February, 1990, pp. 18–33.
3. Rubin, H., Rubin Associates, Pound Ridge, NY, 1991.
4. Pressman, R., *A Manager's Guide to Software Engineering,* McGraw-Hill, New York, 1993.
5. Bouldin, B., *Agents of Change,* Yourdon Press, Englewood Cliffs, NJ, 1989.
6. Humphrey, W., Software and the factory paradigm, *Softw. Eng. J.,* IEEE Publishing, Stevenage, Herts, U.K., March 1989.
7. Rifkin, G., More more defects, *Computerworld,* July 15, 1991, pp. 59–62.
8. Smillie, W., Improving the quality of software development, in *Software Engineering Productivity Handbook,* Keyes, J., Ed., McGraw-Hill, New York, 1993.
9. Corbin, D. S., Establishing the software development environment, *J. Sys. Manage.,* September, 1991, pp. 28–31.
10. Simmons, D. B., Communications: a software group productivity dominator, *Softw. Eng. J.,* November, 1991, pp. 454–462.
11. Burns, A. and Lister, A. M., A framework for building dependable systems, *Comp. J.,* Vol. 34(2), April, 1991, pp. 173–181.
12. Farbey, B., Software quality metrics: considerations about requirements and requirement specifications, *Information and Software Technology,* Vol. 32(1), January/February, 1990, pp. 60–64.
13. Anon., *Software Engineering Productivity,* Hewlett-Packard Company, Palo Alto, CA, 1989.

Chapter 7
Distributed Integration: An Alternative to Data Warehousing

Dan Adler

DATA WAREHOUSING HAS, PERHAPS, BEEN THE MOST COSTLY systems development in the history of financial services. The concept of data warehousing grew out of regional and departmental consolidation projects in which large relational databases were used to store relatively large quantities of data and make these data available to standard query tools such as SQL and various SQL-based interfaces. These queries were very useful in helping departments track customer behavior, P&L, and, in combination with applications written in VB, C++, and S-PLUS, they helped departments and regional entities within financial institutions track market trends, manage risk, and develop predictions.

Many managers, however, when they saw the success of the special-purpose database, were inspired to take this concept to the next level. "If we can do so much with a relational database in one department, I wonder how much value we could extract by representing our entire firm in a relational database?" went the reasoning. And, for expanding global trading businesses that needed to control the risks associated with numerous local portfolios composed of complex financial instruments, the centralized data warehouse containing "everything" was particularly appealing.

At most financial institutions, however, extending numerous departmental and regional data collection projects to create a "firm-wide" data warehouse representing a firm's entire global business just did not work. Wall Street — and retail banking's Main Street — are littered with tales of multi-year, multimillion-dollar data warehousing projects that were killed be-

0-8493-9991-2/99/$0.00+$.50

cause they did not produce anything near what their architects promised. Problems include: transforming data stored in numerous formats, ensuring the data is "clean" and correct, developing and maintaining a firm-wide data model describing interrelationships between different types of data, managing various types of middleware to transport data from place to place, limited network resources, etc. And, of course, users became frustrated waiting for the "warehouse" and it associated promised functionality.

Still, extracting value from firm-wide information and controlling global market risk remain top priorities for financial institutions and their information technology departments, which are struggling to develop alternatives to data warehousing. One of the most promising such developments is Distributed Integration.

Distributed Integration is a new approach to integrating both firm-wide data and analytics based on Internet technologies, such as cascaded Internet servers and data caching. The "Distributed" refers to data and analytics that reside in numerous physical locations. The "Integration" refers to users' ability to access these disparate data and analytics through an *analytic browser,* which can be any application residing on any desktop which maintains an active connection to one or more *Distributed Integration servers.*

This chapter will describe how Distributed Integration solves some data integration problems that data warehousing projects do not always successfully address and show how Distributed Integration leverages existing desktop and intranet technologies to deliver this integrated data (and analytics) to large communities of internal and external users at a very reasonable price point.

THE HISTORY OF DATA WAREHOUSING

The firm-wide relational data warehouse has been proposed as a solution to numerous business issues facing financial institutions during the 1980s and 1990s.

First, in wholesale banking, per-trade margins have steadily declined in the mature foreign exchange and interest rate markets as the number of market participants increased and interest rate markets became more liquid. To respond more nimbly to market movements and to identify long-term trends, "data mining" — in which information is collected and analyzed to identify underlying patterns — became extremely popular. The data warehouse has been proposed as means of conveniently storing large quantities of historical and real-time data in order to facilitate the data mining process.

An important subset of the data mining issue for wholesale bankers and money managers is the management of time series data. These are data that are periodically collected and time stamped. This sort of data is very difficult to store in relational formats because time series records — when expressed in tabular format — are very repetitive. Likewise, time series data are collected more or less continuously. Therefore, they tend to rapidly overpopulate relational databases and reduce performance. So, time series records are more often stored in file format for convenience. Blending time series and relational data for data mining purposes has often been an objective of data warehousing initiatives.

Another trend in wholesale banking has been the development of complex derivative instruments in response to the shrinking margins described above. These more complex instruments, often developed by local trading offices in response to specific customer demands, have raised control issues highlighted by a spate of "derivatives losses" stories in the mid 1990s as banks, corporates, and investment managers recognized the importance of, first, understanding their derivatives exposures in the context of their whole portfolios and, second, keeping a close eye on rapidly expanding foreign offices. Indeed, the downside of extreme decentralization was dramatically illustrated by the failure of U.K.-based Barings Bank. In the wake of the Barings scandal, many financial institutions turned to data warehousing as a solution to their "control and security" issues.

In retail banking, the consolidation and acquisition of numerous banks meant fierce competition, and product innovation and sales became ever more critical. Data mining became very popular in the retail deposit and credit card businesses, wherein effectively dissecting the customer's spending and living habits equals better product development and sales.

Finally, both retail and wholesale financial services providers became increasingly concerned with the rapid distribution and analysis of so-called "real time" data. Indeed, the global bull market, while providing satisfying returns across the board, also makes it more difficult for investment managers to differentiate themselves from the pack or from benchmark indices. Data warehousing capable of handling real data, then, became a Holy Grail for many firms.

CHOOSE YOUR WEAPONS

While data warehousing seemed like a sound solution to many of the above-mentioned business challenges at the conceptual level, the actual implementation of data warehousing solutions did not live up to the initial promise. First, this is because of the many difficulties associated with obtaining, converting, and transporting data that effectively limit the scalability of most data warehousing solutions.

Second, if it is possible to get data into a warehouse, it is often challenging to get the data out of the warehouse and into the hands of end users who need it.

For example, traditional relational data warehouses are built in conjunction with implementation of a large, costly "enterprise" system. Such enterprise systems are typically limited to a certain number of high-priority users. Providing general access to such a system is usually too costly due to licensing fees. And, if the enterprise system performs crucial operations functions, analysts and other nonoperations staff may not be allowed to apply query tools to the data warehouse; if they did, they could slow down mission-critical processes. When general queries are permitted against the data warehouse, they are often very slow. In most cases, specialized query tools must be purchased in order to identify, copy, and manipulate the relevant portion of warehoused data.

There are three major types of data warehousing implementations, and each has different benefits and drawbacks; these are listed below. However, while all of these solutions have been successfully implemented at the local level, none has successfully scaled up to the enterprise level.

Options for Data Warehousing

Numerous Interfaces. This is the classic, old-style data warehouse in which numerous "interface" programs are developed to create even more numerous download files which, in turn, may be uploaded to a centralized data warehouse during nightly, weekly, or monthly batch processing. While the interface method does possess a certain conceptual simplicity and in fact is sometimes the only option available to handle extremely proprietary — or antiquated — bits of data, it traditionally has a low success rate. This is because the sheer number of interface programs which must be successfully run and kept in sync is usually so large. This creates problems because, first, if something goes wrong in any one of these procedures, the entire data warehouse may become inaccurate. Second, these interfaces are often difficult to fix because they are often proprietary and, wherever there is IT turnover, impenetrable and undocumented.

Replication. Data replication can be used to create both a data warehouse and numerous redundant data sources by periodically copying new records across a suitable WAN. For example, let's say bank X, headquartered in New York, has a London office and a Singapore office. Let's also say the data warehouse resides in New York. As new trades are entered in London and Singapore, they are both stored in local relational databases and copied or "replicated" and sent through the WAN to the data warehouse in New York. The same replication procedure can be used to populate a backup data warehouse located in, say, London. While this method is straightforward and has worked well for medium-sized and smaller portfolios, it also has distinct scalability problems. This is often due to excessive network traffic created by the constant copying and transmission of each and every transaction. As the network slows down, it becomes difficult to keep the data warehouse up-to-date, and network failures can result in corrupt, incorrect, or incomplete data.

Middleware. Middleware is a catch-all term referring to "plumbing" software that is typically transparent to the user and may function as an engine for any or all of the following: data transformation, data integrity checking, transaction monitoring, data transformation, data distribution, and/or object/application communication. Some financial institutions have attempted to populate large physical data warehouses through the innovative use of multiple forms of middleware. Others have attempted to link together various types of middleware in order to create their own "virtual data warehouse" in which middleware supplies applications with RAM copies of relevant data.

Regardless of which sort of warehouse one is attempting to create, managing numerous forms of middleware has some substantial drawbacks. These include the extensive effort required to ensure that different middleware packages are compatible with each other and with critical data sources, scalability limits associated with various types of middleware (particularly ORBs when used in conjunction with a "virtual" warehouse), maintenance associated with upgrades, etc.

The Data Mart Variation

In response to the limitations of data warehousing, many financial institutions have abandoned multiyear data warehousing projects in favor of what is known as the "data mart" approach. Basically, the data mart approach refers to a data warehousing projects which is based on a number of local, regional or functional implementations. The prime benefit to this approach is that, unlike the traditional "big bang" style of warehouse building, users in specific regional or functional areas can actually see results within a more predictable period of time. And, for this reason, data mart projects have found a friendlier reception in financial institutions than "old style" data warehousing.

However, the final step of a data mart project is generally to combine all the data marts into a data warehouse by periodically copying these local databases in their entirety into a centralized, relational data warehouse. Often, it is easier to create a data warehouse from data marts than to build one from scratch because data marts are usually built with consistent technology, thus avoiding the need for massive data conversions.

However, these data mart-based warehouses do not usually work well for real-time analysis, in which constant data-copying would compromise performance both at the warehouse and data mart levels. And, a data mart-driven warehouse still comes up against the challenge of distributing the contents of the warehouse in a usable format to those who need them.

DISTRIBUTED INTEGRATION: A NEW WAY

Distributed Integration is a new way to integrate global financial data, analytics, and applications and quickly distribute them to a large community of users. Unlike most traditional data warehousing solutions, this does not require all data to be physically co-located in a single huge database. Instead, the Distributed Integration architecture relies on Internet technologies to create a virtual data warehouse that is optimized for both scalability and the cost-effective delivery of critical data to large user communities.

Data and analytics residing in multiple physical locations behave like a single, integrated virtual environment through Web-enabled *Distributed Integration servers.* These servers take advantage of Internet server cluster organization and data caching techniques and thus are configured for extreme scalability.

End users access the distributed integration virtual environment through a *Distributed Integration workstation,* which simply refers to any desktop which has a direct Internet connection to one or more Distributed Integration servers.

Almost any application (such as Excel™) residing on a distributed integration workstation can be enabled to view and manipulate integrated data and analytics; such applications are referred to *analytic browsers.*

Indeed, for the numerous highly paid analysts at most financial institutions who spend the majority of their time gathering relevant information to feed into their spreadsheets and then verifying that this information is clean, consistent, and correct, the analytic browser is truly a revolutionary concept.

Exhibit 1 provides a quick illustration of distributed integration. It depicts a global financial organization with two or more physical locations separated by a WAN or Internet connection.

The top location, say New York, has an equities group that maintains a database of equities using Sybase. They use a distributed integration server to make the data available to their own clients. They deliver analytics to traders at home through analytic browsers. They also have a group of analysts who write specific analytics and incorporate them into the Distributed Integration server, thus making them available to other analysts and to managers for control purposes.

The bottom location, say London, has a number of other groups that maintain an FX database in FAME and a commodities database in ORACLE. They make the data available to their own traders and analysts through their own Distributed Integration server, which also includes proprietary analytics. This group is also servicing some external clients who are con-

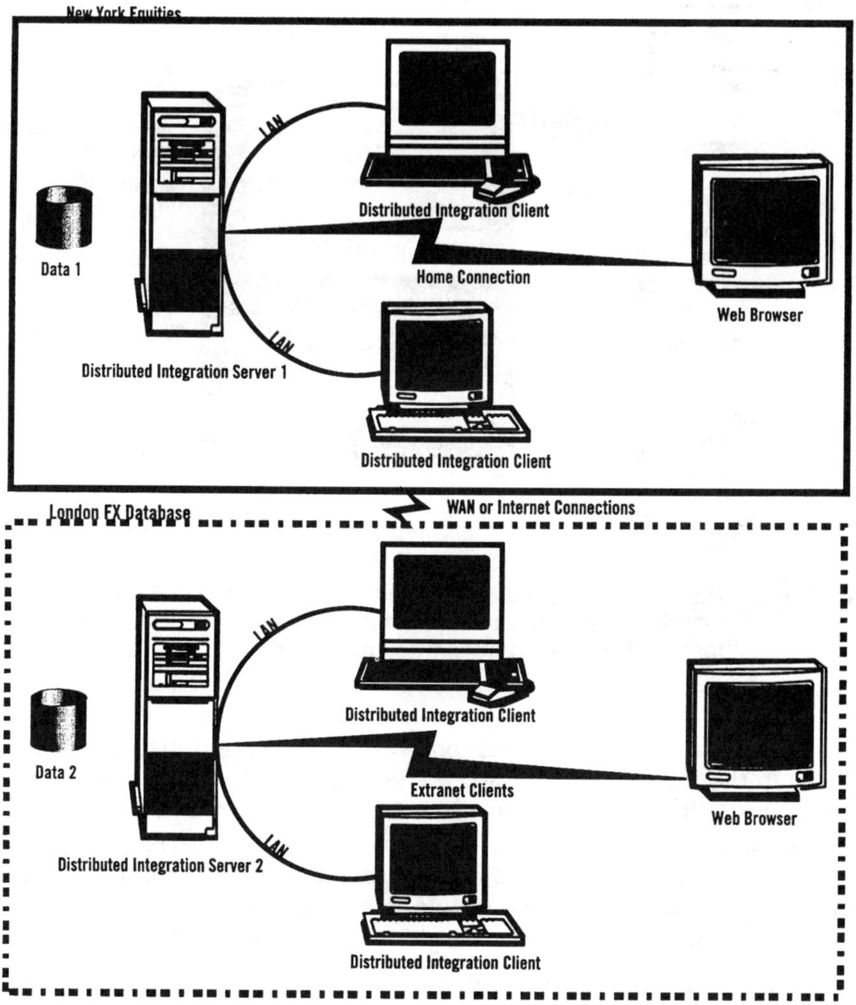

Exhibit 1. A sample of Distributed Integration architecture.

nected to them through the Internet, and get data, analytics, and Web-based applications from them.

LEVERAGING INTERNET/INTRANET TECHNOLOGY

Since the Distributed Integration servers in these two locations can be cascaded, as shown in Exhibit 2, each set of end-users can see the data in the other location. Moreover, since the Distributed Integration architecture is characterized by transparent caching, the access times for local and

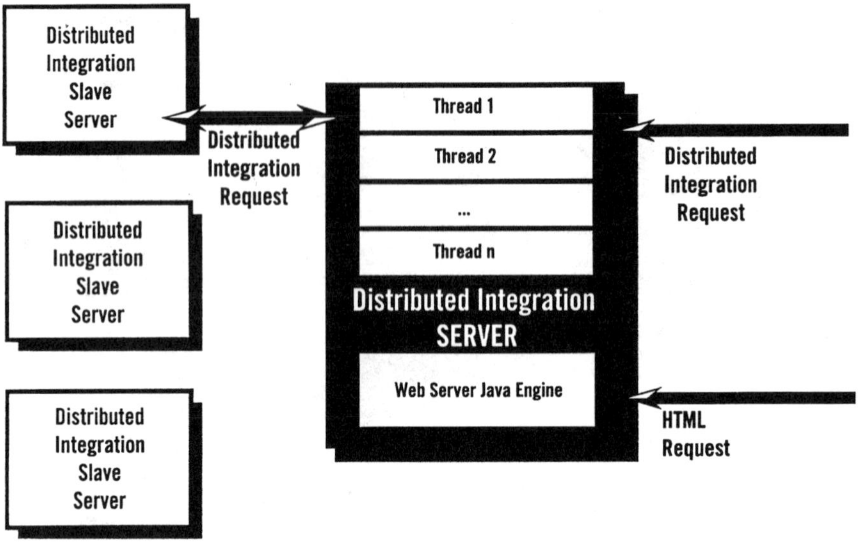

Exhibit 2. Distributed Integration takes advantage of cascaded server technology developed for the Internet to ensure fast and efficient management of Distributed Integration processes.

remote data are almost identical on average. Data are transparently replicated to the location where they are used without significant IT involvement or administrative overhead; this is a far cry from the various data warehousing techniques described above, which require extensive IT resources to implement. As new locations are added with their own Distributed Integration servers, it is a simple step to make those servers known to the existing ones, thereby creating global multidirectional connectivity.

From an administrative point of view, the data, analytics, and applications are being maintained by the group that originated, and most "cares" about them, and they maintain it in whichever database they have chosen. However, because these data are integrated on the server side, local administration and autonomy does not come at the price of effective controls. This is a critical point for risk managers, HQ treasury managers, and compliance managers, who are often strong advocates of data warehousing initiatives which centralize data and in theory enhance controls.

The Distributed Integration server caching will "equalize" the access speed such that the back-end database does not become a bottleneck even if it's a small ACCESS database running on someone's desktop PC. Distributed Integration makes it possible to then selectively share data, analytics, and applications across the entire organization without any additional integration work.

This architecture is highly scalable, since no single point can become a bottleneck as the number of locations increases. Thus, Distributed Integration avoids the scalability pitfalls associated with replication-based data warehousing solutions that tend to "clog up" a company's network.

For optimal scalability, the Distributed Integration server should be configured as a server cluster. This means it is not physically limited to a single process on a single machine. Such a server solution is implemented as a front-end multithreaded cluster manager process, with any number of symmetrical back-end servers that share the same configuration. Moreover, such clusters can always be cascaded amongst themselves, so there truly is no limit to the scalability of the Distributed Integration platform.

THE DISTRIBUTED INTEGRATION SERVER

Distributed Integration servers integrate historical and real-time data, metadata (i.e., data describing data), analytics, and applications. Because the server is capable of handling complex metadata and, by extension, almost any sort of data transformation, Distributed Integration is particularly well suited to address financial institutions' need for integrating time series and relational data.

In order to handle Web-based applications naturally and efficiently, Distributed Integration servers must also, by extension, be Internet servers. Indeed, Distributed Integration servers have been built as plug-ins to preexisting Internet servers. As is consistent with Distributed Integration's reliance on the Web and Web-related technologies, it is most efficient to organize Distributed Integration servers as server clusters.

These Distributed Integration server clusters are stateless and connectionless, just like most Web servers, and should be capable of supporting the HTTP 1.1 keep-alive option for multiple related requests with a single connection for best utilization of network resources. This is also important from a user-functionality perspective; once data have been requested and cached, a user should be able to query that data without recopying it across the network. Likewise, incremental changes should be transmitted without the necessity of replicating the entire data set in which the changes originated.

The server cluster organization is one important reason why Distributed Integration can scale beyond traditional data warehousing solutions. As displayed in Exhibit 2, the front-end Distributed Integration server funnels each request to a number of preconfigured slave servers that actually handle the data and analytical requests.

Scalability is achieved by the fact that any number of slave servers can be added to a cluster, and they are automatically load-balanced by the master server. Fault tolerance is achieved by virtue of the fact that slave servers can be distributed on multiple machines, thereby reducing the chances that a single machine failure will halt the system.

A separate spool of threads handles standard Web server requests such as getting HTML pages, downloading Java applets, etc. This integrated architecture means that application, content, and data can be freely mixed to create a powerful application development and deployment model that is Web-centric and leverages the currently existing infrastructure.

Distributed Integration, it is important to note, performs best in a reasonably consistent hardware environment in which the server machines may be considered more or less interchangeable, and all the slave servers must have access to all the same data and analytics. This implies a shared configuration, as well as shared metadata and data caches. Thus, the user sees the entire cluster as a single server, with one URL address. And this URL address, then, becomes the user's gateway to the firm's total knowledge base.

The Distributed Integration server cluster architecture delivers:

- Performance — through the use of multiple machines coupled with load balancing.
- High availability — through redundancy of slave servers.
- Scalability — you can add more processes and machines as the number of users increases.

THE GATEWAY TO DISTRIBUTED INTEGRATION

Once one or more Distributed Integration servers have been configured to create a single point of integration for data and analytics, the next critical step is to cost-effectively distribute information to a large community of users. This has, in fact, been a challenge for those traditional data warehousing projects that have managed to get off the ground. A Java interface — or Distributed Integration gateway — can be used to connect desktop machines to integrated data and analytics residing on Distributed Integration servers.

When the gateway is active, a machine becomes a Distributed Integration workstation that is capable of "browsing" through all the information that is part of the Distributed Integration environment. Data and analytics can be accessed through a standard Web browser or by building software that connects existing desktop applications to the Distributed Integration environment. Applications that have access to Distributed Integration are called analytic browsers. It is possible to develop Distributed Integration add-ins capable of converting almost any application into an analytic browser.

In the financial services industry, however, one of the most useful applications of the analytic browser will be to connect spreadsheets to the Distributed Integration environment, thus allowing analysts to access integrated data without having to convert files or otherwise participate in the data-cleaning and -collection process. More advanced analytic applications will also become much more powerful when combined with Distributed Integration; indeed, one of the likely benefits of dynamically connecting end-users to an integrated environment is to speed up the pace of financial innovation.

LONG-TERM IMPLICATIONS OF DISTRIBUTED INTEGRATION

Distributed Integration, as it is implemented on a more widespread basis throughout the financial services industry, is likely to have important, even revolutionary, effects on how banks, brokerages, etc. do business in the future. And, as early adopters, the experiences of these financial services firms will serve as a model for other industries. Long-term implications of the Distributed Integration model include the following advantages.

Facilitates Financial Innovation

The desktop PC is synonymous with the modern workplace, and the PC-based spreadsheet application is synonymous with modern finance. However, the demands of today's businesses are straining the practical limits of PC-based spreadsheet analysis. A common illustration of this phenomenon is the fact that numerous highly paid financial analysts spend the majority their time gathering relevant information to feed into their spreadsheets and then verifying that this information is clean, consistent, and correct.

By providing integrated firm-wide data and analytics accessible through spreadsheets — such as Excel™ — Distributed Integration frees financial analysts from time-consuming data management duties and allows them to focus on value-added tasks. End users will also benefit from the opportunity to view and use the sum total of their firms' intellectual capital; they may combine this information in new and profitable ways.

Thus, the widespread adoption of Distributed Integration is likely to foster a new period of rapid financial and business innovation as analysts are simultaneously freed from the demands of data gathering and provided with accurate, integrated information.

Encourages a New Form of Corporate Organization: The Internet Management Model

As the number of Web-enabled workstations within corporations reach critical mass, organizations will be able to learn from the Internet and adopt new ways of managing themselves that go beyond the traditional trade-offs between centralization and decentralization. The Internet Management Model (IMM) is one such method. It applies the Internet philosophy — that information and services are made globally available by the special interests that cherish them at low or no cost across a system which, to the customer, looks consistent, unified, and available on demand — to the corporate organization.

Distributed Integration, which allows local offices to manage and maintain their own mission-critical information while giving everyone access to the entire firm's intellectual capital, is an ideal vehicle for implementing IMM. Thus, rapid growth is sustained while top managers and business analysts have unprecedented access to the "big picture" presented by their firms' collective data and information systems. Islands of data ownership are eliminated.

By allowing firms to track individual and departmental contributions to firm-wide intellectual capital, it becomes possible to identify high- and low-performing areas. Simultaneously, IMM gives individuals and functional units much greater freedom to incorporate new data and analytics into their business activities without obtaining time-consuming approvals from central IT and business planning groups.

Allows Corporations and Financial Institutions to Manage the WHEN Dimension

As businesses' profitability becomes increasingly dependent on the timeliness and quality of the information which serves as the basis for key production, marketing, and strategic decisions, the ability to view, manipulate, and analyze data by time will become a matter of "life and death." Time-centric data, however, is often repetitive and difficult to store in conventional database formats. The Distributed Integration architecture is optimized for the rapid storage, transmission, and analysis of time-centric data as part of an integrated systems environment.

Chapter 8
Distributed Solutions in *n*-Tier Design in the Financial Services Industry

Gregory Dobbin

n-TIER ARCHITECTURE PAVED THE WAY for the development of a front- to back-office software system that conquers the shortcomings of the financial industry's existing technology. This modular system features a single database, which minimizes data entry and allows firms to customize or create their own user interface. Built using Microsoft Distributed interNet Applications (DNA) technology, this system offers users the same functionality on a remote laptop as it does on a networked desktop machine. Finally, its modular design allows firms to use only the parts of the system required to support business practices and gives them the flexibility to increase the size of the system as business grows.

WHAT IS *n*-TIER ARCHITECTURE?

n-Tier architecture differs from the traditional client/server system because it separates business components from the user interface and the database server. A typical system has three distinct tiers: client, business, and database. It is considered *n*-Tier because the architecture can support any number of business tiers between the user interface services and database services.

0-8493-9991-2/99/$0.00+$.50

Client Tier

The client tier contains the user interface code — the portion of an application that gives users access to the system. Until recently, most user interface code was written Microsoft Visual Basic. Today, user interfaces can be built using a variety of tools, including HTML and word processing forms. In a pure *n*-Tier system, very few business processes reside in the user interface code. This separation between the user interface and business processes makes the interface easy to customize and reduces the number of times controls have to be downloaded to client machines.

Business Tier

Business objects represent the real-world objects being automated by the software. The business tier can contain two types of business objects: one that communicates with the user interface, called the client-side object, and one that communicates with the database, called the server-side object. The two types of business objects communicate with each other, thus indirectly linking the user interface to the database.

Client-side business objects are coded to contain business processes as well as business rules and regulations. The server-side business objects translate database concepts into data that can be understood by the client-side business objects. They move data into and out of the database using ODBC, and they contain the SQL statements, recordsets, and results.

Database Tier

At a minimum, the database tier is responsible for creating, updating, retrieving, and deleting data from a data source. In many cases, it also includes more complex features, such as enforcement of relational integrity and other data-related rules.

BUILDING AN *n*-TIER SYSTEM USING MICROSOFT TOOLS

The use of *n*-Tier architecture is an enterprise-wide solution based entirely on Microsoft products, including Windows 95; and Windows 98, Windows NT (Workstation and Server), SQL Server, Microsoft Transaction Server (MTS), Internet Information Server (IIS), Visual Basic (VB), Visual C++, Microsoft Office, and Internet Explorer.

This solution uses Microsoft (DNA) architecture, which allows the capabilities of traditional client/server architecture to merge with the power and accessibility of the Internet. At the heart of Windows DNA are the Component Object Model (COM) and its distributed counterpart, DCOM, which allow for truly reusable code. Since COM and DCOM are language independent, developers can write separate pieces of code that will work together in an application and that can be easily implemented elsewhere in the system. This also means that existing and custom applications interface very simply with *n*-Tier software.

One of the largest shortcomings of client/server architecture is the amount of time, and therefore expense, incurred for client installs of new code and upgrades. Even on a high-speed LAN, upgrading several thousand clients can take a prohibitively long time. Windows DNA solves this problem through the implementation of the browser as the platform for user interfaces. With DNA, all code is stored on the servers and is downloaded to the client on an as-needed basis.

In addition to solving the problem of client code installs, Windows DNA allows the components to run on a LAN, WAN, or the Internet — a truly distributed computing environment. This means that anyone with a computer and Internet access — for example, a broker with a laptop away from the office — has available all of the functionality that in-house users have on their desktop systems. This was an important requirement that could be met only with a system built using *n*-Tier architecture.

Microsoft also provides the Microsoft Internet Finance Server Toolkit (MIFST), which is a set of development tools that allow the development of objects to communicate using Open Financial Exchange (OFX) specifications. OFX is a data format specification that represents financial transaction information that is exchanged among various client and server software packages. OFX supports data transmission for investments, credit, banking, and other financial transactions. MIFST, using OFX, allows the *n*-Tier design to accommodate custom front-end, browser-based applications. Firms using this software could, for example, write their own user interface that uses OFX specifications and implement that interface on the front end of their system. Using MIFST, an object was written that accepts OFX-formatted data, changes the data into *n*-Tier specifications, and passes the data along through *n*-Tier middleware and the rest of the system.

APPLYING *n*-TIER ARCHITECTURE TO THE FINANCIAL INDUSTRY

An *n*-tiered front- to back-office system can use an Internet browser — Internet Explorer, in this case — as the container for the user interface, which allows not only for distribution of code over several machines but also for firms to modify the code distribution to suit their specific needs. An added benefit is that all of the hardware requirements can be satisfied by off-the-shelf machines, at a much lower cost than mainframe systems. And because the *n*-Tier architecture accommodates any size business, firms need only purchase an appropriate number of machines for their activity. As business increases, firms can add machines to their systems to balance the load and keep performance at desired levels.

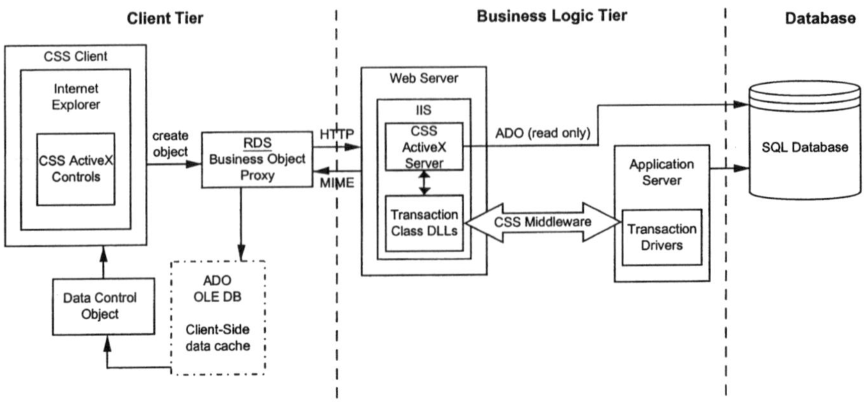

Exhibit 1. The three-tiered model.

The basic architecture of this design is a three-tiered model — client, middle or business logic, and database, as shown in Exhibit 1. Because firms using this system can set up more than one business tier, it is considered *n*-Tier. ActiveX controls on the client machine raise events that create business proxy objects on the client using Remote Data Service (RDS). The business object proxy translates the request into a format that can be sent across the Internet (using HTTP) to the Web server. The request is passed to an API that creates an instance of an ActiveX server, which passes in a SQL statement and data source name information and executes the request using OLE DB.

Most transactions use a Transaction Class DLL to call the appropriate Transaction Driver, which makes the requested reads or updates from the database. Transaction Class DLL refers to a C++ class implementation of a business transaction used to group two appropriate tables with functionality to pack or unpack data for network transport. The Transaction Driver refers to a two-part application that receives and queues messages from clients, processes messages (database requests) and replies to requesting applications, writes error messages to a common location, and sends successful updates to three locations: replication, audit trail, and interface applications. Certain read-only transactions use ADO and speak from the Web server objects directly to the database, skipping the Application server entirely.

Recordsets are packed into MIME format and sent back through HTTP to the client-side business object proxy, which unpacks the results and recreates the recordset. Data are bound to the appropriate client-side controls and displayed to the user.

Client Tier

In an *n*-Tier financial system, a client machine is a basic PC running either Windows 95, Windows 98, or Windows NT Workstation, with Microsoft Office and Internet Explorer installed. Internet Explorer, the system's required web browser, is the medium for the user interface components. HTTP and HTTPS are used for communication to and from the middle tier of the system.

ActiveX controls, which contain user interface code, are downloaded to the client machine on an as-needed basis. As the user navigates through the system, it detects new and changed controls, which are then automatically downloaded from the Web server. There is no need for lengthy, costly client installs; the formerly cumbersome process of installing and upgrading client code becomes automated and transparent.

HTML and ASP pages are called by the business modules, for which these pages contain identification for the required client-side ActiveX controls. For each control, the system takes the class ID, contained in the Object tags, and searches the client machine's registry for that control. If it is not already on the client machine, the system follows the code base to the appropriate location on the server to find the necessary CAB file, unpacks the CAB file and installs its pieces to the client, and registers controls on the client machine. If the control is found in the registry, the system checks the version number, which is contained in the code base, to see if the client has the newest version of that control. If not, the system gets the CAB file and loads and registers the new version.

If the newest version already exists on the client, nothing is downloaded and the control appears to the user immediately. Though the user might notice a slight delay when a new or changed control is loaded, the entire process happens automatically and only when particular controls are needed.

Business Logic Tier

The middle tier houses the business logic and middleware, and is typically divided between two servers, or sets of servers — the Web server and Application server. Using a set of in-house-designed utilities that direct transactions to their appropriate Transaction Drivers, the processes that comprise the middle tier can be divided among more than these two machines for load balancing and performance. For example, a firm might choose to split out the order entry business logic, separate from the rest, since this functionality is more critical than other processes, as shown in Exhibit 2. The middle tier would then consist of a Web and an Application server dedicated to orders and another Web and Application server set for the rest of the system. Firms can split multiple processes out in this man-

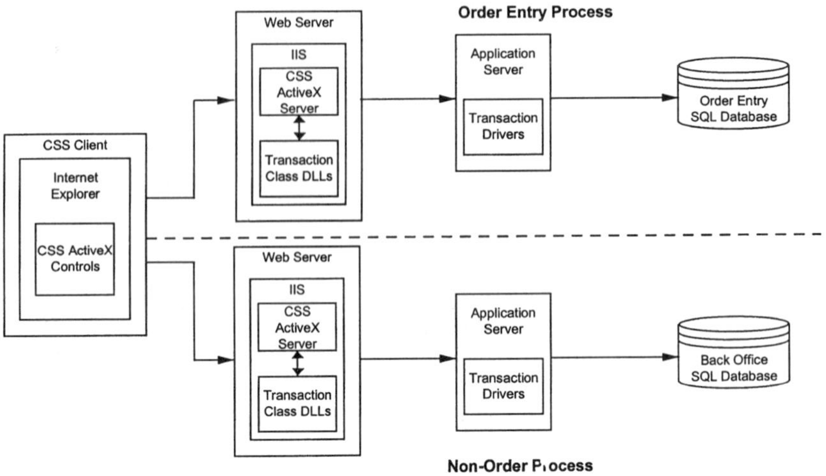

Exhibit 2. Splitting the order-entering processes from the non-order processes.

ner. Another advantage is realized in the area of reliability, since one part of the system could go down without taking the rest with it.

Both the Web and Application servers use MTS to track transactions through the system and to aid in resource pooling. Employing *n*-Tier architecture required the development of NETINF, which is a Message Only Middleware (MOM) component for the business logic tier. NETINF uses User Datagram Protocol (UDP) as its underlying interprocess communications protocol, and many of the *n*-Tier processes use NETINF for sending small message packets that do not require acknowledgments.

The Web server runs on NT Server and uses Microsoft IIS. The Web server houses ActiveX servers, which are invoked during transactions by the client ActiveX controls via RDS. Client controls are also housed on the Web server and are downloaded to the client machines as they are needed. Transaction Class DLLs are created on the Web server and are used to speak to the Transaction Drivers on the Application server, which are responsible for communication with the database.

The Application server runs on NT Server and contains the Transaction Drivers, which are responsible for communication with the database, using ODBC. The Application server also houses *n*-Tier middleware components and the Database Update Control Module (DUCM). DUCM is responsible for assigning a timestamp (discussed later) to every transaction that goes through it to the database, and for creating a transaction log file. As mentioned earlier, there are some processes that do not pass through the Application server, but go instead directly from an ActiveX object on the Web server to the database. These are read-only processes (that do not need to be tracked) and do not pass through DUCM, which means they are not assigned timestamps and are not included in the transaction log file.

Database Tier

The database tier runs on NT Server and uses SQL Server for the database and ODBC for communication. Like the middle tier, the database can be split among several machines to address issues of load balancing and performance. The database itself is third-form normalized, and is an important component contributing to the flexibility and functioning of the system.

Two aspects of the database are important components of the flexible, extensible nature of the *n*-Tier architecture. A system of definition tables, housed in the same database with the rest of the system tables, perform several important functions within the system. Common, reused data, such as a list of the 50 states and their associated two-letter codes, is stored in the definition tables. Every dropdown list in the system that wants a state code reads from a single table that stores that data. Any necessary changes to the list of states would only need to be made one time, in one table.

Definition tables also store codes that impact the functioning of the system, avoiding functionality that would otherwise be hardcoded and would require reprogramming to make changes. A simple example involves the particular screens and information that the firm determines will be required to establish a new account. By modifying definition tables, a firm can determine which of the available screens will be included in the account set-up process and can specify, within those screens which fields are required. Since different firms — even different branches of the same firm — require different sets of information for their business needs, having the ability to change these sorts of parameters without programming can save significant time. Such interaction between application code and the definition tables characterizes *n*-Tier's approach to design.

The other important feature of the database is that tables are updated with new and changed rows, but data is never deleted. Every transaction that is written to the database is given a timestamp, and these timestamps allow the system to distinguish between current and historical rows. This concept of TimeIndependence™ means that historical data is preserved and identified as historical, allowing regulatory and other reports to be generated at a time that is convenient for the firm, typically outside of business hours. Firms can query the database for activity on specific days, at specific times, and accurately recreate activity at indicated times. Rather than tying up valuable processor speed during business hours, firms can run reports at night or on weekends with confidence that the system recognizes the appropriate transactions to include.

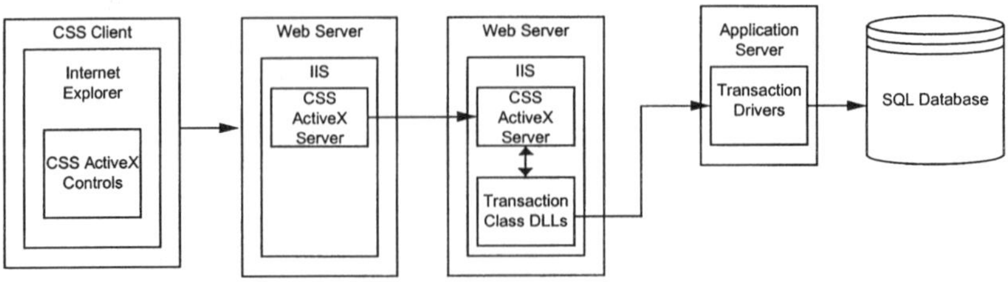

Exhibit 3. Multiple Web servers running in series.

THE BENEFITS OF USING *n*-TIER ARCHITECTURE

The three-tier design offers inherent flexibility because of the distribution of code among the tiers, and, as mentioned, *n*-Tier allows for splitting of the middle and database tiers for better performance and reliability. This design takes the model a step further by allowing tiers to be added to the system. A firm might subdivide a middle tier serially, resulting in multiple Web servers running in series and then to the Application server for a given process, as shown in Exhibit 3.

n-Tier architecture allows the business and database tiers to interface with custom or third-party user interfaces that use OFX. A firm could write its own user interface that uses OFX to communicate with the MIFST piece, which would convert the OFX-based data into *n*-Tier specifications. From there, the transaction would be passed to the middle and database tiers exactly as if it had originated from the in-house-built user interface as shown in Exhibit 4. Any Personal Finance Manager software, or even another Web server, that is OFX-compliant could be used as the front end of the *n*-Tier system in this manner.

Another advantage of the flexibility of the *n*-Tier architecture lies in the ease of extensibility, because of the interaction through OFX and MIFST, and because *n*-Tier design provides the tools to write interfaces to legacy systems. Firms can interface, if they choose, with any legacy back-office system by using a set of available COM objects that can be called by a custom interface application to receive and unpack data from *n*-Tier Transaction Drivers. The data must then only be put into the legacy system. To ensure accuracy when using interfaces, another COM object was developed that can be used to read the DUCM log file and retrieve any message packets that may have been missed. Since all updates are logged by DUCM, interface applications can at any time access thorough data on transactions that have passed through the system.

Because the modules and tiers can interface with existing applications and legacy systems, firms can migrate to an *n*-Tier system rather than con-

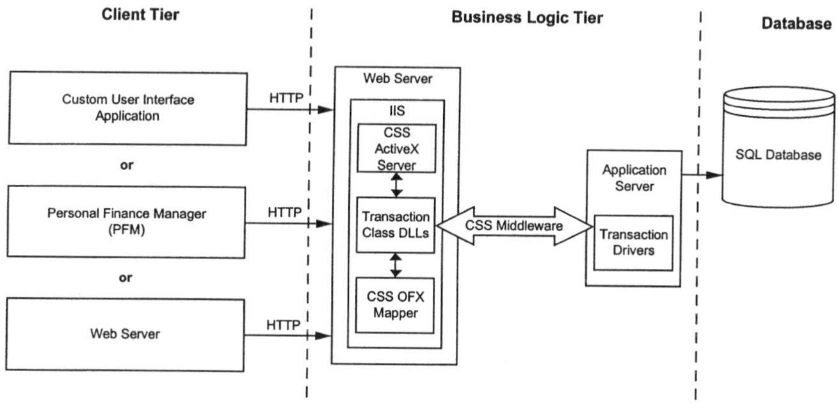

Exhibit 4. *n*-Tier architecture allows the business and database tiers to interface with custom or third-party user interfaces that use OFX.

verting the entire business at once, which could result in significant loss of business and revenue. Firms can implement selected modules one at a time and interface them with their existing legacy system or with their own front end. When those modules have had adequate testing and development time, the firm can then move on to other modules until the entire system (or the portion of the system the firm ultimately wants) is in place. The migration process, because of the system's flexibility, can take place over a period of time that each firm chooses, without disruption of daily operations.

A key drawback of other financial industry solutions is that the inability of separate components to communicate with one another does not allow Straight Through Processing. The interoperability of the parts of *n*-Tier design with each other and with non-*n*-Tier applications allows transactions to pass through the entire system without requiring manual input. Straight Through Processing is faster, more accurate, and more cost-effective than systems that require transactions to periodically come out of the loop because certain applications cannot speak to others.

Chapter 9 Windows Distributed interNet Architecture for Financial Services

Dave Yewman

TO COMPETE EFFECTIVELY IN THE NEXT 3 TO 5 YEARS, retail banks must migrate from monolithic core banking systems to PC-based client/server systems. To achieve this, they need low-risk ways to control costs and integrate existing legacy applications with flexible, powerful, scalable solutions that will enable the integration of multiple delivery channels.

With the recently announced Microsoft® Windows® Distributed interNet Applications (Windows DNA) architecture, the Microsoft Corporation has created a framework that allows businesses to more easily build new systems that take advantage of the capabilities of the personal computer and the opportunities presented by the Internet while integrating with existing systems. This chapter outlines how a new breed of applications can be delivered in retail banking using Windows DNA and the new Windows DNA for Financial Services (Windows DNA FS) while using existing systems and implementing "best-of-breed" solutions.

Windows DNA FS enables legacy computer systems to function in today's high-tech world. Windows DNA FS also works with powerful, scalable client/server computer systems that allow banks to use traditional delivery channels as well as Internet-oriented solutions, customer analysis tools, and load balancing.

INTRODUCING WINDOWS DNA

Windows DNA integrates the personal computer standard, the Internet, and legacy infrastructures by enabling computers to interoperate and cooperate equally well across corporate and public networks. Windows DNA

0-8493-9991-2/99/$0.00+$.50

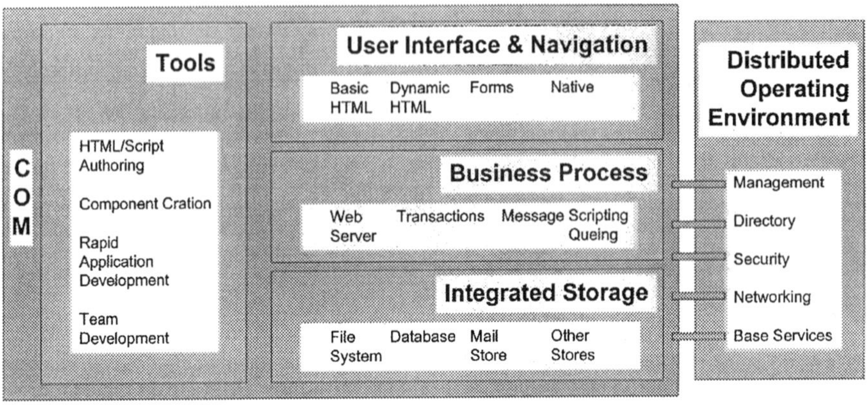

Exhibit 1. Windows DNA.

provides an interoperability framework based on open protocols and published interfaces that allow customers to extend existing systems with new functionality. This same open model provides extensibility "hooks," so third parties can realize new business opportunities by creating compatible products that extend the architecture (Exhibit 1).

Windows DNA applications use a standard set of Windows-based services that address the requirements of all tiers of modern distributed applications — user interface and navigation, business processes, and data storage. The heart of Windows DNA is the integration of the Internet and client/server application development models through the Microsoft Component Object Model (COM). Windows DNA provides a common set of services that are exposed in a unified way at all tiers of a distributed application.

By taking advantage of the capabilities in Windows DNA, developers will be able to build entirely new categories of applications, including electronic commerce and other interpersonal and intercorporate communication applications. Because they can take advantage of standard implementations of networked services and modern, component-based development methods, developers can deliver these innovative applications much more quickly than they could in the past.

These applications will have the potential for wide acceptance because Windows DNA fully embraces an open approach to distributed computing, building on standards approved by bodies such as the World Wide Web Consortium (W3C) and the Internet Engineering Task Force (IETF).

FUNDAMENTAL SERVICES

In the Windows DNA architecture, applications are built as a series of functional components. Microsoft's COM is the glue that is used to knit these components together.

Building applications based on COM components has many advantages for financial institutions. They can reuse business components they built themselves across the delivery channels. They can take advantage of the many prebuilt components available from third-party suppliers. They can tailor one of the many off-the-shelf applications that support COM interfaces to rapidly build new solutions that meet their particular business requirements.

For example, a funds transfer component built in COM can be delivered to a home banking application as an ActiveX™ Control, embedded in branch automation application for tellers to use — without programmatic change — or made available in an ATM running personal computer hardware. The user experience and branding are consistent, and clients recognize transfers in all scenarios immediately.

The net gain for the financial institution is easy to tally: one function, written once, tested once, deployed in many locations — the true promise of reusable programming.

There are currently more than 2000 vendors shipping business software products based on COM technologies. And because COM provides a language-independent component interface, financial institutions have the freedom to pick the best-of-breed suppliers, programming languages, and programming tools. The financial institution can chose a programming language based on developer experience and availability of skills rather than simply according to availability of components, technology vendors, programming tools, or environments. All Microsoft tools, applications, and systems products provide published COM-based extensibility interfaces. In fact, COM is the primary way for third parties to integrate their solutions with Microsoft products. Financial institutions can integrate existing systems through COM. Host- or UNIX-based applications are exposed to the developer in a consistent way through the COM interfaces.

WINDOWS DNA FOR FINANCIAL SERVICES

Traditionally, financial institutions have built separate IT systems and infrastructures to service different delivery channels as business opportunities and demand arose. Typically, this resulted in different IT infrastructures for different delivery channels.

Each infrastructure had its own set of hardware platforms, network protocols, middleware products, development tools, monolithic applications and data stores. Integration was typically at the data stores, leveraging the information itself but not the application logic across delivery channels. This process has resulted in longer development times, less product homogeneity and, when new banking products or services require access across the data stores, ultimately, a less satisfactory user experience — meaning that technology has helped alienate the customer from the bank rather than enhancing the relationship, which was the original intent.

Third parties that build solutions to the Windows DNA FS architecture, however, will allow financial institutions to build a reusable, reliable, scalable delivery channel infrastructure that marries the best of existing systems with the flexibility of new systems and takes advantage of the distributed services provided by the Windows NT® Server operating system and Microsoft BackOffice® family of products.

Financial institutions have long desired what Windows DNA FS promises (Exhibit 2). But in the past, they have had to use different client hardware platforms for each delivery channel, because of the different processing requirements of each channel and the technical limits of existing hardware.

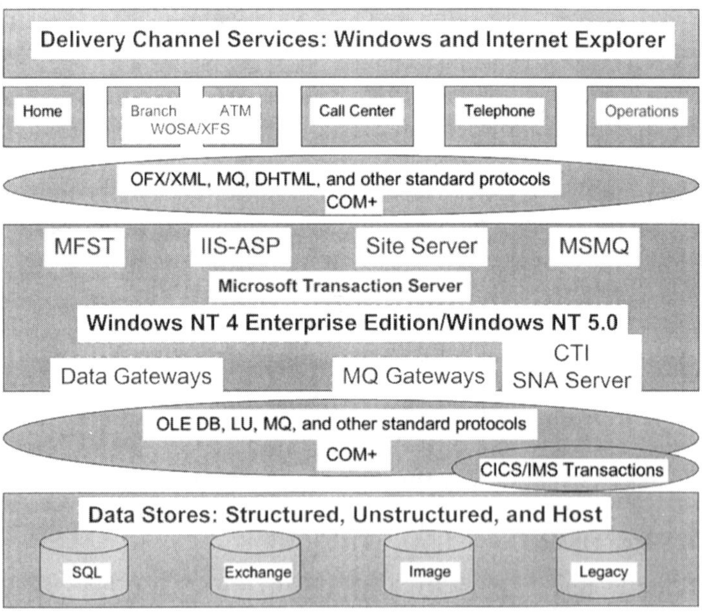

Exhibit 2. Windows DNA in Financial Services for Retail Banking.

For instance, a 3270 terminal connected directly to an account management application served the bank teller who needed to use only that application. However, a loan-processing officer who needed to perform word processing and spreadsheet analysis as well as account management worked with a PC, meaning that from a programmatic standpoint the bank had two incompatible infrastructures. In addition, the bank had a number of client platforms that had to be separately maintained and administered and that had to have applications developed for them. Because each of these platforms is targeted to one particular task, there is little opportunity for flexibility in deploying applications. For example, the loan calculation application that integrates Microsoft Excel and Microsoft Word cannot be used from the teller position even if business process analysis shows that the best way to service loans is through the teller. These issues lead to increased operations, development, and training costs and an inability to adapt quickly to changing business requirements.

The Microsoft Windows operating system family — Windows CE, Windows-based Terminals, Windows 95, Windows 98, and Windows NT Workstation and Windows NT Server — have a consistent user interface and programming model, enabling financial institutions to overcome the technical limitations that handicapped previous systems and to use reusable skills developed by the user, administrator, and developer.

In an integrated infrastructure, the bank teller can now use an account management application running on a Windows-based Terminal or a Windows-based Network PC (Net PC) in Task Station mode. The loans processing officer uses the loan application on a Windows-based PC in Application Station mode. This provides the bank with increased flexibility but lower administration costs. If required, the teller position can quickly and easily be reconfigured by a central administrator to run the loan application without the need for a new hardware platform and operating system. The system administrator has a consistent hardware architecture, and the developer can use a common set of services and development tools across all the delivery channels.

Within the Windows DNA FS architecture, all financial services clients — whether home banking PCs, teller positions, or self-service devices — are connected to Windows NT Server via standard IP-based protocols. This lowers infrastructure costs, decreases systems administration costs, increases reuse of administration skills, and helps lower training costs.

By rationalizing the core messaging protocols used across financial services clients, financial institutions can benefit from economies of scale by deploying one set of application components to support these core-messaging protocols. These components can be used and reused across the financial services clients.

Because of its seamless support for standard network protocols and messaging standards (such as Open Financial Exchange [OFX], XML, HTTP, and TCP/IP), Windows NT Server acts as a gateway to existing delivery channels and the corporate network. This allows financial institutions to preserve existing network investments and migrate to the new standard networking protocols in an evolutionary manner. Microsoft and other industry leaders provide many strategies for preserving investments in middle-tier transaction processing systems — including MVS, AS/400, and UNIX — by integrating them into Windows NT Server-based applications. These applications include CICS, IMS, and XA Support, Microsoft Message Queue Server, OLE DB, database replication from host databases into Microsoft SQL Server™, and Distributed COM (DCOM) support on platforms other than Microsoft.

The ability to integrate with existing systems, together with its support for new technologies such as those underlying the Internet and intranets and a wide range of high-productivity development tools, makes Windows NT a strong application development platform. Developers can produce powerful new applications that tie together existing systems and extend the reach of those systems more quickly and easily than ever.

WINDOWS DNA FOR FINANCIAL SERVICES — SERVICES DEFINITIONS

The Windows DNA for Financial Services framework defines three logical layers (Exhibit 3). Each layer provides the services that allow financial institutions to build the applications that meet their business requirements.

From a logical view, the three services equate to the three tiers in the Windows DNA architecture: User Interface and Navigation, Business Process, and Integrated Storage. Physical implementation of the services can be varied based on the needs of the delivery channel.

Delivery Channel Services

The IT departments of financial institutions are faced with many conflicting demands when deciding how to best serve the delivery channels. On the one hand, they need to service as many delivery channels as the business requires; on the other hand, they want to minimize the development cost of maintaining multiple heterogeneous clients.

Financial institutions can meet these requirements by taking advantage of the broad reach of the Microsoft Windows operating system family and the services provided by the Windows DNA FS architecture.

The Microsoft Windows operating system family, with its consistent user interface and programming model, allows developers to write applications that run on the broadest possible range of hardware configurations (Exhibit 4). From the home through the branch office and onto the trading

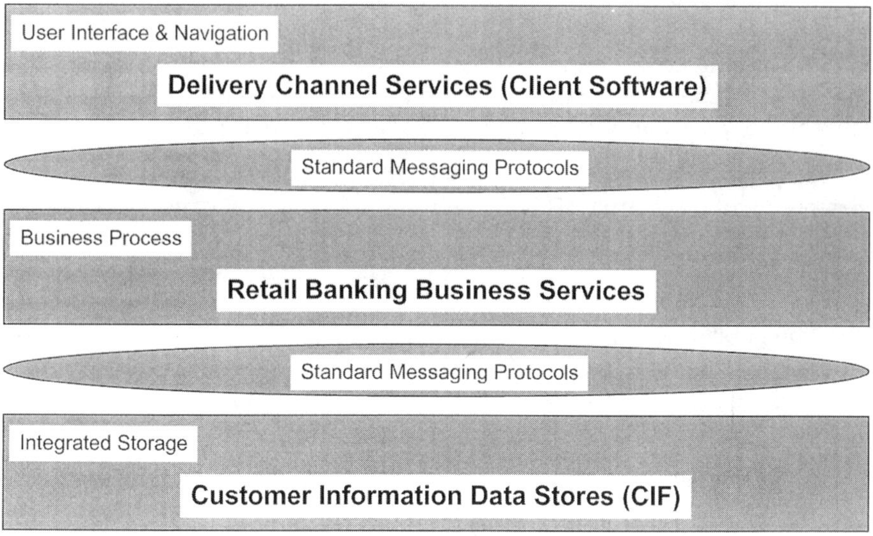

Exhibit 3. Windows DNA for Financial Services.

floor, there are devices based on the PC standard to suit every requirement — all running one member of the Microsoft Windows operating system family.

Financial institutions can build user interfaces using basic HTML to reach the broadest range of clients — PC, Macintosh, and UNIX — running different browsers. Financial institutions can build user interfaces using Dynamic HTML and scripting (the Visual Basic® development system Scripting Edition or JScript™ development software), providing the rich, flexible, and interactive experience users have come to expect from Windows-based applications. Because of the cross-platform support provided

Exhibit 4. Windows devices, like delivery channels, come in various shapes.

by Microsoft Internet Explorer 4.0, such user interfaces can still service a broad range of clients. Financial institutions can encapsulate business logic in scriptable components that can then be deployed on the client or on the server, depending on the client device, because COM and the scripting environment are supported at all layers of Windows DNA FS.

For instance, a home banking application may have a basic HTML user interface and a Dynamic HTML user interface; this will deliver services to all customers but offer a richer experience to customers with more advanced browser software. Microsoft Internet Information Server (IIS) and Active Server Pages (ASP) scripting technology can be used to determine the type of browser the customer is using and deliver the appropriate user interface. The components that verify user input and generate financial services requests run in Internet Explorer 4.0 either on the client or as part of an ASP on the server.

The power and flexibility of Dynamic HTML, combined with scripting and components, allow the user interface for business applications in the branch, the self-service device, the call center, and the back office to be built using this same technology. Developers can reuse business logic and user interface components across delivery channels, reducing the amount of new code they have to write. Developers can use the same tools and techniques for building all of the delivery channel applications, reducing training costs and increasing skills reuse. This reduces the cost of building a new delivery channel application as well as the time to build the application and increases the quality of the application.

For instance, a Dynamic HTML COM component that gathers the details used to transfer funds from one account to another can be used in a browser-based home banking application, in a branch-banking teller application and in a self-service device. By using a common message protocol, such as OFX, to send financial services requests from the client to the server across the delivery channels, financial institutions can reuse the cooperating components that generate those requests.

Financial institutions can use Microsoft Site Server Personalization Services to easily build user interfaces that allow customers to tailor a home banking application to reflect their particular financial needs and interests. By using advanced technologies such as Microsoft NetMeeting™ conferencing software, which allows videoconferencing over the Internet and intranets, financial institutions can offer an even richer service to their customers. For example, if a customer wants to apply for a loan but needs advice, she or he can connect directly to the call center from the home banking application to talk to a customer service representative.

By using the same Internet-based technologies to build the user interfaces for home banking and self-service devices, financial institutions can serve the customer using the same familiar user interface both at home and at a branch or in the supermarket. Not only will the customer be presented with a familiar user interface, but because services such as Personalization and NetMeeting are available, the self-service application can be tailored to reflect the customer's requirements and can offer interactive advice. Such technologies allow the financial institution to provide a wider range of tailored services to customers while reducing the customer's need to visit the branch. It increases the customer's perception of the financial institution's responsiveness and flexibility and therefore increases customer satisfaction and loyalty, while lowering costs by providing these services across the most cost-effective delivery channels.

Business Services

Financial institutions face similar challenges when building the business services that sit behind the delivery channels. They want to service as many delivery channels as the business requires, but they do not want to incur the overhead of maintaining multiple business server infrastructures (Exhibit 5). They want to build an application infrastructure that scales up to Internet banking and scales down to small-branch banking. They want to produce applications that deliver a single view of the customer, but they don't want to re-engineer their existing account-based transaction processing systems. They want to take advantage of the price/performance and choice advantages provided by PC-based servers, but they also want the scalability and reliability that until now have been provided only by high-cost mainframe transaction processing systems.

Financial institutions can meet all these requirements by taking advantage of the services provided by the Windows DNA architecture — Web server, transactions, messaging, and scripting.

Windows NT Server and the Microsoft BackOffice family of products provide the bedrock on which Windows DNA services are built. They offer

Exhibit 5. Separate cooperating application logic.

integrated security and administration, fast file and print, communications, messaging and groupware, database, host connectivity, systems management, Internet, secure proxy, content creation and Web site management, and information retrieval and search services. Microsoft BackOffice server applications, with their familiar Windows-based interface, are easy to install, deploy, and administer. The use of common administration tools across the BackOffice family helps financial institutions reduce training and support needs. Integrated security means that users and their security permissions are defined only once rather than for each service, which reduces administration overhead and the possibility of errors.

Microsoft Transaction Server (MTS), now built into Windows NT Server, provides financial institutions with the services they need to more easily deliver manageable, reliable, scalable COM component-based applications that will service thousands of simultaneous users. MTS manages transaction scope across components, across databases, across machines, and even across heterogeneous systems (Windows NT, UNIX, CICS). It allows developers to build scalable solutions without having to build complex infrastructures or understand arcane programming tools and to build solutions that integrate Microsoft SQL Server, the Internet, and legacy systems via standard COM interfaces. These services allow developers to focus on building business solutions, lowering development costs substantially. In addition, using the symmetric multiprocessor capabilities of Windows NT Server, a COM component can take advantage of a powerful multiprocessor to provide functionality to hundreds or even thousands of clients.

Using the distributed services of Windows DNA FS, developers can build applications as a set of cooperating components. This allows financial institutions to build flexible applications based on components that can be used across delivery channels. For instance, in the past a home banking application and a branch banking teller application would have contained separate but almost identical business logic to transfer funds between accounts. Because this business logic was embedded in the separate applications, there was little or no chance of this logic being reused across the applications and a great chance that common business rules were implemented inconsistently. Now the business logic is encapsulated in a single "financial transaction" component that services both delivery channels, so the business logic needs to be implemented only once. This helps ensure consistent implementation, higher quality, and lower maintenance costs.

This component-based approach allows financial institutions to buy rather than build. In the past, packaged applications could save development time but were either hard to integrate with existing systems and difficult to extend or complicated to set up and deploy. By building their applications to the Windows DNA FS architecture and delivering them as a set of components, third-party developers solve the integration problem for financial institutions. With MTS taking care of transaction coordination and component isolation issues, financial institutions can integrate component-based solutions into their delivery channel infrastructure, and then make use of these same components to build new services.

Financial transaction components can be invoked via the Internet, an intranet or a LAN. Microsoft Internet Information Server and Active Server Pages scripting technology allow financial transaction components to be invoked from Web pages. The Microsoft Internet Financial Services Toolkit (MIFST) provides a framework that allows financial transaction components to be invoked based on Open Financial Exchange requests received from personal financial managers, small-business accounting packages, and browser-based home banking applications. DCOM allows financial transaction components to be invoked directly from applications such as a branch banking teller application. This flexibility gives financial institutions the opportunity to reuse financial transaction components across delivery channels — whether in the home, the branch, the supermarket, or the back office.

By taking advantage of the Windows DNA FS architecture, financial institutions can encapsulate business logic into financial transaction components. A particular component can be used for every delivery channel that needs to implement that business logic, which reduces the amount of new code developers have to write. Because developers can use the same standard tools and techniques for building components for all the delivery channel applications, training costs are lowered and skills are reused. This reduces the cost of building a new delivery channel application, as well as the time to build the application and increases the quality of the application.

By taking advantage of the legacy system integration technologies exposed through COM interfaces in MTS and Microsoft's universal data access technology, financial institutions can build components that gather information from many systems. This allows them to build delivery channel services that present a single view of the customer. The analysis tools built into Microsoft Site Server allow analysis of what pages customers visit on a Web site, how often they go there, and how much time they spend. Combining such information about customer interests with customer information held by financial institutions gives the institutions a uniquely powerful view of the customer that will allow accurately targeted sales and marketing. For example, a customer with $10,000 in her savings account who spends time online looking at information on stocks is a qualified lead for customer service representatives offering investment advice or information on money market funds.

Integrated Storage

Financial institutions need to build applications that present a unified view of customer information and associated relationship information.

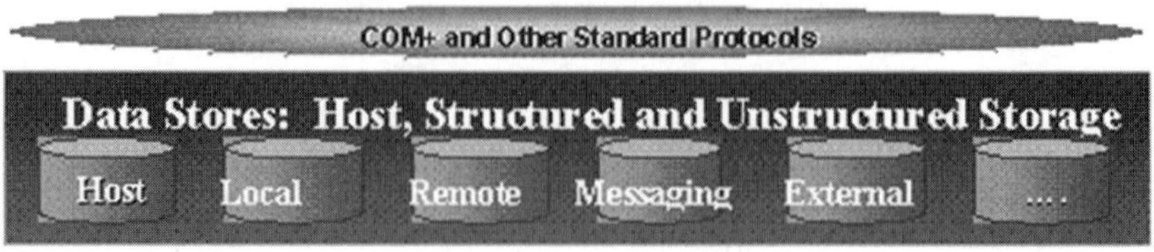

Exhibit 6. A unified view of customer information.

This unified view must transcend system boundaries whether the information lies in a legacy transaction processing system, an e-mail system, or a letter written with a word processor (Exhibit 6).

Microsoft and other industry leaders provide many tools and strategies for preserving existing investments by integrating application transactions, message queuing infrastructure, and data stores into Windows DNA applications. These tools include CICS, IMS, and XA support via COM interfaces in Microsoft Transaction Server and the Component Transaction Integrator, Microsoft Message Queue Server, and DCOM support on platforms other than Microsoft. Integration with these legacy systems preserves existing investment while using the consistent programming model of the Windows family of operating systems.

Microsoft's Universal Data Access Technology, known as OLE DB, allows access to disparate data sources through a consistent COM interface. OLE DB complements ODBC by allowing all data sources, not just relational databases, to expose their data through a common set of COM interfaces. Data from e-mail, files, spreadsheets, and documents as well as databases are accessible through OLE DB. This allows developers to access data from many sources without the overhead of using multiple proprietary data-access APIs.

On Windows NT Server, the Microsoft SQL Server database has outstanding transaction processing performance — holding the top 10 spots in the TPC-c price/performance rankings — and contains high levels of integrity and resilience, built-in data replication, and remote stored procedures. It also supports distributed transaction. Microsoft SQL Server also features intuitive graphical systems management tools that reduce training costs and administration overhead.

Data replication from host database systems into Microsoft SQL Server and distributed transactions, together with low administration overhead, allow financial institutions to distribute data where it adds the greatest value for the customer — for instance, a local branch office.

Financial institutions can use these data access services with Microsoft SQL Server to build components that present a unified view of the customer without the development overhead of using multiple proprietary data access APIs and without mandating a potentially perilous attempt to move all data into a single corporate database.

SUMMARY

Financial institutions have a vision for their future: delivering a flexible and responsive service to the customer — any service, any time, any where. Windows DNA for Financial Services is the first real solution for financial institutions that want to integrate delivery channels in both a networked and Internet-networked world. Windows DNA FS provides a consistent programming model, consistent development environment, consistent distributed services, and consistent application model to the desktop and the server. The core of these features is the Windows family of products and the distributed services built into them.

This vision needs to be supported by flexible, customer-focused IT systems that support multiple delivery channels. These IT systems must take advantage of the power of new technologies without requiring financial institutions to replace their existing transaction processing systems, and they must cost less time and effort to build than in the past. By building to this architecture, financial institutions can more quickly and easily develop delivery channel applications that integrate the new technologies with their existing systems to provide more customer service at lower cost than ever.

WHERE TO GET STARTED?

For more information on Windows DNA for Financial Services, visit the Microsoft in financial services Web site at http://www.microsoft.com/industry/finserv/.

Chapter 10
Evaluation of Financial and Application Prototyping Environments

Charles Bassignani

OVER THE LAST TWENTY YEARS, the emergence of relatively low-cost yet powerful desktop computers has had a profound impact on the financial services industry. The efforts of banks and money management firms to put more computing power on the desktops of traders, analysts, and quantitative researchers has led to the development of sophisticated software packages for research, analytic prototyping, and application development.

Evaluating one analytic and application prototyping environment against another is a difficult task. Diverse feature sets and scope make direct comparisons between packages difficult. The number of packages available is great and it is often difficult to discern which packages are of quality. To make the task of choosing the best environment more manageable, this chapter seeks to build a framework for the systematic evaluation of each environment by identifying the most important features for analytic prototyping and application development.

We will begin this chapter with a discussion of what we mean by the terms *analytic prototyping* and *application development.* We will then proceed with a discussion of important features in both areas. Although we will refrain from discussing particular software packages in detail, we will show examples of the tools available in some of the more common environments. It is important to point out that no single package available on the market today does everything. Each package has its relative strengths and weaknesses.

0-8493-9991-2/99/$0.00+$.50

ANALYTIC PROTOTYPING AND APPLICATION DEVELOPMENT

Having a good analytic prototyping and application development environment is critical to the timely delivery of good software tools for end-users. The term *analytic prototyping* refers to the creation of individual tools which either embody a theoretical model in its entirety, or provide a component necessary for implementation of that theoretical model. The term *application development* refers to the act of packaging analytics, or tools, together along with an interface and some form of data connectivity to create a solution for a real-world problem. An example of application development in this context would the be the creation of a decision support system for fixed income. At a minimum, such a system would consist of a set of tools for valuing bonds, calculating yield to maturity and accrued interest, and for calculating sensitivities such as duration and convexity. This system would probably also include a Graphical User Interface (GUI) and some functionality for retrieving data from and writing data to a database. A good application development environment should support the development of all these components.

The financial application development value chain is a useful framework for understanding analytic prototyping and application development and why selection of a good environment is a critical determinant of competitive advantage in the financial services industry. This value chain consists of activities performed by academic researchers, quantitative researchers ("quants"), application developers, traders, and analysts (see Exhibit 1). In this framework, academics develop theoretical models in the area of fixed income, derivatives, equities, portfolio management, risk management, and foreign exchange. Quantitative researchers take these models and implement them, creating prototype analytics or tools in the process. With the help of the quants, application developers use aggregations of these analytics to create applications which are then tested by analysts and traders. Based on the results of these tests, the algorithms contained in the applications are modified and then retested. From this iterative process, emerges both a set of polished analytics and a finished end-user application. Groups of finished analytics which pertain to the same task or application area in finance are often bundled together into *modules* or *libraries.* Application developers then link these libraries together with other GUIs and an interfaces to a data sources to form even more financial applications.

IDENTIFYING CRITICAL FEATURES

The quality of any analytic prototyping and application development environment (hereafter "prototyping environment") can be assessed along two dimensions: core/functional analytics, and development/development

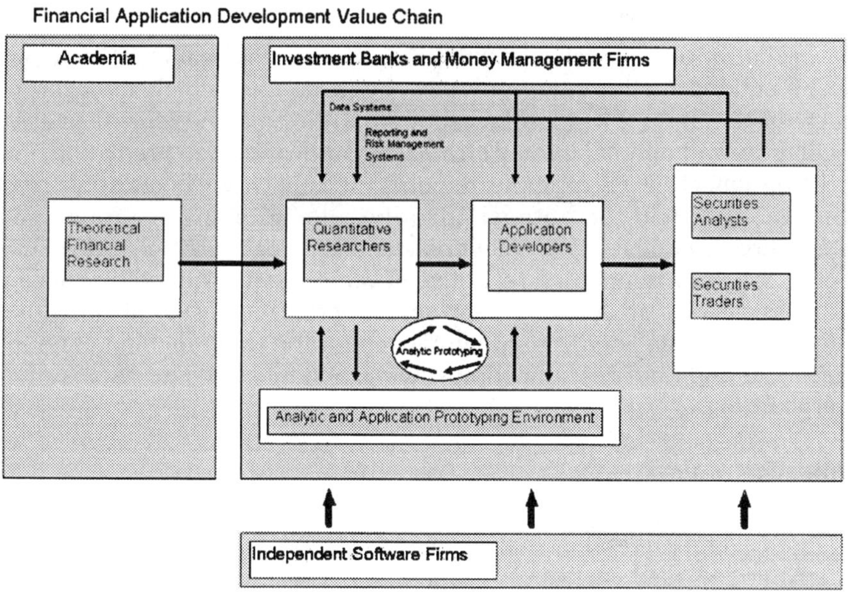

Exhibit 1. The financial applications software development value chain is a useful way to see why having a good prototyping and development environment is critical to the timely delivery of good software tools.

support tools. The terms *core* and *functional analytics* refer to sets of tools designed for specific tasks which arise as a part of the research, prototyping, and development processes. Core analytics include tools for optimization, statistical analysis, and mathematics. Functional analytics include analytics for fixed income, equity, derivatives, portfolio optimization, risk management, and foreign exchange. Development and development support tools refer to the tools and capabilities which specifically support the development of applications from prototype analytics and research results. A good set of development tools will include support for code generation, application distribution, data connectivity, and GUI development.

CORE ANALYTICS

The availability of core analytics is an important concern in choosing a prototyping environment. Especially important are tool sets for optimization, statistics, and matrix mathematics. Tools for sophisticated statistical analysis such as GARCH and an infrastructure for financial time series analysis are desirable, as are tools for spline techniques, symbolic math, neural networks, and fuzzy logic.

Optimization Tools

Optimization involves the minimization and maximization of mathematical functions. Optimization problems frequently arise in finance, particularly in the area of asset allocation, volatility analysis for derivatives valuation, and optimal trading strategy identification and prediction. Portfolio optimization, for example, requires the application of constrained optimization to find the optimal portfolio allocation given a universe of securities to choose from, a covariance matrix for those securities, and a set of constraints, or rules, regarding how and in what quantities those securities can be held. A good feature set for optimization should include scalar minimization, linear programming, quadratic programming, functions for linear and nonlinear equation solving, and functions for least squares curve fitting.

Statistics Tools

Statistics tools are used extensively in finance, from simple descriptive statistical and regression analysis of historical data, to normal cumulative distribution-based analysis in support of Black-Scholes option pricing, to multidistribution-based approaches to Monte Carlo simulation. In addition to tools for basic descriptive statistics and regression, a good set of statistics tools should accommodate analysis based on multiple probability distributions, including normal, lognormal, *t*, binomial, and Poisson. For each of these distributions, the tool set should include tools for deriving and using a probability density function, cumulative distribution function and its inverse, mean and variance as a function of parameters, and random number generation.

Numerical Algorithms

Quantitative financial calculations in support of analytic prototyping requires a broad set of core mathematical functionality. From the interpolation of interest rates for the purposes of developing discount factors for a particular cash flow in time, to root-finding approaches to determining the internal rate of return on a stream of cash flows, to correlation and covariance analysis on a set of assets, to simple sorting, the availability of numerical and mathematical functionality is an important consideration in evaluating a prototyping environment.

Time Series Infrastructure

The term "time series" is widely used in many disciplines. In finance, it has a particular meaning that differs slightly from the concept in electrical engineering or other areas. A financial time series normally consists of a temporally distributed set of prices or price returns for an asset or set of assets. Financial times series will exhibit characteristics that are perhaps uniquely financial, such as data sparseness, volatility clumping, and leverage effects. Since financial time series often contain missing data, some sort of filling or interpolation is normally required as a first step in any analysis. Time series of stock prices may be missing values because trading in a stock was suspended for a particular day, because trading was suspended at midday and the prices are closing prices, or because the stocks are traded in two different geographic markets. Financial statement data, such as earnings, may also be missing values because a company failed to report earnings for one or more quarters or is in the process of restating earnings. This is especially true of publicly held companies that are very small. By contrast, in engineering, time series are normally data-complete and do not require filling or interpolation.

Financial time series analysis itself involves nearly every type of statistical analysis possible, from simple descriptive statistics to more sophisticated analytical techniques such as regression, nonstationary descriptive statistics, principal components analysis, etc. As a result, time series analytics are more an infrastructural concern than they are a set of tools and should be viewed as such.

GARCH

Generalized AutoRegressive Conditional Heteroscedascity (GARCH) modeling is a modeling approach which takes into account the existence of time dependent/conditional variance in a financial time series. In looking at the price behavior of stocks, for example, we see that volatility tends to be clustered, meaning that high price volatility tends to be followed by high price volatility and low price volatility tends to be followed by low price volatility. We also see that a return series typically exhibits "leverage effects," meaning that the impact of positive surprises tends to be less substantial than the impact of negative surprises. GARCH modeling (hereinafter GARCH) allows one to explain and model the time-varying characteristics of risk and uncertainty in a financial time series.

Many derivative securities, such as commodities futures and equity options, derive their value from some underlying asset (hence the term "derivative"). The pricing of these derivative securities depends to a great extent on the investor's estimate of volatility for the price of the underlying asset. For example, the price that one will pay for a corn futures contract which expires 3 months from now will depend on the perceived volatility of corn prices over the life of the option. The price of a call option on IBM's common stock will depend on the recent volatility of IBM's stock price, which will in turn drive investor's perceptions for price volatility over the life of the option. Prior to the advent of GARCH, financial practitioners would model volatility simply as the standard deviation of some historical time series extrapolated into the future. With GARCH, more sophisticated predictions for volatility are now possible.

In addition to standard GARCH, there are several other strains of GARCH being used in finance. Threshold GARCH, or TGARCH, looks at the leverage effect on time-varying changes in volatility above a certain threshold. Exponential GARCH, or EGARCH, gives exponential weighting to the leverage effect on time-varying volatility. Power GARCH, or PGARCH, raises the impact of leverage to a power which, in turn, is statistically estimated from the data. These four types, or strains, of GARCH are important in finance, and any good set of GARCH tools should contain at least these four models. In addition, GARCH can be segmented between univariate and bivariate types. Univariate GARCH involves the modeling of time-varying volatility for a single return series. Multivariate GARCH involves the modeling of time-varying volatility for multiple return series where the covariance of the series is considered. A good set of GARCH tools (see Exhibit 2) should include at least one multivariate model.

Spline Tools

Spline techniques are used extensively for fitting curves to known data points. One of the biggest areas of application for splines in finance is term structure analysis. Interest rate curves, such as zero, forward, and discount curves, are an important input to effective term structure analysis. Because of noisy and incomplete data, curves fitted to data points derived from reported market prices for fixed income securities are often very rough. As a result, these curves are often difficult to use, such as in the case where a rough zero curve leads to instances of negative rates in an implied forward curve, rates which are more an artifact of the poorly behaved zero curve than they are a result of the economic trend in the data. Cubic splines are a popular approach to fitting a "smoother" to these poorly behaved data points. These smoothed zero curves make subsequent analysis based on the information contained in or implied by the curve easier.

Symbolic Math Tools

In addition to tools for numerical analysis, the availability of symbolic mathematical tools is also an important consideration in evaluating an analytical environment. A good set of symbolic math tools should include tools for calculus, linear algebra, simplification, equation solving, and transformations (e.g., Fourier transforms, Z-transforms, etc.). The price of an option is a function of the volatility of the price of the underlying asset. Because estimating volatility as an input parameter to an option-pricing model is a subjective process, analysts often would like to calculate an options price as a function of volatility without having a numeric estimate for that volatility. Symbolic math tools would make such an analysis possible (see Exhibit 3).

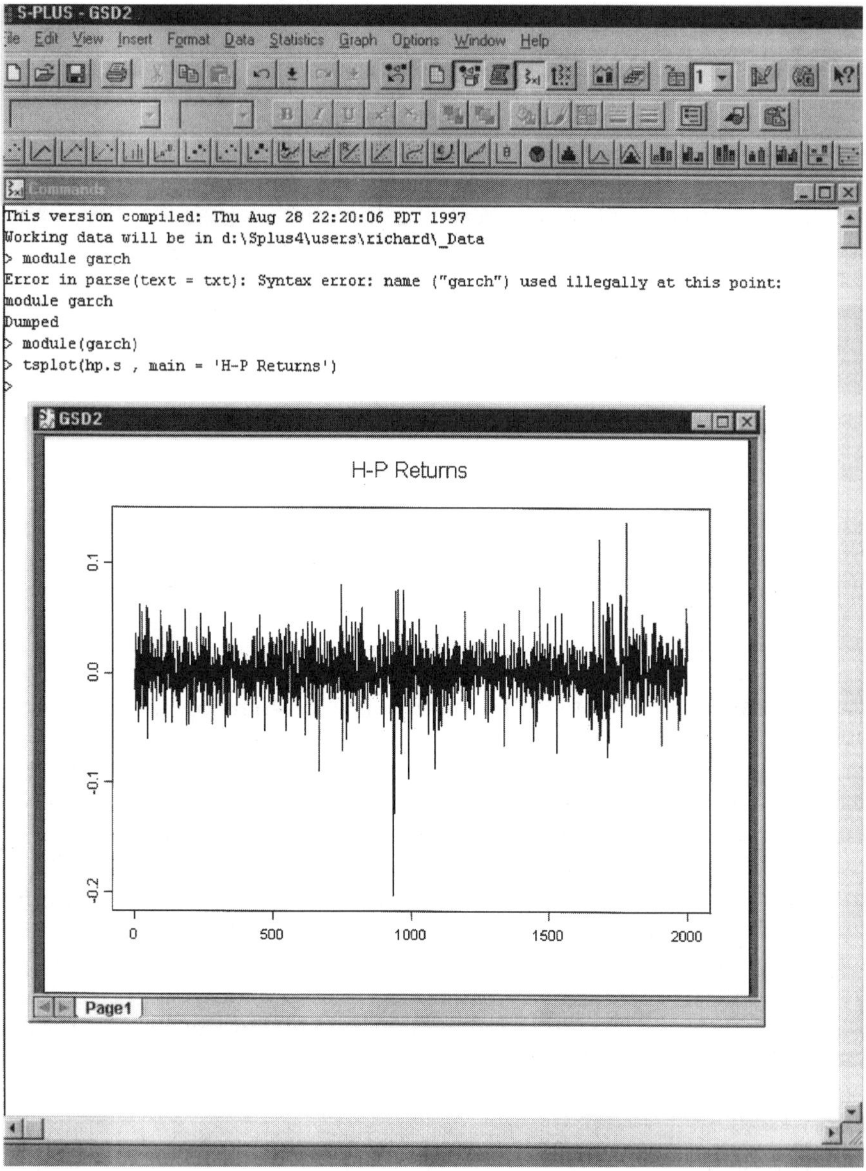

Exhibit 2. MathSoft's S-Plus/S-Garch package provides a powerful platform for doing GARCH-based modeling of volatility.

Neural Networks Tools

Neural networks refers to the application of neural net technology to real world problems. Neural networks are comprised of networks of indi-

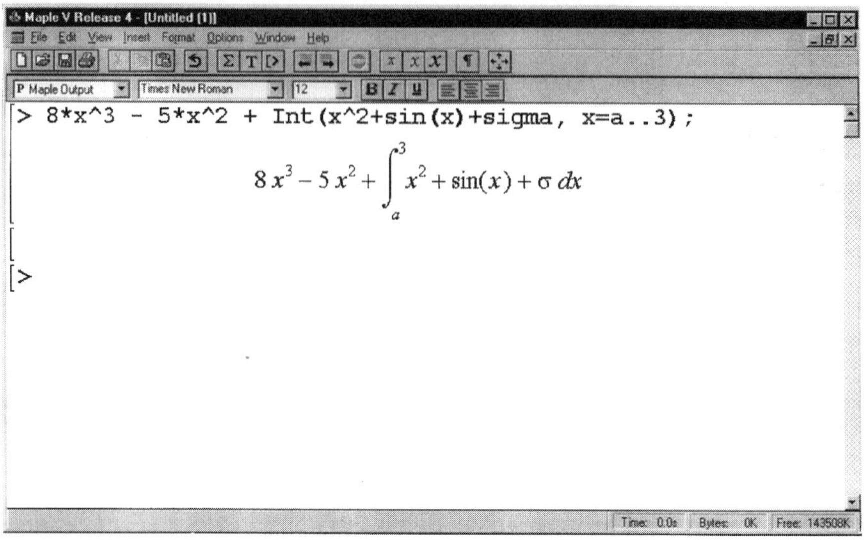

Exhibit 3. Maple V provides a powerful platform for doing symbolic math computations.

---

vidual elements which operate in parallel fashion to recognize patterns or systems in data. Through an iterative approach these elements make continual adjustments to weights until a pattern has been identified within the data set. These patterns are then used to make predictions with respect to future data points. Neural networks have been applied in areas including the aerospace, automotive, defense, and telecommunications industries. In finance, they have proven particularly useful for document reading, credit card application evaluation, real estate appraisal, mortgage lending, market analysis, and any area in which time series analysis is a principal activity. A good neural networks package should include predefined network architectures, like back propagation, and include algorithms for calculating network weights.

Fuzzy Logic

The term fuzzy logic refers to a mapping of an "input space" to an "output space" in which only significant information is used as a part of the mapping process. Fuzzy logic approaches to problem solving involve reducing a problem to its most basic parameters and then using expert or common sense rules for developing a system of solutions to that problem. In finance, fuzzy logic has found application in the area of market analysis and trading rule identification. A good fuzzy logic package should include an editor for creating your fuzzy system. This system editor should in turn include editors for creating membership functions and identifying rules. Finally, the fuzzy package should include a surface view for viewing the resulting fuzzy logic system.

Block-Diagramming Capabilities

Block-diagramming tools have a long history in electrical and mechanical engineering markets. In finance, these tools are gaining increasing acceptance as a means for modeling complex nonlinear securities such as mortgage and asset-backed securities. They also prove useful enabling Monte Carlo-based simulation of the nonlinear components of discounted cash flow models used for equity valuation.

In general, block diagramming enable the modeling and simulation of complex dynamic systems in a graphical manner. A good set of tools should let you build your model quickly, run the model, and make changes to the model on the fly. Since these tools are inherently graphical, the graphical user interface should be intuitive and easy to use. The tool set should include a ready-made block for all commonly used items, such as a cash flow or discount rate, or a standard stochastic process. The tools should also allow for the customization of existing block sets and for the creation of user-defined block sets (see Exhibit 4).

FUNCTIONAL ANALYTICS FOR FINANCE

To be an effective environment for financial analytic and application development, a package should contain functional sets of tools for the main application areas in finance. These areas included fixed income, derivatives, portfolio optimization, equities, risk management, and foreign exchange.

Fixed Income Tools

A set of fixed income tools will include tools for mapping a bond's cash flows, calculating yield and price, calculating sensitivities such as duration and convexity, and for determining total return. Whether a set of tools can accommodate bonds with abnormally short and long initial and ending coupon periods will determine whether the tools can be used to accurately model securities being traded in the marketplace. Tools that cannot correctly model the cash flow structure of a bond in time cannot possibly return correct values for price, yield, duration, and convexity. Therefore, this should be an important consideration when evaluating an environment.

Derivatives Tools

There are many popular models for valuing derivatives (see Exhibit 5). Black-Scholes[1] and simple binomial tree models are common approaches to valuing equity derivatives. Black's Model[2] and Vasicek's Model[3] are pop-

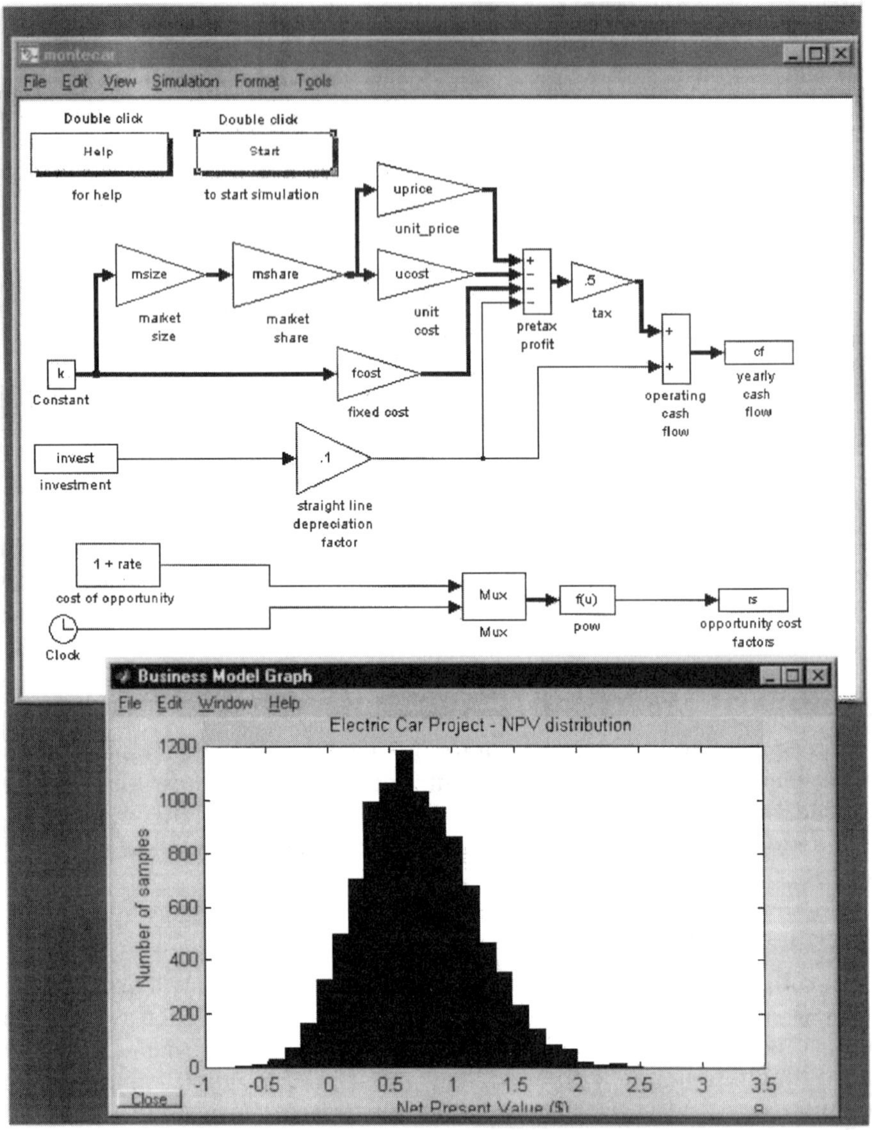

Exhibit 4. **This MATLAB SIMULINK model contains a net present value analysis for an electric car development process. Block-diagramming models such as this make it much easier to understand the complexities surrounding a financial problem.**

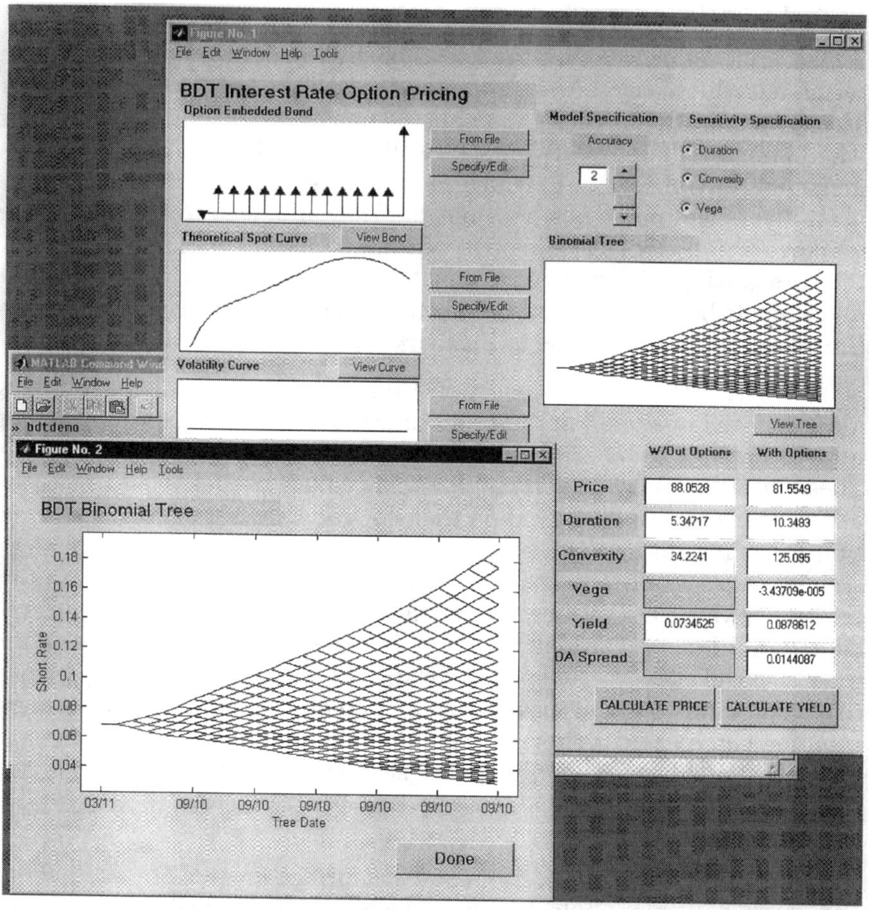

Exhibit 5. Black Derman Toy is a popular tree-based model for valuing interest rate derivatives. Here is an implementation of the BDT model, complete with a GUI, built entirely in MATLAB.

---

ular approaches to valuing interest rate derivatives. A set of tools for analyzing derivatives should contain at a minimum Black-Scholes, a simple binomial tree, and Black's Model approaches to valuing derivatives. In addition to these simple models, a high-quality prototyping environment will make available one or more complex tree-based models for interest rate derivatives such as the Black Derman Toy,[4] Hull White,[5] or Heath Jarrow Morton[6] model. Normally these complex models are only made available as a part of end-user decision support and trading systems costing in excess of $500,000.

Portfolio Optimization Tools

Asset allocation involves the use of portfolio optimization tools for determining which assets to hold in your portfolio and in what quantities. This is an important task for mutual fund managers looking to understand whether or not their investments are well diversified. In the case of actively managed portfolios, fund managers know that they are not holding the most diversified portfolios possible, but they still need to know what the market portfolio looks like in order to understand the nature of the "bets" they are making. Risk managers need to also understand the nature of the investments being made by these portfolio managers in terms of how risky the investments are relative to the market portfolio.

The Markowitz Portfolio Selection Model[7] and the Capital Asset Pricing Model[8] were developed in the 1950s and 1960s as means for determining how to manage asset allocation in the most efficient manner possible. These models underlie nearly all the tools which are being used to determine optimal portfolio allocation today. A good set of portfolio optimization tools should implement these models in some form and therefore should include tools for deriving an asset return time series from a price series, deriving a covariance matrix, and for determining the most efficient allocation of capital among assets. A good set of portfolio optimization tools also will allow you to specify constraints with respect to the portfolio (e.g., limitations on the types of assets or combinations of the types of assets that can be held). They should also allow you to calculate a Value-at-Risk (VAR) number for your portfolio (see Risk Management).

Equity Analytic Tools

The valuation and analysis of equity securities involve both subjective and objective components. Equity analysts spend a great deal of time talking with the management of firms and with competitor companies. They also spend a great deal of time analyzing the industries within which these firms operate. These activities lead to the development of a conceptual framework for valuing a firm. Once they develop this framework, then work begins to develop an objective, analytical framework which embodies their best estimate for intrinsic value for a company's common stock on a per-share basis. Many prototyping environments contain sets of tools for building this analytical framework. At a minimum, these sets of tools contain functions for calculating the present and future value of a stream of cash flows, for calculating the duration and convexity of those cash flows, and for calculating the internal rate of return (IRR) and net present value (NPV) of a stream of cash flows. A good set of tools will also contain functions for determining a firms weighted average cost of capital, for modeling sensitivities with respect to changes in leverage, and for modeling systematic and unsystematic risk components.

Risk Management Tools

Risk management is one of the hottest segments in the financial services industry with respect to the application of technology. Demand for tools for assessing and reporting market risk and credit risk is skyrocketing and many software vendors are scrambling to bring products to market which meet these needs. Demand is being driven by a dramatic increase in regulation both internationally and here in the U.S. with respect to the reporting of market risk exposure.[9] A continual "lowering of the compliance bar" in the area of market risk assessment and reporting and the addition of new regulation in the area of credit risk will continue to fuel demand for risk tools and applications.

In addition to standard financial tools, many prototyping packages contain tools specifically for building risk analytics and applications. These tool sets contain at a minimum tools for calculating Value at Risk (VAR), for doing "fast-valuation" of portfolios of diverse kinds of instruments, and for building the covariance matrices that are input to the VAR calculating tools. The quality of these tool sets is determined by the accuracy of their valuation analytics with respect to the accuracy of the VAR numbers generated. Quality packages will also support various types of reporting with respect to the sources of risk.

Foreign Exchange Tools

As markets become more and more global in focus the need to incorporate foreign exchange issue will continue to increase. This means, for example, that tools for calculating price, yield to maturity, and duration for bonds must now be able to treat foreign bonds and incorporate the foreign exchange rate pertaining to the market in which the security is traded. While a separate set of tools for foreign exchange is not a critical requirement for a prototyping environment, whether a package's functional tools for finance are enabled for foreign exchange (i.e., accept exchange rate data as inputs) is an important consideration. High-quality prototyping environments will have sets of tools specifically dedicated to foreign exchange analysis.

DEVELOPMENT AND RELATED ISSUES

Evaluating a prototyping environment in terms of how well it actually supports application development is, of course, important. Many packages claim to be friendly to both prototyping and application development but then fall short on the development side. To be a good application development environment there are several requirements including:

- The ability to generate stand-alone code.
- The ability to be called as an extension to another application.

- The ability to be distributed using common intranet/extranet technology.
- The ability to interact with live data sources and to interface with databases of standard type.
- The ability to generate GUIs which make other-than-command-line access to the environment possible.

Code Generation

The ability to generate stand-alone C/C++ code from tools, models, and applications built within the analysis and prototyping environment is a critical concern when evaluating prototyping environment. Many good packages include a compiler for generating C and C++ code, and many promise to soon be capable of generating Java code. These packages also make libraries containing compilable versions of core environment analytics.

Compilers. The term compiler refers not to the standard compilers available on the market for generating platform-dependent machine language code from C or C++ code, nor does it refer to the compilers which generate unibyte code from Java which is later interpreted by platform-dependent virtual machines. Instead, the term compiler refers to a tool for translating the procedural language of the analytic prototyping and application development environment into C or C++ code. These compilers also handle the issue of linking in compiled version core analytics which were used in the protoyped tools or models. Some compilers (see Exhibit 6) also allow for the creation of "semistand-alone" code which calls back to the application for needed core functions. Although code of this type requires that the prototyping environment be available on the local machine, it is still useful for enhancing the performance of the environment.

Math and Function Libraries. When you prototype analytics or build applications in a particular technical computing environment, you use many of the core and functional analytics available as a part of the package. When it comes time to create stand-alone versions of your models, however, whether you can "include" compilable versions of these function becomes an important concern. Many environments come with math libraries which can be linked into the stand-alone application when it is built. A few include other functional libraries as well, but in all cases, the user should evaluate the environment on overall library availability since this will significantly affect how friendly the environment will be to application development.

Portability

Here the term "portability" refers to whether the prototyping environment is accessible to other applications. If you choose to build an applica-

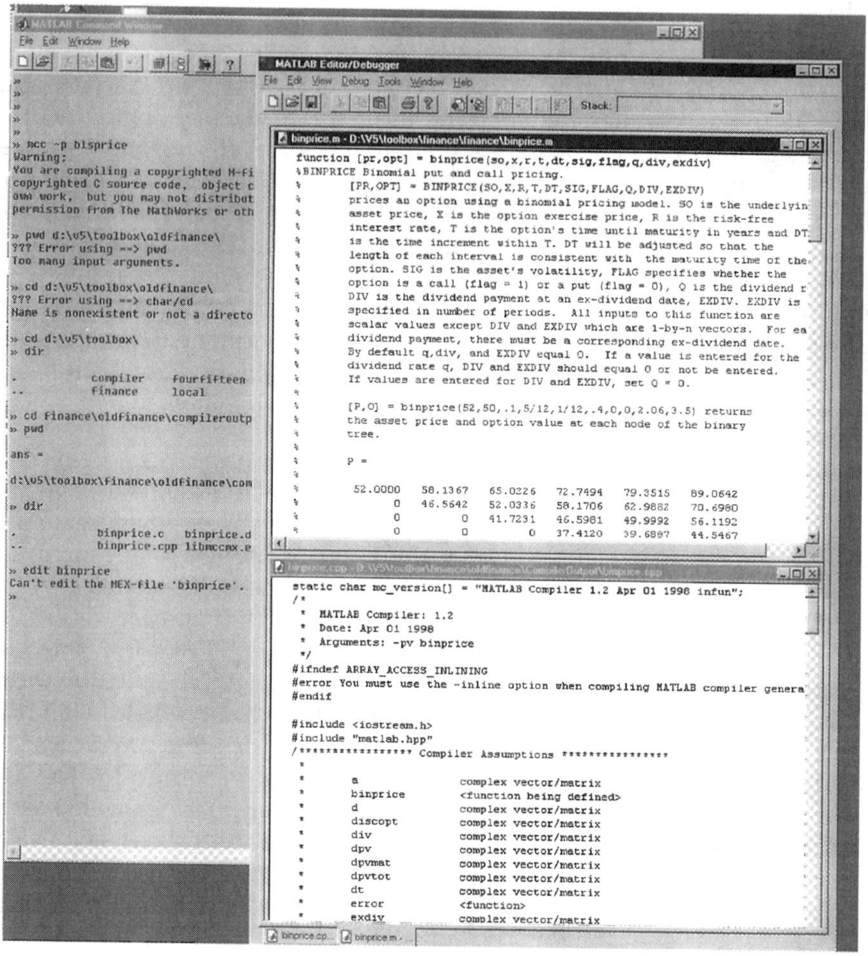

Exhibit 6. The MATLAB Compiler along with the C/C++ Math Library allows generation of a stand-alone C/C++ code version of MATLAB models.

tion within the environment (that is, using the environment's procedural language, core, and functional analytics, etc.) then how well the application can be made to communicate with other applications such as Microsoft Excel and other applications written in Microsoft Visual Basis, or C/C++ will be an important issue. Most applications will have one or more Application Programming Interfaces, or API's, for this purpose. An typical API will include a specification for the capabilities of data import and export as well as enabling calls to a basic environment's "engine" interface via Active X, Dynamic Data Exchange (DDE), or some other standard architecture.

Distribution

Distribution capabilities are an important consideration when developing applications for finance. Markets move quickly. Traders, analysts, and quantitative researchers' understanding of what the correct model for a particular instrument or market are often developed through an iterative process. This means that an application meant to embody those perceptions in a set of tools must also be able to be modified continually and redeployed at low cost. The emergence of intranet/extranet technology has made low-cost, rapid deployment technically feasible, and, as a result, web deployment capabilities are becoming an important quality attribute for any prototyping and application development environment. In addition, the need for rapid, low-cost deployment also has put increased emphasis on the availability of analytic libraries within an environment which can be redistributed at low or no cost.

Web Deployment. The ability to develop analytical tools, models, and applications for finance in a particular prototyping environment and then deploy them over an intranet, or externally over the Internet, is becoming an important consideration in evaluating different prototyping environments. A common solution to the problem of "web distribution" consists of a server and a set of utilities for reading data contained in HTML forms and for dynamically containing HTML forms to hold output data. Functioning within a standard client-server framework, the server which resides on the server machine alongside the prototyping environment communicates with standard browsers using HTML forms. Data are sent to the server from the client machine in an HTML form. The server extracts the data and passes it to a copy of the prototyping environment for processing. Once processing is completed, the server retrieves the data package and sends it back to the client machine embedded in a standard HTML form. The benefit of distribution using this technology is that the prototyping environment need only be available on the server machine. Since many client machines can effectively use the same copy of the prototyping environment there is a significant costs savings, but this savings is limited by performance issues associated with web deployment.

Other Distribution Issues. Another significant issue associated with the distribution of financial analytics, models and applications which were developed in a particular prototyping environment involves the issue of repackaging core and analytic tools. Many vendors requires that royalties be paid on any tools that are repackaged for sale to third parties. In addition, there are often restrictions on how much of a particular set of tools may be repackaged and in what fashion. Normally, vendors want to preclude you from repackaging their tools into anything that resembles a competing product. If deployment of stand-alone versions of models and applications is an important concern, then the repackaging issue should be explored up front.

Data Connectivity

Information is the lifeblood of financial markets. Since the most powerful set of analytical tools in the world is worthless without data to analyze, data connectivity is perhaps the most important characteristics to be considered in evaluating a prototyping environment. As a characteristic, data connectivity can be broken down into two areas: *data feed* connectivity and *database* connectivity.

Data Feed Connectivity. The term *data feed* refers to streams of information which are made available to computing platforms over various types of public and proprietary networks. These streams of information normally contain information on security prices and other metrics, market parameters, and current events. Historically, the data feeds market has been dominated by big proprietary data networks such as Bloomberg, Bridge, and Reuters; however, with the advent of the Internet, many smaller companies have emerged which distribute information via standard intranet/extranet technology. A good prototyping environment should have the ability to import data from one or more of the major information providers who use proprietary networks, as well as import information from Internet-based information providers. These prototyping environments should also enable the packaging of these interface capabilities into applications for deployment to end-users, which means that any core functionality for interfacing with the data feeds should be made available in a compilable format.

Database Connectivity. Database connectivity refers to the ability to interface with standard databases available on the market such as Oracle, Sybase, Microsoft SQL Server and Access, and Informix. Good prototyping environments will have the capability to interface with any ODBC/JDBC[10] compliant database on the market. These environments should at a minimum enable the ability to establish a connection to a database, extract data from that database, and write data to the database. Good environments will also enable database queries involving large data sets, which is an important consideration in finance. They should allow simultaneous connections to multiple databases. They should also provide some sort of graphical user interface for interacting with databases so that the user need not be fluent in Structured Query Language (SQL).

Spreadsheet Connectivity. Spreadsheets are ubiquitous in finance. There are the standard data interface for many quantitative researchers, analysts, and traders. As a result, a good prototyping environment

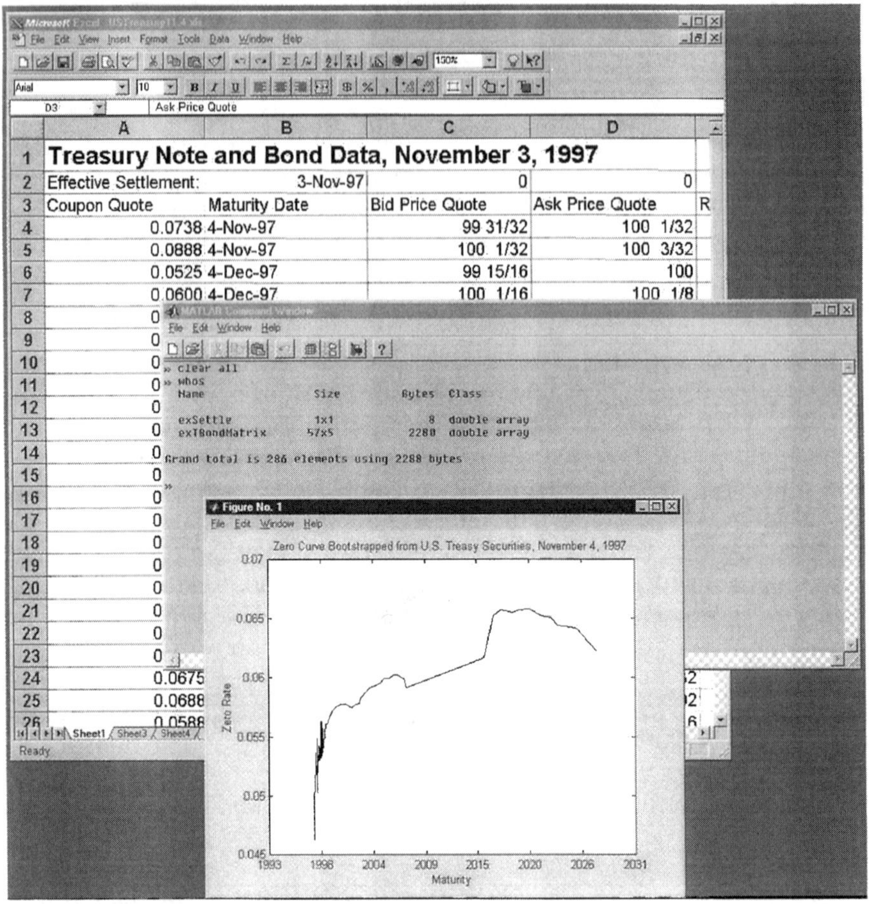

Exhibit 7. Excel link allows users to view MATLAB matrices in Microsoft Excel and to call MATLAB functions from within an Excel spreadsheet.

should support spreadsheet connectivity. Some products support spreadsheet connectivity via an overarching technology such as ActiveX or through a specific set of tools for linking to Microsoft Excel, Applix, or Lotus 123. Regardless off the technology involved, however, the prototyping environment should support use of a common spreadsheet as a data viewing tool (see Exhibit 7). A quality set of spreadsheet connectivity tools should also support use of spreadsheet package printing and report generation facilities. It should also support the calling of functions contained in the prototyping environment from within the spreadsheet itself and vice versa.

GUI Development

Developing effective Graphical User Interfaces (GUIs) is a critical activity in application development. GUIs allow users who lack the technical expertise to work in a prototyping environment from the command line the ability to still use any tools that have been built within that environment. All prototyping and application development environments should support the development of at least basic GUI components. Good environments should support the development of complex GUIs which can be built into stand-alone applications. This normally requires that a graphics library containing the environment's GUI components be available in conjunction with a compiler, math, and function libraries (see the section on Code Generation).

Report Generation

Applications are used in finance directly by traders as a part of their daily activities; however, these applications also function to support the activities of the many analysts and managers whose job it is to support and monitor the activities of these traders. As a result, report generation capabilities are an important characteristic of a prototyping and application development environment. If analysts are working in the prototyping environment directly, then it will be important to be able to generate reports which summarize their results. If analytics which were developed in the prototype environment are going to be packaged into an application which will be used by these analysts and managers, then it will also be important to be able to package the report generation capabilities of the prototyping environment into the application as well.

CONCLUSION

As we have seen, there are several characteristics to consider in comparing one analytic prototyping and application development environment to another. The core and functional analytics that are made available in the platform should be evaluated vis-a-vis the requirements of the tasks to be performed in the environment. Core optimization tools are only important if you are going to be doing research and prototyping analytics in a field were optimization problems arise, such as asset allocation. Derivative tools are only important if the goal is to build tools for valuing equity or interest rate options. Development and development support tools are an important consideration, but the sophistication required for these tools depends on the nature of the applications that will be developed within the environment. Sophisticated data connectivity is not important if the end-user application is only going to accept input typed from the keyboard. Distribution capabilities via the web are unimportant if the applications will only be deployed on the desktops of a few individuals. Evaluation of different environments should be done both to separate the quality packages from the inferior, but also to ensure that the correct package is being selected for the right area of application.

TRADEMARKS

1. Microsoft Inc. — Excel
2. The MathWorks Inc. — MATLAB, SIMULINK
3. Waterloo Maple Inc. — Maple V
4. MathSoft Inc. — S-Plus

Notes

1. This model was first introduced by Black, F. and Scholes, A., The pricing of options and corporate liabilities, *J. Pol. Econ.,* 81: 637–654, 1973.
2. Black's model was first introduced in Black, F., The pricing commodity contracts, *J. Financ. Econ.,* 3: 167–179, 1967.
3. See Vasicek, O. A., An equilibrium characterization of the term structure of interest rates, *J. Financ. Econ.,* 5: 177–188, 1977.
4. See Black, F., Derman, E., and Toy, W., A one-factor model of interest rates and its application to treasury bond options, *Financ. Anal. J.,* January–February, 1990, 33–39.
5. See Hull, J. and White, A., Pricing interest rate derivative securities, *Rev. Financ. Stud.,* 3(4): 573–592, 1990.
6. See Heath, D., Jarrow, R., and Morton, A., Bond pricing and the term structure of interest rates: a new methodology, *Econometrica,* 60(1): 77–105, 1992.
7. The Markowitz Portfolio Selection Model was introduced in two stages in the 1950s in the following article and book:
   - Markowitz, H. M., Portfolio selection, *J. Finance,* March, 1952.
   - Markowitz, H. M., *Portfolio Selection, Efficient Diversification of Investments,* John Wiley & Sons, New York, 1959.
8. The Capital Asset Pricing Model was introduced in a series of three separate articles: Sharpe, W., Capital asset prices: a theory of market equilibrium, *J. Financ,* September, 1964. Litner, J., The value of risk assets and the selection of risk investments in stock portfolios and capital budgets, *Rev. Econ. Stat.,* February, 1965. Mossin, J., Equilibrium in a capital asset market, *Econometrica,* October 1996.
9. On November 21, 1996, in response to recent ammendments to the Basle Capital Accord, a tripartite organization of the Board of Governors of the U.S. Federal Reserve, the Office of the Comptroller of the Currency, and the Federal Deposit Insurance Corporation (herein referred to as "the Agencies") issued an edict known as "The Final Rule on Market Risk." This Rule stipulates that as of January 1, 1998 financial institutions with more than 10% of their assets exposed to market risk (or trading activity in excess of $1 billion) will be required to hold an amount of capital in reserve equal to their exposure. The Final Rule stipulates that this capital charge will be determined via an assessment of value-at-risk (VAR) for the firm, using either an internal VAR model or the Standardized Approach prescribed by the Agencies. In response to the Basle Accord and to the action of the Agencies, the Securities and Exchange Commission (SEC) has also moved to issue its "Final Rules," effective January 1, 1997 require that all publicly held companies comply with their disclosure guidelines by June 15, 1997. The Final Rules require all registrant companies to disclose their exposure to market risk within the context of their financial statements.
10. The abbreviation ODBC refers to the Open Database Connectivity standard for databases. JDBC referes to the Java Database Connectivity Standard. Almost all major databases on the market are ODBC/JDBC compliant.

Chapter 11
Customer Profiling for Financial Services

Monte F. Hancock
Rhonda R. Delmater

DATA-MINING OPPORTUNITIES in financial services abound. As with any information technology (IT) development project, executive sponsorship can be a key element in attaining the necessary resources for a successful project and the commensurate recognition, which in turn enhances opportunities to proceed with subsequent data-mining activities.

ANALYSIS APPROACH

Based on conversations with financial institution executives, several areas may be identified for analysis. It is recommended that the highest-priority subject area be selected as the initial focus of the data-mining project, in order to provide meaningful results from the activity. The target area could be Customer Acquisition Profiling, Customer Retention, Fraud Detection, Liability Prediction, or virtually any area where sufficient historical data exist to support the analysis. If no specific goal is identified, then general data mining pertaining to a selected subject area may be conducted. The focus of this chapter is financial services customer profiling, whether for acquisition or retention purposes. Of course, the target areas that are not initially selected for data mining could be the subject of studies conducted as follow-up activities.

CUSTOMER ACQUISITION PROFILING

A financial institution may select a specific loan product area and geographic region for target market penetration, for example, the commercial loan market consisting of tens of thousands of small businesses in greater Cincinnati. The size of this market is likely to preclude effective, comprehensive (one-on-one) marketing at reasonable cost. If desirable potential customers most likely to move their business to "our" financial institution could be identified based upon available indicators, then marketing could be focused for best return-on-investment.

0-8493-9991-2/99/$0.00+$.50

Using advanced cognitive engineering techniques, a cognitive engine can be constructed that will

1. Use data provided by the financial institution.
2. Select from these data effective indicators of acquisition likelihood (and, possibly, customer desirability).
3. Identify those potential customers whose "acquisition profiles" indicate a higher likelihood of sale.
4. Produce a report which explains the acquisition indicators for each acquisition candidate, and gives a numeric indication of acquisition likelihood.

To support this kind of development, customer data and business history are needed for the financial institution's customers and potential customers, as well as background on the financial institution's previous marketing programs. Some of the data may be simulated or interpolated, if necessary.

CUSTOMER RETENTION PROFILING

Customer retention profiling is similar to customer acquisition profiling, as the objective is to identify predictive patterns. As with all businesses, financial institutions experience some customer turnover each year. Many departing customers do not give detailed explanations of the basis of their decision to leave. This makes it difficult to determine how to modify practices to increase retention.

If customers who are likely to move their business could be identified before a decision to leave has been made, the financial institution would have an opportunity to take action to retain their business. Similar to Customer Acquisition profiling, using advanced cognitive engineering techniques, a cognitive engine can be constructed which will determine effective indicators of retention likelihood, and identify those customers whose "retention profile" indicates high "retention risk." Again, to support this kind of development, customer data and business history are required for financial institution customers as well as their retention status.

FRAUD DETECTION

Another significant area of data mining interest throughout the spectrum of the international financial service community is Fraud Detection. The objective of these systems is to detect fraudulent business transactions, whether they be credit card, insurance, or domestic or international funds transfers.

Prior to automated systems of this nature, banking personnel manually reviewed thousands of transactions per day searching for fraudulent transactions. Although this labor-intensive, tedious process actually detected many fraudulent transactions, a significant number remained undetected, resulting not only in lost revenues but also in exposure for penalties such as fines, etc. Once the knowledge discovery phase of the data-mining activity is completed, an unattended production system can be fielded which combines knowledge-based expert system capabilities and complex fuzzy algorithms to identify transactions of interest (concern). A confidence factor is calculated, and based on user-defined thresholds, a transaction may be allowed to process or be rejected.

A system of this nature can significantly increase the probability of detecting fraud at the same time it reduces the associated costs.

LIABILITY PREDICTION

Again, if an adequate base of historical information is available, a liability value can be predicted based on a new set of data. This type of analysis could be performed to predict the total liability for a population or, based on certain factors, for a specific claim. An example of each follows.

A 10-year history of hurricane claims for South Florida would provide information such as the total number of dwellings by type, the number of claims, settlement value, etc. Combining this information with the weather history and the hurricane forecast for the coming season, model(s) could be developed to predict the near-term liability. (Maybe this is a bad example; I'm not convinced the weather forecasts are that good.) Individual claim liability could likewise be predicted, for example, for Workers Compensation or other Insurance Claims based on feature value patterns in historical data. Information used to predict a settlement value may include age, gender, marital status, income, type of injury, attorney involvement, and so on.

GENERAL DATA MINING

Data mining is an emerging technical discipline which combines conventional decision support methods (classical regression, statistics, modeling, procedural algorithms) with modern machine inferencing technology (neural networks, scientific visualization, adaptive algorithms) to wade through masses of data to extract the residue of information. This marriage of "conventional wisdom" with the best of late-twentieth-century computer science has produced a host of high-end tools to support experts operating in complex domains.

Intuition and utility can be preserved by the application of cognitive tools that can uncover the latent **information** embedded in the growing swell of **data.** Smart tools for making predictions from complex data are a must.

When data volume and complexity reach a certain critical level (which depends upon the domain), end-users can no longer "get their arms around it." Software tools are now available to apply high-end cognitive engineering capabilities to effectively probe the complex data to pinpoint those few critical factors, and their configurations, which yield market intelligence. For example, what is the predictive phenomenology of prospects who are "ready to buy?" These cognitive tools find relationships already present, but obscure, in historical data.

THE TECHNICAL APPROACH

For effective analysis, the subject financial institution must have a substantial database of information on current and past customers. In essence, when properly organized and interpreted, these data constitute a collection of raw descriptions of historical financial institution customers: organizations that, at some time in the past, *made a buy decision* for the financial institution. These data could be collected from various operational systems or could already reside in a data mart or data warehouse.

Once the data source is identified and prepared for analysis, collection of data-mining tools can be applied to the problem of determining refined business profiles for prospects that are *ready to buy.*

Once the *ready-to-buy* profiles have been generated, other cognitive engineering tools can be used to evaluate entries from a database of prospects for a marketing decision. Or, the profiles may be used to manually generate a database of promising prospects.

This process can be further enhanced by the inclusion of general demographic information about the regional market. Though not essential, such information can help with the refinement, interpretation, and exploitation of profiles.

Two important components of an automated decision support systems architecture are the methodology and data-mining software to accomplish analyses as described below. A formal methodology and cognitive systems development tools are essential for successful implementation of a data-mining application. The Cognitive Engineering Methodology (CEM) provides a structured road map for developing decision support systems.

CEM addresses both continuous and symbolic domains. Continuous domains are those where the parameter values have continuous ranges and vary as a function of some criteria such as time or space. Examples of parameter values in the continuous domain include RF signals, temperature, voltage levels, and speed. Symbolic domains are those where the parameter values are discrete and finite. Examples of parameter values in the symbolic domain include words, sentences, parameters, and icons. The

CEM ensures the proper application of intelligent systems technology. It is a spiral process with five phases: Representation, Analysis, Feature Extraction and Enhancement, Prototyping, and Evaluation:

Representation — Establishes the form and syntax of the available information from which decisions are made.

Analysis — Determines what intelligent systems paradigm(s) will be utilized when implementing the DSS. Rule-driven Knowledge-Based Expert Systems and Neural Networks are examples of paradigms that can be applied within specific decision support systems.

Feature Extraction and Enhancement — Determines what measurements or other information should be used to make decisions. Measurements, which serve as the basis for classification decisions are called "features." It is often the case that multiple measurements, which are known as feature vectors, are required to draw effective, consistent, and correct conclusions. Optimizing the selection of features to make decisions is of critical importance in the implementation of a DSS. In addition to the naturally occurring intuitive features that exist in a domain, nonintuitive features can be mathematically derived that simplify and speed the implementation and improve the accuracy of the DSS. Implementation of Knowledge-Based Expert Systems (KBES), which requires the definition of rules, demands extensive discussions with people who are intimately familiar with the problem and its solutions. Contentious issues, disagreements among experts, and addressing unexplored conditions and outcomes are hurdles that must be addressed to field an effective and reliable KBES. Use of a formal interviewing process for acquiring knowledge has successfully supported this methodology on numerous programs. This methodology takes into account aspects of the experts' organization and authority therein, in addition to employing standard knowledge engineering techniques including stream-of-consciousness monologues, single-factor variations, and novel scenarios.

Prototyping — Provides rapid feedback to the engineering staff so that changes can be made to the DSS design before any major investment is made. This mitigates risk substantially. After the first prototype is developed the application can be reviewed and critiqued by the end user. Experience has found that spiral model-based rapid evolutionary development using "real" data is the most effective way to build decision support systems.

Evaluation — The implemented cognitive system is evaluated using blind and operational tests, and sensitivity, comparative, stability, and other analyses are performed to ensure the DSS will function well under all conceivable operational situations.

SOFTWARE SUPPORT

The techniques that can be implemented as software routines for use in data mining can be grouped according to function: Link Analysis, Classification, Clustering, Statistics, Prediction. These are described below, along with specific techniques that are useful in performing each function.

Link Analysis

Link analysis refers to a general collection of techniques that exploit "connections" within a data warehouse. These connections can be based upon time, cause-and-effect, or even random chance. Link analysis is also used to investigate business processes that can be represented graphically. Statistical, graph theoretic, and predictive methods are often used in link analysis. Some applicable terms are

Associations — Collections of facts that occur together (e.g., buyers of product A are often homeowners). Associations are the simplest relationships in a data warehouse, and are often used to suggest hypotheses for data mining: "Among the population of all prospects, are homeowners the most likely to buy?"

Sequential Patterns — Associations that change in predictable ways across a population; these might involve a "time element," and might not (e.g., buyers of product A who own homes often buy product C). Sequential patterns which occur frequently constitute general "rules of thumb": "We should pitch product C to home owners who buy product A."

Sequential Time Patterns — Sequential patterns which have time as the central connection (e.g., "Buyers who file two complaints in a quarter have a 70% chance of dropping their account within the next year"). Sequential time patterns can be used to build predictive models: "Given the outstanding bids and current market, what is the likelihood that next quarter's sales will exceed $2 million?"

Classification

The function of recognizing and assigning an entity to the appropriate class based on feature attributes (or data element values), dividing a set of prospects into high potential vs. others, or classifying financial transactions as potentially fraudulent.

Neural Networks — Mathematical models of animal brains that can be trained to solve difficult problems including classification.

Tree Classification — Following a hierarchical rule structure to determine a classification.

Simple Bayes — An inferencing method that uses Bayes Theorem to estimate the likelihoods and probabilities of certain occurrences. This classical theory is a very well developed, and satisfies certain optimality conditions.

k-Nearest Neighbors — A classification method which bases its decisions on how "similar" the current problem is to all of the previously solved cases: "it's most like the Smith case, so let's try what worked for Smith." The "k" refers to the number of distinct "cases" retained for matching.

Linear Discriminant Analysis — A classification method which creates the best decision method that is attainable by linear functions. LDA has the advantage of simplicity and ease of construction, but is not as powerful as nonlinear decision methods. Sometimes called "linear regression."

Clustering

This is the function of forming subsets of the population based on cohesion.

k-Means Clustering — A method used to recognize patterns in data based upon their population statistics. It can be used to build classifiers which are similar to k-Nearest Neighbor classifiers, but matches only against average "scenarios." It yields, therefore, a classification method which bases its decisions on how "similar" the current problem is to averages of previously solved cases: "it's most like the default scenario, so let's try what works for default." The "k" refers to the number of distinct "scenarios" created and/or retained for matching.

Neural Networks Clustering — Mathematical models of animal brains that can be trained to solve difficult problems including clustering.

Visualization (N-dimensional graphics) — Graphical plotting of feature values which enables a human analyst to see (visualize) natural groupings of the data based on future values.

Principal Component Analysis — Transforms applied to the data identify the most salient features and clusters.

Statistics — Parametric

General Statistics — Values which are calculated to describe a set of data, e.g., population, sample, cluster, etc. Examples of commonly used general statistics include: mean, median, mode, range, standard deviation, etc.

Linear Regression — A mathematical formalism for optimizing objective functions subject to linear constraints, which is used to create models for use in pattern recognition, prediction, etc.

Nonlinear Regression — A mathematical formalism for optimizing objective functions subject to nonlinear constraints; it is used to create models for pattern recognition, prediction, etc. It is inherently more powerful than linear regression.

Tests (T, F, Chi Square) — Statistical values which are calculated for a set of data, often used to determine whether a sample is adequate (in size, etc.) to draw inferences for the population as a whole.

Principal Component Analysis — Transforms applied to the data identify the most salient features and clusters, used in parametric statistics to identify meaningful variations (statistical significance) from the norm.

Factor Analysis — A collection of mathematical methods (typically derived from linear algebra) for identifying and concentrating representational information in complex data sets. It usually reduces the dimensionality of data, and is often applied as a precursor to predictive modeling. Sometimes called "principal component analysis" (PCA).

Statistics — Nonparametric

Knowledge-Based Training (KBT) — The use of adaptive learning algorithms to build decision models which exploit descriptive statistics. An example is expert systems which have a learning capability.

Prediction

One of the most attractive facets of data mining is the development of insight into the business process which makes possible the development of predictive models. In competitive markets, niche selection, product release timing, and marketing focus all stand to benefit from the use of predictive models.

Predictive models can be based upon conventional methods (control charts, GANTT charts, spreadsheets, etc.), but these are largely manual. Emerging applications for high-end "cognitive engines" for predictive modeling are becoming available to commercial users:

Neural Networks Prediction — Predictive models based upon one of the many "neural" paradigms: multilayer perceptrons, Hopfield networks, Boltzmann machines, etc.

Radial Basis Function Prediction — Predictive models based upon one of the many RBF paradigms: partitions of unity, restricted coulomb energy (RCE) methods, adaptive taxonomic classifiers, etc.

Knowledge-Based Expert System (KBES) Prediction — KBES can be built which use heuristics obtained from human domain experts to codify expert knowledge for incorporation into predictive models. These models capture rare, perishable human expertise in executable form, so that it can be retained, copied, and enhanced by successive generations of human experts. This "brain power in a box" will work in any location (or *every* location), can

Exhibit 1. Cognitive Engineering Methodology

Methodology Phase	Financial Institution Project Task
Representation	Task 1: Analysis of requirements Task 2: Knowledge acquisition
Analysis	Task 3: Collect and organize facts and data
Feature extraction and enhancement	Task 4: Apply cognitive engineering tools to financial institution data
Prototyping	
Evaluation	Task 5: Evaluate population Task 6: Delivery

run 24 hours a day, and never asks for a raise. If built with the ability to explain its decisions, such a system can also be used as a training tool.

Fuzzy Logic Prediction — Long popular in Japan and Europe, these systems "mathematize soft" decision-making processes. They work well when information is incomplete, partially incorrect, or imprecise.

Time Series Prediction — A collection of conventional and emerging techniques for predicting the next value of a time series based upon current conditions and prior history (e.g., predicting stock prices).

PROJECT APPROACH

The Cognitive Engineering Methodology described above is essentially a software industry standard "spiral" development methodology for building high-end systems. The amount of effort expended in each of the five phases depends upon the problem. The Prototyping Phase typically constitutes the bulk of the effort. Phases may be reordered, repeated, or eliminated, as required. Every data-mining activity or problem is a little different.

This methodology facilitates a graceful, incremental development that combines substantial user input with high technology, while mitigating risk, as shown in Exhibit 1.

Task 1: Analysis of Requirements

Analytic staff members hold meetings and discussions with financial institution personnel to gather and define preliminary analysis requirements. The purpose of the discussions is to identify long-range program goals, and immediate objectives for the current demonstration task. This includes identifying the initial profiling target area, whether we are targeting new customers or enhancing customer retention. The analysis will include identification and availability of data resources, financial institution participation, and problem statement refinement.

Task 2: Knowledge Acquisition

Meetings are held with financial institution Business Development staff to obtain general background information:

- Descriptions of marketing activities
- Customers
- Heuristics
- Methods
- Resources

Knowledge acquisition methods are then applied, on an as-needed basis. These include visualization exercises, standard scenarios, stream-of-consciousness monologues, etc. These exercises enhance the cognitive engineering team's ability to quickly and reliably capture knowledge needed for the data-mining activities. Meetings also are be held with the financial institution Information Technology staff to obtain detailed technical information including:

- Database format
- Database access
- Hosting information
- Policies and methods
- Limitations

Implementation and design issues will be resolved through these sessions. Timely access to the financial institution's data is of great importance, as the data serves as the basis for all cognitive engineering work.

Task 3: Collect and Organize Facts and Data

An analysis database is then populated with the relevant data and cognitive engineering tools are applied. The analysis database serves as the development and integration repository for all of the data-mining work.

It is not essential to have a data warehouse or data mart to perform data mining, although it is imperative to have confidence that the information used in the data-mining activity is consistent and valid (cleansing, transformation), as would be expected of information of this type.

Meta data, commonly called "data about data" provides detailed definitions of data elements as they relate to specific entities. Understanding the definition of features can aid the analysis in several ways. If data are combined from several sources, it is important that the elements be consistent from each source in definition and in format. For assisted (interactive) data mining, it is also important for the human analyst to understand the nature of the data.

Task 4: Apply Cognitive Engineering Tools to Financial Institution Data

Enhancement and Data Preparation. The data are enhanced by the application of tools that find and emphasize information-bearing aspects. Data enhancement tools allow users to determine which data items are "most significant," can rank-order data items by predictive power (salience), and can apply transforms which concentrate information into the smallest number of features. This allows the development of optimized prediction engines, the creation of highly discriminating visualizations, and the suppression of irrelevant factors during data analysis. Data enhancement was applied to all of the analysis tasks in this report, with great benefit.

The data are prepared for cognitive engineering through the following processes:

- Registration: proper formatting, placement of data items.
- Normalization: making disparate data commensurable by suppressing irrelevant components of data items.
- Feature extraction: effective representation of information within records.
- Statistical analysis: analysis of data distribution in feature space.
- Correlation: exploitation of similarities and differences within data.
- Clustering: discrimination between disparate data items, and aggregation of similar data items.
- Profile generation and refinement: synthesis of information content, distribution, similarities, and differences to generate a consistent mathematical description of the commercial loan prospect population.
- Build customer/prospect classifier: once the data have been prepared and enhanced, classification engines are applied to create a prospect profiler. The profiler is a software routine that accepts as input a prospect record, and produces as output a measure of "marketability" (likelihood of buying) for that prospect. Once the profiler has been built, it can be rapidly applied to any number of prospects.

Task 5: Evaluate Population

The Profiler is applied to the prospects in a test database. Each prospect is given a numeric rating for "marketability." These ratings are compiled into a marketability roster, which will be included in the Final Report.

Task 6: Delivery

Final Report. A final report is prepared to describe the tools and methods applied, and will include the results of the "marketability" experiment.

Presentation. Typically, it is important to present the results of the data-mining analyses to financial institution executives in order to promote the value of the activity and ensure follow-through with the application of the knowledge gleaned from the effort into a production system.

Demonstration. The presentation may include a live computer-based demonstration of the software for processing and profiling prospects.

Schedule Estimates. A project of this type typically ranges from 3 to 10 months, with check points to determine whether and how to proceed based on the "results to date."

SUMMARY

Like many businesses in the 1990s, commercial banking is becoming more competitive. Businesses grow in such an aggressive economy in two primary ways:

1. They increase existing market share.
2. They create or penetrate new markets.

Both methods are effective if good "business intelligence" is available; market information about *who is ready to buy.*

A financial institution may have a limited market share in a particular loan type and geographic area, and wants to increase its market penetration. The market itself is likely to be large and diverse, which is both good and bad.

The opportunity is obvious. Large, diverse markets offer tremendous potential for out-year growth, with many avenues for market penetration and the development of a broad, stable customer base.

The challenges are equally clear. Large diverse markets are inherently difficult to reach. Market diversity ensures that focused niche marketing techniques (journal ads, association contacts, etc.) will not have good coverage, while market size makes comprehensive marketing techniques costly and time-consuming. The result is poor return-on-investment.

The Solution

A solution to this problem is to apply advanced cognitive engineering tools to help the financial institution generate "business intelligence" from its existing data. In this way, the institution can focus on marketing (for reduction of expense) across all customer types (for good coverage). In other words, tools can be developed and applied that identify those customers whose backgrounds and situations indicate that they are most likely to respond favorably to a marketing contact.

Chapter 12
Business Rule Systems

Henry Seiler

THIS CHAPTER IS INTENDED FOR THE BENEFIT of financial and business analysts who may be called upon to participate in the specification and design of new business software systems or the redesign of legacy software systems. The intent is to familiarize business analysts with the new emerging software development methodologies of business rules and knowledge management, with the goal of helping them become better stewards of the business systems knowledge inherent in today's software applications.

Business rules represent the codified policies and decision-making practices of an organization. Historically, business rules have been coded directly in the program logic of an application. Today, the terms business rules and knowledge management are used to describe the isolation of business policies and decisions from application logic.

Production rule systems provide a better alternative for implementing business rules than embedding them in application logic or implementing them as database triggers. Production rule systems will allow you to achieve the benefits of business rules while avoiding the problems inherent in entwining application logic with business logic.

The processes of business rule development, knowledge management, and application development are intimately linked. They are focused on solving the problems of how to represent business knowledge and how to manage the use of this knowledge as a part of business applications. The goals of knowledge management are first, to isolate the business rules of an application into identifiable and separate components of the system rather then allowing the knowledge contained in an application to be dispersed throughout the programming of the application. And second, to represent knowledge in a fashion that is appropriate for the modeling of business decision knowledge, as opposed to program control.

0-8493-9991-2/99/$0.00+$.50

Production rule systems address these goals of isolation and knowledge representation with the use of component-oriented architectures and production rule systems technologies, respectively.

PRODUCTION RULE SYSTEMS

Production rule systems differ in basic computational style from traditional procedural systems such as C++ or Basic; the main difference being the production system's use of unordered data-sensitive rules as the fundamental unit of computation. This is in stark contrast to the sequenced instructions used by traditional procedural systems. Production rule systems are most appropriate when the knowledge to be represented naturally occurs in rule form, where the relationships between rules are extremely complex, and where frequent changes in the business knowledge are anticipated. The key to production rule systems' success in modeling and processing business knowledge is in their ability to represent knowledge explicitly in chunks (i.e., rules) that are just the right size for capturing the small units or steps business analysts naturally use when solving complex problems.

Architecture of Production Rule Systems

The architecture of production rule systems is comprised of five primary components:

- Data. The facts and values of the knowledge problem.
- Rules. The If Condition-Then Action representation of the knowledge.
- Inference Engine. The underlying executor that matches data and rules.
- Knowledge Representation Language. The representation grammar for data and rules.
- Knowledge Component Objects. The packaging of rules and data into a component-reusable entity for use by an application. A package of data, rules, and inference engine is called a RuleSet.

Production System Data

The data of a knowledge problem can be considered the inputs and outputs for the set of rules used in solving the problem. Production rule systems model problem domain data as objects, which represent the things and events of the problem. The set of all data objects and their current values is collectively referred to as the context. Data values come into being in the following ways:

1. The data is statically declared in the RuleSet and initialized upon program activation of the RuleSet.
    - The data is provided to the RuleSet by the activating application.
    - The data is changed or created by the rules of the RuleSet.

- The RuleSet requests the data in an ad hoc fashion from either the controlling application or an interactive user.

2. A less obvious but most critical role that data plays in production rule systems is that it is the only means for rules to communicate with one another. The state of context data is the primary means of control of the production system. Control passes from one rule to another not by explicit linear step-wise execution or subroutine call, but by changes in the data values of the context.

Production System Rules

Rules in a production system consist of a collection of If Condition-Then Action statements. Each rule has a left-hand side, or IF part, and a right-hand side, or THEN part. The IF part of a rule comprises the conditions or antecedents of the rule. The THEN part is the action part of a rule and is often called the rule's consequent or conclusion.

The IF part of a rule is comprised of one or more clauses, or expressions, combined with the Boolean operators AND, OR, and NOT. An expression or antecedent usually is a restriction, or relational expression, on some value or attribute of some object of the context data. The object may, for example, be an object of the problem domain such as a customer or inventory item, or internal variable used for directing problem solution strategy, such as a goal.

Rules in a production system are thought of as having direction. Direction being implied by whether the IF part or the THEN part is the means by which the rule becomes active. Rules that are activated by the IF part are said to be data driven or forward chaining rules and rules that are activated by the THEN part are said to be goal driven or backward chaining rules.

Production System Inference Engine

The inference engine of production systems acts as the "unseen hand" or executor which causes processing to take place. Processing here is defined as the combining of supplied data with rules to create inferred data. It is the inferred data that is the desired end result of the production system processing.

In a RuleSet control is based on cyclical re-evaluation of the state of the context, not on any explicit ordering of instructions. There is no explicit transfer of execution control between rules as there is in traditional program statements. Rules communicate with each other only by way of the data values of the context. This complete separation of execution flow, provided by the executor from problem knowledge represented as rules, is the key to the representational and processing power of production systems. The author of a RuleSet need only be concerned with the representation of knowledge explicitly as rules, constructing the small units or steps one would naturally use when solving complex problems. The process of choosing, ordering, and connecting the steps for problem solution is carried out by the executor or inference engine.

The inference engine provides two primary problem-solving engines relevant to production systems: the forward chaining engine and the backward chaining engine. Production systems may possess additional secondary computational engines for method and command processing.

The simplest distinction that can be made between the forward and backward chaining inference engines is one of direction. The problem-solving process of a production system can be thought of as a search to find a path from an initial situation to a solution. The starting point for the search may be either the initial state or the final solution; the choice of search strategy is dependent on the nature of the problem at hand and the programmatic ease with which initial state data can be provided or final solutions can be proposed.

- Forward chaining inference processing starts from an initial data state and produces final goals or conclusions.
- Backward chaining inference processing starts from a proposed or desired goal or conclusion and proceeds to seek data in support of that goal.

These distinctions between forward and backward chaining are not mutually exclusive. It is possible, and often desirable, to use both modes of processing in a problem solution.

FORWARD CHAINING SYSTEMS

Forward chaining systems process from initial information that is provided to a final state or goal as shown in Exhibit 1. Starting from an initial or current set of data, the forward chaining inference engine makes a chain of inferences until a goal is reached. In forward chaining the data values of

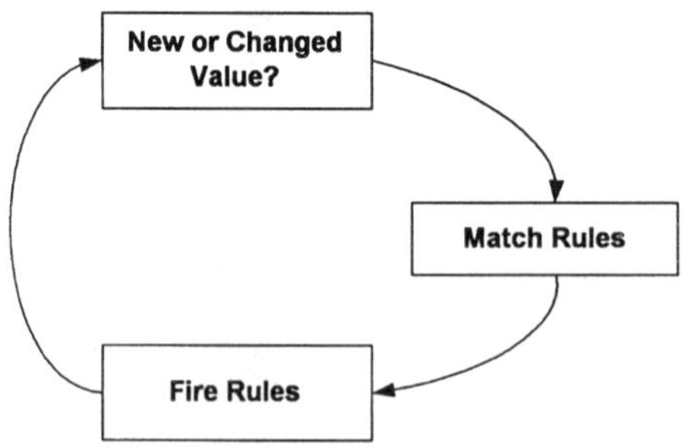

Exhibit 1. Forward chaining inference processing.

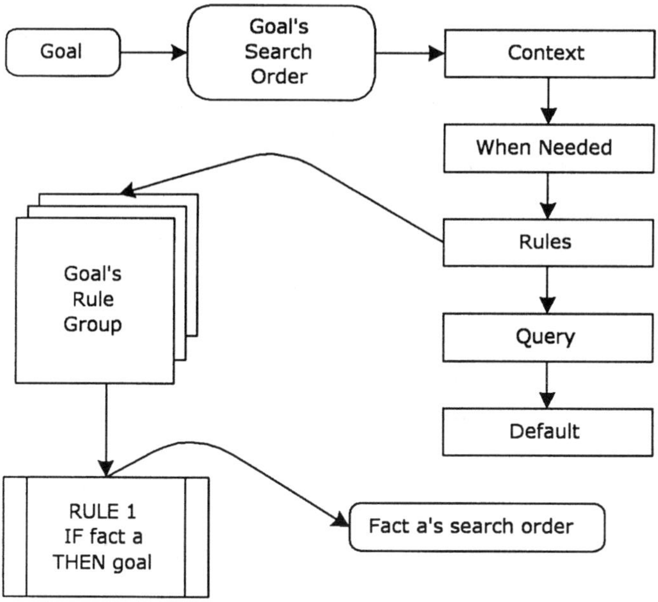

Exhibit 2. Backward chaining inference processing.

the context are matched against the IF parts, or left-hand sides, of rules. If a rule's IF side matches the context then the inference engine executes the THEN part, or right-hand side of the rule. If the execution of the THEN part of a rule changes the data values of the context, then the inference engine repeats the entire match-execute cycle again using the new state of the context data values as a new initial set of data.

Forward chaining systems are most appropriate when the initial data are well defined by a single set of characteristics and many possible concluding goal states exists.

BACKWARD CHAINING SYSTEMS

Backward chaining systems process from a required final goal and obtain context data as needed to support that goal, as shown in Exhibit 2. Starting from the overall goal the inference engine breaks down the goal, into simpler subgoals. The process of subgoal decomposition continues, producing additional subgoals or context data facts for which a value can be immediately obtained. The backward chaining inference engine uses rules to facilitate the process of goal to subgoal decomposition. The THEN parts or right-hand sides of the rules are matched against currently active goals. If a rule's THEN part matches an active goal, the IF part, or left-hand side, of the rule then provides a new set of active subgoals. This process of

THEN part to IF part backward chaining decomposition continues recursively until no rules can be found whose THEN part matches any of the currently active subgoals. At that point the backward chaining inference engine matches the set of currently active goals with the data values of the context. If there is a match, then the rule that provided the subgoals executes and the inference engine then uses the context data values provided by executing the rule to the next set of subgoals. This process continues until the inference engine asserts, denies, or is unable to determine the original goal.

Backward chaining systems are most appropriate for problems such as diagnostics, or categorization. These problem types share the characteristic of a single goal which can be consistently stated, in conjunction with an undetermined and/or large amount of initial information that would pose a severe burden to provide all at once, as an initial data state.

The backward chaining inference engine solves the problem of a difficult to provide complete initial data state by actively requesting context data values only when and if they are needed. In contrast the forward chaining inference engine only processes on the data values provided and never requests additional information.

PRODUCTION SYSTEM KNOWLEDGE REPRESENTATION LANGUAGE

The rule language of production systems is generally a high-level grammar for business problem representation and abstraction designed specifically for the specification and processing of business rules. A RuleSet may contain class declarations and methods, forward chaining rules, backward chaining demons, and an agenda. Thus, the major components of a production system language are

- Objects in a knowledge base are created via class declarations.
- Class declarations define the structure of the objects contained in a knowledge base. As instances, classes hold and retain the application's data values. An object's structure is defined by its class and attribute declarations.
- Rules and Demons describe the operational logic, rules-of-thumb, and cause-and-effect relationships needed to make decisions, and trigger certain events or actions during processing.
- An agenda schedules the main events and the sequences of events or procedures in pursuit of goals.

PRODUCTION SYSTEM KNOWLEDGE COMPONENT OBJECTS

For a problem-solving RuleSet to contribute effectively to a business application it must be packaged and made available to the tools being used for creating business applications. A production system's RuleSet packag-

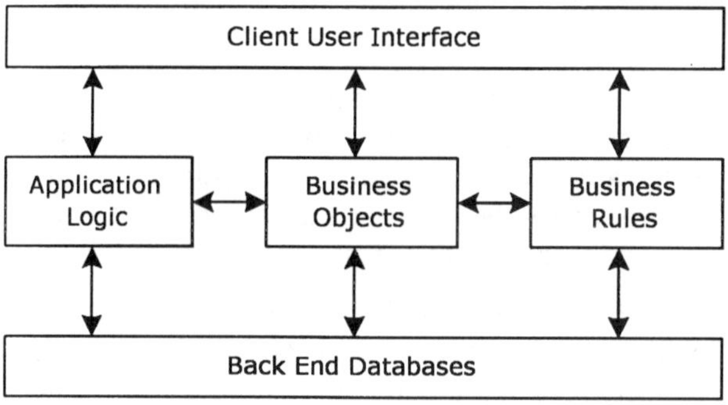

Exhibit 3. Business rules as part of the component development process.

es problem-solving rules by means of the industry standard Component Object Model (COM).

KNOWLEDGE MANAGEMENT

The packaging of a set of problem-solving rules into a RuleSet allows for the management and reuse of knowledge within and among software development projects. The effect of this packaging is to isolate the business rules of an application into identifiable and separate components of the system, rather than allowing the knowledge contained in an application to be dispersed throughout the programming of the application. Thus, the process of knowledge management is a cooperation of both the enabling technologies of knowledge component packages, and the design and development methodologies of business rule isolation as shown in Exhibit 3.

Component-oriented production systems provide, for the first time, the necessary enabling technologies for knowledge management methodologies to become an integrated part of modern business application design and development. Component-oriented production systems address each of the primary criteria of successful knowledge management.

Isolation — Production systems enforce complete isolation of business rule logic and processing from application logic processing. This allows development teams to partition design and implementation into distinct efforts for application logic vs. business logic.

Integration — Business rules are encapsulated in business objects called RuleSets. As COM Automation Servers, RuleSets achieve the highest possible degree of industry standard application and language interoperability.

Reuse — Because business policies and practices often apply to all of an organization's applications, isolated business rules can be reused.

RuleSets can be reused without modification in multiple production applications.

Rapid Response to Business Change and Simplified Maintenance — Developers no longer have to review an application's lines of code to identify business rules and then change and test them. Isolated business rules can be changed very rapidly. And because they're not embedded, testing them doesn't mean retesting the entire application.

Increased Developer Productivity — Production systems are designed specifically for the specification and processing of business rules. Their use can save developers significant time and effort compared with using 3GLs and 4GLs that do not include the specialized constructs and the functionality for business rules.

APPROPRIATE USES OF PRODUCTION SYSTEMS

It is true that business rule logic can be implemented with equal process outcome in either conventional programming languages or production rule systems. The stark differences between these two means of representing and processing business logic requires the use of some discerning criteria when considering the appropriateness of one method over another. This section will discuss the types of business application problems that are best solved with production rule systems, and the further reaching benefits production rule systems bring to the life cycle of such business applications.

Background

Historically, the application of production rule systems to a problem solution was considered a high-risk, high-return endeavor. The causes of the high-risk perceptions of production rule system undertakings was not due to any intrinsic shortcoming of production rule problem representation, but rather was due to limitations imposed by the development methodologies and technologies available at the time. The key limitation was the lack of methodologies and technologies that easily enabled software interoperability.

Without any standardized methods or tools to develop applications that could share or access the capabilities of other existing applications, each program had to implement all of its required applications elements. The primary components of these application elements were user interface, database access, and client-server capabilities.

The early commercial vendors of production rule or expert system products had not only to implement their particular rule authoring, representation, and processing components, but also all the other components required to enable developers to create complete applications. The resulting products were not just production rule systems but also complete development environments for user interface, database access, and client-server applications.

The end result of expert system vendors having created complete application development environments is that prospective users of expert systems would have to choose to accept the limitations of the application development tools that housed the production rule system. The risks in using these systems were high. At a time when corporate IS was just beginning to accept the use of RAD tools from the major software vendors, choosing to use a less capable RAD tool from a not so major vendor, for the sole purpose of gaining access to the production rule system that it housed, was risky indeed. The resulting reluctance to use these tools for anything but the most complex of problems was understandable.

This legacy has left us with several misperceptions about the applicability of production rule systems in today's business applications:

- Rule system projects have a low success rate.
- Commercially available rule system tools are closed environments.
- Rule systems should only be used for extremely complex, "unsolvable" problems.

Today, packaging of rules into industry standard component reusable objects not only dispels these myths but allows us to make the following assertions regarding the appropriateness of production rule systems in today's business applications:

- Projects using component reusable production rule systems can have a higher success rate compared to projects that fail to isolate business rules.
- Component reusable rule systems are completely open and are usable by all modern RAD tools.
- Rule systems should be used for all business logic processing, regardless of the perceived simplicity or complexity of the problem.

SUITABLE PROBLEM CATEGORIES

Problems that are generally appropriate for production rule systems can be grouped into two major categories: analysis problems and synthesis problems. Naturally, the real world is never quite so black and white. It is often the case that problems contain elements of both. Nevertheless, considering them separately gives us considerable explanatory leverage.

Analysis Problems

Production rules systems are especially adept at the representation of all varieties of analysis problems. Analysis can be considered a broad umbrella term for problems categories such as diagnostics, classification, fault determination, and situation assessment. Such problems are generally solved by backward chaining systems, although forward chaining rules may be used as well. Authoring rules for analysis problems is relatively easy, since there usually is a clearly identifiable goal, e.g., a diagnosis, which yields readily to subgoal decomposition via backward chaining rules.

It is the properties of diagnostics and classification problems that make them so easily solved by production rule systems. The process of classification begins by identifying all the possible problem solutions. These become the goals of the production system. Each possible goal of the classification then becomes a relatively independent subproblem. For each subproblem, one must identify all supporting evidence necessary to assert the goal of the subproblem. The supporting evidence and associated goal are naturally modeled by the IF part and THEN part of production system rules.

Analysis systems are extremely easy to enhance and maintain. Additions or modifications to analysis systems can be localized to the set of rules associated with the subgoal of interest.

Synthesis Problems

Problem categories such as design and scheduling are considered to be synthesis problems. These problems are among the most specialized and obstinate problems known to computer science. Synthesis problems are almost exclusively solved with forward chaining production systems.

Forward chaining production systems have the ability to cyclically transform an initial context state into a series of synthesized solution steps as shown in Exhibit 4. The production systems for synthesis problems con-

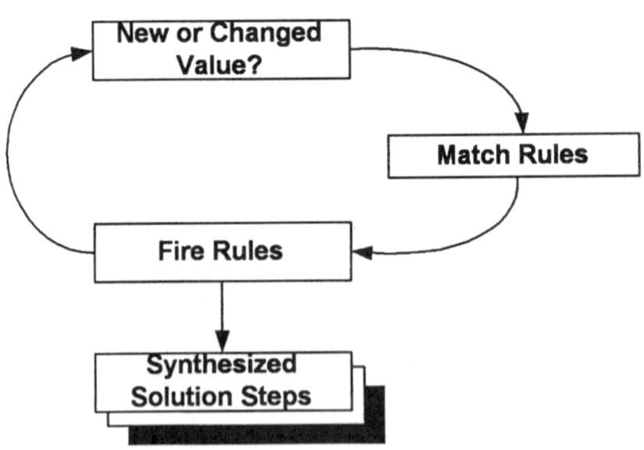

Exhibit 4. Forward chaining as used in synthesis problems.

sist of one or more groups of rules, each of which is responsible for a given transformation of the context data to a new valid state. The new state of the context data then becomes the attention of some other set of rules which "knows" how to transform the context data into yet another valid state. Each intermediate transformed state and the temporal order in which it was generated, represents the synthesized steps for the problem solution.

Unsuitable Problems

There are many parts of a typical business application where production rule systems should not be used. These include the application components iterated above: user interface, database access, and client-server communication. Additionally, it is undesirable to use production rule systems in the routine management of general application control. That is not to say that production rule components should not be called upon by these application components to assist in, or add intelligence to these application processes.

Another obvious category of problems unsuitable for solution by production rule systems would be mathematical or algorithmic processes that have existing and well-codified solutions. These are best solved using traditional procedural languages.

GENERAL PROBLEM CHARACTERISTICS

Whether a problem can be categorized as analysis or synthesis, it's appropriateness for solution by production rule systems should be subject to the general criteria of knowledge representation. If the problem lends itself to a representation by knowledge chunks, that is, a set of loosely coupled problem solution steps, then that logic within the overall system is best implemented by production rule systems.

A Small Example

A common business transaction is customer credit authorization. Such an application would contain the typical software elements of the presentation layer, database access layer, and physical database layer. Traditional implementations of this common business application would also contain the company's "rules" of credit authorization loosely distributed across these three layers.

Explicitly applying knowledge management discipline to the design and development methodology for our hypothetical credit authorization business application would result in the isolation of all credit decision logic in a single RuleSet.

```
!==================================================
RULE 1 authorize against outstanding balance
IF new outstanding balance <= CreditLine OF Customer
THEN authorize outstanding balance

RULE 2 authorize against outstanding balance
IF new outstanding balance <= CreditLine OF Customer * 1.15
AND Preferred Status OF Customer IS Good
THEN authorize outstanding balance

RULE 3 authorize against outstanding balance
IF new outstanding balance > CreditLine OF Customer * 1.15
AND new outstanding balance < CreditLine OF Customer * 1.25
AND Preferred Status OF Customer IS Outstanding
THEN authorize outstanding balance
ELSE Reason OF CreditAction IS Credit Limit Exceeded
!==================================================
RULE 1 overdue payment
IF Months Overdue OF Customer = 0
THEN authorize overdue payment

RULE 2 overdue payment
IF Months Overdue OF Customer = 1
AND new outstanding balance < profile.crline * 0.1
THEN authorize overdue payment

RULE 3 overdue payment
IF Months Overdue OF Customer >= 1
AND Months Overdue OF Customer <= 4
AND CreditLine OF Customer >= 10000
AND new outstanding balance < Bank Balance OF Customer
THEN authorize overdue payment

RULE 4 overdue payment
IF Months Overdue OF Customer > 1
AND new outstanding balance < Bank Balance OF Customer
AND Management authorization of overdue IS yes
THEN authorize overdue payment
ELSE Reason OF CreditAction IS Overdue Balance
!==================================================
RULE 1 for authorize amount
IF PurchaseAMt OF Customer <= Order Limit OF Customer
THEN authorize amount

RULE 2 for authorize amount
IF PurchaseAMt OF Customer > Order Limit OF Customer
AND Management authorization of large amount IS yes
THEN authorize amount
ELSE Reason OF CreditAction IS Amount Too Large
```

```
!===============================================
! CreditAction Authorization — Main Rule
!===============================================

RULE 1 for credit authorization
IF authorize amount
AND authorize outstanding balance
AND authorize overdue payment
THEN CreditAction IS Authorized
ELSE NOT CreditAction IS Authorized
```

The backward chaining set of rules shown in Exhibit 5 represents the credit policies of our hypothetical company. A business application would use this RuleSet to authorize a customer's credit for a purchase transaction. The goal of this RuleSet is "CreditAction IS Authorized." Using backward chaining the inference engine would find the rule that can conclude the goal. This would cause the rule "RULE 1 for credit authorization" to be evaluated. Each of the terms of the IF part of "RULE 1 for credit authorization" would become subgoals for determining "CreditAction IS Authorized."

It is an easy exercise to follow the back chaining process through each of the subgoals: "authorize amount," authorize outstanding balance," and "authorize overdue payment."

In integrating the credit authorization RuleSet into a business application the traditional software component elements of presentation layer, database access layer, and physical database layer would be expanded to include a business layer. The business layer would gather the necessary information required, evoke the credit authorization RuleSet, and then act on the RuleSet's conclusions.

This example, though simple, exemplifies the development methodologies of business rules and knowledge management. Consolidating all the rules governing the customer credit authorization into a single component simplifies the specification as well as the ongoing revision of critical business policies.

CONCLUSION

Business software systems often contain hidden knowledge about how companies do their business. Today's need for rapid adaptation and change dictates that this hidden knowledge becomes isolated, exposed, and manageable. Businesses can no longer afford to allow the rules governing their business practices to be poorly codified and hard to change. The adaptation of production rule systems, business rules, and knowledge management as a standard part of the business software life cycle will dramatically improve the ability of companies to specify, maintain, and adapt the business knowledge within their software systems. This will in turn allow companies to rapidly adapt to changing market pressures and business opportunities.

Exhibit 5. Credit Authorization RuleSet

```
RULE 1 authorize against outstanding balance
  IF          New outstanding balance <= CreditLine OF Customer
  THEN        Authorize outstanding balance
RULE 2 authorize against outstanding balance
  IF          New outstanding balance <= CreditLine OF Customer * 1.15
  AND         Preferred Status OF Customer IS Good
  THEN        Authorize outstanding balance
RULE 3 authorize against outstanding balance
  IF          New outstanding balance > CreditLine OF Customer * 1.15
  AND         New outstanding balance < CreditLine OF Customer * 1.25
  AND         Preferred Status OF Customer IS Outstanding
  THEN        Authorize outstanding balance
  ELSE        Reason OF CreditAction IS Credit Limit Exceeded
RULE 1 overdue payment
  IF          Months Overdue OF Customer = 0
  THEN        Authorize overdue payment
RULE 2 overdue payment
  IF          Months Overdue OF Customer = 1
  AND         New outstanding balance < profile.crline * 0.1
  THEN        Authorize overdue payment
RULE 3 overdue payment
  IF          Months Overdue OF Customer >= 1
  AND         Months Overdue OF Customer <= 4
  AND         CreditLine OF Customer >= 10000
  AND         New outstanding balance < Bank Balance OF Customer
  THEN        Authorize overdue payment
RULE 4 overdue payment
  IF          Months Overdue OF Customer > 1
  AND         New outstanding balance < Bank Balance Of Customer
  AND         Management authorization of overdue IS yes
  THEN        Authorize overdue payment
  ELSE        Reason Of CreditAction IS Overdue Balance
RULE 1 for authorize amount
  IF          PurchaseAMt OF Customer <= Order Limit OF Customer
  THEN        Authorize amount
RULE 2 for authorize amount
  IF          PurchaseAMt OF Customer > Order Limit OF Customer
  AND         Management authorization of large amount IS yes
  THEN        Authorize amount
  ELSE        Reason OF CreditAction IS Amount Too Large
CreditAction Authorization – Main Rule
RULE 1 for credit authorization
  IF          Authorize amount
  AND         Authorize outstanding balance
  AND         Authorize overdue payment
  THEN        CreditAction IS Authorized
  ELSE NOT    CreditAction IS Authorized
```

Chapter 13
Customer Data Quality: The Foundation for a One-to-One Customer Relationship

Jody Lyon

IN TODAY'S COMPETITIVE FINANCIAL MARKET, every day brings new challenges for customer acquisition and retention. To stay ahead, financial services companies are turning to decision support solutions to help identify and manage their customer relationships. Solutions such as data warehouses or data marts provide a solid foundation of accurate information upon which they can base their decisions. Accuracy is one of the biggest obstacles blocking the success of many data warehousing projects. In fact, data quality is the number one challenge facing financial institutions as they implement their data warehouses. It is not unusual to discover that as many as half the records in a database contain some type of information that needs to be corrected. One of the most crucial areas of data quality is customer information. For the most accurate information to support your financial services business, you will need to incorporate data quality into each critical step — extraction, transformation, consolidation, and maintenance. Data quality is especially important to accurate consolidation because it allows you to recognize and understand customer relationships. As a result, you can gain a clear picture of your customers, analyze their buying patterns, and predict future sales.

Which data is most important to your company? Before you evaluate data quality solutions, you need to determine the type of data that is most important to your company. Will you focus primarily on customer informa-

0-8493-9991-2/99/$0.00+$.50

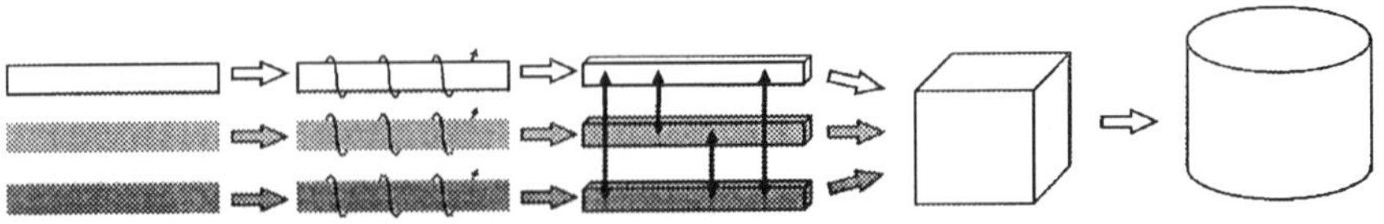

Exhibit 1. Data quality is achieved in three stages: cleansing, matching, and consolidation. In the data cleansing stage, the data are parsed, corrected, enhanced, and standardized for accurate matching. In the matching stage, comparisons are made within and across the data sources to locate similar information. Finally, the matching data elements are consolidated and placed into a data warehouse, data mart, or other data staging area.

tion, or are you most concerned with data such as price trends, dates, and probability scores? Once you make this decision, you can choose the data quality products most appropriate for your applications. In either case, you will find that most data quality and consolidation products fall into one of two categories: data-referenced solutions which combine reference tables with sophisticated algorithms, and non-data-referenced solutions which rely on algorithms alone. In data warehouses where customer data are essential, data-referenced software is more effective. This type of software features an extensive knowledge base of empirical data, which allows you to enhance and improve the quality of your information.

Building data quality into a data warehouse involves six key elements as shown in Exhibit 1: parsing, correction, enhancement, standardization, matching, and consolidation. This chapter will help you discover the principles and inherent problems of data quality and data consolidation, and the available solutions to help you manage them.

PARSING: DO YOU KNOW THE CONDITION OF YOUR DATA?

Parsing is the first critical component in data cleansing, as shown in Exhibit 2. This process locates, identifies, and isolates individual data elements in your customer files. These components may include such data as a customer's first name, last name, title, company name, street address, city, state, or ZIP code. Parsing makes it easier to correct, enhance, standardize, and match data because it allows you to compare individual components, rather than long strings of data.

Parsing the Elements

There are several obstacles to parsing that may later hinder successful matching. Perhaps the most pervasive problem is discrepancies in the

Input Data
BETH CHRISTINE PARKER, PURCH MGR
REGIONAL PORT AUTHORITY
FEDERAL BUILDING
12800 LAKE CALUMET
HEGEWISCH IL

- - - - - →

Parsed Data	
First Name:	BETH
Middle Name:	CHRISTINE
Last Name:	PARKER
Title:	PURCH MGR
Firm:	REGIONAL PORT AUTHORITY
Firm Location:	FEDERAL BUILDING
Range:	12800
Street:	LAKE CALUMET
City:	HEGEWISCH
State:	IL

Exhibit 2. Parsing is a vital step for the cleansing and matching stages. This example shows how parsing identifies and isolates the individual elements of an input record.

---

metadata — information about the data in your database. For example, the information in a field may not match its metadata profile. Inconsistent definitions and multiple data sources make it difficult to determine if fields possess the same characteristics from one source to the next, as shown in Exhibit 3.

Other obstacles include:

- *"Misfielded" data* — Data that is placed in the wrong field, such as name data in an address field.
- *Floating data* — Customer data that may be contained in different fields from record to record, resulting in data "floating" between fields.
- *Extraneous information* — The data may contain irrelevant or blank fields.
- *Atypical words* — Records may include ethnic, multicultural, and hyphenated names; unusual titles; abbreviated business names; industry-specific acronyms; etc.
- *Inconsistent structures and formats* — Operational, purchased, and exchanged data sources may be formatted differently from each other or from the data warehouse.

Field Format		***Field data***
First-middle-last-title	- - - - →	Juanita Alvarez, Trustee
Last-title-comma-first-middle	- - - - →	Alvarez Trustee, Juanita E.
Last-comma-first-middle-title	- - - - →	Alvarez, Juanita E. Trustee

Exhibit 3. Inconsistent field formats, such as those indicated above, present an obstacle for unparsed data, making it difficult to combine all data sources into one data warehouse.

First Name:	BETH
Middle Name:	CHRISTINE
Last Name:	PARKER
Title:	PURCH MGR
Firm:	REGIONAL PORT AUTHORITY
Firm Location:	FEDERAL BUILDING
Range:	12800
Street:	LAKE CALUMET
City:	HEGEWISCH
State:	IL

Corrected Data	
First Name:	BETH
Middle Name:	CHRISTINE
Last Name:	PARKER
Title:	PURCH MGR
Firm:	REGIONAL PORT AUTHORITY
Firm Location:	FEDERAL BUILDING
Address:	12800 SOUTH BUTLER DRIVE
City:	CHICAGO
State:	IL
ZIP:	60633
ZIP 4:	2398

Exhibit 4. The record on the left has an alias street name and a vanity city name. The record on the right shows how these elements were corrected.

CORRECTION: HOW DO YOU KNOW YOUR DATA ARE ACCURATE?

Once you've parsed your data, you are ready to begin the next phase of the data cleansing process — correction, as shown in Exhibit 4. Customer information is the most difficult type of data to cleanse and validate. If your data comes from a variety of sources, you may encounter:

- Variations in abbreviations, formats, etc., because of individual preferences of the person entering the information.
- Misspellings caused by phonetic similarities during telephone data entry.
- Outdated information due to name and address changes.
- Transpositions resulting from keying errors.

Correcting the Elements

The only way to intelligently correct and verify your data is to use software that references a reliable secondary data source. In many instances, correction is used only to prepare data for matching — the original records remain unchanged.

For instance, some neighborhoods have "vanity" city names (i.e., "Hollywood" vs. "Los Angeles") or "alias" street names (i.e., "Valley View Mall" vs. "Highway 16"). Some residents living there may prefer to use one city or street name over the other, and therefore may be more likely to respond to an offer bearing the name they prefer. However, by recognizing that both names refer to the same location, you have a better chance of identifying matches.

Corrected Data	
First Name:	BETH
Middle Name:	CHRISTINE
Last Name:	PARKER
Title:	PURCH MGR
Firm:	REGIONAL PORT AUTHORITY
Firm Location:	FEDERAL BUILDING
Address:	12800 SOUTH BUTLER DRIVE
City:	CHICAGO
State:	IL
ZIP:	60633
ZIP 4:	2398

Enhanced Data	
First Name:	BETH
Middle Name:	CHRISTINE
Last Name:	PARKER
Title:	PURCH MGR
Firm:	REGIONAL PORT AUTHORITY
Firm Location:	FEDERAL BUILDING
Address:	12800 SOUTH BUTLER DRIVE
City:	CHICAGO
State:	IL
ZIP:	60633
ZIP 4:	2398
Marital Status:	M
Age:	34
# Credit Cards:	3
Est. Income:	$45K

Exhibit 5. Once the data have been corrected, the record may be enhanced with additional information.

ENHANCEMENT: DO YOU HAVE ALL THE DATA YOU NEED?

Enhancement, the next process in data cleansing, adds new data and appends missing information as shown in Exhibit 5. The new data provides you with information to help you better understand your customers and predict their buying, investing, and saving behaviors. This information may include data such as age, household income, presence of children, marital status, number and type of credit cards owned, and loan histories. Missing information that may be appended includes apartment numbers, missing address elements, telephone numbers, latitude/longitude information, county codes, and political districts.

Enhancement may be accomplished by sending your customer data to an outside firm for processing, purchasing an outside source of customer data, or surveying your customers and manually updating their information. These alternatives, however, may present some additional challenges:

- External processing may be time and cost prohibitive.
- Financial customer records may be too sensitive to send to an outside firm for processing.
- Internal resources and expertise may be insufficient to integrate an external data source.
- Customers may be difficult to reach or unwilling to provide additional information.

There are many outside data sources available to perform enhancement. It is important to select a solution that contains the type of data best suited for predicting the behavior of your customers.

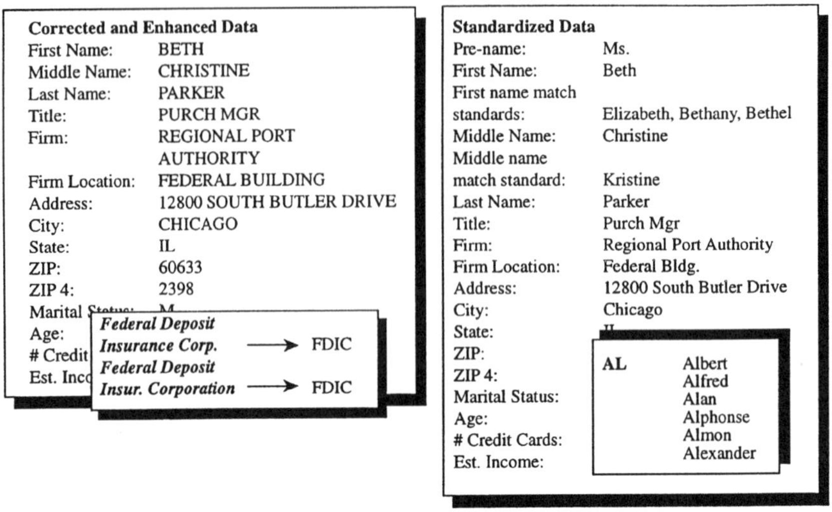

Exhibit 6. Once data have been corrected and enhanced, the elements undergo further cleansing. The data are standardized according to the established criteria. These same criteria will come into play later in the matching stage.

STANDARDIZATION: IS YOUR DATA READY FOR MATCHING?

Standardization, the final step in data cleansing, allows you to arrange customer information into a preferred and consistent format as shown in Exhibit 6. Some of the biggest challenges for accurate standardization of customer data include:

- *Inconsistent abbreviations*, such as International Investment Incorporated, Internat'l. Investmnt. Incorp., Int'l. Invstmnt. Inc.
- *Unusual titles*, for example, joint tenant with rights of survivorship (jt wros); power of attorney (poa); universal gift for minors act (ugma).
- *Misspellings and variant spellings*, i.e., Kwik, Quik, Quick.

Software solutions that integrate secondary data sources perform more effective standardization, and allow you to make business decisions with confidence. For example, some software is certified to standardize addresses using the most widely accepted data source — the U. S. Postal Service's National Directory. It is important to create separate fields of standardized information and not to overwrite the original data.

Standardizing the Elements

Some software can also standardize other customer information, such as pre-names, post-names, titles, and business locations ("Doctor" to "Dr.," "Junior" to "Jr.," "Floor" to "Flr.," etc.). It may also identify genders, based on empirical name data, to give you a better understanding of your customers for one-to-one marketing.

MATCHING: CAN YOU FIND THE DUPLICATES IN YOUR DATA?

Matching allows you to identify similar data within and across your data sources. This is the "heart" of data warehousing. Using cleansed information and match standards, you can eliminate duplicate representations and consolidate all information about each individual customer or an entire household. This will help you to:

- Truly "see" each customer or household, and generate accurate data about them.
- Enhance response rates of marketing promotions.
- Reduce the risk of offending customers with repeat offers.
- Identify trends and patterns to accurately target new prospects.

One of the greatest challenges in matching is creating a system that incorporates your "business rules" — criteria for determining what constitutes a match, as shown in Exhibit 7. These business rules will vary from one company to another, and from one application to another.

In one instance, you may require that name and address information match exactly. In another, you may accept wider address variations, as

---

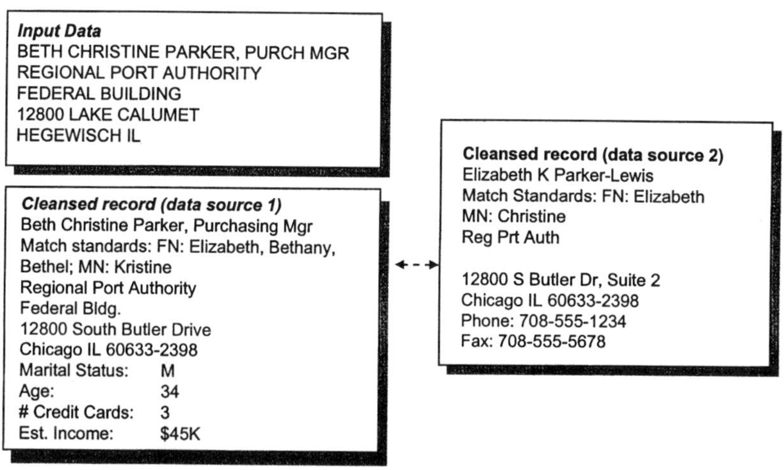

Exhibit 7. Parsing, correction, enhancement, and standardization are the bases for accurate matching. This example shows how data cleansing has prepared the original input record for matching against a record from another data source. Sophisticated standardization software can assign match standards to facilitate more successful matching for elements such as personal and business names.

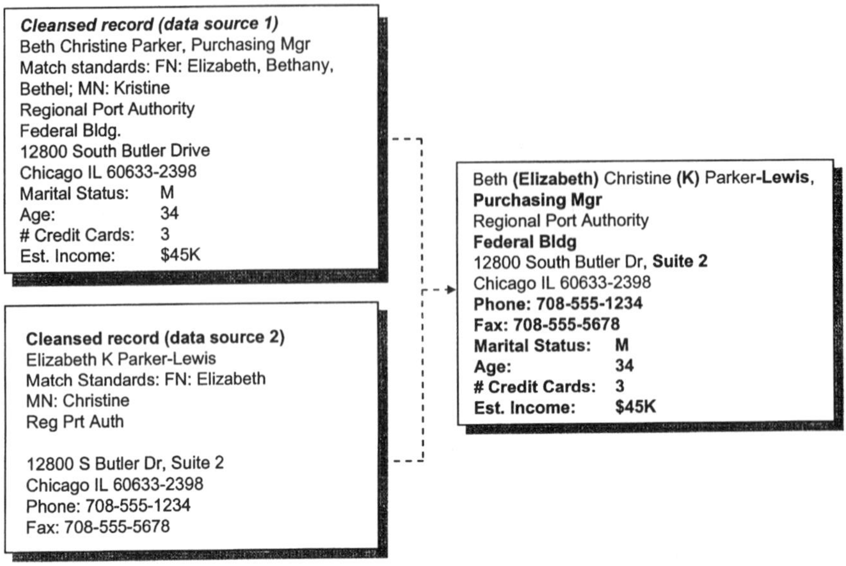

Exhibit 8. Consolidation combines the elements of matching records into one complete record. The information in bold type in the final record was not originally contained in the two cleansed records.

---

long as the name and phone number match closely. Some additional challenges to matching business-to-business data include:

- Company mergers, acquisitions, or corporate name changes.
- Relationships between divisions, subsidiaries, and parent corporations.
- Business acronyms (i.e., NASDAQ or NYNEX).
- Initialisms — the first letter of one or more words in a title or phrase that are sounded one by one (i.e., CFO or SEC).

CONSOLIDATION: YOU'VE MATCHED YOUR DATA — NOW WHAT?

Once you've located the matching records in your data, you can identify relationships between customers and build a consolidated view of each as shown in Exhibit 8. This critical component of successful one-to-one marketing allows you to gain a clearer understanding of your customers. "One-to-one marketing allows organizations to better serve the customer at every point of contact," according to Tom Hurley, vice-president of database marketing and research for Invesco Funds Group. When you base marketing, telemarketing, sales, customer service, and accounting decisions on clean and accurate data, you can more easily retain customers by anticipating their needs.

There are two methods for consolidation, both of which are essential for most financial services data warehousing and one-to-one marketing applications. The first consolidation process combines all of the data on any given customer using all of the available data sources. The second process — customer relationship identification — reveals links between your customers.

There are two common types of customer relationship identification: householding and business grouping. Typically, householding links consumer records that contain the same address and last name. Another type of householding identifies customers with a joint ownership or interest in an account or investment. Business grouping combines business records that share such information as company name, address, department, or title.

By identifying the characteristics and buying habits of a group or household, you can create special offers and better target direct marketing efforts. As you combine your data on each customer, you will need to determine priorities between data sources and specific data fields. For example, some records may contain more complete information, but may be from an unreliable source (see the Consolidation Systems section later in this chapter).

DATA CLEANSING SOLUTIONS: WHAT ARE YOU GOING TO DO ABOUT IT?

As previously mentioned, most data quality tools fall into one of two categories: data-referenced and non-data-referenced. Both systems allow you to reformat your data, but data-referenced systems go a step further. *Data-referenced solutions* combine reference tables with sophisticated algorithms. In most cases, this type of solution deals better with the challenges posed by customer-centric data warehousing applications. By accessing the empirical data in their reference tables, these solutions can intelligently parse, correct, enhance, and standardize your critical customer information, rather than simply format it. *Non-data-referenced solutions* rely on algorithms alone. These solutions can handle less-challenging data, such as account balances, dates, product numbers, or credit rating scores.

In either case, you should choose a data integrity solution that includes:

- Customizable standardization options.
- The ability to retain original data and save corrected information.
- Flexible output options.

Data-Referenced Systems: Best for Customer Data

For customer-centric data warehouses, the most effective systems use empirical information. They provide the foundation for logically consolidating multiple, diverse databases. The best systems for address cleans-

Processing with non-data-referenced software	
JERRY BENSON, EXECUTOR 704 MARTIN LUTHER KING BOULEVARD PRINCETON FLORIDA 33031	Jerry Benson, Executor 704 Martin Luther King Blvd Princeton FL 33031

Processing with data-referenced software	
Jerry Benson, Executor	**Mr.** Jerry Benson, Executor First Name Match Stds: **Jerome, Jerald,** **Jeremiah, Jerilyn**
704 MARTIN LUTHER KING BOULEVARD PRINCETON FLORIDA 33031	704 **SW 4th St.** **Homestead** FL **33031-6914**

Exhibit 9. Non-data-referenced vs. data-referenced software. Non-data-referenced software offers limited functionality and flexibility compared to data-referenced software. The bold type highlights the information that data-referenced software appends and standardizes over non-data-referenced software.

ing use the National ZIP+4 Directory developed by the U. S. Postal Service (USPS). They are designed with high-speed engines that are certified as being 99% or more accurate. By leveraging the USPS' multimillion dollar, multiyear investment, they offer the most comprehensive source for address parsing, correction, enhancement, and standardization. The most effective data-integrity software can also parse names, titles, business locations, business names, and financial terms such as trustee, retired, and deceased. By using empirical data and user-modifiable tables, these systems can more accurately locate floating, unfielded, or incorrectly parsed data. Because they are founded on actual data, you can properly process ethnic, hyphenated, or atypical names; and recognize business name and location data.

Data-referenced software can also perform enhancement for a more complete customer view, as shown in Exhibit 9. This information may include gender codes, salutations, geographic information (i.e., geo-census codes, county codes, and county names), and demographic data. When choosing data-referenced data cleansing systems, look for the ability to:

- Recognize formal and informal street names, multiple addresses (reflect different addresses for account owner and beneficiary) and vanity city names.
- Minimize users' learning curve using a significant base of predefined data — you should not need to train the product.
- Flag outdated or invalid address data (i.e., rural-route address converted to 9-1-1 address, or a nondeliverable address).
- Access and modify reference tables.
- Assign match standards.

MATCHING AND CONSOLIDATION SOLUTIONS: HOW WILL IT ALL COME TOGETHER?

If your data consist of unparsed data strings, you are in danger of missing many matches or of erroneously consolidating different customers. However, corrected and standardized data in discrete fields allow most matching systems to successfully detect:

- Transposed, missing, or extra characters.
- Transposed words.
- Phonetic errors.
- Acronyms and abbreviations.

Matching Systems

There are several varieties of matching systems available, each offering a different way to arrive at a match:

- *Key-code matching* performs identical comparisons using the first few characters in one or more fields. This primitive method is rarely practiced because it uses only a small subset of the data, which can result in many false matches.
- *Soundexing* detects phonetic similarities, such as "f" and "ph" or Quick and Kwik. These errors often result from data received over the telephone, particularly with data that can't be standardized. However, soundexing is inadequate as a sole solution because it can only detect phonetic errors.
- *Similarity matching*, also referred to as "fuzzy matching," can identify matches by computing a degree of likeness between two discrete components. Because identical matches are not required, it can adjust for spelling, phonetic, typographical, and transpositional errors. Similarity matching, as shown in Exhibit 10, is widely considered the best matching method. It is especially valuable for data that cannot be standardized, such as last names, business names, and house numbers. It considers all characters in a field and their position to determine the degree of a match. In this example, the degree of the match is indicated by the similarity score.

In the address 1001 Rose St.:

1001 and 101 have a similarity score of 85%
1001 and 1010 have a similarity score of 75%
1001 and 1025 have a similarity score of 50%

Exhibit 10. Similarity matching.

- *Weighted matching* can be used in conjunction with soundexing or similarity matching. It allows you to indicate the relative importance of fields that determine a match.
- *Special purpose algorithms*, which are extensions of similarity matching, apply exception logic (if/then rules) to traditional match rules. There are four categories of special purpose algorithms:
- *Special-case field logic* customizes matching techniques for specific fields. For example, these algorithms are used to identify matches between acronyms or initialisms and their full business names, or numeric components within names.

Special-Case Field Logic. With special-case field logic, you can identify a match between a full name and its initialism, or between numbers in a name and their full spelling.

- *General-case field logic* applies additional match logic when it encounters certain anomalies, such as blank fields. In comparing discrete components, it allows you to specify when blank fields should be considered matches against fields that contain data.
- *Special-case multi-field logic* adjusts weighting, which depends on the data found in specific sets of fields. When householding, for instance, this method would assign a higher value to the "name" field when the address is an apartment complex and the "unit number" field is blank.
- *General-case multi-field logic* performs a second match when it encounters specific anomalies, regardless of the fields in which they are found. For example, it could search for elements with low parse-confidence scores, concatenate them, and compare the resulting data strings.

A combined approach — incorporating similarity, weighting, and special purpose algorithms — is usually best. As many as 6 to 10 levels of matching may be necessary for complete data consolidation or maintenance.

When using a combined approach, you need the flexibility to modify business match rules. This is important as the reliability of certain data may vary between records and sources. For instance, people who move often have unreliable contact data. When this happens, your combined solution should provide the flexibility to use alternate fields as match criteria, such as social security number, credit card numbers, account numbers, and date of birth.

Consolidation Systems

The data cleansing and matching processes lead to one end result: accurate data consolidation. To build on this foundation, you'll need a flexible consolidation solution to combine existing operational data and maintain incoming data feeds. Some key components of proven consolidation solutions allow you to:

- *Prioritize incoming data sources.* In-house databases are usually more reliable than purchased or rented data because they tend to be more up-to-date.
- *Prioritize fields.* Fields that have been cleansed and verified tend to be more reliable than those that have not. Again, the source and recency are important considerations.
- *Maintain sources of original data.* Complete metadata allows you to trace data errors or discrepancies back to the source.
- *Identify unreliable or missing data.* Once identified, if it is economically feasible, you can request information directly from the customer or from a valid outside source.

Depending on the scope of your project, you may wish to approach consolidation one step at a time. If you don't have the resources to build an enterprise data warehouse, you may choose to start with a data mart. With each small success, you will gain expertise, confidence, and continued support for completing your data warehouse.

DON'T OVERLOOK THE FOUNDATION

As you implement your data warehouse, don't overlook its foundation — data integrity — which is essential for quality matching and consolidation. It is critical to first determine which data are important, and to choose the most appropriate cleansing tools. When working with customer data, a data-referenced solution is best. With a variety of matching solutions available, look for one that combines different types of matching algorithms. This will allow you to more accurately locate, understand, and target your customers. By building parsing, correction, enhancement, standardization, matching, and consolidation into your system, you can meet your goals, which may enable you to:

- Make better and more immediate marketing decisions.
- Increase market share.
- Increase revenue.
- Increase profitability.
- Detect fraud more accurately.
- Improve customer service.
- Ensure clean feeds to online analytical processing (OLAP) and data-mining tools.
- Implement your solution faster than building your own.
- Understand your customers.
- Guarantee the success of your project. The best course of action is to choose tools that offer the flexibility and accuracy your project demands. By implementing these tools, you will secure a solid foundation for building one-to-one customer relationships.

Chapter 14
A History of Knowledge-Based Systems in Financial Services

Jessica Keyes

ONE OF THE REASONS why the computer hasn't produced the spurt of productivity that we all expected is that we are still dealing with bits and bytes of information. We still haven't learned how to turn it into certifiable knowledge. That's because most of us are still building traditional systems, that is, systems that provide merely tactical information, rather than smart systems that provide competitive advantage — systems that provide knowledge.

Financial Services has always looked beyond the ordinary toolset in an attempt to develop systems that would not only process data but turn the data into this elusive thing called knowledge. What many MIS types new to Financial Services might not realize is that the "road to smart systems" has been well traveled by the industry.

This chapter is a summary of the development of the some of the most highly publicized and eloquent knowledge-based systems of the past two decades. It's worthwhile to know where we've been in order to develop a plan to get to where we want to go.

TRANSFORMING INFORMATION INTO KNOWLEDGE

Perhaps the industry with the largest share of traditional systems is the banking industry. No one personifies banking more nor has done more for the banking industry than Citicorp's chairman emeritus Walter Wriston. In his many years as chief executive officer he revolutionized the international banking environment. And one of the tools in his toolbox of change was the computer. With over a trillion dollars a day changing hands in the New

0-8493-9991-2/99/$0.00+$.50

York market alone, the banking industry has really geared up for an alliance between technology and strategy. Wriston envisioned a banking environment where the interface between man and machine permits easy access to complex information. Artificial intelligence (AI), predicts Wriston, will become the norm and not the exception. He looks forward to a day when he can walk up to a smart system in a bank lobby that will be able to answer complex questions about his account: "Can I invest in a tax-free fund? Can I do brokerage transactions?"

Quaker Oats in Chicago was one of the first consumer goods marketers to realize the potential of strategic technology. More than 15 years ago it set up its own computer program to analyze some 2 billion facts about different products and competitors. Use of this system permitted Quaker Oats to understand the data and to draw insights from it. This led it to the number one spot in such product categories as Rice-A-Roni and the ever-popular Aunt Jemima Pancakes. More recently it began to realize that new technology was making the system obsolete. So without hesitation out it went and in came a much more high-tech analytical tool. With it Quaker Oats can perform the intricate "what if" analyses that will keep it number one.

This brand of filtering methodology is a technology very much in vogue as more and more entrepreneurial start-ups compete to slay the information dragon. MIT has stepped in to become knights in shining armor when they devised a novel way to separate the e-mail wheat from the chaff. For many of us, electronic mail messages rate right up there with junk mail. The MIT system found a novel way to categorize messages as top priority if they come from certain people or if the message implies that it needs a response within a few days. Joining the Knights of The Round Table is a former LOTUS development executive. He started a company called Beyond Inc. based just on this technology. LOTUS itself has its own mail sifter. NOTES uses graphical displays to permit senders to imprint distinctive logos on their electronic missives. You can direct your mailbox to turn up its nose at certain logos and permit others access. I suppose some enterprising start-up company will find a comfortable niche in producing counterfeit logos for gate-crashing. Or will we call it logo-crashing?

Filters work for more than just turning up your nose at uninvited electronic guests. It also is a mainstay in the marketing arena. For years marketers used technology to filter relevancies out of the information glut. It started with the first totally computerized census back in 1970. The Census Bureau created demographic data on computer tapes. This provided a plethora of information on neighborhoods right down to your very own city block. By the time the 1980 census rolled around these stats had ballooned into 300,000 pages of statistics. And a whopping 10 times that amount sat patiently on computer tapes. Today the personal computer has put this same information on a desktop.

Many in the financial industry quickly followed suit. Investors Services, out of Bridgeport, CT has been collecting data for some 30 years. Today it manages Worldscope, an international database containing a wealth of information on some 5000 companies. The key here is smart filtering.

Individual Inc. sifts through full text articles and pinpoints items of interest to its subscribers. They describe themselves as operating an information refinery that takes a broad stream of raw data and turns it into actionable knowledge.

Dean LeBaron agrees to this approach. He was very much in the *avant-garde* in the middle 1970s. That's when he preached the use of computers to improve the quality of investing. Batterymarch Financial Management is one of Boston's leading money management firms with a portfolio of over $11 billion. LeBaron runs Batterymarch as one large expert system. It's "designed to operate the way an intelligent institutional investor would operate if put on a silicon substrate."

Wriston, LeBaron, and the rest of these folks recognized early on the advantages of using smarter technology. And each revels in "number one" spots in their respective marketplaces. These companies have learned to distinguish between information and knowledge. The rest of this chapter will profile several "smart systems." Hopefully the reader will begin to discern a pattern in developing these systems that can be applied to his or her own organization.

AI ON WALL STREET

What better place to start then the den of the money lions. Wall Street grabbed onto the idea of intelligent systems in a big way back in the early 1990s. Their goal? To make more money, of course. The financial markets are the most complex of systems, characterized by literally thousands of variables. While there are some shrewd wheeler-dealers around who trust their own intuition, for the most part Wall Street relies on superintelligent systems to handle and make sense out of all that chaos.

Oh, the joy of it all. To be on the floor of the New York Stock Exchange is to be at the center of the universe. The roar of the crowd and the scent of a fresh kill quickens the pulse and flushes the cheeks. But let's exit through the side door and walk down any street. Look, over there, in that tall gray limestone building, that's where all the real action is.

Behind locked doors a blinking, whirring gray box chugs away uninterrupted. A few feet away a shirt-sleeved denizen of the Wall Street canyon stands watching this magic box perform its magnus opus. Suddenly the printer began its dance and the Wall Street trading fiend scrambles to rip the report, ink still wet, from the printer. Running to the phone, our intrepid but frazzled, ivy league investment banker screams into the phone, "BUY DISNEY."

In October 1987 even the kitchen sink was in jeopardy as the market dropped over 500 points in the largest one-day decline in Wall Street's history. And now that shock wave is behind them, Wall Street has revved up spending on the iron and the stuff that goes in them. All in an often frustrating attempt to deal with market volatility, increasing globalization, and the proliferation of products that litter the market. So its no wonder that some formerly heretic disbelievers are increasingly turning to artificial intelligence to get the upper hand. Expert system applications not only will be used, but will be necessary to respond to the enormous amount of data generated by changes in the European and Asian financial markets, predict the traders who have invested lock, stock, and barrel in these technologies.

Morgan Stanley Dean Witter & Company uses an expert system on their profit and loss desk to solve what had been a costly dilemma. When a trader is busy, often the time can't be taken to review the real-time ticker and make sure that the trade just made is quoted. One of the best-known expert systems on the street, this system's goal in life is to look at all the information and figure out the likelihood that the trade hit the ticker.

Perhaps the best applications for smart systems are on the other side of the ticker. Almost every Wall Street firm has one or more projects underway to provide the trader with a toolset that will provide real-time insights and a Wall Street type of expertise. There are few people on Wall Street who don't believe that computers and automation of investing, hedging, and tracking will yield strategic leverage.

To do this, firms large and small are investing in a combination of smart systems and advanced workstation technology. Most analytics folks are looking for a minimum 50 to 100 MIPS (millions of instructions per second). Combining artificial intelligence and the speed of workstation technology gives the trading room a heady combination. Smart systems account for one out of every seven workstations sold. Citicorp, in New York, ordered 3000 DEC workstations way back in the mid-1990s. The purpose of this grand scheme was to tie its traders into a global network. This network provides each Citicorp trader with the ability to see prices on several markets. It also performs instantaneous portfolio analysis and even automatically executes orders. Yes, the integrated AI workstation approach is a potent weapon with everyone up and down the street clamoring to get a piece of the pie. Paine Webber Group's Hedging Assistant prototype made use of this strategy as does the Chicago Board of Trade's Aurora system.

Perhaps the best use of AI would be as an embedded component in a quantitative investment algorithm. This could, in fact, change the face of the street.

Fourteen years ago Charles Dym pioneered a new quantitative investment theory that butted heads with the three theories most widely held: the Modern Portfolio Theory, the Efficient Market Theory, and the Random Walk Theory. Dym's approach combined pattern recognition and probability theory. A test pilot of this theory did so well that it ranked in the second percentile of the annual Becker rankings. Fourteen years later Dym joined Larry Geisel with the goal of taking this 14-year-old theory and adding two additional components: the experience of the last decade and the ITG expert system.

Not every Wall Street smart system needs to run on a workstation or needs the power of Charles Dym's theories. The most widely used smart systems are those that come off-the-shelf and many of them run on PCs. Incline, a Nevada-based AIQ Systems company markets a trio of products — IndexExpert, StockExpert, and MarketExpert — popular with the stock-buying set.

And the list goes on. As early as 1987, Coopers & Lybrand worked with the now-defunct Drexel Burnham group to develop an expert system that would have the capability of recognizing patterns in auditing trading data. Another innovator, Manning & Napier Advisors out of Rochester, NY, long ago found a novel way to handle their ever-increasing trading volumes. Their novel approach included the use of the now-defunct Wang VS computer to build a rule-based system that guides the trader through the process of determining how many shares to buy and for what accounts. The system tracks many variables including market value, position size, and objectives of the account Not only does the system permit Manning to take advantage of smaller commissions and reduced commission rates, but it's much faster than the old way of doing business. They like to quote the statistic of the new 1.5-hour program vs. the old 7.5 hours it took to complete a trading program. Even venerable old Merrill Lynch uses an off-the-shelf expert trading package to assist in making buy/sell recommendations.

There's great potential here. From front office to back office, the expert system is being used to stem the information crunch in the same way the computer itself was used to stem the great paper crush of the early 1970s. Perhaps the most exotic use of all is on the floor of a stock exchange.

TRADING THEORIES TAKE ON A NEW ALLY — AI

"Computers Challenge the Stock Market Gurus." "Bold New Theory Could Make Investors' Day." These are headlines in the trades. Everybody, from the chairman on down to the mailboy who dabbles in securities on the side, is waiting for smart trading systems to take their bow.

Our friend Charles Dym was a pioneer 14 years ago and he's a pioneer today at the Pittsburgh-based Intelligent Technology Group. With his AI-analytic approach to trading that seems to outperform the S&P 500, AI is getting a really good name on the street.

THE WATCHDOG

Northwestern National Life Insurance Company decided to use an AI solution to solve the problem of analyzing the bond market to minimize losses and maximize revenues.

Before the decision was made to proceed with development of the system, two senior financial analysts were given a seemingly impossible task. This was to screen voluminous and quite complex financial data on individual companies of interest. This process required the use of some 15 ratios to be applied. These analysts searched out increases and decreases of these ratios in an attempt to predict future performance. They attempted to discover causes for ratio fluctuations. They then used this information in their evaluations for each company, which then led to Buy-Sell recommendations. The financial analysts really needed some tool to help them do this process faster and better.

The resulting system was developed to act as an assistant to the not-very-computer-literate financial analysts. It had to be able to access external files such as a commercially available database containing current information on over 7000 companies. It needed to have a robust form of knowledge representation and inferencing mechanisms to perform the type of financial ratio analysis that was now being set down by the expert analysts.

For each of the 7000+ companies, the user would have the option of selecting different time periods to narrow the financial analysis. At this point, the system would analyze the performance of each company using the same methodology that the human analysts had been performing for years. This in-depth financial analysis is coupled with the subjective judgment of the human analysts. This was obtained during the knowledge engineering sessions with outside consultants. In addition, the knowledge base was made even smarter by loading in the determined causes of previous ratio fluctuations. The system's output is a screening report which shows changes in performance of each company in various sort categories as well as more detailed reporting on each specific company.

The system was configured into five integrated knowledge bases. Three of the five knowledge bases contain explicit information on how the financial analysis is performed. The fourth and fifth control the user interface and the current state of the entire system, respectively.

The credit knowledge base contains information about the companies which are to be analyzed. Since an object-oriented design was used, the objects were used to great advantage by defining each company as an instance object. Each company object contains both financial and human judgment about the company.

The data knowledge base contains the specifics of the methodology of financial analysis. Showing its well-integrated nature, it is able to access the credit knowledge base to access financial data about a particular company. Once obtained, the financial analysis of the company can be performed. Here, demons are employed to activate the actual calculation of the financial ratios.

Upon completion of financial analysis the results need to be analyzed to determine a company's financial performance over time and projection of financial performance into the future. This normally human subjective analysis is performed by employing the rules knowledge base which uses production IF...THEN rules to approximate the formerly manual judgment applied by the human experts.

The development team spent under $100,000 and less than 3 months in creating a system that had immediate and enormous payback. A human analyst takes over 100 hours to perform this set of procedures for 80 companies. Watchdog takes under one hour, proving the point that a little money and a lot of expertise and creativity can go a long way.

THE BANKING CONNECTION

From Citibank's natural language money transfer system, to Chase Lincoln's financial planning system, to credit analysis, to real estate appraisal, to mortgage loan analysis, the depth and breath of these applications is staggering. That's probably because the type of work that banks do and the numbers of transactions that flitter through their systems are staggering, too.

A survey from the National Council of Savings Institutions displays some pretty interesting statistics. This survey looked into the back offices of 409 member institutions with assets between $50 million and $5 billion. It showed that the banking industry is, and has always been, very reliant on computer technology to service their vast information needs. More than 65% of these banks use automated teller machines. And a whopping 79% have automated their platform areas, showing a banking emphasis of placing smart technology within a customer's reach. In today's hostile banking environment banks are no longer assured of the profits of the past and are faced with regulatory changes, competition and unending mergers and acquisitions. Technology is needed for more than just competitive advantage — it's needed for survival.

Banks need to push away from the tactical data processing of the past. Here the emphasis is in pushing reams of paper through the bank. They need to look to strategic computing. Clark and Wolfarth[1] make recommendations to apply technology in the areas of managing customer information, developing asset-quality tracking, and in the area of expense control. Perhaps tracking asset quality will provide the biggest bang for the buck in application of technology. Here the overriding concern is to control risks and evaluate asset alternatives. Using technology for competitive advantage can also be applied in evaluating asset alternatives, monitoring nonperformance, and in performing impact analyses on customer activities.

AN EXPERT FOREIGN EXCHANGE SYSTEM

Money. A delightful topic. Walking about a Foreign Exchange trading room and hearing the babble of the trading — 50 million in Deutsche Marks, 100 million Yen — makes a visitor tingle with anticipation. The amounts are so astronomical and the pace so rapid-fire the uninitiated get the distinct impression that this is just so much monopoly money.

The Foreign Exchange Environment

For the foreign exchange trader this is serious business. The world of the trader is small. Very often, a lot of people are crammed into, small dealing rooms. Shoulder to shoulder they sit, stand, and sometimes jump up and down, acting and reacting to people and blinking equipment. A stressful environment, this. Sometimes six screens are simultaneously flashing information on currency rates and other market data. Pages upon pages of information streaming by. Under the glow of these displays are the trader's connection to the outside world. Oftentimes 120 line telephone boards are not even enough so the intrepid trader installs yet new outside lines to reach clients quickly.

And it is quickly that these traders must react, for they cannot afford the luxury of deep analysis. In the bat of an eyelash they must scan and understand volumes of data, assess the historical trend of these data, discard unnecessary information, and finally reach a simple yes or no answer: to sell, to buy.

No equanimity here. Traders have been known to skip lunch, glued to their displays, eyes red and bulging, waiting for an opportunity. And when it comes they seize it and are pleased with being right somewhere around 60% of the time. It's the other 40% that's the killer, however. Traders have been known to go out for an innocent lunch to find, upon their return, that the market did a turnaround and a large amount of money was lost. So many telephones have been ripped out of trading rooms by furious traders that the telephone company has a franchise on the trading floor.

It was to this environment that Manufacturer's Hanover Trust, now part of the Chase Manhattan banking conglomerate, decided to look for technical innovation. The development of the TARA system (Technical Analysis and Reasoning Assistant) is a case study in how to do everything right in building an AI-based system.

Foreign Exchange trading is a prime banking profit center. It's a legal form of gambling in which you try to forecast which way the price of a particular currency is going. Forecasting is a tricky process. Traders have two techniques that they use to peer into the crystal ball. Using fundamental analysis, such esoteric factors as the world economy, political events, and even market psychology are studied to predict the supply and demand for a particular currency. On the flip side, technical analysis uses the techniques of charting and statistical methodologies to forecast based upon historical trend analysis. Neither method is practiced to the exclusion of the other by the trader and neither approach has any set formula and often rely on the experience and gut instinct of the individual.

It's these gut instincts that Manufacturer's Hanover wanted desperately to capture. So a team of heavy hitters was established that could bring the dream TARA to life.

The Technology

Back in the late 1980s, the trading room management team took Tom Campfield off the line. Tom, a vice-president in the investment banking sector, was one of the more senior traders at the bank. His goal was to seek out innovative

technological solutions to the problem of enhancing the trading process. This one act — taking Tom off the line — set Manufacturer's Hanover up for the success it ultimately achieved. Tom represented the highest level of knowledge in the trading area. He was a most valuable resource with his "hands-on" experience plus his academic credentials in international finance and electrical engineering.

A few miles away, the technology department at Manufacturer's Hanover offered a position to Elizabeth Byrnes. With her doctorate in clinical psychology, the bank bought themselves an expert in eliciting knowledge from human confusion. The successful development of TARA began with the joining of forces of the trading and technology departments.

The newly formed TARA team decided to do an experiment. They knew that expert systems had been developed successfully before. They had some, but not all, of the ingredients of success. They did have a recognized and willing expert in Tom. The area of knowledge they wished to capture was limited to foreign exchange trading, which was a nice narrow domain. And they possessed substantial documentation on the process of trading. What they didn't have was a manageably sized database. With live data feeds of thousands of pages a day, the problem of data access within a reasonable window of time became a *cause celebre* within the team. And what they had too much of was fuzziness. In the world of trading, no two experts often agree, each relying on his or her intuition. In fact many traders are so superstitious that the dealing room is filled with fuzzy bears, Gumbys, and the like, which are rubbed, patted, and tossed into the air for luck.

So sifting through this haze of superstition, gut instincts, and inarticulate traders was stupendously hard.

> "Why did you sell Deutsche Marks?"
>
> "Because I had the feeling it was going to depreciate."
>
> "Why did you feel it was going to depreciate?"
>
> "Well, I just spoke to my friend, Joe, at Solomon Brothers and he said ... and then I spoke to my friend, Mary, at Chemical who does a lot of dealings with Deutsche Marks and we just got this feeling that the DM was going to go down."

The fearless TARA team spent 3 months interviewing the traders; 3 months of pulling methods out of the words of the traders. In the year of the prototype the foreign exchange trading department had a comfortable income of $161 million. Management decided that if the system could have an impact of as little as a 1% increase to this income, TARA could survive. Manufacturer's Hanover also knew that virtually every foreign exchange dealing room on the street was looking into AI. So they decided to pursue TARA for two simple reasons: honest GREED and competitive advantage.

The TARA team set about looking to enhance the prototype to boost the deal success rate of the trader from the level of 60% it now hovered at. Their team motto was, "Maximize good trades and minimize bad trades." But the team had a problem, impatient management. They needed to install a working system by the end of the year. A very short time-frame indeed. To accomplish a very complex undertaking in a very short amount of time they needed to make quick decisions and sometimes compromise on solutions that were less than perfect.

Luck was on their side, however, during the initial prototype period. They did make the correct decisions. They had selected a high-powered and expensive Symbolics workstation. With its 19-inch monitor, TARA was able to process all of that streaming trading data in as many as 50 windows at a time. That's a lot of machine power. The psychological and technical considerations were overwhelming. Data were coming into the system in video form. Previously these data were for display only. Now they had to be captured and stored in the appropriate window so the trader could activate the screen on whim. The data also had to be made accessible to the expert programs that used these feeds as input to the "smart forecaster" that was the core of the TARA system. And all of this had to be done in a window in less than 3 seconds.

To accomplish this end the team used heavy-duty software. While most of TARA was written in LISP, Intellicorp's KEE Expert system shell was used for inferencing and knowledge representation. The knowledge representation scheme used was the rule. At the outset of the project this knowledge base consisted of some 350 rules, of which about 175 were related specifically to currency trading. The rules analyze both technical and economic factors. The technical factors can be considered the do's and don'ts of trading while economic factors use modeling algorithms. It is only after both analyses, both technical and economic, are completed that a trading recommendation is made. KEE's ability to both backward and forward chain through the rulebase is used to great advantage when the trader wants to review the rationale behind the expert system recommendation.

And sandwiched between the knock-your-socks-off workstation display and the state-of-the-art software was the trader. All dealers have their own styles. Some use the Gumby approach to trading, some use analytical methods. So TARA had to be flexible enough to open all sorts of doors and windows so the dealer could use the system in many different ways.

Using a rich graphical interface to simulate the foreign exchange trading environment, TARA can be used in two modes: as a skilled assistant and as an experienced colleague. With its knowledge base of both technical and fundamental trading strategies, TARA can assist in evaluating any of the 30-odd technical trading models stored in its innards. It tracks multiple currency, bond, and interest rates, runs algorithms, and fires rules to interpret these models. TARA makes recommendations whether to buy, sell, or hold a particular market position. As the price of a currency changes, TARA is instantly made aware of it through the diligent monitoring of the live data feed. Appropriate rules and algorithms are triggered and recommendations and alerts are flashed across the workstation display.

Like a game of tic-tac-toe, a technical model of any particular currency is composed of X's and O's. The X's representing increases in price and the O's a decrease. The model filters out insignificant price movements to permit the trader to zero in on the beginning and end of the trend. Each X or O represents a unit of price.

Manufacturer's Hanover didn't want to spend huge sums of money on just mimicking currently existing technical charting programs. They wanted to lay a foundation of knowledgeable analysis of the data by encoding technical trading rules which knew how to use these charts to trigger a Buy-Sell-Hold recommendation.

THE CITIBANK MONEY TRANSFER PARSER

Yen. Dollars. Pesos. What a nice ring to these words. And sometimes words have a way of getting all jumbled up on messages. Do you remember the movie *Close Encounters of the Third Kind*? In this classic sci-fi, the skies were darkened by the enormity of an alien spacecraft. It was kind of common as spacecraft go. You know, oval with blinking lights. What was different was its attempt to communicate with us lowly earthlings. The aliens, which turned out to be skinny little bald creatures, attempted to speak to us via blinking lights and music. This message was a sort of an intergalactic Morse code. Well, the humans on the ground looked up at this monster spaceship in awe and scratched their heads trying to figure out just what the aliens were getting at.

Getting At The Gist

Getting at the gist of the message was terribly important to our sci-fi crowd for it meant world peace and galactic harmony. Back on Earth, getting to the gist of the message means money to hundreds of banks that wire billions of dollars in the thousands of funds transfer messages that are Telexed or Swifted criss-cross the globe each day.

At Citibank the crew in the Institutional Bank International Service Management department would have done marvelously well in interpreting the musical message of our little alien visitors. Each person in this unusual entourage seems to have a musical alter ego. The lead ego plays keyboards and acts while the rest of the group either act, sing, or play the harp. This isn't as unusual as it sounds.

Expertise in the artificial intelligence branch of natural languages requires a unique perspective. After all, what kind of person likes to sit and look at a word and say to themselves, "I know that this word means these two different things in these two contexts. What are all the other contexts?"

The precision of musicianship coupled with the love of the fluidity of the human language makes for fireworks in the application of natural language. Why is natural language needed for funds transfer? In a word, the answer is marketing. A second word here is customers. Bank customers like to take the easy way out. They're paying big bucks to the banks to move money from one account to another. They want to do this transfer as easily and quickly as possible. They do not want to be encumbered with rigid formats and procedures. They just want to type an English message on a Telex and press GO.

> "Pay through Chase for the account of San Juan Bank to the account of John Doe."
>
> "Pay to John Doe of San Juan Bank through Chase."

There are as many ways for a message to be written as they are tentacles on aliens from Mars. Conventional programming systems, those that do Accounts Payable and Human Resources, can't cope with the vagaries of the English language. When the study of AI opened the door for use of natural languages in business, the big banks did a jump-start and forged ahead into the heady world of international funds transfer.

Citibank jumped into the deep end of the pool in the institutional banking area in the middle 1980s. The forward-thinking Citibank management decided that natural languages could be the answer to the question of how to process the thousands of garbled fund transfer messages received by the group each day. They wanted to develop a smart system that could determine who to debit, who to credit, what reference numbers to use, what account numbers to use, and all within a short period of time. So an AI project was funded.

Picking out the right city in a money transfer message is even more difficult than figuring out the right bank name. The secret of a successful money transfer is the interpretation of both bank name and city. You get a message, "Swiss Bank Zurich pay through Chase New York." A person viewing this message would immediately interpret the message as pay through the Chase New York bank which is a bank name. For the computer, it's not so easy. Remember it's looking for two banks and two cities. In this case it could interpret New York as a designation rather than as part of the bank name. And then there's the problem of messages that contain complete addresses and the street names within these addresses that contain cities. How about New York Avenue, Chicago, Illinois. As in all things automated there is a danger that this smart system is too smart and will spell-correct these addresses into something totally different from what it's supposed to be. To compensate for this, Citibank provides human staff members to verify each one.

An average money transfer message is one page long. All messages that are routed over the Telex are unstructured, free-form English of approximately one page in length. SWIFT is another method of sending instructions across the wire. The SWIFT service forces a structure on messages sent across the wire. Given the structured SWIFT format and the unstructured Telex format, bank customers sometimes garble the two. So what you get is pseudo structure typed into the Telex. Since the SWIFT format is a bit like English Morse code, there is a great potential for system confusion. So the team wrote what they call a shunt program to determine which format the message is in and pass it to the appropriate processing program.

With all this expertise in money transfer message deciphering it's no wonder that the bank decided to expand their horizons and use natural language technology in reimbursement claims message understanding. Here the system analyzes a rather free-form message of the ilk, "I didn't get my money." The system determines whether or not this claim is a new one or old one and then routes the message to the appropriate human staff member at Citibank.

AND NOW FOR CREDIT ANALYSIS

Open any person's wallet and out will fall two American Express cards, one personal and one corporate, two Visa cards, two Mastercards, and a slew of various department store charges. Americans have taken to buying things on credit like an oinker takes to a mudbath. We revel in it.

A trillion. That's how many dollars we owe to banks, finance companies, and assorted other credit grantors. And quite a large portion of this debt can be considered deadbeat. So what's a poor financial company to do?

Banks, finance companies, and the like are in a tight bottleneck in their race to compete for mortgage, credit card, business ... ad infinitum ... credit dollars. The bottleneck occurs when the loan goes out for credit review. While these credit institutions really do want to grant you the loan, they need to be extra cautious just to whom they grant credit.

The art and science of projecting the credit worthiness of individuals and investors is called credit analysis. Here the underwriter attempts to piece together a financial puzzle consisting of many, many pieces. If it's a mortgage you're after the underwriter looks at such things as your income, debts, as well as the type of neighborhood the house or apartment is in. If you're a business the underwriter looks at revenue, assets, liabilities, cash flow, and a host of other minutia. The object here is to the grant the maximum number of loans with the minimum percentage of bad debt. This takes time and experience to accomplish. There have always been automated credit analysis systems. But now there are expert credit analysis systems.

Several vendors have jumped on the expert system bandwagon, knowing a good opportunity when they see one. First Security Bank of Idaho in beautiful downtown Boise has been innovatively using Financial Proformas' FAST credit analysis software for years. Financial Proformas, based in California, built a system revolving around 550 proprietary rules in its goal to create a system that produces historical analyses and forecast assumptions.

Another California company assists loan officers and credit analysts in assessing risk. Syntelligence's Lending Advisor was written to combat the experience void: 50% of the people making loans today have under 5 years of experience. Using expert products gives these 5-year-and-under babes in the woods the experience level of 30-year veterans and speeds up the process by 30 to 50% to boot.

How do these systems work? The secret inner workings of an expert corporate credit management system was unveiled by two professors who developed a prototype crediting granting system for a nameless Fortune 500 company.

When Venkat Srinivasan was the Joseph G. Reisman Research Professor at Northeastern University and Yong H. Kim was CBA Fellow Professor of Finance at the University of Cincinnati,[2] they set out to develop a robust, working expert credit grantor. Prototypes of this nature are often more interesting than ones in the industrial segment since academic models tend to involve leading-edge ideas. In addition, the mix of individuals involved and the numbers of reviews that this project was subjected to ensured the viability and completeness of the finished system.

Development of the system was divided into two segments. As in most expert system development projects, the first step is to elicit the knowledge from a base of one or more experts. In this case our two academics had the cooperation of a participating financial entity. A multitude of in-depth interviews of a credit management staff was performed over a period of time. To ensure that they obtained all viewpoints of the credit granting process, the team made sure that they had interviewed diverse staff members across the management hierarchy. They also did a detailed analysis of the actual decisions that were made.

Credit Granting Defined

Their analysis, which was necessarily iterative, found that the credit granting process was composed of two different processes. The granting institution must first determine a line of credit which is reviewed on an annual basis. There are always exceptions to the rule and these must be handled to the satisfaction of both the customer and the credit institution. In the Fortune 500 company that participated in the prototype the rule was that all major credit lines, defined as greater than $20,000, are to be reviewed once a year. Upon review, credit limits can be increased pending analysis of updated information on the customer. The exceptions to this rule are new customers and customers who have exceeded their credit limits.

Procedural rules for the granting of credit are heavily dependent upon the amount requested. At our friendly Fortune 500 company requests for less than $5000 are quickly approved after a cursory review of the application form, while requests for credit up to $20,000 includes review of bank references. And when more than $20,000 is requested, then watch out for that Dun & Bradstreet report.

There are so many subjective decisions to be made that it's a wonder any credit is granted at all. Let's say you stop by the friendly Moolah National Bank for a $30,000 line of credit for your new business. You sit down opposite someone in horn-rimmed glasses who grills you for over an hour on such things as, "What's the growth potential of your business?" "How are others doing in your location?" "How good is your management prowess?" "What are your bank references?" "What's your market position?" "What is your order schedule like?" "What about the other products that you market?" "What's your payment record like?" "How long have you been in business and have you ever filed for bankruptcy?" and on and on until your shirt is as wet as a sponge and your nerves turn to jelly.

The Prototype

The Srinivasan-Kim system was designed around two phases. The first is a customer evaluation phase where all of the information collected in our little scenario above would be evaluated. This entailed the design of both a database and knowledge base to support this grand plan. Once evaluated, a credit limit determination model would be deployed.

While the overall design of the system is interesting and quite insightful, as it is rare to find such a complete specification of an expert-type system, it is the rule bases that we are most interested in.

The rule base for the both the customer evaluation component and the credit line determination component is really a series of interconnected rule bases. Using 11 different classifications such as financial trend rules, business potential rules, and liquidity rules, the large rule base was able to be logically segmented. Each segment contained rules specifically for that category. The academics shared several of their rules, which are presented in Exhibit 1.

The judgmental conclusion of rule evaluation is ultimately passed into the credit limit model. Towards this end what is known as the AHP-based model was chosen to assist in making this all-important financial decision. The AHP model had been used in the past in areas such as predicting oil prices, planning, and marketing. AHP, based on the concept of tradeoff, works in the following way. First, the problem is broken down into a hierarchy composed of a set of elements and subelements. The very bottom level of this hierarchy is composed of the specific courses of action or conclusions that are under consideration. Each element is assigned a relative weight using a 9-point measurement scale with 9 being of absolute impor-

Exhibit 1. Credit Granting Customer — Evaluation Rules

Profitability	
IF	Sales trend is Improving
AND	Customer's net profit margin is greater than 5%
AND	Customer's net profit margin trend is improving
AND	Customer's gross margin is greater than 12%
AND	Customer's gross profit margin trend is improving
THEN	Customer's profitability is excellent
Liquidity	
IF	Sales trend is improving
AND	Customer's current ratio is greater than 1.50
AND	Customer's current ratio trend is increasing
AND	Customer's quick ratio is greater than 0.80
AND	Customer's quick ratio trend is increasing
THEN	Customer's liquidity is excellent
Debt Management	
IF	Sales trend is improving
AND	Customer's debt to net worth ratio is less than 0.30
AND	Customer's debt to net worth ratio trend is decreasing
AND	Customer's short-term debt to total debt is less than 0.40
AND	Customer's short-term debt to total debt trend is decreasing
AND	Customer's interest coverage is greater than 4.0
THEN	Customer's debt exposure is excellent
Overall Financial Health	
IF	Customer's profitability is excellent
AND	Customer's liquidity is excellent
AND	Customer's debt exposure is excellent
THEN	Customer's financial health is excellent

Source: Adapted from Srinivasan, V. and Kim, Y. H., *Financial Management,* Autumn, 1988, pp. 32–43.

tance and 1 being of equal importance. You will note that the rules in Exhibit 1 make frequent mention of the word excellent. For the purposes of this prototype an excellent rating was assigned a value of 9 on the 9-point measurement scale. A weight of 3 indicates weak importance of one over another, 5 indicates essential importance, and 7 indicates demonstrated importance. The in-between numbers of 2, 4, 6, and 8 are just that — intermediate values between two adjacent judgments. These pair-wise comparisons are then evaluated such that global priority levels or weights are determined. In other words, the decision-making system is required to respond to such questions as "What is the relative importance of customer background over pay habits?" What this all boils down to is a decision to either grant or deny credit.

In comparison to the nonexpert system mode of credit approval, the prototype developed in this academic exercise was deemed to be correct

97% of the time, which is quite impressive. Although the prototype omitted many other credit granting components such as keeping track of collateral maturities, it provides an interesting insight into the way an expert system is developed in an area of great complexity. Here, a detailed rule base was gleaned from expert users and associated with a statistical model to achieve the desired goal of accurately and consistently granting maximum credit with minimum losses.

AMERICAN EXPRESS — A GREAT EXAMPLE OF CREDIT ANALYSIS

Another company that lives by the maxim, "Max credit, Min losses" is American Express. It's hard to categorize American Express into any of the three slots that describe the financial services industry. What is American Express, anyway? For me American Express is my ticket to exotic places such as Tahiti, Paris, and China. They are better known for their unique type of credit card which is low on the credit (since you can't really carry over a balance unless you have a line of credit with an associated bank) and high on the bells and whistles, such as no preset credit limit on the gold card. This can get a body into scads of trouble in a duty-free port such as St. Thomas in the Virgin Islands, where the town is virtually littered with jewelry stores.

Why Expert Systems

Since American Express provides the most popular and prestigious of the credit cards, the gang at the home office is always on the prowl searching out the new and better.

One of the new and better tools that they discovered was a technology tool. They knew that they had a problem. This problem was not unique to the industry. Banks have dealt with this for centuries. It's call bad debt and fraud. In American Express' case, with their huge number of cardholders, it's easy to understand why their losses from bad credit authorizations and fraud would be substantial. Since conventional computer systems didn't make much of a dent in reducing this problem, the idea of an expert system became more and more appealing.

American Express began development of their expert system, to be called Authorizer's Assistant, in the early days of commercial expert system acceptance. Since few companies tread where American Express dared to go they developed new techniques which, years later, many other financial companies have endorsed in their own forays into expert systems.

One of these strategies was to create a corporate group that would coordinate this new technology among its several subsidiaries. These subsidiaries were already tackling other expert system projects in such diverse areas as trading, customer service, back-office support, and insurance underwriting. This reflects the wide variety of American Express business interests.

The Authorizer's Assistant was destined to become the *piece de resistance* of the American Express company and perhaps the single most visible expert system anywhere in the annals of financial services.

In a nutshell, the system assists operators in granting credit to cardholders based on a review of the customer's records. Since there is no preset credit limit, this process can be a bit tricky. The Authorizer usually is called into the picture if the customer is making a purchase outside of the limits of the normal computerized system. This means that small purchases can be approved by using the ubiquitous telephone automatic approval device. Here the store clerk slides your card through a slot which picks up your card number, enters the amount, and waits for an approval code. It's when the amount is over a certain level, which is different for each store, that Authorizer's Assistant goes into play.

Developing The Prototype

In developing the system, American Express choose the path of utilizing an outside consulting firm. In this case the firm was the vendor of the product that they choose to use during prototype mode. Inference Corporation sells a heavy-duty expert system shell called ART or Automated Reasoning Tool. They also sell their services as knowledge engineers. American Express took the package deal.

The goal was to build a system that would assist, but not replace, the human credit authorizer. Using the five best senior Amex credit authorizers, Inference Corp's knowledge engineers went to work at eliciting their knowledge. Their knowledge allowed them to determine whether a current transaction should be approved.

In making this determination the senior credit authorizers reviewed many items such as customer's outstanding charges, payment history, and (my favorite) buying habits. You see, the American Express philosophy is that you can charge anything as long as you pay your bills on time. Gradually, over the years that you have your credit card, you can build up the amount that you spend on your card until one day they permit you to charge a Mercedes on it. Some people have.

The system required over 4 months to prototype and consisted of about 520 decision rules. It ran on a stand-alone Symbolic workstation. Using a forward-chaining inferencing strategy, the system permitted the authorizers to speed up their review of the customer's files to grant that request faster. This assistant has the capability of guiding the authorizer through phone dialogues with merchants and cardholders. If the situation warrants, it prompts the authorizer for an appropriate inquiry to make of the customer. In addition, as is the forte of expert systems, the system can display its line of reasoning, which is a marvelous in the training of new authorizers.

While the prototype contained 520 rules, the pilot contained over 800 rules. When it came time for American Express management to review this pilot and provide a yea or a nay for wholesale deployment, they reviewed astonishing statistics. They found a 76% reduction in bad credit authorizations. They also found the system to be accurate 96.5% of the time as compared to the human rate of 85%. Management gave the nod and the team started to plan for deployment of this system to the 300-odd authorizers.

In order to make this system work the expert system had to be connected to the mainframe as a coprocessor. The system also had the constraint that the hardware currently used could not be changed. The original authorizer workbench consisted of a 327X IBM terminal connected to an IBM mainframe. Since American Express already had made a huge investment in this hardware, it was decided to keep it and "embed" the expert system. In embeddable expert systems the expert system component is called by the conventional mainline processor. It's not obvious to the user that this is an expert system, they just notice that extra ingredient of intelligence.

THE CITIBANK PENSION EXPERT

It's not the ides of March that scare us but the ides of April. The specter of taxes causes weak knees and fits of despair in the strongest of us. We spend the days before April 15 mired in a cocoon of pencils, calculators, and self-help tax books. Fortunately, April 15 comes but once a year for the mere mortal; but the processors of those giant pension funds are not so lucky. For these banking institutions, withholding taxes need to be calculated on a daily basis for hundreds of thousands of pensioners. For them, this is taxes with a twist.

Citibank is one of the largest banks in the world. Their data processing functions were decentralized long ago. In fact, they have more data centers and more dollars invested in technology than a fair- to middling-sized foreign country. Citibank is segmented into several diverse business lines including Individual Banking, Investment Banking, and Institutional Banking. A common thread among these three diverse areas is the Corporate Technology group. It is these gurus who set the standards and make recommendations; but it was the hot shots in the line area that really got expert systems heated up.

Pensions are big business to any bank. Hundreds of thousands of checks are processed and mailed to retirees every working day. What sounds like a simple process is complicated by the complex structure of the differing tax laws in our country. The Feds are one thing, but each state and local government is different. Any pension system must be able to process a check with the correct deductions depending on where Joe actually lives and how many exemptions he takes. If Joe lives in New York with a wife and three kids, his pension check will look different than had he moved to Kalamazoo, MI.

In 1986 Citibank realized that they had a problem. They got the news that California had passed a new tax law that was to have a profound effect on Citibank's then Cobol-based pension processing system. This Cobol system had only the capability of processing federal taxes. The specter of adding the differing, and quite complex state tax laws was quite unnerving. The Cobol system was dutifully modified. It was a 120-man-day effort for the state of California alone. The estimation for adding the remainder of the states to the system made Citibank think there had to be a better way.

Lesser men (and women) would be mortified at having to learn a new tool and new techniques as well as implement a real, not a prototype, system in a 6-month effort. The Citibank-IBM team was apparently up to the job. Citibank had one constraint, the system must be developed on their IBM 3084 MVS/XA system, forcing the developers into the untried domain of mainframe expert system shells. Around this time, the majority of expert systems were being deployed on AI workstations or personal computers. Given the hundreds of thousands of transactions and the very large databases filled with tax and pensioner information, the mainframe platform was the only game in town. The IBM mainframe expert system shell, Knowledgetool, was selected as it exhibited the richness of toolset that was necessary for the system. Using a Consulting paradigm, Knowledgetool employed forward and backward chaining as it processed each DOLS transaction by residence of the pensioner.

The Knowledgetool inference engine, written in PL/I, is touted to be a high-performance expert system shell. It uses a very efficient, but proprietary, algorithm for pattern matching. Astute users of the tool do well to employ the OS PL/I optimizing compiler on their applications as this serves to increase throughput. Citibank found that use of this tool actually enhanced the performance of the system over the more conventional Cobol approach. Remember, they already had a good benchmark completed with the Cobol system only recently redesigned for the state of California. In fact they determined that they had a decrease of 14.3% in clock time in the running of the expert system version of California.

How do the guts of Knowledgetool work? It processes a knowledge application in a RECOGNIZE-ACT cycle (or for you conventional programmers, loop). The inference engine matches rule conditions to existing class members and updates the conflict set with the instantiations recognized. We now have a set of rules ready to fire. This is the heart of the process and Knowledgetool uses an IBM version of the OPS5 algorithm, one of the fastest available. During the second step of this process the inference engine attempts to resolve the conflict set. Here it chooses which rule, amongst many, to fire next. Citibank took the option of controlling or predetermining the order of rules, which is a Knowledgetool feature. In the last step of the cycle, the rule selected is executed, or to use expert system parlance, fired. The rule fired is procedural and might add, change, or delete class members or might even fire a nested RECOGNIZE-ACT cycle for a nested block of rules.

Like most large MIS shops, Citibank's programming language of choice was COBOL. In fact, only one staffer had ever used PL/I. Knowledgetool, written in PL/I, had structured its development environment using a syntax similar to PL/I. So when the project was begun, Citibank was far behind the eightball. They were unfamiliar with AI, unfamiliar with Knowledgetool, and unfamiliar with PL/I. Here's where IBM stepped up to the gate. Since this was a flagship project, they supplied large doses of technical help. IBM was right there to assist with everything from installation, to knowledge engineering, to training.

The project team consisted of three full-time staff members, one consultant, and one intrepid IBMer. Since PL/I was virtually unknown at Citibank, the group spent 1 week learning the fundamentals. Another 3 days was spent in Knowledgetool training. Armed with the desire to succeed and all of this technical know-how, the team spent 2 intensive weeks on the design. At the end it took 3 months to develop the entire system, soup to nuts. They averaged five to six complex rules per day to find a total reduction of manpower usage in the range of 12 to 13% in comparison to the Cobol version. Since the original senior level management goal was to find tools to increase productivity, they appeared to have found a winner in Knowledgetool.

At the heart of the project was the expert and his knowledge. The system goal of this expert system was to apply the tax law at the federal, state, and local level uniformly and accurately during the processing of pension checks. The stated user goal was to automate and integrate all tax processing. The unstated goal was to eliminate the System's department interference and let the business unit run with the ball. A high-level end-user from the Pension Disbursement department at Citibank acted as disseminator of tax information. It was this person who created the rules, based on information from the Tax Department. And it was the end-user who was heavily involved in testing the accuracy of a system that would need to pass muster with the auditors.

Since this system would deal with disbursements of millions of dollars each evening, the team tested and tested and tested some more. A case history approach to validation of the system was used. This is a tried and true method of testing for expert systems as it permits a parallel test of the expert system vs. the current system or the manual method, whichever is applicable. In this case, the team jointly worked on a representative sampling of test cases. Each test case was run through the expert system and then compared with the results arrived at manually. The user painstakingly compared all test results. After all, one misguided rule could result in Grampa John in St. Petersburg receiving a surprising windfall. Testing completed, the user department gladly signed off with a flourish.

DOLS

The DOLS knowledge or rule base contains over 100 rules. Since some of these rules were generic, that is they apply to all states, the total knowledge base can be considered to contain over 200 rules. The team, practicing the "art of structured design" and having learned from the much publicized mistakes of several of our forerunner expert systems such as DEC's XCON, organized the rules by state of residence or jurisdiction. This method provides for easy maintenance. In the case of DEC's XCON, a system which assists in the configuration of DEC's one-of-a-kind computers, the knowledge base was composed of more than 10,000 rules. Rules were entered into the system in no particular order, making it a nightmare when a rule needed to be modified or erased. The new and enhanced version of XCON now contains such structure — but DEC paid dearly to have it enhanced. Fortunately for Citibank, the design team combined their conventional data processing experience, which is characterized by a love for the organized, with the new black art of expert system design to create a structured knowledge base.

DOLS can be considered a two-tier system. On the front lines is the user interface, or "Chinese menu," permitting users to modify the tax parameters in the knowledge base. Bringing up the rear is the overnight processor. Issuing hundreds of thousands of checks is by no means a real-time application. In the dead of night the conventional component of DOLS performs mundane processing routines. On ready standby is the DOLS expert system, carefully embedded into the system architecture, eager to make decisions about withholding amounts for these complex check disbursements. Pension data is stored on a standard IBM VSAM file. One of Knowledgetool's strengths is the ability to integrate easily into the standard IBM VM or MVS batch or online environment. Interfaces exist for the IMS/VS, DB2, and SQL/DS databases as well as "hooks" for the PL/I, COBOL, FORTRAN, Pascal, and Assembler languages. This permits Knowledgetool to integrate fluidly with any existing application through one of the interfaces or hooks, as was the case with Citibank. In effect, the expert system acts similarly to any other called application, the only difference being in the sophistication of the processing.

Notes

1. Clark, C. and Wolfarth, J. H., A new era in bank data processing: managers look to DP for strategic capabilities, *Bank Adm.*, January 1989, pp. 22–28.
2. Srinivasan, V. and Kim, Y. H., Designing expert financial systems: a case study of corporate credit management, *Finan. Manage.*, Autumn 1988, pp. 32–43.

Chapter 15
The Unfolding of Wireless Technology in the Financial Services Industry

Michael A. McNeal

HARVARD'S JOHN KENNETH GALBRAITH IS QUOTED as saying there has been no innovation in financial services in the last 500 years. Whether you can agree or not, there should be little doubt that the financial services arena needs to innovate in response to the dramatic changes in customer needs.

Certainly, the market for financial products is more competitive than ever before. This gives customers a distinct advantage to demand new and better service for less money. The resulting business environment is extremely turbulent, with hundreds of bank mergers per year, insurance industry regulation, and unforeseen shifts in the global stock market.

To add to the challenge, lines have blurred between pieces of the "financial service pie." Life insurance firms now compete against banks, brokers, and online agents. On their web sites, both American Express and Fidelity offer annuities through e-commerce, and another firm offers online quotes and applications.

All these trends boil down to one fundamental point. While financial businesses realize they have to change they don't always know how. Clearly, they will be forced to rely on technology to help them work "smarter." This includes eliminating inefficiency, reorganizing the way people work, and acting on opportunities that emerge from the technology itself.

That's where wireless computing has already gained rapid appeal in these markets. The broad genre of wireless applications and devices from simple personal digital assistants (PDAs) to advanced software for elec-

0-8493-9991-2/99/$0.00+$.50

tronic messaging will provide financial companies a special edge to compete, as well as to achieve many core objectives.

The following topics will be discussed in this chapter: the unfolding of wireless technologies in securities, insurance, and banking; the pathways to implementing a wireless infrastructure; and potential implementations in the areas of two-way paging, electronic messaging, and other future market applications.

WIRELESS AS A MEANS TO INNOVATE

Historically, new technologies tend to succeed in vertical markets first. Despite the relative youth of the wireless industry, the demand for customized solutions is strong. Banks, brokerages, and insurance companies are prepared to spend money to obtain a competitive advantage, and are willing to learn the technology from the ground up.

The mobile data market initially grew from vertical market demand. Courier, dispatch, and truck fleet companies account for an estimated 65% of this market. (*Wireless Computing,* Ira Brodsky, 1997). Federal Express and United Parcel Service, for instance, use wireless devices to dispatch trucks and to track the progress of packages from shipper to recipient.

It didn't take long for wireless computing to make its way into the financial services market. For claims adjusters, sales agents, and stockbrokers, real-time information is the key to best serving customers. In certain examples, which will be cited later, wireless can sometimes be the only answer to specific communication needs.

Today, it's no longer strange to see someone reading e-mail on a digital phone or sending messages with a two-way pager. Personal digital assistants, which fall somewhere between an electronic day planner and laptop computer, are also an effective tool for the day-to-day activities of mobile field employees.

WIRELESS COMPUTING

The following section will provide a brief overview of wireless hardware and software, with the exception of cellular, PCS, or smart phone technologies. This information should serve as a basic guide as to essential classifications regarding a broad range of wireless products, including:

- Handheld PCs (HPCs)/PDAs
- Laptop and Notebook Computers
- One- and Two-way Pagers
- Ruggedized Terminals

Wireless technology is purely a different medium through which we can push voice, data, and video transmissions. One can think of it as an invisible cable, with the potential of being stretched through increases in bandwidth and compression technologies in order to accommodate a particular application's required speed of delivery.

Handheld PCs/PDAs

Handheld PC vendors will readily admit that their devices are not meant as full-time notebook replacements. The target user is someone who needs quick access to specialized corporate data, reasonable access to e-mail, and the ability to view and edit small files.

These devices are broadly enabled computing machines of relatively limited speed, power, memory, and functionality. They are durable in nature, and offer advanced features as pen-based input, bar code scanners, and wireless modems integrated into a lightweight, sealed, and shock-resistant chassis.

Laptops and Notebooks

Such devices were also designed for field use, and feature heavy-duty cases of magnesium or high-impact plastic. They come with shock-mounted circuit boards, and a minimum of connectors. They optionally support CDPD, RAM, and ARDIS, but only one network per device. It's important to consider which designated service provider you prefer.

Full-sized laptops with integral radio modems are still scarce in the marketplace. In fact, it's very rare to find a conventional portable computer incorporating a built-in wireless modem. The only portable computers so equipped are large-format ruggedized terminals. Integral modems are popular within this category simply because outboard modems or card-mounted modems are more vulnerable to damage.

Pagers

Pagers have evolved from being a fairly generic product category to being highly differentiated in terms of capabilities and performance features. Traditional paging was designed purely to notify field professionals when a telephone call or message was waiting for them. Today, with the growth of alphanumeric, full-text paging, there is much more information being sent over paging networks.

Recent paging technologies include FLEX, ERMES, narrowband PCS, and two-way paging. Pagers have the capability to transmit e-mail, Internet information, and digital voice messages. In the future, alphanumeric pagers are expected to surpass numeric pagers in popularity as businesses demand more data-intensive features.

Two-way wireless messaging certainly represents the natural evolution of paging. Paging has actually always been two-way; until recently, the land-line phone was the only practical return link. Technological progress is the key to growth. Many vendors have invested substantially in the development of cross-industry solutions. These solutions have already impacted the financial services market.

Ruggedized Terminals

Wireless-enabled ruggedized data terminals are actually specialized computers. Small, compact, and durable, these devices sport large keyboards and displays and have high-capacity batteries. Local area network (LAN) or wide area network (WAN) operation tends to define specific subtypes within this category, and relatively few devices incorporating modems are offered to the user with a choice between private and public network modems.

A ruggedized terminal should be evaluated according to the same criteria that would be applied to any portable computer. The speed, processing power, and overall system capabilities must be considered in the light of current and future applications within the enterprise, and the usefulness of the terminal must be weighed against price.

THE NEXT GENERATION OF WIRELESS SOFTWARE

Handheld PCs, laptops, and other wireless devices wouldn't be of any use unless the software to run the applications existed. In the area of paging and messaging software, one can integrate just about any office communication system with pagers. Wireless software applications allow users to be automatically paged, for instance, whenever they receive an e-mail. This type of software can also redirect coming e-mail to alpha pagers and allow users to screen incoming communications to only receive messages from certain individuals.

Other software turns pagers into a vital part of monitoring systems. Monitoring and telephony-based alerts can automatically be forwarded to the pagers of managers, technicians, and other people who need to stay informed of a system's status. Immediate pager-based alerts translate into immediate responses to malfunctioning systems and critical situations.

In wireless software applications, the term, "middleware" comes up frequently. This term simply refers to software that is intended to make a network transparent to a given application. Some wireless networks have been designed with middleware built into the transport protocols, examples being CDPD cellular and Reflex two-way paging.

An important element in wireless applications, middleware software can help to solve the idiosyncrasies of wireless transmissions. Special performance features include least-cost routing, where the middleware chooses between two or more networks, and intelligent agents, which manage the user's network by prioritizing messages. In short, this software helps to guarantee the delivery of messages and reduce redundancy.

THE CONVERGENCE OF INTERNET AND WIRELESS TECHNOLOGIES

Given the high percentage of large banks and insurance companies with sophisticated "wired" infrastructures (AS/400s, distributed computers, and networked personal computers), an optimal wireless solution should be able to bridge the gap between diverse computing environments. It should also have superior performance, reliability, and be scalable to the enterprise.

Today, there are software packages available to provide wireless communications with environments that include computing, telephony, and monitoring systems. They support the Internet (TCP/IP) protocol as an internal networking backbone; centralize users, groups and wireless carriers; and provide connectivity throughout the enterprise.

The coupling of "wired" and wireless technologies provides significant benefits to the end-users in the financial services industry. Recently, the Mutual Group (TMG) of Canada deployed a wireless solution to centralize their paging into one solution and upgrade them from numeric to alphanumeric paging. The corporate giant insures one in every 10 Canadians, with 5800 employees and 125 offices.

Another excellent example of a wireless success story occurred at one of the nation's largest banks. Every year, this bank processes 5 billion online transactions; produces 125 million statements and letters; issues 15 million credit cards; and responds to 200 million phone calls. To deal effectively with this volume, a sophisticated technological environment is required.

The bank recently deployed a centralized wireless messaging solution as a plug-in to their existing legacy environment. They use the software for network management, to reach their paging technicians, for general alphanumeric paging, and automated alarms from Windows NT and UNIX servers. With 545 paging users and 55 groups, their paging capabilities now allow them to send anywhere from 100 to 500 pages per hour.

In summary, the purpose of wireless software is to facilitate an individual's connectivity to necessary information at any location, whether one is on-site, down the street, or thousands of miles away. For the financial services industry, this translates into increased revenues, whether the company has local, national, or international communication needs.

WIRELESS IN THE SECURITIES INDUSTRY

In the past, brokers potentially jeopardized a client's stock position by leaving their terminals for lunch or breaking away from the office. Today, they can use wireless tools to monitor what's happening with a client's portfolio.

For the stockbroker on the trading floor, person-to-person communication is critical. There's no time to check e-mail or voicemail. Trades for thousands of dollars occur every second.

The demand for information is crucial in the securities business, and wireless data access provides the competitive edge to the demand. One of the major benefits of wireless is that it works indoors in areas lacking suitable phone jacks. In essence, it enables true peer-to-peer messaging.

As slaves to the smallest stock fluctuations, financiers can now fully capitalize on the mobility of data in fund management. In addition, using a laptop with a wireless connection to the Internet, stockbrokers can find out the latest market activities without having to be at their offices.

A Broker in Every Laptop

Wireless services in the securities industry can offer traders a combination of personalized attention of a portfolio manager with the technology necessary to keep them on track toward meeting their client's goals.

Based out of New York, a company called Wireless Financial Services offers a product called Universal Trader. It provides investors real-time prices for equities, futures, and options, and current headlines wirelessly or via the Internet. Compared to 800 numbers or cellular phones, the wireless trader dramatically reduces communications costs.

The average response time for a portfolio quote is under six seconds, and less than one second over the Internet. Some of the benefits are cross-functionality as both an order entry and quote service; freedom from client visits; the ability to send broadcast messages to clients using e-mail; and an increase in commissions by being able to serve more clients.

The Wireless Trading Floor

Few business environments are more mission-critical than those involving the flow of dollar bills. At a major stock exchange, where the flow of millions of dollars occurs per hour, the circumstances are perfect for the deployment of wireless communications. Stock exchanges are vast two-way auctions, with orders to buy and sell securities constantly flooding the trading floor.

The NYSE recently launched a $100 million integrated technology plan, designed to carry it into the next century. As part of the plan, the exchange spent $10 million on two wireless applications, after carefully evaluating all their options. They had initially considered infrared technology, but ruled it out due to the fact that infrared lacks range.

In the first application, 200 reporters were equipped with wireless touch-screen terminals. About half of all trades (stock name, price, and volume) are monitored every day by reporters. The purpose of this application was not stock comparison, but to deliver information to the outside world to facilitate further trading.

In the past, reporters used pencils with preprinted cards. Today, they are equipped with pen-based, handheld computers that have wireless LAN adapters. The adapter consists of a PC card plus a separate radio and antenna module. The unit is fastened to the EHT-30 and connected to the PC card by a short cable.

The main application equipped about 3000 brokers with wireless terminals for both data collection and comparison and settlement. The wireless LAN ensures the timely flow of information, improving the NYSE's competitive position, and eliminating deferred data entry, which reduces errors.

For wireless data users in the financial markets, new options mean more flexibility. Today, businesses can utilize the power of wireless computing to make their day-to-day activities flow much smoother.

Software developers will continue to provide niche market applications that will justify wireless technology over wire-line service. The more brokers are freed from being tethered to an office or desk, the more efficiency and productivity a securities firm will realize.

AN EFFECTIVE "FIELD PARTNER"

The major issue today for insurance companies is whether or not they will be able to compete 10 to 15 years from now. One of the keys to success will be the deployment of more efficient systems to distribute information to claims adjusters, sales agents, and other field employees.

Insurance companies were "early adapters" of wireless technology to improve their businesses. Sales agents who relied on e-mail as a means to managing customer relationships now forward their e-mail to pagers or handheld PCs. With wireless e-mail services, agents save on mobile phone costs, and keep business transactions private.

Technology for the Field

In 1995, State Farm equipped its field agents with pen-based computers to automate the processing of property claims. The hand-held PCs featured a database that allowed the company adjusters to estimate property damages and settle claims. Upon evaluating these properties, adjusters were able to wirelessly retrieve material costs for repairs, labor, and other pertinent data.

In case of disaster, mobile solutions can significantly reduce the time it takes claims adjusters to process claims. When landline communications go down, American Family Insurance rolls out a "disaster recovery trailer." Fitted with a 2.4-meter satellite dish, the trailer has 11 workstations, each with a telephone and computer, printers, copiers, and fax machine. A satellite dish links to a mainframe at company headquarters.

In the area of field sales, a London-based insurance company has had great success with mobile solutions. After equipping 1000 sales agents with laptops, they were able to have more productive client meetings. The mobile PCs allowed agents to track policy history and product preferences, as well as conduct a needs analysis on-site to determine optimal policies based on the customer's requirements.

The payback for the laptops has been reduced sales cycles. It also gives agents the ability to give policy quotes at the time of the client visit. Instead of a previous week-long process, time has been drastically cut by bypassing the need to mail in orders and signed confirmations.

REMOTE BANKING

The progress of wireless communications in banking has been mild at best. Software applications for internal use are quite common within large banks, as cited above in the section on Wireless Software.

When it comes to financial transactions with bank customers, however, possibilities for the deployment of a large-scale wireless application will be driven by strong customer demand. That's the way it's been historically, and the development of the "smart card" is a perfect example of what is to come.

An example of a potential banking application of the future is, for instance, a day when you can have your bank balance forwarded to you, wirelessly, by entering a series of numbers into your two-way, alphanumeric pager's keypad.

As a matter of fact, the basic two-way paging technology to run that application exists today. But the day when it becomes widespread is probably several years into the future. That's mainly due to the fact that software and hardware vendors are just beginning to work together on vertical solutions for the banking industry.

WET (Wireless Electronic Transactions)

With the implementation of satellite and terrestrial wireless services, electronic transactions will be conducted on a global basis. For example, if you need to use your VISA card in the Gobi Desert to pay for bottled water and a tent, in the future you will simply have your card swiped and, *voila*, you'll be able to receive your transaction approval in seconds as the whole process is wirelessly transmitted around the globe via a low-Earth-orbiting (LEO) satellite system.

The Mobile Bank Branch

By the year 2000, analysts predict that up to 75% of all routine banking will be conducted outside of the branch. Remote banking services have been around since automatic teller machines (ATMs) became widespread in the late 1980s.

The most logical extension of the ATM is (naturally) the wireless ATM. Wireless ATMs are becoming increasingly popular, because they can be placed at nontraditional locations such as cruise ships, state fairs, trade shows, and any other location where there's a need for mobility. They maintain the functionality and speed of landline-based ATMs.

It works by replacing phone links with a digital air link. The solution sends data over a CDPD network to a land-based gateway that converts the wireless data to the bank's preferred protocol, and then passes it to the processing center's host computer.

Super mobile branches will be possible with C-WAN (Cellular-Wide Area Network) technology, which enables mobile units to process transactions at a much faster rate than typical mobile units.

For Barnett Bank, while an actual branch office was being built, a "mobile branch" was deployed in a South Florida community. The mobile unit was also used to offer banking on-site at special events as well as a back-up to branches when computer lines were down.

To stay profitable, banks will have to continue to evolve their remote banking services. Joint partnerships between hardware or software vendors and large banking institutions will shape the future of banking in the year 2000. Though progress is being made, it may take years before bank customers widely accept the idea of completing account transactions via smart cards or a handheld PCs.

CONCLUSION

Wireless and mobile products are becoming an increasingly attractive option for many industries, in part because of cost reductions and continued improvements in the technology itself. The ability of wireless to allow people to move freely in their work activities will have as strong an impact on business in the future as the provision of a telephone on every desk did in the middle of the twentieth century.

Unfortunately, wireless communications won't revolutionize financial services overnight. The applications available have only scratched the surface of potential market applications for large- and medium-sized banks, insurance companies, and securities firms. The industry is still a toddler, but once it "grows up," business people in these industries will be able to capitalize on instant information to help them do their jobs even better.

Keeping up with change is paramount in the financial marketplace. We've seen automatic payroll deposits and ATM cards become ubiquitous in the space of about five years. That's what customers wanted, what they valued, and that's why it's here today.

The Future

The wireless hardware and software of the future could become one standard dataphone, as portable as your watch and as personal as your wallet. It would be able to recognize speech and convert it to text. But for now, that is still only part of a Star Trek episode.

Looking ahead, wireless technologies and applications will continue to evolve. For future generations, the one thing we will never have to replace or upgrade is the wireless medium through which information is distributed — the airwaves.

Advantages for individual financial organizations vary, but the returns are the same: gains of productivity, timely distribution of data, and improved customer service. More importantly, once wireless becomes widely accepted, the financial industry as a whole will realize tremendous gains to their own bottom lines.

Chapter 16
Personal Financial Appliances

Greg Crandell
David Williams

THE OPPORTUNITY FOR THE DEVELOPMENT OF INNOVATION in online financial services could not be better. Key standards are falling into place, and the Internet continues to grow and mature. New Internet platforms are proliferating, thus lowering the investment required for establishing a Web presence. While savvy financial service companies are offering customers more options for how service may be accessed, the challenge of providing solutions that meet the requirements of most users remains.

Most of the activity in the area of online financial services has focused on infrastructure development. This is extremely important, as the success of these services will depend on robust, scalable, and most importantly — secure solutions. But lets suppose that the infrastructure is, or soon will be, in place to enable anyone real-time access to banking, investment, and other personal financial information online. What delivery mechanism will become dominant? The options available today include browser banking, with its high availability but relatively limited functionality. These browser-based transactional Web sites don't extend the financial institution's existing delivery system. They offer little more capability differentiation than ATM or debit card access.

Existing personal finance management (PFMs) software like Quicken and Money, which combine offline financial tools with online financial support, limit the user to a single desktop. Additionally, they are "hard branded," thus subordinating the very financial institutions who will increasingly depend on this desktop presence as their primary point of contact with a growing customer segment.

Strategic differentiation will be driven by the approach the financial institution takes in investing in an innovative digital presence — a presence innovative in its value proposition for the consumer and in its integration

0-8493-9991-2/99/$0.00+$.50

and presentation of the products and services offered across the financial institution.

Survey findings suggest users place a low value on the benefits of existing home banking solutions.[1] Financial institutions, looking to implement solutions for these users, are put in an interesting position. Users are not enamored with existing Web solutions and PFMs are hard to use and limit the financial institution's choices. With success hanging in the balance, these are tough issues.

The potential rewards are compelling, however. By building Internet-type distribution channels, and facilitating consumers' and merchants' entry into electronic commerce, financial institutions can place themselves in a nearly unassailable role for facilitating payment and settlement. They can open new avenues for the creation and delivery of information-rich products, and protect their role as the primary providers of financial services. In this scenario, account balances rise, transaction costs fall, and revenues grow.

What follows are some of the issues and challenges that software developers and financial institutions must face if they are to meet the needs of this rapidly evolving and increasingly "wired" customer base. Specifically, we discuss a new class of client software we have termed the Personal Financial Appliance (PFA). The readers will learn what a PFA is and how it might work for them in meeting their online financial services challenges. We believe PFAs hold the key to mass acceptance by a user audience not yet addressed by existing solutions.

INTERNET AT THE CROSSROADS

> The birth of the web marks not just another hot information technology, but the emergence of an entirely new domain of human economic life.
>
> — Michael Rothschild, *Upside Magazine,* February, 1996.

To best understand where we are, we need to understand where we have been. Over the last 5 years the Internet has come from being a curiosity, used only by the cognoscenti, to become part of the daily activities of increasing numbers of average everyday people.[2] That the Internet has come of age is no secret, but how it will turn out in the end is anyone's guess. We are still just opening the door to what is expected to reshape the boundaries of our lives more fully than any single technology event has ever done before. While we can't say specifically what these changes will be, we can say with absolute certainty that, at least in the area of electronic financial services, things have already changed forever.

THE NEW BOSS

Today, the Internet is an amorphous collection of data sources, billboards, communities, places, people, organizations, books, libraries, newspapers, museums, stores, malls, myths, and legends. It is all of these things and more. What it will evolve into, no one knows. But, we have learned a few things about the Internet that can help us understand how and along what lines it will evolve. It is in looking at *application* development that we can learn the most about how and where the Internet is going. It is important to place application development in some larger context. The next wave can be broken down into three MegaTrends: Information Access and Management, Relationship Management, and Electronic Commerce.

Information Access and Management

No one doubts the enormous reservoir of information that is available everyday over the Internet. Consider that the earliest successful Internet entrepreneurs focused on search engines as a way to add value to a user's Internet access. Key developments to pay attention to in this area include:

- Search and retrieval engines — provide better query languages and concept extraction.
- Agent/filtering algorithms — provide better and more functional agent communities, and more precise filtering of responses.
- Web push/pull — better methods for multicasting and streaming media. Push is great; however, it suffers from poor network response and a lack of good tools for managing active content development.
- Computational media — computational media or "just-in-time" media that is rendered in real time on the user's screen. Examples include personalized news services and collaborative environments such as virtual world communities.

Relationship Management

The Internet brings relationships to a completely new level. On the Internet the notion of relationships and relationship management will need to be rethought. Key capabilities that we see users wanting include:

- Friends and family — financial institutions already view account holders in terms of households. Solutions will enable users to better manage their financial relationships with the reality of complex account ownership.
- Subscribers/customers — solutions are needed that understand the requirements of servicing online customer/subscriber communities. Financial institutions and merchants, acting as online service providers, will require new tools which enable them to nurture, grow, maintain, and *mine* their subscriber base for new business and services.

- Online financial institutions and merchants — solutions that link purchase and transaction histories to correspondence with a specific financial institution/merchant. This is critical for users to manage the various types of relationships that they may have online.

Electronic Commerce

This is the Holy Grail of the current phase of Internet development. If we can standardize the right communication and security technologies, and deliver better tools and applications for performing commerce, we believe the commercial promise of the Internet will be realized. The benefits of open access and universal availability will drive usage of the Internet for commerce precisely because it is inexpensive, always there, always open, always ready to do business. No other medium can offer this power. Key capabilities we believe users will want in this area include:

- Online banking, bill pay, and bill delivery. These are the basic capabilities that users need to automate and simplify their banking chores.
- Online investment. Trading and brokerage are considered the current instance for true empowerment. In this application, users are able to take direct control of their trading resources and make changes as required.
- Online shopping and electronic funds transfer at point of decision (EFT@POD). Online shopping is expected to grow dramatically over the next few years and lots of examples of secure credit-card transactions already exist today. But true online shopping by the masses will have to wait for a more standard method for performing it. On the other hand EFT@POD denotes a new capability which, we believe, will evolve out of online shopping. This capability gives users the ability to move funds anywhere, anytime, for any purpose the user decides.
- Online asset management. This is another new capability that we expect to become important as users develop relationships with multiple financial service providers, such as insurance companies, financial institutions, credit unions, brokers, and financial planners. They will want to consolidate these accounts into a single place where they can make decisions that could ripple through their financial world.

THE CHALLENGE

> It is an indictment of the industry that the only way I can do business with Amazon.com is with my credit card.
>
> — E. Alan Holroyde, executive vice-president, Wells Fargo & Co., as quoted in the *American Banker.*

The Internet allows financial institutions to play a larger role in point-of-sale payment initiation (EFT@POD). In the past, financial institutions have developed and/or relied upon third parties and networks to capture and initiate the payor's payment instruction, leaving the financial institution with the less attractive task of settling the payment. Financial institution-provided Internet point-of-sale services can allow financial institutions to earn more on transactions, while playing a larger role in the commerce activities of both consumer and commercial customers. This is a major opportunity for financial institutions, but one that could be lost if they don't focus on the correct battleground, i.e., if they don't start focusing on the opportunity to capture their current and prospective customers' "Internet eyeballs."

Specifically, where should financial institutions be looking? The next great steps in electronic commerce are coming through satellite, cable, and telephone company initiatives that will boost the speed and functionality of home and workplace communication devices such as telephones, televisions, and personal computers. These newly forming channels represent a genuine opportunity for financial institutions to regain the technological high ground — to lead the development of interactive commerce services, especially payment and settlement; and to lead the migration of merchants and consumers onto the information highway.

Strategically, the focus moves from service desks and sales counters to the focal points of remote electronic banking — screens and phones — where new products, new distribution channels, and new competitors converge. At these remote convergence points, value lies with information — on accounts, transactions, and services. It is here that the PFA positions the financial institution to both lead Internet commerce payment and build stronger customer relationships. Deploying PFAs will allow financial institutions to take a preeminent position in their retail and commercial customers' daily commerce activities. PFAs will open the door to direct access to demand deposit accounts, but in a way that empowers customers without risking the security of banking transactions. Exhibit 1 is an example of how an electronic funds transfer could transpire at the point-of-sale, allowing for real-time, guaranteed funds transactions.

If consumers use a financial institution-distributed PFA, they will be capable of purchasing online without a credit or debit card. They will be able to request payment from their financial institution, and have their checking account debited while having the merchant receive a "guaranteed funds" message, allowing for completion of the online transaction. Payment clearing and settlement can take place in a traditional fashion, but the PFA environment creates the opportunity for real-time, guaranteed funds transactions at the point-of-decision, something no other Internet commerce payment solution has successfully addressed.

FINANCIAL INSTITUTION AS AN ONLINE SERVICE: THE NEW "WIRED" CONSTITUENCY

One important legacy of the Internet will be its role in training a new class of "wired" customer. This new wired constituency is accustomed to

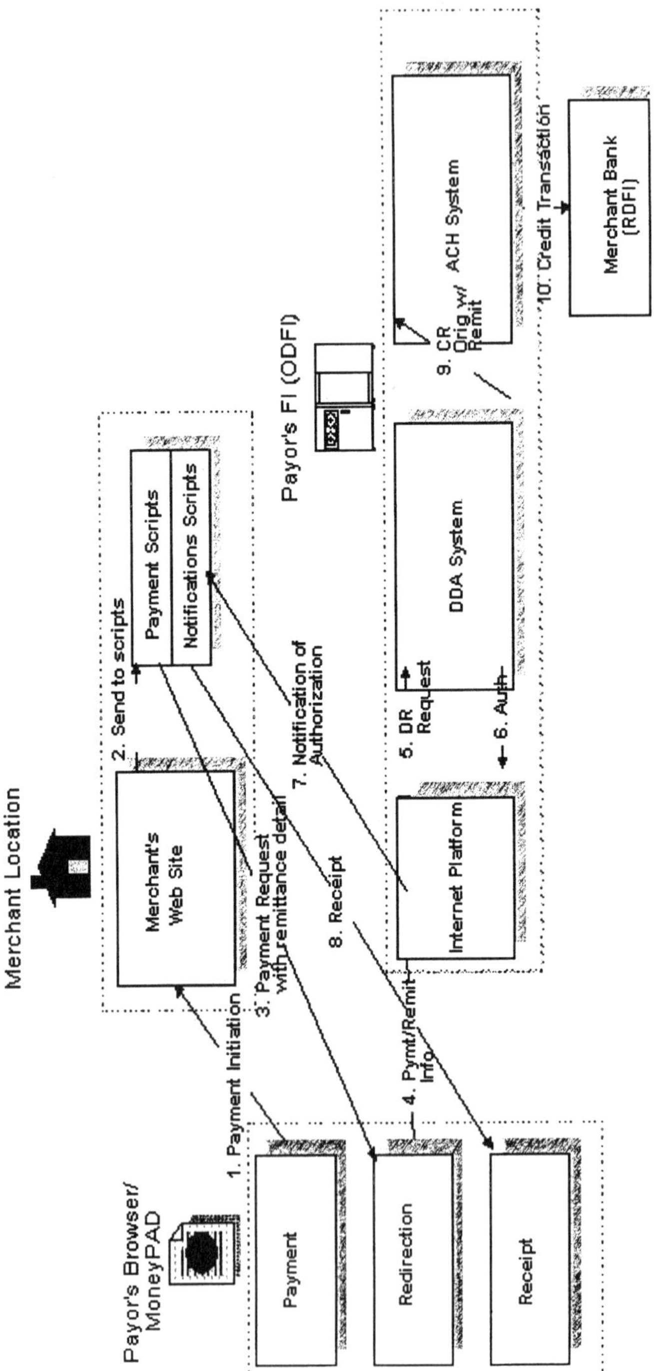

Exhibit 1. Internet EFT at Point-of-Decision (EFT@POD).

using the Web to select, transact, and in some instances, fulfill their requests online. These customers are demanding that their vendors offer more of their services online. This means financial institutions that are looking to grow their businesses must adopt new methods that have no precedent in existing practice.

Financial institutions need to understand their business as an online service and themselves as online service providers. That is, the financial institution is no longer just a brick and mortar establishment that occupies a specific, however elegant, space in the community. The notion of space for business in the physical world must be extended to space for business in the virtual world.

Now, financial institutions must view themselves as online service providers, and view their access points as virtual access spaces which are available 24 hours each day, 365 days per year. Users may access these services from anywhere on the net, at anytime. Continuous availability is just one of the major paradigm shifts from the traditional view of business hours.

The New Battleground: The Convergence of the Internet, the User Interface, and Payment Services

> For years bankers have said they would never allow customers to move money online, but that attitude simply leaves the door open for others to step in and serve financial institution customers. I want to be the first screen my customers see. I want to build a relationship with them that allows me to provide for all of their financial needs.
>
> — A Senior Vice-President of Internet Commerce, a $30 billion financial institution.

Financial institutions are not sitting still. They are stepping up to the challenge of providing Internet-based browser banking to their customers, both retail and commercial. The number of financial service firms offering online transactional services is growing at a rapid rate. As recently as 1994, there were only 20 banks or credit unions with Web sites, and none of them offered account access to their customers. By year-end 1998, it is estimated there will be 4800 bank/credit union Web sites, and 625 of them will offer account access. Looking to the future, the General Accounting Office (GAO) estimates 4800 financial institutions will provide online sites by year-end 1998. Separately, Online Banking Report (OBR) projects 8000 financial service institutions will provide Web sites within 4 years, and 4500 of them will offer account access to their customers.

Financial institutions entered the online remote banking space by working with technology providers to provide a link between customers' banking services and the technology providers' *client* software. It proved to be an expensive service to deploy and maintain. And rapid adoption of Internet technologies made the financial institutions' early online efforts nearly obsolete before the programs were even in full flight.

Internet technology eliminates two parts of the home banking equation: front-end software and private network connections. While, this technology is making financial institutions' initial investments in online services look like poor ones, it has opened the playing field for financial institutions to develop branded end-user experience and to develop bank-centric payment processes, reducing the need for third-party payment processors, and increasing the opportunity for financial institutions to play a central role in online commerce.

Online Branding, Brand Control, and Other Issues Unique to Online Services

Branding over the Internet continues to be one of the most critical activities within which a Financial Service Provider can participate. Online branding, however, differs from traditional branding in interesting ways.

Online branding differs from traditional branding primarily in the methods used to implement it. Look and feel elements that people take for granted in the real world need to be specifically created in the virtual world. That is, the elements of brand in the online world need to be understood and used by the service provider to maximize the capabilities of the new medium.

In the same way, architecture, product support, and the attire of tellers contribute to the brand image of the branch financial institution, the experience of online branding is defined by the unique sights and sounds of the interaction. Online branding requires that all of the elements of the interaction be used for brand identification. Taking advantage of images, sounds, interactive dialogs, jingles, and animations as elements to be exploited by service providers seeking a differentiated experience that uniquely bonds the user to them.

Related to branding is the issue of who manages it. Who has control? Does the financial institution manage the experience of the user? Does the user's application manage the brand? Is the financial institution subordinate to the application's brand? Control of brand is a big deal as it shapes the end-user's idea of value and who is providing it. To be successful, the financial institution must grab and maintain control of its brand throughout the online financial experience. This will necessarily require the financial institution to become a more involved player in providing the online solution.

Relationships in the Screen-to-Screen World

Historically, financial institutions served their customers face to face. Personal relationships were possible and sought after as a way of better serving the customer. In the online world, of course, the face is the user interface that is presented to customer visitors. This carries tremendous responsibility on the part of the online service provider. Interfaces must be developed which communicate their function while, at the same time facilitating the brand investment necessary to retain the long-term relationship with the user. When users are a mere click away from their financial institution's most distant competitor, one must know how to keep the customer from clicking away!

Online relationships differ from standard customer relationships precisely because one may never actually meet the person with whom one is interacting. Online relationships are more like pen pals. The parties that make up an online relationship may, in fact, meet, but a strong online relationship can be developed without face to face contact. To the user the financial institution is a service, and hopefully a friend. The user is a subscriber, a visitor, a supplier, or perhaps even a competitor to the services provided by the financial institution.

Active Content (Advertising and Info Channels)

Support for advertising and access to information are often taken for granted as natural elements of online practice. However, methods differ on how this is accomplished and with what flexibility it may be used.

Active Content, or action-enabled content, refers to content the user may interact with. Trigger points in product usage, like loan retirement, should link to selling messages encouraging evaluation of new loan programs. Dynamic evaluation of competitive information available in bill payment records should drive specific related selling instances. Other examples include advertising that enables the user to seek increasingly more levels of detailed information regarding a product or service. This can also be built into the news/advertising stream that users can receive. Or, it could take the form of wizard-based help which the user can navigate to complete a task. Active content is critical to creating an engaging and memorable online experience.

Active Advertising refers to the ability for active advertising content to be broadcast to users where interaction, on the part of the user, is integral to the service offering. A desktop presence that incorporates a dynamic information/advertising channel tied to active content will be required to realize the potential of online selling. When users are informed of something that interests them, they expect to be able to interact with the message to get more information. Ultimately users expect to be able to execute a transaction.

STANDARDS CREATE OPPORTUNITY

Much has been written about the emerging standards of Open Financial Exchange (OFX) from the consortium headed by Microsoft, Checkfree, and

Intuit, and the Gold Message Standard (Gold) from the Integrion consortium, supported by IBM. We have an agnostic view of these standards, in that we believe PFAs can be supported within both.

OFX and Gold have been viewed as competing specifications, although the two are complementary in many respects. For instance, OFX focuses on *client* (front-end) *to server* messages, while Gold holds many *back-end-oriented* message sets that have no counterpart in OFX. OFX is perceived to have a PFM bias, while Gold is seen as having a thin client bias.

We fully expect these two standards to converge successfully, removing any confusion as to their uses. We believe this is a nonissue for financial institutions and fully expect the convergence of the two standards will make PFAs easier to adopt and deploy.

THE USER DILEMMA — MANAGING FINANCE CHORES

Despite all of the gains technology has contributed to the lives of its users, most individuals do not look forward to time spent reconciling financial institution accounts and paying bills. It is a chore that all must deal with and deal with on a regular basis. *Financial institutions must realize that for most people, managing finances is a drag.*

There are two categories of end-user customers: **Transactors** and **Analysts.** Each has different needs and therefore may require different solutions. **Transactors** are primarily concerned with executing transactions and include the HTML users that today make use of browser-based solutions. These solutions offer the financial institution a low cost of entry and the market is growing. These solutions, however, are poorly differentiated and do not offer much in the way of performance, richness, or interactivity.

Those who use PFMs characterize **Analysts.** These solutions are rich and offer many features for analysis. They also suffer from feature overload that is threatening to many users who are already in fear of using computers. Most users of these packages use only a small percentage of the functionality offered. While needed, these features offer a way to deal with the user's problems. When they are not needed they place a burden on the part of the user by complicating their lives with needless functionality. Increasing evidence suggests that these solutions are already slowing their penetration which, we believe, is due to adequacies in addressing the needs of the average user. This is particularly true for the wired user. Note that these solutions were originally designed for stand-alone use and only recently has Internet access been grafted on.

"After a decade of near-total failure, the online banking industry needs to begin working with innovative software developers to help make the combined online banking/money management experience less onerous and complex," stated David Fenichell, author or FIND/SVP's *Online Banking.*

The challenge for financial institutions has as much to do with *how* the customer does something, as with *what* they are doing. The task is not just home banking, *its home banking in a context and manner that best matches the customer's needs and abilities.* In the area of financial services, this is particularly difficult, as the average user already considers finance a complex subject. Thus, the financial institution must educate the customer in addition to providing a service.

Financial institutions must become online service providers, in this they have no choice. Do they also need to become software developers, thereby having to develop a new set of competencies? Current solutions do not permit a solution provider to establish a dominant brand.

The financial institution's dilemma is characterized by the need to offer a solution that gives the users a simple method for dealing with their finance chores, while growing the institution's online service offerings in a brand-managed way.

THE SW APPLIANCE PARADIGM

Enter the Software Appliance. Appliances bring convenience to user's lives by performing specific tasks exceedingly well. That is, a toaster makes toast, it does not make coffee, nor does it play your CDs. When users turn to use of appliances they do not want to think about how the appliance works; only what it can do for them and the specific task at hand.

Software appliances perform a single function, but do so far easier and more intuitively than programs that cover a broad range of functionality. Like appliances in the physical world, software appliances perform well a limited set of functions. We believe users will resonate with the appliance metaphor. The **Personal Financial Appliance** is designed specifically to mitigate the finance chores of average people. The PFA will give financial institutions the ability to deal with creeping complexity by containing the functionality their customers need most.

Reducing complexity for users interacting online has got to be a major concern for financial institutions intending to grow their businesses through online financial services. Users just want to focus on the task at hand, not the software that they need to complete the task. Our experiences in developing software for people draw heavily on the notion of appliances. We are trying to reduce the tasks of home banking to that of a simple appliance that users can quickly adapt to their needs, and that easily gives them the features they need to perform their tasks. Internet banking solutions that enable the financial institution to support existing PFM users while concurrently offering a brandable solution of their own is what the PFA is all about.

Personal Financial Appliance Solutions For FIs

A Personal Financial Appliance (PFA) can reside on a user's desktop, running as a browser plug-in or as a stand-alone object that provides interactive real-time banking functionality via the Web. Unlike traditional HTML and PFM applications, a PFA can support interactive objects, multimedia effects, and user-controllable functions. PFAs can be designed to support core banking transactions and, when bundled with an OFX-compliant server, offer financial institutions a turnkey transaction presence via the Web.

PFAs will allow graphics and information that do not require secure transmission to be directed to other server sources, increasing load ability on the active data server. Use of applets will allow the customer to view the same data in a variety of formats and combinations, thus eliminating another session to the server for reformatting of data. PFAs can be designed using an authoring tool that enables the creation of a highly customizable PFA. This tool gives the financial institution a quick and easy method of creating and protecting a brand and a proprietary customer relationship.

PFAs will support the following types of features:

- Real-time access to account information such as checking, money market, savings, line of credit, and credit card.
- Real-time intrabank funds transfers between authorized accounts.
- Ability to schedule single or recurring bill payments to any OFX-compliant bill payment provider.
- Interactive communication between the customer and the financial institution by use of e-mail messaging.
- Integrated interactive help library.
- Active content for interactive advertising control window defined by the user's placement within the control or by defined analytics on the user's data history.
- Interact with any OFX-compliant server, thereby providing the ability to route various transactions appropriately.
- Use of applets which eliminate additional server requests and enable parsing of data not requiring encryption to other sources.

ANATOMY OF AN APPLIANCE

An early version of a PFA that is available today offers five key features working together to help users manage their finances. The user interface can be customized with enhanced features, graphics, and navigation that differentiate the financial institution. The PFA can be offered for download from the financial institution's Web site and is organized in feature bundles as is compatible with other products as shown in Exhibit 2. The baseline transaction set offers core banking, bill payment, brokerage, and e-mail messaging. The environment features a unique look and includes an Interactive Ad Control feature.

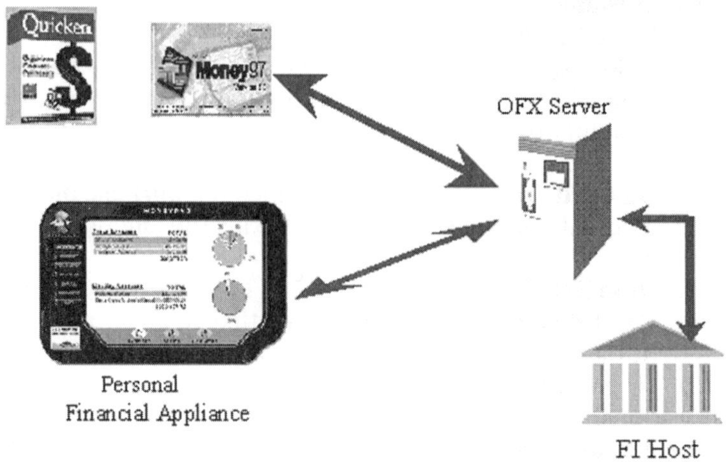

Exhibit 2. Personal Financial Appliance transaction set compatibility.

Exhibit 3 highlights some of the key areas available for branding. A description of these areas is listed below. Note that the entire look can also be changed per the requirements of the financial institution.

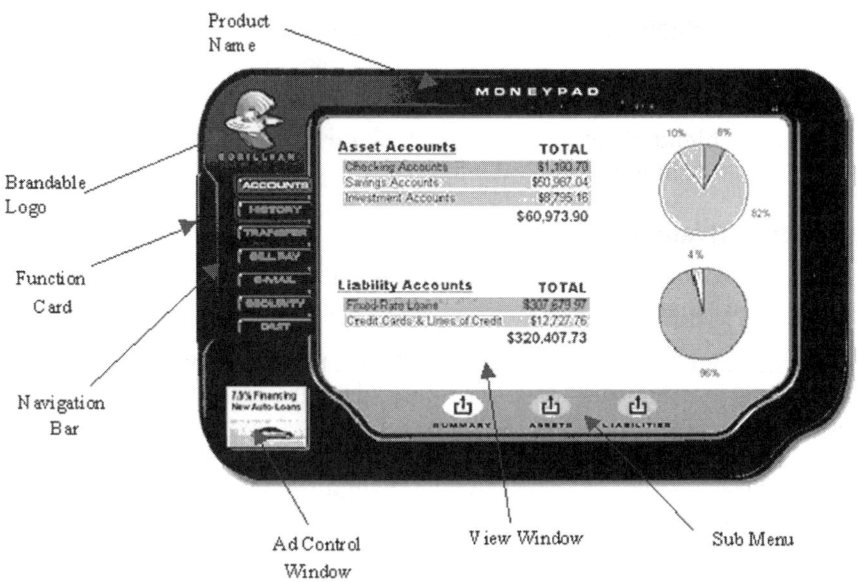

Exhibit 3. A typical Personal Financial Appliance.

1. **Product Name.** The Financial Service Provider's name or the name they give to the PFA.
2. **Brandable Logo.** The space reserved for the Financial Service Provider's logo. Note that it can be implemented as "active" giving the user the ability to link to a place of the financial institution's choosing.
3. **Function Card.** The function card defines the purpose of the appliance. Different functions can be added using the function card as the control.
4. **Navigation Bar.** The primary navigation facility with which the user interacts. It defines the key operations that the user may perform; account data, transfers, etc. It works in conjunction with the **Sub Menu.** Together, these two features guide the user through the PFA's operations.
5. **View Window.** The view window is the primary viewing window for the user. Information coming from the financial institution is displayed here. In addition, when the user interacts with the ad control, the view window can be used to display the advertising in the foreground.
6. **Ad Control.** The ad control is a special feature of the PFA. It can be used to provide real-time information, interactive advertising content, or help information to the user as part of their online experience. The authoring tool would be used to develop content for this control.

PERSONAL FINANCIAL APPLIANCES VS. BROWSER AND PFM BANKING

Exhibit 4 illustrates how the PFA is positioned — between existing HTML solutions on the low end and PFMs at the high end. We believe the PFA provides a good blend of functionality that includes some of the analytics of the PFM with the online transaction immediacy of standard browser banking.

Product Motivations

Many issues motivate the development of PFAs, while assuring their deployment and market success. Key among the motivations are the following:

Ease of Use (EOU). EOU is a "catch all" term referring specifically to ease of install, ease of learning, ease of using, and finally, ease of maintaining and performing a task on a computer. Ease of use has been an issue since the dawn of computers. Even sophisticated users are still daunted by computers. To better understand this aspect of computer usage lets break it down into its key facets.

Ease of Install. The installation process is the first time a user looks at a product. This is particularly true when they are selecting it from an online

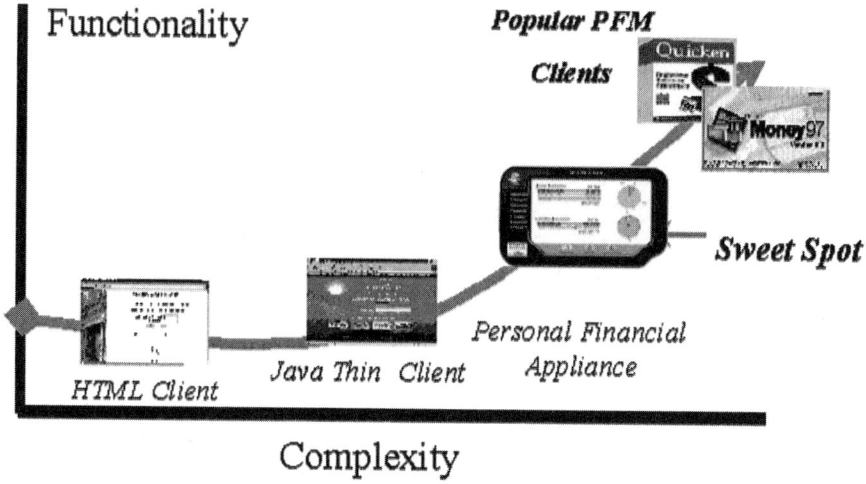

Exhibit 4. Personal Finance Appliance positioning.

display. There is no box to look at and no manuals to peruse, so they are at the mercy of the install program. We believe that installation is a critical time for new users and thus needs to be understood in the context of the first look.

Ease of Learning. After installation, the user must now learn how to use the application. This is where most users are at their highest state of discomfort with a new application. Is it obvious what it does from looking at it? Does the user need to configure it before use? Is there ready help for common problems? These all must be confronted.

Ease of Using. After learning the basics, is it easy to use on a daily basis? Do trade-offs made in the learning phase translate into boring usage? Many solutions that are extremely easy to learn can degrade into boring and non-interesting usage once learned. Users need to be able to tell the system whether they are new users or experienced users and the system must accommodate these usage requirements to keep it interesting for the user.

Ease of Maintaining. With the increase of Internet usage, many users are well aware that updates are a part of the software experience. That is, the application in use today will eventually need to be updated. Questions that need to be addressed include: Does the application know that an update is available? Does the service provider enable the user to upgrade at their leisure, or is it forced upon them? Can the system be updated in the background?

Ease of use and all its facets must be fully comprehended by anyone who would develop solutions for online use. PFAs can incorporate all aspects of ease of use into their design.

By engaging User Interface (UI), we are speaking of the experience provided by the application. Does the application engage the user as part of the experience of using it? The experience of an application is largely subjective. Nevertheless, there are aspects of the UI that can actively engage the user as part of the experience of using it. In an early PFA development, we took it as axiomatic that simply making the application functional was not sufficient to make it engaging.

Online Computational Media and Active Content

The Internet has opened up many new possibilities for delivering information in a way that is "just in time." That is, the user makes a request and the information is sought out and delivered in a rendered manner as if someone had actually spent time "producing" it for the user's consumption. However, it is rendered *on-the-fly* by the user's machine using conventions set by the programmer and, in some instances, by the behavior of the users themselves. We refer to information that is rendered "just in time" by the computer as computational media.

The Internet provides an excellent environment for the development and delivery of computational media. In fact, the information repository that is the Internet would not work if every request had to be produced by hand before users could access it for consumption. Computational media makes it possible for content providers to put content on the Internet without any knowledge of how it will be used or accessed. The clients and servers that make up the Internet perform this function under program control.

This distinguishes it from traditional media where the *design* and *development* of the content is separate from the *distribution* of the content. In computational media, the creation and distribution happen at the same time. Examples of the uses of computational media are to be found in many of the current personal news services like *my.yahoo.com* or *my.excite.com*. These services provide "just in time" snapshots of what's happening in the news and they can be tailored to meet specific interests and profiles of a single unique user.

Active Content is interactive in nature. Both computational media and active content are extremely useful for dynamically creating a compelling information experience for the user. An early version of a PFA incorporates computational media and Active Content specifically as a method for users to be informed of new services and for financial institutions to target specific messages for customer consumption. This feature is critical if financial institutions are to grow their service offerings within the Internet retail channel.

Asset Consolidation from Multiple Financial Institutions

Asset consolidation will become one of the key features that users require on the Internet. Asset consolidation refers to the ability to consolidate account information from multiple financial institutions for the purpose of analysis, making decisions, and taking action.

Most financial institutions today accept the fact the customer is likely to have relationships with multiple financial institutions. This stems from the fact that only recently have financial institutions been deregulated enough to give them the ability to offer the range of financial services that a user is likely to need or want. The new competitive environment of online financial services will then revolve around who or which financial institution has primacy, if not exclusivity, with the user. Asset consolidation from multiple financial institutions will then be a user requirement for some time to come.

Internet Delivered and Updated

The ability to use the Internet as a delivery mechanism is well known. It offers financial institutions the ability to proliferate changes and updates using the same medium the user uses to interact with the financial institution. Unlike PFMs, which are too large for online delivery and updates, PFAs can be easily distributed, changed, and updated over the Internet. This flexible delivery model should be considered a key requirement for Internet service solutions.

CONCLUSIONS

The world of online finance is just beginning to be realized. However, enough progress has been made for financial institutions, looking for entry into online financial services or expansion of their existing online offering, to implement solutions that will work. We have shown that the ability to meet increasing needs of online customers requires some new ways of thinking in several key areas; branding, online relationships, and simplified functionality. We believe that PFAs hold the key to growing the installed base of online customers. PFAs are simple to use, considerably more engaging for users, and can be used by the financial institution to inform and sell new services. Early versions of PFAs represent the first of a new class of software designed from the ground up as an Internet software appliance; we expect more PFA types will enter the market as financial institutions respond to the needs of their broader market base.

Notes

1. Forrester Research, Inc., Is Quicken Obsolete?, March, 1997.
2. Steve Perlman, founder of WebTV, commented that, when he saw the Campbell's Soup Company announcing its Web address in a TV commercial, he knew we had turned a corner on the Internet.

Chapter 17
Putting Inbound Fax Automation to Work in the Financial Organization

Jerry Rackley

SO MANY OF THE KEY MESSAGES AND TRANSACTIONS that drive our commerce are still conveyed on the simple yet essential piece of paper. Many of these are sent and received as faxes. Indeed, the fax machine has become the most ubiquitous printing device in the enterprise. Financial organizations and their customers favor fax transmission as a much faster way to exchange key documents: credit applications, purchase orders, invoices, credit reports, transaction confirmations, sales quotes, and many other time-sensitive documents. Not only does fax provide a faster way to distribute documents, but it provides the sender with positive confirmation of receipt. If you are a customer or consumer, fax is the easiest, fastest, and cheapest way of getting a document to its destination.

For the enterprise, the world of high technology has provided us with computer-based automated fax servers. These solutions have been around for years and are capable of accepting documents destined for printing and mailing, but instead are now transmitting them as faxes. Often the length of time required to experience return on investment in these fax servers is as little as three months. Millions of pages of faxes are reliably transmitted through fax servers every year, but until recently, computer-based fax solutions only solved half the problem associated with faxes.

The real problem with faxes is that they end up at fax machines. This is not a problem if you're dealing with the outbound side of fax distribution. But the more complex side of the fax equation is on the inbound side. How do organizations who receive hundreds or thousands of faxes a day receive them and route them to the proper recipient? For most organizations that

0-8493-9991-2/99/$0.00+$.50

are buried in faxes every day, the answer is simple: in a very low-tech fashion. Until recently, technology has failed to provide a solution to automating this mission-critical inward flow of documents.

The most common approach is to maintain a sufficient number of manual fax machines to accommodate the inbound fax volume and employ "runners" to take received faxes and deliver them. In fact, some organizations have their runners on roller skates to speed up the process. While this approach can certainly be made to work, it is far from ideal. Tremendous productivity and even competitive business advantages exist for organizations who can automate this aspect of document handling. There are now commercially available solutions that solve the problems of handling high volumes of inbound faxes and route them securely to the intended recipient. In the balance of this article, the problems associated with handling inbound fax traffic and a strategy for automating it will be explored.

The sheer volume of faxes many organizations receive in the course of a day's work makes handling them difficult. Unlike a piece of mail, a fax carries with it a certain sense of urgency. Persons on the receiving end of a fax typically are not content to let it be handled like a piece of mail — they want it now! The larger the volume, the bigger the problem it is for the organization to manage. A typical scenario is a credit processing center or order processing center where applications and purchase orders are received by the thousands each day. On average, it takes 1 minute to transmit or receive 1 page of fax over a single phone line, yielding a theoretical capability to receive 480 pages over an 8-hour shift. If you have a requirement to receive 5000 faxes per day during an 8-hour period, you would need to maintain at least 11 fax machines, assuming little excess capacity.

Receiving the faxes, however, is the easy part of the process. Getting those 5000 faxes routed to where they should go within an acceptable time frame can prove more challenging. In addition to the complexity involved in managing this deludge, it doesn't scale well. Should business growth drive your inbound fax volume up, your only option is to add more phone lines and manual fax machines. One financial services organization sought an automation solution when 69 fax machines were no longer enough to allow them to receive credit applications and process them within 15 minutes. The complexity associated with managing these inbound faxes increases exponentially as the volume and number of recipients increases.

Perhaps a bigger problem than just receiving a large volume of faxes is routing them. Getting these faxed documents in-house is not enough, they must end up in the hands (or under the eye) of the persons for whom they were intended. Determining who should receive a fax is not always a straightforward affair. Processing and service centers that have heavy fax volumes don't always receive documents addressed to a specific person. They may be addressed to a department, for example. Or the correct recipient may be determined by the type of document, the time of day it was received, the location from which it was sent, or even the order in which it arrived. To compound this distribution problem further, once the fax is received in paper form, it cannot easily be routed through the organization in electronic form without rescanning it first — yet another step in an already lengthy and complicated process. It will probably have to be routed via runner or in-house courier.

Perhaps the greatest concern with manually faxed documents is security. The opportunity for the wrong eyes to see sensitive or confidential information on a manually faxed document is greater than it would be for mailed documents. In fact, the concern for security has prevented some organizations from using the fax for document exchange when otherwise it would be quite advantageous. But now there is good news: the issues of volume, routing, and security have been addressed in new, second generation fax automation solutions now in the marketplace.

Fax automation came into its own in the early 1990s. These first generation fax servers allowed a computer-generated document that ordinarily would be printed to be delivered instead as a fax. As the marketplace evolved, two strata of fax solutions emerged. The first is the familiar LAN-based solution designed to meet the needs of users generating documents from their word processors, spreadsheets, or other desktop applications. The second strata is the enterprise-wide fax server. These solutions are engineered to distribute documents generated by enterprise applications. They can handle high volumes and attach to multiple host systems simultaneously. Most also offer a LAN client solution. It was the customers of these high-end enterprise-wide fax solutions who had the need for an automated solution on the inbound side of fax. The result is AIR, or Advanced Inbound Routing. Exhibit 1 illustrates the possible destinations in a corporate LAN environment for a fax received by a fax server equipped with AIR.

The premise of AIR is pretty straightforward on the surface: receive high volumes of fax transmissions and route them securely through the enterprise. The receiving part is not a problem. Many vendors in this product space offer solutions capable of attaching multiple high-volume T1 (24 fax channels) communication links to their systems. What separates the best from the rest is a robust architecture to route faxes through the enterprise. Faxes can be AIR'ed based on the transmission or communications information available at the time of receipt, like ANI, DID, RSCID, DTMF, T.30 subaddressing, and other identifying data. AIR solutions can also deliver faxes based on a wide variety of attributes about the fax itself including: day of week fax was received, length of fax, time of day fax was received.

Of course, there are AIR options designed specifically for the service or processing center, like round-robin routing when it doesn't matter which processing agent handles the fax as long as it gets handled in time. You can

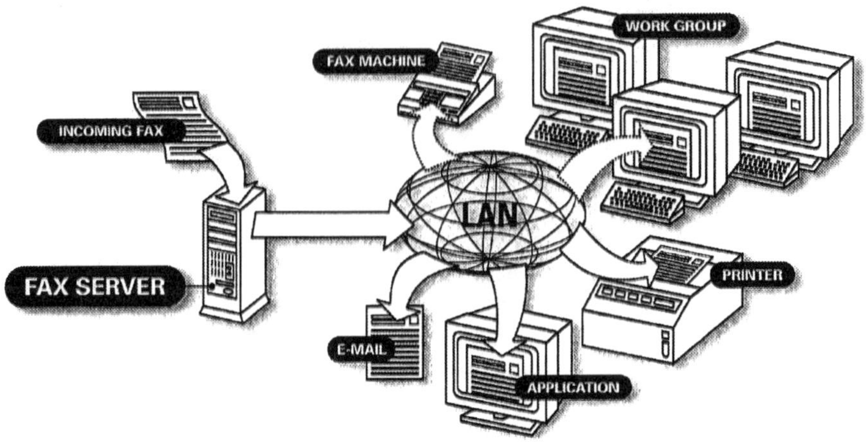

Exhibit 1. Destination of a fax in a corporate environment.

also exploit Optical Character Recognition (OCR) or Image Character Recognition (ICR) software to interpret recipient names, phone numbers, or other identifying information to use for routing purposes. Although this is not a 100% reliable approach with today's technology, it can still be used in certain situations.

A major benefit of AIR is security. Because faxes are received and stored as images, they may never have to appear in the form of a printed page. These faxes can be routed through the electronic infrastructure of an organization directly to the intended recipient. The most common way of doing this is through the corporate e-mail network. Faxes AIR'ed in this way appear as a normal message in the user's e-mail in-box. The fax is attached as an image file that can be viewed using the e-mail image viewer or the one supplied by the fax server vendor. More advanced implementation of AIR have faxes integrated with key business applications like order entry, often through some sort of image application. AIR provides a secure environment with many options for processing faxes.

The best way to understand the benefits of AIR is to look at examples of how companies are exploiting it. One financial services company uses AIR to receive applications for credit. Prior to automating this process, they received faxes manually and routed them via runners to their credit processing center. AIR had a significant impact on their ability to meet their target of processing credit applications within a 15-minute window. They were able to reduce their processing window from 15 to 7 minutes using AIR. A major office products retailer is using AIR to receive and route over 30,000 orders per month. The benefits are lower costs, higher productivity, but most of all a customer service advantage, all of which came with a 2-month return on investment. Insurance companies are using AIR to receive claims and commit them directly into host image applications for processing. Where organizations struggle with large volumes of inbound fax, AIR is making a big impact and providing a fast payback.

If you receive large numbers of faxed documents that must be routed and processed in a timely fashion, automated fax servers with AIR are probably in your future. Fax volumes are going nowhere but up — it is the preferred way for consumers and customers to communicate with the enterprise because it is so easy. Now, it is easy for the enterprise to automate all aspects of fax document flow, particularly the inbound side of the equation. AIR is being used as a competitive weapon by many leading-edge organizations. If you receive faxes that require some form of processing and they contain time-sensitive information or impact a customer service transaction, then its time to look at putting AIR in your arsenal.

Chapter 18
VPNs for Financial Services

Evan Kaplan

THE FINANCIAL SERVICES INDUSTRY has always needed fast, reliable, and secure access to information, and that holds true today more than ever before. As we move toward a global economy, this industry grows increasingly complex and brokerage firms, investment banks, credit card companies, insurance firms, and the like are looking for better ways to procure information. Many organizations are looking to leverage the Internet as a means to gain a competitive advantage. The fear of security risks, however, has prevented mainstream businesses from taking advantage of the Internet's potential. Virtual Private Networks (VPNs) are rapidly eliminating that obstacle.

THE RAPID EVOLUTION OF VPNs

Traditionally, companies have had to invest in expensive dedicated leased lines or direct-dial remote access software and hardware to have secure server-to-server or client-to-server communication. VPNs, which have only been available for the past couple of years, have just recently matured enough to offer "one-to-many" security so that corporations can share confidential information and applications with branch offices, partners, consultants, clients, and remote employees. Not only are VPNs more affordable than traditional dial-up or leased lines, but they are more secure, they scale better, they are easier to manage, and they have greater flexibility. By utilizing the Internet as the backbone for secure communication, VPNs can easily and affordably link corporate networks to each other and their end-users, offering more versatility for multiple platforms and rapidly expanding environments.

VPN technology has caught the attention of a broad spectrum of hardware and software vendors, which have rushed to incorporate VPN capabilities into their products. Not all VPN solutions are equal, but the market is quickly legitimizing the notion of private networking over the Internet.

Many respected analyst firms agree VPN adoption will be aggressive over the next few years. According to an independent study conducted by

0-8493-9991-2/99/$0.00+$.50

Forrester Research in July 1997, the estimated total annual cost for a private 2000-user remote access infrastructure was $3.016 million, whereas the cost for an Internet-based VPN solution for the same number of users was estimated at just $1.193 million. The annual savings resulting from a VPN approach to remote access totaled $1,823 million — over 60%. More data need to be gathered to give an accurate estimate of potential savings, but in almost every instance VPNs offer a fast return-on-investment, significant long-term savings as compared to traditional internetworking methods, and the potential to gain a competitive advantage and increase profits.

HOW VPNs ARE BEING USED TODAY

The potential benefits of VPNs are increasingly being recognized by a diverse array of financial services companies, though differentiating the myriad VPN products available today can be challenging. To simplify the hype, imagine three broad VPN categories:

- LAN-to-LAN communication over a relatively trusted network, such as between a corporation and its branch offices.
- Encrypted tunneling for employee remote access.
- Mission-critical business communication between a corporation and its partners, clients, consultants, and remote employees.

In each scenario, the VPN can reduce bandwidth charges, lower network operations costs, simplify administration, reduce capital expenditures, and increase scalability and flexibility. The most important scenario for the financial services industry is that of the extranet VPN.

Sample Implementation

To understand how an extranet VPN works, imagine a full-service brokerage investment bank that makes its money from trading shares globally for hundreds of small, independent brokerage firms. The more firms who utilize their services, the more money they make. The best way to earn and retain business from these firms is to provide them with immediate, easy access to information and services. The best way to do that is by extending the investment bank's service applications to the Internet. Before that can happen, however, security must be ensured. An extranet VPN can provide that security by authenticating the individual brokers and portfolio managers, applying access control based on their association with a particular firm and department, and then encrypting all data that crosses the wire. The VPN effectively becomes the manager and conduit for secure connectivity, and the Internet becomes the private backbone.

The initial solution might look something like this:

Users — 1000 Customers, about 200 trading partners, and almost 500 remote employees, each with varying levels of access to information on multiple systems, including mainframes, enterprise resource planning systems, and databases accessed through a Web interface. Dozens of applications need to be secured to provide information on a self-service basis without exposing confidential data to anyone other than the intended recipients.

Infrastructure — The VPN proxy server sits on a UNIX machine behind the company's fire wall. The client software is preconfigured and made available for download to end-users through a Web site.

Security options — 128-Bit SSL encryption is used along with user-based authentication through hard token cards. Access control is defined to a very granular degree with the VPN's administration tool. The complete solution enables the company to reduce remote access costs, retain and attract customers, improve service, increase revenues, and lock in strategic partnerships.

HOW TO IMPLEMENT A SECURE VPN

Historically, when people thought about securing their networks, fire wall technology for "perimeter defense" came to mind. Today, with the deployment of intranets and extranets, security is not just about perimeter defense. It is about controlling access to many different information systems, implemented in a variety of network environments.

In this era of the extranet — where organizations provide remote access to approved network resources for trading partners, resellers, and customers — the complexity of networking has grown exponentially, posing significant management and support challenges. Companies need a network that can survive a merger, grow to tens or even hundreds of thousands of remote users, and accommodate users with different access permissions, equipment configurations, points of network entry, and geographic locations. Managing thousands of modem banks and rooms full of networking gear is not a workable option for most network administrators in the financial industry. And most MIS administrators agree that if they had a choice, they would opt to tap into the Internet to simplify configuration and management of remote users, regardless of location and service needs.

Before beginning any serious evaluation of products and services, companies should consider the nature of the connections they will be making through the VPN both today and in the future, because having a long-term vision of the VPN will save time and money. Companies should consider the nature of those connections in terms of trust relationships and Information Technology (IT) governance issues. Are the users entirely trusted employees of the organization, or is there a mixture of employees, consultants, business partners, and clients? If there is a mixed population using the VPN, then features like tiered access control and strong, user-based authentication are critical. In many cases, financial organizations want to connect select users from an untrusted network without connecting back to them. This requires strongly authenticating users, not simply configuring a VPN such that anyone from a specific IP address range is allowed in. Furthermore, when a VPN services a population of mixed trust status, the VPN must have robust, user-based access controls to strongly govern what the user is able to do once authenticated.

Evaluating VPN Solutions

The most essential criteria to use when evaluating VPN solutions include:

Strong Encryption. Encryption is one of the more complex aspects of VPN selection. Encryption standards are many and can be difficult to differentiate, even by the seasoned Information Systems (IS) professional. The best products allow organizations to use multiple methods of encryption and key management so that they can make changes and scale their system gradually over time. More sophisticated organizations will want to look for products that will allow them to embed proprietary or "home-grown" ciphers using the GSS (Generic Security Services — RFC 1961) API. VPNs that allow this kind of customization will provide further flexibility and potentially greater security.

Tiered Access Control. Once a VPN has authenticated a user, it should be able restrict that user's activities on the host network based on a combination of factors including the user's credentials, the port being requested, the server or subnet being requested, the time of day of the connection, and the location from which the user is connecting. VPNs that only restrict access on source and destination cannot be as tightly controlled. The VPN should have some way to cache the user's credentials and pass them transparently with each connection to avoid basing decisions on IP addresses. More advanced VPNs will also be able to modulate access privileges based on other factors, including the strength of encryption being used or the type of authentication employed. For example, a given user authenticating to the VPN using a hardware token might receive his entire set of access privileges. The same user authenticating using a simple password might get only a subset of those privileges since they are authenticating using a less robust technique.

User-Based Authentication. The strength of a VPN's authentication is perhaps the greatest measure of the overall security of the system. Authentication should always be done on the basis of a human attribute, not a machine attribute. In other words, primary authentication should be based on the user coming in, not the machine's IP address. Any VPN not providing user-based authentication should be removed from consideration.

Comprehensive Auditing. Auditing should provide the identity of the user connecting, the method of authentication used, the strength of encryption, IP address, the identities of any accessed servers, port used, byte count, time and date of connection, and duration of connection. The VPN should also have some means of letting the administrator capture custom information through an API or management tool.

Easy for the End User. Rather than users having to re-authenticate with each new connection, they should be able to sign on once and be assured that the entire session will be secure. Stay away from client software that alters the TCP/IP stack or replaces important DLLs. This could have a negative effect on the desktop. Also, examine how the client software affects other connectivity traffic in the user's LAN and on the public Internet. Ideally, the VPN will allow all local area and Internet traffic to run as usual while maintaining a secure connection to the host network.

Simple, Centralized Systems Management. The easier it is to manage a VPN, the less chance for human error. All incoming and outgoing connection requests should go through a single point of control, just as all user records and authentication data should be controlled through one centralized database, preferably a database that is replicable. The VPN should incorporate a secure technique for accessing and monitoring the VPN and making updates as necessary. The VPN should have a method for performing load balancing, and the system should allow real-time traffic monitoring across the system.

Guaranteed Interoperability. The solution should be able to work with multiple standards and adapt to emerging standards. The solution should also be able to integrate with existing networking environments and leverage available equipment.

Fire Wall Independence. Determine thoroughly how the VPN allows traffic to pass through multiple fire walls, and more importantly, disparate fire walls. What is required of a fire wall administrator to allow traffic to pass out across the fire wall? Does it entail opening ports that the administrator would prefer remain closed? Answering these questions will help you judge the suitability of a given VPN for servicing clients, consultants, and partners.

Value-Added Services. Since a VPN manages incoming traffic from the public network, it is in a position to perform value-added services above and beyond its security function. A well-designed VPN should also incorporate functions such as virus scanning, active content management (including Java and ActiveX), and query filtering. Virus scanning should be applied to the entire inbound data stream, not simply to select applications. Filtering should be based on specific application traffic.

Open APIs. The application programming interfaces, or APIs, used in the VPN should be well documented, usable, and publicly accessible in order to allow for adaptability and customization. The VPN should be designed in such a way that it can easily service a growing and changing population of users. The system should also be able to incorporate new authentication, encryption, and filtering techniques as they become available.

PROs AND CONs OF DIFFERENT VPN APPROACHES

The perceived lack of security associated with doing business on the Internet is the number one reason financial institutions hesitate before doing mission-critical business online. VPNs are the key to making the networks safe for e-business applications. Many financial companies have a vested interest in taking advantage of the Internet beyond Web browsing and e-mail. They need to secure access to custom and legacy applications as well. The argument for implementing a VPN to distribute information to brokerage firms and/or clients is compelling. The remaining question is how to select the best VPN solution.

There are numerous software, hardware, and carrier-based VPN products and services available today, and all of them employ various authentication, encryption, and authorization techniques to deliver the required security. How those three criteria are tied together determine the merits of how secure the VPN approach is. A well-architected VPN will scale well, provide tiered access, and interoperate with multiple security technologies. One fundamental aspect of a VPN architecture is the OSI (Open Systems Interconnect, an international standards body) layer at which the VPN operates.

The core security technologies being deployed today include: IPSec, PPTP, L2TP, and SOCKS v5. Each technology roughly maps to a different layer of the OSI networking model, bolstering its respective layer's strengths and weaknesses. In general, higher-layer solutions, as defined by the OSI model, provide greater security and access control because they have access to more information about the applications running above them than do the lower-layer solutions. A simplistic rule of thumb is that security increases moving up the hierarchy, and performance improves moving downward. Most VPN vendors have introduced products that straddle the line between security and speed, offering different trade-offs for different deployments.

IPSec, which is strongly supported by the router and VPN hardware vendors, is expected to be an integral component of IPv6, becoming the default standard for securing IP traffic and facilitating interoperability among routers and other internetworking devices. It does not require a client piece of software unless security needs to be extended to the desktop, so it provides appealing solutions for companies that want to extend their WAN to remote offices and subsidiaries. It is well suited for creating IP-based LAN-to-LAN VPNs, which are used most often in situations where both sides trust each other, like a brokerage firm and its branch offices.

Point-to-Point Tunneling Protocol, or PPTP, was initiated by Microsoft and is often talked of in the same breath as its future offspring, L2TP, which is a combination of PPTP and Cisco's Layer Two Forwarding, or L2F, protocol. Both protocols can support multiple, simultaneous tunnels for a single client, and both offer the unique capability of supporting non-IP traffic like IPX and Appletalk. The greatest benefits of PPTP and L2TP are their cost and availability. They are ready-made to work with any Microsoft-centric environment and virtually free because they are embedded into Windows operating systems. PPTP is available on Windows NT 4.0, Windows 95, and above operating systems. L2TP is expected to ship with the release of Windows NT 5.0. Because of client-side ubiquity, analysts predict that PPTP and L2TP will play a dominant role in the Internet-based remote access market, as long as limited encryption and authentication are sufficient. Financial services companies could use this method to provide independent brokers with timely information, as long as it does not have to be tightly secured.

SOCKS v5 is a session-layer standard that can stand alone or run on top of the other protocols, adding access control and circuit-level proxying capabilities to strengthen security. It was originally championed through the IETF by NEC Systems Laboratory as a standard protocol for authenticated firewall traversal, but is effectively used in a VPN context where security is a priority. Unlike the tunneling protocols, SOCKS v5 uses a directed architecture, which essentially protects resources by proxying traffic between source and destination computers. It also hides the address structure of the network, making it more difficult for confidential data to be cracked. Analysts expect that because of its firewall traversal capability, flexibility, and added security, it will be adopted by companies that need to provide highly secure, client-to-server connectivity for building supply-chain or partner extranets. This scenario most appropriately addresses the financial services industry.

The VPN protocols will continue to be refined and standardized, resulting in greater interoperability among products and improved communication between companies and their clients. Currently, the best way to securely share data across an intranet, the Internet, or an extranet is to combine solutions that offer the best of different network layers into one security framework. For the financial services industry, that framework should be built around a directed architecture, which is the opposite of an encrypted tunnel that establishes a bidirectional communications link. In many cases, financial companies do not want to assume two-way trust because bidirectional connections can be exploited, putting both the visitor and the host network at risk. For example, a credit card company hosting a VPN may be connected to numerous companies at once, some of whom may be in competition. It is in the interest of the visitors and the host network to avoid scenarios that allow one company to connect to the host and then exploit a connection from the host network out to a competitor — essentially to use the VPN as a "hacker's bridge." This can be avoided by implementing a VPN that supports only unidirectional connections, which is only possible with the higher layer, client-server solutions like SOCKS v5.

LOOKING AHEAD

As financial companies enable users to work remotely and share information globally, VPNs will provide cost-effective, ironclad network security. Financial companies can gain an immediate competitive advantage by using the Internet in a seamless and secure fashion for activities such as loan syndication and providing clients with account information and stock performance reports. By adding VPN security to an extranet, companies can easily define which network resources are available to end users. VPN solutions that will survive the market's rapid changes will be built on open standards and a modular-directed architecture that can easily incorporate the latest authentication and encryption standards.

In short, a top-of-the-line VPN should be highly secure, easy-to-use and administer, affordable, and flexible enough to work with multiple operating systems, protocols, and future security markets. If the VPN being evaluated can pass this checklist, then the Internet can be used as a revolutionary communications medium for financial brokers, lenders, representatives of credit card companies, and other professionals from anywhere in the world.

Chapter 19 Designing a High-Performance, High-Availability Network Infrastructure

Chris Marino

AS THE FINANCE INDUSTRY EXPANDS its deployment of open systems and embraces intranet/Internet-based computing, IS teams and network managers face an increasing challenge in ensuring that their company's vital information is readily and constantly available. Beginning in the 1980s through mid-1990s, enterprises have been moving from "legacy" mainframe, SNA, and similar applications to what we'll refer to as "traditional" client-server applications, in order to improve productivity, reduce administrative costs, and provide wider access to corporate data. Today, the latest network and application designs are based on a tiered server deployment which makes use of:

- Database and application servers in the back office.
- HTTP and other open systems which act as middleware to serve data to open, standards-based clients.
- End-user client applications (Exhibit 1).

These designs bring new customers directly to Web-based storefronts, more easily disseminate corporate information to employees, increase site performance, and reduce application development costs by adopting open, industry standards. In ensuring constant data accessibility and availability in this new model, the network administrator and CTO must be concerned with more than simple bandwidth allocation.

0-8493-9991-2/99/$0.00+$.50

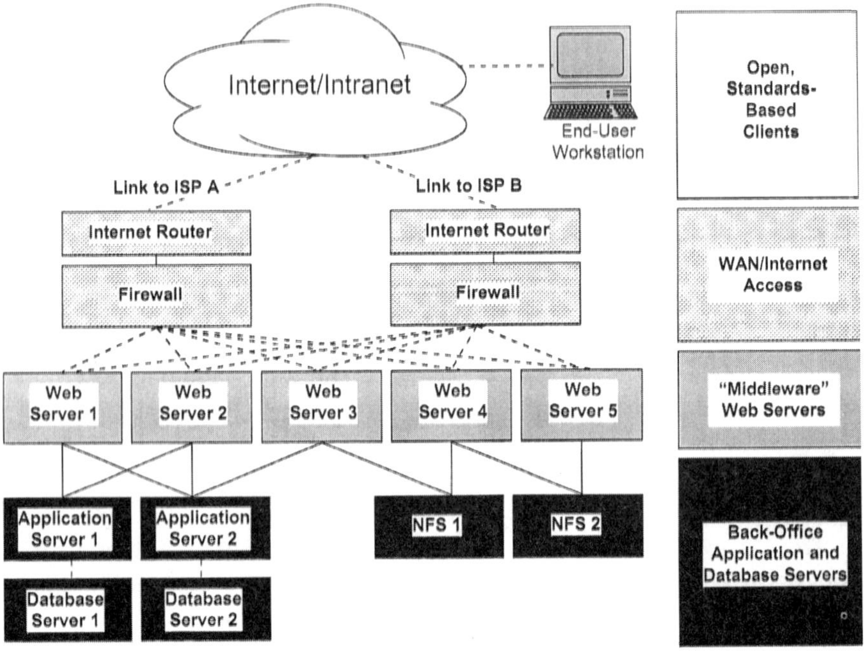

Exhibit 1. Areas of focus in evaluating traditional network performance.

While bandwidth is still a metric to be monitored, the more pertinent performance metrics for today's networks are application throughput and application response times.

WAN AND ISP CONSIDERATIONS: SERVICE LEVEL AGREEMENTS AND POLICY-BASED NETWORKS

In the tiered network model, each layer can be analyzed from a performance and reliability perspective. The first level to evaluate is the top level identified in Exhibit 1. This level provides access to and from the corporate infrastructure to the Internet or intranet. Considerations at this level involve evaluating Internet Service Provider (ISP) offerings, consideration for multiple points of presence (POPs), and evaluation of hardware solutions. As with all layers, fault tolerance is designed in by eliminating all single points of failure — this applies to Internet, as well as WAN connectivity. The network designer should strongly consider a minimum of two POPs for externally accessible data, as well as multiple access points to the Internet provided via multiple ISPs.

There have been a number of instances where an entire POP goes down due to fire, power outage, user error, or a natural disaster. Existence of a second POP in an alternate location provides enhanced system reliability, and when tied to a traffic management solution, offers the ability to load balance between POPs.

And while it is rare for a service provider to go down system-wide, the reality is that these events do happen. In addition to maintaining redundant links to the Internet via multiple POPs, the network administrator or CTO may wish to consider using multiple ISPs. If a single ISP has a major system outage and cannot route traffic to the Internet, the second POP from the alternate ISP can maintain site availability, allowing network transactions to continue as normal.

ISPs also offer various service levels to address the needs of business customers. Varying service levels can give priority to network traffic for critical applications. To accommodate service-level traffic prioritization, network equipment providers are building more intelligence into their hardware. This intelligence allows individual network components (routers, switches, etc.) to establish and enforce network policies that support the desired service levels. Service levels can be established when the network administrator classifies user groups and priorities, monitors traffic flow, changes traffic patterns to meet response requirements, and prioritizes packets (high priorities for packets involving designated users, video, and other real-time applications; low priorities for e-mail and nonurgent requests).

Establishing guaranteed service levels typically require homogeneous networks comprised of intelligent network devices from a particular vendor. These homogeneous networks, however, are often not suited or capable of optimizing application performance over the heterogeneous networks that make up today's wide-area networks and the Internet.

The answer to the problem of application performance optimization lies beyond intelligent hardware, and centers instead on building intelligence into and throughout the network. Ideally, for thorough optimization, an enterprise-wide, network traffic management solution spans all layers of the network. The solution must not be limited to just the network devices (since these approaches cannot adequately monitor application-level activity) or the application level (where it becomes impractical to incorporate intelligence about the lower levels). Independent of lower-level products and topologies, high-level traffic management tools optimize information flow and the performance of client-server applications by overseeing the entire infrastructure and intelligently allocating each request to the most appropriate resource.

Such a solution can cross over department lines to effectively manage all parts of the infrastructure, and to deliver enterprise-level performance benefits. By monitoring and adjusting overall traffic and application activity, a high-level traffic management solution optimizes corporate productivity. Reliability and high availability of corporate data services and other resources can be maximized by a traffic management solution that monitors the status of individual servers, services, or even points of presence, and reroutes to avoid any trouble spots. The solution must also scale, spanning LANs, WANs, and the Internet to keep pace with corporate growth.

HARDWARE AND APPLICATION-SPECIFIC SOLUTIONS

Today, routers (Layer 3 products) can look at packet information and provide network managers with real-time behavior information needed to enforce policy-based networks and support multiple service levels. Cisco and 3Com have extensive lines of switches, routers, and other network devices which offer various aspects of policy-based networking. Over-provisioning network bandwidth and bandwidth conservation techniques are positioned as methods for managing increasing traffic. However, since the network vendors are building in intelligence at only the device level, their policy-based solutions can not take an enterprise-wide view or include any significant intelligence for evaluating application activity; they strictly focus on packet traffic.

Some router (Layer 3 devices) manufacturers are incorporating Layer 4 functionality into intelligent routers. While this may seem advantageous, this creates a significant problem in secure environments — typical in many financial businesses. In these environments Layer 4 information maybe encrypted (IPSEC), and if routers incorporate Layer 4 functions, the protection offered by encryption is lost at every router in the network. This behavior severely compromises security and sensitive data cannot be adequately protected.

An alternative to hardware intelligence is application-specific embedded intelligence. This short-term bandaid forces application developers to become networking experts and results in less than optimal traffic management solutions. As with hardware-specific solutions, application-specific optimization cannot optimize traffic from end to end. If a POP, router, or Web server goes down, or is overburdened, application-specific optimization cannot redirect traffic, and cannot ensure that data reaches the end user. Neither network devices nor applications can communicate effectively among levels to analyze information from all three tiers and appropriately adjust all network parameters. Standard network equipment may keep traffic flowing, but it does not necessarily direct traffic to the optimal resource or server for the fastest and most reliable access.

Likewise, applications with embedded networking intelligence fail to offer an acceptable solution. Applications-based packages do not adequately consider the traffic within the entire intranet/Internet infrastructure and are not inherently compatible/testable across mixed-vendor environments.

A BETTER SOLUTION

A network design based on multitiered traffic management offers the ideal solution (Exhibit 2) for building a high-performance Internet and intranet infrastructure. A sophisticated software-based solution can deliver traffic prioritization, load-balancing, and service-level availability, ensuring optimized end-to-end performance on a high-availability network.

Stated most simply, these software solutions optimize, coordinate, and manage TCP traffic across all three levels — WAN, server, and application. The software intelligently performs in heterogeneous environments and will accommodate the inevitable change to and growth of the infrastructure.

Solutions in this space are dominated by companies whose sole focus is on providing these capabilities. When evaluating software traffic management solutions, consider the following criteria:

WAN-based scheduling — This product or module should direct requests to the POP that offers the best performance at that time for the end user initiating the request. For optimal performance, the WAN scheduler should service requests based on at least three metrics: current client-server latencies, real-time server load, and server availability. A robust WAN scheduler lets network administrators and ISPs easily establish traffic policies and priorities, as well as guarantee high availability and high performance to users on the distributed network.

Server-level scheduling — This component of the traffic management solution lets IT organizations deploy multiserver environments that are highly responsive to client requests. Each site should appear to users as a single virtual site, even though its servers may actually be distributed across subnets and firewalls. Software-based server-level scheduling optimizes the use of server resources to respond to TCP requests. More than a

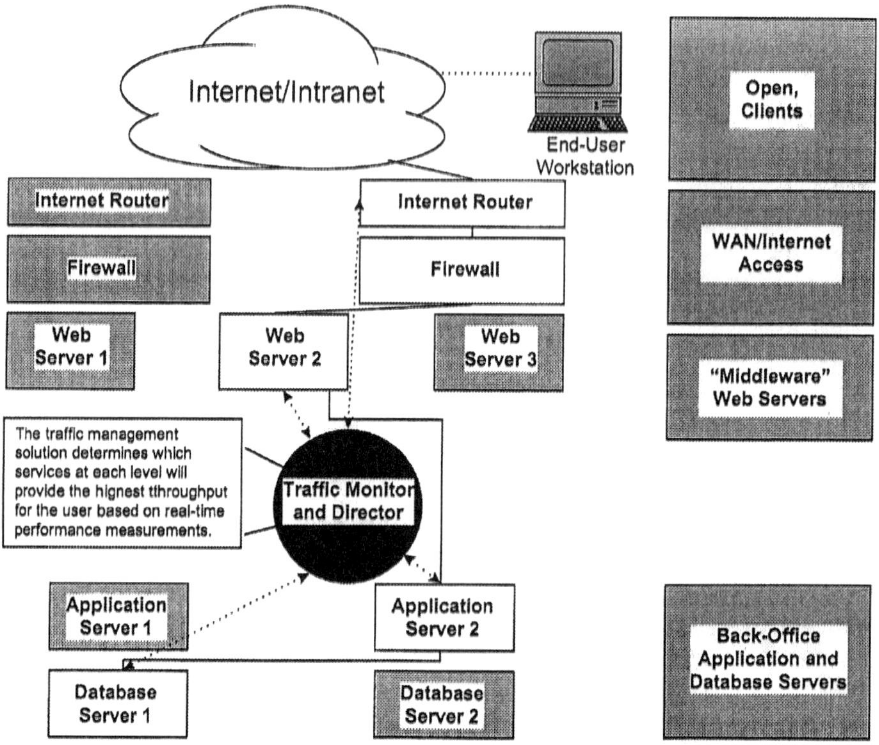

Exhibit 2. Network-wide traffic management solution.

simple load-balancing product, this software should provide immunity to server failure by detecting problems and redirecting traffic, without requiring dedicated hardware that would introduce a new point of failure.

Application server scheduling — Application servers deliver critical user programs such as database and other business management services. An intelligent application dispatcher can coordinate server resources to respond as efficiently as possible to client requests for applications. As with other scheduling components, the application dispatcher should be transparent to users. It should support uninterrupted service, giving priority requests the highest attention. To manage resources for the wide variety of individual application programs used throughout an enterprise, this scheduler should support all industry-standard application interfaces.

Although some vendors offer one or two of these functions, the optimal software solution integrates all three levels, providing the highest infrastructure performance possible while requiring the least amount of intervention from the IT staff. Real-time feedback from network resource monitoring should provide the basis for dynamic traffic allocation and policy updates that will help keep critical business operations running smoothly.

Exhibit 2 illustrates how a total traffic management solution can operate. By analyzing directly or in conjunction with server-based agents the traffic "director" determines application throughput end-to-end from the user's workstation to a database or application server and back. Based on measurable criteria including response time, CPU utilization, server availability, WAN/Internet latency, and other specified rules or policies, the director (with backup director) can ensure that data are available in the shortest time. A traditional implementation simply accounting for device "hop count" does not consider application server attributes (CPU utilization, open sessions, or server load) or rapidly changing WAN attributes (latency, response times, and POP availability).

Additionally, all software components should blend as seamlessly as possible into the existing environment. For example, traffic scheduling services should be running from any location on the network. As the network changes or grows, the software should easily scale to accommodate the changes, without requiring complex modifications or installations. A Java-based management GUI can simplify operation and reduces the requirements for special IT training.

A powerful multitiered software networking solution benefits everyone accessing data on the corporate infrastructure. The right architecture also helps IT administrators, Web masters, and CIOs tasked with creating and managing the network. Not to be overlooked, the software-based solution enables more efficient allocation of hardware assets. Rather than over-allocating hardware to ensure availability and data redundancy, IT organizations can distribute hardware in the manner best suited to the usage patterns of users.

SUMMARY

Careful consideration of the issues presented will help you design the right long-term solution and avoid some costly short-lived investments. The following four basic steps will keep you heading in the right direction:

1. Deploy or upgrade network segments and backbones to the highest-speed technologies appropriate.
2. Incorporate redundant systems at every level in the network, including Internet/WAN access, "middleware" web servers, and back-

office database, file, and application servers. A single point of failure at any one level of the network obviates the benefits established by redundant systems at every other level in the network.

3. Select hardware products with embedded intelligence, which can accommodate policy-based service-level networking and work in homogeneous (mixed-vendor) environments.
4. Incorporate traffic management solutions into your infrastructure, choosing those that support the features discussed in this chapter — features that will ensure long-term solutions in a dynamic, heterogeneous environment.

By designing a network which includes the latest in traffic management solutions, the CIO and MIS department will ensure users will always have rapid access to corporate data resources, while minimizing investment in additional infrastructure purchases.

Chapter 20
Applications of GIS Technology in Financial Services

Donald F. Cooke

MANY YEARS AGO, when asked why he robbed banks, Willy Sutton replied, "Because that's where the money is." Bankers and other financial services managers who deal with consumers also need to know where the money is. Do you know who your most profitable customers are? Do you know where they live? Can you locate other people like them? While you know where your branches and ATMs are, do you know where your biggest competitive threat is? How many of your customers live nearer to a competitor than one of your branches? What is the most promising location for a new ATM or branch?

GIS — the science of where — is the key to answering these questions. GIS (Geographic Information Systems) is a technology that allows computers to deal with location: where your customers are, where the competition is, and where the best prospects are located. This chapter describes how GIS works and how it can help you improve profitability and productivity.

GIS

Geographic information, which has been stored on paper maps for centuries, can be encoded and processed in computers. Since the mid-1960s GIS technology has developed from a government research tool to a maturing discipline which can have a direct, positive effect on the operations and profitability of financial institutions.

GIS works because computers can now analyze maps — stored as databases — as easily as they can compute a payroll. What makes GIS work for businesses is a detailed nationwide computer map database called TIGER, which is maintained and distributed by the Census Bureau along with census data. TIGER provides the computer with the same locational knowledge as is shown on a very detailed street map. TIGER and GIS allow the

0-8493-9991-2/99/$0.00+$.50

computer to pinpoint each bank account and calculate market penetration and driving distance from each account to any bank facility.

Two decades ago, GIS was an exotic discipline reserved for hardy pioneers with big budgets for computer time and expensive plotters to display maps. Nevertheless, by the late 1970s, hundreds of large banks measured branch performance, market penetration, and customer demographics using rudimentary GIS techniques, even if the analysis only took the form of counting customers and products sold by Census Tract.

In the 1980s government regulators effectively mandated GIS use through CRA and HMDA reporting compliance requirements. CRA and HMDA reports are actually GIS applications: locating and summarizing various types of bank product use by census tract areas.

Nowadays, a $799 computer from Staples provides more power than the leading innovators had available 20 years ago. Since GIS technology can consume a lot of computing resources, the advent of powerful and inexpensive personal computers is a welcome development.

But you need more than a powerful computer to benefit from GIS. A computer doesn't do anything but consume electricity if you don't have useful software to run on it. Though you can buy wonderful GIS software packages capable of unlocking strategically useful information from operational data, it takes an experienced, technically oriented specialist to operate most of this software.

This is the state of adoption of GIS technology as the 1990s draws to a close; plenty of computing power, plenty of GIS software, lots of opportunity for benefit, but because of technical complexity, only a glimmer of true usability of GIS technology by banks. However, changes in the GIS industry will shortly make GIS an inexpensive and rewarding technology for even very small community banks.

SITUATION

Banks today operate in an environment of unprecedented threats and opportunities. Big banks can take advantage of economies of scale and expand their influence with strategic acquisitions. Small banks can use their knowledge of the community they serve, either to compete effectively against their larger competitors or to preen and position themselves for acquisition.

All banks need strategic information to operate effectively. Knowledge of many aspects of a bank's operations is essential for survival. Each bank's CEO or marketing officer should be constantly asking: Are my products priced right? Who are my most valuable customers? Where do they live? What are we doing to retain them? Can we upgrade our middle tier of customers and make them more profitable? Can we change product offerings or pricing to reduce the liability of lower-tier customers? Are our branches strategically sited relative to where our customers live and work and drive? Where should we open the next branch or ATM? Many of these questions can be answered by GIS technology.

Applying GIS technology to banking is a bit like cooking a meal: you need the right mix of ingredients and processes. The main ingredient of GIS analysis is the bank's own data. In fact, much of the value of GIS technology lies in revealing patterns of profit and opportunity from operational data. GIS works by processing routine operational data in ways that will reveal a bank's profit patterns.

The second key ingredient is the computerized street map of your area. This is essential for the "geocoding" process, for calculating driving access to banking facilities, and to permit visualization of geographic relationships in map form. While some business GIS users find the public-domain TIGER street maps sufficient, most use a privately maintained one like Dynamap/2000 from Geographic Data Technology, Lebanon, NH. Having a current and complete digital street map is especially important for processing bank customers who live on relatively new streets.

The other essential ingredients are commercially available data about households, businesses, and banking facilities:

- Household data, for example, R.L. Polk's TotaList file, are compiled from many sources such as vehicle and product warrantee registrations. TotaList serves dual purposes as a source of household prospects and the key to obtaining a demographic profile of your customers. While it's customary to profile customers by geographic areas like tracts and block-groups, it's clearly worthwhile to discriminate between the 300-odd households in a block-group by using the power of a household-level database like TotaList
- Business files, from Dun & Bradstreet (D&B) or American Business Information (ABI) provide commercial prospects and profiling information for commercial accounts. Finally, bank information, available from Thompson or Sheshunoff, is the key to analyzing competition.

THE PROCESSES

Several key processes cook these data ingredients into a nutritious strategic marketing meal.

The most important process is a well-calibrated profitability model. Good models go far beyond "Fed Functional Costs," and use all aspects of fee and interest income in balance with cost of funds and transactions of various types. It may be a surprise that the pricing model does not have to balance with the General Ledger to be useful. It is essential to be able to rank accounts from most to least profitable, based on accurate calculations.

The next essential process is householding. Householding allows the computer to pull together various different accounts for each household, based on similarities of name and address along with other clues such as social security number and telephone number. Householding allows the computer to consider all accounts owned by a household and calculate an aggregate profitability ranking at the household level.

The same householding process also matches customer households to TotaList households. This provides two benefits: customer profiling by appending TotaList's household-level demographic and lifestyle codes to customers, and identifying and tagging Totalist households which are already the bank's customers. This step automatically "merge-purges" the prospect file so you can prospect for new households excluding existing customers.

The GIS process is "geocoding," where each customer and prospect address is matched to the proper spot on the digital street map. Each address receives a unique latitude/longitude coordinate value which locks it into its place on the face of the earth. Geocoding is the foundation of GIS technology. Once all addresses have been geocoded, the power of GIS technology can be unleashed.

Finally come the GIS and analytical processes. GIS technology can show you graphically where profits are coming from and where you're losing money. GIS can define the areas of influence of your branches and those of your competitors. GIS can identify territorial advantages and weaknesses, suggesting opportunities to site new facilities or pointing out where your own branches are competing with each other. Best of all, GIS can identify areas where potentially profitable households are clustered so your marketing efforts can lure new accounts to your bank.

ACTION OR ANALYSIS?

Too often, banks and consultants use GIS technology just for analysis. While it is useful to find out about a bank through the window of GIS, if that's all that is done, the GIS becomes simply a cost burden. The analysis must lead to action if the bank is to improve its operations.

All productive use of GIS must begin with an understanding of the actions a bank can take to make changes in operations. GIS can support a wide array of decisions and actions: opening and closing branches, siting new ATMs, targeting a direct mail campaign, evaluating merger and acquisition opportunities, and selecting new prospects near a branch or in neighborhoods with high profit potential.

A banker who considers these actions in full knowledge of product profitability, cross-sell opportunity, competitive strengths and weaknesses, and other strategic factors, will outperform a banker who operates by the seat of his pants. The key is knowledgeable action, where the spatial dimension is understood and considered. Business reengineering may be necessary and it may take months to create a sales culture, but without strategic marketing knowledge, actions may just be random or futile.

Bankers should not underestimate the cost, complexity, and risks of plunging into GIS. While a fair amount of data, software, and computer power must be acquired, the main cost of a GIS operation will be staff time. Unfortunately, GIS competence is a scarce resource, and banks may have trouble recruiting or growing GIS personnel, or — worse — they may find that staff turnover gets hard to manage as GIS specialists "graduate" to higher paying jobs at other organizations.

GIS is not just another systems area that a typical IT department can acquire and master, though support of a GIS effort by IT will be essential to its success. GIS remains largely a strategic marketing function and the expertise and technology should reside there. Because of its technical nature and the day-to-day demands of running a small bank, until recently GIS has been used mainly by the largest banks, with occasional application in smaller banks through the efforts of consultants.

Everybody has seen computerized maps in various forms, from animated weather maps on TV to PC-based street maps and trip planners such as Expedia Streets '98 from Microsoft or StreetFinder from Rand-McNally. Why shouldn't GIS technology be as accessible to bankers as these mapping products are to consumers?

Geographic Information Systems is a technology that is emerging from the early adopters and is inching its way into mainstream conservative markets. Given the pressure on financial institutions of all sizes, GIS analysis leading to strategic action is likely to become a staple of bank operations in the next decade.

Chapter 21
Designing and Implementing a Virus Prevention Policy in Financial Services Organizations: Key Issues and Critical Needs

Pat Bitton

COMPUTER MANAGERS IN FINANCIAL SERVICES COMPANIES realize that computer viruses are a major threat to information security. Many have found that virus infection can be costly in time, resources, and productivity. But all too many do not know what to do about the threat of viruses. Before developing a company policy that addresses their security concerns, many computer managers want to know what questions they should be asking as well as what issues they should address.

This chapter provides a step-by-step process for developing corporate anti-virus policies by highlighting virus entry points in a company network, identifying key issues, and listing tasks. Products, people, and procedures are discussed, with an eye toward protecting companies from viruses transmitted via electronic file exchange — by far the most common method of virus distribution today. Using this chapter as a guide, computer managers in the financial services industry can tailor an anti-virus policy to their company's specific needs.

0-8493-9991-2/99/$0.00+$.50

BACKGROUND

Computer viruses are a major threat to information security in all companies, but are of special concern to financial services companies. In fact, many large financial services companies based in the U.S. are currently investing heavily in reliable and secure electronic commerce and home banking applications all over the globe.

As viruses become more prevalent, the threat becomes more real, with somewhere between 8000 and 20,000 viruses existing in the world today. According to a survey released in April 1997 by the International Computer Security Association (ICSA), formerly the National Computer Security Association, almost every medium- and large-size organization in North America has experienced at least one computer virus infection firsthand. The survey also indicated that about 40% of all computers used in the surveyed companies would experience another virus infection within a year.[1]

Computer viruses (any program or code that replicates itself) are insidious. Without virus detection or protection, users typically do not know their systems are being infected until they see results that can range from annoying to catastrophic. And virus infection is on the rise. Despite a significant increase in the usage of anti-virus products, the incidence of computer virus infection in corporate America nearly tripled in 1996.[1]

Although several factors are behind the rise in computer virus infection, the main one is the meteoric rise in popularity and use of the Internet in business. The Internet can be thought of as an information highway — an evolving global electronic mode of communicating, providing information, and obtaining information. Two important ways of enabling this communication are e-mail for exchanging mail, and the file transfer protocol (FTP) for exchanging files. Growing at a staggering rate, the Internet is an unprecedented link between more people in more countries than ever before.

But along with these Internet capabilities comes a major problem. As the Internet becomes more popular as an e-mail and file transfer medium, users are at a growing risk from the many viruses that can be spread via e-mail attachments and FTP downloading/uploading. The ICSA survey reports that e-mail attachments as a source of infection tripled from 1996 to 1997 — from 9% of all infection sources to over 26% of infections. At the same time, virus infection via downloading of files from the Internet increased from 10% of all infections to 16%.[1]

To make matters worse, a relatively new class of viruses, called macro viruses, are now taking advantage of widespread Internet usage to spread like wildfire. In fact, these viruses are spreading faster than most anti-virus software makers can find ways to detect and remove them. Macro viruses are now the most prevalent form of computer virus in the world, representing 80% of all infections in North America in 1997, compared to 49% a year ago.[1]

This prevalence is largely due to the new way in which they spread. Because they are written in Microsoft® Visual BASIC, they can insert themselves into the macros used in word processor and spreadsheet documents, which often are transmitted as e-mail attachments. And now, a new type of malicious code, carried by ActiveX and Java controls that spice up web pages, poses the potential for PC damage simply by users browsing the web.

Before widespread Internet popularity, viruses spread slowly from one part of the world to another. For example, the Michelangelo virus that appeared in Asia in 1991 did not appear prominently in Europe until 1992 and the U.S. 1 year later. Today, viruses migrate much faster than this rate of one continent per year. The Concept macro virus that became prominent in the U.S. in August 1995 appeared in Asia only 2 months later. On the Internet, an e-mail attachment alone can transmit a virus from one country to another in less than a minute, and the number of files now transmitted through the Internet each year may number in the billions.

What this means is that if you do not have an anti-virus security policy, you need one, because inaction can be costly. Depending on the size of the infection, a virus infection incident can cost between $2000 and $500,000 in data loss and loss of productivity.[2] One study showed that the average cost of recovering from a virus infection on a network is $15,000 and that 85% of those sites were reinfected within 30 days.[2] You can estimate the cost of an e-mail virus infection at your company using the attached Excel worksheet.[3]

PRODUCTS, PEOPLE, AND PROCEDURES

Certainly, products such as anti-virus software are needed to thwart computer viruses. But even product vendors agree that, while a valuable part of the puzzle, products alone do not solve problems. People do. And if people understand the need for virus protection and the benefits of that protection, they are more likely to take appropriate steps. Defining these specific operational steps, "procedures" completes the triad. Through procedures, people make best use of available products to achieve the goal of comprehensive virus protection.

Exhibit 1 illustrates the important distinction between procedures and overall corporate policy. Charles Cresson Wood, an independent information-security consultant, defines policy as "high level statements intended to provide guidance to those who make decisions ... typically including general statements of goals, objectives, beliefs, ethics, and responsibilities."[4] Conversely, Wood defines procedures as "specific operational steps

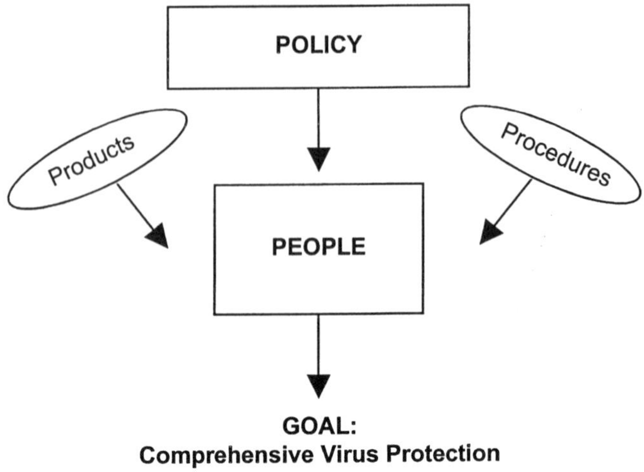

Exhibit 1. Products, people, and procedures are needed to thwart computer viruses.

that workers must take to achieve goals — goals which are often outlined in the policy."[4] Hence, any discussion of a corporate policy must also address procedures — the way the policy is to be implemented.

VIRUS ENTRYWAYS

The most effective way to ensure that your internal network remains virus-free is to monitor all entryways for viruses. While a detailed treatment of these entryways is beyond the scope of this chapter, Exhibit 2 illustrates virus entry points: through Internet gateways, groupware and intranet servers, LAN servers, and desktops.

THE HUMAN ELEMENT

The key players, and of course, the ultimate target, in an anti-virus policy are the users and managers inside the company. Understanding the attitudes of the company's staff towards information exchange and an awareness of the history of virus infection and corresponding action taken will go a long way towards enabling you to understand your organization's unique "corporate culture." And this understanding is critical to the ultimate development of a policy that is right for your company. Two companies with different corporate cultures are likely to develop different policies. And beyond policy development, these two companies may very well implement their policies in different ways.

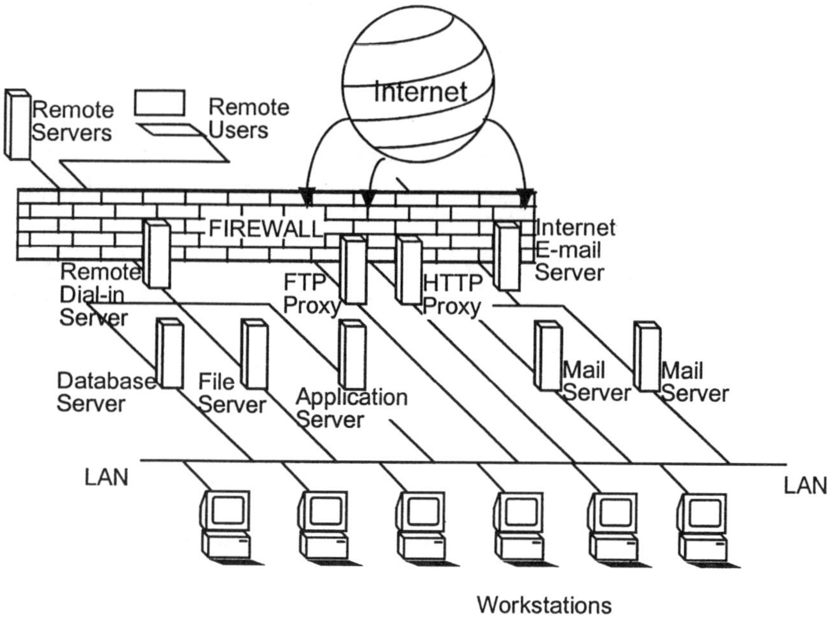

Exhibit 2. Virus entry points on a typical network.

Let's examine two very different company cultures and how their approaches to virus protection policies are closely linked to those cultures.

Company A, which grew quickly from a small banking firm to a medium-sized one, is quite open with its data and information. Few, if any, procedures have been established regarding information exchange, either between employees or with those outside the company. Moreover, resistance to formalized procedures is high, as the company fosters a relaxed working environment as an alternative to the typical office environment of its competitors.

So far, Company A has been lucky. Its only virus experience has been a couple of isolated run-ins with a relatively benign macro virus that was quickly eliminated from a floppy disk that had come in from an outside client. The employee had recently installed desktop anti-virus software that was able to detect the virus on the floppy before it could be copied to a hard disk. Both the employee and management reacted calmly to the virus detection, and no disciplinary action was regarded as necessary.

MIS professionals at Company A face the challenge of a workforce that is highly resistant to the kinds of procedures they view as necessary to reduce the virus threat. Employee motivation to act is low, since they have not experienced the stress and frustration of recovering from a major infection. Company A needs a campaign to promote awareness of the virus threat, reinforced by high-level corporate commitment for this endeavor. Orientations and training seminars for all employees on the virus threat and of measures to be taken to minimize it, both initially and later to remind them of the need for compliance, will go a long way toward elevating their knowledge and understanding.

Through this education process, Company A employees will learn that they can retain their relaxed working environment by taking a few simple precautions and following some procedures that require little time. Company A also needs a highly visible show of support by top management for efforts to minimize virus infection from the beginning of the policy adoption process. This can be done most easily by placing a management statement of support upfront on the anti-virus policy document.

In contrast, Company B is an established stock trading organization, with conservative employees. Company B's employees are accustomed to rules and regulations, and have come to value them for their assistance in minimizing problems. Most aspects of employee tasks are carefully organized to maximize productivity. The company has encountered macro viruses several times, without resulting in any major loss of productivity. But recently, Company B was infected by a virus received via an e-mail attachment from one of their customers that cost them considerable loss of productivity over several days. The employee who received the virus, but for whatever reason did not detect it, feared he would lose his job, and management was upset over the incident.

Company B requires less training on the need for an anti-virus policy, but more emphasis on how to implement such a policy. Less computer savvy than their counterparts in Company A, Company B employees need periodic training to learn how to combat the threat. They are already motivated to comply with procedures, given their virus encounters, and they would have no problem in adapting to the inclusion of one more set of procedures in their work environment.

PUTTING IT TOGETHER WITH PROCEDURES

While the approach taken in developing an anti-virus policy is likely to vary from company to company, some issues must be addressed in all cases — issues best addressed with a corporate policy that includes specific procedures. For example, procedures are needed for making best use of selected product and service solutions, such as how to install and set up software to take advantage of automatic configuration and deployment, how to customize the level of protection appropriately for different types of users and, most importantly, how to ensure that regular updates are obtained and deployed to all the workstations. New viruses are appearing at a rate of 250 or more every month. Operating too long without virus pattern updates unnecessarily exposes your company to new viruses "in the wild" — particularly when product families like Trend Micro's can deliver these updates to fit your schedules, in the background without interrupting work, and use a single file to update both server and workstation-based protection.

But procedures go beyond product and service solutions. Procedures must address how new behaviors can be integrated into corporate culture to replace past practices that may have exposed the company to viruses. While centralized, server-based virus protection is important, it must be supplemented by commitment from the workforce to ensure a virus-free environment.

One way to encourage this distributed responsibility is to establish a virus response team. Similar to an emergency response team or other cross-disciplinary group in an organization, a virus response team can be assembled from many different departments, then trained and empowered to deal calmly, effectively, and professionally with any virus incident. One advantage of such a team is that when an incident does occur, specific people are already selected to immediately tackle cleanup. Of equal importance, providing team members with a specific identity and status sends a message to all employees that virus protection is important and that it involves more than "the guys in MIS." Another way to draw attention to an anti-virus policy after its adoption is to periodically review and revise it to reflect changing conditions. An annual review is usually sufficient and serves to reinforce an important issue that may not have been discussed for some time.

One particularly sensitive issue is dealing with policy noncompliance. The key is to foster an environment that encourages personal (and group) responsibility and that rewards honesty. Consider, for example, an employee who promptly reports the appearance of a virus on his or her machine, probably because of downloaded unauthorized software from the Web. If this is a first-time occurrence for this individual, a formal meeting to discuss and reinforce anti-virus policy and procedures is appropriate, but further disciplinary action would discourage prompt reporting of virus incidents, allowing viruses to potentially spread unchecked through an organization. Of course, repeat offenses would call for more stringent actions. The idea is that failure to comply with anti-virus policy and procedures should be treated in a manner consistent with violations of other company policies.

Using the two hypothetical companies described in the previous section, Company A employees who detect a virus would probably not suffer an overreaction from management to a virus detection. Dismissal would not be considered for a first-time offender. Promoting awareness of the potential magnitude of the virus threat would promote understanding of the seriousness of violating anti-virus policy.

Conversely, managers at Company B might consider dismissing an employee who violated an anti-virus policy and cost the company significant loss of productivity, even if it was a first offense. At this company, taking advantage of the situation to demonstrate to others that management encourages virus reporting would reinforce anti-virus procedures and have a more positive impact than dismissing the employee.

CONCLUSIONS

It is recommended that you address a series of issues before developing an anti-virus policy. These issues can be captured in the form of questions organized in three groups — corporate culture, anti-virus product/service status and use, and virus incident history. These questions encourage you to address issues specific to your company, enabling you to tailor an anti-virus policy to meet your company's unique needs and situation, and are shown below:

Corporate Culture

1. How would you characterize the openness of information exchange in your organization?
2. Are your employees open or resistant to formalized procedures?
3. Do any formalized procedures exist that regulate information exchange in your company? If so, to what extent do they explicitly address virus protection?
4. Has management made any mention of anti-virus policy or procedures in formal announcements to employees? Any mention of other security issues?
5. Do new employees sign an agreement that includes any mention of anti-virus policy? If so, what are employees' responsibilities?
6. Does your company have a virus response team? If so, what are their responsibilities? How widely is it represented across the company? Are team members given a different status in any way?

Product/Service Status and Use

1. What anti-virus products or services does your company currently employ?
2. What virus entryways are protected with anti-virus products or services? (Refer to Exhibit 2 for virus entryways.)
3. Are anti-virus software products periodically updated? If so, how often?

Virus History

1. Has your company experienced any virus incidents? If so, how many in the last year?
2. What type of impact did the infection(s) have on operations?
3. How widespread within the company was knowledge of the incident(s)?
4. How did the employee(s) who reported the incident(s) react? Did they downplay its importance or were they highly concerned?
5. How did management react to the incident(s)? Was any disciplinary action taken against the employee(s)?

The policy you develop must integrate anti-virus products/services, people, and procedures in a manner consistent with your corporate culture, mission, and goals. The resulting policy must be clear, concise, and consistent with other corporate policies. Several references contain suggested outlines of security policies, which can be used as a model for your anti-virus policy.[4-6]

Exhibit 3 lists the steps necessary to address issues prior to policy development: develop a policy, maximize the chances of its successful implementation, and periodically review and reinforce it. After policy development, review, revision, approval, and distribution, further steps might include developing an anti-virus procedure manual, assembling and empowering a virus response team, upgrading anti-virus product/service use, and beginning an employee awareness campaign.

Anti-Virus Policy Development and Adoption Tasks

1. Assess corporate culture.
2. Evaluate current anti-virus product/service use.
3. Review corporate virus history.
4. Draft policy.
5. Review and revise draft anti-virus policy.
6. Approve and distribute anti-virus policy.
7. Draft, review, revise, approve, and distribute anti-virus procedure manual.
8. Name members of virus response team.
9. Upgrade anti-virus product/service use.
10. Begin employee awareness campaign.
11. Periodically review and revise anti-virus policy.
12. Periodically reinforce importance of policy.

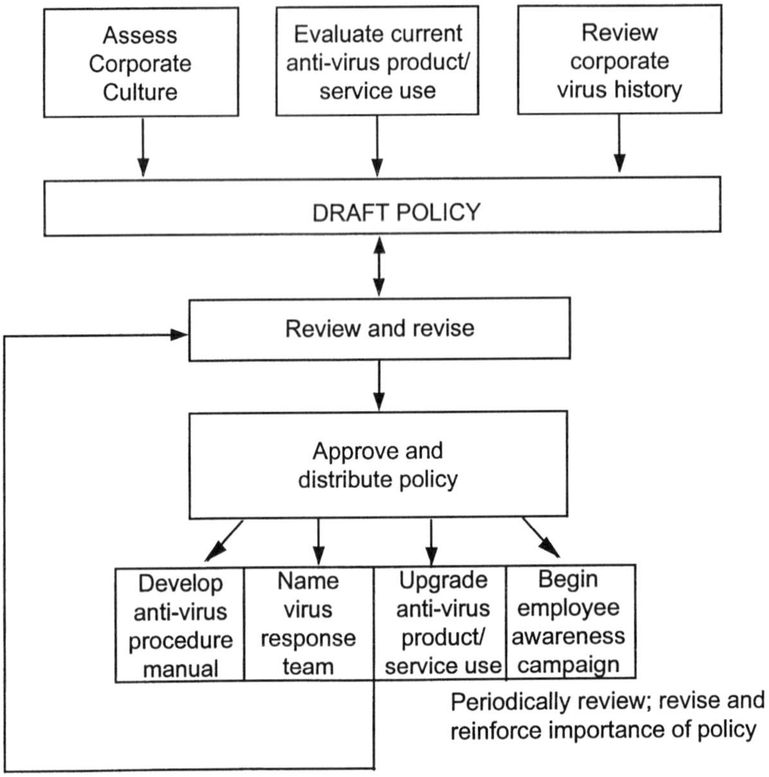

Exhibit 3. Effective virus prevention goes beyond anti-virus policy development.

Notes

1. ICSA(r) 1997, Computer Virus Prevalence Survey, International Computer Security Association, available at http://www.antivirus.com/corporate/white/index.htm.
2. Dataquest Survey, 1994.
3. Cost Analysis: Return on Investment, Trend Micro worksheet, www.antivirus.com/products/vcost.html.
4. Policies From the Ground Up, Charles Cresson Wood, *Infosecurity News,* March/April 1997, pp. 24–28.
5. Trend Micro Delivers the First Free On-line Virus Scanning Service, Trend Micro press release, May 7, 1997.
6. Policy Format and Structure, Gerald W. Grindler, *Infosecurity News,* March/April 1997, p. 29.

Chapter 22
Voice Over ATM

Gary Mangus

FOR ANY NATIONAL OR GLOBAL INDUSTRY dependent on quality and current communications, the push has begun to migrate to wide area networks (or WANs). The communication speed and delivery using legacy equipment is one of the keys to deploying any new network technology. Asynchronous Transfer Mode networking, or ATM, has been around about 5 years. It is gaining momentum in the present for its ability to handle large amounts of traffic and to really deliver the traffic. IP and frame relay networks have been the buzz of the communications industry, but these network protocols are revolutionary by design — there are no guarantees of service in quality of transmission or in delivery of the communication.

So the argument in new network technologies, like ATM, becomes more focused. Why migrate to a new type of network when it lessens the quality plus there are risks of losing transmitted communications? This argument becomes more heated when talking about "voice" traffic being transmitted over a data network. Most companies are accustomed to having the computer network go "down," but a voice network — no way!

This chapter will provide an overview of Voice over ATM and why this technology should be deployed today. The answer is not a technical one, but is strongly supported financially. ATM provides the quality of service like no other new network can. The financial community depends on networking much like the U.S. Government — it functions because of the information available. Financial institutions, whether a regional banking operation to a finance company or Wall Street brokerage house, have more remote sites to connect. The larger the operations center, the more likely multiple T1/E1(or even higher-speed) leased lines are involved. This chapter will discuss networks where ATM is already available for the data side of the network and the voice network has remained separate.

INTRODUCTION

If your campus or enterprise network already has an ATM network installed it may only be serving the data communications needs of your organization. Because ATM is equally adept at supporting video, voice, and data, the maximum utilization of your network can become a cost factor in

0-8493-9991-2/99/$0.00+$.50

today's communications decisions. Whether your ATM network is installed or simply under consideration, many vendors offer ATM network managers a unique opportunity to send voice over ATM while providing substantial savings on operational dollars through the reduction or elimination of leased lines dedicated to voice traffic.

One of the key ATM applications for an ATM switch or multiplexer is the consolidation of voice traffic over ATM by interconnecting multiple PBXs across an ATM network. To address this application, a business case is made in this chapter for using DS1/E1 Circuit Emulation — available in ATM switches as an additional module or in ATM access multiplexers, which allow for provisioning of other network interfaces.

TODAY'S ENVIRONMENT

Today's typical customer will have multiple site operations or multiple buildings on a campus. In many cases, data and voice requirements will be large enough to require more than one T1/E1 leased line between sites. These network sites can be categorized into two broad groups.

The first organization has islands of ATM networks in place for its data needs. To connect these ATM islands, it may have an ATM WAN or it may be using one or more leased lines (T1/E1 or greater) for the interconnectivity across the WAN. It may also be using additional T1/E1 leased lines for interconnecting PBXs between its sites. In other words, multiple networks may already be in place to support different services. Exhibit 1 is a representative example configuration.

The second organization has no ATM networks installed, but has multiple T1/E1 leased lines in place between sites to support its voice and data traffic. Exhibit 2 is a representative example configuration. Both organizations can be better served with a voice consolidation solution, provided there is a need for multiple site interconnection.

PBX ENVIRONMENTAL DESCRIPTION

To provide a solution for voice consolidation over ATM, the Circuit Emulation (or CE) module will interface to a PBX. A PBX, which is a small telephone switch, will have analog (or digital) connections to individual telephone handsets within a facility. These handsets are connected to the public telephone network through the PBX, via a digital trunk which is typically at the T1/E1 rate of 1.544 Mbps or E1 rate at 2.048 Mbps. Depending upon the size of the PBX and the number of calls to be supported simultaneously by the PBX, multiple T1/E1 trunks may be used to connect the PBX to the public telephone network. Exhibit 3 illustrates a PBX environment with one T1/E1 trunk attached to the public telephone network. If your organization has multiple sites, refer to the telephone network in Exhibit 4.

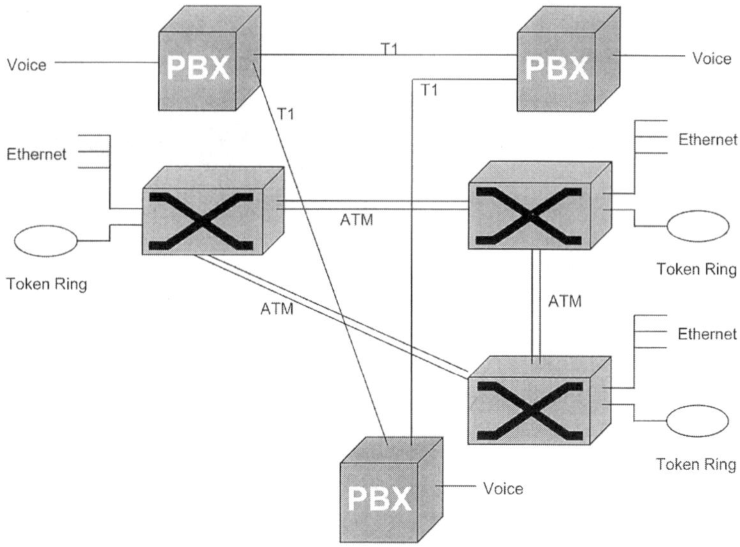

Exhibit 1. Multiple ATM networks.

The ATM CE Module makes practical the transport over ATM of a class of services called Constant-Bit-Rate (CBR). CBR sources are characterized as devices which generate traffic at a constant or nonvarying rate. A typical device which requires CBR service is a PBX. Exhibit 4 illustrates the telephone network in an organization with multiple sites.

Other types of communications equipment which require CBR service, and therefore can benefit in the same way with ATM, are T1/E1 multiplexers and channel banks.

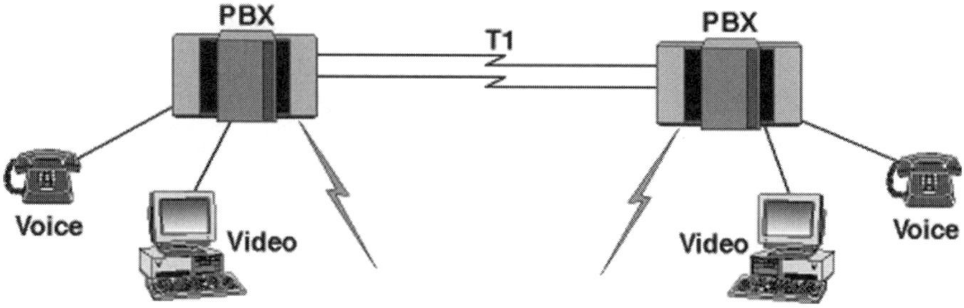

Exhibit 2. No ATM networks, multiple T1/E1 leased lines.

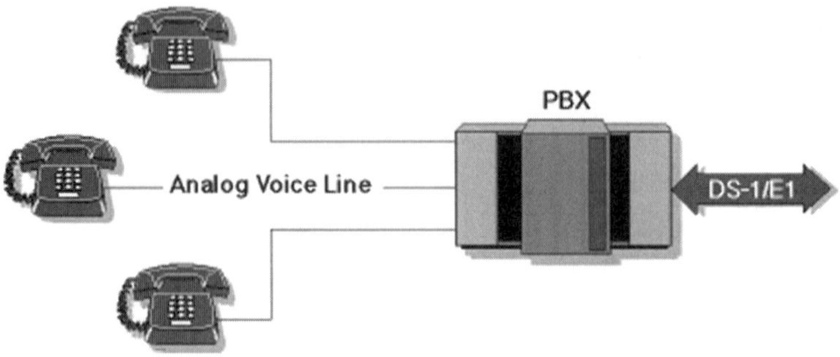

Exhibit 3. PBX environment with one T1/E1 trunk.

BUSINESS CASE ANALYSIS

Exactly how much can you save by consolidating your leased lines? If you already have or are planning to use ATM for data communications, then you may save all of the costs that are now being spent on leased lines for voice. In this case, the cost for deploying ATM is already absorbed in the data communications infrastructure. By adding PBX transport for voice to your data-only network, you can further enhance the justification for the ATM network because the costs for the T1/E1 leased lines for handling the PBX traffic are eliminated. Even if you don't have an ATM network installed for data, the time is right to consider ATM for interconnecting PBXs. Voice over ATM is a solid financial business decision.

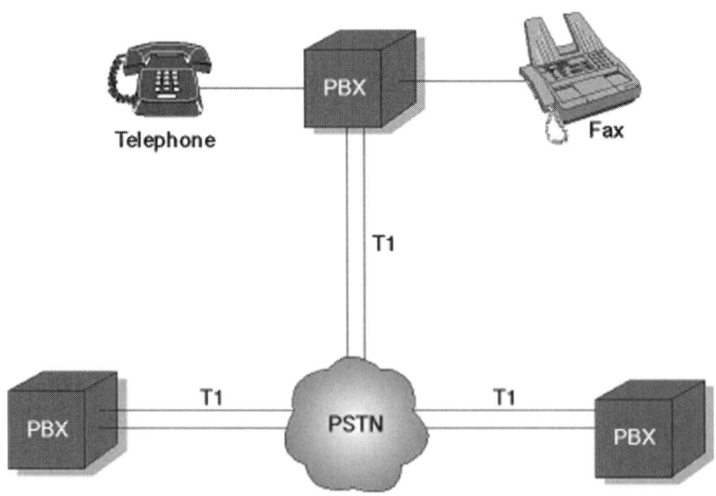

Exhibit 4. PBX network with multiple sites.

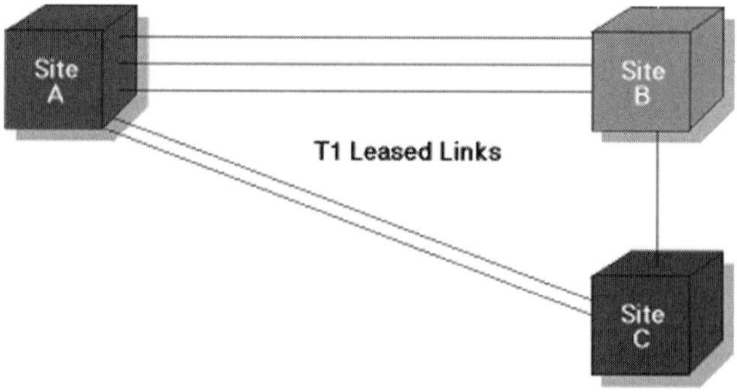

Exhibit 5. Three-node leased line network.

Local service providers charge variable ATM service rates depending upon your region of the country. The financial advantage of moving to a consolidated system is based upon the difference between your current costs for existing T1/E1 leased lines and ATM implementation costs. This difference reflects your monthly operational savings achieved when you deploy an ATM network.

A simple three-node system may help to illustrate the comparative process. The example below represents a case where you may wish to eliminate costly leased lines being used for voice traffic and replace them with an ATM network. The current leased line network may look like the example in Exhibit 5.

Exhibit 6 demonstrates how the three-node network of Exhibit 5 may be connected over an ATM infrastructure that requires only one ATM drop per site.

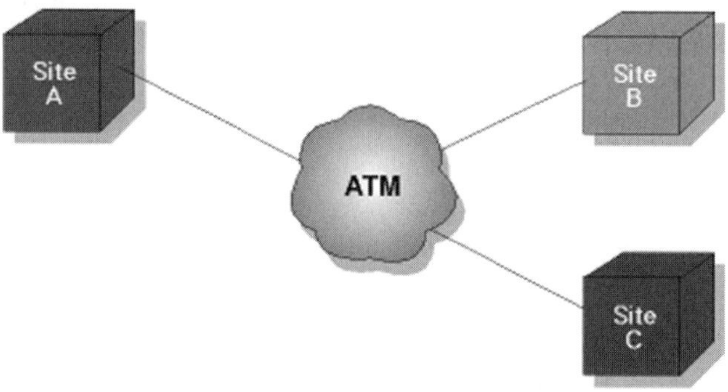

Exhibit 6. One ATM drop/site network.

Exhibit 7. Cost of an ATM Line

Site Connection	# of T1/E1 Lines Replaced	T1/E1 Line Cost per Month	Extended Cost per Month	ATM Line Cost per Month
A-B	3	$2500	$7500	$4200
B-C	2	$2500	$5000	$4200
A-C	1	$2500	$2500	$4200
		Total	**$15,000**	**$12,600**

U.S. COST ANALYSIS

Although the specific cost for a T1/E1 leased line may vary from region to region, a typical monthly fee is $2500 per line, per month. Similarly, a typical ATM line cost for an OC-3c is $4200 per month. The financial analysis is summarized in Exhibit 7.

Therefore, in this analysis, it is evident that your operational cost savings per month is $2400 and you can recover the cost of the Circuit Emulation equipment in about 18 months. This example illustrates the minimal PBX interconnection network only. If you are interested in replacing more T1/E1 circuits in your network, the payback period decreases dramatically.

Exhibit 7 demonstrates a process to compare operational cost savings for an ATM solution that consolidates T1/E1 leased lines based on voice traffic alone. If your application uses T1/E1 leased lines to support data communications requirements, the total cost of the ATM solution would remain the same and the operational savings would increase even more substantially.

FUTURE PROOF

Without question, ATM will be the basis upon which communications will be built in the future. It represents the first practical solution for integrating voice, data, and video information onto the same network. An investment in ATM today will be an investment in tomorrow's technology.

Benefits of the Circuit Emulation for Voice over ATM

Flexibility. Structured and unstructured circuit emulation service is available from most vendors. Support for structured emulation enables users with PBXs or any other channelized services such as T1/E1 multiplexers and channel banks to be connected across PVCs on an ATM network. Unstructured services are suitable for the transport of signals from video codecs or other equipment with unchannelized interfaces where nonstandard framing is used by the end equipment.

Minimize ATM Bandwidth. Rather than sending a full T1/E1 bandwidth over the ATM network, which is the case with unstructured service, the user can save ATM bandwidth by sending only the T1/E1 time slots that are actually needed to support the desired service.

Save on Leased Line Costs. With up to 4 to 8 ports available on most modules, networks with private PBX transport between sites may be consolidated onto the ATM network. For example, the multiple T1/E1 leased lines connecting PBXs to other PBXs may now connect over a common ATM network infrastructure. This can save significant operational dollars.

Interoperability. Standards-based technology. The standards created by the ATM Forum ensure product interoperability. CE modules in ATM switches have talked to ATM access CE modules and vice versa. Nonproprietary solutions conform to the ATM Forum Circuit Emulation Service Interoperability Specification (CES-IS) version 2.0.

Quality of Service. All traffic on an ATM network is assigned to an AAL layer, or an ATM Adaptation Layer. AAL-1 receives the highest priority on the ATM network. It is transmitted first and the traffic cannot be dropped — unlike frame relay networks. Circuit Emulation for voice over ATM travels on AAL-1. The ATM Forum is preparing to release AAL-2, the greater spectrum for Voice over ATM. Today's problem lies in the recognition of AAL-2 in already installed or manufactured equipment. ATM switches and multiplexers understand AAL-1. And the circuit emulation modules understand PBXs, video conferencing equipment, and routers like CSU/DSUs, the existing equipment in the network.

SUMMARY

The concept of Voice over ATM has changed and emerged as the winner in the "voice over " networking technologies. Voice over ATM makes strong financial sense and it delivers quality voice transmissions over the network. Analyze your network today and you will see how well Voice over ATM fits into your infrastructure.

Chapter 23
Toward a More Perfect Union: The European Monetary Conversion and Its Impact on Information Technology

Information Technology Association of America

EUROPE IS BEING FACED WITH A CHALLENGE that could significantly impact its development and change the face of the global economy. Sovereign states are beginning a multifaceted process aimed at moving them into European economic and monetary union (EMU). As of May 1998, 10 countries have been confirmed in their EMU membership. On January 1, 1999, EMU member states will see the rates of their respective currencies irrevocably fixed to a new currency, the euro. On that day, the euro will become a functional legal currency within these countries. During the next 3 years, public and private sector entities will prepare for the cut over to this new currency, while conducting business in both the existing national currency (such as Deutsche Mark or Franc) and the euro. On January 1, 2002 the process of actually replacing national physical currencies with the euro will begin, with the 76 billion coins and 13 billion bills of the old currencies being with-

0-8493-9991-2/99/$0.00+$.50

drawn from circulation and coins and bills of the new currency going into circulation.

The Maastricht Criteria for Admission to EMU consists of:

- Budget deficit of no greater than 3% of GDP
- National debt no greater than 60% of GDP
- Inflation no greater than 1.5% above the average of top performing countries
- Limits on interest rates

The move to a single currency will affect member states who join EMU immediately. It will also have a major impact for European nations which delay their entry as well as countries around the world which trade with Europe. This chapter examines the implications of this sweeping conversion for Europe's business community — a move estimated to cost in excess of $100 billion. In particular, this chapter examines the impact of EMU on the information systems which support this commerce. These implications will be explored from three principal perspectives: business strategy, information technology operational considerations, and IT supplier community concerns.

EMU and a single currency will pose difficult strategic questions for many businesses. For instance, banks realizing substantial revenue today from currency exchange operations may see this line of business diminished, perhaps even eliminated. Other firms may see traditional patterns of trade or consumer purchasing dramatically altered as price variations across national boundaries are made more transparent and potentially narrowed. In light of these new realities, information technology must be harnessed to facilitate the customer's changing business strategies; to deploy into new lines of business; to achieve a smooth transition from legacy systems, data, and operations; and to provide potential new competitive advantages.

From an operational point of view, most firms will be forced to modify or replace financial systems in order to handle the introduction of the euro. These changes will be necessary whether or not an enterprise alters its strategic course in response to the monetary conversion. Here, we will review some of the key considerations in moving to information systems with euro-enabled capabilities. Successful EMU conversion may be defined by forces external to the technical fixes involved. The Year 2000 software conversion, a process which requires extensive repairs to enable proper computer functioning after the century rollover, is being conducted in the same time frame. This head-to-head competition for corporate attention and technical resources could spell doom for organizations lacking a highly disciplined approach to the management of systems and software.

Many U.S. software firms enjoy more than 50% of sales from overseas markets. These software packages can be banking and finance applications, or other types of programs with finance-related features and functions. Because much of Western Europe represents a computer-intensive community, the region is an important marketplace for high-end IT consultants, system integration firms, outsourcing companies, and other value-added service providers in the U.S. Both software and services firms must have a euro strategy in place. At a minimum, this strategy must accommodate basic EMU conversion requirements as commercial products are developed or enhanced, as custom-designed systems and software are implemented, or as outsourcing workloads are processed. Savvy IT providers may find new opportunities in helping overseas clients adjust to the euro, reengineering business processes, adding new levels of integration, and containing or avoiding risks.

STRATEGIC APPROACHES TO EMU

The euro conversion may represent strategic opportunities for business development, force business process reengineering in key functional areas, require new approaches to the marketplace, and improve communication with customers, suppliers, and other trading partners. The new euro will not be just another currency, but a base currency against which all other currencies will be measured and compared. At a business level, changes in strategic direction may be needed to accommodate and leverage:

- Exchange rate stabilization
- Elimination of redundant activity (such as treasury operations)
- Price transparency
- Market expansion and improved trade opportunities
- New product and service opportunities
- New competitive pressures
- Reduced currency risk
- Simplified transaction costs
- Improved access to capital
- Greater economic stability and predictable monetary policy
- Supply chain changes
- New accounting regulations, directives, and procedures
- Shifting consumer demand patterns
- Human resources management
- Customer and employee education and training
- Electronic business and commerce opportunities and growth

In a highly fluid situation, organizations will be forced to determine which elements of the enterprise will require changes, how they will be changed, and in what time frame. Internal modifications will have external manifestations. As a result, euro conversion must be synchronized to meet the needs of both the enterprise itself and its business partners.

The 3 years between January 1, 1999 and January 1, 2002 are a "transition period," in which both national and euro currencies can be used concurrently. As a matter of strategy, an organization might elect to adopt a very aggressive approach to the euro conversion, fielding a wide array of euro-enabled products or services as quickly as possible. Companies might elect this route to demonstrate technical sophistication, to gain early market share over competitors, to acquire the longest possible learning curve, to enjoy cost efficiencies while demand is low, or to achieve other advantages. Conversely, an organization might decide to take a very conservative approach to the conversion, learning from the mistakes of others, testing the political wind, waiting for a more predictable regulatory and business environment.

The schedule of events for euro conversion is as follows:

- **May 1998:** Selection of first group of countries in compliance with Maastricht criteria to join the euro
- **1998:** Production of euro coins and currency begins
- **January 1, 1999:** Exchange rates irrevocably fixed, dual currency period begins, changeover commences, European Central Bank conducts and coordinates single monetary policy in Europe
- **January 1, 1999 to January 1, 2002:** Dual currency period
- **January 1, 2002:** Euro becomes legal tender
- **January 1 to July 1, 2002:** Euro coins and banknotes go into circulation. Old national coins and banknotes withdrawn

Each strategic approach to conversion has its attendant risks and rewards; all must be carefully considered. For instance, companies must determine how long they might support transactions in either or both national and euro denominations. Decisions must be made in terms of incoming and outgoing activity. A firm may conclude, for example, that it will only accept payments in the national currency during the transition period, while being forced by other parties to make payments in one or both currencies or to interface with systems which accept only the euro. A firm might also wish to offer its customers the choice of denomination for a transaction, and would need system changes to deal with these alternatives. Importantly, because organizations will convert systems at different times, constant communication between parties is critical to assure a smooth transition and clear identification of the denomination in use at any given time.

A "big bang" conversion — the immediate switchover of systems to euro — may mean higher risks as hidden programming errors and unforeseen integration issues emerge all at once. Organizations running behind schedule on euro conversion programs may have no alternative. More disciplined firms may take this approach to avoid the need to support both national and euro currency units in their information systems. A phased-in approach allows the enterprise to build and test on an incremental basis, containing the risks of failure. But even this strategy is not risk free. Organizations electing a phased-in strategy to euro conversion will be faced with "bridging" between converted and nonconverted systems, similar to the strategy now common in Year 2000 software programs. Bridge building requires expenditure on resources which will be discarded after the conversion is complete. Coexistence of converted and nonconverted systems also raises the possibility of data contamination, either as test data flows into production systems or as euro denominated data is mistakenly run into a production system still set for the national currency unit.

Timing and transition scheduling decisions must also factor in the organization's critical accounting and reporting requirements. For many companies, implementing the cut over from national currency to euro denomination will make most sense at fiscal year end. At this point, the enterprise is likely to be "closing the books" and going to special lengths to eliminate bookkeeping discrepancies. The year end constitutes a logical juncture for making the transition, whether in terms of a big bang or in select mission-critical systems.

Strategic decision-making goes beyond timing concerns. Some organizations may be tempted to rely heavily, perhaps even completely, on key vendors to perform the euro transition successfully. For competitive reasons, most IT vendors will view the euro as a critical customer requirement — a requirement which must be efficiently and cost-effectively addressed if that customer is to be retained. From a management perspective, however, overreliance on vendor performance is never a good idea. Even in situations where the technical work of converting information systems or software is delegated to the vendor, organizations must remain engaged with a variety of strategic considerations:

- Determining whether to replace or repair existing systems
- Deciding whether manual "patches" or parallel processing alternatives are realistic
- Assuring that euro-enabled functionality meets corporate requirements
- Mapping vendor timetables with organizational priorities and scheduling
- Providing adequate test scenarios and time frames
- Preparing contingency plans
- Monitoring vendor performance

Business processes and applicable regulations may require the use of historical data for auditing and other reasons. An abrupt break in corporate financial records from one currency to a second may potentially be unacceptable to auditors, tax officials, and others. Importantly, the conversion event will make it particularly difficult to correlate archival documents with corporate data. As a result, organizations may need to be able to express historical records in both the new and old currency. Euro conversion requires not only determining what applications must be changed, but what data — and with what functionality.

The euro conversion may place small companies with limited or no export base at a competitive disadvantage. These firms are most likely to deal in a single currency at present. As a result, such companies are the least likely to have experience developing or maintaining multicurrency systems. Such firms are also the least likely to have the "deep pockets" necessary to perform the necessary changes. Without dramatic changes in strategic marketplace approach, small companies are also the least likely to benefit from new market opportunities, risk reductions in currency fluctuation, lower transaction costs, and the like.

Vision, strategy, and strategic planning draw the best and worst from organizations. Certainly, the strategic implications of a complete transition in national currencies are profound, exceeding the bounds of a single white paper to elaborate. Common sense suggests, however, that organizations consider the strategic impact of the euro transition on existing and planned operations before launching major technical corrections to support the new currency.

THE EURO TRANSITION: IMPACTS ON INFORMATION SYSTEMS

Not every organization will elect to perform a full systems conversion to support the euro. As noted, manual workarounds or duplicate systems may be an acceptable alternative, at least in the short term. This discussion assumes, however, that the enterprise has decided to make the necessary modifications or replace existing resources with euro-enabled systems solutions.

The euro transition effectively forces financial information systems to become bilingual. Once able to operate in a single "language," now the system must be able to accept information in either (or both) the national denomination and the euro; to output in either or both; perhaps to process information in both denominations; and to interface with systems which understand only one or the other. In most systems, financial information can be input in the national currency and converted to the euro (the base unit). If required, it will be converted from euro to national currency for output. Conversion from national currency to the base unit and back again can, however, cause rounding differences. Systems able to process in two base units, both the euro and the national denomination, allow these differences to be traced and give the enterprise greater flexibility in determining when to cut over to euro operations. Such systems are apt to be more expensive, with the additional functionality relatively short-lived.

Attention to currency conversions and rounding rules are of particular importance to systems transitions. An exchange rate is computed by multiplying the euro base unit by a fixed value in national currency. To calculate amounts from one national currency to a second national currency generally requires triangulation — determining the value of the first in terms of euros, then using this amount to determine the value of the second. Other approaches should be used with caution. Regulations disallow using inverse exchange rates. The inverse exchange rate computes a conversion amount by multiplying the base unit of the national currency by its fixed value in euros. This method generates rounding differences. Even though the differences may be very small, from an accounting viewpoint system adjustments must be made to eliminate them.

Rounding errors are of special significance in dealing with historical data, particularly in cases where both detailed and aggregate data are stored. Systems in transition to the euro may pick up rounding discrepancies (and therefore performance errors) as incremental data converted to the euro no longer matches the cumulative total. Ultimately, converting all data to euro and operating in a single currency will address these issues. In the interim, this solution may be unrealistic. To avoid rounding differences and the accompanying accounting difficulties, organizations may wish to formalize a series of rules in system design:

- Agree on the number of decimals to be specified
- Anticipate discrepancies between individual and cumulative transaction amounts
- Adopt a base currency with the lowest possible increments
- Expect rounding differences and, where feasible, utilize other criteria for transaction matching
- Establish criteria for clearing rounding differences

As noted earlier, system interfaces are a key consideration. With thousands of organizations making the transition to the euro on different schedules and utilizing divergent approaches, the need for electronic bridges between enterprises is apt to be unavoidable. At the operational level, special attention must be given to coordination among electronic business partners. In short, partners must communicate on their transition strategy and modify interfaces as necessary.

Other contingencies deserve brief discussion. For instance, not all national currencies in Europe use decimals. One euro will be worth 100 cents, similar to the U.S. dollar. Information systems in countries such as Italy, without coins representing fractions of a base unit, will need to be modified to operate in at least three decimals (to support rounding). Similarly, internal controls of some information systems may need to be adjusted to support the euro. The new currency expression may trigger certain threshold actions, from running reports to denying credit requests. In many instances, dual display of currency amounts may be necessary. This capability will require attention to report formats and screen layouts. Systems must also be capable of inputting, displaying, and printing the euro currency symbol.

Not all euro impacts will occur in centralized information systems. Desktop systems such as spreadsheets and databases can be used to make important financial computations and, if left uncorrected, may be the source of conversion problems in larger corporate systems.

Software and Hardware Impacted

- Enterprise Resource Planning
- Finance
- Accounts Payable and Receivable
- General Ledger
- Point of Sale
- Human Resources
- Automatic Teller Machines
- Vending Machines
- Electronic Data Interchange
- Electronic Funds Transfer
- Shipping and Receiving
- Ordering
- Sales Support
- Database Management Systems
- Spreadsheets
- Operating Systems
- Distributed Platforms

The euro transition is often compared to the Year 2000 software conversion. In the latter situation, a *de facto* two-digit date standard for representing years in code poses a serious threat to computer operations after the century rollover. No longer able to assume a twentieth-century reference, computers may respond to these incomplete dates by computing the wrong answers or by aborting operations. In the euro vs. Year 2000 debate, discussion often focuses on which situation is bigger, more important, more costly, and other similar irrelevancies. Unfortunately, both conversions spring from real conditions and both must be addressed in a timely manner with a clear emphasis on prioritization and pragmatism.

In setting priorities and forming work plans to confront these twin issues, organizations may wish to balance the absolute completion deadline imposed by the Year 2000 rollover with the more gradual schedule offered by the euro's three-year transition period. Striking an appropriate balance will be critical because the twin conditions inevitably compete for corporate mindshare, technical staff availability, budget dollars, test facilities, and other resources.

In effect, successful euro conversion is aided by a variety of factors: European Union regulations mandate that organizations in member states have this capability; the euro conversion ties directly to the ability of organizations to conduct commerce in the European Union; and currency conversion within member states is a relatively commonplace commercial activity. Even with these forces in its favor, however, the euro transition is likely to fail if the software on which it depends cannot correctly process dates.

Organizations faced with performing the euro and Year 2000 conversions in roughly the same time frame must take a highly disciplined approach. Whether the actual conversion programs can be combined in a single enterprise-wide initiative is debatable. Regardless of whether or not this step is taken, organizations should not ignore the inherent synergies and overarching corporate considerations. These include:

- Setting program schedules which recognize internal deadlines, EU time frames, vendor compliance statements, and customer requirements
- Delaying, deferring, eliminating, or outsourcing internal projects which compete for resources and make it more difficult to test baseline configurations
- Leveraging common processes and methods to the maximum extent possible. Possible areas for productivity gains include business process analysis, inventory evaluation, configuration and program management, auditing, testing, information sharing, and external interface management
- Building common infrastructures, such as repositories for software objects, source code, software designs, test procedures, and documentation
- Coordinating on testing schedules, both internal to the enterprise and, as necessary, with industry groups
- Mission-critical system contingency planning which assumes one or both conversions fail to take place as scheduled
- Reusing successful recruitment and retention strategies for technical personnel

The euro and Year 2000 conversions are unavoidable business realities with substantial costs and risks. Failure at either task could mean drastic changes — even elimination — of the business involved. Organizations must avoid the tendency to view one as more important; rather, every enterprise with European operations, customers, or partners must tailor a management and technical approach which balances corporate resources, requirements, and opportunities.

THE EURO MARKETPLACE: CONSIDERATIONS FOR SOLUTION PROVIDERS

The euro transition represents a variety of challenges and opportunities for IT companies. Like the Year 2000 conversion, the euro situation is causing organizations to revisit certain aspects of their information systems deployments. Like Year 2000, organizations are confronted with repair, upgrade, retire, or replace decisions. Such determinations will drive new business opportunities, both for commercial software vendors, custom software developers, and systems integration firms. For instance, organizations with financial systems now capable of processing in only a single base currency may wish to upgrade and process in both euro and national currencies. Customers may demand new capabilities, such as database tools which allow easy conversion of historical data and efficient traceability back to transaction records, or new functionality for the dual currency period. And organizations may decide to achieve the new functionality by replacing legacy systems with new commercial products — a step that could directly impact vendor competition for IT budget dollars.

As in the Year 2000 situation, some IT companies will be more tactically focused, developing product and service solutions aimed primarily at getting customers over the euro hurdle. Because the euro transition is, like the century rollover, a discrete event, such IT companies may find it more difficult to demonstrate an extensive track record in the area, document success stories, generate customer references, or leverage a broad base of past experience. Other IT firms will view the euro transition in more strategic terms, looking at the situation as one more opportunity to build an ongoing relationship with the client, to better understand the customer's business processes and information systems operations, and to gain competitive advantage for downstream product and service offerings.

To be successful, IT companies will need to be acutely attuned to the customer's changed business realities. A single currency may, for instance, be the stimulus to force some firms to become pan-European or to modify transnational business and pricing strategies. Global IT firms have extensive experience helping customers identify and accommodate regional differences in business operations. Like the Year 2000 conversion, the euro will have an extensive "ripple effect" for multinational organizations, particularly in the area of supply chain management. The euro transition may represent an excellent opportunity to revisit the customer's approach to electronic commerce and supply chain interfaces, introducing business process improvements while assuring the ability of relevant systems to convert to and from euros. The ripple effect will also find its way to intranets and the Internet. Firms selling on the Internet, whether in Europe, Asia, North America, or elsewhere, may be forced to offer a payment in euros option. Likewise, multinationals may be required to insert euros into the intranets serving divisions, subsidiaries, and other business units.

Changed customer circumstances may also require IT companies to consider the downside this situation represents for some firms. As noted earlier, the euro will eliminate some business functions, particularly in areas like arbitrage and currency trading. For these customers, the euro transition comes as a two-headed hydra, bringing substantial new costs as well as lost revenue opportunities. IT consultants and systems integration firms will be challenged to help such firms redefine operations and redeploy assets to respond to the new business environment.

As with Year 2000, IT companies offering euro solutions are challenged to agree on a definition of "compliance." For a number of reasons it may be preferable to restrict any notions of "compliance" to EU-regulated matters such as precision, conversion, rounding, and triangulation rules and the euro symbol. The EU has specific regulations on rounding calculations, but other facets of euro compliance are still open to interpretation. For instance, a euro-ready solution might operate in both the national currency and in euros. Or it might operate only in euros. Similarly, a converted system may be required to show a retail customer pricing information in two currencies.

Customer expectations about euro features and benefits may vary. Some may view the introduction of euro capabilities as adding value and be willing to pay for it. Others may see it as fundamental to the operations of a software program, like offering commands in English or French. Segmenting the marketplace may also be a significant challenge. Countries are participating in the common currency on different timetables. Even those that adopt the euro in the next few years will operate in a transition period. Meanwhile, customers inside and outside the EU may realize the need to be euro enabled on schedules dictated by their own strategic business and technical considerations. Business expansions in response to a more predictable currency may trigger the need for new system architectures and new computing platforms. Such factors may leave IT vendors guessing as to when to introduce euro-capable products, to which industry sectors, on what platforms and in which countries.

Workforce availability is also a key issue for IT vendors. Unlike the Year 2000 conversion which requires more generic skill sets, the euro conversion will be performed by technical personnel with a specific understanding of financial systems. Studies suggest that most firms have difficulty recruiting appropriately trained software professionals. The schedule competition between Year 2000 and euro conversions exacerbates the problem. And in lining up the euro conversion workforce, employers may find that the talent pool is by definition smaller still.

CONCLUSION

The euro transition clearly poses a broad range of strategic and operational considerations for IT vendors and their customers. Perhaps overshadowed in North America by the Year 2000 conversion, the euro will nevertheless have major implications for organizations in and out of the EU. While the time frame for implementing the euro is more fluid than the "hard" deadline of the century rollover, fluidity poses its own problems, fostering a tendency to postpone the work and making it more difficult to determine how and when the cutover will take place.

The euro transition may cause many firms to reevaluate their approach to implementing information systems. Companies adept at strategic planning will use the technology to leverage new opportunities. This may require changes in business structure and process as well as redeployment of IT architectures and capabilities. As with the Year 2000, time is of the essence. Pragmatism will carry the day, and close attention must be paid to both business processes and their underlying and enabling information technology infrastructures. Euro-savvy IT vendors able to assist customers reach strategic goals, both in terms of technology planning and implementation of flexible solutions, will have a significant competitive advantage. Euro-savvy enterprises, similarly, will more effectively map out their post-euro business strategy and be able to enhance and create their competitive advantages.

Recommended Reading

Preparing Information Systems for the Euro, Pieter Dekker, European Commission, Directorate General XV,
http://www.ispo.cec.be/y2keuro/

KPMG Euro Overview,
http://www.kpmg.co.uk/uk/services/manage/emu01.html

The Single Currency: Everything You Ever Wanted to Know, Gillian Tett, *The Financial Times*, November 12, 1996.

Switch to Euro is Tech Challenge, Lamia Abu-Haidar, *CNET,* October 24, 1997.

Banks: Anxiety over EMU Starts to Creep In, *The Financial Times*, December 3, 1996.

Euro: Creation of a New Currency, Anne Knowles, *Datamation*, November, 1997.

Chapter 24 Systems that Build Themselves: Anatomy of a Development Before the Fact Software Engineering Methodology

Margaret Hamilton

THE PURPOSE OF A BUSINESS PLAN is to state what an organization will accomplish over a time frame. Its operational plan states how it will be done. Before such plans are created, what is often lacking is a true understanding of an organization's goals and therefore a means to accomplish them (what the true business plan should be). If goals (the organization's requirements) were better defined, business plans (specifications) and its associated operational plans (detailed designs) would be more realistic and the company in question would have a much better chance to be on the right track. Otherwise what is the system (the company) that is being developed or transitioning to and who are its users (the marketplace)?

We have worked with several software organizations to define goals and to determine how each organization can best meet its goals. These goals were defined as part of an enterprise model using the Development Before the Fact (DBTF) formal systems theory[1-4] and a system design and development environment based on DBTF.[5]

0-8493-9991-2/99/$0.00+$.50

Part of defining goals is to show how they relate to each other; for example, if a goal is not accomplished with some success, other facets dependent on it have less chance of being accomplished successfully.

Interesting things surfaced during this process. For example, it quickly became clear how dependent the bottom line can be on seemingly unrelated or distantly related areas. A decision such as who is chosen to manage and build the software, what software processes and methods and tools are selected, what axioms are at the very foundations of the methods selected, how one module in the organization is designed, or what a property of an object is in one of the application systems would be taken more seriously by upper management if they realized the significance of such a decision on the bottom line. Even before this kind of exercise, one would no doubt conclude that such decisions could impact the quality and cost of building the software. What is not so apparent is that it affects the organization in many not so obvious ways ranging from what kind of people are attracted to your business to what kind of business you will ultimately have.

GOALS FOR COMPANY X

Recently we worked with Company X, a software developer who develops financial and communications systems for its customers, to define its business goals. The market leader of a rapidly growing vertical market, Company X is at a crossroads and must decide whether to keep things the way they are now or whether it should change its way of doing business.

Many goals of Company X are similar to other software development companies. For example, making a profit. Other goals, in particular those at a lower level, could be quite different. One company may be interested in data base-only applications (still others in the use of a specific vendors product such as Oracle- or Sybase-only data base applications), another in real-time applications for manufacturing, another in applications for only PC NT or only UNIX, and another in GUIs for travel agencies.

Company X builds reasonably complex to quite complex systems for a large vertical market for its end users, which includes specialized hardware and software components with a “man in the loop.” These systems have both real time distributed and data base requirements. Until now the company has been building systems the traditional way using a commercial proprietary GUI builder for screens, two competing data base products for data base portions, and hand coding in C or C++ for the rest of its software development process. These systems reside on several platforms including UNIX, PC, and mainframes.

Standards are not in common use at this company and every project does things differently. The company is growing too fast and is having trouble delivering on time. When it does deliver, the systems are not working and it takes months longer than anticipated to turn them into production quality for its users. Everything depends on a handful of experts and there are not enough experts to go around. Even though this company is its market leader and continues to bring in new business at a startling rate, it is losing money, also at a startling rate. It could soon begin to lose market share to a company that has less baggage to cope with. Company X now has some hard decisions to make, particularly in how to build its software.

Changes have to be made in order to avoid such problems in the future. The question is what to do and how and when to get from here to there.

OPTIONS FOR COMPANY X

Company X has several options, ranging from one extreme to the other:

1. Keep things the same.
2. Add tools and techniques that support business as usual but provide relief in selected areas.
3. Bring in more modern but traditional tools and techniques to replace existing ones.
4. Use a new paradigm with the most advanced tools and techniques that formalizes the process of software development while at the same time capitalizing on software already developed.
5. Same as the previous option except start over from the beginning.

Choosing an option becomes an easier task once the company's goals are understood and agreed upon (Exhibit 1). Below is a discussion of how DBTF and an automation of it can be used to address these goals. Note that when a goal (e.g., GOAL#2) refers to another goal (e.g., GOAL#13), the goal it refers to becomes one of its reusables.

HOW THE GOALS IMPACT EACH OTHER

Each company goal is better understood if its relationships to other goals are understood. GOAL#1, to maximize short and long term profits, is ultimately accomplished by reaching all other goals, i.e., GOALS#2 through #13. Similarly, meeting GOAL#2, be strategic, is dependent on meeting other goals including GOAL#9 and GOAL#13. High-level goals such as making a profit and preparing for the future are directly dependent on which methods and tools are used for building the company's software.

It becomes clear that GOAL#3, which is to put in place a mechanism for handling fast growth, will not be satisfied if the company keeps doing things the way it does now. Upon further analysis of this goal, to formally understand Company X in its "as is" and "to be" states means defining views of the company's enterprise as an evolving system. This requires methods and tools to effectively perform such an analysis (note that this part of GOAL#3 depends on GOAL#8, which depends on GOAL#13). In

Exhibit 1. Software Company Goals

GOAL#1: Maximize short- and long-term profits (GOALs#2–#12)

GOAL#2: Be strategic: prepare for now and the future
- Understand everything as a system (GOAL#8)
- Use strategic methods and tools (GOAL#13)
- Capitalize on reuse (GOAL#9)
- Do no more, no less (GOAL#7)
- Always apply a preventative philosophy (GOALs#3, #4)
- Eliminate problems (failure to deliver, lost profits, business lost to competitors, exit of critical personnel) before they happen

GOAL#3: Create mechanism to handle fast growth
- Cohesive plan with strategic supporting technologies (GOAL#13)
- Formally understand "as is" and "to be" states of Company X (GOAL#8).
- Hire (and keep) the best people (GOAL#5).
- Standardize throughout corporation (GOAL#6)
- Capitalize on reuse (GOAL#9)
- Transition without going backwards (GOAL#11)

GOAL#4: Prepare for the shortage of good, experienced developers and the large turnover issue that challenges our industry today
- Attract/keep good people by being the best (GOAL#5)
- Use techniques to accelerate learning
- Depend less on individuals. Replace manual with automated processes (GOAL#13). Reuse knowledge already captured (GOAL#9)
- Standardize (GOAL#6)

GOAL#5: Be the best
- Use the best methods, tools, and relationship with vendors (GOAL#9, #10, #13).
- Hire top people (incentivized with the best)
- Maintain market share and ensure lead
- Build the best systems (GOAL#12)
- Underbid the competition without sacrificing quality and profit

GOAL#6: Standardize throughout Company X, facilitating personnel to move from project to project and phase to phase. Reusables created on one project can be immediately used elsewhere and communicated on the same terms. Use same language, methods and tools (GOAL#7, GOAL#9, GOAL#13) for defining (and developing)
- Applications and reusables for all levels and layers of abstraction
- Requirements, specifications, designs, tests
- Views of development (e.g., user model)
- Hardware, software, peopleware
- Projects and project plans
- Processes of development (e.g., management, analysis, design, build, test)
- Enterprise models for Company X and its customers

GOAL#7: Apply the "no more, no less" rule to reach corporate goals
- Use true reuse; avoid reinventing the wheel over and over again (GOAL#9)
- Use true automation that does "real work" and does not propagate "make work"(GOAL#13)

Simplify necessary tasks
Eliminate redundant and unnecessary tasks and resources
When possible, convert manual tasks into automation

GOAL#8: Understand everything as a system: the business, development processes, applications, reusables, user models, customer enterprises, development environment, and management
Formally define each system with strategic methods and tools (GOAL#13)
Formalize planning and analysis for parameters such as cost and risk
Formalize from the beginning starting with requirements
Trace from requirements to implementation and back again
Requirements are implemented as a possible set of specifications, each of which is implemented as a possible set of implementations
Everything understood in terms of its relativity

GOAL#9: Capitalize on reuse (GOAL#13). Mechanize by standardization (GOAL#6) and effective automation. Reuse only things that:
Work
Are inherently part of, become installed as part of, or is derived from the chosen technology
Evolve with change
Can be shared across projects

GOAL#10: Work with vendor(s) who understand Company X's current and future needs
Vendor uses his own product(s) when applicable in the way that he markets it
Is able to demonstrate highest priority lifecycle areas using Company X systems
Can successfully support transition to new methods and tools without going backwards (GOAL#11)
Use strategic technologies (GOAL#13)

GOAL#11: Transition to new methods and tools without going backwards (no time or money lost and less risk than before)
Relatively fast learning curve
Can be used to replace, evolve with, or evolve from existing technology
Need for high productivity of new tools to make up for learning curve
New approach should be a considerable improvement to justify its entry into Company X
Use approach that can evolve immediately with Company X's legacy software (GOAL#9)
Use as much as possible of what already exists to get jump started
Use strategic technology, with features like an open architecture, to minimize risk (GOAL#13).

GOAL#12: Build better applications with faster, cheaper development
Make prudent "make or buy" decisions for the components in the applications
Use no more, no less rule (GOAL#7)
Strategic technologies should be used for both make or buy applications (GOAL#13)

GOAL#13: Choose an integrated set of strategic methods and tools (only use "point" products if they can become an integral part of the strategic products) that:
Is based on a before-the-fact philosophy that inherently avoids problems
Inherently capitalizes on reuse (GOAL#9) and the "no more, no less" philosophy (GOAL#7)
Treats everything as a system (GOAL#8) resulting in a system-oriented object (SOO)

Exhibit 1. Software Company Goals *(Continued)*

Can be used selectively on a system-wide or module basis
Can be used at any phase of development
Is formal, but friendly
Does not lock in Company X or its customers
Can interface to other technologies and legacy code
Evolves and provides a means to evolve a system with changing technologies and requirements
Provides a means to reconfigure and automatically regenerate to diverse architectures from a given set of requirements
Allows one to build in terms of it, maintaining the same formal properties
Can integrate with old and new developments should one choose to add to the vendor's environment
Automatically does real work (instead of supporting unnecessary manual processes which can create extra work)

addition, capitalizing on reuse depends on GOAL#9 which again depends on GOAL#13.

In a similar way GOAL#4, preparing for the shortage of developers, ultimately depends on the methods and tools selected. The first subgoal is optimistic. In preparing for the shortage of good developers, they must not only be attracted but incentivized to stay as well. Good developers are attracted to companies who excel. Part of excelling means using better methods and tools. Within an exciting development environment, developers and their managers are proud of their accomplishments and more motivated since they can deliver better systems, relieved from grinding out inaccurate code, often by hand. Managers appreciate faster throughput, reliability, and cost savings.

The subgoal of depending less on individuals is the more pessimistic one. No matter what, developers are going to leave even when good developers are easy to find. This means a company must be less dependent on an individual. Gone are the days when it is acceptable to have an entire organization depend on one individual who is the only one who knows how to design a particular component of an airplane. An organization can depend less on individuals by reusing knowledge already captured.

With respect to GOAL#5, using the best methods and tools, if they are new to the company they require a supportive and knowledgeable vendor (GOAL#10). It also means other things like hiring the best people, being the market leader, and building the best systems. Again, GOAL#5 is dependent on GOAL#13.

GOAL#6, the standardization goal, is constrained further than at first meets the eye by having the same language, methods, and tools be used for building all aspects of software and related systems. This means, for example, that the same language is used for defining the requirements for a financial system as that which defines its specifications or designs; this same language could also be used to define the process of developing the financial system, the enterprise of the user, and the enterprise of the project or corporation responsible for developing the software. Having the ability to successfully accomplish this depends on satisfying GOAL#13.

Coming up with an arbitrary set of standards just to have standards is not within the spirit of GOAL#6. For example, to mandate a standard of using the same vendor's tools as those used by a neighboring project when such tools do not support the project as well as other tools, is an example of not satisfying this goal. Subgoal constraints such as using the same language, tools, etc. for all aspects of definition help to prevent a loose and misguided interpretation of GOAL#6. This illustrates the importance of formally defining these goals.

Satisfying GOAL#7 means applying the "no more, no less rule." This means doing what is necessary to reach the company's goals, but not doing anything unnecessary. Unnecessary work happens when meetings or paperwork are created for walkthroughs of results from manual tasks that could have been automated (such as the manual creation of code and its analysis); learning more than one language for different phases or for different tools when it is not necessary; doing extra work because of being locked into the wrong tool; doing redundant work because work done to use one tool cannot be transitioned over gracefully to another tool that is needed to complete the task.

Satisfying GOAL#7 also means not making things more difficult than necessary. Most everyone learns from their own experiences, whether developing real-world systems or just getting through each day, that there are difficult (sometimes impossible) solutions to problems and very straightforward solutions to the same problem. For example, it is more difficult to perform long division with Roman numerals than with the Arabic number system.

Sometimes things can be simplified by creating solutions that will help recover from what appears to be the effect and not the cause of a source problem (but, in fact, is the source relative to the problem being solved). For example, dealing with a concept of recovering from the loss of computer memory is simpler than dealing separately with all of the things that might cause such a thing to happen such as lightning, the computer being mishandled by the user, etc. Here, relativity becomes a consideration in simplifying the solution. In this case the source of the problem that is being solved resides with the computer, not the outside world which has lightning and careless users. In a sense, this is the ability of an object to have self preservation.

Often, a solution derived for one problem solves other problems. The trick then for doing no more work than necessary is to recognize when you have solved more than one problem with a solution. For example, we developed a system that could be reconfigured in real time to more effectively respond to and recover from errors and to deal with changing priorities by going from a synchronous to an asynchronous operating system. We then realized we had also found a much better and less error-prone way to have the same kind of flexibility with the development of that system. It worked because the actual system being developed had been evolved into a more modular system to accommodate the asynchronous processes of development, where a change to a process or functional area was separate and apart from another process. This significantly accelerated the application's development and maintenance process.

Reducing unnecessary tasks is not only a savings in time and money, but it also eliminates a dependency on processes, methods, and tools that are no longer needed. More importantly there is no longer a dependency on what could become for some businesses armies of people needed to support obsolescence. And today armies of people are hard to find.

Reaching GOAL#7 and GOAL#8 (understanding everything as a system) becomes more successful when GOAL#13 is satisfied. GOAL#8 is all encompassing and cannot be satisfied overnight. Many directions can be taken such as formally defining something from the very beginning and maintaining such formalism to its completion; evolving the system formally throughout all of its lifetimes; or formally defining all systems that the target system (the application in question) has a relationship with (including the business that develops it, the methods used to design and develop it, and the processes, including analysis, design, and management used to develop it).

GOAL#8, carried to its ideal, means defining systems to have a future. Defining requirements that can be implemented in terms of a possible set of specifications or a set of specifications that can be automatically implemented in terms of a possible set of implementations (for example, to different languages, communications protocols, operations systems, data bases, legacy code, etc.) means that these systems are all defined up front with an open architecture approach and evolution will not become an issue later.

EVERYTHING IS RELATIVE

To truly understand a system means to understand it in terms of relativity. Everything in the world of any of these systems is relative. One person's requirements are another's implementation; one person's application is another's operating system.

On one project, two development groups argued for weeks about which definition for requirements was the correct one. Upon further analysis, they were both correct since they were both talking about a different target system. One was a system for the end user. The other was a system about that system used for developing the end-user system.

To capitalize on effective reuse (GOAL#9) means to satisfy GOAL#13 since reuse will only work if the objects that are reused, work and can evolve. Effective reuse is a possible way of alleviating a potential disaster, since it can be a powerful tool in addressing goals such as GOAL#2, which is to be strategic. Part of meeting the reuse goal is to mechanize by standardization (GOAL#6) and effective automation, both of which are inherent forms of reuse.

Reuse in the true sense of the word is a systematic process (see again GOAL#8). It starts from the beginning with requirements that allow for diverse projects with an option for different specifications where each specification allows for different implementations (for example, one project with code generated to interface with Informix and another with Oracle; or one project with the client server and another with the mainframe) which can be automatically generated from each of that requirement's possible specifications.

To be successful, reuse needs to be an intelligent and formal process, under control. A mechanism can be set up by management to support all development projects in the sharing of a common set of reuse modules — itself a system. This could be a core product from which all applications could jump start their developments (what NASA refers to as reusable productization[6,7]).

It is important to work with vendor(s) who have an understanding of the company's development needs both for now and the future (GOAL#10). Such an understanding can be verified by having the vendor in question demonstrate its abilities by designing and developing part of the company's system with the vendor's products.

Company X would benefit by defining its current process of building software starting from the definition of requirements and going all the way to final production of code and maintenance with all of the steps and tasks that it goes through to develop an application. Then the vendor can be asked to go through the same steps with its solution (or equivalent steps to accomplish the same functionality) and demonstrate where the vendor's method is superior (or inferior). Company X will determine if the amount of improvement justifies a transition to the vendor's methods and products and also learn what it is like to work with that vendor in the process. If a vendor actually uses its own technology and products to do for itself what it is selling to the customer, this should be an excellent sign.

To transition to new methods and tools without taking a step backward (GOAL#11) — no time or money lost and less risk than before — by its very nature depends on what the new methods and tools are and how they are applied. Many things need to be taken into consideration. A learning curve that fits into a project's schedules is important, but if the benefits such as the increase in productivity using the new methods is great enough to justify it, then a longer learning curve may be justifiable. To counter risk, it is also important to have a means to evolve from the existing methods to the new ones at a safe pace should it become necessary or desirable to do so. It is important, for example, that the new approach provides a means to reuse what has already been developed at Company X. By using a strategic technology with features like an open architecture, risk is minimized (GOAL#13).

To make sure that the transition is a smooth one, it helps to start off with one or more forward-thinking technical leaders at the company. They will inspire others and can help train them as well. In addition, it helps to define a process for the others that shows one way to get started, using a company project as an example of how to accomplish this.

The result of reaching GOAL#12 is better applications with faster, cheaper development. This goal will be satisfied if goals #7 and #13 are satisfied and #7 and #13 will be satisfied if goals including #8 and #13 are satisfied.

With GOAL#13, choose an integrated set of strategic methods and tools, "point" products are used only if they can become an integral part of the strategic product. Such a technology and products should be used only if they support the philosophy of preventing as many things as possible from going wrong before they do go wrong. All objects in a system, whether they be for hardware, peopleware, or software (or some combination thereof) should be treated systematically from the start to the deployment of that system, GOAL#8). Such a technology solution inherently capitalizes on reuse (GOAL#9) and applying the "no more, no less goal" (GOAL#7) and can be used at any phase of development.

This technology should be formal so that its semantics and the semantics of the system it is used to develop are well understood. Although the properties of being formal are inherently part of the methods and associated tools, it must also be "friendly" enough to be placed into practical use.

What does not often surface in the beginning that should surface when considering a technology is its durability, i.e., its ability to adapt to changing technologies, market conditions, and requirements. It is safe to say that never should a technology be adopted that locks a corporation in. The product should be able to interface to others and provide for others to interface to it. A product that locks you in compromises your choices of functionality, hardware, and software products you can use (including your own reusables) both now and in the future.

With a product that locks you in, the result could be at best a significantly greater effort if you want to change your mind in the future. An example is a product that can only generate to client server applications but not to mainframe-based applications. Another is a product that can only use its own GUI environment but does not allow its users to take the advantage of additional capability from another GUI environment in the marketplace when there is a requirement to do so. Or a product that once it automatically generates its application for one data base environment cannot turn around and automatically generate that same application for another data base environment.

A strategic product should be able to interface to other technologies (call or be called by, or generate to other technologies) as they come into the marketplace, and to existing legacy code on an as-needed basis. It should provide a means to evolve from and with legacy code now and later to newer technologies and application requirements as they become available; it should provide a means to automatically generate (and then reconfigure and regenerate) diverse implementations and architectures from a given set of requirements.

A strategic product should be able to evolve and allow one to continue to build on top of it and in terms of it, maintaining the same formal properties. It should allow one to integrate with old and new developments should one choose to add to the vendor's environment.

What is important is that the product automatically does the real work, instead of automatically supporting unnecessary manual processes and thereby sometimes actually creating extra work. In addition, it should provide the ability to build effective reusables that will evolve with change. With properties such as these, the reliability of the software is maximized and the cost to build it and the time to market it is minimized.

Exhibit 2 contains a sketch of goals as types of objects in Company X's enterprise model. Among other things, we show in this model the goals discussed above and their relationships, including dependencies. In this sketch the goals are presented with a slightly different view than in Exhibit 1. Here the relationships in the TMap sketch are more explicitly shown in terms of being direct or indirect. In addition we begin to make more use of reusables to express the goals. These goals are sketched with a partially filled in Type Map (TMap). The TMap is one form of model using DBTF's system language. The models are created with the use of a systems design and development environment, an automation based on DBTF.

In this TMap sketch, the top node type is Maximize Profit (see upper left-hand corner). This sketch has been decomposed a few levels in order to illustrate some of the types of relationships in this system. The types on all

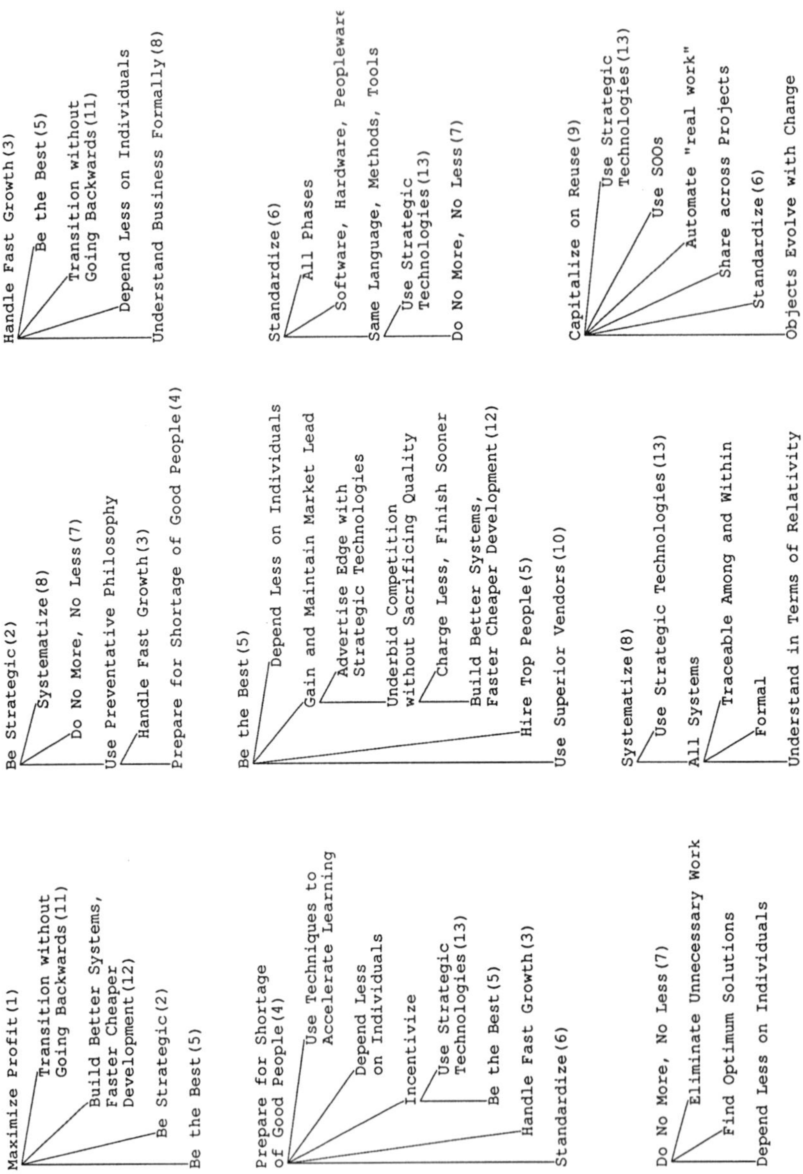

Exhibit 2. TMap sketch of goals.

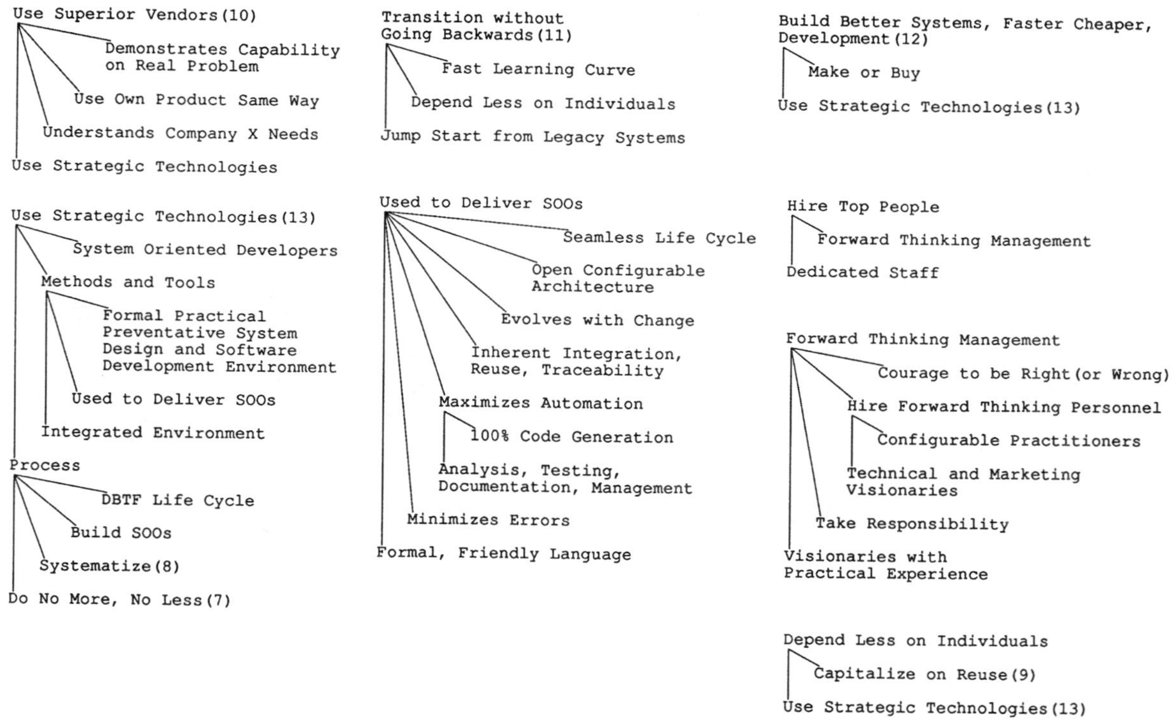

Legend: Development Before the Fact (DBTF)
System Oriented Object (SOO)

Exhibit 2. ***Continued.***

of the other nodes are needed in this definition to define how to Maximize Profit. Several other TMap sketches are contained in this model, each of which is a reusable for at least one TMap. See, for example, TMap Be the Best, which is used in Maximize Profit, Handles Fast Growth, and Prepare for the Shortage of Good People.

One of the interesting findings in examining this model is that every goal, if you drive it down to a low enough level, is dependent on GOAL#13, including GOAL#13 itself since it is recursive. Similarly, all of the goals are dependent on GOAL#9, including GOAL#9 itself. Clearly, if they are not already, the reuse and technologies strategies used within the corporation should take on the highest of priorities in determining if the company is in fact meeting the requirements that are important for all of its goals, including maximizing short- and long-term profits for the corporation.

A RADICALLY DIFFERENT APPROACH FOR STRATEGIC TECHNOLOGIES (FULFILLING GOAL#13)

The means to fulfill GOAL#13 may well be found along nontraditional paths through innovation — which means creating new methods or new environments for using new methods. In fact, the road to success may well exist within past mistakes. If this is the case, Corporate X is in the right place at the right time to take advantage of such a moment.

The first step to a new approach is to recognize the problems that are truly at the root, and categorize those problems in terms of how they might be prevented in the future. Deriving practical solutions comes next, and the process can be repeated again and again as we look to solve new problems with the benefit of what we know from our new solution environment. With Corporate X, for example, this can be accomplished by saying what is needed (defining the goals), realizing what is therefore missing, and filling in the void by satisfying the goals, including coming up with the right methods and tools.

What if the kind of thinking needed to satisfy GOAL#13 would govern Corporate X's development? What if there were a different way to build systems that would significantly and positively affect Corporate X's financial picture — one that concentrated on preventing problems that surface in a typical development environment rather than fixing them after they've surfaced at the most inopportune and expensive point in time (see Exhibit 3). How might it work? Wouldn't it require a radical revision of the way Corporate X does its software?

Radical, indeed, because it would have to provide a formal framework for doing things right the first time. Such is the case with Development Before the Fact (DBTF).

Exhibit 3. Problems of Traditional System Engineering and Software Development Environments

Too Late, If At All	Compromised Quality, Late to Market, $$$ ... Wasted
Integration: Mismatched methods, objects, modules, phases, application types, architectures, and products.	Left to devices of a myriad developers well into development. Hard to understand. Cannot trace objects. No correspondence to real world.
Elimination of errors: Methods encourage systems to be defined as ambiguous and incorrect.	System out of control, incompatible interfaces, propagation of errors throughout development.
Flexibility/unpredictability: Systems not defined to handle open architectures/processes, changes, or error recovery.	Porting is new development. Maintenance is costly and risky. Critical functionality avoided for fear of the unknown.
Reusability: No properties in definitions to find, create, and use commonality. Focus is on implementation.	Redundancy a way of life. Errors propagate accordingly.
Automation: Supports manual process instead of doing the real work. Limited, incomplete, fragmented, disparate, and inefficient.	Most of the development process is manual and therefore error prone and inefficient. Manual processes needed to complete unfinished automations.

The DBTF paradigm is about beginnings. It was derived from the combination of steps taken to solve the problems of traditional systems engineering and software development. What makes DBTF radically different is that it is preventative rather than curative.

We can make an analogy to a human system to explain the difference. John goes to the dentist because he has a cavity and the dentist determines that a root canal is needed. Had John gone sooner, the dentist might have been able simply to fill the cavity, which — because now a root canal is necessary — would have been curative with respect to the cavity and preventative with respect to the root canal. Had John eaten properly and brushed regularly, he might have prevented not only the root canal, but the cavity as well.

If we add in the cost of dental care, this analogy becomes particularly instructive with respect to systems development. To treat a cavity with a root canal — that is, after the fact — is expensive. To fill a cavity on time is far less expensive. And to prevent the cavity in the first place — that is, before the fact — is even less expensive again.

Another illustration comes from our own experience in developing systems. A few years ago, one of the students in training in our group was in awe of one of the developers because he could "program so fast." But this developer's stuff was full of bugs and impossible to understand. In fact, we spent a lot of time redeveloping his application to make it work, because it wasn't done right in the first place.

There was another developer in the group who was not nearly as fast, but almost everything he did worked and was easy to understand. The time we spent redeveloping the "fast" developer's work exceeded the time this "slower" developer spent on his stuff.

A third developer in the group got little attention from this student. He was always deep in thought, looking for ways to abstract, looking for ways to build more generic software. He often took even longer to program than the "slower" developer above. On more than one occasion, he found out that it was not necessary at all to develop the program in question because he had already created reusables. In the end, the third developer was really the "fastest," because his approach was more "before the fact" than the others.

The first developer — the one with whom our student was in awe — might learn to develop modules for the rest of us to reuse. But what would be missing without the benefit of the right experience, or reusable knowledge, is that deep thought the third developer put into his work.

THE DBTF PHILOSOPHY

Reliability is at the heart of Development Before the Fact. DBTF treats all objects as complete systems. It provides an initial and logical framework using mathematics within which objects, their structure, behavior, and interactions with other objects may be captured. The philosophy behind DBTF is that its objects are recursively reusable and reliable. Reliable systems are defined in terms of reliable systems (Exhibit 4): only reliable systems are used as building blocks, and only reliable systems are used as mechanisms to integrate these building blocks to form a new system. The new system becomes reusable for building other systems. All levels and layers of a system have to be reliable for a system to be reliable.

DBTF is based on a set of axioms and on the assumption of a universal set of objects. Each DBTF system is defined with properties that control its own design and development throughout its life cycle(s), where the life cycle itself is an evolving system that could be defined and developed as a target system by using this approach. The emphasis on defining things with the right methods the first time prevents problems before they happen. An integration of function and object-oriented, DBTF is based on a unique concept of control of a system's objects (including control of organization of objects, timing, priority, resources, data flow, and data).

From the very beginning, a DBTF system inherently integrates all of its own objects (and all aspects, relationships, and viewpoints of these ob-

Reliable Systems
are Defined in Terms of Reliable Systems

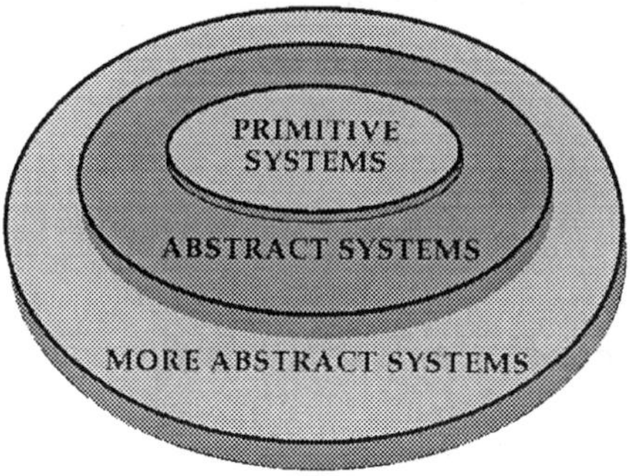

- Use only reliable systems
- Integrate these systems with reliable systems
- The result is a system(s) which is reliable
- Use resulting reliable system(s) along with more primitive ones to build new and larger reliable systems

Exhibit 4. Reliable systems are defined in terms of reliable systems.

jects) and the combinations of functionality using these objects. A DBTF system maximizes its own reliability and flexibility to change; capitalizes on its own parallelism; supports its own run-time performance analysis; and maximizes the potential for its own reuse and automation. It is defined with built-in quality, built-in productivity, and built-in control.

Our concept of automation is central to this whole discussion. When you think about it, automation itself is an inherently reusable process. If a system can not be reused, it certainly can not be automated. Consider, for example, the process of software development used within a particular organization. Were that process mechanized it could be reused again and again. That in itself implies the process could be automated.

Again, a DBTF system achieves its high level of quality through a preventative rather than curative approach. Whereas the curative approach requires continuously testing the system until the errors are eliminated, the preventative approach of DBTF means not allowing those errors to appear in the first place. Whereas accelerating a particular design and development process under the curative scenario means adding resources, be they people or processors, the preventative approach finds a more efficient way, capitalizing more on reusing or eliminating parts of the process altogether.

DBTF is centered on doing things right in the first place by using a unique yet straightforward way of definition. A starting point is concept formulation and requirements definition, done in a way that eliminates many of the common problems of traditional software development.

This method concentrates on how one can define a system model that captures, to the greatest extent practical, goals such as reuse, portability, and interoperability. Engineering judgment is useful in determining when to use which type of modeling, and how these sides of a system should play together depending on the requirements of the target system. Under this scenario, "design" and "programming" become relative terms. Higher-level "programming" becomes design to lower layers. The focus is a systems viewpoint keeping in mind that even lower levels of a program can be defined as a set of models.

With DBTF, we model objects from the real world with a formal but friendly graphical language and then use that model to build an implementation-independent design around those objects. We describe a set of system-oriented concepts and a modeling technique that can be used to analyze problem requirements, design a solution to the problem, and then automatically implement that solution in terms of an architecture of choice (e.g., choice of operating system, programming language, graphical user interface, communications protocol, database, or legacy code).

We see effective reuse itself as an inherently preventative concept. Reusing something that has no errors, to obtain a desired functionality, avoids the errors of a newly developed system; time and money will not be wasted in developing that new system. Reuse can be successful only if the system is worth reusing. The functionality requirements of each have to be equivalent to the system being reused. This means starting from the beginning of a life cycle, not its end — as is typically the case with traditional methods. From there, a system can be reused for each new phase of development. No matter what kind, every ten reuses saves ten unnecessary developments.

Because DBTF systems can be developed with properties that control their very own design and development, the methodology results in the creation of reusable systems that promote automation. Each system definition models both its application and its life cycle.

It has been our experience that the requirements definition for a software-based system determines to a great extent the degree to which the development of that system is a success. Not only should the requirements be defined to state the user's explicit intent, but they should also support the process of defining themselves and the systems implemented from them. These are underlying concepts of DBTF.

With an automation of DBTF, the same concepts and same notation can be used throughout the entire systems design and software development process. There's no need for the software engineer to translate into a new notation at each development stage.

The DBTF approach includes a language, an approach, and a process, all of which are based on a formal theory.

Formal but Friendly Language

Once understood, the characteristics of good design can be reused by incorporating them into a language for defining systems. The DBTF language — meta-language, really — is the key to DBTF. It can define any aspect of any system and integrate it with any other aspect, whether it is used to define highway, banking, library, missile, or enterprise systems; Internet based, real-time, client server, or database environments; across industries, academia or government. The same language can be used to define system requirements (where the language supports and accelerates the collective thinking process before concepts are well understood), specifications, design, and detailed design for functional, resource, and resource allocation architectures throughout all levels and layers of seamless definition, including hardware, software, and peopleware.

Although syntax independent, every syntax shares the same semantics. Overarching this is that all of these aspects are directly related to the real world and that the language inherently captures this.

DBTF's language is used to define system-oriented objects. A system-oriented object (SOO) is a system that is both object oriented and function oriented. Its function-oriented definitions are inherently integrated with its object-oriented definitions. With SOOs, every object is a system; every system is an object (Exhibit 5).

Unlike traditional approaches, DBTF concentrates on delivering formal and reliable systems as its main focus. Whereas traditional tools support a user in managing the process of developing software, DBTF's automation develops the software. In fact it developed itself.

DBTF is used throughout a life cycle, starting with the formulation of concepts and interviewing the user, and continuing with the definition of requirements, analysis, simulation, specification, design (including system architecture design), algorithm development, implementation, configuration management, testing, maintenance, and reverse engineering. Its users include end users, managers, system engineers, software engineers, and test engineers.

Modeling a System-Oriented Object

Every SOO model is defined in terms of functional hierarchies (FMaps) to capture time characteristics and type hierarchies (TMaps) to capture space characteristics (Exhibit 6). The TMap, a static view of the structure of the objects in a system, describes the types of objects in a system and the relationships between them. The FMap describes the functions in a system and the relationships between them — including the potential interactions among objects in the system as they change state and transition from function to function. Exhibit 7 contains an example of a very small view of

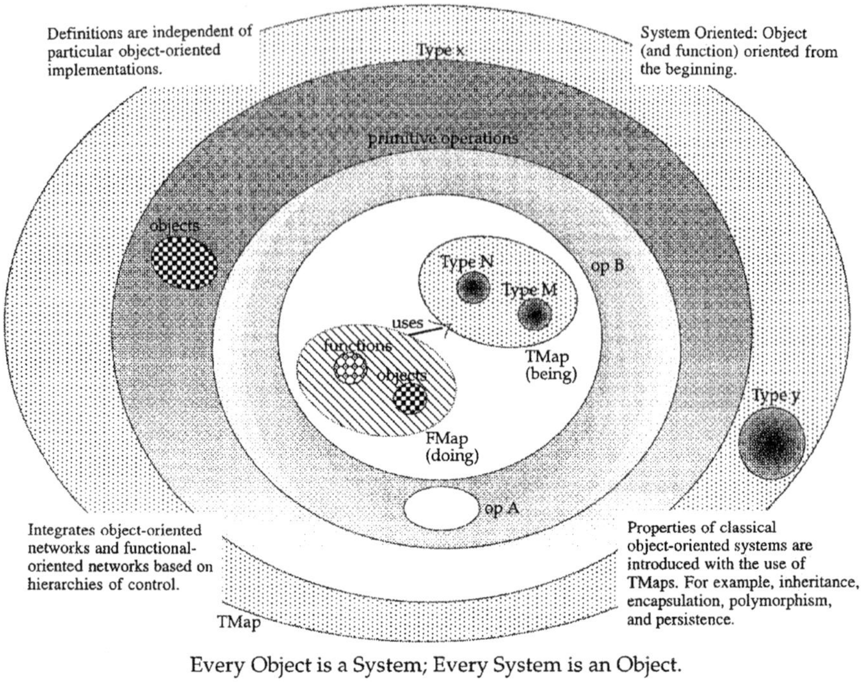

Exhibit 5. Every object is a system, every systems is an object.

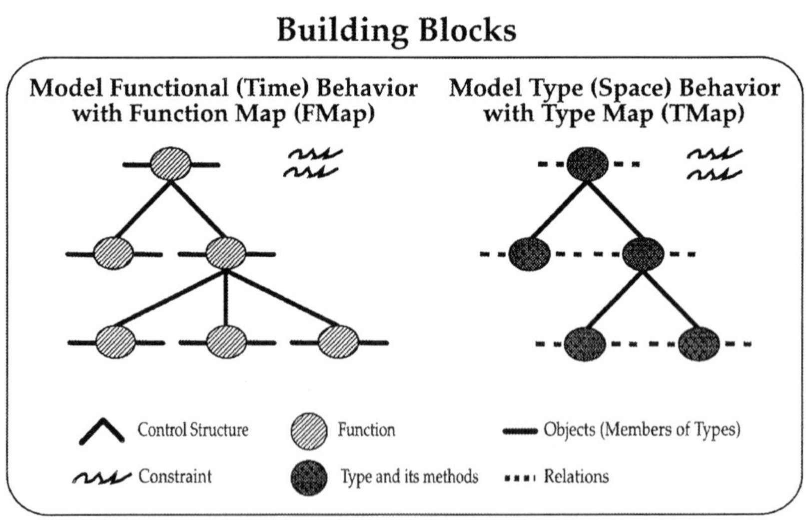

Exhibit 6. Building blocks.

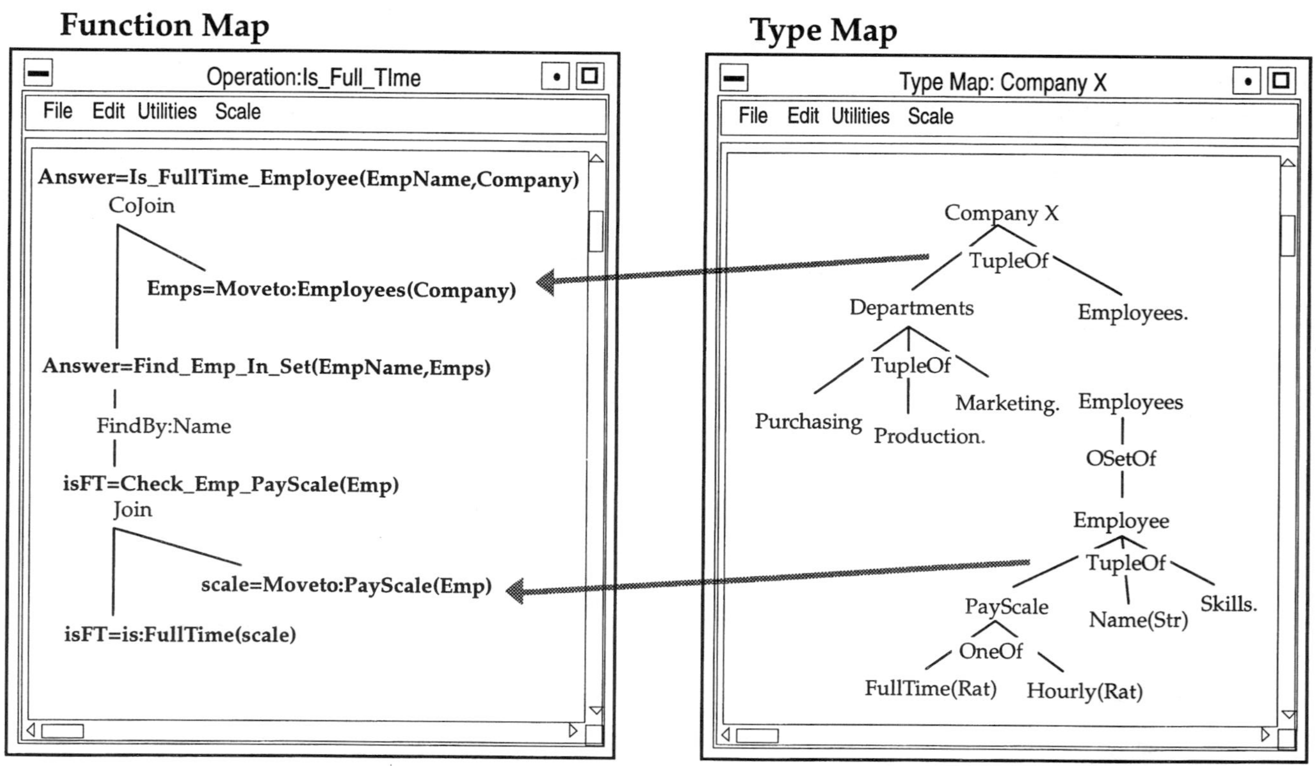

Specific Abstract Types inherit methods from Parameterized Types and are applied as leaf functions in FMaps

Exhibit 7. A system: the integration of FMaps and TMaps.

Company X's enterprise model (which has only one FMap and one TMap). In this model the TMap defines the objects having to do with kinds of employees and departments and the FMap is used to determine if a given employee is full-time or not.

Using an FMap, the functional model describes the dynamics or aspects of a system that change over time, including data flow, control flow, and the functional mappings (data transformations) that take place within a system. An FMap is an hierarchical network or graph whose nodes are functions, any of which could be assigned to a process. A parent's relationship to its children is defined in terms of a function structure. A function structure is a type of function with unspecified function nodes in its definition, but when the structure is used the nodes, as with the Tmaps, are specified or filled in.

FMaps and TMaps guide the designer in thinking through his concepts at all levels of system design. With these hierarchies, everything you need to know (no more, no less) is available. All model viewpoints can be obtained from FMaps and TMaps, including those mentioned above: data flow, control flow, state transitions, data structure, and dynamics. Maps of functions (FMaps) are inherently and naturally integrated with maps of types (TMaps).

Each function on an FMap node is defined in terms of and controls its children functions. For example, the function — Build the Table — could be decomposed into and control its children functions — Make Parts and Assemble. Each function on an FMap has one or more objects as its input and one or more objects as its output. All inputs of any function in an FMap as well as all outputs are members of types in a TMap. On a TMap there is a type at each node that is defined in terms of and controls its children types. For example, type, table, could be decomposed into and control its children types, legs, and top.

A TMap is a hierarchical network (control hierarchy or networked relations between objects) or graph whose nodes are object types. Every type on a TMap owns a set of inherited primitive operations. For every function (operation) within an object's domain there is an associated function control hierarchy (i.e., an FMap). Each object type node, as a parent, controls its children types; as a child, each is controlled by its parent. A parent's relationship to its children is defined in terms of a type structure. A type structure is a type of object with unspecified type nodes in its definition; when the structure is used, the nodes are specified or filled in.

The relationship between a parent and its children is determined by the type structure chosen to define it. A type structure encapsulates a set of operators to be applied to the relationships between the parent objects

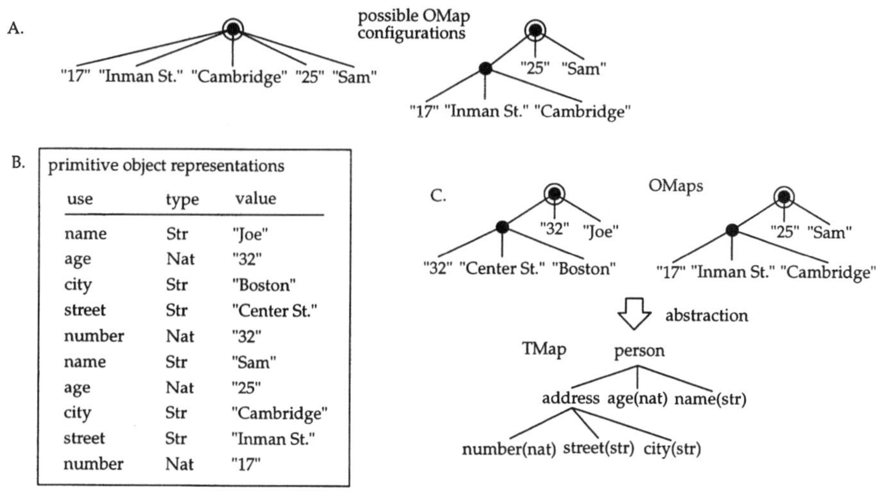

Abtracting OMaps into TMaps

Exhibit 8. Abstracting OMaps into TMaps.

and their children objects. A type structure may also include other encapsulated object types. Every type has a set of operations associated with it.

There are other types of control hierarchies for SOOs. For example, an object map (OMap) — which is an object control hierarchy — is an instance of a TMap. John's green truck represented by an OMap could, for example, be an object instance of object type, truck, represented by a TMap. In Exhibit 8 Joe, in one of the OMaps, is an instance of person on the TMap and Sam, on the other OMap, is an instance of the same type. Each object (a member of a type from a TMap) is an instantiation of a TMap type and resides in an object hierarchy (OMap).

FMaps are inherently integrated with TMaps by using these objects and their primitive operations. FMaps are used to define, integrate, and control the transformations of objects from one state to another state (for example, a table with a broken leg to a table with a fixed leg). Primitive functions corresponding to primitive operations on types defined in the TMap reside at the bottom nodes of an FMap. Primitive types reside at the bottom nodes of a TMap. Each primitive function (leaf node) on an FMap is a primitive operation of a member (object) of the TMap.

In this context, primitive does not imply low level; rather it is a term that describes the encapsulation of behavior and data behind a well-defined interface, raising the level of abstraction of a system. New primitive types are

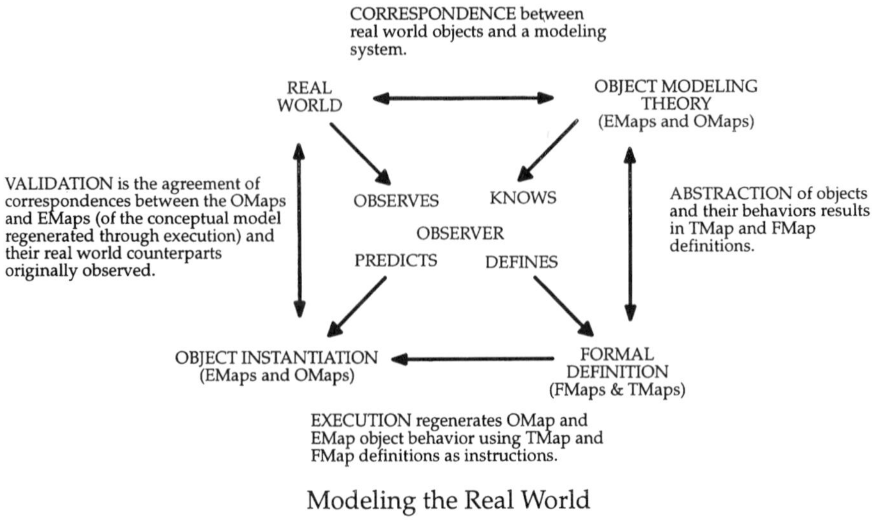

Exhibit 9. Modeling the real world.

defined and recursively reused in new DBTF systems. Primitive types are also used to define boundaries between a DBTF system and other existing systems (such as database managers or existing legacy systems). When a system has its input object states instantiated with values plugged in for a particular performance pass, it exists in the form of an execution hierarchy (EMap).

A way to begin designing a SOO is that an observer (or modeler) compares the behavior of real-world objects to the known tools that support the DBTF object modeling theory (Exhibit 9). Objects and their behaviors are represented in the object modeling theory in terms of OMaps, each of which is an instance of a TMap, and EMaps, each of which is an instance of an FMap, as tools. An OMap is a hierarchical network of objects and their relationships. An EMap is a set of functions instances and their relationships.

A history of instances of OMap and EMap model constructions (which are really based on an underlying control theory, upon which the modeling theory is based) can be simplified by abstracting them into formal definition as TMaps and FMaps, respectively. An OMap derives the control of its objects from a TMap. Likewise, an EMap derives the control of its actions from an FMap. Once a modeler has a formal definition, it is then used to run (or regenerate the OMap and EMap instances of) the system. Since the object instantiation is to be a prediction of the original real-world correspondence that was defined, it is validated by comparing it to the original real world with the object instantiation. If it matches, it is an accurate depiction of the real world and the observer's intent has been satisfied.

Models and Their Integration

Relative to OMaps and EMaps, TMaps and FMaps are reusables for capturing an object's structure and behavior. Whereas an OMap depicts an actual instance of an object's behavior, a TMap depicts one of a possible set of instances of an object's behavior. Whereas an EMap depicts an actual execution instance, an FMap depicts one of a possible set of execution instances. An object is an instance of a type. An action is an instance of a function. Conversely, when one executes a definition consisting of FMaps and TMaps, the FMap abstract definition is instantiated as one or more EMaps and the TMap abstract definition is instantiated as one or more OMaps.

An FMap (Exhibit 10A) is a definition of a system of object events and their possible interactions. The FMap integrates with the TMap to specify the event types and the specific function (as an instance of a primitive operation of a TMap type) to be performed on each object. The FMap controls the sequencing and activation of events — the event structures — in terms of what we call primitive control structures, which define all the possible ways in which events may functionally interact. As we discussed earlier, the concept of a structure is applied to both FMaps and TMaps.

A TMap (Exhibit 10B) defines the potential organization of objects for its OMap instances, the potential relations, and the interactions which an object may have with other objects. The TMap is sometimes thought of as a blueprint for object construction. These potential interactions are defined for each parent type as a set of primitive operation definitions. When used in an FMap, a primitive operation defines how the parent may interact with other objects in a particular functional context as with a primitive function.

An EMap (Exhibit 10C), an instantiation of an FMap, indicates within a particular time interval the lines of active control over actions that are in force for a set of co-occurring events and their associated OMap objects. Primitive functions of an FMap become primitive actions on an EMap. An action, once activated with its input events, transitions their associated OMap objects to output events. As new events come into existence, new lines of control are formed to bring future actions under control. When events and actions are no longer needed and they recede into the past, their lines of control are withdrawn. An EMap is always only in the present, while the FMap represents all the potential activations of the system of events and actions over all time.

An OMap (Exhibit 10D), an instantiation of a TMap, indicates the current state of interrelationships of the set of objects of which it is in control.

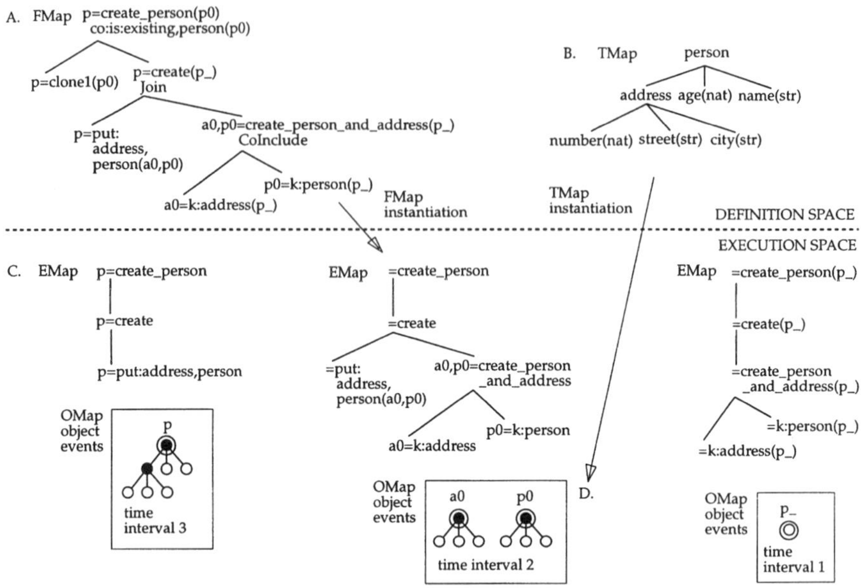

Relationship Between Definition and Execution

Exhibit 10. Relationship between definition and execution.

OMap objects and their relationships are subject to the actions of the EMap. As actions in response to object events are managed by the EMap, their corresponding OMap objects (referenced by an event) evolve, appear, change (having relations with other objects and severing relations), and disappear. OMap objects take on a shape or structure as constrained by the blueprint of combinations which are allowed in the TMap.

A Design Scenario

Typically, a team of designers will begin to design a system at any level (this system could be hardware, software, peopleware, or some combination) by sketching a TMap of their application. This is where they decide on the types of objects (and the relationships between these objects) that they will have in their system. Often a Road Map (RMap), which organizes all system objects (including FMaps, TMaps, and other RMaps) will be sketched in parallel with the TMap (Exhibit 11).

As we've been told by several SOO designers: "the FMaps begin almost to fall into place once a TMap(s) has been agreed upon by the design team because of the natural partitioning of functionality (or groups of functionality) provided to the designers by the TMap system." The structure of a TMap by its very nature defines several universal mechanisms that sup-

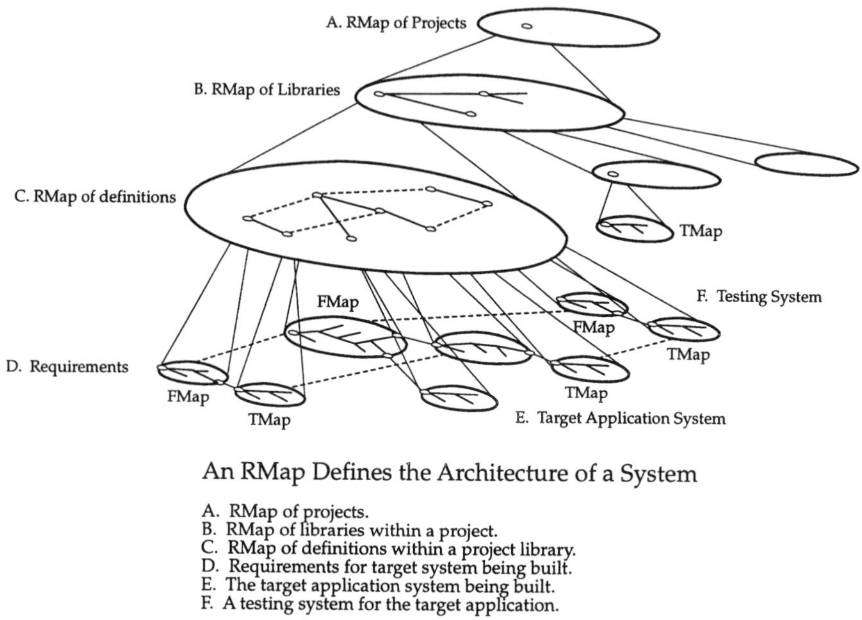

Exhibit 11. An RMap defines the architecture of the system.

---

port its life cycle. For example, a TMap has an inherent way to be instantiated, to be populated using a GUI, to be stored persistently, etc. The TMap provides the structural criteria from which to evaluate the functional partitioning of the system (for example, the shape of the structural partitioning of the FMaps is balanced against the structural organization of the shape of the objects as defined by the TMap). With FMaps and TMaps, a system (and its viewpoints) is divided into functionally natural components and groups of functional components which naturally work together; a system is defined from the very beginning to inherently integrate and make understandable its own real-world definition.

All FMaps and TMaps are ultimately defined in terms of three primitive control structures: a parent controls its children to have a dependent relationship, an independent relationship, or a decision-making relationship. We say "ultimately" because, as we'll see below, more abstract structures can be defined in terms of the primitive ones. A formal set of rules is associated with each primitive structure. If these rules are followed, interface errors — which typically account for up to 90% of all system errors — are removed before the fact (that is, during the definition phase) by preventing them in the first place. In a traditional development these errors would not even be discovered until testing. Using the primitive structures and their derivatives supports a system to be defined from the very beginning to inherently maximize its own elimination of errors.

The TMap provides universal primitive operations of type, Any, which are used for controlling objects and their object states which are inherited by all types. They create, destroy, copy, reference, move, access a value, detect and recover from errors, and access the type of an object. They provide an easy way to manipulate and think about different types of objects.

With the universal primitive operations, building systems can be accomplished in a more uniform manner. TMap and OMap are also available as types to facilitate the ability of a system to understand itself better and manipulate all objects the same way when it is beneficial to do so.

TMap properties ensure the proper use of objects in an FMap. A TMap has a corresponding set of control properties for controlling spatial relationships between objects.

Any system can be defined completely using only the primitive structures, but less-primitive structures can be derived from the primitive ones and accelerate the process of defining and understanding a system. Nonprimitive structures can be defined for both FMaps and TMaps. They can be created for asynchronous, synchronous, and interrupt scenarios used in real-time distributed systems such as those found in Internet applications. Similarly, retrieval and query structures can be defined for database management systems within a client server environment. Nonprimitive structures can also be created for more vertical market-driven reusables, for example for a cash management or accident reporting system.

PROPERTIES OF SYSTEM-ORIENTED OBJECTS FOR BETTER, FASTER, CHEAPER SYSTEMS

The goals defined for Company X are the requirements for its enterprise as a target system. DBTF can then become part of the specifications for meeting those goals. As discussed above, DBTF is a systems theory for defining, designing, and developing software systems in terms of SOOs. Within this context, we'll discuss further the properties of SOOs in order to show how they can support the goals of Company X, as part of supporting GOAL#13.

The DBTF system-oriented approach has many properties required for a system to be conceptualized in terms of objects. They are discussed in terms of system-oriented objects. They serve as requirements for the analysis and design phase as well as all of the later phases, such as implementation.

Above all, a system-oriented object is about quality. And quality systems are systems that are both reliable and affordable (Exhibit 12). Whenever a

Exhibit 12. System-Oriented Object Properties of Development Before the Fact

Quality (better, faster, cheaper)

Reliable
Affordable

Reliable (better)

In control and under control
Based on a set of axioms
- domain identification (intended, unintended)
- ordering (priority and timing)
- access rights:incoming object (or relation), outgoing object (or relation)
- replacement

Formal
- consistent, logically complete
- necessary and sufficient
- common semantic base
- unique state identification

Error free (based on formal definition of "error")
always gets the right answer at the right time and in the right place
- satisfies users and developers intent

Handles the unpredictable
Predictable

Affordable (Faster, Cheaper)

Reusable
Optimizes resources in operation and development
- in minimum time and space
- with best fit of objects to resources

Reusable

Understandable, integratable and maintainable
Flexible
Follows standards
Automation
Common definitions
- natural modularity
  - natural separation (e.g., functional architecture from its resource architectures);
  - dumb modules
  - an object is integrated with respect to structure, behavior and properties of control
- integration in terms of structure and behavior
- type of mechanisms

Reusables *continued*

- function maps (relate an object's function to other functions)
- object type maps (relate objects to objects)
- structures of functions and types

category
- relativity
  - instantiation
  - polymorphism
  - parent/child
  - being/doing
  - having/not having
- abstraction
  - encapsulation
  - replacement
  - relation including function
  - typing including classification
  - form including both structure and behavior (for object types and functions)
- derivation
  - deduction
  - inference
  - inheritance

Handles the unpredictable

Throughout development and operation
- Without affecting unintended areas
- Error detect and recover from the unexpected
- Interface with, change and reconfigure in asynchronous, distributed, real time environment

Flexible

Changeable without side effects
Evolvable
Durable
Reliable
Extensible
Ability to break up and put together
- one object to many: modularity, decomposition, instantiation
- many objects to one: composition, applicative operators, integration, abstraction

Portable
- secure
- diverse and changing layered developments

Exhibit 12. System-Oriented Object Properties of Development Before the Fact *(Continued)*

Flexible *continued*

open architecture (implementation, resource allocation, and execution independence)
plug-in (or be plugged into) or reconfiguration of different modules
adaptable for different organizations, applications, functionality, people, products

Automation

The ultimate form of reusable
Formalize, mechanize, then automate
it
its development
that which automates its development

Understandable, Integratable and Maintainable

Reliable
A measurable history
Natural correspondence to real world
persistence, create and delete
appear and disappear
accessibility
reference
assumes existence of objects
real time and space constraints
representation
relativity, abstraction, derivation

Understandable, Integratable and Maintainable *continued*

Provides user friendly definitions
recognizes that one user's friendliness is another user's nightmare
hides unnecessary detail (*abstraction*)
variable, user selected syntax
self teaching
derived from a common semantic base
common definition mechanisms
Communicates with common semantics to all entities
Defined to be simple as possible but not simpler
Defined with integration of all of its objects (and all aspects of these objects)
Traceability of behavior and structure and their changes (maintenance) throughout its birth, life and death
Knows and able to reach the state of
completion
definition
development of itself and that which develops it
analysis
design
implementation
instantiation
testing
maintenance

Note: All italic words point to a reusable.

Taken from Hamilton, M., Software Design and Development, *The Electronics Handbook,* CRC Press, Boca Raton, FL, 1996, Chap. 122.

property in the table is underlined it refers to a section that is a reusable. This table is a TMap-like definition; it was first created as a TMap sketch and has a corresponding TMap to go with it. For example, the object "affordable" has children objects "reusable" and optimizes resources in operation and development.

Whether a system or application is viewed as an object with its functions or as a function with its objects is not the issue. One person's object can be another person's function. Either can be viewed as a system; it's just a matter of perspective. What does matter is how these objects and their functions (or functions and their objects) are put together and, ultimately, how they will work together as a family of systems — both now and for future reuse.

The properties of system-oriented objects in DBTF include those which the object-oriented world has come to expect (the desirable ones, that is), and more. The DBTF notion of system-oriented objects can be represented by a simple equation.

quality system = reliable and affordable system
= better, faster, and cheaper system

A reliable system is in control, is based on a set of known axioms (i.e., assumptions), on the assumption of a universal set of objects, has properties of being formal, and is error-free. An error free system always gets the right answer at the right time and in the right place and satisfies the intent of the developers and the users.

Each axiom defines a relation of immediate domination. The union of the relations defined by the axioms is control. Among other things, the axioms establish the control relationships of an object for replacement or invocation, input and output, input and output access rights, error detection and recovery, and ordering, during its developmental and operational states of existence.

A SOO can be reliable and still handle the unreliable. It is predictable, yet, it can handle the unpredictable. By predictable is meant that its behavior and structure can be understood in terms of its relationships, without ambiguity.

Predicting the Unpredictable

To handle the unpredictable, an object must be able to operate under all conditions — including that which is off nominal — without affecting unintended areas, both in development and during system operation. This means the object must be able to change and reconfigure when necessary, as well as detect errors and recover from the unexpected. If required, the object will operate in, simulate, communicate with, respond to, and interface with other objects within an asynchronous, distributed, real-time environment.

Consistency is Critical

The formal rules behind SOOs ensure that an object is consistent and logically complete, and that an object is unambiguous and there are no interface errors — that is, conflicts of timing, priority, and sharing of objects — within and between objects.

An object is consistent if it does not contradict any other object within its internal and external environments. Associating incorrect properties or behavior with an object is an example of an inconsistency. For instance, if John is inadvertently assigned to a mail carrier rather than a passenger aircraft for his flight home, one could conclude that the properties of mail were incorrectly assigned to John.

Timing, data, and priority conflicts are examples of inconsistencies. For example, John and Mary might be assigned to the same seat at the same time in a passenger aircraft — which would be a timing, data, and priority conflict all at once.

An object is logically complete only if it completely satisfies a set of requirements and its meaning is well understood. If an airplane's requirements are that it must fly in the air, and it has a propeller and wheels but it has no engine, then it probably does not fulfill its original requirements — unless something other than an engine will perform in an equivalent manner.

With formality comes the property of minimality — the ability to define necessary and sufficient information about an object. In other words, the minimality of an object refers to the ability to say everything one needs to say about an object to understand it, but no more than is needed. Albert Einstein was an advocate of minimality.

The formal rules behind SOOs ensure they share a common semantic base with each other. The formal rules also ensure the property of single reference and single assignment, resulting in object states that are uniquely identifiable. This property is very important for traceability.

In and Under Control

Control is a pivotal property of system-oriented objects. A SOO is both in control of its children objects and under control of its parent object — just as objects in the real world. For instance, the CEO of a corporation is in control of the people who work for him, but is under the control of the board of directors. A parent bank controls its subsidiaries but is under the control of the Federal Reserve. One could model a truck to be in control of the parts of which it is made and/or of the passengers and driver, which could be part of the truck as an object (depending on how the truck is modeled). The function of truck — Drive the Truck — can be modeled to be in control of its children functions, Drive Left and Drive Right, where there is a choice to drive in either of those two directions. SOOs are both in control and under control throughout all phases of their development and operation.

In DBTF, basically everything is an object, including every function. Every object has behavior (that is, function — including its dynamics), belongs to a type, and has structure. Control of objects and functions is accomplished with FMaps and TMaps. In a TMap, every object type on the hierarchy is in control of its children types and every object type on the hierarchy is controlled by its parent. For every function (operation) within an object's domain there is an associated function control hierarchy (i.e., an FMap).

As mentioned earlier, an object can be either a parent or child depending on the role it plays. A parent object (e.g., trip) controls its children objects (e.g., plane and passengers). Each child (e.g., kind of plane) in turn is controlled by its parent (plane).

Parents can control children in different ways. A parent object might control a pair of its children to be independent of each other. For example, plane would probably be modeled to be independent of passengers. Another parent can control a pair of its children to be dependent on each other. The morning schedule, for instance, might be modeled to be dependent on the evening schedule.

A parent can also control a pair of its children objects where one of the children is selected to represent that parent. In the trip system we've been discussing, there is a decision as to whether the plane chosen to represent the parent will be a mail carrier or a passenger aircraft. If for example, the mail carrier is selected then it will represent its parent.

Other forms of control can be derived in terms of these more primitive kinds of control. For example, there are cases where a parent can control more than two children with combinations of independent and dependent relationships. Each parent is completely replaced by its children as we move down the hierarchy — as in the case where "trip" is replaced by "plane" or "passengers" — except that the parent always remains in control.

How Axioms Can Help Objects

We mentioned earlier that part of being reliable is being based on a known set of axioms. A SOO has these properties of control precisely because it is based on a set of control axioms.

Replacement is the ability of an object to be replaced in some manner (e.g., in terms of functionality) by one or more objects while remaining in control. In addition to having properties of control of replacement, a SOO has properties of control of access rights, ordering, and domain identification. A real-world example would be the supervisor at your job, who can turn over some of her functions to those who work under her while still remaining in control of the process.

The property of access rights is the ability to locate an object from a set of objects and, once located, the ability to reference or assign the value of that object. A parent is in control of its childrens' access rights, just as the supervisor is in control of the access rights of her workers. A password is an implementation example of a mechanism for granting such access rights. The supervisor is also responsible for providing access to objects for her workers while other things are off limits (what we call incoming objects or relations) and for providing a place for the workers to put them (outgoing objects or relations).

Ordering is the ability to establish a relation in a set of objects, with one element preceding the other element so any two object elements are comparable. Ordering includes priority — the ability to determine which object is more important than any other object — and timing. In the case of our imaginary supervisor, she would determine which worker uses a given machine first (priority) and would establish schedules and deadlines (timing). It is not unlike defining a list of things to do to make sure that they will eventually get done and prioritizing that list to make sure that the things that should get done first do get done first. Some objects' priorities are influenced by their dependencies. If, for example, it is necessary to go to the bank to get money before you eat, the bank trip is a higher priority process than eating.

With the property of domain identification, an object is responsible for determining whether it will be able to perform its own intended function. The object is able to identify intended from unintended phenomena as part of its domain, and is therefore responsible for its own error detection and recovery. As an object, the supervisor is similarly responsible for completing her own function, which is the task at hand she performs for her parent or supervisor. If the supervisor works for a bank and she handles only European transactions and if someone asks her to work on an Asian transaction, she would reject that request and send it back to go where it belongs.

Having the means to define boundary conditions for an object provides the ability to safely exclude invalid states of an object. This provides every object the potential to perform its own error detection and recovery.

Although formal, a SOO is also practical in that it is affordable to build and use. Being affordable depends on (that is, inherits the properties of) being reusable. This optimizes resources — but to optimize resources requires that an object is efficient to develop, maintain, and operate.

What do we mean by efficient development and maintenance? Minimum time to complete, minimum use of resources (such as people), minimum physical space of all kinds, the best fit between development functions and resources without compromising the object's integrity — all these are indications of efficient development and maintenance. Similarly, efficient operation means the best fit between functions and resources, as well as execution in minimum time and space.

Common definition mechanisms are also pivotal to SOOs, and especially to their reuse. Just because something is called an object or because it follows some of the rules of object orientation does not necessarily make it a candidate for reuse. A SOO that is reusable depends on being flexible, understandable, integratable, and maintainable. It follows standards, is made up of common mechanisms, and the process of using it, relating to it, generating from it, inheriting it, and so on can all be automated once it has been mechanized.

Automation is the ultimate form of being reusable. The first step in the process of automation is to formalize, then to mechanize. In a SOO environment, not only the object but its development and that which automates its development should be actualized as automated SOO objects as well.

Common Definition Mechanisms

Relativity (which includes polymorphism), abstraction (which includes typing — of which classification is an example — and encapsulation), and derivation (which includes inheritance, inference, and deduction) are examples of properties of types of use of common mechanisms for a SOO. These are discussed below.

Relativity. Relativity is the ability for an object to change roles depending on such things as how, when, and with respect to what it is being used or viewed. For example, an object can be in a "being" (i.e., static) or "doing" (i.e., dynamic) state. A dog looking at his master is in the state of "doing." A grocery store — from the "being" or static point of view — might comprise freezer cases and clerks as part of its physical make up. From the "doing" or dynamic perspective of "running the store," the object grocery store could take in customers, food, and money as input and provide profit as one of its outputs. An object can be in a being state and a doing state at the same time — for instance, the dog might be described by his master as a Shepherd that can talk (and as such the dog is in a "being" state), while at the same time the dog already is looking at his master (that is, the dog is in a "doing" state).

We could give dozens more of examples of an object changing its role depending on how it is viewed. An object could be viewed as the one in control (that is, as a "parent") of another object, or that same object could be viewed as being controlled by another object (that is, as a "child"). For instance, the master as an object type is in control of the dog as an object type — the object being controlled — but the dog at the same time can be in control of the biscuit as an object.

An object also can have and not have at the same time. Again, consider the dog, which can be defined such that she is able to eat food and drink water. But at any given moment the dog might have water and not have food. Plus, depending on one's perspective, we could be referring to different dogs here. For instance, from Jane's perspective the dog being referred to is Fido. For Ron, the dog being referred to is Clark within one time frame and Rei another time. From one person's perspective the same dog could be viewed as small by John and large by Jane. It's similar to a development process, where requirements (an object) for one group are specifications for another group or even implementation by still another group. Such differences in perspective are part of the reason people fight and countries have wars. They do not realize that they can all be right and wrong or stupid and smart at the same time.

Having, which is another property of relativity, is a object's ability to have a child, a sibling, a set of proper values, and an architecture, for example. Conversely, belonging, another property of relativity, is an object's ability to belong to another object in terms of a defined relationship. Examples are belonging to a parent where the relationship is one of control, or a type where the relationship is one where the object is an instance of a type.

Polymorphism. Polymorphism, which provides the ability for a particular operation to behave differently on different types of objects, is also an example of the use of the property of relativity.

The implementation selected for a given object depends on the type of object using that operation, and there can be more than one implementation for an operation. The get operation, for example, may behave differently on type employee than on type paragraph. A specific implementation of an operation on a type is similar to a method or member function in an object-oriented programming language. Because an operator is polymorphic, it may have more than one method implementing it.

Methods should be transparent to the designer, since each object knows how to perform its own operations. The issue of methods need be addressed only when new operations are added to a type, or a new type is added. It should be noted that designers usually think in terms of operations, not methods.

Abstraction. The property of abstraction is the ability to recognize commonality among a set of objects and then identify a new object for which any of the original objects can stand. Examples of abstraction include typing, relations, encapsulation, and replacement — all of which help separate out levels of thinking.

To understand how abstraction works, think about how one designer for a given system definition might choose to focus on different parts of a problem than another for the same application. For example, a clock could be defined as digital or analog, with or without its hands, and whether those hands are black or white — leaving out or adding other details. Or the definition could be any device for telling time, such as a sundial with "clock" becoming a particular form of implementation for such a device. From a SOO perspective, an analog clock with hands is more general than a clock with numbers since there is no need to know how to read numbers on the analog clock.

Unlike with the use of SOOs, abstraction can potentially lead to loss of control of objects within a traditional environment. Aspects that are dealt with in an algorithm such as traceability and event priority control of ordering can inadvertently be removed during the abstraction process to make a reusable for the sake of ease of use. Such problems with events surface, for example, in applications with call-backs function where the user is not fully in control of the priority of events. To base such abstractions on a common set of rules which is updated to correct problems as they surface is one way of coping after the fact. But it is far better to avoid such problems from the beginning by the very way a system is defined, where events and the rules which they abide by come built into the language used to define that system.

This abstraction process separates out the what from the how of the thinking or design process. There can be as many levels or layers as needed, depending on the different views considered desirable or necessary to define and implement an application.

Abstraction helps the designer delay decisions as long as possible or not to have to deal at all with certain properties within an application. Before real operating systems became available, the details of scheduling were necessarily embedded in an application. Likewise, before GUIs were available, GUI aspects were embedded in an application. With system-oriented objects, any kind of detail (except for that which is always required by the language to maintain control) can be removed from any kind of application; it is no longer necessary to embed details that can be saved as a reusable for later use. This greatly increases the potential for reuse within other architectures: the more that implementation details can be removed or abstracted for a given application, the greater that potential.

If abstraction is successful each layer lives on throughout all of its lower layers of design — with each layer containing more implementation detail than any of its higher layers. Of course, one designer's application is another's architecture or resource. One designer's design is another person's implementation.

Encapsulation. Encapsulation (or containment) allows an object to have an inside not accessible to other objects and an outside which is accessible to other objects. To the outside objects, the inside comprises implementation details of the object in question. From a practical view, it involves packaging-related object instances and operations together. The outside view of an object may be completely replaced by the inside view of the object in question.

Encapsulation is desirable because it prevents the massive ripple effects caused by small changes to programs that are too interdependent. The implementation of an object can be changed — to fix errors, port to a new architecture, increase performance, or evolve to cleaner code or better-written code — without affecting the applications that use it.

For objects, encapsulation is a natural extension of the information-hiding strategy developed in structured languages years ago. The Motif and Windows GUI environments are examples; users of Motif and Windows operations are not affected by changes in new releases of Motif or Windows since all of these changes — from the perspective of the user — are made to the inside of the objects. Operating systems, which have been around for years, are an earlier example.

Abstraction comes in different forms, including object behavior, object structure, functional behavior, and functional structure. Object behavior refers to the common relationships that hold for members of a type of object. For example, the linear ordering relationship for members of object type "time" is a behavioral characteristic of time. All derived object relationships are traced to common semantic primitives.

Object Structure. Object structure refers to the common relationships (control is such a relationship) among members of an object type. Abstraction of object structure refers to the common relationships among members of an object type without specifying particular instances that fit the pattern. As an example, a rational number can always be replaced by an object structure of two integers.

Typing. Typing is the ability to group objects together according to common functional behavior and object structure. This means that objects with the same attributes and functions (operations) and behavior are grouped into the same object type. Money, corporation, bank, customer, engine, truck, doctor, hospital, paragraph, and book are all examples of types of objects. A type of object is an abstraction of an object. For example, type "doctor" is an abstraction of Dr. Jones and Dr. Goldberg. Each object is an instance of an object type. Dr. Jones is, therefore, an instance of type "doctor."

A type describes objects important to a particular kind of application. Any choice of types is arbitrary and depends on the application. Each type describes a set of objects which could be infinite or finite. Each instance shares the same types of attributes and general behavior, and has the same operations as any other instance of the same type, but it has its own values for its specific behavior and attribute. Although two banks are of type bank, one could be located in New York and another in London.

A type can be divided into subtypes, forming a type hierarchy. Every object belonging to that type (instance of that type) along with its sub objects exists as an object hierarchy and abides by the control rules of its type hierarchy. For every object there is a type, and every object knows to which type it belongs. For example, the bank in New York knows that it is a bank and what the characteristics of a bank are such as location, owners, type, etc.

With the use of types, issues of data and behavior (i.e., dynamics and function) are combined. A modeler does not need to get involved with implementation issues such as how an operation on an object is implemented, or how many implementations exist for a particular operation. Changes made to the implementation have no effect on the modeler.

Functional Behavior. When we speak of functional behavior, we are referring to the relationship between the input and the output of an object's function. The function that states the relationship between input and output is an abstraction with respect to an algorithm for implementing such a relationship.

Whereas object behavior refers to the common relationships between members of a particular kind of object (green car and red car are members of a kind of object, car), functional behavior refers to the relationship between the input and the output of a function of an object. If a function "drive the car" takes "driver" and "car" as input and produces "driver in car" as an output, it doesn't matter whether the car is green or red: the function of driving either car takes in a car and a driver, and ends up with a driver in the car structure. Functional structure refers to the relationships between functions (see above). Abstraction of functional structure refers to the ability to define common patterns between functions without specifying the particular functions that fit the patterns.

With structure, there is the ability to distinguish between relations which have properties of dependence, independence, and decision making within, between, and about objects, both in terms of types of objects and functions of types. Every relation between and among objects and between and among an object's functions and its relations is defined in terms of a structure: type structures for TMaps and function structures for FMaps.

Derivation. Reuse can be also be accomplished through derivation. One form of derivation is inheritance — the ability of an object to derive behavior in terms of other objects. Other forms include those which are more indirect: deduction, the process of reasoning in which a conclusion follows necessarily from already existing premises; and inference, which is reasoning from the general to the specific.

Attributes, behavior, and operations are shared between types of objects based on the relationships between the types of objects as defined by a type hierarchy. A type can be defined as abstract or as broadly as desired and then refined into successively finer and less abstract types. When an abstract type is decomposed from a parent into its children on a type hierarchy from the standpoint of a class, subclass relationship — such as that of a truck to a dump truck — each subclass may inherit all of the properties of its superclass along with its own unique properties. Not every parent-child relationship on an object type hierarchy is a class, subclass relationship. This relationship depends on how the designer designs his application.

Classification. Classification is the potential of a particular type of object to share an overlapping set of properties — that is, functional behavior and structure in common — with other objects which are subtypes of that type. A class is a particular kind of type which is divided into subtypes (subclasses) — each of which shares an overlapping set of properties. We refer to this as a class hierarchy.

The ability to share common properties among several classes within a common superclass can greatly reduce wasteful repetition within the design process. This is illustrated with the example of a dump truck. Whereas it would probably be modeled to be a subclass of class (type) truck, an engine type contained within a truck type on a type hierarchy would probably not be modeled to be a class, subclass relationship but a different kind of relationship on the type hierarchy. Then, the dump truck could inherit all of the properties of class "truck" — such as its ability to be driven and its having an engine. But it would not make sense for the engine to be modeled to inherit its properties from a truck, or at least the same truck as the one that was the superclass of the dump truck.

Building Blocks

The use of common building blocks is important for effective reuse. We have discussed two kinds of common mechanisms that are needed to define and then reuse a system-oriented object: object types and object functions. They capture the properties of a definition as well as follow the path of natural modularity.

Flexibility. When an object has the property of flexibility, the user can break it up and to put it together again without compromising its integrity. A flexible object is portable, extendable, evolvable, and changeable without causing side effects. With a flexible object, one may change his or her mind both with respect to changing requirements for what the object is supposed to do as well as where that object can reside or how it is implemented.

Portability. A portable object can work in different environments, as a layer within a changing, diverse, and multilayered system and within a secure application. Security is an object's ability to keep its behavior and/or structure secure from objects which do not have the "need to know."

A portable object can work within different groups of people, organizations, functionality, products, or applications. It can be a plug-in for another object, or another object can be plugged into it. It can be used for different implementations, resource allocations, or executions within sequential, multiprogrammed, or distributed environments. A portable object can be implemented with the language or operating system of choice; executed by a computer, robot, or human; and be interfaced within a reactive client-server system or mainframe environment.

Breaking Objects Up and Putting Them Back Together Again. It's important to be able to combine objects with other objects to form a new object, or to divide the object into a set of objects. There are many ways to break up an SOO and put it back together again.

Breaking something up and putting it back together again has an important practical use. One can use these processes to define distinct objects for the various architectures in an environment, including the functional architecture (for example, the software for the cash management system), its potential resource architectures (Windows or UNIX platform), and the mappings from the functional architecture to each of its potential resource architectures (where each mapping itself is an architecture and therefore represented by an object). Such flexibility makes it possible to work with each architecture and make changes to it without affecting any others.

An example of such a flexible system is an enterprise model. The functional architecture might describe a corporation's financial processes. The resource architecture includes the people (e.g., the accountants and the computers that perform financial calculations); the resource allocation architecture includes the assignment of tasks to the people and computers for performing the functions of the corporate processes.

Composition and Decomposition. Composition is the process by which a set of objects becomes a set of children to another object, their parent. Decomposition is the ability to identify one of the possible sets of subordinate objects, each set of which could replace an object in terms of its behavior. This is one of several inverse processes of abstraction. Once a set of subordinates has been chosen, the decomposition has taken place. The abstraction for this chosen set — as well as for the other possible sets — is the original before it was decomposed. The abstraction, composition, is the inverse of decomposition.

Again, take our truck type of object: it could be decomposed into wheels and engine, or it could be decomposed into a choice of a green or blue truck. In both cases, "truck" is an abstraction of each set of its decomposed objects. Similarly, the function type of object — Drive the Truck — can be decomposed into subtypes Drive to the Store and Drive Home. In both cases, the abstraction of these functions is Drive the Truck. Any object can be viewed as a "what" with respect to a set of objects into which it has been decomposed (the "how").

Integration and Modularity. Having the ability to integrate objects into larger objects (or configure a larger system out of smaller systems) is a reverse property to separating an object into smaller objects.

Integration is the processing of connecting one object to another object, both statically and dynamically. Modularity is the ability to separate parts of an object in a way that allows its subparts to stand alone as objects while maintaining the same system-oriented properties (including those traditionally associated with being modular, such as portability, flexibility, and reusability).

With these mechanisms, there is natural modularity. Objects are "dumb" in that they do not know anything about their users or parents. Further, they provide the ability to separate parts of a system such that only those parts that need to be changed are changed when a part of the system is changed. An example is having the ability to separate a functional architecture from its resource architectures, so a change to the resource does not change the functional architecture unnecessarily — and vice versa. Another example is when an object type is changed, thus making known every impact (and only those impacts) to its functions and the functions of the objects to which it relates. With these mechanisms an object is integrated with respect to structure, behavior, and properties of control.

Just as a car does not know who is driving it, a system-oriented object does not need to know who is using it, for what purpose it is being used, or where it is going. This holds for objects as well as for functions within an object. This makes for models that are user-, intent-, and application-independent.

SOOs are also resource-independent; for example, a module does not need to know under which operating system or server it will be running. Different resources can be applied to a module depending on different constraints in the use of a module. This is important, because in a given system time may be more important than space, or money may be more important than time. A module is also syntax-independent. Like the sport of orienteering — which has a common semantics whether one is in Japan, Timbuktu, or Ohio — a SOO's semantics is not bound by artifacts of a particular syntax within which one chooses to state the object. A module is also independent of its implementation.

Applicative and Computable. The property of relating one set of instances (domain) to another set of instances (range) is called applicative, while computable is the property of relating these instances, one pair at a time. Applicative applies to objects when one type of object is related to another type of object. It refers to functional in the mathematical context of function — that is, the relationship of input to output. Both the input object and output object exist. The function is the relation such that each input corresponds to one output. A computation (or performance pass) is an instance of a function. An object is an instance of a type of object. For example, in the function

Total income = add (salary income, consulting income)
= salary income + consulting income

there is always a unique total income for a selected combination of salary and consulting incomes.

If an object or an algorithm can be established to be allocated to each unique definition object so that it is set up to execute correctly on a resource (e.g., machine), then that definition is computable or able to be performed. Instantiation is the process of performing or executing a system. An object can be an instance of a type of object. An algorithm can be an instance of a function. Timing is the ability to instantiate an object at a given time or a given event or when an object has been given a new state.

Understandability

Many things are important if a SOO is to be understandable. The property of being reliable is a key. First the SOO is defined with an integration of all the objects (and all aspects of these objects) of which it is composed, each of which is a SOO and shares its same SOO properties. Relations within the structure of an object provide the ability to relate it to any other object in terms of the real world. Both its behavior and its structure are traceable everywhere and at any point in and throughout time, within each phase and between and among phases, both during its development and its operation. For example, one can tell where all independencies, dependencies, and decision making takes place in every object — thus allowing a user to capitalize on these properties in making decisions (e.g., where to use distributed resources).

The traceability property provides the ability to trace the birth, life, and death of an object and its definitions, as well as its transitions between definition and instantiation; to trace changes and know the effects of an object on all other objects in a system; and to trace patterns (e.g., distributed patterns), control, and function flow (including data, priority access rights, and timing). A SOO is defined to be as simple as possible but no simpler, with "user-friendly" definitions derived from a common semantic base, each of which hides unnecessary detail. One way to hide unnecessary detail is through encapsulation, a form of abstraction (discussed above).

User-Friendly Objects. One user's paradise is another's nightmare. It is therefore important that the language used for the definition of an object provide for a user-selected syntax. A SOO can be communicated in terms of common semantics to all entities, objects within and outside of its domain, all levels of users, developers, and managers, as well as computing environments and automated tools.

An understandable object is defined with a natural correspondence to the real world, and it provides a history that is measurable. An understandable object also provides a means to know when it is in a state of completion, which is the ability to determine when an object is, for example, completely defined, developed, or instantiated.

Real-World Properties of Objects

A real-world object exists by its very nature and depends on the use of the formal mechanisms of being reliable to enable us to talk about it and understand it from all of its possible viewpoints and the possible viewpoints of its observers. Many of the real-world properties include the reusable properties such as relativity, abstraction, and derivation.

A real-world object must be created in order to talk about it (and relate to and represent it) and deleted in order to simplify a particular problem domain. To be "real world," one has to be able to reference and uniquely identify an object, as well as be able to assign properties of "belonging" and "having" to objects. The identify property is part of the property of typing under abstraction.

Persistence is another real world property. Persistence — or healthy existence — is the ability of an object, no matter how complex, to live a full life throughout all its states of being and doing. This property has definite advantages. For instance, it allows for a complex object to be found or put away at will, without having to recreate the object each time.

Identification is the ability to identify an object as a distinguishable entity with respect to its structure, its behavior, and its relationships — both in its development phases and during its operational phases. Objects can be concrete — such as a physician or the engine in our truck — or they can be concepts — such as a management policy in a manufacturing enterprise, an idea in one's thoughts, or a value of TRUE in a Boolean. Each object has its own unique identity. Two objects are distinct even if they have the same values: consider two people, each with the same name and birthdate.

To create a SOO means to recognize, for the first time, particular structural and behavioral properties of a real-world object as an object that exists. Deleting that object unrecognizes that object and returns the system to a new state — that is, one without that object. A SOO can be created and deleted; it has the ability for itself and all of its influences to be destroyed. It has the ability to appear into and disappear from a user's domain.

Once created, an object must be able to be referenced (the ability to use or mention that object). Because the object is unique, there is always the ability to select or find that object. With the property of accessibility, there is always the ability to access an object safely in all its states of existence. For example, a person object may have a name and address in one state but not a phone number. In another state, that same person object does have a phone number.

Representation is the ability for an object to have a natural correspondence to the desired aspects of the real-world object of which it is a model. Real time and space constraints provide the ability to realize an object in terms of its physical existence.

From Definition to Execution

From the perspective of relativity, the development process is an integration of many viewpoints including an object's being, doing, controlling, and having for a particular time interval. The functional architecture as an object is a being with respect to the resource architecture as an object that it resides on for implementation and operation. From this view, the resource allocation architecture as an object is in its doing state when it maps the functional architecture to a chosen resource architecture. A TMap defines the possible states of being of an object and its relationships to other objects in terms of controlling and being controlled. An FMap defines an object in its doing state along with its relationships to other objects in their doing state in terms of controlling and being controlled. The integration of an FMap and TMap takes place when the objects in an FMap do something with objects whose being properties are defined by a TMap.

Analysis of an object is completed when all of its possible interfaces to other objects separate and apart from its resource architecture (including being, doing, controlling, being controlled, having, and being had) are consistent and logically complete. System design of an object is completed when the process just described also includes the chosen resource architecture and implementation strategies.

Object design is the same process as system design, only with more details added to relate more directly to the object's implementation environment. Implementation is the process of preparing an object for a particular execution environment to potentially have everything that belongs to it. The execution of an object is completed when every object within its domain has everything that potentially belongs to it (throughout its past, present, and future states) as a result of its associated resource architecture(s) having references to it as part of the objects of the architecture(s) to be had. The performance testing of a system is completed when all of the execution passes that have taken place or will potentially take place produce states of "has" and "being had" for each object that is correct according to the original requirements of the system. The maintenance of an object is another round of analysis, design, implementation, instantiation, and testing.

There is nothing magical about DBTF. It's just common sense, with a duality of control and flexibility in the process of organizing one's thoughts and recording them — so automation can take over and finish the job.

An Embodiment of DBTF

To capitalize fully on the properties of a SOO a suite of automated tools based on DBTF is needed for supporting its development. One such automation is a full life cycle systems design, engineering and software development environment encompassing all phases of development starting with the definition of the meta process, and the definition of requirements. Part of this environment concentrates on developing the system by working with the definition space of a system in terms of FMaps and TMaps, and the other part concentrates on understanding a system in terms of OMaps and EMaps (see Exhibit 12). With this environment, everything is a system. It could be an individual software module defined and automatically generated for, say, a turnpike software application or it could be a module defined and simulated for the requirements for the entire turnpike system which might include, hardware, software, and operators. All of these "systems" are defined (and if software, automatically developed) as SOOs (see Exhibits 13 and 14).

Using FMaps and TMaps, any kind of system can be designed and any kind of software system can be automatically developed, resulting in complete, integrated, and fully production-ready target system code (or documentation) configured for the language and architecture of choice. Also provided is a means to observe the behavior of a system as it is being evolved and executed in terms of OMaps and EMaps.

Every system developed with this environment is a DBTF system, including itself. This is because it was used to define and generate itself. Although a full life-cycle design and development environment, it can coexist and interface with other tools. It can be used to prototype a system and/or to develop that system fully.

All models within this environment are defined with the DBTF formal systems language resulting in SOOs. This modeling process could be in any phase of the life cycle, including problem analysis, operational scenarios, and design. Models are submitted to a data flow structure calculator to provide automatically the structures, with an analysis of the local data flow for

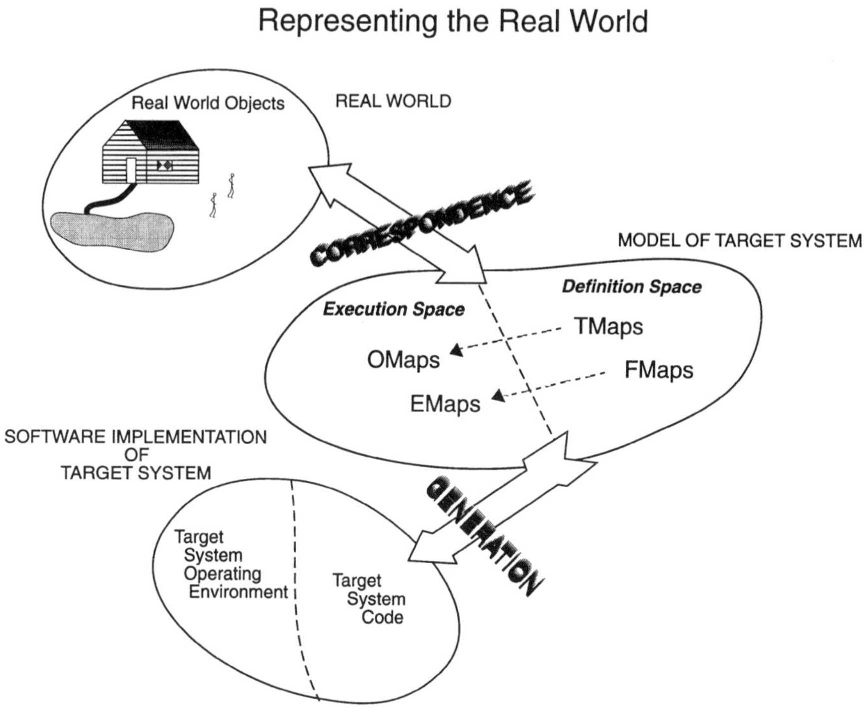

Exhibit 13. Representing the real world.

---

a given model. The analyzer can then be used to ensure that each model or set of models was defined properly. This includes static analysis for preventative properties and dynamic analysis for user intent properties.

Once a model has been decomposed to the level of objects designated as primitive and analyzed successfully, it can be handed to the generator. The generator automatically generates a fully production-ready and fully integrated software implementation for any kind of application, consistent with the model, for a selected target environment in the language and architecture of choice.

The generator is generic: it can be configured to interface with language, database, graphics, client/server, legacy code, operating system, communications systems, Internet-based systems, and machine environments of choice. If the selected environment has already been configured, the generator selects that environment directly; otherwise, the generator is first configured for a new language and architecture.

The type part of the generator generates object type templates for a particular application domain from one or more TMaps. The code generated

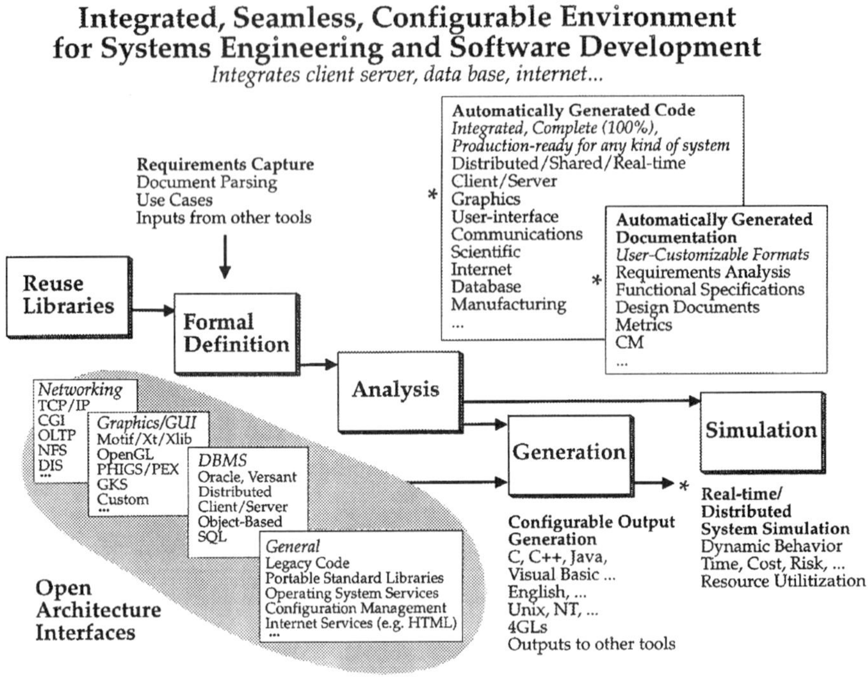

Exhibit 14. Integrated, seamless, configural environment for systems engineering and software development.

by the functional part of the generator is automatically connected to the code generated from the TMap and code for the primitive types in the core library, as well as, if desired, libraries developed from other environments.

Once the generator is configured for a new environment, a system can be automatically regenerated to reside on that environment. This open architecture approach provides more flexibility to the user when moving from an older technology to a newer one. For example, one system automatically generated C code for part of an application, Ada for another part, and FORTRAN for another. The system was then executed with executables generated from three different languages, all executing concurrently, communicating via TCP/IP protocol to perform a coordinated multiprocessing task. The user-configurable generator has been configured for several languages including C, FORTRAN, COBOL, Ada, and English and is soon to be available with Java and Visual Basic.

The DBTF environment has a completely open architecture that allows a user to put wrappers around a set of capabilities so that it can be configured to automatically generate to an architecture of choice. It can be configured to interface to a system at all levels, from high levels such as a DBMS API to low levels such as operating system calls (e.g., POSIX). With a user-configurable open architecture for interfacing to databases (e.g., Oracle, SQL Server), operating systems (e.g., UNIX, NT, OpenNT), user interface (e.g., Motif, Windows), communication protocols (e.g., TCP/IP, SNMP, SNA), web packages such as Front Page and legacy code of choice, there is no need to lose time to market and spend unnecessary resources to port to a new environment.

Examples of interfaces currently available are UNIX, Motif, and TCP/IP as well as cross targeting from UNIX to Windows console applications. With this facility, there is a choice of code generation using a single solution specification (also user configurable). There is no need to port to a new environment. Once the generator is configured for a new environment, it will automatically regenerate the new system to reside on that environment. Thus the generator becomes an agent of reuse across its target code implementations.

The generated code can be compiled and executed on the machine where the DBTF environment resides where those platforms have been configured or can be ported to other machines for subsequent compilation and execution. User-tailored documents and metrics — with selectable portions of a system definition, implementation, description, and projections such as parallel patterns, decision trees, and priority maps — can also be configured to be automatically generated by the generator. Once a system has been generated, it is ready to be compiled, linked, and executed.

To maintain traceability, the source code generated by the generator has the same name as the FMaps and TMaps from which it was generated. Once generated, a system is ready to be executed. If it is software, the system can undergo testing for further user intent errors. It becomes operational after testing. As part of the execution and testing phase an OMap editor is provided — a run-time system which automatically creates a user interface based on the data description in the TMap.

Run-time constraint tests that validate correct object manipulation and construction as well as unit test harnesses for testing each object and its relationships are automatically generated. The automatic user interface is provided with the OMap editor for populating and manipulating complex objects, including storage and retrieval for persistent objects. This provides the ability to test the target system at any input-output interface with predefined object test data sets.

In addition, the generator automatically generates test code that finds an additional set of errors dynamically. For example, it would not allow an engine to be put into a truck that already had one, nor allow an engine to be removed from a truck with no engine.

To support testing further, the developer is notified of the impact in his system of any changes; those areas that are affected (for example, all FMaps that are affected by a change to a TMap) are demoted.

The GUI environment (as well as its interface to the Internet) is tightly integrated with the development of an application. The user interface is graphical and displayed in terms of RMaps, FMaps, and TMaps (using a tree-like representation of models). RMaps at a library and project level are used as a high-level organizational tool to support user coordination and support user understanding of the organization of the system.

GUI (e.g., Motif) support is provided while preserving traceability and interface integrity and control seamlessly between the GUI part of the application and the other parts of the application. Its automatic, data-driven interface generator supports rapid program evolution. Layers of loosely to tightly coupled GUI integration are provided. At the lowest level of integration, a set of primitive data types is provided to access the power of Xlib, Xt, and the Motif windowing system. Each of these layers is defined with primitive operators and types that match the API for that layer. At this layer, all of the raw power of the windowing system may be accessed.

An intermediate layer above these base level APIs (called GUI and GUIELEMENT) is provided that encapsulates most of the repetitive operational aspects of Widget management and construction of X widgets. Since this layer was defined as SOOs, it's object editor can be used to specify and view information about the window hierarchy. In addition, the GUI objects may be persistently stored as OMaps to be used during the initialization, modification, or analysis stages of GUI development.

The highest layer is tightly integrated with the TMap system. It is at this layer that the object editor is always available to an application to populate and manipulate objects based on the TMap. The object editor has standard default presentations as well as a set of primitive operators that allow a user to use the OMap editor presentation features to develop interactive GUIs that are tightly coupled to the TMap (e.g., automatic generation of a system of menus from a TMap description).

Other screen description technologies (e.g., WYSIWG GUI builders) may also be used in conjunction with a translator of their export capabilities to a DBTF GUI specification. An example translator was developed to go from Motif UIL as an output of ICS's Builder Xcessory product.

In addition to the above GUI layers, users can define their own primitive type interfaces to user-chosen APIs, providing the end user with freedom and flexibility of choice. Throughout all of these choices the APIs are integrated with the use of FMaps and TMaps, a part of DBTF's systems language.

FMaps and TMaps can be executed directly by a system analysis component that operates as a runtime executive, as an emulator, or as a simulation executive. A definition is an executable specification in that it has information in it for its simulator to understand its behavior and dynamically analyze it for things such as risk, timing, and cost; and a higher-layer operating system to execute it. For software, that same definition can be used as input to the automatic code generator. The result is a rapid prototype for a system designer or a production-ready system for a software developer. That which is simulated by the DBTF simulator can be integrated with that which is automatically generated by the generator to a very fine or loosely grained level.

As an executive, resources are scheduled and allocated by the systems component to activate primitive operations. As an emulator of an operating system, it dispatches dynamically bound executable functions at appropriate places in the specification. As a simulator, it records and displays information. It understands the real-time semantics embedded in a SOO definition by executing or simulating a system before implementation to observe characteristics such as timing, cost, and risk based on a particular allocation of resources. If the model being simulated has been designed to be a production software system, then the same FMaps and TMaps can be automatically generated for production.

The analysis component can be used to analyze processes such as those in a business environment (enterprise model), manufacturing or software development environment (process model), as well as detailed algorithms (e.g., searching for parallelism).

The documentation environment is tightly integrated with the definition of the system. In fact documentation can be automatically generated from a SOO definition by the generator, wrapping in the user's own comments should it be desirable to do so; and that same definition can itself become part of that same generated document. Documentation from the various model viewpoints of a system can be collected and integrated into the documentation of the system. This means, for example, that a resulting document could also include descriptions of the requirements, the testing, developer's issues, and developer's decisions made about a definition of a system.

The baseliner facility provides version control and baselining for all RMaps, FMaps, TMaps, and user-defined reusables, including defined structures. The build manager configuration control facility's primary role is to manage all entities used in the construction of an executable. This includes source files, header files, and context information about the steps taken to produce the executable. This facility also provides options for controlling the optimization level, debugging information, and profiling information of the compiled code.

The requirements component provides users with more control over their own requirements process. In addition to generating metrics, it allows users to enter requirements into the system and trace between those requirements and corresponding FMaps and TMaps (and corresponding generated code) throughout system specification, detailed design, implementation, and final documentation.

With the requirements component a user can define any relationship between objects and describe the complex dependencies between these objects. This allows the user to query, for example, on the relationships between a set of requirements and its supporting specifications and implementations.

A session manager component is provided for managing all sessions, the project manager for managing all projects, the library manager component for managing libraries within one project, and the definition manager component for managing definitions within a library.

The project manager component is the system management interface for all projects and users. It lets the user create, enter, and delete projects, and maintains a list of file system mount points on which projects may reside, watching them for adequate space. For each project, the project manager component also maintains a list of users who may access the project and enforces these access privileges.

The library manager component is the system management interface for a single project, where each object it manages is a library. The library manager allows the user to create, enter, and delete libraries within that project. Libraries may also be linked together into subtrees; this enables one library to use the definitions in another. Library utilities work on the currently selected library to provide error recovery, environment configuration, searching, and other useful support.

The definition manager component is the system management interface for a library, where each object it manages is a definition. Maps may be created, edited, and deleted, as well as taken through their respective life cycles.

The definition editor component of the definition manager component is used to define FMaps and TMaps in either graphical or textual form. Each manager manages an RMap (Road Map) of objects, including other managers, to be managed (refer again to Exhibit 11). An RMap provides an index or table of contents to the user's system of definitions; it also supports the managers in the management of these definitions, including those for FMaps, TMaps, defined structures, primitive data types, objects brought in from other environments, as well as other RMaps. Managers use the RMap to coordinate multi-user access to the definitions of the system being developed. Each RMap in a system is an OMap of the objects in the system used to develop that system within each particular manager's domain. The Road Map editor is used to define RMap hierarchies.

THE PROCESS IN ACTION

Using the DBTF automated environment, an organization can select a management process that works for its type of environment. For example, some projects may wish to manage the process of managing the development of a system by following the traditional waterfall model. Others may choose a spiral development model. Below we discuss some aspects of a system design and software development process which can be applied in either type of management model.

Requirements Capturing

A typical development process begins with the capturing of requirements which are usually in the form of a customer-supplied English document. As part of this process, the requirements component is used to automatically parse a requirements document. Key expressions (for example, "cash management system") and key words (for example, "shall") are then filtered from the requirements.

An RMap is then automatically generated which essentially is an outline of the sections in the requirements document. Each node in the RMap corresponds to an FMap and its automatically generated functions which continue to outline the paragraphs of a section of the requirements document. An FMap leaf node function under a parent function associated with a paragraph is associated with a requirements sentence. Each requirements sentence is uniquely identified and is numbered with a requirements identifier used to make correspondences to the target system which will be defined by the user during the design process. Each FMap corresponds to a requirement based on keyword/key phrase matching of sentences in the requirements document.

Those statements with the key words and expressions (i.e., the requirements statements) are attached to functions in an FMap belonging to a node in the RMap (which corresponds to a section in the original requirements document) along with information the user chose for the purpose of establishing traceability and gathering metrics throughout the life cycle. As part of the design process, reusables can be used to fulfill some of the requirements associated with the nodes on the RMap. For others, some FMaps and TMaps may already have been defined for this system. Others are yet to be defined.

A requirement in a definition (e.g., the currently selected requirement in an FMap or a TMap) can be graphically connected (via RMap model relationship connectors) by the system designer to other definition nodes (e.g., another set of requirements or a target system model) for the purpose of tracing requirements to testing and target system functions. A traceability matrix is automatically generated based on traceability between different model types information classifications.

The requirements editor allows the user to specify, query, and report on a database of information about a model and its relationships. This information, together with its formal definition, is used for gathering metrics about the system and its development (such as who is responsible for the object in question, constraints, TBDs, requirements from the user, etc.), providing a mechanism to trace from requirements to code and back again, ensuring that the implemented system meets the requirements. The generator can use this information to generate reports on the progress or state of the development of the current target system and its relation to the original requirements. This includes information about the development process, issues, and information about the contents of the model object itself.

The requirements are modeled by the development of FMaps and TMaps to match a users initial set of English requirements. The automatic import facility reads a user's requirements document and builds an RMap of FMaps matching the requirements is used to get a head start on the development of these FMaps and TMaps. Changes to the requirements could then be made to the FMaps and TMaps which are a formal and consistent representation for the requirements. Once the requirements are in this form the analyzer is able to automatically determine if all of the requirements are consistent and logically complete and traceable. If a user makes incremental changes to the requirements document and then re-imports it by generating a new RMap of FMaps for those requirements, the requirements component will allow for requirements document changes and then re-import those requirements with a minimum of disturbance to the established RMap of FMap requirements models and their associated links to other models (e.g., testing systems or the target system under development).

Following is an RMap excerpt taken from the system, agent001db (Exhibit 15). agent001db is used to manage the interaction of agents and objects being traded between them. Within this system there are producers and consumers. Consumers can specify objects (and their characteristics) that they need and producers can identify objects (and their characteristics) that they can provide. The agent data base automatically provides a trading service which matches supply and demand. When a producer specifies the items that they can provide, a listing of all potential consumers is provided to the producer so that he may have the option of selecting the consumer. The agent001db will automatically selects a consumer for the producer, if he

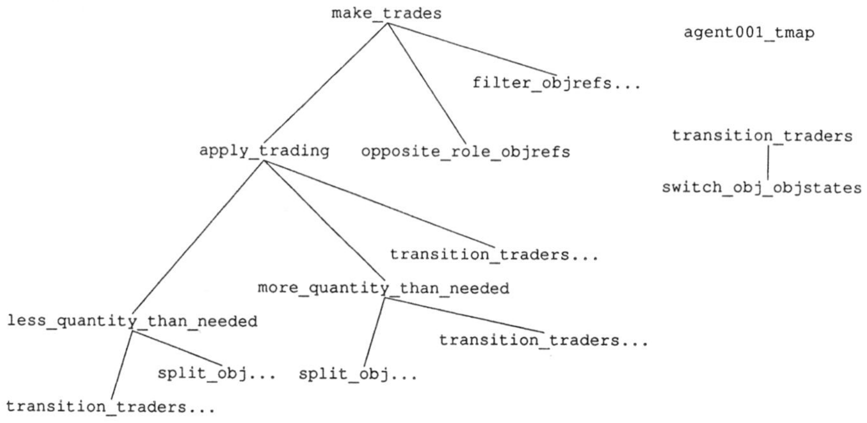

Exhibit 15. RMap sample from agent001db.

does not select one. In addition to providing trading services, agent001db provides general-purpose search and presentation services.

Requirements Tracing

For requirements tracing, RMap relations are automatically and visually drawn between model types on the RMap which is then printable as an RMap diagram. A traceability matrix can be automatically generated for any combination of RMap model relationships to provide traceability information.

Code Coverage

The need for code coverage testing is minimized with the use of SOOs. The use of the formal language for defining the system ensures no interface errors which means that there will be no logic in danger of not being used properly due to interface problems in the models since the model, if it had an interface error, would be caught by the SOO analyzer before the code was automatically generated from that model. This eliminates the need for wire-tracing-oriented tests for analyzing generated code.

Since all of the code is automatically generated from the FMaps and TMaps of the target system by the generator, the chance for a human to miss either creating the code for part of a model or interface incorrectly to the other code in the system is eliminated.

Additional test coverage analysis can be performed by configuration of the generator to generate coverage analysis FMap calls to provide user-definable monitors in generated C code. Decision information inherent within FMaps and TMaps can be used for test case initialization for these numbers.

Software Design Modeling

With this development environment, complete life-cycle development is based on formal methods using a formal language from requirements to code generation. Following are excerpts of FMaps, TMaps, and OMaps taken from the agent001db system as well as an excerpt of C code that was automatically generated by the generator from the set of FMaps and TMaps that these were taken from (Exhibits 16, 17, 18, and 19). Notice that the FMap, apply_trading, is an FMap node on the excerpted RMap.

Debugging

We have already discussed how run-time constraint tests that validate correct object manipulation and construction as well as unit test harnesses (at the granularity of an FMap), or how testing each object and its relationships, are automatically generated by the generator. An automatic user interface is provided with an object editor for populating and manipulating complex objects, including storage and retrieval for persistent objects. This provides the ability to test the target system at any input-output interface with predefined object test data sets.

Debugging is done at the code level with the users native debugger. The code is generated with variable and function names that closely match to their corresponding name in the design specification. The debugger is used to set breakpoints and examine values of simple object variables. The OMap editor (with a Motif windowing interface) is used to examine complex OMap objects (from within the debugger) and to modify their values or load other OMaps having test values. Testing is also supported by ASCII output generation of OMap objects from the debugger.

In addition, code regression testing can be defined in FMaps to perform comprehensive analysis of any subsystem portion of the system at the granularity of an FMap model. A unit test harness interface is automatically generated upon request for any FMap operation in the system. This test harness provides access to data sets corresponding to the inputs of the FMap in order to drive the regression testing. The resulting outputs of these test data sets can then be validated for correctness.

Much of the testing is no longer needed when using this environment since the semantics of the formal systems language not only supports the user to think, design, and analyze his system's requirements in an organized manner, but it eliminates errors from the very beginning, and its analyzer automatically ensures that the language was used correctly so that such errors are indeed eliminated. Systems are defined to safely handle changes both during development and operation, increasing flexibility and

Exhibit 16. Excerpted from agent001db FMaps.

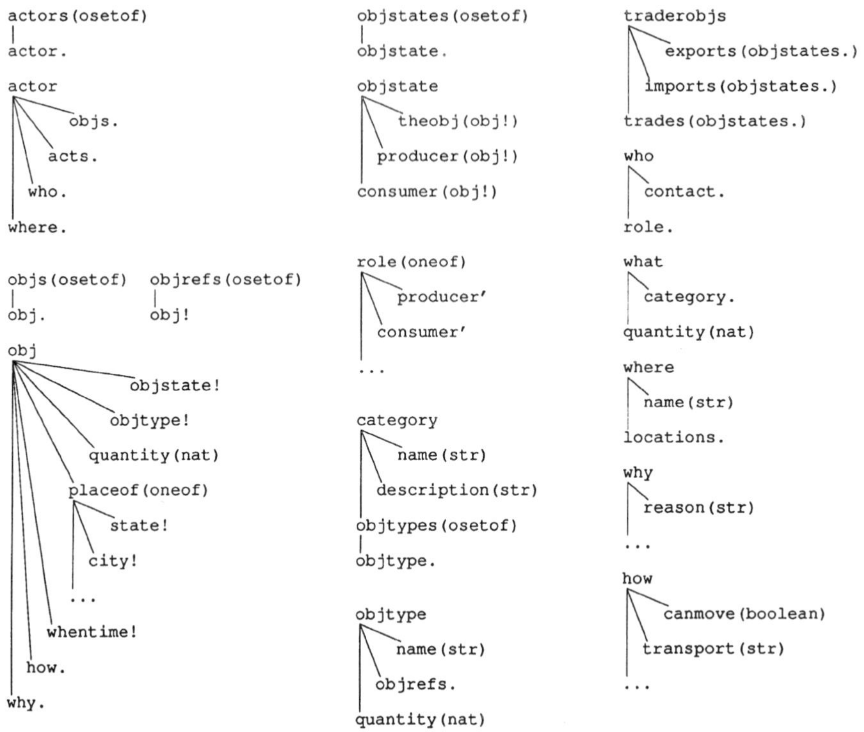

Exhibit 17. Excerpted from agent001db TMaps.

reducing unpredictability. All interface errors are automatically found, starting with the definition of a system (over 75% of all errors found in a traditional environment at testing time, after implementation, are found before implementation with the DBTF approach, and more are found automatically by tests generated by the DBTF generator). All objects in a system are under control and traceable; again, obviating the need for another set of tests that are needed in a more traditional setting.

Code Generation

Code is automatically generated (or regenerated) for any part or type of model in a system (and for any part of the system that has been changed, obsolete code is automatically replaced and integrated into the new and changed code) whether it be GUI, database, Internet-based, communications, real time, distributed, client server, multi-user, or mathematical algorithms. There is no manual work to be done to finish the coding task. The generator is accessible to a user to tailor it for his own brand of generated code, if needed. This generator can be used to provide output information

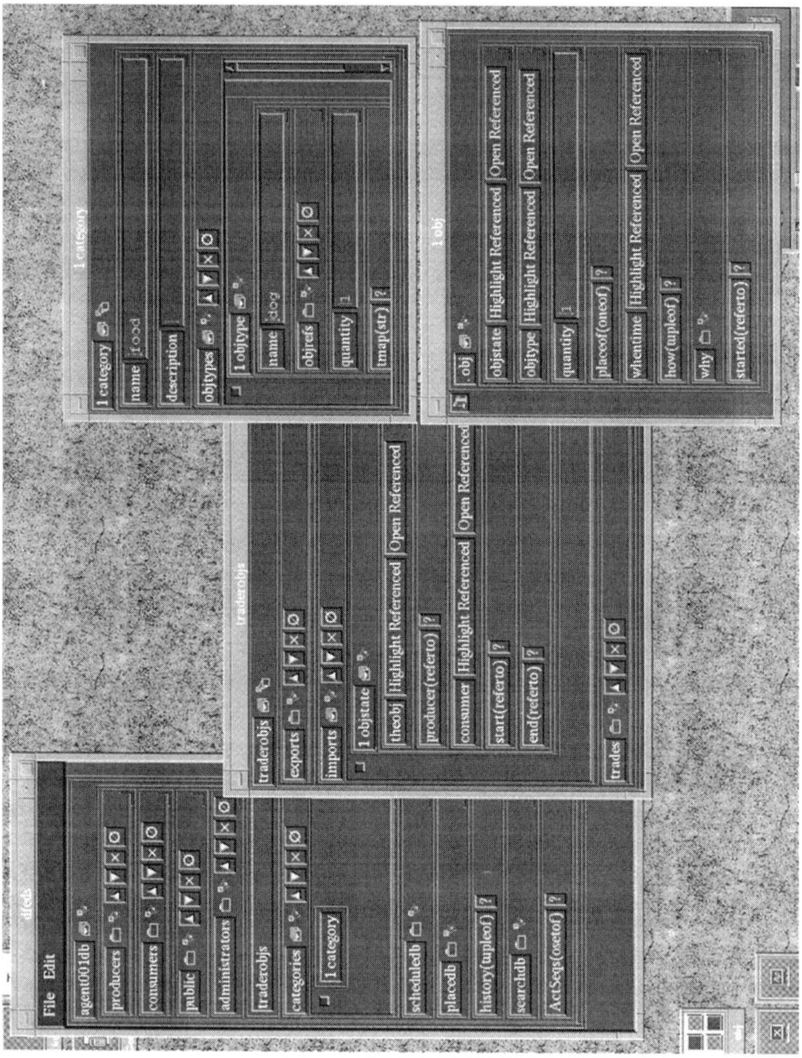

Exhibit 18. Excerpted from agent001db OMaps.

```
/*  001-Generated C code for functional specification 'APPLY_TRADING'
       VERSION: 3.2.3.9 C-RAT
        AUTHOR: Hamilton Technologies Inc. Copyright 1991.
     OPERATION: APPLY_TRADING
     GENERATED: Wed May 27 15:58:38 1998
        SCCSID: @(#) %M% %I% of %G%.
*/
#include "AGENT001DB.h"
...

fAPPLY_TRADING(V0DB0,V0INITIATOR0,V0TRADERS0,
               V0DBN,V0INITIATORN,V0TRADERSN)
IDECLARE_AGENT001DB(V0DB0)
...
{                /* __LOCAL_VARIABLE_DECLARATIONS__ */
DECLARE_NAT(C1)
...
                 /* __FUNCTION_SOURCE_CODE_BEGINNING__ */
...
rec1_0REPEAT=1;
while(rec1_0REPEAT--){
   ATNULL_OBJREFS(V0TRADERS1,V1_0ATN)
   COPY_BOOLEAN(V1_0ATN,D1_D10)
     if(D1_D10<1)
 {if(D1_D10 == REJECT_BOOLEAN) {REJECT_TEST_BOOLEAN()}
   MOVETO_OBJ_OBJREFS(V0TRADERS1,V2_PO)
   CONVERT_OMAP_OBJ(V2_PO,V2_POOM)
   JUMP_REFERTO_OMAP(V2_POOM,V2_OBJOM)
   CONVERT_OBJ_OMAP(V2_OBJOM,V0TRADER)
   MOVETO_QUANTITY_OBJ(V0TRADER,V0TRADERQ)
   MOVETO_QUANTITY_OBJ(V0INITIATOR0,V0INITIATOR_Q)
   EQ_NAT(V0INITIATOR_Q,V0TRADERQ,D0D7)
     if(D0D7<1)
 {if(D0D7 == REJECT_BOOLEAN) {REJECT_TEST_BOOLEAN()}
   LT_NAT(V0INITIATOR_Q,V0TRADERQ,D0D8)
     if(D0D8<1)
 {if(D0D8 == REJECT_BOOLEAN) {REJECT_TEST_BOOLEAN()}
   fMORE_QUANTITY_THAN_NEEDED(V0DB0,V0TRADERS1,V0INITIATOR0,
                              V0TRADER,V0TRADERQ,V0INITIATOR_Q,
                              &V0DB,&V0INITIATORM,&V0TRADERSM);
}/*FALSE*/
else{/*LESS_QUANTITY_THAN_NEEDED*/
...
}/*FALSE*/
else{/*0INITIATOR_QUANTITY_EQ_TO_OTHER_TRADERS_QUANTITY*/
   fTRANSITION_TRADERS(V0DB0,V0INITIATOR0,V0TRADER,
   &V0DB,&V0INITIATORM,&V0TRADER1X);
   LOCATE_OBJREFS(C1,V0TRADERS1,V0TRADERSM)
...
return;
}
/*  -------------- end of source ------------------*/
```

Exhibit 19. Excerpted from code automatically generated from agent001db FMaps and TMaps.

that can be used as input by other tools or as output for testing (such as showing all of the decision points in the system). This feature can also be used as another means of rapid prototyping for systems design studies.

The quality of the generated code has been given high marks by its users since it inherits all of the SOO qualities including interface correctness and traceability, from and to the requirements and design from whence it came and within the code layer itself.

While the task of configuring the generator is in process, the user can develop his systems using a current generator configuration to automatically generate his applications. Once the new configuration of the generator is prepared the user can automatically regenerate his system for the newly configured architecture. Once this new configuration is completed it can be used over and over again as a reusable for other projects.

Detailed Design Document Generation

A change in a DBTF specification is followed by an automatic regeneration of the code that has been impacted with the change using the generator in order to guarantee that the code matches the integrity of the specification. Because DBTF's documentation environment is tightly integrated with the definition of the system, a new document or portion of a document can be automatically generated by the generator from a specification that has changed. Documentation (e.g., detailed design documents generated from the SOO models) can be automatically generated (when analysis is completed or when needed) from those same specifications, making them always consistent with the generated code.

Documents can be generated to match document templates or document artifacts corresponding to those for other phases. This documentation (partial or complete) can then be imported into, for example, WORD for processing and/or direct incorporation into the other phases.

In the DBTF development process, changes to the requirements are made in the requirements FMaps and TMaps. Any relationship connections between models are automatically maintained. For example, if a requirement FMap has a dependency relation to a supporting target system (software) model and the requirement FMap is deleted, then the dependency relation is removed. Test models can be evolved as needed and regression tests performed as needed. The design information is extracted and put into the document based on a document configuration of the generator.

A definition can have additional information about it and its relationships provided by the user. This information, together with its formal definition, is used for gathering metrics about the system and its development, providing a mechanism to trace from requirements to code and back again, ensuring that the implemented system meets the requirements. The generator can use this information to automatically generate reports on the progress or state of the development of the current target system and its relation to the original requirements.

Mapping Changes to Code

With DBTF, maintenance is performed at the specification model level. Target changes are made to the definition or model, not the code. Target architecture changes are made to the configuration of the generator environment, not the code. All changes are traceable. If, for example, a TMap is changed, all of the FMaps impacted by that change are demoted. With traditional products, after the shell code or partial code has been generated, it is necessary for programmers to add or change code manually; as more code is written, it becomes less possible to regenerate the shell or partial code from changes in the requirements, because the manual code would be destroyed or made obsolete. The maintenance process using traditional products becomes increasingly manual and therefore error prone as the software evolves. With the DBTF approach, the user doesn't ever need to change the generated code, only the specification, and then regenerates (automatically) only that part of the system that has changed. Once again the system is automatically compiled, linked, and executed without manual intervention.

Integration with Legacy Systems

Because the architecture of the DBTF environment is open, it allows for interfacing to existing or future legacy code. Several options exist for such an interface. Wrappers can be placed around existing or legacy code to create primitives for the generation environment to automatically interface to; systems can be defined to have FMaps that directly call legacy code and legacy code can send input to DBTF-generated code at execution time; the generator can be configured to generate language specific statements that interface to the legacy code; or shell scripts within the environment are open to end-user modification (e.g., modification of link and compile scripts).

Prototyping

A DBTF system can be presented before the fact to end users as a rapid and evolving prototype starting with a skeleton "show and tell" or "mock up" of what is to come for the user. DBTF enables design and modeling of any concept that humans can envision. It could, for example, be the target system, the testing system (including the operational model), a model of the development process for building target systems, a model of the end-users' enterprise, or the enterprise of the developer organization itself.

FMaps and TMaps are used to model regression tests that are used in the testing system. These test cases are stored as OMap files and then code is automatically generated from the test system models by the generator. The regression tests are then ready to run. The results are captured as OMap files. Regression testing is related to coverage analysis by a test case.[11] Regression testing includes the use of the generator code generated for coverage analysis. In addition, any special analysis functions can be developed as a part of the test system to analyze the results (i.e., output objects) of a test case with the input objects for that test case.

As these scenarios illustrate, the DBTF environment automates the development process within each phase and between phases, beginning when the user first inputs his thoughts and ending when testing his ideas. The same language and the same tools can be used throughout all phases, levels, and layers of design and development. There are no other languages or tools to learn. Each development phase is implementation independent. The system can be automatically generated to various alternative implementations without changing its original definition.

Traceability is backwards and forwards from the beginning of the life cycle, to implementation, to operation, and back again (for example, the generated code has names corresponding to the original requirements). There is also traceability upwards and downwards, since it is a seamless process from requirements, to specification, to design, to detailed design. A primitive in one phase — say, requirements — becomes the top node for a module in the next lower-level phase, specifications. The environment takes advantage of the fact that a system is defined from the very beginning to inherently maximize the potential for its own automation.

If the real system is hardware or peopleware, the software system serves as a simulation upon which the real system can be based. Once a system has been developed, the system and the process used to develop it are analyzed with tools such as simulation together with metrics to understand how to improve the next round of system development.

A new set of alternatives is provided for the different disciplines associated with the traditional development process. Take, for example, reverse engineering. Redevelopment is a more viable option, since a system can be developed with higher reliability and productivity than before. Another alternative is to develop main portions of the system with this approach, but hook into existing libraries at the core primitive level and reuse portions of existing legacy code that are worth reusing, at least to get started. In the future, for those systems developed within the DBTF environment, reverse engineering becomes a matter of selecting the appropriate generator configuration or of configuring the generator environment of choice and then generating to the new environment.

MEETING COMPANY X'S GOALS WITH DBTF

We have already concluded that we will go a long way towards maximizing profits (GOAL#1) if we address the other goals successively. In a similar way GOAL#2 and GOAL#3 depend to a large extent on meeting many other goals, each of which if we address, we are helping to address these goals. But part of satisfying goals #2 and #3 is to take the initiative in other areas such as eliminating problems within the company before they happen (for GOAL#2) and having a strategic plan that includes how, for example, the company will apply those aspects realized in terms of other goals (e.g., how to apply strategic technologies for GOAL#3).

With a DBTF environment, both developers and managers can be proud of their accomplishments and be more motivated since they can deliver. With the current critical programmer shortage plaguing our industry today, it is clear that Company X is not as dependent on individuals with an environment such as this at their disposal — in particular since it can be set up to not only do a major part of the programmer's work (for example, generate 100% of the code), but to make it easy to reuse. These are additional contributing factors for reaching GOALS#4 and #5.

The fact that a SOO definition can describe any kind of system and not just a computer-based target system is a valuable consideration for both GOAL#6 and GOAL#8. It could be any system; for example, a human-based system such as a development work plan. In this case the functions are implemented by people as resources and the simulation analyses the system behavior in terms of how they would execute the plan. It could also be the testing system (including the operational model or user model), a model of the development process for building target systems, a model of the end users's enterprise, or the enterprise of Company X.

Although meeting GOAL#13 can support GOAL#8 in many ways, it is important that Company X take the initiative to use a strategic technology that will accomplish, for example, tracing requirements in the systems it has defined to understand itself as an organization. The DBTF environment's ability to trace from requirements, to design, to code, and back again in fulfilling GOAL#13 can be used directly to fulfill GOAL#8.

FOLLOWING THE "NO MORE, NO LESS" PATH (GOAL#7)

The formalism behind DBTF enforces many aspects of the "no more, no less" rule, a prime example of which is reuse. That is, it inherently makes objects that are system oriented for the modeler, which include properties of being both object oriented and function oriented. All SOOs are inherently reusable and integratable and as such are tinker-toy or lego-like in their use.

Following the "no more, no less" path means getting rid of everything that is truly no longer needed (no more), but it does not mean getting rid of things that are needed just to show that money is being "saved" (no less). With strategic methods, and tools that follow the "no more, no less path," a multitude of processes, methods and tools are no longer needed. With one formal semantic language to define and integrate all aspects of a system, diverse modeling languages (and methodologies for using them), each of which defines only part of a system, are no longer necessary.

No longer is there a need to reconcile multiple techniques with semantics that interfere with each other. Why, for example, learn C, followed by a replacement of C with a more modern C++, followed by a replacement of C++ with Java? Each is a major step which requires significant training and reverse engineering. One could instead use — and continue to use — a single-definition language and automatically generate the latest implementation environment.

The fact that DBTF-developed systems will not lock an organization in means that unnecessary work can be avoided. They incorporate a structure and process for the continuous evolution of any or all parts of a system. Not only can the models, as well as their automatically generated implementations, be reused, but new implementations can be regenerated from any model and this can be done by using reusable architecture configurations.

The fact that the DBTF approach does not lock an organization in to process, architecture, design, or implementation becomes even more important with today's rapidly changing technologies. The user has designer freedom without compromising integrity of the system. The only constraints imposed are those that support the designer in making a reliable system. In fact the designer can abstract to as high (or as low) a level as he would like.

Techniques and tools for transitioning from one phase of the life cycle to another become obsolete. Dealing with all of the paperwork that is either manually or automatically generated to support the manual processes of development when they could be automatically developed can be eliminated. Techniques for maintaining source code as a separate process are no longer needed, since the source is automatically generated from the system specification. Verification, too, becomes obsolete. Techniques for managing other paper documents give way to entering requirements and their changes directly into the requirements specification database. Testing procedures and tools for finding most errors are no longer needed because those errors no longer exist. Tools developed to support programming as a manual process are no longer needed when programming is automatic.

No longer needed are tools that focus on the measurement of complexity. Instead of measuring it, it becomes minimized. Complexity does not increase with the size of the system since all objects are under control, integrated, and traceable. No longer is it necessary to do what is unnecessary over and over again or to keep adding on after the fact when there is a way to do it right the first time.

With respect to GOAL#9, Reuse succeeds only if what is reused works and is under control. Such is the case with SOOs. Every defined model becomes inherently a candidate for reuse. Reuse is supported in FMaps by operations, universal operations (those containing polymorphism), and user defined FMap structures (functional templates with or without polymorphism). Reuse in TMaps is supported by the automatic generation of abstract types using a set of predefined parameterized types (i.e., type templates); leaf types defining: container extension, external references or relations (pointer-like), recursive objects; user-defined primitive types (at code level or layered onto FMap and TMaps); user-defined layered types, and user-defined paramaterized types.

Reuse naturally takes place throughout the DBTF life cycle. Objects, no matter how complex, can be reused and integrated. Environment configurations for different kinds of architectures can be reused. A newly developed system can be safely reused to increase even further the productivity of the systems developed with it.

Inherent reuse with SOOs recursively and safely raises objects to a new and higher level, inherently integrating aspects such as the GUI, database, and communications side of a system with all of its other parts. They can be object oriented, function oriented, or an integration of both. Software fails because of what we do not learn from history. Learning from history is a form of reuse. Towards this end, reuse with SOOs culminates in automation itself.

With respect to GOAL#10, we mentioned above how a vendor's understanding of the company's environment can be verified by having the vendor in question demonstrate its abilities . Our staff defined a portion of Company X's requirements for one of its projects and simulated them; designed and developed to operational status a part of a target application with our environment; defined formally the process (itself as a system) of developing a Company X system in a scenario where the company and we would work together in this process. The output of this process was a developed module for Company X's customer. Company X personnel were trained in the technology, and a set of reusables was developed that could be used in common on company projects.

FMaps and TMaps were used throughout for all steps from formally defining parts of the target application to formally defining the steps of developing it as well in order to illustrate how all of these processes can be viewed and developed as formal systems.

If a vendor actually uses its own technology and products to do for itself what it is selling it to the vendor for, this should be an excellent sign for the customer. The fact that the DBTF environment was used to completely define and generate itself is significant because it means that its developer is its own user (or customer). Over 7 million lines of code have been generated by the DBTF environment to generate its own major versions. It has been important for both ourselves and our users that we use our methods and tools in the same ways we have our customers use them.

The learning curve of DBTF is relatively short. A week's introductory course proves sufficient to start using its environment. Internships are typically used to teach in-depth techniques that are applied to solving problems in a particular application area. Internships reinforce that which is taught in the introductory course. One can become quite productive after a month of regular use. The learning curve is relatively fast. This is because the process is intuitive, there is only one language and only one set of integrated tools to learn for the life cycle, it is straightforward, everything else is derivable from the initial concepts, its formalism enforces the "no more, no less" rule, and the modeler concentrates on the objects in a system and how to relate and use them, not on how to make them be object oriented. All of these aspects contribute to meeting the transition goal, GOAL#11.

With respect to another aspect of GOAL#11, transitioning from another environment to a new one, this can be done with for example, by using the DBTF environment for creating wrappers around legacy code, including code generated by other tools, and turning it into DBTF primitives which can then be automatically generated to by the generator. If other chosen tools support openness, the code generated by the generator can be integrated with or accessed by these other tools.

To make sure that the transition was a smooth one, our staff defined the process of working together with the company, formally, with FMaps and TMaps. Such a plan was defined (and parts of the system simulated) to show how the organization will not lose time, but gain, even though this would be a transition to a new, more formal and systematic way of doing things.

The DBTF environment has been shown to significantly cuts expenses and time to market while building better systems resulting in unprecedented productivity savings (GOAL#12). This is because of all of the benefits that can be derived from SOOs which collectively result in better software and faster, cheaper development. We have analyzed the results of using DBTF and its automation on many projects on an ongoing basis to understand more fully the impact properties of a system's definition have on productivity in its development. Productivity was analyzed with several systems and then documented. Compared to a traditional development, the productivity of DBTF-developed systems has been shown on many system by many different kinds of users to be at least an order of magnitude greater.

When we carried this analysis further, we discovered that productivity was higher the larger and more complex the system — the opposite of what one finds with traditional systems development. This is in major part because of the high degree of DBTF's support of reuse and therefore the use of reuse on larger systems. Measuring productivity becomes a process of relativity, relative to the last system that was developed. Older methods for measuring productivity are no longer applicable.

But there are other reasons for this higher productivity as well, such as the savings realized and time saved due to tasks and processes that are no longer necessary with the use of this approach. For beginners there is less to learn and for everyone less to do — less analysis, less testing, less to manage, less to document, less maintenance, little or no implementation, and less to integrate since a major part of all these areas has been automated or they inherently take place because of the nature of the language.

With respect to GOAL#13, integration in all forms is key. One of the problems that can occur with traditional systems, including the object-oriented ones, is the difficulty in integrating all the parts. The process is error prone and time-consuming. This is not the case with DBTF since all of its parts are by their very nature formally integrated. The result is an integrated seamless design and development environment. There is no longer an additional expense for integrating diverse products for developing different parts of a system, phases of the system, or for integrating the modules or views (e.g., data flow, timing, state transition, and object types) of a module created with or resulting from these disparate products.

Systems are defined to handle changes both during development and operation. All objects are system oriented, under control, and traceable. All aspects of system design and development are integrated with one systems language and its associated automation.

As mentioned earlier, all of the goals are dependent on the reuse and strategic technologies goals (i.e., GOAL#9 and GOAL#13). We have discussed many ways in which DBTF and its automated environment support these goals.

THE RIGHT OPTION FOR COMPANY X

It is high risk for Company X to keep doing things the way it has been. With any organization change is not easy, but Corporate X knows that change will be necessary in order to save itself. Option 1, therefore, should not be an option. To do so would compromise reaching the company's highest priority goals. The second option of applying a more or less quick fix would at best address only some of the problem areas and then only on a temporary basis. Maybe worse yet is bringing in an entirely "new" but traditional approach. Not only does it take the time and effort to transition from one approach to another but the new approach still suffers from the basic core problems of the one being used by the company today.

In order to reach the goals as defined above, the company would need to choose the fourth or fifth option of evolving to the use of tools and techniques that formalize, preventatively, the company's process of software engineering. The fourth option is probably most practical from a short-term consideration. The fifth option, although most desirable from a long-term view, would take more time and should be chosen if such time, including lead time, is available on the project that will first apply the new technology.

DBTF and its automation address in major part the subgoals defined for the strategic technologies goal (GOAL#13). Should it not have all of the components desired by Company X's developers either now or in the future, it has an environment that is completely open. Open to interface to other products or to be interfaced to by other products. Open to allow for enhancements to be developed, brought in from the company's existing or future legacy code and interfaced and or added to the DBTF environment by the company itself. Not only can it be configured to generate to any language, architecture, OS, communications, data base, etc., but it could be configured as well to automatically generate to a special-purpose environment (such as a language of another product or specialized embedded code).

In today's market it becomes increasingly important for a product to be able to interface to others and for others to interface to that product. A product that locks you in compromises your choices of functionality, hardware, and software products that you can use (including your own reusables) both now and in the future.

It may not always be considered realistic for a project to develop a particular application from the standpoint of a pure systems viewpoint, where in the ideal world the requirements are understood first as a system before later phases of development. Should this be the case, the DBTF approach has the flexibility of either supporting its users in defining such an application from its beginning or in starting to use it in defining such an application in a later phase of development, such as with one of its software module subsystems (for example, the host software) in a detailed design phase. The software implementation would then be automatically generated from the design of this subsystem.

It becomes evident that what is really needed for Company X is a way to create durable systems. Durable because they incorporate a structure and process for the continuous evolution of any or all parts of a system. Durable because they provide a way to productively, instead of destructively, manage change to a system — change in the businesses they support and change in the technologies used to implement them. Once durable systems are able to be developed, the company will be free to safely make the key decision of when and how it transitions what it has today to what it needs tomorrow.

Such a transition as would take place with Option 4 or Option 5 presents a major opportunity — an opportunity to take a step back and examine the underlying process used to design, build, and deploy software and examine where the next introduction of modern (in the real sense) technologies and products truly fit within the company's systems development framework.

Despite everything, two things remain constant at Company X. Its systems and software fail often and change is inevitable. This is only compounded in an atmosphere of rapid growth. Change in the software industry needs no introduction. But it is this facet of our industry which has provided at best a foundation of quicksand for the systems deployed to date. We cannot do anything about changing change, but we can do something about dealing with it. A transition from the old to the new which uses a formal, before the fact, systems approach will go a long way towards addressing this issue.

CONCLUSION

Analysis of Company X's goals shows a strong dependency between all of them and the software approach it uses; or, putting it in another way, a strong dependency on the properties in the software it develops. Decisions made today about the company's software methods and tools could be the deciding factor as to whether its business will succeed or fail.

Once organizations like Company X begin to understand the degree to which a technology affects them, software will be given its due respect. The right strategic approach and the technology that executes it forms the foundation for better, faster, cheaper software, the answer to success in business, certainly in a business which delivers software.

Within today's commercial enterprise users demand much more functionality and flexibility, which includes durability, in their systems than before. Models are distributed, including Internet models which are a popular form of distribution in use today. And given the nature of many of the problems to be solved, their systems must be error free. These environments and object-oriented projects begin to sound like the earlier days of real-time, distributed environments where complexity gave rise to new kinds of problems, including those having to do with interface and integration issues. The issue should not, for example, be whether an approach is object oriented or one that the competitor is using, but rather whether it will be what is needed to meet the highest-priority goals of the organization.

Collective experience strongly confirms that quality is maximized, and cost and time to market are minimized with the increased use of DBTF's properties and its automation.[8-11] Its preventative philosophy, to solve a given problem as early as possible, means finding a problem statically is better than finding it dynamically. Preventing it by the way a system is defined is even better. Better yet is not having to define (and build) it at all. Only then have we satisfied the reuse goal, the other one that needs to be satisfied to successfully achieve all of the other goals in the business.

Although change is difficult for any organization, changing from a traditional environment to an environment like Development Before the Fact is like transitioning from the typewriter to the word processor. There is certainly the need for the initial overhead for learning the new way of doing things, but once having used word processors would we ever go back to the typewriter?

Following the "no more, no less" rule, becomes the deciding factor. Yet, if we think about it, it is a matter of common sense. Not only does it result in using the best strategic technologies, but it makes sure that they are used the way they should be, capitalizing, for example, on reuse and treating everything systematically. One result is that of removing the need for armies of people that are no longer needed to support obsolescence. This brings freedom — both for the people who should not be locked in to using obsolete methods and to the corporation who should not be losing profits by doing unnecessary work. At the end of the day, freedom is the most valuable commodity of them all, for without it we lose control of our destiny.

True, many software companies today are doing quite well using traditional, informal, and after-the-fact development techniques. Relatively speaking, that is, when it comes to making a profit. But how long will this last? As with anything, it is usually a matter of time and timing. And as we said earlier, every system is relative. What works for success today may not work tomorrow, especially if there are known weaknesses in the system.

Others will catch on that there is a better way to do business after all. Especially those who have less to lose. They could well leave the so-called successful ones behind in the dust.

Notes

1. Hamilton, M., Development before the fact in action, *Elec. Design,* June 13, 1994.
2. Hamilton, M., Inside development before the fact, *Elec. Design,* April 4, 1994.
3. Hamilton, M., Zero-defect software: the elusive goal," *IEEE Spec.,* 3(23), 48–53, March 1986.
4. Hamilton, M. and Hackler, W. R., *Object Thinking,* McGraw-Hill, New York, 1996.
5. Anon., The 001 Tool Suite Reference Manual, Version 3, Hamilton Technologies, Inc., Cambridge, MA, 1993–1998.
6. Hornstein, R., Willoughby, J., Hamilton, M., Heuser, W., LoPinto, F., and Hawkins, F., From Space Systems R&D to Commercial Products: Technology Transfer Initiatives to Benefit Small Satellite Missions, NASA Headquarters, Fall of 1997.
7. Hornstein, R. S., A Cross-Cutting Agenda for Achieving a Faster, Better, Cheaper Space Operations Infrastructure, AIAA Workshop on Reducing the Costs of Space Operations, Arlington, VA, 1995.

8. Keyes, J., (Refer to the 4 chapters on 001-developed systems for the Internet), *DataCasting: How to Stream Data Bases Over the Web,* McGraw-Hill, New York, 1988.
9. Krut, B., Jr., Integrating 001 Tool Support in the Feature-Oriented Domain Analysis Methodology (CMU/SEI-93-TR-11, ESC-TR-93-188), Software Engineering Institute, Carnegie-Mellon University, Pittsburgh, PA, 1993.
10. Anon., Software Engineering Tools Experiment — Final Report, Vol. 1, Experiment Summary, Table 1, Page 9, Department of Defense, Strategic Defense Initiative, Washington, D. C., 20301-7100.
11. Ouyang, M. and Golay, M. W., An Integrated Formal Approach for Developing High Quality Software of Safety-Critical Systems, Massachusetts Institute of Technology, Cambridge, MA, Report No. MIT-ANP-TR-035.

Chapter 25
Multimedia-Based Training (MBT) for Financial Services

Barbara Sealund
Tim Brock

WHEN THINKING OF MULTIMEDIA, one often associates it with slick interfaces, interactive widgetry, hyperlinking, branching, and a plethora of user access and controls. Multimedia-Based Training (MBT) can also use a multiplicity of media: text, image, audio, video, and animation. Media can be used simultaneously, sequentially, and interactively to train users on systems as well as to convey conceptual information. MBT can support conventional instructional strategies ranging from guided tours, matching exercises, drill and practice, questions and answers, to simulation, scenarios, games, and more.

WHY MBT?

Numerous studies have proven that the more senses activated during a learning session, the greater the retention. In addition, if the media is merged to create a believable "virtual" environment — a learning environment that conjures a kind of theater of the mind — then a greater opportunity for "mental practice" can improve performance. The idea of electronic performance-based training is certainly not new, but the use of multimedia to enhance the user experience — creating a more realistic or engaging performance environment — is just beginning to be fully developed.

Multimedia can be used to create interfaces that suspend disbelief so that users are motivated to try things over and over until mastery is achieved. When talking to professional athletes or musicians about their skill, many say it is 80 to 90% mental. For the football player, the ability to mentally previsualize a physical response to the coming play is the key to his success. Proper mental rehearsing is fundamental. For the musician, mentally hearing and anticipating the note before it actually happens is of-

0-8493-9991-2/99/$0.00+$.50

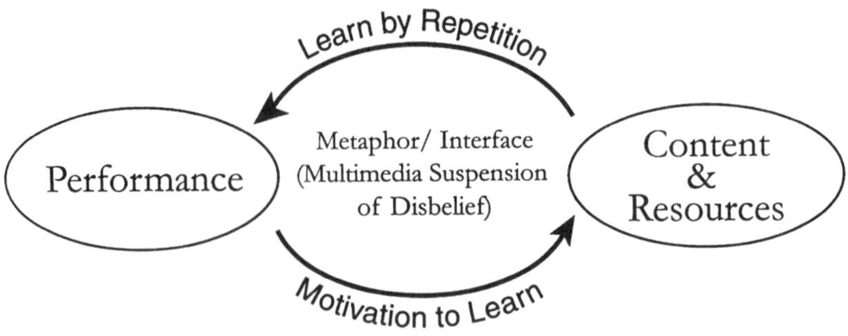

Exhibit 1. MTB can provide the focus and motivation for repetition of a job function by creating a "virtual rehearsal place."

ten 90% of the effective act. One Los Angeles-based concert violinist will not perform a concerto in public without first "playing" the piece several times in her mind without the instrument. Good mental rehearsal habits for both the athlete and the musician are fundamental to professional quality performance. MBT can provide the focus and motivation for repetition of a job function by creating a "virtual rehearsal place" (Exhibit 1).

DEVELOPMENT ISSUES: EXAMPLES IN FINANCIAL SERVICES INDUSTRY

The onset of rapid application systems development brings with it many challenges for training. MBT is one answer to the challenge of "how can we train the multitudes of people globally who need to use our new online banking application?"

Bank executives today face the new challenge of being able to effectively and successfully implement new application systems, which seem to roll out more frequently than ever before. In addition to rapid application systems development, technical teams are becoming more sophisticated in developing systems that meet the specifications of their user. These systems often impact not only an employee base, but the bank's customer base as well. To add to the complexity of implementation, often the systems will be rolled out globally across multilingual and multicultural environments. All too often, training is not considered an integral part of the initial deployment, thus failure of a well-designed application system becomes imminent.

It is important to acknowledge that training will make a significant impact on the successful implementation of new application systems and that the earlier the involvement of the training team, the better. In fact, a well-designed training solution will run parallel with the application development, even to the point of common deliverables. For example, a thorough analysis of the new application should be completed with the first deliverable, which is a Project Analysis Report for the training project plan.

It is from this analysis phase that the training team along with the systems deployment team can make the best decision for an effective training solution. Without this critical phase of the project plan, you will begin the journey without a road map and perhaps with an undetermined destination.

The good news is that with appropriate analysis and planning of the training, the training team can become a dynamic and motivational part of the project team as well as bring value to the successful implementation of the application system.

While MBT is one of the most instructionally dynamic media, it is not always the best training solution. Each individual implementation and environment needs to be carefully reviewed before decisions can be made on the most appropriate training media for the specific application. Again, the due diligence spent at the analysis phase will save volumes in time and dollar savings at the implementation phase.

A high end Custom Training Team tends to view each project at the level of:

- What is the training issue/problem/challenge
- What can we do to help
- What will we do to support

Oversimplified:

- Business Need
- Business Solution

The following examples illustrate various business challenges that customers have been faced with, and how a selected Custom Training Team supported the business need with a successful training solution.

Case Study A: System Conversion Affecting 38,000 Employees

Business Need. One of the largest financial organizations in the West was converting 990 branches to an integrated banking application system. The conversion would affect 38,000 employees, all of whom would require training to perform their job function. Accomplishing the task with classroom training was virtually impossible considering the size of the audience, geographic location throughout the U.S., the aggressive schedule, and the lack of expertise.

Business Solution. The Custom Training Team had the systems conversion experience, training experience, and the systems expertise that would ensure a successful conversion and implementation of the training materials. The Training Team designed and developed a Total Training Solution which encompassed 27 fully-integrated Computer-Based Training (CBT) courses totaling 43 hours of instruction, 7 days of Classroom Training for Train-the-Trainer, including Leader and Student Guides, Self-Study Workbooks, Job Aids and Pre/Post-Test and Scenario Handbook utilizing Computer-Managed Instruction. The training materials provided step-by-step instructions on how to perform system functions and emulated the system so learners could practice in a nonthreatening environment. The implementation of the training materials was a tremendous success.

Case Study B: Market Terminology for Global Audience

Business Need. One of the world's largest banks required training for a very large and diverse audience. The training would need to familiarize the audience with market terminology covering areas such as securities, buzzwords, and accounting/taxation.

Business Solution. The Custom Training Team designed a menu-driven CBT course to allow students to select areas of terminology relevant to their job function. The course contained four main categories: buzzwords, markets, securities, and miscellaneous. Within each category terms were listed in alphabetical order and were accessed via a sub-menu. Upon selection of a term, a tutorial would appear along with an example. At the end of each category the student could select a testing segment to ensure their knowledge of the terminology presented. The course was highly successful and used worldwide.

Case Study C: Standardization for Bank Card Division

Business Need. One of the nation's largest banks, located in the northeast, desired to standardize training for its three geographically dispersed training sites. The training sites conducted intense three-week courses to train customer service representatives on their role and responsibilities within the bank card division, as well as how to use the division's computer system. At the time, the training varied not only from site to site, but from trainer to trainer. Standardization was a major goal for the bank card division, not just in training, but in all aspects of the business.

Business Solution. The Custom Training Team conducted in-depth training analysis with all three sites to reach a consensus of the topics to be covered as well as the best training approach. The Training Team then designed a 3-hour CBT course which provided instruction relative to the organization, the bank card industry, and the customer service representative's role and responsibilities.

Included in the customer service representative's role and responsibilities was product knowledge, calculations such as average daily balance, minimum monthly payments, finance charges, and ensuring customer satisfaction. The trainers could then concentrate on systems training and role-playing. The CBT course was a big success and helped give the customer service representatives a positive self-image related to their role within the organization.

Case Study D: Major HR System Impacting Over 500 HR Managers

Business Need. More than 500 Human Resources managers and input clerks in a major bank were being prepared to convert to computerization of all personnel records. The system would cover inquiries, updating personnel records, payroll, and changes to the bank's personnel records. Generic software was to be customized for the massive, 2-year project.

Business Solution. The Custom Training Team stepped in at the start to develop custom computer-based training for each unit. The CBT was ready at least 4 weeks before the new software was to go online, so that employees had ample time to learn the system before implementation. Records on more than 30,000 employees were computerized in the ongoing project, which continues today.

Case Study E: 800 Relationship Managers Selling Bank Services

Business Need. Managing the relationships between a major travel and entertainment credit card company and its corporate clients was the job of more than 800 relationship managers who received computer-based training created by the Custom Training Team.

Business Solution. The 1-hour training explained the benefits of the credit card marketing program, enabling them to sell their package to major clients.

Case Study F: Graphical Interface Increases Retention

Business Need. One of the nation's largest insurance companies was trying to find an efficient method of disseminating information with respect to a business resumption policy that was being implemented. An additional goal was that those employees to whom the information was distributed be able to "try out" the new mechanisms: first to see how the new plan would work, and second to ensure that they understood the new policies and procedures.

Business Solution. The Custom Training Team studied the plan, analyzed the client's goals, and developed a highly interactive Multimedia-Based Training module. Users were given an overview of the plan and specific procedures for completion of the necessary paperwork. Throughout the module, users were required to answer questions to test retention of the material. Finally, the user was given an opportunity to practice "filling in" the forms on the computer screen. The module would then inform the user as to the correctness of their work. Graphics and animation were used consistently throughout the module to maintain user interest.

MBT APPLIED TO FINANCIAL SERVICES

Interface Issues

Analysis is vital for creating an effective MBT interface. Analysis reveals the business needs for training. Those needs then direct the development of an effective metaphor/interface. Below is a general synopsis of the corporate banking learning environment, including a brief analysis of corporate culture, the audience, and performance tasks.

Corporate Culture Analysis

The corporate banking culture is changing quickly. These changes are happening on global and local levels. Banking applications are merging and moving online. Employee time is precious. The training paradigm is changing from instructor-led to user independence — online, just right and just in time. As currencies begin to merge, questions arise within the corporate culture about these trends and their future impact on banking. In short, the culture is changing rapidly and customers as well as employees are looking with some uncertainty to the future.

Audience Analysis

The training audience in banking includes internal and external customers from around the world. They range from high level decision makers to end users. The internal/external clients may be senior managers (decision makers), security managers, information technologists, sales representatives, and end users. Computer experience and subject familiarity encompass a wide range. End users for example may have a high level of exposure to systems. In summary, the banking audience requires a fast, global, modular training solution with a broad-based appeal.

Task Analysis

Task analysis is crucial for defining the MBT interface requirements. This is where the core performance skills are clarified and from which scenarios are created. Performance tasks are either based on using an existing system or are based on mastery of conceptual content.

APPLYING AN MBT INTERFACE

These two mastery types have different interface requirements. If performance on an application system is needed, then the interface requirements could be minimal, since using the system is the instructional focus. If mastery of specific conceptual information is needed, then the interface could be more robust, but should serve the need of those conceptual requirements.

In addition, the business need could require both systems and conceptual skills. A sales manager may be required to know the global features of a new banking application as well as know how to use the system. For example, this new banking application may feature online banking anywhere, anytime, just enough, and just in time. It may have certain online performance standards that would require "hands-on" scenario practice. The MBT interface solution for this training need could be a virtual internet "palm-top" Personal Digital Assistant (PDA) with real-time access to assets, foreign exchange, and settlement functions — demonstrating a "hands-on" modular, online banking experience — from anywhere in the world.

CREATING A REALISTIC INTERFACE

Interfaces really are the machines that make MBT work. The more consistent and believable the machine, the greater the suspension of disbelief and the more engaging the training. If the interface simulates a chest of drawers or a filing cabinet for example, then the drawers should open like drawers, they should sound like drawers sliding on wood or steel. If the interface metaphor is based on a particular Picasso painting, then buttons should appear and function in a cubist multiple-view style. If the interface is a walkie-talkie or cell phone, then the Liquid Crystal Display (LCD) panel should light up with green upper-case san serif letters and the audio should sound like its coming through the phone's speaker. In other words, realism helps bring the interface to life — all for the purpose of engaging the user.

There are numerous ways to create immersive interfaces, but one of the most powerful tools is 3D animation. Three-dimensional (3D) modeling and animation can greatly support MBT interface realism. Information in the "real world" is rarely conveyed in two dimensions (2D) only — even paper has a thin 3D quality. If interfaces are to be realistic, evoking an immersive "theater of the mind" quality, then 3D modeling and animation can help add this 3D value to MBT.

PUSHING THE "Z" (DEPTH) AXIS

Most users and some designers see a blank screen as a 2D flat surface with only an X and Y (cross) axis. Some perceive paintings as 2D shapes and colors and most people perceive text as flat 2D strokes and shapes. However, if those 2D letters extrude and become 3D objects then the Z (depth) axis is now active. With the activation of the "Z" axis, designers have a powerful metaphor for building not only two-dimensional shapes but 3D forms such as cubes, spheres, or cylinders. These 3D forms can become extended surfaces for organization of information. Text can be "mapped" not only onto the front plane of a cube, but also can be mapped onto to the side, back, top, or bottom of the cube. The 2D surface expands to 3D for organizing more information on multiple surfaces within a 3D multimedia space.

PUSHING THE "T" (TIME) AXIS

If a 3D space can draw one into a static "mindscape" of information, animation can cause that landscape to come alive and can be used to actually transport users to other "information objects," rooms, or "mindscapes." Also, animation can further economize the use of space and help imprint a lasting impression on the mind. Gravity and time can be manipulated to simulate the desired effect. Reality can be "changed" to economize space and kinetic objects can be "loaded" with content.

Movement involves time and sequencing. Nothing draws attention like movement. This is a TV/film-saturated culture. This cultural immersion in the language of movement can provide an incredible reference for interface designers who wish to attach information and content, not only to static objects, but to kinetic objects as well.

AUGMENTING REALITY

Once an interface is plausible, effectively engaging the user, the next stage of development can be very exciting: augmenting or exaggerating portions of reality. Just like in motion pictures or in cartoon animation, the exaggeration or augmentation of reality can take us somewhere. Disney's flying elephant Dumbo, for example, has enough reality to draw us into the story, but when the little elephant's ears fill with air and Dumbo flies — reality is exaggerated. Augmenting reality can evoke our imaginations and help greatly with retention and motivation. Other forms of augmentation may include humor, the miraculous, time travel, and futurism.

FUTURISM — PUSHING THE INTERFACE PARADIGM

Futurism can be great fodder for augmenting reality in MBT. Believable interfaces in a virtual multimedia environment can easily shift into the next paradigm. Future trends in technology can be experienced through simulation, exaggerating reality to engage users. For example, in online banking MBT, realistic interfaces could project future applications of personal real-time banking transactions between individuals and institutions across the globe. Just think of it, real-time currency foreign exchange transactions between hometown, U.S.A. and Peking, China. These extensions of reality can be a form of "intertrainment." In short, just like cinema, MBT interfaces should take us to a place we've never been.

TRUSTEE TRANSFER - PARTIAL
EXERCISE FLOW CHART

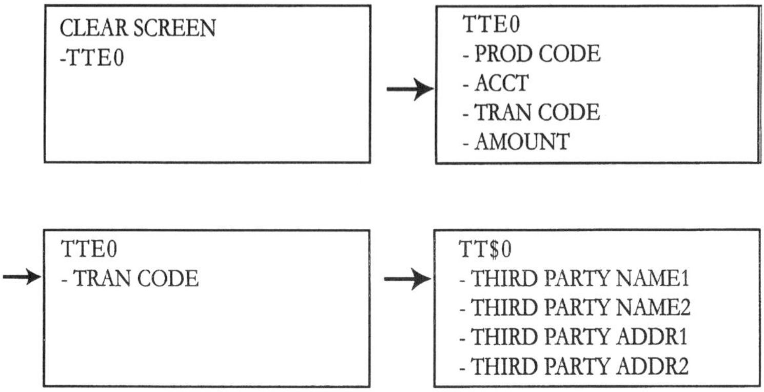

Exhibit 2. A simple example of a transactional task in banking — a trustee transfer transaction.

ONLINE BANKING: MBT INTERFACE SCENARIO EXAMPLE

To bring all this back to financial services, the following flowchart (Exhibit 2) is a simple example of a transactional task in banking — a trustee transfer transaction. The current task is expanded to a typical scenario practice exercise (Exhibit 3). The original computer-based training screen (Exhibit 4) shows the original mainframe systems environment where the scenario exercise was to be practiced by an end user. The original computer-based training (CBT) interface simulates the systems application environment, which is purely text-based. The user is prompted to enter a transaction code, select the transaction function, and enter another code to select a third-party beneficiary.

Practice Exercise

Osama Suliman has decided to transfer part of REA 473023689432165 to Got Rocks National Bank, P. O. Box 99999 Littleton, CO 80120. You are responsible for transferring the $10,000.00.

Exhibit 3. The current task is expanded to a typical scenario practice exercise.

```
                    ____ TTEO 3 IDS  REA TRUSTEE TRANSFER INQ   95/04/19 08.55.40
APMU        CO  9999 OP                    MS         ACTION SUCCESSFUL
ACTION               COID
PROD CODE  REA   ACCT  473023598432165   SHORT NAME


TRAN CODE       6628                     CURRENCY
AMOUNT        10000.00
EFFECTIVE DATE                                  ENTER TRAN CODE FOR INQUIRY
                                                  6627 - WITH PENALTY
PAYMENT AMOUNT                   .00              6628 - WITHOUT PENALTY
WITHHELD AMOUNT                  .00
ACCRUED INTEREST                 .00            ENTER TRAN CODE TO POST
PENALTY AMOUNT                   .00              6593 - WITH PENALTY
                                                  3085 - WITHOUT PENALTY
PROJECTED LEDGER BALANCE                    .00

AIP MADE      AIP ADJ AMT                   .00
              +----------------------------------------------+
              | Complete the required fields on TTEO to      |
              | determine the effect of the partial          |
              | withdrawal on Dr. Suliman's account balance. |
PF:           +----------------------------------------------+
```

Exhibit 4. The original computer-based training screen shows the original mainframe systems environment where the scenario exercise was practiced by an end user.

The following screens (Exhibits 5 through 8) apply an MBT interface to the same scenario exercise, providing a "virtual rehearsal place" for user performance.

The MBT interface reflects a corporate bank environment with marble pillars and a surreal 3D representation of time (Exhibit 5). It features a global "hand-held" device with a futuristic twist, displaying an imbedded screen (Exhibit 6) suggesting online Internet/global access. The interface is dimensional, and combines present-day familiar browser elements within a futuristic "palm-top" globe-like device.

Within the interface, the scenario exercise is represented as if it is an online transaction (Exhibit 7) — possibly a real-time event. Osama Suliman is signed on and engaged in a trustee transfer to a third-party person. As the scenario plays out, the user is taken to the next screen (Exhibit 8) showing the third-party beneficiary, Gozde Kucuk — either a video representation or a real-time telepresence representation — an individual touched by the transaction. The scenario is applied in an exaggerated reality. The user is immersed and transported to the world of "online" banking.

MBT for Financial Services. Who says training for banking has to be boring?

Exhibit 5. Providing a "virtual rehearsal place" for user performance scene 1.

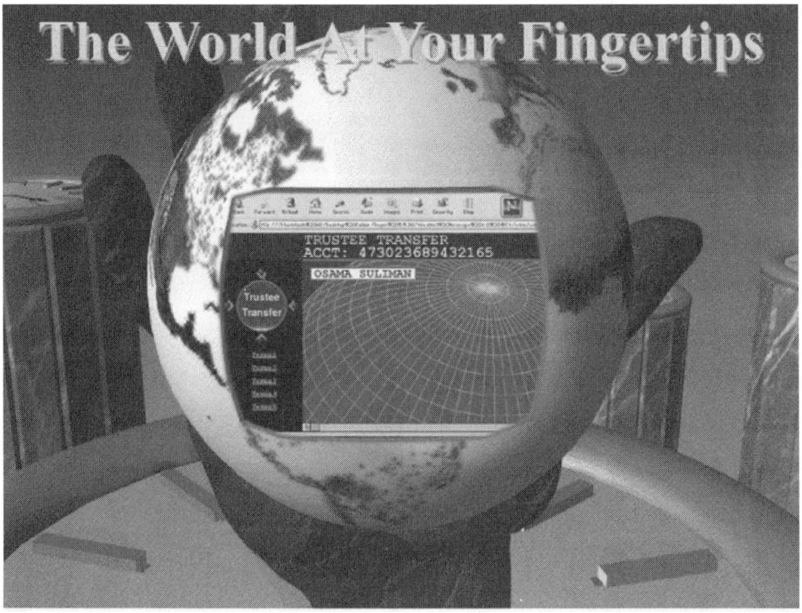

Exhibit 6. Providing a "virtual rehearsal place" for user performance scene 2.

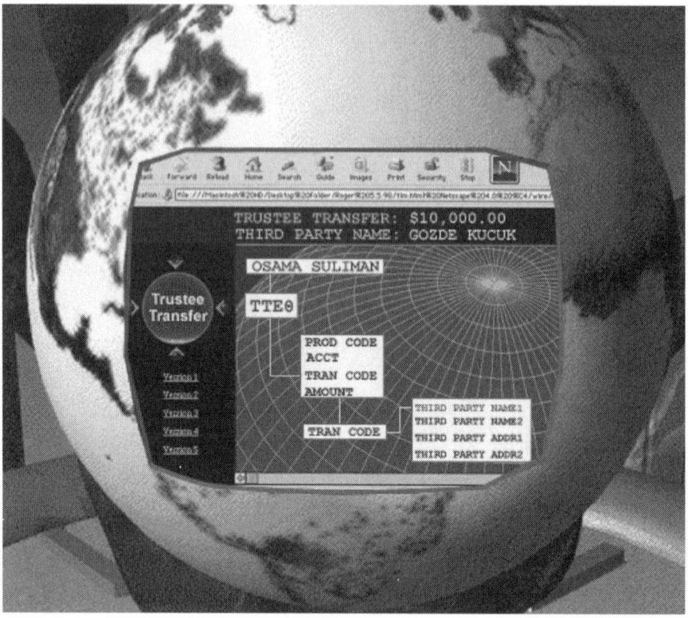

Exhibit 7. Providing a "virtual rehearsal place" for user performance scene 3.

Exhibit 8. Providing a "virtual rehearsal place" for user performance scene 4.

Chapter 26
Law (or the Lack of It) on the Web: A Primer for Financial Services Technology Managers

Federic M. Wilf

THE INTERNET APPEARS TO BE A "WILD WEST" circus that is above or unconnected to the law. The reality is that the Internet is pretty wild, but the law of each and every country, state, province, county, municipality, town, and borough applies to the Internet, and its most-famous aspect, the World Wide Web ("Web"). Web site developers, programmers, users, and others (this chapter uses the term "webmaster" for convenience) all need to be aware of the mechanisms of the law so as to get the maximum amount of protection for her work, while making sure that she does not trip over someone else's rights by mistake.

WHY THE WEB IS DIFFERENT FROM A LEGAL PERSPECTIVE

The law responds to each new technological challenge by first studying it, and then, if appropriate, doing something about it. For example, the Copyright Office started accepting copyright registrations for computer programs as early as 1964, but it was not until 1980 that Congress amended the U.S. Copyright Act to explicitly protect computer programs. Moreover, when the law initially confronts an issue, it usually does so in fits and starts.

The law tends to pigeon-hole issues. The Internet breaks all of the pigeon holes as it is a different form of communication that, in itself, can carry virtually all prior forms of communication. Distinctions that make sense

0-8493-9991-2/99/$0.00+$.50

in hard copy or on television may be irrelevant on the Internet, while the technology of the Internet creates new distinctions that do not apply to any other media. A single Web site may contain text, photographs, artwork (two-dimensional and three-dimensional), music and sound recordings, video, software, scripts, databases, and so on, all of which have been altered and arranged to form a single integrated work.

The law deals with Internet legal issues by analyzing each element that goes into a Web site as if the element were by itself. An element-by-element analysis may take a little more time to complete, but, as you will see, you do not need a lawyer to conduct this analysis. Much of this you can do yourself.

WHAT THIS CHAPTER COVERS

This chapter discusses legal issues that webmasters should be aware of under U.S. law. For example, if a webmaster would like to copy and use a photograph from another Web site, and there is no copyright notice, can the webmaster do this legally?

Suppose a webmaster has completed a Web site that consists of text, video, and sound, as well as searching software. How can the webmaster protect the work, or at least have the right to sue anyone who pirates the work?

There are fairly simple techniques to protect what the webmaster has created, as well as methods to enforce that protection. The other side of the coin is that the webmaster does not want to unwittingly infringe the rights of others, so a basic understanding of common legal problems can be helpful.

This chapter briefly discusses copyright, privacy and contract law as they apply to Web sites.

WHAT THIS CHAPTER DOES NOT COVER

This chapter discusses a number of legal issues that webmasters face, but it does not cover every legal issue. Nor does it say everything that needs to be said for each issue that it does cover.

This chapter discusses the law in the U.S. Except for a few brief references, it does not discuss international law or the law in any other country. More importantly, many issues in U.S. law (such as contract law) are a subject of state law, which means that the law will be different from one state to the next.

This chapter does not provide the "final word" on the state of the law. The law continues to change. One example is the U.S. Copyright Act, which was completely rewritten in 1976. However, Congress has seen fit to amend the Copyright Act several times each year since then. All of the areas of law discussed in this chapter are also subject to constant change.

Finally, this chapter does not provide legal, accounting, or other professional advice. If legal advice or other expert assistance is required, the services of a competent professional should be retained.

DO'S AND DON'TS

Normally, a list of do's and don'ts would be placed at the end of a chapter. We place it at the beginning, so that you have the answers while you read the details.

Do

- Consider patents.
- Use "SM" (service mark) and "TM" (trademark) for your marks for services and goods.
- Consider filing trademark applications with the state, federal, or foreign governments.
- Place copyright notices.
- File copyright applications for your Web sites.
- When multiple companies or parties work on a Web site, agree beforehand in a written document who will own the copyright and other rights.
- Review contracts with your attorney before signing them, and use an attorney to develop written agreements with your customers.
- Investigate the law of every country in which your Web site is used to provide services or sell goods.

Don't

- Mail HTML or software files, or other works, to yourself to secure rights (it's an urban myth).
- Wait until after signing an agreement to call your attorney.
- Assume the law doesn't apply to you because you're on the Internet.
- Assume the First Amendment protects you throughout the world (as one pundit likes to say, the U.S. Constitution is a local ordinance in cyberspace).
- Assume that the law in other countries is like that of the U.S.

COPYRIGHT LAW

Copyright law is the primary means to protect Web sites. Copyright law is designed to protect "expressions" of ideas, while making available to others the underlying ideas, facts, and information. Copyright law defines what is and is not protected, as well the methods by which protection is enforced.

Owning a Copyright as Opposed to Owning an Object

When a person buys a book or a record, that person then owns the physical object — the book or record. Owning the book or record does not give the purchaser the right to copy the book or record, or make new versions of the book or record.

So, if you purchase a videotape of a 10-year-old movie, you can watch that movie and show it to your friends. However, you cannot copy scenes from the movie into your Web site that is your guide to cinema without the permission of the person or company that owns the copyright to the movie.

As for the videotape, you can also sell it to another person (so long as you don't keep any copies for yourself). In copyright law, this is called the "first sale doctrine." Once the physical copy embodying the copyrighted work is sold, the purchaser can use or dispose of that copy any way she likes, so long as she does not make copies of the work (or portions of it).

Source of Law

The United States Copyright Act is the sole copyright statute in the U.S. This has been so since Congress pre-empted the field with the Copyright Act of 1976, which became effective on January 1, 1978.

No state is allowed to legislate in the area of copyright law, so there is no state copyright law. Nor is there a "common law" (judge-made) copyright law, so that judges will not create new rights or responsibilities, as they can in other areas of the law. Judges may interpret the U.S. Copyright Act, which means that a judge can create explanations and structures for resolving disputes where the Copyright Act is ambiguous, unclear, or incomplete.

For those who have access to federal statutes, the Copyright Act may be found in Title 17 of the United States Code. When this chapter refers to a section number, it will be to a section number of Title 17. For example, the definitions of copyright terms are found at Section 101 of the Copyright Act.

Definitions of Key Copyright Terms

Copyright law is whatever Congress says it is. Key to an understanding of copyright law is the terms that Congress uses in the Copyright Act. The definitions are important because a particular term will have one meaning in copyright law and a different meaning in a different area of the law. For example, the term "publication" in copyright law means dissemination to the general public; while "publication" in libel law means any dissemination of libelous matter to any other person, in public or private.

The following are key terms defined in Section 101 of the Copyright Act.

"Work". A "work" in the copyright lingo is any embodiment that contains expression that may be protected under the copyright law. Works include building designs, drawings, books, or any kind of text, two-dimensional and three-dimensional art, computer programs, movies, etc. All of the things protected by copyright law and discussed in this chapter are called "works."

"Audiovisual Works". An audiovisual work is a series of related images and any accompanying sounds that are intended to be shown by the use of machines, such as projectors or electronic equipment, including computers and televisions. It does not matter whether the audiovisual work is embodied in tape, on film, on floppy or CD-ROM, or in an MPEG file.

"Derivative Work". A derivative work is a work that is based upon one or more preexisting works, regardless of the type of preexisting work. The derivative work can be in any form in which a work may be recast, transformed, or adapted. Digitizing a photograph creates a derivative work (the digital version) of a preexisting work (the film-based or analog photograph). A derivative work can constitute an original work of authorship that is separate and distinct from the preexisting work. As noted above, however, the copyright owner can control whether a person is allowed to make derivative works of the copyright owner's work.

One key issue involving derivative works is the point at which a derivative work is no longer considered derivative. For example, if you digitize a photograph, that creates a derivative work that can be recognized as a copy of the original. If you then alter the digitized version to the point where it is no longer recognizable in any way as a derivative of the original, then you have created a new work.

Think of it as melting down a bronze statue. If you melt it down partially, and part of the original is still recognizable (even a small part), then you have a derivative work. However, if the bronze is melted completely into a liquid and then poured into a new mold, an original work is created that no longer owes anything to the prior work, except for the raw material.

Thus, if you take a photograph on print film of the White House, that is an original work. If you digitize the print, you have created a derivative work. If you then use the digital version (the first derivative work) of the White House photograph to create new images, such as a Blue House, a Pink House, a Green House, a Fuchsia House, each of these variations would be a separate derivative work, owing to the original print-based work. However, if you so changed the digital version of the photograph that none of the original work is recognizable, then the newest version is no longer a derivative work of the original work.

"Fixed in a Tangible Medium of Expression". The Copyright Act automatically protects all works — including Web sites — as soon as they are written on paper, stored on a disk, or saved in some other medium. As an example, if one person talks to another person face-to-face, no copyrighted work is created. However, if one person records the conversation on audiotape or videotape, or in an MPEG or WAV file, then a copyrighted work is created.

"Copyright Exclusive Rights". The Copyright Act grants five exclusive rights to a copyright owner, who may: (1) copy or reproduce the work, (2) prepare derivative works, (3) distribute copies, (4) perform the work, and (5) display the work. Thus, the owner of the copyright can control who copies the work, who can make new versions of the work, who can distribute copies of the work by hard copy, mail, or e-mail, who can perform the work on stage or screen, and who can display the work on the walls or monitors of an art gallery.

"Author" and "Owner". The "author" is the person who creates a work. The creator of the work is called an "author" even though the creator may be creating a photograph, a videotape, a sound recording, or a Web site.

The "owner" is the owner of the copyright at any given time. Initially, the author and the owner are the same person, because the author is the initial owner of the copyright. Then, the author may transfer the copyright to another person, who becomes the owner. Often, the terms "copyright owner" and "copyright holder" are used interchangeably.

"License". A "license" is a contract by which the copyright owner allows another person to exercise any one or more of the five exclusive rights. An "exclusive license" means that only the licensee can exercise the licensed rights. A "nonexclusive license" means that the owner is free to allow people other than the licensee to exercise the licensed rights.

"Assignment". A document by which the copyright owner transfers all of the exclusive rights to another person, who then becomes the copyright owner.

"Publication". Distribution of a work by sale, rent, or lending copies of the work. Generally speaking, any distribution of a copyrighted work to the general public is deemed a publication of the work, regardless of whether copies the work are sold by mail order, door-to-door, or while standing on a street corner. As soon as a Web site is publicly available on the Web, it is "published" for the purpose of copyright law.

WHEN COPYRIGHT ATTACHES

Copyright law automatically protects any copyrightable work that is "fixed in a tangible medium of expression" (see above). Another way to think of it is that copyright law protects any work that has some physical embodiment, even if it is only a series of magnetic blips on a tape or disk.

You do not have to register your copyright, although registration is recommended for most works that can be copied and which are worth more than the few dollars it costs to register the copyright with the Copyright Office. (See Copyright Registration later in the chapter.)

WHAT COPYRIGHT PROTECTS

At its most basic form, a copyright is a right to copy. The owner of the copyright can control who can have a copy and what can be done with it.

The copyright owner can allow one person to have five copies, another person to have three copies, and refuse to allow a third person to have any copies.

The copyright owner of a photograph can allow one person to make a copy of the photograph and incorporate it into a Web site, allow another person to use the same photograph for advertising purposes only, while licensing a third person for the sole purpose of distributing e-mail copies of the photograph to Internet addresses that begin with the letter "q."

The Idea/Expression Dichotomy

Copyright law does not protect ideas, but only expressions of ideas. If there are many ways to express an idea, then copyright law will protect one expression from being copied or incorporated into another expression without the permission of the copyright owner. In copyright lingo, this separation of ideas and expressions is called the "idea/expression dichotomy."

If there is only one way, or just a handful of ways to express an idea, then the Copyright Act may not be used to protect that idea, and other people may use any expression of that idea.

The problem with drawing a line between ideas and expressions is that the line is drawn at a different place for each work. Thus, for one computer program, the line may be drawn in one place, while in another computer the line is drawn in a different place. Moreover, since most copyrightable works contain many elements and pieces, each element is separately evaluated for the purpose of drawing the line between idea and expression.

So, if a brochure contains photographs, text, and drawings, then each photograph, each paragraph of text, and each drawing constitute a separate element that must be evaluated to determine where the line is drawn between idea and expression. Is one photograph an unadorned picture of a man in a business suit? If so, then anyone can use the idea of photographing a man in a business suit, but this particular photograph cannot be copied or reproduced without the permission of the copyright owner.

WHO IS THE COPYRIGHT OWNER

Under Section 201 of the Copyright Act, ownership of the copyright goes to the person or persons who created the work (the "authors" of the work). Thereafter, the copyright owner may transfer ownership to another person, partnership, corporation, or other entity that can own property.

The exception to this general rule is "work for hire," which has two distinct and different definitions found in Section 101 of the Copyright Act.

Work for Hire in Employment Relationships

Under the first definition of "works made for hire," an employer is deemed to be the "author" of all works created by an employee within the scope of his or her employment.

It does not matter whether the work was created at the office or at the employee's home, and it does not matter whether the work was created when the employee was being paid, or was on a lunch break. As long as the type of work created falls within the broad boundaries of the tasks the employee performs, then the employer automatically owns the copyright to that work. No written documents are necessary.

As an example, if a person who works as an accountant as an employee of a large accounting firm creates a rock video Web site at night, then that accountant would personally own the copyright to the Web site. Creating Web sites is not within the "scope of employment" of the accountant.

By contrast, if a person is employed to create Web sites of all types by day, then her employer may own the copyright to any rock video Web site she creates at night.

Work for Hire in Independent Contractor Relationships

The first definition of "works made for hire" is limited to employment relationships. By contrast, the second definition of "works made for hire" is completely different in that it applies to independent contractors who create certain types of copyrightable works, and requires that each contributor sign a written document.

The second definition of "works made for hire" states that the copyright in specially ordered or commissioned works will be owned by one party where all the parties expressly agree in a written document or documents signed by all of them that the work to be created is a work for hire.

This definition is limited to (1) contributions to collective works, (2) parts of a motion picture or audiovisual work, (3) translations, (4) supplementary works, (5) compilations, (6) instructional texts, (7) tests, (8) answers to tests, and (9) atlases. These nine classes of works may be thought of as "commissioned work for hire." This definition of work for hire does not apply to any other type of work. A Web site can be a "work made for hire" under this legal definition if the Web site is instructional, and if the contributors agree in writing beforehand that the Web site is a work for hire.

Where Work for Hire Does Not Attach

Work for hire does not apply to self-employed individuals who are creating copyrightable works by themselves. A person working alone (and not as an employee of anybody else or of any partnership or corporation) will own the copyright and will be called the "author" of the work.

Work for hire does not apply to independent contractors creating works that are not commissioned works for hire (see above). So, a photographer who takes photographs of a product for an advertising campaign does not come under either definition of work for hire, and the photographer will own the copyright for each photograph. Photographs are not one of the nine types of commissioned work for hire discussed in the Copyright Act, even though the photographer was commissioned by someone else.

Work for hire does not apply to independent contractors creating commissioned works for hire where there is no written agreement. If 10 people agree to contribute to the making of a film, but there is no written document signed by them, then the film is not a work for hire. Instead, all 10 people who contribute will be joint owners of the copyright in the film.

How to Ensure that Only One Person or Company Owns the Copyright

The Copyright Act defines who will own the copyright by default. However, the default may be changed at any time by use of a written document signed by the parties.

Regardless of whether either definition of "work for hire" applies to a type of work, you can always write and sign an agreement among those who contribute to a work that one person or company owns the copyright. Thus, an independent Web site developer can assign her copyright to her client in writing. An employee and an employer can even agree in writing that the employee will own the copyright to everything she creates, regardless of whether it is within the scope of her employment.

COPYRIGHT NOTICE

Section 401 states that copyright notices are optional, but, if you are going to use them, then the notice should consist of three parts: (1) "Copyright," "Copr." or "©"; (2) if the work is "published" (see above), then include the year of first publication; and (3) the name of the copyright owner. Copyright notices are still strongly recommended, but are no longer required.

Under the Copyright Act, if the author places a copyright notice on a work, and then later sues an infringer, the infringer cannot claim in court that she did not know the work was protected by the author's copyright.

Prior to 1989, any work published without a copyright notice ran the risk of losing its copyright protection. This approach allowed readers and users to assume that any published work that did not bear a copyright notice was in the public domain, and thus available for re-use by everyone else. Now that the law has been changed, you must assume that all works are protected under copyright law, regardless of whether or not the work bears a copyright notice. The good news is that it is tougher to lose a copyright, but the bad news is that you must assume that everything is protected by copyright law, unless you are told otherwise.

COPYRIGHT REGISTRATION

The first thing that you should know about copyright registration is that it is optional, but recommended for many works. Section 408 will tell you that. The second thing that you should know about copyright registration is that you do not need a lawyer to do it for you. The Copyright Act does not say that, so I will. Registering a copyright is a fairly simple and painless process.

Congress uses a "carrot and stick" approach to copyright registration. The "carrot" is that if you file the copyright application early enough, you get additional rights should you need to go to court and sue an infringer. The "stick" is that you cannot file a copyright infringement lawsuit unless you have received the certificate of registration, or at least have filed the copyright application.

Why You Should Register Your Copyright Early and Often

Copyright registration is recommended for any work worth more than the filing fee (presently $20), and for any work that may be stolen or otherwise infringed. If the work is worth less than the filing fee, why bother? If the work cannot be stolen or infringed (which is not the case for most works), then there is no need to bother.

There are several reasons why early registration of copyrights is recommended. First, under Section 411, you need to have a certificate that shows the copyright is registered before you can sue anyone for infringement (although Congress has been debating removing this requirement). Since it normally takes several months to receive the certificate of registration, you would have to wait several months before suing an infringer, or you would have to pay an additional fee to get the certificate of registration back in a week. By filing early, you will already have the certificate of registration in hand in case you have to sue someone.

Second, in a copyright infringement suit, under Section 412, the copyright owner may get attorney's fees and additional types of damages if the copyright application was filed prior to the start of the infringement, or shortly after publication (i.e., within 3 months of the date of first publication). If the copyright is registered after the infringement begins, then the copyright owner cannot ask for attorney's fees or additional types of damages called "statutory damages" (see Damages and Remedies, below). Congress has been debating removing the filing of a copyright application as a prerequisite for attorney's fees and statutory damages, but Congress had not passed a bill changing this part of the law as this book went to press.

How to Get and File an Application for Copyright Registration

You should not need a lawyer to file a copyright registration. Unlike federal trademark and patent applications, the process is simple.

Call the Copyright Office at (202) 707-3000 for free copyright application forms and instructions, or download them in Adobe Acrobat (.pdf) format from <http://lcweb.loc.gov/copyright>. The telephone number currently is an extensive voice-mail system that will allow you to leave your name and address, and the Copyright Office will mail you forms and instructions on how to fill them out. It usually takes 4 to 6 weeks to receive the forms. Once you have the forms, you can always make more forms for yourself by photocopying the hard copy forms onto a good quality white bond paper. This will make the Copyright Office happy because they don't want to mail out any more forms than they have to. Of course, if you download the forms and instructions, you will not need to wait 4 to 6 weeks to receive them and you can print an unlimited number of copies without having to photocopy them.

To register a copyright, you need to send the completed application (two sides of one piece of paper), a check for the filing fee (presently $20), and a copy or other specimen of the work. Different forms are used for different types of works, and the specimen will also be different from one type of work to another. For most Web sites, the specimen of the work is one copy of the site printed on paper, plus up to 50 pages of code or scripts used on the site.

Once you file the application, it often takes 3 to 8 months to receive the certificate of copyright registration. Neatness counts on the application because the Copyright Office will make a few marks on the application, and then photocopy the application onto a nicer piece of paper to create the certificate of copyright registration. If you can't easily read the application, neither will anyone else, least of all a judge who is trying to enforce the registration as shown on the certificate. If you later lose or misplace the certificate that you receive, you can always get another from the Copyright Office for a small fee.

TRANSFER OF COPYRIGHT

A copyright owner may transfer all or part of a copyright by a written document, or by bequeathing the copyright in a will like any other family heirloom. A copyright may not be transferred by an oral agreement, although the parties can make an oral agreement effective by following it up with a written document.

If the copyright is transferred by a written document, the person transferring the copyright needs to sign the document. The person receiving the copyright may sign the document, but it is not effective unless the person transferring the copyright signs the document.

A copyright is "divisible" which means that the owner of all five exclusive rights can transfer one of the five rights to one person, another of the rights to a second person, and the rest of the rights to a third person. This often makes it difficult to track down who owns which rights when the copyright has been parceled out among several owners.

COPYRIGHT TERM

Knowing the copyright term is useful, since it allows you to plan how long you will have rights to your own work, as well as help you determine whether another person's copyright has expired.

Works Created Since 1978

Under Section 302, for all works created by individuals since 1978, the copyright is good for the life of the author, plus 50 years. If two or more individuals are the creators of a work, then the copyright expires 50 years after the last author dies. Thus, if a particular work is created by a webmaster in 1999, and the webmaster dies in the year 2030, the copyright will be good until the year 2080.

For all anonymous works, pseudonymous works, and works made for hire, the copyright is good for 75 years from the date of first publication, or 100 years from the creation of the work, whichever occurs first.

Thus, for a Web site where all the contributors signed "work for hire" agreements, the copyright will last for 100 years from the date that it is created, or 75 years from the date that it is first made available to the public, whichever term is shorter. Another example is where an employee creates an intranet Web site for her employer in 1999, and the work is not made available outside the company, the copyright will be good until the year 2099.

This assumes that the Copyright Act is not changed again in the interim; however, the Copyright Act will likely be changed on this issue. It seems likely that Congress will change the length of copyright protection for individuals from life-plus-50-years to life-plus-70-years. The term for anonymous works, pseudonymous works, and works made for hire would be extended to 95 years from the date of first publication, or 120 years from the creation of the work, whichever occurs first.

Works Created Before 1978

During the period 1909 through 1977, the copyright on a published work was good for 28 years, and then had to be renewed (by filing a paper with the Copyright Office) for another 28 years. Unpublished works received unlimited protection. Just to complicate things, Congress wrote in Section 304 that the copyright in any work published prior to 1978, but still protected as of 1978, would be protected for up to 75 years. As you might expect, this led to confusion that made a lot of work for copyright attorneys.

Unpublished works under prior law were protected so long as they were not published. Thus, a personal diary written in the 1860s would be protected from copying forever under prior law, so long as the diary remained unpublished. However, under Section 303, all works not published by 1978 remain protected under the Copyright Act, but that protection would terminate no later than 2002 if the work remains unpublished, or no later than 2027 if the work is published between 1978 and 2002.

As a rule of thumb, you "should" assume that any work published before about 1922 is in the public domain (which means that anyone can use it), and that any work created (published or not) in or after 1922 is protected by the Copyright Act, unless proven otherwise.

THE REAL MEANING OF "PUBLIC DOMAIN"

In the copyright context, the term "public domain" means that nobody owns or has a claim to a particular copyrightable work. Thus, anyone can use, copy, or make derivative works of a public domain work. Some people confuse the "public domain" with "published work" or "publication." A work that is publicly available or published via the Web or otherwise is not necessarily in the public domain.

When a copyrightable work enters the public domain, it never leaves the public domain. However, anyone can take a public domain work, add new expression to it, and claim a copyright in the new work. However, the copyright in that circumstance covers only the new expression (the aspects that were added), so the original work will continue to be in the public domain for anyone else to use.

As an example, the stories of the Brothers Grimm are now in the public domain because they were published well before 1922. Anyone can copy the original stories, translate them into English, edit them, add new art work and video, and publish the result on a Web site. Copyright law will protect the new art work, the video, the new translation (translations of human languages are considered derivative works), as well the editing if the editing is more than trivial. If anyone does copy the Web site or protected elements of the Web site, then that person can be sued for copyright infringement. However, copyright law will not prevent anyone else from going back to the original stories, making their own translation, and publishing them with other art work on their own Web site.

INFRINGEMENT OF COPYRIGHTS

Once you have a copyright, you may need to sue a pirate. On the other hand, you may need to know what you face if someone accuses you of being a copyright pirate.

Filing a Copyright Infringement Action

As noted above, U.S. citizens cannot file a copyright infringement action unless they have received a certificate of copyright registration from the Copyright Office. Although Congress has debated removing this requirement, it was still in effect when this book went to press.

By contrast, a French citizen who created a Web site in Germany for a Japanese company that hosts his Web site in Sri Lanka can file a copyright infringement suit in Peoria, Illinois without first obtaining a U.S. copyright registration.

You should always have an experienced attorney represent you in court. Like the television commercials that show professional race car drivers on race tracks, you should not try litigating a copyright infringement case by yourself.

Damages and Remedies that a Court May Award

Under Section 504 of the Copyright Act, the copyright owner asks the judge to award either "actual damages" or "statutory damages." Actual damages is measured by taking the money lost by the copyright owner and adding to that the amount of money made by the infringer as a result of the infringement.

Statutory damages means that the judge picks a number in a range (presently $500 to $20,000) per work infringed and awards that amount as damages. Moreover, if the judge finds that the infringement was committed "willfully," then judge picks a number from a larger range (presently $500 to $100,000) per work infringed. Statutory damages are usually chosen when the infringer has not lost much money as a result of the infringement, yet needs to teach the infringer a lesson by making the damage award much higher. Unfortunately, statutory damages are available to copyright owners only when the copyright is registered prior to the beginning of the infringement, or shortly after the work is first published.

The judge can always assess court costs and order the seizure and destruction of all infringing copies. The judge can also issue injunctions. Under Section 505, if the copyright was registered prior to the infringement, the judge has the option of making the infringer pay the attorney's fees and expenses of the copyright owner, which can total tens or hundreds of thousands of dollars.

FAIR USE OF COPYRIGHTED WORKS

Certain uses of a copyrighted work may not be prosecuted. One set of uses is called "fair use," which is defined in Section 107 of the Copyright Act. Fair use is not a magic formula that instantly turns copying into a permitted use. Rather, it is a set of guidelines that balance the rights of the copyright owner with other rights and needs, including First Amendment concerns and the need to give students and teachers additional leeway for educational purposes.

Fair use is limited to a handful of certain types of uses, mostly related to teaching, comment, and criticism. Four factors are weighed to determine whether a particular circumstance is a fair use or an infringement.

In one case, several publishers sued a nationwide chain of copy shops located on college campuses. College professors assembled copies of articles from magazines and journals into a sort of text book, and left the copies at the copy shop. The professors then told their students to go to the copy shop and pay for one copy of the hand-made textbook. When the publishers sued the copy shop, the copy shop claimed that it is allowed to make copies as a fair use because the professors wanted the copies for teaching purposes. The courts sided with the publishers because the professors did not bother to ask permission from the copyright owners before copying the articles, and because the hand-made text books competed with text books sold by the publishers. Similarly, if the professors had posted the same text on a Web site for reading by their students, the outcome would likely have been the same.

Types of Uses Recognized as Fair Uses

The making of copies without permission is excused as a fair use only when the purpose of the use is criticism, comment, news reporting, teaching (including multiple copies for classroom use), scholarship, or research.

The purposes are fairly narrowly constrained. So, teachers can invoke fair use when they make copies for their classroom, but publishers of classroom books cannot claim fair use, because the book publishers are not directly teaching students.

First Factor: Purpose and Character of the Use

The first factor weighed is the purpose and character of the use, including whether such use is of a commercial nature or is for nonprofit educational purposes. Thus, if the person making the copies is doing so for a profit, that weighs against fair use. However, if the person is making copies for teaching at church, this factor will weigh in favor of fair use.

Second Factor: Nature of the Copyrighted Work

If the copyrighted work is one that generates large amounts of money, such as advertisement-funded Web sites that receive a great deal of traffic, popular books, records, or movies, then any copying will be closely scrutinized. If the copyrighted work is not a money-maker, then fair use is easier to prove.

Third Factor: Amount Used

It is an axiom of copyright law that an infringement occurs when even a small part of a work is copied, especially if the portion copied is of high quality or is important to the rest of the work.

The third fair use factor recognizes that by weighing the amount and substantiality of the portion copied in relation to the copyrighted work as a whole. If one paragraph is copied from the text of a large Web site, then the portion is not substantial. However, if 20 seconds are sampled from a two-minute song, that is substantial, especially if the 20 seconds contains the chorus of the song.

Fourth Factor: Effect on the Market

One of the primary purposes of the Copyright Act is to ensure that authors of copyrighted works are compensated. So it is not surprising that the fourth factor of fair use is the effect of the copying on the potential market or value of the original, copyrighted work. If each copy made without permission replaces a copy that would have been sold, then that weighs against fair use. If the copies made do not affect the sales of the original, then this factor weighs in favor of fair use.

Application of Fair Use

Initially, the use of the copy should fit into one of the categories (criticism, comment, etc.) stated above. Then, all four of the factors are weighed together. Some factors can be more important than others. There is no mechanical application of "three-out-of-four factors wins."

For example, what happens when a publisher creates a Web site containing the copyrighted works of a living playwright without the playwright's permission? The Web site contains all of the text of all of the playwright's plays, plus full-motion video of one play that the publisher captured off a television rebroadcasting an old movie version. The Web site is intended for students who pay $2 each time they access the Web site. Is this a fair use?

First, you must consider the type of work. Teaching, scholarship, and research are all included as fair use purposes, so the Web site should be weighed under the four factors. The first factor cuts against a fair use. The publisher is making money in this venture, even though the purchasers may be nonprofit educational users. Second, the nature of the copyrighted work consists of highly profitable works (plays and movies, which are subject to video rental income and broadcast royalties), even though the sales of texts of plays probably do not generate large amounts of income for playwrights or other copyright owners (since the producer of the movie may own the copyright to that production).

The third factor also cuts against fair use because the Web site contains an entire movie and the entire text of each play. Finally, the fourth factor also cuts against fair use since each access to the Web site potentially replaces one copy of each play manuscript that could have been sold, as well as one copy of the movie that could have been sold. So, this is not a fair use, and the publisher should seek licenses from the playwright and the owner of the copyright in the movie.

INTERNATIONAL COPYRIGHT LAW

The U.S. has signed a number of treaties over the years that grants protection of U.S. copyrights in other countries, while protecting in the U.S. copyrighted works created in other countries. At this time, the number of countries that are not a party to a copyright treaty to which the U.S. also belongs is fairly small. Accordingly, you must assume that works created outside the U.S. are as well protected as works created inside the U.S. Similarly, works that are created in the U.S. are protected outside the U.S.

Most of the better-known copyright treaties use "national" treatment, which means that Web sites created in Germany are protected in the U.S. as if they had been created in the U.S. by U.S. citizens, while U.S. Web sites are treated in Germany as if they had been created by German citizens in Germany. The details of the laws do change from one country to another, so caution is urged before marketing your products in any country that does not have a tradition of protecting copyrighted works.

COPYRIGHT COLLECTIVES, STOCK HOUSES, AND AGENCIES

You should consider what permissions, if any, you need for a Web site long before you begin development. You may find that a piece of music or a video clip is either unavailable for licensing, or is so expensive that it may as well be unavailable. License fees are negotiated based on the type of use, the market that you are selling to, and the number of years you expect to use it.

You can license the use of copyrighted works from others by using stock houses, copyright collectives, and other agencies. Each agency has the right to license the use of copyrighted works to others on the basis of a set scale of fees, or they have the power to negotiate fees with you on behalf of the copyright owner.

The agencies provide a large selection of works to choose from, which makes it easier to conduct one-stop shopping for licenses to use copyrighted works in your Web sites presentations. If your work needs only one or two permissions, for example to use the music and lyrics of a few popular songs, which you are personally performing for inclusion on your Web site, then you should contact the copyright owner or collective agency yourself and negotiate the transaction. By contrast, if you need permissions to use dozens of works, and you intend to sell your work commercially around the world, then you should consider hiring a permissions company to track down the permissions and negotiate on your behalf.

There are hundreds of agencies from which to choose. Several agencies have offices around the country. The names and principal addresses of several of the better-known agencies follow.

PERMISSIONS AGENTS

A Web site is at its best when different types of elements are juxtaposed. However, using preexisting elements requires that you seek and obtain all necessary permissions. A permissions agent or company can do the work for you, and probably be more efficient, which helps your budget. One of the better-known permissions companies is

BZ/Rights & Permissions, Inc.
125 West 72nd Street
New York, NY 10023
(212) 580-0615

TEXT

Most text can be licensed directly from the author or the publisher. Terms are generally negotiable, although the license fees vary widely. The Copyright Clearance Center was formed to help collect royalties on a variety of journals and other hard copy publications, and more recently has started licensing online rights. The Center may be reached as follows:

Copyright Clearance Center, Inc.
222 Rosewood Drive
Danvers, MA 01923
(978) 750-8400
http://www.copyright.com

Licensing of Original Music Compositions

The licensing of music is broken down into several categories based on the type of music-related work, and the type of license sought.

Web sites works may need (1) an original composition license if the final product includes covers of original compositions not previously recorded, (2) a mechanical license to cover a previously recorded song, and (3) a synchronization license where music is combined with video.

Original compositions are the sheet music and lyrics written by composers and lyricists. Anyone who wants to record or perform an original composition should contact the appropriate rights organization for this purpose. Two of the best known are

American Society of Composers, Authors and Publishers (ASCAP)
One Lincoln Plaza
New York, NY 10023
(212) 621-6000
http://www.ascap.com

Broadcast Music, Inc. (BMI)
320 West 57th Street
New York, NY 10019
800/366-4264
(212) 586-2000
http://www.bmi.com

Mechanical and Synchronization Rights

Once a music record or CD is made available to the public for private home use, any song (original composition) on that record or CD can be recorded by another webmaster or group. This is required pursuant to Section 115 of the U.S. Copyright Act. The type of license is called a "mechanical license" (because records used to be considered "mechanical" reproductions) or a "compulsory license" (because the Copyright Act makes it difficult for the copyright owner to refuse permission). Mechanical licenses do not apply to music used for movies, television, or other visual images.

"Synchronization licenses" are licenses to use music in combination with visual images in movies, television or home video. Synchronization licenses are negotiated on a case-by-case basis, and are not subject to compulsory license rates.

The agency best known for mechanical, synchronization, and related licenses is

The Harry Fox Agency, Inc.
National Music Publishers' Association, Inc.
711 Third Avenue
New York, NY 10017
(212) 370-5330
http://www.harryfox.com

PHOTOGRAPHY

Photography is often licensed through stock photography agencies, one of which can be found in virtually every city, and many large towns (check the phone book).

Almost all of the stock agencies are aware of digital uses, and many offer images in digital form in popular binary formats. License rates depend on the type of use and how many people are likely to see the photo or other image.

One agency on the cutting edge of digital uses of images is

Media Photographers Copyright Agency (http://www.mpca.com)
American Society of Media Photographers, Inc. (http://www.asmp.org)
Washington Park, Suite 502
14 Washington Road
Princeton Junction, NJ 08550-1033
(609) 799-8300

MOVIES AND VIDEO

Several stock houses that handle still photography also license video stock. Movies and television video can be licensed directly from the copyright owners (usually the production firms) or their distributors.

You have to be careful about using movies and television, because like other audio-visual work, they incorporate the copyrighted works of others, including music and still photographs. The copyright owners of the movies may not have the right to license to you the background music or other preexisting works incorporated into the movies. In those cases, ask the copyright owners for their licensing information so that you can get all of the permission that you need in writing.

TRADEMARK LAW

A trademark is anything that designates the source of goods or services, including words or terms, drawings, graphics, sounds, and even colors in some cases. Certainly, domain names can serve as trademarks. In creating your Web sites, you must be careful not to infringe someone else's trademark by associating your Web site with the other person's trademark.

Trademark law is a matter of commerce. Trademark law is not concerned so much with originality as with the commercial impression created by the trademark owner. If you place on your home page a roaring lion above the phrase, *Ars Gratia Artis,* then MGM's present owner may sue for infringement of their trademarks, which includes both the roaring lion and the Latin phrase.

SOURCES OF TRADEMARK LAW

Unlike copyright law, there are several levels of trademark law in the U.S. A "common law" trademark is one that accrues rights merely through use. If you adopt a distinctive term for your business and promote it, then you gain common law trademark rights on a "use it or lose it" basis. Your rights do not begin until you start using it, and are limited to the goods you sell or services you provide, in the geographic area in which you provide them, and last only so long as you continue to provide them. The price is reasonable, however, since there is no application and no filing fee.

Each of the states has adopted a trademark law. Any trademark registered with a state agency receives additional rights within that state, but those rights do not extend outside the state of registration. State trademark registrations are useful for marks used within only one state, and which are not worth the additional cost of filing a federal application for registration. Most states use simple application forms, and the filing fees tend to be between \$50 and \$150.

The third source of trademark law is Congress, which in 1988 substantially revised the federal Trademark Law (also known as the "Lanham Act" after Rep. Walter Lanham). A federal trademark registration provides the trademark owner with the right to sue any infringer in federal courts throughout the U.S., and provides substantial remedies in favor of the trademark owner against infringers.

Unlike common law trademarks, where rights do not accrue without use, an application for a federal trademark registration can be filed without any use of the mark. Called an "intent to use" or "ITU" application, the ITU application allows the trademark owner to gain a reservation on the trademark long before the goods are ready for market, but the registration does not issue unless and until the applicant files another document stating that the applicant has begun use of the mark on goods or in connection with services in some form of commerce that Congress can regulate, usually by selling goods from one state to another. Applications can also be filed on an "actual use" basis, which means that the goods or services have been sold across state lines, or between the U.S. and another country.

Federal trademark applications are more extensive than state applications, and the filing fee is, as this book went to press, $245 per class of goods and services. Web sites are in one class, while packaged software is in another class. Unlike copyright applications, trademark applications are difficult enough that you should consider retaining an attorney to file and prosecute the application.

STRENGTH OF A TRADEMARK

The more distinctive a trademark, the "stronger" it is. Trademarks are characterized by their strength. Stronger marks provide better protection and can be enforced against a wider range of other marks for different goods or services. Weaker marks can only be enforced against virtually the same mark for virtually the same goods or services. The spectrum of trademark strength follows.

Generic Terms

A generic term or design is one that is used for a category of goods or services. A generic term cannot be protected as a trademark, because it is needed for the purpose of classification. The term "Web site" is generic.

Descriptive Terms

A descriptive term or design is one that describes the goods or services but is not generic for the goods or services. A descriptive term cannot be used as a trademark unless it gains a "secondary meaning," which means that when people hear the term, they think of a particular source or set of goods, rather than all goods with that characteristic. The term "WINDOWS" is descriptive of all software that uses windowing technology, but the term "WINDOWS" has gained a secondary meaning, that of Microsoft's operating environment, "Microsoft Windows."

Suggestive Marks

A suggestive term or design suggests what the goods or services may be, but is not descriptive of them. The term "MICROSOFT" suggests microcomputer software, but the term does not describes the products of Microsoft Corporation. Suggestive trademarks are protectable and make for good trademarks.

Arbitrary Marks

An arbitrary term or design has a real meaning to most people, but the meaning is different from the goods or services it is associated with. The term "APPLE" by Apple Computer Corp. is a good example of an arbitrary mark because most computers are not made of apples. Arbitrary terms and designs make for excellent trademarks.

Coined Marks

A coined term is one that has no meaning except that it is associated with the goods or services. The term "BORLAND" is a good example of a coined term as the term has no meaning outside of the fact that Borland International uses the term on its software. Coined marks are on the opposite side of the spectrum from generic terms.

TRADEMARK NOTICES

Any good you sell or service you provide can bear a notice in the form of "TM" ("trademark") or "SM" ("service mark"). It doesn't cost anything, but it puts the world on notice that you claim your trademark rights.

The circle-R character ("®") is reserved for owners of current federal trademark registrations. It cannot be used by owners of state registrations (unless they also have a current federal registration). Similarly, filing a federal application is not sufficient to use the "®" symbol; a federal certificate of trademark registration must first be issued.

Each of your works may also contain a notice that "[your trademark] is a trademark of [name of your company]." If you have a current federal registration, you can state that "[your trademark] is a registered trademark of [name of your company]."

If you are properly using the trademarks of another, then you should include a trademark notice. For example, if you prepare a training CD-ROM called "How to Use Microsoft Windows," then you should include the trademark notice that "'MICROSOFT' and 'WINDOWS' are registered trademarks of Microsoft Corporation." You can use the approach for each trademark of which you are aware. Many works also bear a catch-all trademark notice; "[your trademark] is a [registered] trademark of [name of your company]. All other trademarks are trademarks or registered trademarks of their respective owners."

LIKELIHOOD OF CONFUSION

Trademark infringement is generally a matter of determining whether the consumers of the trademark owner are "likely to be confused" by a trademark used by another. In determining "likelihood of confusion," a court will consider how close the marks are in sound (since trademarks are often passed from person to person by word of mouth), how close the goods or services are, and whether the goods or services are provided in the same way or in the same "channels of commerce."

For example, the trademark "EXCEL" is a good one for both Hyundai and Microsoft. However, there is no likelihood of confusion, because consumers will not mistake a Hyundai Excel car with a Microsoft Excel spreadsheet.

TRADE DRESS

In addition to the protection trademark laws provide to names and logos, the law also protects the distinctive nonfunctional packaging of a product. The totality of a distinctive product's packaging is known as trade dress.

This total package includes the look of the product, the packaging, and can even include the design and shape of the product and its packaging. Trade dress can be protected by two different methods: (1) if distinct enough it can be registered on the Principal Register of the U.S. Patent and Trademark Office; and (2) if it has achieved a secondary meaning in the marketplace it can be protected under the guise of unfair competition.

CHARACTERS

Trademark law will protect the use of two-dimensional and three-dimensional characters, and terms associated with the characters, so long as they are associated with goods (such as videos, T-shirts and other clothing, lunch boxes) and services (e.g., cable services).

A well-designed character such as Mickey Mouse can be protected under trademark law indefinitely, so long as the character continues to be used on goods and associated with services. With the power of Web technology, it is tempting to copy well-known characters from cartoons, animation, and toys. However, almost all such characters are trademarks of their owners, and their use without permission from their owners is to invite a trademark infringement suit. The Walt Disney Co. and the rights owners of children's cartoons have been especially active in policing their marks against infringement.

TRADEMARKS ON WEB PAGES

Trademarks are part and parcel of a company's marketing and advertising efforts. The World Wide Web has proven to be one of the most effective communication mediums since the invention of television. So it's no surprise that many companies are using the World Wide Web to advertise their wares and display their trademarks.

There is little doubt that the use of a trademark on a Web Page connected to the Internet is used in interstate commerce for the purpose of advertising services to generate goodwill. As noted above, use of a mark in connection with a service generally means that the mark is placed on advertising or marketing materials, or other materials that may be associated with the provision of services, such as letterheads and invoices. Use of a service mark on a Web Page will also qualify as a service mark for use in interstate commerce so long as the Web site is associated with the provision of services. Even the simplest of "brochureware" Web sites that contain service marks will be deemed to be a good use of the service mark in interstate commerce.

Use of a mark for goods on a Web site is generally unlikely to be deemed use of that mark in interstate or other commerce. Marks for goods (unlike marks for services) must be placed on the goods or packaging for the goods. Even in the case of packaged software (which is considered a goods, not a service) sold via Web site by downloads to users, the placement of a mark on the Web site will not be a good use in commerce. Instead, the mark should be in the software itself (e.g., on a boot-up or "splash" screen) since software downloaded from a Web site will not have any hard copy packaging.

TRADEMARKS UNDER WEB PAGES

Search engines on the Web, such as Yahoo!, AltaVista, Lycos, Webcrawler, and HotBot, do not actually search the Web each time that a user enters a query. Instead, each search engines create an index of Web sites by reviewing each Web site that it finds or is told about, and then builds an index of terms that it deems relevant. Most search engines look at keyword meta tags to help create the index, because keyword meta tags indicate what the author of the Web page considers important.

Of course, some Web page authors fill the keyword meta tags with terms that they consider important to attract the type of users they would like, as well as repeating certain key words dozens of times in the hope that the search engines will rank their page as more "relevant" than those of their competitors. And then there are the Web pages in which the keywords in a Web page will include terms and trademarks of the author's competitors in the hopes of attracting users away from the competitors' Web pages. This has led to several law suits.

There have been several cases in which the author or owner of a Web page placed trademarks belonging to others in the keyword meta tags of the page in the hopes of attracting users who are interested in the trademarks. In each of the cases so far (as of this printing), some or all of the defendants consented to removing the plaintiff's trademarks, and notifying the search engines to re-index the defendant's Web site, so as to remove the plaintiff's trademarks from each search engine's index of the defendant's Web site.

TRADEMARKS ON SOMEONE ELSE'S WEB PAGES: LINKING AND FRAMING

In several cases, the owner of one Web site has sued the owner of another Web site because the first Web site includes links to the second Web site. Generally, the allegation is that the link on the first Web site associates the contents of the second Web site with the goods or services offered by the first Web site, especially when the link is not clearly marked to show that the user will be obtaining a document from a different Web site.

For example, one newspaper in the Shetland Islands sued and obtained a preliminary injunction against another newspaper in the Shetland Islands on the allegation that the defendant's Web site misled users into thinking that the defendant was the source of the some of the articles accessed from the defendant's Web site, when, in fact, the defendant was linking to discrete articles on the plaintiff's Web site. Although initially couched in terms of copyright law, the claim sounds better in trademark law as a claim that the defendant was passing off plaintiff's information reportage as its own. The parties subsequently settled.

In another case filed and subsequently settled, *The Washington Post* and several other large news organizations sued a small Web site owned by a company called Total News with numerous allegations of trademark infringement and unfair competition. A user who surfed on over to the site would receive a frame that contained the first site's own content and advertising in several windows, plus buttons that served as links to *The Washington Post* Web site, CNN Web site, Fox News Web site, and so on. A user who clicked one of the buttons would receive the content of *The Washington Post* or other Web site in one large window of the frame on the user's screen, but the first site's buttons and advertising would remain in the other windows of the frame. Unfortunately, the first site had never asked for permission from any of the news organizations because it believed that it did not need permission. After all, all that the first site did — so it argued — was to establish the frame and the buttons, and it was the user who downloaded the content of the other Web sites by clicking on a button. The parties settled, and the first site as of this writing is still linking to some news organizations, presumably with their express permission.

DOMAIN NAMES AS TRADEMARKS

A domain name can serve as a trademark for the goods or services provided or advertised by a company on the Internet at its domain name, so long as the domain name is used as more than just the computer address for a Web or other Internet site.

A domain name can be registered as a trademark, so long as it used as more than "just" an Internet address or URL. Since each domain name (usually a combination of top-level domain and second-level domain) must be unique for the domain naming system to work, domain names are generally issued on a first-come, first-served basis. The result is a number of lawsuits filed by plaintiffs who claim that they should have the sole right to use a domain name registered by the defendant.

To illustrate the connection between domain names and trademarks, a writer by the name of Josh Quittner registered the domain name "mcdonalds.com" and established an e-mail address for himself as "ronald@mcdonalds.com." His article, Billions Registered (*Wired*, October 1994, at page 50) sounded the charge for others to register trademarks they did not own as their domain names in the hope that the trademark owner would then ransom the domain name. Quittner's own demands were relatively modest; McDonald's complied with Quittner's demand that it pay to have one public school in New York City connected to the Internet.

Many who followed Quittner's lead did so by registering large numbers of domain names incorporating the trade names and trademarks of well-known companies. Unlike Quittner, they did not offer to turn over the domain name in response to an act of charity, but sought payments of large sums of money. Called "domain name arbitrage," "cybersquatting," "domain piracy," "domain grabbing," and any number of other terms, the practice has led to many suits against domain name owners by trademark owners claiming that the domain name infringes or dilutes a trademark. Several of these cases have alleged dilution of famous trademarks under the federal and state dilution statutes.

In cases where the domain owner does not compete in any way with the trademark owner, the dilution claims have been more successful, although the courts have strived mightily to find that a plaintiff's trademark is "well-known" to fulfill the condition precedent of the dilution statutes. In what appears to be a self-fulfilling prophecy, if not a matter of circular logic, the courts note that the domain name owner had hoped to sell the domain name to the trademark owner, thus suggesting that the mark must be sufficiently "well known" to attract this unwanted attention.

The use of a domain name can also lead to a tarnishment claim. Thus, the use of a domain can reduce the value of the trademark owner's right in its trademark. In one case, the owners of the TOYS 'R' US trademark sued the owners of the "adultsrus.com" domain name on the grounds that the domain name was associated with the advertising and sale of sex-related products on a World Wide Web site at <http://www.adultsrus.com>. The court expressly held that defendant's use of the second-level domain name "adultsrus" for sex-related products tarnished the rights of plaintiffs in the 'R' US family of marks for children's toys and clothing.

PRIVACY AND PUBLICITY LAW

The rights of privacy and publicity are two sides of the same coin. The rights of privacy and publicity apply even if you photograph or record (video, audio, or both) a person out-of-doors in a public location, such as a park, town square, or walking down the street. The law deems that a person has the right to control how her image is used.

This is a growing area of law that is more closely related to trademark law. California and New York have passed statutes that protect privacy, and other states are likely to follow.

DON'T MAKE PRIVATE PEOPLE "PUBLIC" WITHOUT THEIR PERMISSION

If the person is a private person, then she may prohibit the use of her image for your profit or gain. A private person has the right to remain private.

CELEBRITIES HAVE THE RIGHT TO CONTROL THEIR PUBLICITY

If the person is a public person or celebrity, she may be able to prohibit your use of her image without proper compensation, primarily because she is deemed to have a property interest in her image. In other words, she can make money from her status as a celebrity, so you cannot use her status to help sell your product without her permission.

One good example of the right of publicity is the Bette Midler case. A car manufacturer wanted to run a series of commercials that featured Ms. Midler's singing. Ms. Midler decided not to participate, so the car manufacturer hired someone else who sang just like Bette Midler. Ms. Midler sued and won about $400,000 because people who listened to the commercials thought that she was singing in the commercial. Even though no image of Ms. Midler was used, her vocal style was sufficiently distinctive to serve as her trademark. Since everyone agreed that Ms. Midler's vocal style helped sell cars, Ms. Midler was held by the court to have the right to control when her voice and vocal style could be used to help sell cars.

RELEASES

There is no better way to ensure that you have all the rights that you need to use a person's image or other distinctive features than to get a release. Professional photographers use releases all of the time. You may need to consult an attorney to ensure that the release you would like to use is enforceable under the law of the states in which you will use the release, and to make sure that the release covers every type of use that you contemplate.

WHEN YOU CAN USE THE WORKS OF ANOTHER PERSON

There are several ways in which you can use and incorporate the works of others into your Web sites. Ask yourself a few questions.

First, is the work in the public domain? As discussed above, public domain means that nobody owns the copyright or other rights to the work. If you have access to an original Leonardo da Vinci painting or manuscript of a Mozart concerto, then make your own copies without fear of copyright violation.

Second, if the work is not in the public domain, can you get a license to use or copy the work? The saying goes that "it is easier to beg forgiveness afterwards than to ask for permission beforehand." However, for copyrighted works, permission is often easy to get and costs very little, while forgiveness is very expensive. At the very least, forgiveness (including legal fees, court costs, and damages) costs a great deal more than permission.

Third, will any original work that you copy be recognizable as a derivative work? As noted above, a derivative work remains a derivative work only so long as any part of it is still recognizable as originating with its predecessor.

Fourth, does the work affect anyone else's privacy or publicity rights? If a person can be recognized by her looks, voice, or other distinctive attributes, that person can request compensation. So long as you have appropriate releases from each individual, or the person that you have licensed the work has the appropriate releases, then this will not be an issue.

Chapter 27
Using Net-Based Interactive Technology for Online Marketing, Sales, and Support of Financial Services Firms

Steven Semelsberger

> We're going to integrate the Internet completely into the Schwab organization.
>
> — *Charles Schwab,* Chairman and Co-CEO, Charles Schwab & Co.

THE IMPORTANCE OF IMPLEMENTING SOFTWARE SOLUTIONS to improve customer service and provide operational efficiency has been well documented. Most likely, you've already experienced several waves of euphoria as vendors have promised significant returns on investment from the latest in software gadgetry. From the mainframe boom of the 1970s through the UNIX and client/server explosion of the late 1980s to the "thin client is in," multitiered approach to computing in the 1990s, solutions have come and gone as application writers and software manufacturers have pushed each other to develop robust, easy to implement, highly scalable solutions for critical business functions.

0-8493-9991-2/99/$0.00+$.50

While applications from currency exchange, to account maintenance, to options pricing have all become automated and computerized, most leading investment banks, brokerage houses, and diversified financial institutions have yet to move beyond the branch or the telephone as a means to actually interact with their customers. A few companies have adopted online banking services to allow customers to perform simple tasks, such as pay bills or check balances, over the Internet. Many have established a marketing presence on the Web, utilizing the easy access of the Internet to hawk products and services. Others, spurned into action by up and comers like e*Trade, have invested heavily in the infrastructure needed to carry out online trades.

Still, actual Web-based customer interaction has been limited to a few basic frequently asked question (FAQ) sections and an occasional "e-mail for more information" link. Only a few visionaries in the financial services industry have truly embraced the Internet's potential for a complete array of interactive services.

When one examines the usual customer life cycle, it becomes evident that the rise of the Web offers companies an unsurpassed opportunity for efficient, effective, and personalized interactive service. The Internet provides a significant opportunity for four key functions:

1. Community building. The interactive nature of the Web enables companies to give their customers a global forum to express ideas, concerns, thoughts, and demands, both with each other and with company representatives. While the idea of these "many-to-many" forums can be daunting for some, as Hagel & Armstrong noted in their 1996 manifesto on virtual communities, *NetGain,* interactivity is the most proven means to develop a sense of allegiance to an online destination or brand. Ongoing threaded discussions and interactive chats are two proven methods to bring customers together around a concept, product, or service. Each will be discussed in detail below.
2. Marketing events. The Web also creates new opportunities for financial service providers to hold interactive events in a "one-to-many" manner. Individual customers, spread across boundless geographies, can now have access to high-ranking company officials who may have never been reachable through traditional communication channels. Video streaming in conjunction with moderated chats has given rise to a new era in communication and will be explored below.
3. E-Commerce. With Forrester's prediction for Internet commerce to rise to $327 billion by 2001, most organizations are scrambling to unlock how they can utilize the Web to efficiently and effectively increase top line revenue. While specific e-commerce payment and tracking systems are discussed elsewhere in this book, this chapter

will focus on how interactive communication mechanisms can be utilized to increase purchase conversion rates and enable cross-selling and up-selling. Specifically, live interaction, offered as a main component of a corporation's Web site, (through interactive text conferencing, screen synchronization, telephone callback, and even voice and video over IP), provides the human touch that is often needed to encourage a purchase decision.

4. Customer support. Once an individual has become a customer, it is critical that he or she receives an appropriate level of service and support. The Internet offers a multitude of new, efficient, interactive support channels, ranging from self-service options all the way through a multitude of live communication channels. The Internet-enabled customer support process will be explained in an upcoming section.

The four pillars of Web-based customer interaction can be summed up in the diagram shown in Exhibit 1.

This chapter will focus on describing applications to enable organizations to effectively build Internet communities, market to their customers, interact with prospects to sell products and services online, and finally, provide efficient customer service and support. It will also serve as an in-

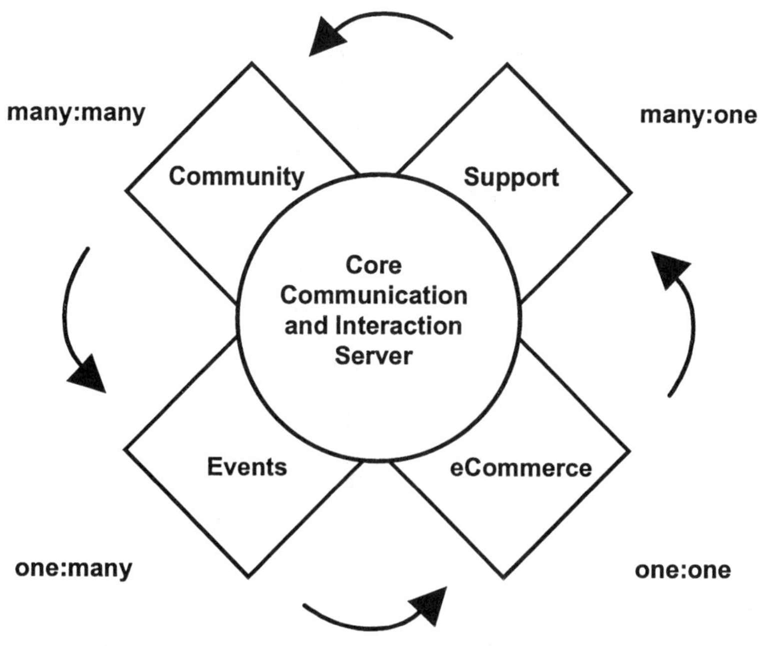

Exhibit 1. The four pillars of Web-based customer interaction.

troduction to specific software vendors and to set basic expectations for technical and human resource requirements to implement and maintain interactive forums.

BUILDING AN INTERNET COMMUNITY: MANY-TO-MANY DISCUSSIONS

At this point, many Web sites are vast arrays of "brochureware," or jumbles of pages of marketing materials. However, analysts and executives alike have realized the need to improve both information and interaction if they are to fully realize the potential of the Internet. John McCarthy, an analyst at Forrester, says that corporations need to be thinking about how to provide a compelling experience for their customers. "Static Web pages that you have to go and fetch just aren't going to make it," says McCarthy. McCarthy stresses that the next wave of Web sites will focus on "intelligent interactivity." These effective applications will draw customers in with engaging content, collect information, and use the information to direct clients to products and services of targeted interest.

A major component of these intelligent sites will be the use of interactive, threaded discussions and live chat. Both offer compelling advantages and can be used as stand-alone solutions or as an integrated system.

THREADED DISCUSSION SERVERS

Users of Usenet servers are quite familiar with the concept of threaded, topical discussions. The idea is simple: a customer, community member or corporate representative initiates a thread with a question or statement posted in an online "bulletin board" accessible by other community members. Individuals who visit the thread can then post follow-up statements and replies, or initiate new conversation threads.

An example of a threaded discussion (also frequently called message board) environment is shown in Exhibit 2.

In this instance, iBank, a fictional Internet financial services corporation, has set up a threaded discussion environment to provide user forums where individuals can search for information, browse, and post questions about various topics of interest such as car loans and online banking. Threaded discussion servers have several key benefits:

- Information posted is accessible by all future users, increasing knowledge transfer.
- Website visitors can view information in a self-service mode, decreasing their reliance on live bank representatives for information.
- Threaded discussions can be viewed from within the browser, allowing easy integration into existing Web sites or corporate intranets.

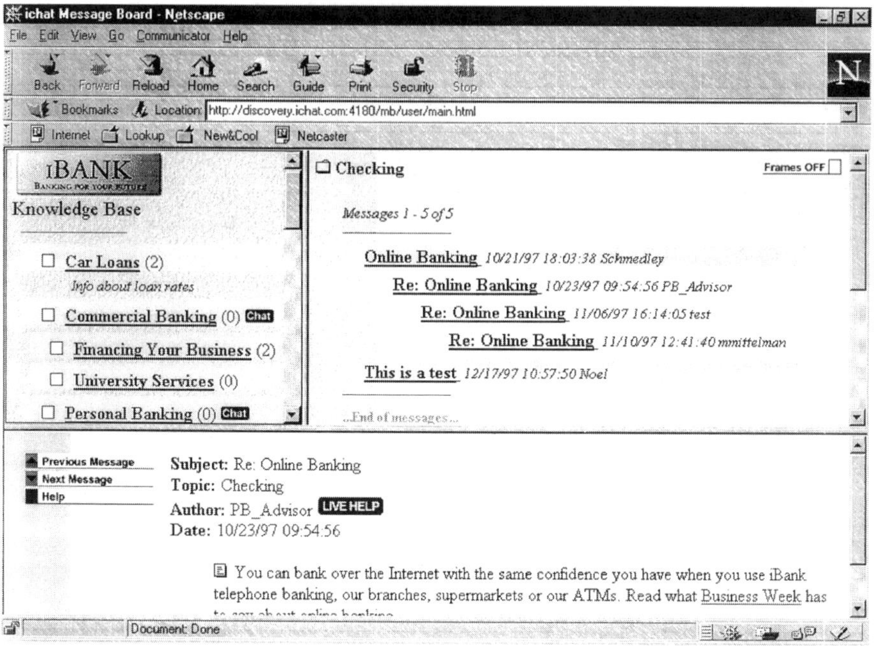

Exhibit 2. A threaded discussion group.

- A sense of community can be quickly established without having the constant site traffic that chat requires (see below for information on text-based chat).
- Users can visit and post messages and replies at their convenience, without having to meet at predetermined times.

THREADED DISCUSSION REQUIREMENTS

Generally, threaded discussion servers are fairly quick and easy to set up. The majority of the effort can be in maintaining and monitoring threaded discussion topics. Depending on the level of human filtering, threads and posts can be monitored by a single individual on a daily basis, or could become a multiperson full-time task.

Most message board applications work with major Web servers (Microsoft IIS, Apache, and Netscape Enterprise Server), post information in straight HTML (meaning that firewalls shouldn't pose a problem), and support numerous databases, including SQL, LDAP, and ODBC compliant storage applications. Windows NT 4.0 and Sun Solaris 2.x are by far the most popular operating system versions available.

While vendors have a variety of requirements for system memory, 32 MB should get you started. Plan on setting aside plenty of disk space (100 MB just to get off the ground) as growth in message posts can quickly fill up a hard drive.

CHAT SERVERS

Long a key "late night" component of proprietary online offerings such as CompuServe and America Online, chat exploded onto the Web in early 1996. Since then, chat has become a must-have for major Internet destination sites. Initially, text-based chat was seen as a gimmick to draw traffic to a Web site and allow users to banter about frivolous topics of discussion.

However, the rise of several prominent discussion areas on the Web quickly ended any preconceived notions about the application of chat to the financial services arena. The Motley Fool and Yahoo!'s financial forums (shown in Exhibit 3) have drawn substantial attention, serious, worthwhile discussions, and even advertisers' dollars.

As the Yahoo! screen shot exemplifies, text-based chat is a simple, flowing process that entails users entering into conversations in an open fo-

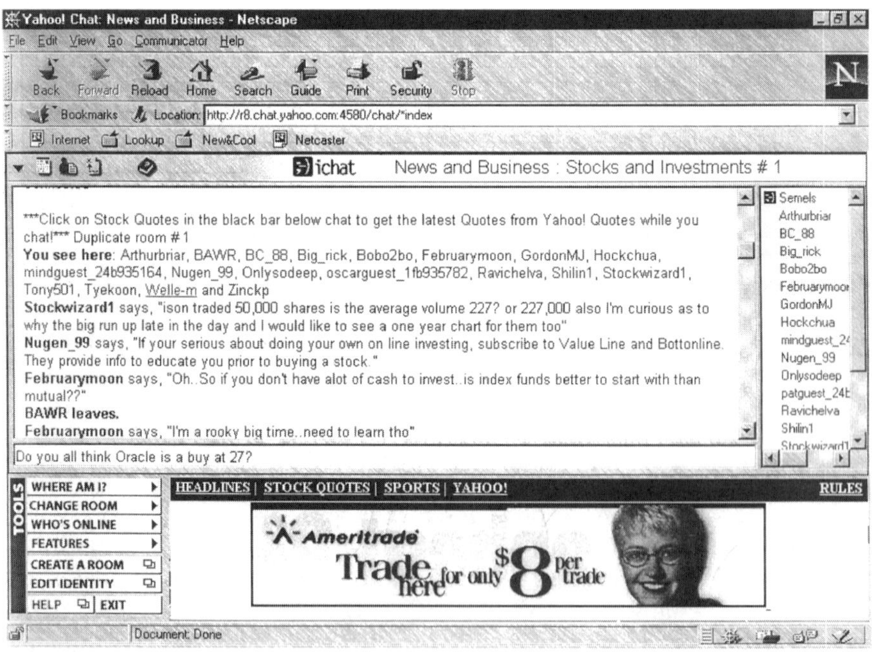

Exhibit 3. Sample financial forum on the Web.

rum. Conversations are often dynamic and spontaneous, and regular users are quite often outspoken and critical. Yet no other application has demonstrated to have as effective a draw for Web users: *Business Week* estimates that chatters stay on Web sites for up to three times the 10-minute average and chat-enabled Web sites report up to 50% increases in traffic.

For financial services corporations, open chat rooms can also be utilized as ad hoc meeting areas, enabling distributed teams to collaborate on problems, discuss market trends, and work on projects — all in real time.

The major benefits of adding chat capabilities to your Web site include:

- Increased user loyalty — users who develop a community perspective around your Web site have a significant probability of returning to your online forum.
- Immediate information exchange — sites have the ability to find out issues of importance and major customer concerns immediately.
- Logging user feedback — information exchanged in chats can be stored for future reference.
- Captured eyeballs for advertising — chat rooms, with their long, average visit times, provide an excellent forum for advertisers.

Chat Server Requirements

Most chat servers handle both administrative functions and user sessions from within a standard browser environment. Setup and configuration time is generally minimal, but can become quite lengthy, requiring up to a few days if user loads are anticipated to go above 1000 concurrent chatters, the company has an extensive firewall setup, or the site desires extensive user interface customization.

Most chat servers work with major Web servers (Microsoft IIS, Apache, and Netscape Enterprise Server). Firewalls can be tricky, since the chat information is often passed through a port other than the standard :80 port open for HTML transfer. To counteract these concerns, major chat vendors have developed firewall proxy servers to encapsulate chat text in straight HTTP.

Various chat servers come with proprietary user information databases or support standard apps, including SQL, LDAP, and ODBC compliant storage databases. As with threaded discussion servers, Windows NT 4.0 and Sun Solaris 2.x are by far the most popular operating systems available.

While vendors have a variety of requirements for system memory, 32 MB should get you going. Storage requirements are not as great as needed as message boards, since (unless you leave logging options on) information transmitted is not stored. Plan on a minimum of 20 MB to get started.

Case Study: Citicorp (www.citibank.com)

Citicorp firmly believes in offering user forums to build a sense of community around its products and services. The bank has added both threaded discussion and real-time chat capabilities to provide customers with an interactive resource to learn about investment options and bank services from company representatives and other users. Additionally, the Web site utilizes guides who host financial subject areas such as mortgages, credit cards, and pension plans. At each customer information section, the guides answer questions, steer users to information, write columns, and moderate chats.

The bank's embrace of real-time, interactive communication software represents a paradigm shift in the corporate approach to the Web, says Forrester analyst Emily Green. "Service companies are starting to grasp the intimacy aspects of the Web," she says. "With the size of the investments that they make online, [banks] need to make sure people stick around."

ONLINE EVENTS: ONE-TO-MANY DISCUSSIONS

While threaded discussion boards and open chat rooms create community forums that encourage users to return to share information on their latest and greatest investment recommendation, moderated online events are an excellent means to bring targeted customers together to exchange information in a controlled manner.

Internet events are the "Larry King Shows" of the Web — users have an opportunity to submit questions directly to the individuals running the event. Usually, a group of screeners will filter and edit incoming questions. Appropriate and interesting inquiries are then presented to the speaker and to the audience as a whole — to be answered in real-time. Exhibit 4 demonstrates the normal flow of an Internet event.

While Internet events are typically run using special moderating add-ins to leading text chat software packages, many organizations have turned to a blended multimedia offering for their online discussions. For example, using video-streaming technology, an investment bank could bring one of their sector analysts online to present his or her conclusions about a specific investment vehicle or market trend.

During the course of the presentation, the analyst could also present slides, graphics, and charts to the audience. Since the entire event is pushed out to the users' browser (generally by breaking the browser into frames for text content, video, and presentation graphics), the attendee won't need any additional software or hardware (such as microphones, Internet phones, or video cameras) to receive a multimedia-rich experience. Although outside of the scope of the financial services industry, the screen shot shown in Exhibit 5 demonstrates an online event that was held by Jeff

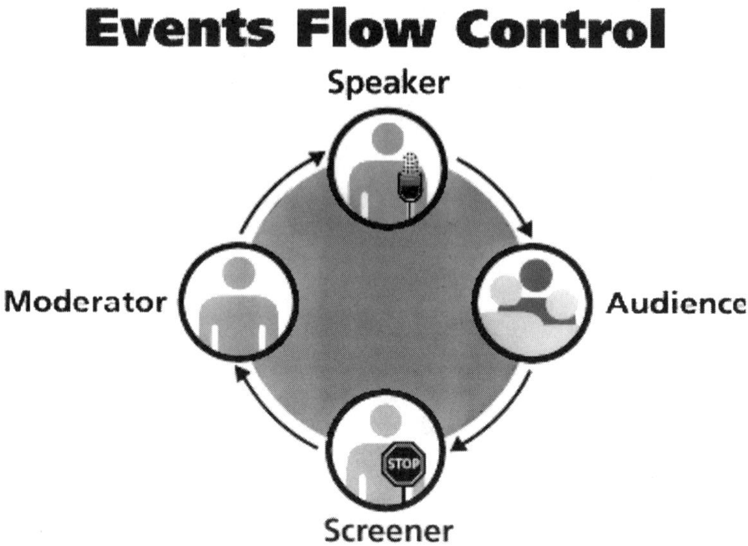

Exhibit 4. The normal flow of an Internet event.

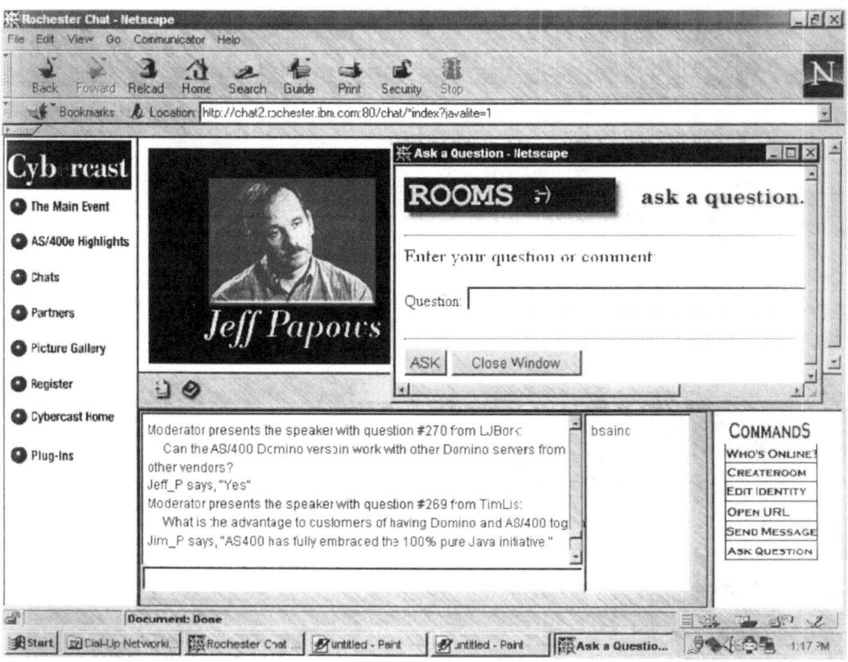

Exhibit 5. The IBM Web event.

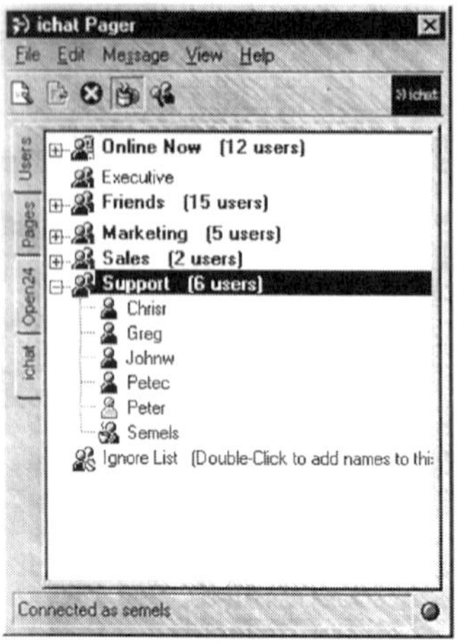

Exhibit 6. Instant messaging.

Papows, president and CEO of Lotus, to introduce the new IBM AS400e server.

One of the major challenges of running online events is actually communicating to the targeted audience the location, time, and content of the event in a manner that draws significant attention and ensures participation by audience members. Instant messages, generally text-based announcements that pop up in the forefront of open windows on users' computers, are a great way to invite targeted participants to online forums.

Using instant messaging technology, clients can be notified the second that critical new investment information is available. They can then join a real-time, interactive discussion in a moderated chat environment. For instance, as Federal Reserve Board chairman Alan Greenspan is testifying, a broker can send instant messages to her clients, inviting them into a closed session with leading analysts and company economists who offer insight and advice into appropriate market plays. An example of an instant message is shown in Exhibit 6.

Online Events Requirements

Hosting online events requires more human intervention and thought than merely providing an open chat forum. Still, most event moderating tools are quite simple to use and can be installed and running in a few hours. Systems and technical requirements are comparable to the chat server section discussed above.

Case Study: Merrill Lynch

With nearly $1 trillion under management, Merrill Lynch realizes the importance of providing exceptional services that will enable them to continue to strengthen their customer relationships. For example, they were one of the first major financial services organizations to utilize e-mail for more efficient client interaction.

During the fall of 1996, Merrill Lynch began to look for a software solution that would allow them to hold moderated events where their technical and financial experts could conduct online seminars. After reviewing various products and considering proprietary, online service companies, they chose an open, Internet solution. Joe Corriero, director of interactive technology, summed it up this way: "After we experimented with events on America Online, we realized that we would never reach our targeted customer base through AOL's closed community business model. We clearly saw the Web as the future for our customer interaction needs."

Online events represent a logical progression of the use of Internet technology and mark an exciting new opportunity for Merrill Lynch customers to interact directly with leading company minds. Merrill Lynch actually holds three types of online events:

- Public events — industry luminaries present their predictions on market trends and technological innovations.
- Private events — financial consultants interface with their key clients over the Web to discuss investment strategies and appropriate market moves.
- Financial consultant-only events — financial consultants gather together for training and focused discussions.

E-COMMERCE: ONE-TO-ONE DISCUSSIONS

With Web-based transactions expected to grow to more than U.S.$220 billion by 2000 (source: International Data Corp), the returns for investments in technology that provide the means for customers to gather information and make informed purchases will be enormous.

With extended economic prosperity, the opportunities for financial services organizations that provide investment services to high net worth individuals are exceptional. As John F. Snyder, portfolio manager of the John Hancock Sovereign Investors Fund, puts it: "We're in the seventh year of an economic expansion and inflation is 2% and falling. Things really are different."

Additionally, the extended bull market has increased assets in 401(k) plans — at a compounded annual rate of 18% over the past decade — to around $810 billion, according to Access Research Inc. in Windsor, CT.

With equity markets on a run that has no foreseeable end in sight and average customers with 65% of their financial investments allocated to equities, communication between high net worth individuals and their financial consultants is of the utmost of importance.

The Internet is an exciting new communication channel for e-commerce-motivated interaction. Where companies and customers were once locked to the phone or face-to-face meetings to correspond, the Internet enables customers to set up accounts, monitor market activity in real-time from their office or home, and research and conduct trades.

What's been missing until recently has been a means to actually communicate with a company representative online for advice during the course of a purchase evaluation. Many would-be buyers have left very slick Web sites in disgust after they've been unable to find the answer to an elusive question. To make sure that prospects receive information without having to suffer through a tedious phone call or wait for an e-mail response, several new solutions are being offered.

Text-Based Conferencing, Screen Synchronization, and Web ACDs

Chat solutions, either in open forums or in specific one-to-one, channeled environments, create the capacity for instant correspondence. Upon clicking on a "live help" button, a prospect can be given the opportunity to enter into a text dialogue with a sales rep who can then push information such as investment portfolio charts, diagrams, and product/service descriptions (through browser screen synchronization) directly to the customer. Exhibit 7 represents one potential application for text-based conferencing.

While several stand-alone chat applications can function for basic live support, the integration of a Web-automated call distributor (ACD) to route requests for help to appropriate agents based on customer attributes, work flow rules, and agent availability will be needed to handle heavily trafficked call centers that wish to complement their telephony commerce efforts with Internet-based, e-commerce support.

CTI CallBack

Offering a callback mechanism for customers is another option for live correspondence. While a button that allows a customer to submit a request for a phone call brings one close to true Internet interactivity, the delays inherent in actually routing a call to the appropriate agent in conjunction with the limits for customers with a single phone line (such as an investor dialing in from a hotel room) make CTI callback a secondary option at this point.

Voice and Video Conferencing

H.323-based voice and video transmissions have been heralded as major new breakthroughs in Internet telephony and conferencing. However, the band-

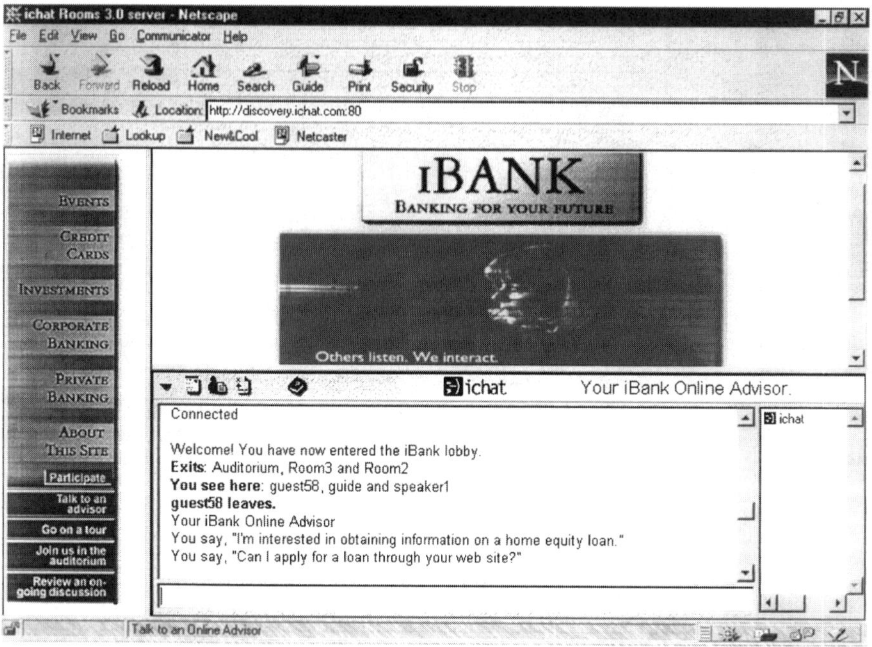

Exhibit 7. An example of text-based conferencing.

width, processing power, and hardware requirements to actually run a video transmission, and the limited quality still inherent in live, packet-switched communications, make this option one to consider on a limited basis.

BENEFITS OF LIVE INTERACTION

Live interaction, through singular applications of the technology described above or through a multioption, mutlichannel communication center, offers several benefits to e-commerce efforts, including:

- Higher closure rates.
- Higher average sales prices due to agent cross-selling and up-selling activity.
- Improved customer satisfaction due to live human availability.

Live Interaction Requirements

Each of the applications described above requires a variety of hardware and software depending on the scope of the project and the integration into telephony support processes. In most cases, it is recommended to work with the vendor and a leading e-commerce and/or call center system integrator such as Cambridge Technology or TSC to develop the optimum solution for your efforts.

Once launched, live Internet interaction can be run as a stand-alone environment, or integrated into telephone-based sales efforts. Human requirements can range from a single, part-time agent to monitor activities all the way through, to a multihundred rep call center to handle thousands of concurrent transactions. An additional benefit to consider with text-based conferencing is the multitasking capabilities and voice breaks that text correspondence enables agents to experience.

Case Study: Pristine Capital Management

Pristine Capital Management (PCM) was named Baron's number one day trading site on the Web for 1997 and is an outstanding example of a start-up Internet company that has successfully utilized chat to create an e-commerce-driven business model. PCM believes that their short-term trading style (2 to 5 day holding period) takes advantage of a very profitable market niche overlooked by most active investors. Too brief for large institutional concerns to take advantage of and, at the same time, too lengthy for floor traders (who typically don't hold positions overnight) to be comfortable with, this time frame offers the perfect opportunity for independent traders who possess the expertise necessary to profitably exploit it.

In June 1997, Pristine launched a real-time trading room on the Web — revolutionizing the financial trading industry. This virtual trading room, using interactive text-based conferencing technology, provides live, ongoing stock recommendations and market commentary throughout the trading day, effectively bypassing end-of-day services and cumbersome intra-day phone messages.

Members with access receive a steady flow of real-time trading ideas, just as if they were sitting in the private trading room of the editors. Breakouts and stocks that are on the verge of exploding to the upside are recognized in a matter of seconds, allowing users to act quickly. Subscribers also get pre-market commentary moments before the markets open, and informative post-market remarks are made to summarize each day's events.

By charging a monthly membership fee of $525, Pristine has seen a dramatic return on their investment in live, text-based conferencing technology. "Within 1 month of launch, we signed up over 150 customers," Tony Nunes, Director of Technology for Pristine stated. "Real-time, Web-based text conferencing has provided the means for us to launch an extremely profitable service."

CUSTOMER SUPPORT

As discussed thus far, Internet-based interactive technology can be used to bring a prospect to a company's Web site to participate in ongoing discussions and debates over various investment instruments. It can also be used to hold major online events, further closing the gap between an individual's transition from prospect to customer. Live interaction then can be the critical element in e-commerce initiatives, as customers seek to buy everything from specific equities to new insurance plans online, and often need assistance before actually conducting a transaction.

The final piece of the customer life cycle arises from the support side of the equation. Customer service is at the forefront of most organizations' concerns. With support labor costs escalating and customer expectations for immediate, personalized attention rising, financial services innovators are turning to the Internet to serve as a new channel for customer correspondence.

Through both interactive self-service and live help, organizations hope to reduce their share of the $60 billion that Brean Murray Institutional Research estimates is spent on support labor costs. According to Forrester Research, increased self-service, better distribution of information, and more efficient agent utilization can enable organizations to experience a 43% decrease in labor cost per customer contact through deployment of Web-based customer interaction solutions.

Internet-Based Customer Support in Action

One easy method to envision Web-based customer interaction is through a description of a customer's experience on a major financial services site. Research indicates that over 80% of customer call center inquiries are routine questions, so the support process starts by giving customers easy self-help options, allowing valuable support agents to focus on more complicated inquiries, premium customers, and sales opportunities. Browsable and searchable self-help options including dynamic frequently asked question (FAQ) and knowledge base searching capabilities where customers can easily find answers to investment questions, account status, or portfolio position.

If they are unable to locate the support information required, customers can then have the option to send an e-mail inquiry or enter into a live help mode. Automated e-mail routing and response capabilities ensure a timely response in conjunction with escalation to a live agent if the question is unrecognized.

Should the customer request live help, dynamic queuing mechanisms route the request to the appropriate agent or group, based on customizable business rules and attributes such as customer profile, question urgency, and agent availability. Ideally, the agent and customer will have multiple options for live interaction, including text-based conferencing, synchronized browser screens, phone callback, and voice and video con-

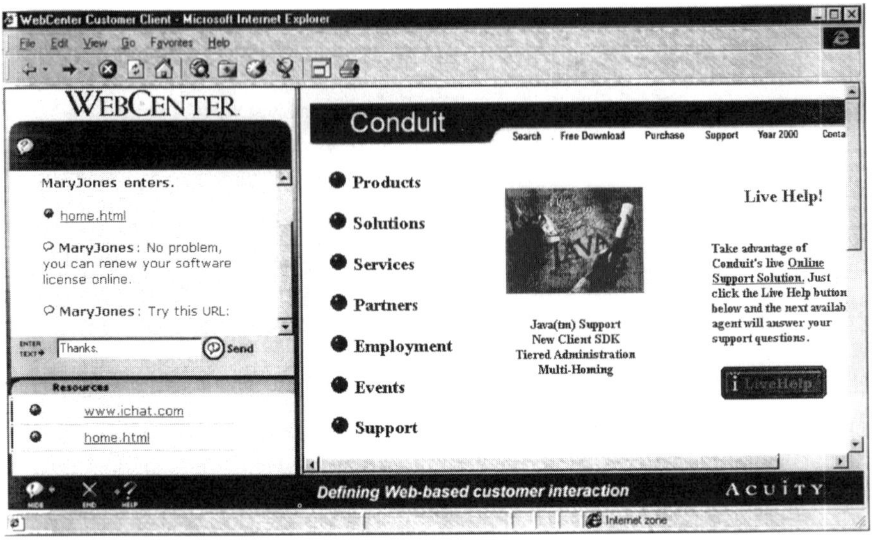

Exhibit 8. Text-based customer interaction.

---

ferencing (see the e-commerce section above for descriptions of each). Exhibits 8 and 9 below demonstrate a text-based interaction session from both a customer and agent perspective.

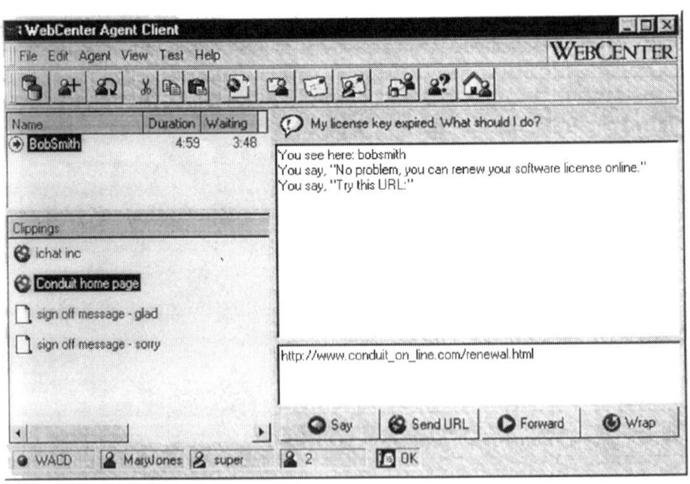

Exhibit 9. Text-based agent interaction.

Following the live help session, customer and session data can be automatically stored in a third-party customer management system, posted in the organization's knowledge base for future self-service sessions, and when requested, e-mailed directly to the customer. With the live help option, customers can be guaranteed a response in real time, without having to log off from a company's Web site to pick up the telephone.

Customer Support Requirements

As with major e-commerce undertakings, each of the applications described above requires a variety of hardware and software, depending on the scope of the project and the integration into telephony support processes. In most cases, it is recommended to work with the software vendor and a leading customer support and/or call center system integrator such as Cambridge Technology or TSC to develop the optimum solution for your efforts.

Case Study: Charles Schwab & Co.

Schwab's help desk group, responsible for supporting 700 distributed financial executives, uses Web-based, interactive technology for self-service and live help. At Schwab, employees are given the option to search and browse various online FAQs and knowledge bases to discover new investment vehicles, analyst recommendations, and HR information. They also have the ability to receive technical support online in a self-service mode. If the employee wishes to click into a live help session, Schwab's interactive, net-based system enables text conferencing and browser screen synchronization. "Web-based customer interaction is the foundation of Schwab's leadership position," says Rick Washburn, VP Customer Technology, Charles Schwab & Co. "Our vision for delivering an outstanding client experience through efficient self-service, online delivery and personalized, real-time, interactive support, has created an excellent environment for efficient, effective service."

CONCLUSIONS

As described in the opening section, Web-based interactive software enables financial services organizations to effectively build communities, hold online events, assist their customers during the purchase decision process, and provide appropriate levels of support ranging from self-service through to live assistance.

With Forrester's claims that Web-based customer interaction software can lead to a 43% decrease in labor cost per customer contact, and vendor claims that live help on a Web site can increase sales margins by 15 to 25% through up-selling, cross-selling, and efficient content distribution, the return on investment (ROI) for interactive initiatives can be substantial. Pristine Capital Management, as described above, experienced an ROI of several hundred percent during 1997. Forrester envisions that a $650 million company will save approximately $1 million through the deployment of interactive customer support software.

With these types of figures and a new array of outstanding products from a multitude of vendors, now is the time to turn your static Web site into a major interactive marketing, sales, and support system.

Chapter 28

Internet Security Analysis Report: An Executive Overview

Mary Rose

THE RAPID GROWTH OF THE INTERNET has prompted companies in all industries to look closely at the significance of the Internet and question if a presence should be developed, and if one is developed, what it should be. One of the key issues surrounding an open system like the Internet is security: security of data, e-mail, and financial transactions. Some business managers troubled by recently publicized security breaches have decided to take a wait-and-see approach.

While this reaction is understandable, the major drawback is the loss of a window of opportunity, a key competitive edge. Although the Internet may seem intimidating, it can be a marketing advantage in that it offers equal footing on which to compete. Smaller community financial institutions can effectively compete with the larger national players via the Internet the world over. Security is a valid concern, but many of the risks are viewed as greatly overrated by some industry analysts. In addition, there are software programs and hardware systems to reduce the risk.

However, in spite of this concern, the financial services industry is experiencing rapid growth on the Internet. Nontraditional competitors are continuing to take market share. Financial institutions who do not offer PC-based online services are consistently reporting losing customers. It is imperative that financial institutions become quickly educated with the Internet possibilities. Those who do and develop a viable presence will remain competitive and be seen as players who intend to stay around. Financial institutions have historically maintained carefully controlled and audited systems. The idea of an open system is in direct conflict with fiduciary relationships. However, the possible enormous gain can far outweigh the risks. It is our opinion that if certain precautions are taken, the risks can be minimal.

0-8493-9991-2/99/$0.00+$.50

Most financial institutions have found that internal theft by employees constitutes the majority of losses. Thus, secure systems must have internal and external controls. Education is the key to understanding and controlling potential exposure.

INTERNET VS. INTRANET

An increasing number of corporations and financial institutions are installing Web servers on internal corporate networks (intranets) for private purposes such as human resources information and internal databases. In this case, the server is not attached to the Internet. As the applications are increasing in diversity, access by nonemployees such as bank clients are continually being added.

Web servers on the Internet are considered to be much more vulnerable because of the worldwide access to them. Thus, software that provides security or as it is commonly referred to, fire wall software, should be considered essential when placing a Web server on the Internet (see Exhibit 1).

Internet/Intranet Choice

Financial institutions have the choice of installing banking software products on the Internet, an open system, or on a proprietary, closed, intranet system. If an institution chooses not to offer Internet access to client accounts, the system can be installed as an intranet where clients dial a private phone number to connect to the Web server, as shown in Exhibit 2. This option allows a financial institution to provide remote client account access with the option of migrating to Internet access at any point in the future.

SECURITY DESIGN

Basic security measures should be used for intranet installations. For Internet installations, fire wall software and a router are used for additional security.

Basic Security Measures

Security should consist of multiple layers of protection. Basic security design is broken into five categories described below.

For Client Security. Financial institution customers are required to have secure browsing software such as Netscape or Microsoft Internet Explorer. Attempts to connect with a nonsecure browser will be rejected. These clients are provided with an Identification Code and a Password that are required to successfully connect to the system. Financial institutions must carefully instruct their customers on the importance of protecting their sign-on security information. Both identification code and password will be

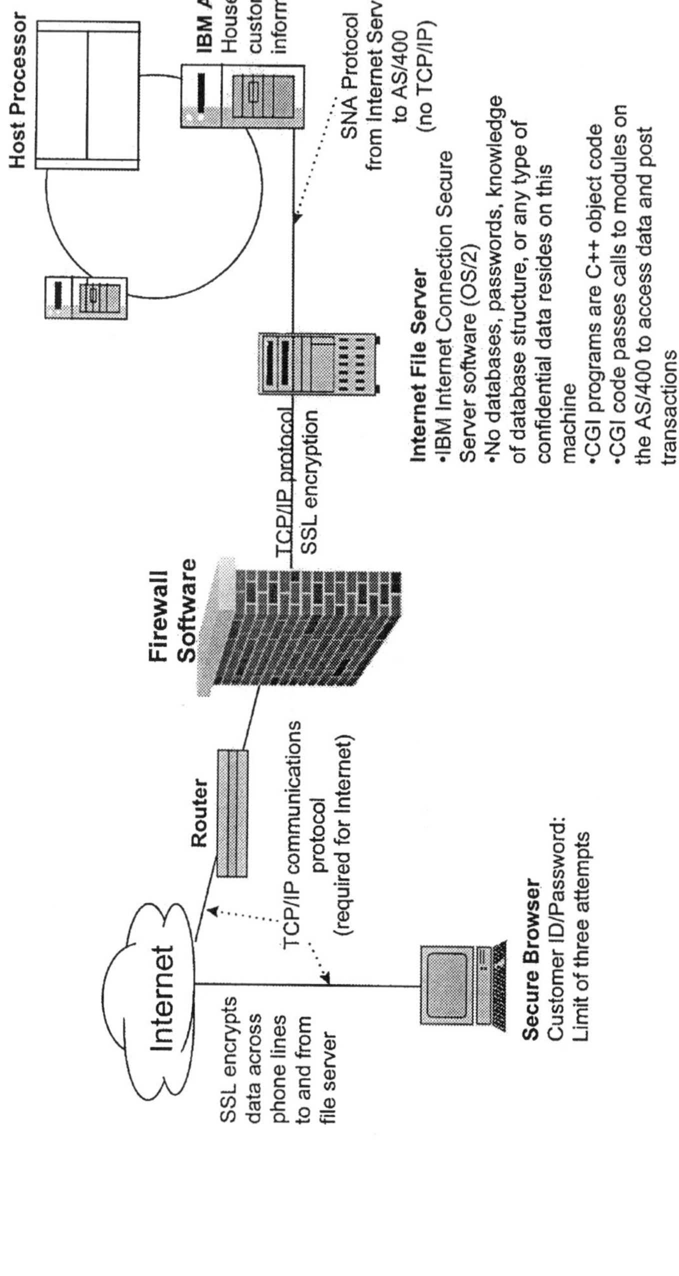

Exhibit 1. Fire wall software.

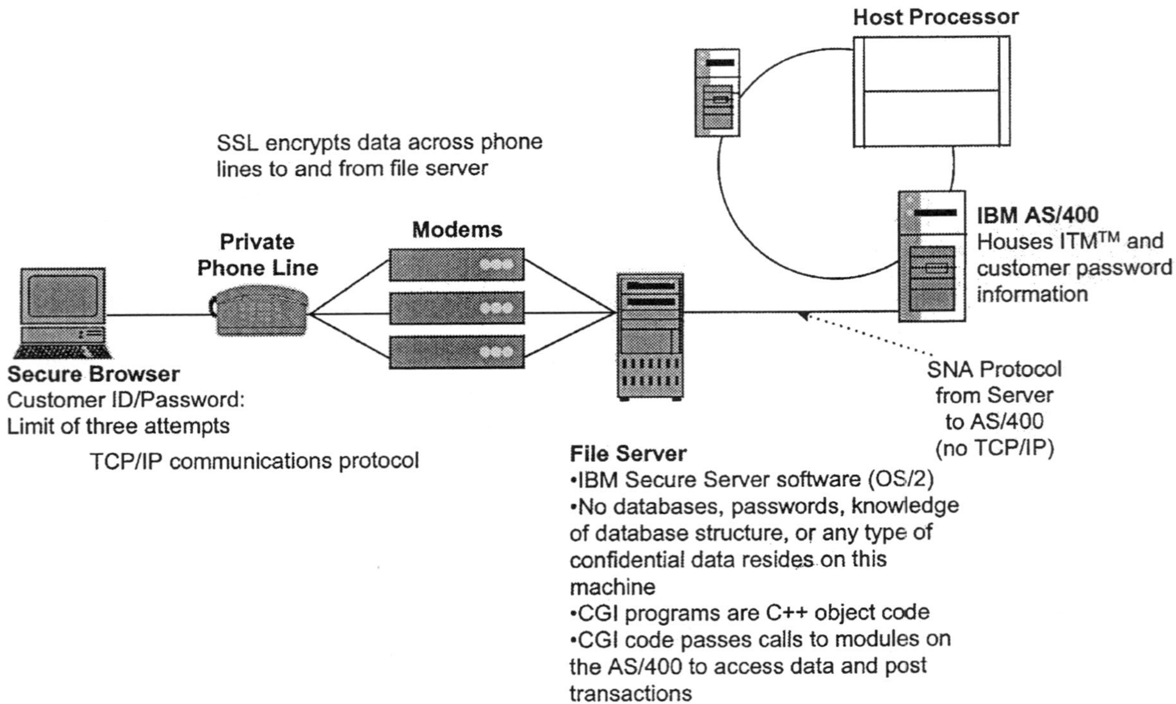

Exhibit 2. The system can be installed as an intranet; clients dial a private phone number to connect with the Web server.

designed to be difficult to access randomly, and will contain a combination of letters and numbers.

There is protection against repeated unsuccessful attempts to sign in to the system. Three unsuccessful attempts will lock the customer out of the system, requiring contact with the financial institution to reestablish service. This is for the obvious protection of both parties. Audit reports of these incidents are printed for review. When a customer has successfully signed on, the request received by the server is checked to ensure the customer has signed into the system, thus making it difficult for an intruder to masquerade as a customer by attempting to bypass the security screens.

For Phone Line Security. All transactions that are passed across phone lines are encrypted using SSL (secure sockets layer). Therefore, customers must use a secure browser to successfully connect to the system. Encryption prevents eavesdropping on phone lines to obtain information.

For Web Server Security. Banks will be required to place the server in a secure physical location that prevents unauthorized access to it. A password will be required to access the server console. All unnecessary TCP/IP services are disabled on the Web server, such as login and Telnet. [Financial institutions should disable the capability to FTP (upload files) to the server.] Virus detection software will be installed on the server to minimize the risk of infection and its potential damaging consequences. Audit files are backed up daily.

The Web server houses absolutely no identification/password information or customer account data. There is no information on the server that can provide any degree of insight into the customer information which resides on the AS/400 or other host processor.

For Host Data Security. Databases on the host processor are accessed only by call modules requiring specific parameters and called by a program on the Web server. The module performs additional integrity checks such as ensuring all account numbers involved in the request belong to the client.

In many cases, all transactions are memo posted to host databases so that clients have up-to-date account information. Transactions can be posted online if the financial institution prefers. The host should have additional checks that can limit the number of fund transfers and limit the total amount of funds transferred in a 24-hour period. Evening processing could provide audit and balancing reports prior to posting the transactions to the host databases (memo posting only). Any suspect transactions would then be held and examined prior to posting.

For Internal Network Security. TCP/IP protocol is the favorite and most powerful tool used by intruders to break into a network. TCP/IP must be used between the client and the Web server. Financial institutions should not use TCP/IP between the Web server and the AS/400. SNA should be used instead. The typical intruder who may manage a connection to the Web server will have a tremendous challenge in reaching the AS/400.

Beyond the AS/400, there are additional internal security measures a financial institution has the option of implementing. As previously stated, internal theft/fraud by employees constitutes a major percentage of losses by financial institutions. There are software applications that encrypt all data traveling across internal networks. Access by each individual workstation and/or employee can be carefully defined. Thus, internal theft/fraud can be greatly reduced, if not eliminated.

FIRE WALL SOFTWARE FOR INTERNET IMPLEMENTATIONS

Because definitions of a fire wall vary, the concept is initially confusing. The term fire wall is sometimes used in reference to fire wall software, but such software is only one piece of an overall fire wall system. *For the purposes of this chapter a "fire wall" is defined as all techniques utilized to prevent unauthorized traffic from moving through a Web server.* The objective is to present multiple and difficult obstacles for confronting potential intruders. It is important to note that fire wall software cannot protect a site from all forms of intrusion, specifically:

- Viruses which can't be detected by fire wall software. Virus software is available.
- Internal attacks that are on the other side of the fire wall and inside the financial institution.
- Back doors into the network such as dial-in connections that do not pass through the fire wall.

For financial institutions or enterprises who choose to implement products on the Internet, using highly rated fire wall software is imperative. When a Web server is attached to the Internet without security, literally anyone in the world can access it. It is important to offer customers the choice of a Unix or Windows NT fire wall platform for several reasons:

- Many financial institutions do not have in-house Unix expertise. Windows NT is a common and popular operating system.
- Unix-based fire wall packages cost more and require more expensive hardware.
- Some financial institutions have Unix expertise and prefer to use it despite the cost and skill required.

SUMMARY

An Internet presence must not be ignored by the financial services industry. While the Internet is an intimidating concept, it offers the opportunity to compete with other financial services providers on equal footing. Benefits of acting now outweigh the concerns of security risks.

Many industry analysts believe that Internet security concerns are greatly overrated. While security issues must be taken seriously and safety measures must be investigated and implemented, financial institutions should not postpone Internet development plans due to these fears. Secure account access can be provided for customers.

Security should be designed in layers to present multiple, difficult obstacles for a possible intruder. Categories of security include customer security, encryption of data over phone lines, Web server security measures, host data protection, and internal network techniques.

Financial institutions who do not offer customers the ability to offer PC-based online account access in an intranet or Internet environment (or both) are losing customers to those institutions who do.

Chapter 29 Multicast Applications and Technology for the Financial Services Industry

C. Kenneth Miller

MULTICAST NETWORKING TECHNOLOGY and applications can greatly benefit the financial services industry. Unlike other vertical markets for multicast technology and applications, there are clear compelling reasons in the financial services sector for all of the multicast categories of applications.

There is a wide variety of multicast applications as shown in Exhibit 1. Many associate real-time multimedia synonymously with multicast; in reality, there is a whole spectrum of multicast applications as Exhibit 1 displays. With the exception of the top left quadrant, real-time multimedia, virtually all of the applications above require reliability, i.e., data must be complete at the receiver to be useful. This is in contrast to real-time multimedia delivery, where the loss of some data is acceptable.

With multimedia delivery, timeliness is the important parameter; the multimedia flow must come with minimal timing variation, which is called *jitter*. Some loss of data is acceptable as long as the flow of data is constant. The killer one-to-many multimedia applications for businesses are remote training and multimedia events which would most often use a corporate intranet rather than the public Internet as the underlying network infrastructure. Video conferencing is an important many-to-many multimedia application.

0-8493-9991-2/99/$0.00+$.50

	Real-time	Nonreal-time
Multimedia	• Video server • Video conferencing • Internet audio • Multimedia events	• Replication: – Video & web servers – Kiosks • Content delivery – Intranet & Internet
Data-only	• Stock quotes • News feeds • White boarding • Interactive gaming	• Data delivery – Server-server – Server-desktop • DB replication • SW distribution

Exhibit 1. Multicast applications.

With the rush of technology overwhelming us, training becomes more and more important, and it is not always convenient to be trained in the same location. Similarly, multimedia events are looked at as being an important new tool to facilitate communications between management and employees in large organizations.

The financial industry has been one of the early adopters to embrace the use of multimedia to view events over networks in real time; they wish to know of business news such as mergers and acquisitions as well as other fast-breaking business news as soon as it happens, while observing the body language of the presenter as well as the words associated with the event. For them, there could be much money to be made by correctly judging the real message of the event. To be able to do this, you need high quality video and audio, which means bandwidths of at least 1.5 Mbps. Starlight Networks, an early multimedia solution provider, is targeting the financial industry to provide high quality multicast multimedia streaming solutions.

The set of reliable multicast applications has widely varying requirements. The two non-real-time quadrants contain applications where timeliness is not very important. Additionally, these applications are typically one to many rather than many to many. Data-only real-time applications (the bottom left quadrant) have two basic types of application; collaboration, such as network gaming and data conferencing which are many to many, and data streams, such as ticker tape and news feeds which are one to many.

The data-only real-time applications have a sense of timeliness, i.e., the amount of latency allowed is relatively small. For example, a collaborative game or data conference cannot afford to have a latency that exceeds the tolerance of the human being playing the game or participating in the conference. Ticker tape feeds also have data that need to be delivered within a small time window as the data are quite volatile.

These applications also have different scaling requirements. Collaborative applications have modest scaling requirements, usually involving 100 or less in the group. In contrast, one to many applications can have very large scaling requirements of thousands, or even possibly millions of simultaneous recipients.

The data-only real-time application that is most interesting to the financial industry is ticker tape streams. There are different requirements for the ticker tape stream depending on the consumer of the information. If it is a casual user, the stream does not need to be absolutely reliable, as the stream is continually refreshed by updated trades. However, if the consumer of the stream is an actual trader, the requirements are very stringent; reliability, timeliness, and concurrency are all needed.

The simultaneous requirements of reliability, timeliness, and concurrency cannot be satisfied without resorting to an over-designed network which is guaranteed to not be congested and has redundancy built in. This is in fact how this is accomplished today. Most of these "feeds" have not been designed using reliable multicast, but reliable multicast and multicast IP networks could be used to advantage in this application.

There are a number of non-real-time multicast applications that are of interest to the financial industry. The financial industry is characterized by many remote offices to whom information needs to be disseminated rapidly. It is also desirable to have the information disseminated to these offices relatively concurrently, so that all offices are synchronized, i.e., are dealing with the same up-to-date information.

The same thing can be said for the software running on the computer resources at the remote offices. Not only is it desirable to have all computer systems in synchronization with the latest software, but also it is cost effective to have centralized management of computer resources in many cases. Both of these can be accomplished by the ability to reliably multicast software and business information to these remote offices.

Download of multimedia files for replay off a local server may also be desirable in some instances. In this case, the multimedia content is sent as a file via reliable multicast to a local server for replay later.

TECHNOLOGY

The TCP/IP protocol suite is shown in Exhibit 2. TCP/IP provides two choices for the transport layer (layer 4), TCP and UDP. The transport layer is responsible for end-to-end delivery of data from one host to another.

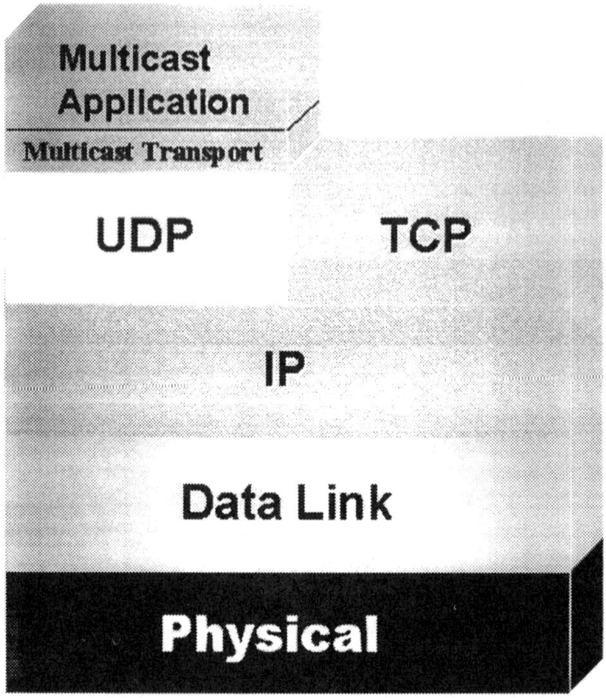

Exhibit 2. TCP/IP protocol suite.

Most applications, e.g., File Transfer Protocol (FTP) and HyperText Transport Protocol (HTTP), operate over TCP because of the rich services provided: error correction, packet ordering, congestion control, and port multiplexing. UDP, in contrast, provides minimal services; only error detection and port multiplexing. If a UDP packet is detected in error, it is simply discarded.

However, TCP operates only in a point-to-point (unicast) manner from one host to another host. Thus, most multicast applications operate over UDP as shown in Exhibit 2 and provide their own specialized transport in the application. Additionally, multimedia applications cannot use TCP in any situation, as TCP is designed for data and is not capable of delivering the constant flow required.

Multimedia applications have settled on the Real Time Protocol (RTP) and it's companion Real Time Control Protocol (RTCP) to be the transport of choice for multimedia transport. RTP is a simple protocol framework, and there are a number of companion specifications for carrying different payloads, e.g., MPEG (Motion Picture Experts Group) for high-quality video, H.261 and H.263 for video conferencing quality, and a variety of audio formats. Given that the financial industry wants high quality for media events, the MPEG payloads are most important.

Unlike the case where multimedia streaming has standardized on RTP/RTCP as a specialized transport, no such protocol or protocols have been standardized for reliable multicast. The subject is now being studied in the Internet Research Task Force (IRTF). The decision to have the subject of reliable multicast be studied in the IRTF rather than the Internet Engineering Task Force (IETF), the body that works on Internet standards, was that the technical issues are complex and basic techniques should be recommended before standardization.

Nevertheless, there are a number of commercially available reliable multicast products available — tool kits from Globalcast supporting Scalable Reliable Multicast (SRM), Reliable Multicast Transport Protocol (RMTP), and Reliable Multicast Protocol (RMP), and application products and tool kits from StarBurst Communications which support the Multicast File Transfer Protocol (MFTP). MFTP also includes a mechanism for setting up groups, as well as providing a reliable transport protocol.

Additionally, Cisco announced at the IP Multicast Summit in February, 1998 support for Pretty Good Multicast (PGM). PGM is a reliable multicast protocol that supports all multicast applications and thus can act as a multicast equivalent of TCP. PGM gains scaling by assistance of network elements, i.e., routers in the network infrastructure. PGM was first publicly documented in an Internet Draft in January, 1998 and products incorporating PGM along with Cisco routers with PGM code for scaling will likely be available in 1999. PGM looks to be a significant offering in land-line networks with Cisco routers in the infrastructure. However, alternative network infrastructures such as satellite will not benefit from this scaling.

Additionally, TIBCO is a company that provides messaging middleware software, called TIB/Rendezvous, targeted to the brokerage sector of financial services. This software includes a proprietary reliable multicast protocol that is not publicly described. However, this proprietary protocol is not that scalable, and has therefore primarily been implemented over LANs. TIBCO is heavily embracing PGM to be its underlying reliable multicast protocol for the future that scales to the wide area network.

Two concepts have been heavily promoted by TIBCO, *publish/subscribe* and *subject-based addressing*. Both are relevant to brokerage applications. Publish/subscribe is really synonymous with send and receive. Subject-based addressing provides a mechanism to identify content in a message stream based on subject. This can, for example, be used to pick out particular types of stocks in a ticker tape feed and even redirect a piece of a ticker feed to consumers desiring it, based on subject.

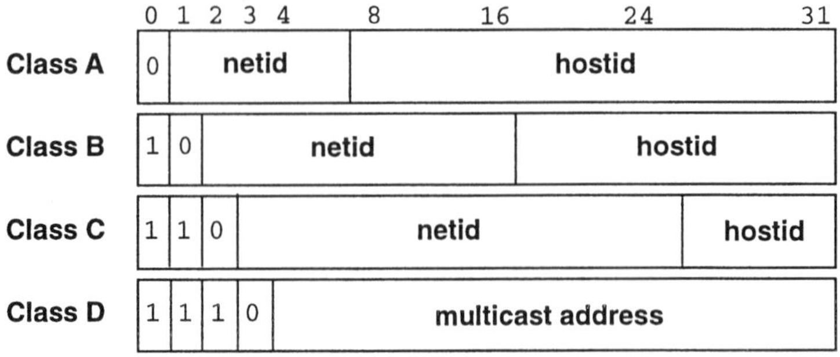

Exhibit 3. IP address types.

IP MULTICAST NETWORKING

Multicast IP uses different IP addresses than are used for point-to-point communications, as shown in Exhibit 3. Class A, B, and C IP addresses used for point-to-point communications have a host and network component; in contrast, Class D IP addresses used for multicast transmission to a group simply have one address space indicating the multicast group.

Class D addresses also differ in that often the address is only used on a session by session basis, as opposed to the semipermanent nature of Class A, B, and C addresses.

The multicast address space occupies the range from 224.0.0.0 to 239.255.255.255. The Internet Assigned Numbers Authority (IANA) maintains lists of registered users and assigns new numbers for new uses. The range from 224.0.0.0 to 224.0.0.255 is reserved for permanent assignment for various uses, including for use by routing protocols.

Joining particular multicast groups is receiver initiated using the Internet Group Management Protocol (IGMP). IGMPv1 (the version most implemented) is specified in RFC 1112,[1] and defines a dialog that occurs between routers supporting multicast routing and hosts on a subnet attached to that router. IGMP has since been upgraded twice, and IGMPv2 is specified in RFC 2236.[2] IGMPv2 has, as its primary enhancement, facility to reduce group leave latency. IGMPv2 is now starting to be implemented in new versions of operating systems and in routers, but remains backward compatible with IGMPv1. IGMPv3 is still a work in progress.

IGMP

IGMPv1 is defined in RFC 1112. This defines the protocol and the dialog that occurs between a host in a multicast group and the nearest router supporting multicast, as shown in Exhibit 4. Multicast routers that are

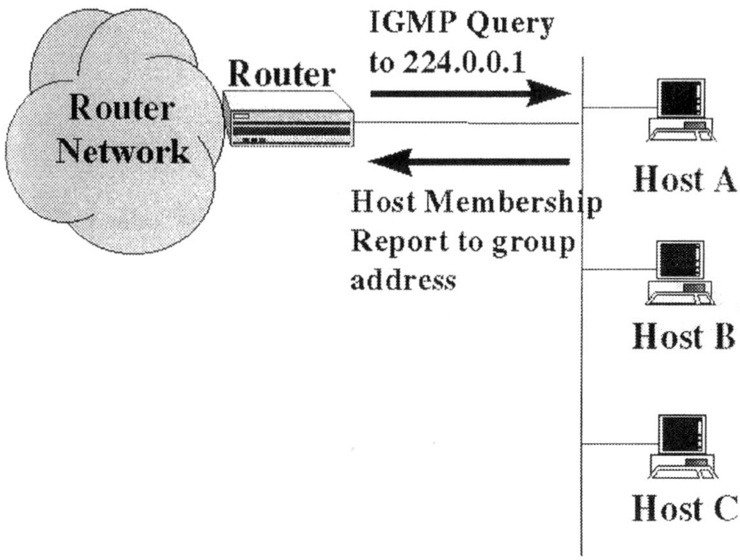

Exhibit 4. IGMP dialog.

chosen to be the *designated router* (DR) for a subnetwork periodically transmit Host Membership Query messages to determine which host groups have members on their directly attached subnetwork. Host Membership Query messages are sent to the "all hosts group" (224.0.0.1) and have an IP time-to-live (TTL) of one. This means these messages are confined to the directly attached subnetwork and are not forwarded by any other multicast routers.

When a host receives an IGMP Query message, it responds with a Host Membership Report for each group to which it belongs. These messages are sent to the group address to which it belongs. Thus, if a host belongs to multiple groups simultaneously, it must send multiple Host Membership Reports to each group. Host Membership Reports likewise have an IP TTL = 1 and are thus confined to the local subnetwork.

Host Membership Reports suppress redundant messages by means of random backoff timers. Each host generates a random backoff time, after which it sends the Host Membership Report(s). If, during the timeout period, a host hears a Host Membership Report identical with one it was about to send, it suppresses its response. Multicast routers do not need to know the exact host in the group in that subnetwork; it only needs to know that there is at least one host in that group on that subnetwork. This feature serves to reduce the traffic required to be sent on that subnetwork.

Even though the nearest multicast router is not in the host group being reported, all multicast addresses must be received promiscuously by all of their interfaces. The sending of the Host Membership Report on its group address also is a convenient mechanism to allow other hosts in that group on that subnetwork to listen and suppress identical Host Membership Reports from other hosts on that subnetwork.

Multicast routers periodically transmit IGMP Queries to the subgroups to which they are attached. Hosts do not send Host Membership Reports except when queried by a router with one exception; when a host first joins a group. At this time, a host sends a Host Membership Report without waiting for an IGMP Query. Thus, joins to a group are immediately reported to the nearest DR multicast router, whereas leaves from a group are only determined by a timeout, i.e., no response to an IGMP Query. Polling intervals for IGMP Queries and timeout to declare a leave are both configurable parameters.

The total latency in setting up a group is dependent on the sum of the time to notify the nearest router of the join, plus the time to set up the multicast routing by the routers in the network. Typically, this is seconds. The latency to leave a group is longer, as the timeout needs to expire based on no response from an IGMP Query to declare a leave. Then that leaf of the multicast tree needs to be torn down by the routers. This total time may approach a minute for typical configurations. IGMPv2, as its primary enhancement, adds explicit leave messages so as to reduce the leave latency and make it closer to the join latency.

MULTICAST ROUTING PROTOCOLS

Multicast routing protocols are used by routers in a network or internetwork to optimally route multicast packets through the network or internetwork from the source to the multiple destinations that consist of the members of the multicast group. This is analogous to the unicast (point-to-point) routing protocols that are the backbone of operation in all TCP/IP networks including the Internet.

Unicast routing protocols use two basic techniques: *distance vector* or *link state*. Earlier routing protocols were distance vector, such as Routing Information Protocol (RIP) and IGRP (Cisco proprietary). Open Shortest Path First (OSPF) became the dominant link state routing protocol. Link state routing protocols converge quicker, important considerations for networks that may change dynamically.

Some multicast routing protocols are derived from distance vector or link state unicast routing protocols. However, a new category of *shared tree* protocols has also been introduced for multicast. Thus, multicast routing protocols come in three basic flavors; distance vector, link state, and

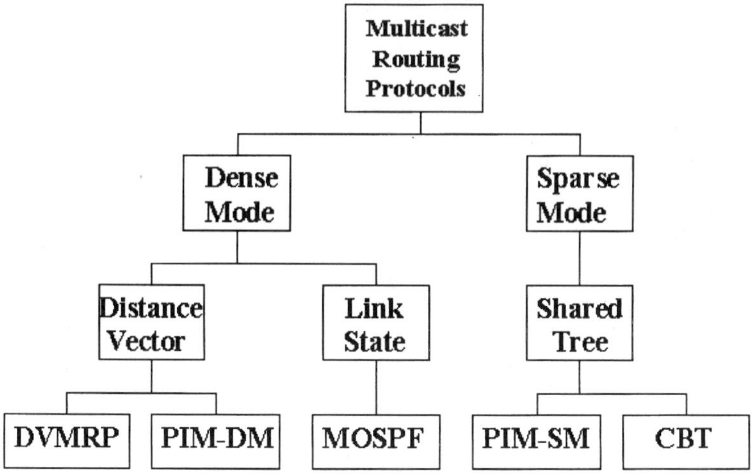

Exhibit 5. Multicast routing protocol family tree.

shared trees. Distance Vector Multicast Routing Protocol (DVMRP)[3] and Protocol Independent Multicast — Dense Mode (PIM-DM)[4] are distance vector based, Multicast Open Shortest Path First (MOSPF)[5] is link state based, and Protocol Independent Multicast — Sparse Mode (PIM-SM)[6] and Core Based Trees (CBT)[7] are shared tree based.

DVMRP, PIM-DM, and MOSPF have been called *dense mode* multicast routing protocols, as they require some form of flooding of datagrams to the network to find multicast routes and this is most suitable for areas with dense concentrations of group members, such as campus networks. In contrast, the shared tree protocols, PIM-SM and CBT have been called *sparse mode* multicast routing protocols, as they are best suited for widely dispersed group members in a wide area network. The family tree of multicast routing protocols is shown in Exhibit 5.

All multicast routing protocols need to set up *distribution trees* to route datagrams to the members of the group in an optimal way. The challenge is to create multicast routing protocols that can set up these distribution trees quickly, efficiently, and without excessive network traffic. The different multicast routing protocols each have their strengths and weaknesses, as discussed further below.

The *dense* mode protocols, DVMRP and PIM-DM, are relatively simple in concept and create optimal source-rooted trees for distribution of data from the source. DVMRP and PIM-DM are both independent of the unicast routing protocols used in the network; DVMRP includes its own unicast routing protocol and PIM-DM uses the routing tables from whichever uni-

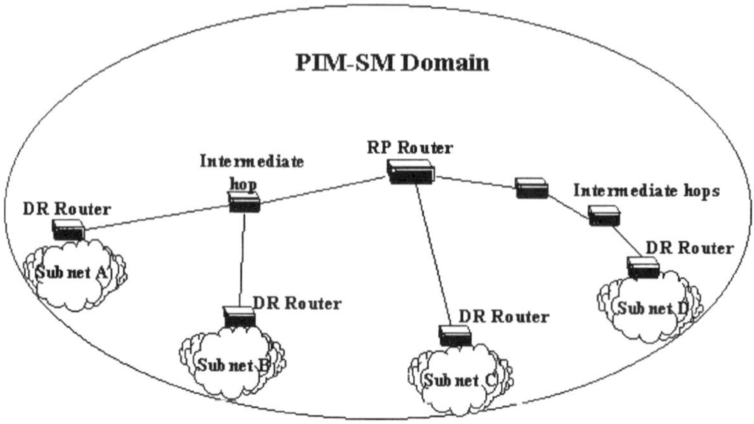

Exhibit 6. PIM-SM showing RP.

cast routing protocol is being used. These unicast routing protocols help the multicast routing protocol figure out the optimal routes.

MOSPF is also a dense mode routing protocol, but it is an extension of the popular OSPF unicast routing protocol and as such is dependent on it being the underlying unicast routing infrastructure. MOSPF, like DVMRP and PIM-DM, calculates optimal multicast distribution trees rooted at the source.

All of the dense mode routing protocols depend on periodic flooding of packets to determine routes. As such, they are viewed as being most appropriate for networks where the group members are densely packed in the network, such as in a campus network.

The *sparse* mode protocols, PIM-SM and CBT, create shared trees based on selection of a *rendezvous point* (RP) in PIM-SM or a *core* in CBT. This is illustrated in Exhibit 6 for PIM-SM.

The *designated router* (DR) for each subnet determines which rendezvous point (RP) or core should be selected for a particular multicast address and joins to that RP or core. All traffic to the group then passes through the RP or core. No flooding to determine routes is performed and the same shared tree is used, independent of the source of traffic. Additionally, much less state is required of the routers to keep track of multicast routes. The only negative is that the tree is not optimal from the point of view of number of hops. The RP or core can be located far from the bulk of the members of the group. PIM-SM has the optional facility to switch to a source-routed tree based on some criterion, such as overload of the RP, to help gain the best of both worlds.

All of the major router vendors support one or more of these multicast routing protocols in their most recent software releases. DVMRP is the earliest multicast routing protocol, and is also supported in a program called *mrouted* which is available in many Unix host platforms.

All of the above multicast routing protocols are *interior gateway* protocols, i.e., they are used within one *autonomous system* which is a routing domain under one administrative authority. A major hole is the lack of a standardized *exterior gateway* multicast routing protocol, which would be used for multicast routing between autonomous systems in similar fashion as the Border Gateway Protocol (BGP) is used to route between autonomous systems with unicast routing.

The InterDomain Multicast Routing (IDMR) working group of the Internet Engineering Task Force (IETF) is working on this problem and presented the first proposal for an interdomain multicast routing protocol, to be called Border Gateway Multicast Protocol (BGMP),[8] at the December, 1997 IETF meeting. Thus, this problem is on the way to be solved, but is still work in progress.

All of these multicast routing protocols were developed assuming a mesh-like land-line network infrastructure, such as is present in today's Internet. However, a second alternative networking infrastructure is being proposed by many as a risk averse way to gain high-speed multicast services. This approach is a hybrid satellite/land-line network as shown in Exhibit 7. The satellite is inherently a broadcast medium, and multicast is therefore a subset. The satellite is also a one-hop network that can be delivered anywhere without having to string cable.

This approach is also very cost effective if the number of remotes is large, as the recurring charges are typically independent of the number of remotes. For example, one satellite carrier has tariffs for satellite coverage in the U.S. shown in Exhibit 8.

Additionally, remote equipment needed is on the order of $1000 per remote receive site. Since the tariffs are fixed, this provides a very cost-effective solution if the number of remotes becomes large.

However, a low-speed land-line connection to the sender is needed to insure reliability. This can be very inexpensive; zero if there is already an Internet connection in place and on the order of about $70 per month for zero CIR frame relay service. Additionally, a dial modem connection or ISDN connection could be used whose tariff would consist of a monthly charge plus a usage charge.

There is an issue with this scenario, however. Static routing is needed as standard routing protocols do not automatically work with this network in-

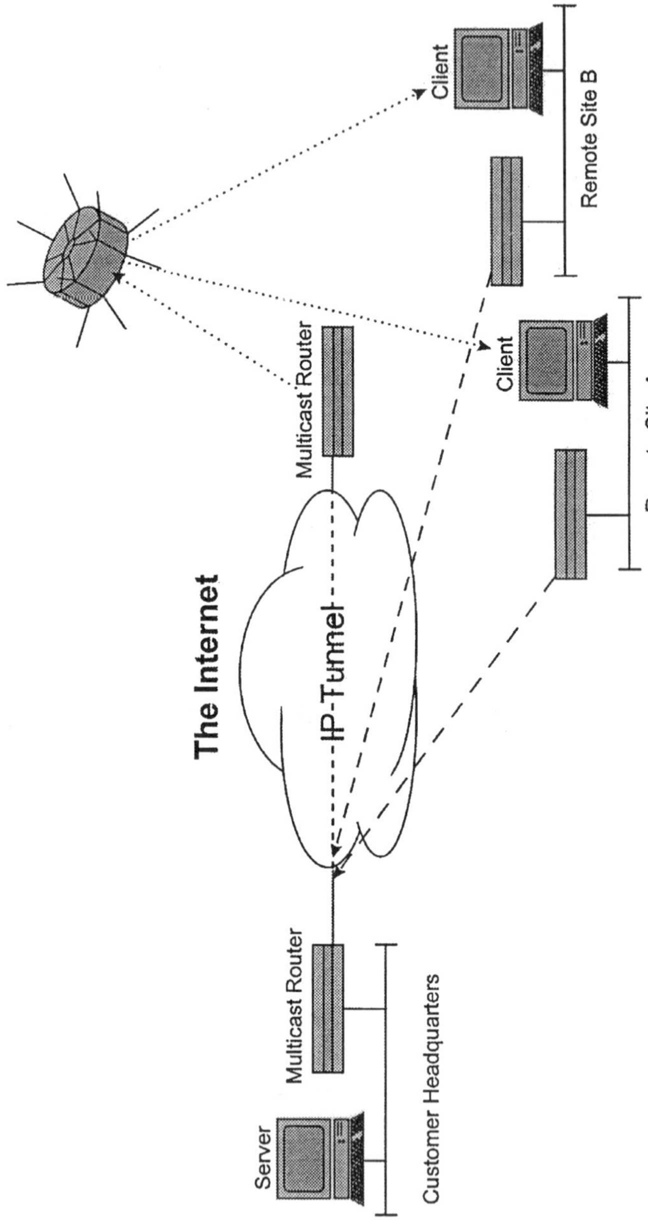

Exhibit 7. Hybrid satellite/land-line network infrastructure.

Exhibit 8. One-Way Satellite Tariffs

Date Rate	Price/Month	Price/Receiver (100)	Price/Receiver (1000)
38.4 Kbps	$8746	$87.46	$8.75
56 Kbps	$9546	$95.46	$9.55
64 Kbps	$9746	$97.46	$9.75
128 Kbps	$10,746	$107.46	$10.75
256 Kbps	$13,746	$137.46	$13.75
512 Kbps	$16.746	$167.46	$16.75
1.0 Mbps	$22,246	$222.46	$22.25
1.5 Mbps	$33,846	$338.46	$33.85
2 Mbps	$42,846	$428.46	$42.85

Source: Microspace Communications Corporation, Raleigh, NC.

frastructure. The UniDirectional Link Routing (UDLR) working group in the Internet Engineering Task Force (IETF) is working to correct this deficiency.

The digital satellite broadcast industry is also viewing the ability to provide high-speed one-way multicast data services as a new opportunity, and tariffs could be even lower in future.

MULTICAST APPLICATIONS TARGETED TO THE FINANCIAL INDUSTRY

As mentioned earlier, the financial services industry has a need for all classes of multicast applications as shown in Exhibit 1.

Multimedia Applications and Associated Protocols

In the real-time multimedia class (upper left quadrant of Exhibit 1), multimedia events are of particular interest. The Real Time Protocol (RTP) documented in RFC 1889[9] is the protocol that has been created to transport multimedia streams over IP networks. It's companion, the Real Time Control Protocol (RTCP), is used to monitor and control RTP sessions. RTP is on standards track in the IETF.

RTP operates over UDP, as shown in Exhibit 9. The multimedia stream file format (e.g., QuickTime or Microsoft's ASF) and the Codec, e.g., MPEG, and the actual application operates over RTP.

RTP is a protocol framework that is deliberately not complete; companion "profiles" need to be specified to completely document how a specific application will be handled within RTP. The MPEG1/MPEG2 profile was first documented in RFC 2038 and was recently updated in RFC 2250[10] and is the one that would be most important to the financial industry in being able to deliver high-quality video and audio for events. MPEG streams typically need to flow at data rates of 1.5 Mbps or higher.

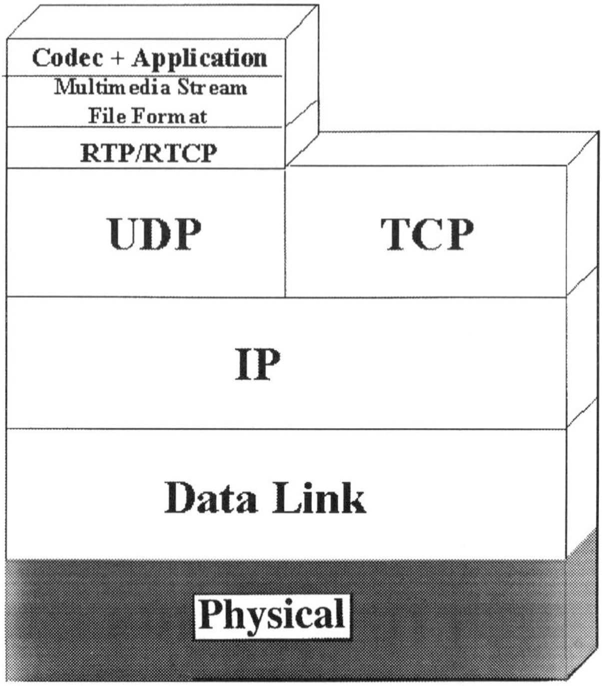

Exhibit 9. RTP in TCP/IP protocol suite.

Multimedia streams (also called “flows”) need to recover their time relationship at the receiver, i.e., jitter needs to be removed to be coherently received. This is accomplished by buffering real-time data at the receiver for a sufficient time to remove the jitter added by the network and recover the original timing relationships between the media data. In order to know how long to buffer to achieve synchronization, each packet must carry a time stamp which gives the time at the sender when the data was captured.

Each RTP flow is supplemented by Real-Time Control Protocol (RTCP) packets. There are a number of different RTCP packet types. RTCP packets provide the relationship between the real-time clock at a sender and the RTP media time stamps, and provide textual information to identify a sender in a conference from the source ID. RTCP session messages are restricted in rate, so that as a group grows in membership, the rate of session messages remains constant, and each receiver reports less often. A member of the group can never know exactly who is present at a particular time from RTCP reports, but does have a good approximation of group membership.

QUALITY OF SERVICE (QOS) AND THE RESOURCE RESERVATION PROTOCOL (RSVP)

Multimedia streaming applications require a minimum bandwidth for the stream or "flow." The Resource ReSerVation Protocol (RSVP) was created to allow a flow to reserve bandwidth, hop by hop, from the receiver back to the source, i.e., provide a quality of service (QoS) for the flow. Note that receiver initiation is the same methodology as that of joining a multicast group, which is also receiver initiated. RSVP is documented in RFC 2205[11] and is now on standards track within IETF.

Multimedia flows must be delivered on a certain schedule (rate) or the data become useless. If delivered too late, multimedia traffic is worse than useless, as it impedes delivery of later multimedia data. QoS techniques have been proposed to reserve bandwidth for multimedia flows, as the best effort characteristic of TCP/IP networks otherwise makes multimedia viewing quality poor, especially when the flow is at a high speed as would be expected with MPEG flows.

RSVP is the first documented specification to address QoS needs for real-time multimedia traffic, where the host application requests the QoS from the network. A number of router vendors, including Cisco Systems, are supporting RSVP in their router products.

Reservation requests are originated at receiving hosts and passed upstream to the sender(s). Reservation requests are unidirectional, i.e., from sender to receivers. At each hop upstream to the sender, reservation requests are made. The RSVP process passes the request to *admission* control and *policy* control, both of which are local decision modules. Admission control determines if the node has sufficient resources to supply the requested QoS. Policy control determines if the requester has the administrative permission to make the reservation. If either test fails, the reservation is rejected and suitable error messages are sent to the receiver(s). If both succeed, the node is set to select the data packets defined by the reservation request and interacts with the appropriate link layer to obtain the desired QoS. As flows hit a replication point at a network node, they are merged together as one flow to proceed with reservation requests back to the source.

There are a number of issues with RSVP. As it now stands, admission control and policy control are both locally administered. This means that there is not any coordination between routing nodes in the network (unless performed manually), increasing the probability that a reservation request at one of the hops upstream to the source may refuse the request. If this happens, there is no mechanism to try to find another route back to the source that can accept the request, meaning the application could get shut out and not get any service. This problem was discussed in a Data Communications article last year. A recent Internet Draft[12] discussed scaling issues of RSVP and questioned its use in high-speed backbones.

These issues are less important in Intranet or private network scenarios, where one network manager can set QoS policies uniformly in the routing nodes throughout the network and can work to insure that there is sufficient resource allocated for multimedia flows. Scalability is also less of an issue in these environments.

An adjunct protocol used with multimedia streaming applications is the Real-Time Streaming Protocol (RTSP) as defined in a recent Internet Draft.[13] RTSP is a control protocol very similar to HTTP/1.1 that is used to establish and control either a single or several time-synchronized streams of continuous media such as audio and video. It does not typically deliver the continuous streams itself, although interleaving of the continuous media stream with the control stream is possible. Essentially, RTSP acts as a "network remote control" for multimedia servers, similar to a VCR control for television.

A number of companies offer multicast multimedia streaming applications based on RTP and a number of multimedia profiles, including StarLight Networks, Precept, Icast, RealNetworks, and Microsoft in their NetShow application, which is included in Internet Explorer, Microsoft's Internet browser. Many of them also support RSVP. StarLight has targeted the financial industry as one of its key markets.

More information on these companies may be found at their Web sites as follows:

StarLight Networks:	www.starlight.com
Precept Software:	www.precept.com
Icast:	www.icast.com
RealNetworks:	www.real.com
Microsoft:	www.microsoft.com

RELIABLE MULTICAST APPLICATIONS AND ASSOCIATED PROTOCOLS

Unlike multimedia streaming applications, reliable multicast protocols are not yet standardized nor are any on a standards track as of yet. It is being studied in the Internet Research Task Force (IRTF) which is tasked to recommend techniques to be used by a working group in the Internet Engineering Task Force (IETF) to create a standards track reliable multicast protocol.

The issues viewed as most difficult by Internet researchers are those of congestion control and "fairness" to TCP traffic. Most Internet traffic is TCP, as it provides for error correction and packet ordering and thus ensures that the data received for an application is correct. TCP combines four different algorithms; slow start, congestion avoidance, fast retransmit, and fast recovery. Slow start and congestion avoidance are the two properties that are most relevant to determining behavior of a reliable multicast protocol so as to be "fair" to TCP.

However, that does not mean there are no reliable multicast products or protocols available commercially. There are a number of research protocols, and a number of products and toolkits available commercially. The protocols used, however, are not viewed by the Internet research community to be sufficiently able to handle congestion and fairness in the global Internet, but are very suitable for use on private networks and intranets over which most data in financial organizations traverse.

There is a wide range of reliable multicast applications with different requirements for transport, as can be seen from Exhibit 1. The real-time applications in the lower left quadrant are also varied in themselves. Data conferencing and network-based games, which are many to many collaborative applications, have low latency requirements along with small group sizes. Data streaming applications such as ticker tape and news feeds, which are one to many, need only semireliability sometimes and group sizes can be large — in the tens of thousands or even millions.

The non-real-time applications depicted in the right half of Exhibit 1 all involve delivery of data where low latency is not important. This is often described as *file transfer*, where the data to be transferred reside on a hard disk or other permanent memory and is delivered to another host and written on another hard disk or permanent memory. The data to be sent can be of any form; multimedia, software executables, documents, or images.

There are three primary companies that offer reliable multicast software products that reside in hosts: Globalcast Communications, TIBCO, and StarBurst Communications.

Globalcast offers protocol toolkits to allow application software vendors or IS departments to incorporate reliable multicast capability into their product or application. Globalcast offers three different protocols as follows:

Reliable Multicast Protocol (RMP)
Scalable Reliable Multicast (SRM)
Reliable Multicast Transport Protocol (RMTP)

RMP has the oldest origins and has limited scaling capabilities, so is probably of least interest to the financial community. SRM[14] is the darling of the Internet researchers and was originally designed to operate with the wb whiteboarding data conferencing tool that was created by researchers at Lawrence B. Livermore Laboratories. SRM is set up to be a framework protocol much like RTP is in the multimedia world. Neither of these has been deployed to any great extent in commercial applications.

RMTP[15] was originally developed by Bell Laboratories researchers who became a part of Lucent Technologies when Lucent was divested from AT&T. Lucent licensed RMTP to Globalcast which is offering it as a toolkit.

RMTP has not had much commercial deployment as yet either, but has been implemented for a message billing application inside a major carrier. RMTP supports both data streaming applications and file transfer and gains scaling in routed networks by adding hierarchy.

TIBCO and StarBurst Communications both offer applications as well as an underlying reliable multicast protocol. TIBCO has specialized in reliable message streaming applications with its TIB/Rendezvous software. The current reliable multicast protocol used in TIB/Rendezvous is proprietary, and not publicly documented. It is thought to not scale very well over wide area networks, with the result that TIBCO products today have been mostly installed on local campus networks. However, they have participated with Cisco Systems in the creation of a new reliable multicast protocol just documented in an Internet Draft in January, 1998 called Pretty Good Multicast (PGM).[16] PGM appears to be the protocol of choice for TIBCO in the future. PGM depends on assistance from routers in the network infrastructure to achieve scaling.

TIBCO has heavily marketed two intertwined concepts, *subject-based addressing* and *publish/subscribe*. Information is sent (published) on a subject name. Interested parties listen for (subscribe to) specific subject names. This has been used to benefit in financial trading systems. For example, securities data feed handlers can "publish" the latest stock prices to hundreds of traders on a trading floor simultaneously using TIBCO technology.

StarBurst Communications specializes in multicast file transfer with software that can provide centralized multicast group setup and control as well as reliable delivery to up to tens of thousands of receivers. The protocol used is the Multicast File Transfer Protocol (MFTP) documented as an Internet Draft[17] originally in February, 1997 and updated in March, 1998. MFTP was created by StarBurst Communications and refined with the help of Cisco Systems.

MFTP is more than just a reliable multicast protocol, as it is also a group setup and management protocol. Groups can be set up at a central location and critical information can then be "pushed" to the group members that have been set up.

Recall that joining a multicast group using IGMP is receiver initiated. This has resulted in most group setup procedures occurring similar to broadcast television; content is advertised somehow about its availability and receivers "tune" in, similar to the way television watchers tune their TV to desired programming. The sender has no knowledge of who is listening. This model is satisfactory for the sending of noncritical information but is not very satisfactory for the delivery of critical information, where the sender wants confirmation of delivery.

StarBurst created a "Closed Group" model as a part of MFTP. A group is created at the sender. At the start of a session, the sender directs the group members to join using "Announce" messages. Those directed to join respond with "Registrations" to tell the sender they are available. After all register or after a user-defined timeout, transmission of the file(s) commences. At completion, all receivers confirm delivery with essentially one positive acknowledgment called a "Done" message, which is confirmed.

This model has proven attractive to the financial industry. Financial Publishing/Thomson Financial uses an "Extranet" to deliver daily 40 to 60 Mbytes of derivative financial information for a fee via the network to their customers. Their customers are paying for this information, so it is essential that there is a record of delivery at the central site. The Ohio Company delivers the company's 300- to 400-Mbyte electronic financial database of financial properties to its 200 investment executives at 50 offices in 5 states. This database is updated immediately as inventory changes to make sure that all investment executives have up to date information.

Exhibit 10 summarizes the reliable multicast applications and the companies that can provide solutions. GlobalCast does not have application products, but have underlying reliable multicast toolkits, hence is shown

	Real-time	Non-real-time
Multimedia		Delivery of multimedia content as files StarBurst (GlobalCast)
Data-only	Message streaming apps., e.g. tickertape TIBCO (GlobalCast)	Critical data delivery, e.g. databases, sw StarBurst (GlobalCast)

Exhibit 10. Reliable multicast applications and companies with products.

in Exhibit 10 in parentheses. More information on these companies may be found at their Web sites as follows:

StarBurst Communications:	www.starburstcom.com
GlobalCast:	www.gcast.com
TIBCO:	www.tibco.com

SUMMARY AND CONCLUSIONS

Multicast IP as a networking technology and the various applications and associated protocols can provide very valuable tools for productivity for financial organizations. The applications are very varied from multimedia events to ticker tape and news message streams to critical information update to multiple remote offices. In all cases, IP multicast technology can save money over alternative solutions in its ability to conserve both server and network resources. In other cases, the application cannot even be applied without using multicast technology.

Historically, many financial technology solutions have been customized, leading to expensive solutions. Multicast IP and the protocols associated with the applications are either standardized or are publicly documented and available for support by multiple organizations. Early financial organizations who are pioneers have started to use multicast IP technology to benefit in their organizations. All financial organizations should at least investigate it to see how it can benefit their enterprise.

Notes

1. Deering, S., Host Extensions for IP Multicasting, RFC 1112, August, 1989.
2. Fenner, W., Internet Group Management Protocol, Version 2, RFC 2236, November, 1997.
3. Waitzman, D., Partridge, C., and Deering, S., Distance Vector Multicast Routing Protocol, RFC 1075, November, 1988.
4. Deering, S., Estrin, D., Farinacci, D., Jacobson, V., Helmy, A., and Wei, L., Protocol Independent Multicast Version 2, Dense Mode Specification, Work in Progress, Internet Draft, *draft-ietf-idmr-pim-dm-05.txt,* May 21, 1997.
5. Moy, J., Multicast Extensions to OSPF, RFC 1584, March 1994.
6. Estrin, D., Farinacci, D., Deering, S., Thaler, D., and Helmy, A., Protocol Independent Multicast — Sparse Mode (PIM-SM): Protocol Specification, Work in Progress, Internet Draft, *draft-ietf-idmr-pim-sm-specv2-00.txt,* September 11, 1997.
7. Ballardie, T., Core Based Trees (CBT version 2) Multicast Routing, RFC 2189, September, 1997.
8. Estrin, D., Meyer, D., and Thaler, D., Border Gateway Multicast Protocol (BGMP): Protocol Specification, Work in Progress, Internet Draft, *draft-ietf-idmr-gum-01.txt,* October 31, 1997.
9. Schulzrinne, H., Casner, S., Frederick, R., and Jacobson, V., RTP: A Transport Protocol for Real-Time Applications, RFC 1889, January, 1996.
10. Freed, N. and Kille, S., RTP Payload Format for MPEG1/MPEG2 Video, RFC 2250, January, 1998.
11. Braden, R., Zhang, L., Berson, S., Herzog, S., and Jamin, S., Resource ReSerVation Protocol (RSVP) — Version 1 Functional Specification, RFC 2205, September, 1997.
12. Mankin, A., Baker, F., Braden, B., Bradner, S., Romanow, A., Weinrib, A., and Zhang, L., Resource ReSerVation Protocol (RSVP) — Version 1 Applicability Statement Some Guidelines on Deployment, RFC 2208, September, 1997.

13. Schulzrinne, H., Rao, A., and Lanphier, R., Real Time Streaming Protocol (RTSP), Work in Progress, Internet Draft, *draft-ietf-mmusic-rtsp-09.txt,* February 2, 1998.
14. Floyd, S., Jacobson, V., Liu, C., McCanne, S., and Zhang, L., A Reliable Multicast Framework for Light-weight Sessions and Application Level Framing, ACM Transactions on Networking, November, 1996.
15. Paul, S., Sabnani, K. K., Lin, J. C., and Bhattacharyya, S., Reliable Multicast Transport Protocol (RMTP), *IEEE J. Sel. Areas Comm.,* April, 1997.
16. Farinacci, D., Lin, A., Speakman, T., and Tweedly, A., PGM Reliable Transport Protocol Specification, Work in Progress, Internet Draft, *draft-speakman-pgm-spec-01.txt,* January 29, 1998.
17. Miller, K., Robertson, K., Tweedly, A., and White, M., StarBurst Multicast File Transfer Protocol (MFTP) Specification, Work in Progress, Internet Draft, *draft-miller-mftp-spec-02.txt,* February 13, 1997.

Chapter 30
An Introduction to the Internet for Financial Services Developers

Jessica Keyes

BEFORE THE "INFORMATION HIGHWAY" BECAME SYNONYMOUS with the brave new world of video-on-demand, high-powered multimedia, and 24-hour home shopping, it was a road well traveled by those needing an efficient and productive way to keep on top of their business.

For those in the financial services area, the information highway, or information services as it was known pre-Al Gore, offers a wealth of information that will help you do your job faster, better, and smarter. And in spite of all the hubbub about it, it has been easily accessible for more than a decade.

The difference is that today it's no secret anymore. While not everyone knows how to get to it, everyone at least knows it's out there. Most organizations are quickly realizing that they simply don't have a choice any longer. Not hitching a ride on the information highway (IH) is becoming a distinct competitive disadvantage.

The IH is really a misnomer (at least for now). Look at a map of the U.S. and you'll see what I mean. While there are some major arteries criss-crossing the country, the map is really a spider's web of roads all connected together to enable you to go from any one point in the U.S. to any other point in the U.S. It's the same with the IH — really a collection of interconnected networks. Understanding how to navigate it enables you to get from any one point in the IH to any other point in the IH.

While the IH probably has more information nuggets tucked into its hard disks than the New York Public Library, for some strange reason it's e-mail that seems to have captured everyone's attention. The ability to communi-

0-8493-9991-2/99/$0.00+$.50

cate with millions of people across thousands of computers across seven continents is no mean feat. It's also a productivity booster.

Of course, the IH is far more than e-mail. It's also a series of databases and bulletin boards. Both provide sources of information that are worth looking into. Bulletin boards are exactly what they sound like, places to post information. Public forums are open to anyone who has a urge to take a look-see. For example, many of the software companies have bulletin boards that enable users to file trouble reports and/or download "fixes" to those troubles.

The most interesting of bulletin boards are those that are maintained by the various special interest groups that have sprung up on the IH. Sometimes referred to as forums, these are veritable goldmines of camaraderie and information. For example CompuServe, now a part of America Online, has a Legal forum where I've been able to get assistance that would have cost me thousands of dollars if I had spoken to a nondigitized attorney.

CompuServe's Finance forums are similarly well endowed. The Investors Forum's libraries, for example, include such esoteric items of interest as stocks/bonds, fixed income, option trading, futures, commodities, newsletters, theories, charting, and technical analysis.

There's also all that shareware. CompuServers are a "sharing" lot so there's quite a bit of "free" software. (Shareware is, for all intents and purposes, free. However, you are often asked to make a donation of a rather nominal sum for the care and feeding of the developer of the program you are using. Payment is optional, but always appreciated.) If you were to access the charting and technical analysis library of the aforementioned Investors Forum, you could download QCharter 1.3, which is a shareware program for historical quote charting. Similarly, you could download useful ratios, macros, and text files such as an index of the SEC's EDGAR database.

While shareware software and databases dominate the forums, the database research services of the IH are the real prize here. Knowledge-Index (KI) , the night-owl version of Dialog's very expensive professional research database service, is a veritable gold-mine of financial information. For a paltry $16 an hour (after 6 p.m. and all weekend), you get access to dozens of databases including: Books in Print, Business Dateline, Business-Wire, Pr NewsWire, Harvard Business Review, practically all of the computer news and business publications (including Pravda), as well as Standard & Poor's Daily News and Corporate Descriptions.

If you recall our earlier discussion comparing the IH to a network of interconnected roads, you'll begin to understand how it works in relation to the services on CompuServe. When you sign on to CompuServe you log on to CompuServe's computers, but when you request access to KI, CompuServe actually passes your request across a bridge to Dialog's own computer — hence the accurate analogy of a series of connecting roadways.

CompuServe offers numerous other financially oriented services (i.e., bridges). Basic Quotes provides delayed quotes for items such as stocks, options, indexes, exchange rates, and mutual funds. Citibank's Global Report, which happens to be the primary information resource for many large corporations, integrates and organizes news and financial data including real-time foreign exchange rates, spot commodity prices, and industry news. Commodity Markets and Pricing offers exactly what its title says it offers.

Company Analyzer provides public company information including income statement, balance sheet, and ownership information from Disclosure (which is also available) and an S&P estimate on future earnings. All you need is the company name, ticker symbol or CUSIP number.

It wouldn't be feasible to describe the myriad other services offered on CompuServe. They run the gamut from D&B's Business Directory to Fund-Watch Online to Thomas Register Online to TRW Business Profiles to Investext, which is a full-text online version of all the research reports done in the last 2 years.

America Online and MSN all offer commensurate services. Of course, Financial Services firms will benefit from providing information on services such as American Online and its rivals. As shown, Citibank, S&P, D&B, and a host of others have already made an investment in just such an undertaking. Today it is possible to use these non-Internet service providers to provide services to existing customers, to market to prospective customers, and to even provide information for a fee to whoever wants it.

For the most part, systems development in this venue is surprisingly easy and affordable. For example, CompuServe provides free access to an online area where the organization can develop its service as well as access documentation for software with which to build the service. The developing organization is merely responsible for the time and labor necessary for creating, maintaining, and promoting its database, including transmitting and reformatting the product during the developmental stages.

CompuServe, and its parent, America Online, approach all Information provider relationships as a partnership. They provide sufficient training, documentation, connect time, and disk storage for product development at no cost. They also provide the full support of their marketing and technical staff to assist in development of the organization's product to its full potential.

Interestingly, programming knowledge is not necessary, though it is helpful to be familiar with videotext services and menu-driven formats.

The actual format for the product will depend upon the nature of the information. CompuServe makes available, at their cost, several programs to facilitate the service's delivery:

Menu-driven display — This program can be likened to an electronic magazine, whereby menus serve as the "table of contents" and lead the user to articles of information. This works well for concise factual information.

Keyword search — This program enables the developer to assign keywords to each entry and allows the user to enter the word(s) he or she wants to find. It is particularly appropriate for dictionaries, access to information by state, date, or special interest, and other reference material.

Gateway arrangement — This is where information resides on the organization's host computer and the user is "transferred" to the host computer to access the information. This is particularly appropriate for information that requires immediate responses or minute to minute updating, such as stock prices.

Wire service — This CompuServe program gathers a continuous stream of information and makes the information available to users as soon as it is received. Information is dynamically added to menus in reverse chronological order. This continuous updating is typically used for news wires which require timely processing of large amounts of data.

Developers can transmit information to CompuServe by various means. With a terminal and a modem the developer can dial CompuServe's network and directly type the information into a CompuServe database using a CompuServe word processing program. Other means available are uploading and submission of diskettes and tapes to CompuServe's computer center.

A host of savvy financial services organizations have been using these Information Superhighway service providers for years for definite competitive advantage. But with the thousands of articles and growing interest in the Internet, most of these organizations are looking to the Net as well. But what they're finding is that the Internet is as different from the proprietary service providers as night is from day from a development perspective.

Where CompuServe works as a partner to help the organization deploy its service — going as far as providing access time and disk space — development on the Internet means going it alone. As you'll see in the rest of this chapter, there are many choices as well as issues that need to be grappled with if the financial services organization is to use the Internet successfully.

USING THE INTERNET

A commonly asked question is "What is the Internet?" The reason such a question gets asked so often is because there's no agreed-upon answer that neatly sums up the Internet. The Internet can be thought about in relation to its common protocols, as a physical collection of routers and circuits, as a set of shared resources, or even as an attitude about interconnecting and intercommunication. Some common definitions given in the past include:

- A network of networks based on the TCP/IP protocols.
- A community of people who use and develop those networks.
- A collection of resources that can be reached from those networks.

Today's Internet is a global resource connecting millions of users that began as an experiment over 20 years ago by the U.S. Department of Defense. While the networks that make up the Internet are based on a standard set of protocols (a mutually agreed upon method of communication between parties), the Internet also has gateways to networks and services that are based on other protocols.

In many ways the Internet is like a church: it has its council of elders, every member has an opinion about how things should work, and you can either take part or not. It's your choice. The Internet has no president, chief operating officer, or Pope. The constituent networks may have presidents and CEOs, but that's a different issue; there's no single authority figure for the Internet as a whole.

The ultimate authority for where the Internet is going rests with the Internet Society, or ISOC. ISOC is a voluntary membership organization whose purpose is to promote global information exchange through Internet technology.

The council of elders is a group of invited volunteers called the Internet Architecture Board, or the IAB. The IAB meets regularly to "bless" standards and allocate resources, like addresses. The Internet works because there are standard ways for computers and software applications to talk to each other. This allows computers from different vendors to communicate without problems. It's not an IBM-only or Sun-only or Macintosh-only network. The IAB is responsible for these standards; it decides when a standard is necessary, and what the standard should be. When a standard is required, it considers the problem, adopts a standard, and announces it via the network.

No one pays for the Internet. Instead, everyone pays for their part. The National Science Foundation pays for NSFNET. NASA pays for the NASA Science Internet. Networks get together and decide how to connect themselves together and fund these interconnections. A college or corporation pays for their connection to some regional network, which in turn pays a national provider for its access.

Many big corporations have been on the Internet for years. Up until now, their participation has been limited to their research and engineering departments. Businesses are just now discovering that the Internet can provide many advantages to their bottom line:

1. Providing information to end-users is less expensive than with the proprietary networks such as CompuServe which normally charge a royalty on profits made.
2. There are many more users of the Internet than on all the proprietary networks combined. At last count there are were 22 million users of the Internet compared to less than 5 million on proprietary networks.
3. Advances in technology have provided the ability to build visual storefronts which include liberal use of images and even video and sound. This is made possible through deployment of the browser graphical user interface and use of the Hypertext Markup Language (HTML) which has quickly become an Internet standard.

Perusing the glossary at the end of this article demonstrates the great variety of capabilities that the Internet provides organizations looking to it to provide information. Although browser interfaces currently dominate the press, the readers should be aware that the Internet was successfully disseminating information long before Netscape Navigator or Microsoft Internet Explorer was ever developed.

Essentially the Internet is being used by organizations in five venues:

1. E-mail — Organizations are making good use of e-mail to correspond to clients and staff members. Updates and notices can be inexpensively and quickly routed to all four corners of the world.
2. FTP — One of the oldest of the Internet technologies, File Transfer Protocol, enables organizations to provide databases of files (i.e., text files or programs) that others may download to their personal computers.
3. Gopher — A distributed information service that makes available hierarchical collections of information across the Internet. This service uses a simple protocol that allows a single Gopher client to access information from any accessible Gopher server, providing the user with a single "Gopher space" of information. Public domain versions of the client and server are available.
4. Telnet — This technology enables those outside of the organization to remotely log in to a host computer as a guest to access information that resides on that host.
5. World Wide Web — The newest of Internet technologies, when used in conjunction with the browser graphical interfaces provides the ability to store hypertext and images for use by current and future customers.

Financial Services firms are using all of these technologies to take advantage of what is, for now at least, a practically free worldwide network.

Using FTP and E-Mail for Support

Network Software Associates (NSA) is a consulting firm that supports the government and industry — including financial services. With offices on the West and East coasts, NSA needed to find a way to better support their customer base. For NSA, the solution turned out to be the Internet.

NSA found that a large percentage of customer support traffic comes from the user requesting help in locating information or help in performing a certain function. The other important task in customer support was in providing timely software updates and fixes.

If the request is not time-critical, the user can be trained to e-mail a request for help to the customer service group or, alternatively, to other users. This second option is a form of e-mail known as Usenet.

Both the IS organization and the user community can greatly benefit from setting up Usenet discussion groups. In essence, Usenet is Internet e-mail with a twist: It is a mailing list to which users subscribe where a message is sent not to one individual, but to the entire mailing list of individuals.

Starting a Usenet. NSA is one of many who have opted to start its own Usenet group on the Internet. Although an organization doesn't require permission to start a discussion group, it does require some special intelligence and some computer resources.

In the tradition of the Internet, the software to manage the Usenet mailing list is provided on the Internet itself. The software, known as Listserv, can be downloaded free of charge using the Internet's File Transmission Protocol (FTP).

Usenet enables NSA customers to solve some of their own problems. Responding to questions and problems from the user community is only half of NSA's customer support problem the other is providing fixes, patches, and software updates. NSA feels there is no reason to use sneakernet anymore when you can distribute software to users through the network. (Sneakernet is the network created by physically walking from location to location to deliver software to users.)

Using FTP. To accomplish this, NSA decided to implement an FTP server. The support of NSA users is handled using FTP for file transfers. NSA places the files in a common access location and then sends users an e-mail to inform them of the latest release, thereby giving them the option to obtain it or not.

According to NSA, becoming an FTP server is not as straightforward as it would be if one were dealing with a centralized organization complete with tech support personnel. Connecting to the net is no easy task and requires developing a careful plan (see below). NSA didn't, and, as a result, suffered from it. For example, NSA did not accurately predict the high level of customer usage of its Internet-based services. As a result, they had to increase capacity by installing a higher-speed line.

That this was so difficult a task is the result of the Internet relying on physical numerical addresses called IP addresses. IP, or Internet Protocol, is the network layer for the TCP/IP Protocol Suite. It is a connectionless, best-effort packet-switching protocol. For example, a server that we know as ns.uu.net has a physical address of 137.39.1.3. Since getting a higher speed line also requires a new address, there is a big conversion effort that must be undertaken to change the mapping between logical and physical addresses.

Implementation Considerations

There are a plethora of implementation issues that the NSA had to consider when opting to create an FTP server.

Hardware. The first decision was to consider the type of hardware to be used as the FTP server. Most organizations opt for high-powered, Unix-based workstations since they understand that the higher the number of users the more powerful the machine must be.

NSA opted for a Sparcstation and the Unix operating system since the number of users was large. However, most companies starting out can get by with a 486-based IBM PC-compatible.

Software. Unix is the operating system of choice for most servers since most of the software running on the net (i.e., FTP itself) is Unix based. In addition, of all the server-based operating systems, Unix is the most robust in the client/server arena.

In addition to the operating system, the organization must also ensure that telnet and FTP software is available on that server. While telnet is your basic remote telecommunications software readily available from a variety of sources, FTP comes in a couple of flavors. The traditional flavor of FTP is simply a series of Unix commands. This can be confusing to non-Unix users. Vendors have recently come out with a more graphical form of FTP, but there is a high financial cost associated with it. So instead NSA decided that, although difficult to use, a bit of training and support would go a long way towards alleviating the problem of dealing with the Unix shell.

Phone Line. The organization must order, install, and test the circuit or phone line that is connected to the server. Before this can be accomplished, however, a model of the expected usage of the Internet must be developed to accurately determine line capacity. Model variables include number of users, number and type of services being used, and amount of data being uploaded and downloaded.

NSA uses a dedicated connection to hook the FTP server to the Internet. This requires a dedicated, point-to-point telecommunications circuit and an IP router, which is a dedicated networking device, linking the organization to the Internet. Line speeds usually range from 9.6 kb to 45 Mb, with the most common connection speeds being 56 kb and 1.54 Mb. NSA ultimately required a 65-kb line to assure good response time for its users.

An alternative is to use a dial-up connection. This method uses a regular phone line and a workstation. When a network connection is needed, the workstation is used to establish a connection over the modem and phone line. At the end of use, the connection is broken. Line speeds range from 9.6 kb to 56 kb, with lower speeds being most common. Obviously slower than a dedicated connection, this solution is used by organizations which have fewer users dialing into the network. The trade-off here is increased response time vs. lower costs.

Costs. Depending upon the number of users and the hardware configuration, the cost of implementing an FTP server ranges from $1000 to $5000 per month with a one-time hardware and phone line installation cost averaging $13,000.

What you will wind up paying is really dependent upon the number of servers you use, the number of customers you have, what they're doing and the amount of time they spend on the net, the type of software you're running, and the speed of your line.

INTERNET SECURITY CONSIDERATIONS

Ten of the largest buy- and sell-side firms, including Scudder, Salomon Brothers, and Goldman Sachs & Co., have joined together to establish the Financial Information Exchange or FIX for short. FIX is a common protocol for sending and receiving equity trading information including orders, execution details, fill reports, and account allocations.

With the goal of eliminating the proliferation of proprietary order routing systems, one standard industry protocol means that brokers will be able to reach multiple clients while buy-side traders can reach multiple brokers.

Since April of 1994, Fidelity has been communicating with Goldman Sachs & Co. and Salomon Brothers using the FIX protocol. According to all indications, these firms are experiencing a tremendous surge in productivity because these brokers no longer have to manually key in the information. From a liquidity point of view, sells and buys can be more quickly matched.

FIX allows customers to see on-screen multiple inbound indications from different brokers on the same stock, and fill information coming back on multiple orders. The most intriguing aspect of FIX is that the protocol to enable open communication between firms has been written to allow messages — including equity trade orders — to be sent over the Internet.

Security Risks

Wary of Internet hackers, those participating in FIX over the Internet have deployed stringent security measures including data encryption as well as strong fire walls. Internet subscribers can receive FIX information over the Net at fix@world.std.com. Included are the FIX protocol specification, FIX committee meeting minutes, application notes, and FAQ (frequently asked questions).

The Internet poses a particularly high level of security risk. Few need to be reminded of the case of Cornell University graduate student Robert Morris, Jr., who programmed an Internet worm that single-handedly brought down 6000 machines. In November of 1991, the U.S. General Accounting Office reported that computer hackers from the Netherlands broke into military computers. More recently a group of students known by the name The Posse have been taking down systems just for the thrill of it.

Setting security policies and procedures really means developing a plan for how to deal with computer security. A procedure for creating a security plan includes the following steps:

- Look at what you are trying to protect.
- Look at what you need to protect it from.
- Determine how likely the threats are.
- Implement measures which will protect your assets in a cost-effective manner.
- Review the process continuously, and improve things every time a weakness is found.

Most organizations utilize several of the following methods to ensure security.

Passwords. Many organizations are lax in enforcing password assignment and maintenance for users of their mainframes and other in-house servers. Shadow passwords, which means that no public password files are available for the casual browser, is the preferred method.

Of course, all of this is worth nothing if security isn't an intrinsic part of the corporate mind-set. Security begins with the individual. There has been more than one instance of employees giving out Internet IDs and passwords to friends — incidents usually immediately followed by a few break-in attempts.

Data Encryption. Encryption is perhaps the most popular method of security for financial firms using the Internet. But it comes with its own set of problems.

Other than a lack of standards in the industry, there remains the problem that people need to have some way of decrypting the message. If the messaging is done internally (i.e., over the organization's own network), or between two or more cooperating organizations (e.g., securities firms transmitting buy and sell information between each others' computers), then a private encryption key can be used. But if you're messaging on the Internet and a customer needs to transmit private financial information, a public key needs to be sent along with the message. The problem is that this public key needs to be decrypted at the receiving end of the message.

Fire Walls. The hardware and software that sits between the computer operation and the Internet is colloquially known as a fire wall. Its specific mission is to examine Internet traffic and allow only approved data to pass through. One type of fire wall is a software-driven filter in the network connection. An organization may have 60 machines handling Internet e-mail; however the use a software filter makes it appear to the outside world that they only have one. It is also a good idea to strip the organization's host address. In this way it is possible to lock out those who would attempt to get into a system through e-mail.

A second approach to building a fire wall is to use computers as routers or gateways. The main thrust of this solution is to route all Internet traffic through what is sometimes referred to as a bastion (i.e., bastion meaning wall, as in a wall between the main computer and the Internet) host. Essentially, this technique is simple. The bastion host is a server which is connected both to the Internet and the organization's main computer installation. Only users and/or information with the proper security clearance are routed through the bastion host to the organization's computers.

USING THE BROWSER

A variety of organizations are using a combination of the World Wide Web and a browser-type interface — in the guise of either Netscape Navigator or Microsoft Internet Explorer — to do everything from providing information to enabling catalog shopping.

The World Wide Web is a hypertext-based, distributed information system created by researchers at CERN in Switzerland. Users may create, edit, or browse hypertext documents — either in a text-based format or using a graphical user interface. As with most Internet technologies, software to run a Web site as well as develop graphical user interfaces is freely available on the Internet itself.

First Union Corporation, with headquarters in Charlotte, NC, is a bank holding company made up of eight financial institutions that is seriously interested in contributing to the free flow of information on the Internet.

First Union's vision of the future lies in its commitment to the delivery of what they refer to as Cyberbanking[SM] to its customers and strategic partners. Although, like most financial services firms First Union is just getting started, they plan to enable their customers to buy products and services over the Web without worrying about security issues and having the money directly debited from the customer's checking or credit card account.

First Union has created what they call the First Access Network. Although today it contains information solely about the bank, First Union soon hopes to provide its commercial customers with the ability to build virtual storefronts. Even without these virtual storefronts, First Union's Web network is impressive for the amount of information it provides. This includes:

Corporate Mission
History of First Union Corporation
Financial Information
Investor Relations
Stockholder Account
Stock Listings
News Media Contact
Career Opportunities
Products and Services
Checking Accounts
Savings Accounts
24-Hour Service
Credit Solutions
Loans and Leasing
Buying and Refinancing Your Home
Mortgages
Equity Loans
Relocation Services
Investing for the Future
Brokerage Services
Estate Planning
Retirement Services
Insurance Services
Business Services
Consumer Reference Library
Career Opportunities
The Consumer's Guide to Credit
Using Credit
Basics of Credit
What Every Consumer Needs to Know about Credit Cards
VISA Home Page
History of the Credit Card
History of the Banking Industry
First Union and the Community

Each of these items, which appears on First Union's Home Page, is a link to a separate hypertext document which contains information about the titled subject.

Creating a Web document requires marketing and artistic skills as well as technical skills. Since an HTML (hypertext markup language) document is hypertext-linked, developers often have to draw a storyboard to keep track of where there are going.

Web document designers really have to understand the ramifications of designing a document that will be displayed in a networked environment. The general rule of thumb is to keep documents relatively small, and relatively uncluttered. Don't put large images in the document because it would take a long time to download these images over a slow link although the text comes very fast.

The major impediment to using the Web is speed. Most users of the Internet are accessing it using fairly slow 28,000 bps modems, so downloading images that are typically 200 kb can be painstakingly slow. The point here for developers is to be well aware of what your prospective users will be using as their graphical user interface.

Most developers limit their use of graphics to thumbnail images with the ability for the user to request a full screen image. Since these images are stored on the organization's host (unless this work is contracted out to one of the many Internet service providers), careful deployment of imagery will prevent a network disaster. If you have a large document with many, many images, you can take a major hit on the net by requesting these images all at once.

Programming the Web is really a misnomer. Developing an HTML document is more akin to word processing than programming. And, in fact, major vendors such as Microsoft have provided HTML extensions to their word processing packages at no additional cost.

HTML (Hypertext Markup Language) is really a rich text formatted document which looks like the example below (from First Union):

```
<ul>
<li> <a href="#mission">Corporate Mission</a>
<li> <a href="history.html">History of First Union Corporation</a>
<li> <a href="financial.html">Financial Information</a>
<li> <a href="financial.html#investor">Investor Relations</a>
<li> <a href="financial.html#account">Stockholder Account</a>
<li> <a href="financial.html#stock">Stock Listings</a>
<li> <a href="financial.html#media">News Media Contact</a>
<li> <a href="careers.html">Career Opportunities</a>
```

HTML enables the developer to embed images as well as provide for hypertext links to other documents and even other Web sites such as the Visa Home Page.

There are really two halves to creating an online presence on the World Wide Web. You have to create one or more documents using HTML and then you have to develop a way to present those documents to someone looking for them on the Internet. In other words, you have to become a Web server.

Becoming a Web server requires some careful planning. Additional software, itself available free on the Internet, needs to be obtained and configured. In addition, the organization needs to estimate the bandwidth of the telecommunications line as well as the required capacity of the hardware. This is all dependent upon the amount of information to be disseminated and the number and workload of the users using the system.

Internet Users' Glossary

Address. There are three types of addresses in common use within the Internet. They are e-mail address; IP, internet, or Internet address; and hardware or MAC address.

Anonymous FTP. Anonymous FTP allows a user to retrieve documents, files, programs, and other archived data from anywhere in the Internet without having to establish a user ID and password. By using the special user ID of "anonymous" the network user will bypass local security checks and will have access to publicly accessible files on the remote system.

Archie. A system to automatically gather, index, and serve information on the Internet. The initial implementation of archie provided an indexed directory of filenames from all anonymous FTP archives on the Internet.

Archive Site. A machine that provides access to a collection of files across the Internet. An "anonymous FTP archive site," for example, provides access to this material via the FTP protocol.

Cyberspace. A term coined by William Gibson in his fantasy novel *Neuromancer* to describe the "world" of computers, and the society that gathers around them.

Dial-up. A temporary, as opposed to dedicated, connection between machines established over a standard phone line.

Electronic Mail (e-mail). A system whereby a computer user can exchange messages with other computer users (or groups of users) via a communications network.

E-mail Address. The domain-based or UUCP address that is used to send electronic mail to a specified destination.

Encryption. Encryption is the manipulation of a packet's data in order to prevent any but the intended recipient from reading the data. There are many types of data encryption, and they are the basis of network security.

File Transfer Protocol (FTP). A protocol which allows a user on one host to access and transfer files to and from another host over a network. Also, FTP is usually the name of the program the user invokes to execute the protocol.

Gopher. A distributed information service that makes available hierarchical collections of information across the Internet. Gopher uses a simple protocol that allows a single Gopher client to access information from any accessible Gopher server, providing the user with a single "Gopher space" of information.

Internet. While an internet is a network, the term "internet" is usually used to refer to a collection of networks interconnected with routers.

Internet. The Internet (note the capital "I") is the largest internet in the world. Is a three-level hierarchy composed of backbone networks (e.g., NSFNET, MILNET), mid-level networks, and stub networks. The Internet is a multiprotocol internet.

Internet Relay Chat (IRC). A worldwide "party line" protocol that allows a person to converse with others in real time.

Internet Society (ISOC). The Internet Society is a nonprofit, professional membership organization which facilitates and supports the technical evolution of the Internet, stimulates interest in and educates the scientific and academic communities, industry, and the public about the technology, uses, and applications of the Internet, and promotes the development of new applications for the system. The Society provides a forum for discussion and collaboration in the operation and use of the global Internet infrastructure. The Internet Society publishes a quarterly newsletter, the Internet Society News, and holds an annual conference, INET.

Point-to-Point Protocol (PPP). The Point-to-Point Protocol provides a method for transmitting packets over serial point-to-point links.

Serial Line IP (SLIP). A protocol used to run IP over serial lines, such as telephone circuits or RS-232 cables, interconnecting two systems.

Telnet. Telnet is the Internet standard protocol for remote terminal connection service.

Wide Area Information Servers (WAIS). A distributed information service which offers simple natural language input, indexed searching for fast retrieval, and a "relevance feedback" mechanism which allows the results of initial searches to influence future searches.

World Wide Web (WWW or W3). A hypertext-based, distributed information system created by researchers at CERN in Switzerland. Users may create, edit, or browse hypertext documents.

Chapter 31 Introduction to e-Commerce

David Peterson

ANOTHER MONDAY MORNING ARRIVES. You quickly make a list of the things you have to do today. The list includes buying a gift for your nephew and having it delivered, checking on airline reservations for a trip the following month, and making a change in your 401k deductions. You want to get the latest novel by Tom Clancy. You need to scan your checking account balance and transfer funds from savings to cover a check you will write today. You want to check the latest stock quotes for your held securities portfolio. You need to send a note to your brother who lives in an adjoining state regarding the upcoming family reunion. If you have access to the Internet and World Wide Web, all of these tasks can be accomplished from the comfort of your home in a fraction of the time it would require otherwise.

Welcome to the bold, new world of electronic commerce. Today anybody can access the ever-growing world of online information, transactions, and purchasing. This introductory chapter shows you, the financial institution, how to identify opportunities in the electronic access market, capitalize on those opportunities, and develop a strategy for providing solutions to current and future customers.

For the purposes of this chapter, electronic commerce is defined as your customers' ability to access your institution remotely to (1) get information, (2) perform transactions on existing accounts, and (3) sign up for additional services. While many banks are rapidly expanding their online offerings to include insurance, brokerage, trust, and other financially related services, these are merely other types of activities to which the ensuing discussion may also be applied.

Today's customer is faced with many challenges. The amount of time that individuals have to take care of their personal finances is severely limited. Today it is common for both parents to work. To accommodate the resulting limitation on families' time, financial institutions now provide access to services at nontraditional times and places.

0-8493-9991-2/99/$0.00+$.50

Banks are usually open only when most people are at work. Therefore, typical bank operating hours are not convenient for most banking customers. With the proliferation of the personal computer and other electronic channels, however, banks may make their services available whenever and wherever it is convenient to the customer.

More checkbooks are balanced at 10 p.m. than 10 a.m. Late at night, when a customer discovers a missing check item, and therefore cannot balance her checkbook, the bank's access and delivery channels, or lack thereof, become most real to her. When earlier surveyed, this very customer may not have indicated a desire for accessing the bank via electronic channels, but now having experienced the need for late-night access, that desire materializes. Some customers are so accustomed to their financial institution's limited accessibility that they are not aware other means of access exist. The simple act of balancing the checkbook, however, may feed the customer's need for electronic access more than any other.

The typical business customer's needs differ from those of the typical consumer. Businesses want to know what's happening with their accounts on a daily basis. Almost all small businesses today operate on a cash basis. From this standpoint, businesses need to know exactly what items hit their accounts from the previous day's work. They maintain a list of their issued items, and, once the items have cleared the bank businesses know exactly which outstanding items may post against their accounts in the future.

Regardless of whether we are talking about late-night access for the retail customer or daily access for the business customer, customers today have wants and needs that require more than traditional banking hours and access can accommodate.

So, is the brick and mortar bank branch an endangered species? No. The bank lobby is there to sell other products and services, such as individual retirement accounts, trust services, specialized lending services, and so forth. The "lobby" has tremendous value as a service delivery channel. But for traditional "bank lobby" questions, such as balance inquiries, account transfers, loan payments, year-to-date interest inquiries, etc., electronic channels provide a higher level of service than is delivered when the customer comes in the bank, sits, and waits for the next available bank representative.

THE "PROFITABLE" CUSTOMER

Banks are increasingly focused on the profitability of their customers. Profitability studies indicate that the most profitable relationships, both personal and business, are those with customers who are looking for online services. In general, profitable customers represent 20 to 25% of your total customer base. These are the customers on which your financial institution must remain fiercely focused, and these are generally the customers who are most interested in electronic commerce and electronic banking.

TYPES OF ELECTRONIC DELIVERY SYSTEMS

There are differences between providing customers electronic access via a private network vs. an open network such as the Internet. Private network access provides a direct connection between a customer's access device, such as touch-tone telephone or PC, and the financial institution. The Internet, however, is an open network. The Internet was originally designed to prevent a foreign enemy from being able to knock out U.S. computer networks by creating an extensive web of telecommunications routes and connections over which information may be routed. It was created to facilitate the free flow of information between numerous PCs and mainframes. Therefore, information flowing over the Internet is accessible to everyone connected to it.

Which kind of delivery system do financial institutions need? It depends on the financial institution, the sensitivity of the information being delivered, and the security (or perception of security) being implemented. For example, if a wire transfer instruction is sent to the bank via a private network, that instruction travels directly through a connection from the customer's access device to the bank, without travelling through any other system. If, however, the wire transfer instruction is routed through the Internet, the connection to the financial institution is not direct. The instruction can and is routed through several different PC servers on its way to the bank.

Today, the Internet's ability to provide secure information sessions has greatly improved. In fact, there is very little evidence to suggest that a transaction performed during a secure session over the Internet is substantially less secure than a transaction performed over a private network. But the perception of a lack of security still exists, and customers who are not accustomed to the Internet may still prefer private networks. This perception is changing rapidly.

Realize that the bank already has multiple delivery systems in place. Branches are delivery systems where customers come in, buy products, and execute transactions. The ATM is another delivery system. Many banks now participate in credit and debit card programs that provide yet another delivery system. Rather than treating each individual access channel or delivery system as a separate product, these channels and systems should be evaluated together to determine how successful they are in luring and retaining profitable customers.

If a customer desires to use online systems, then that customer will gravitate to the type of financial institution that provides such systems.

The issue then is not whether a particular product is profitable, but whether the institution is meeting its most profitable customers' needs. What happens when those needs are not met? Generally, if one institution does not meet a customer's need, there is another institution ready, able, and willing to do so.

ONLINE VS. OFFLINE ACCESS AND DATA CENTER VS. IN-HOUSE PROCESSING.

As you investigate various electronic banking services, you must address whether a new service should be online with your current host system. Your host system, whether an in-house system or one processed by a third-party service bureau, houses most of the information your customers want and need. Many customer requests are processed on that host system. Smaller financial institutions who are not online post their transactions at the end of the day in a batch mode, and information is then made available the following day. This can lead to "untimely" information for the customer. It is important for banks to clearly disclose any aspects of their technology that affect its customers. Customers must be aware of any time lapses between when requests are submitted and when they are performed on the host system. Depending on the access device, a disclosure to this effect may be played or displayed automatically to prevent any confusion.

Other issues also arise with offline services. For systems that are solely dependent on online information, the customer's offline request cannot be fielded, and the financial institution must communicate, in an appropriate way, that the information is not currently available. Also, if a financial institution offers online services, there must be a mechanism for information delivery at times when the host system is not available. This can be achieved by downloading information from the host system and populating a database at the electronic delivery channel level. This database may be updated on a regular basis so that information is available to the customer at all times, even when the host isn't available.

SHOULD A BANK HOST ITS OWN SYSTEM?

Security concerns, one of the biggest reasons banks do not host their own systems, are slowly diminishing as security devices called routers and fire walls make the Internet a safer place to conduct business.

Additional security issues arise when a bank installs its own access to the Internet. For this reason, and the increased expense of maintaining and securing such access, many financial institutions have found it prudent to have third parties provide the Internet access.

Should financial institutions then choose an in-house or hosted processing option? It really depends on whether they have the interest and expertise required to provide Internet access themselves. In many cases, the decision is based on which type of Internet access the institution wants to provide its in-house staff, and other activities in which the financial institution may be engaged.

PLANNING AND IMPLEMENTATION CONSIDERATIONS

Another important consideration when implementing an electronic banking system is the attitude of senior management. It is important that the decision makers be literate when it comes to electronic commerce. Often, the Internet and the speed at which electronic commerce is progressing may go unnoticed by senior management.

The Anti-Mirage

Why does it go unnoticed? You might call this the "anti-mirage" effect. A mirage is something that you can clearly see but that is not real. As you get closer and closer to it, it disappears. An anti-mirage is something that you don't see or can't see but that is very real. It's there, but it's invisible.

The electronic community is an "anti-mirage." A bank executive might see traditional development, construction projects, and a growing commerce base. Because these are visible, the executive can assimilate the information and assess whether each may be an area worthy of a branch or other access device. The same philosophy should be applied to electronic commerce.

Senior management must be challenged to go out and explore these systems and virtual communities for themselves. Every financial institution should have at least one PC connected to the Internet, and this PC should be made accessible to all employees, if for nothing more than to conduct research and foster awareness. At a minimum, both management and staff should have the opportunity to experience the information and communities of interest and commerce that now exist on the Internet.

Once senior management understands — once they have realized that the Internet is something real and vital to the bank's future growth — the financial institution — from top to bottom — will ultimately embrace the idea.

THE IMPLEMENTATION TEAM

Once the financial institution has decided to pursue electronic commerce options, the next step will be to involve individuals from the various sectors of the financial institution. These individuals will form the implementation team.

This team should address all areas of the bank, concentrating on the operations area where the actual computer systems will be implemented. A member of the senior management team, a member of the client services team (such as a customer service representative), and most importantly, a member of the marketing department should be involved. Good communication must be established so that as the project moves forward all of these individuals move in sync. At the time the product or service is ready to be rolled out, a well-organized team will ensure that the implementation is smooth.

Choosing a Good Technology Partner

One of the keys to entering e-commerce successfully is selecting a good technology partner. It is a given that most financial institutions cannot, and should not, implement these systems on their own. Even in the area of the Internet, where it is presumedly simple to create a Web site, it is prudent to have professional assistance.

The technology partner should be rooted in the knowledge of electronic access. The institution would do well to find a technology partner that can provide multiple pieces of the puzzle, even if it is not going to implement everything at once. In the future, when the financial institution wants to incorporate additional pieces of the technology pie, it will want to go back to the same vendor and have a continuity relative to the implementation and performance of the system.

The bank needs a technology partner that is going to provide multiple device access. It should use a vendor that can, for example, process both business and retail customers through the touch-tone telephone, through direct PC access, and through the Internet. All of these access channels may not be needed initially. A good first step is touch-tone telephone access and direct PC access for performing basic banking functions. The institution should ensure that the vendor also has an Internet product available so that when the institution is ready to implement Internet access, it can get it from the same vendor. That vendor should be able to provide a sound technology plan that gives the financial institution a blueprint for long-term implementation.

Education and Training

One thing that cannot be overemphasized in rolling out any type of electronic banking initiative is the education and training necessary for both staff and customers. Staff education is something most banks have on their "to do" list, but often never get to it even though it is invaluable.

Consider the analogy of the farmer. One of the greatest assets the farmer has is the farm equipment he utilizes. If the farmer leaves his equipment sitting in the field and never performs even the most rudimentary maintenance, his equipment will certainly deteriorate. To safeguard his investment, the farmer must ensure his equipment is regularly maintained and in prime condition to harvest his crops. It isn't any different for a bank and its employees. Employees are the bank's most important assets. Training employees is the basic maintenance that ensures the bank will advance technologically and operationally.

What are the best ways to train? First, every employee should have a PC on which they may install and use the bank's software products and access the Internet. Many employees do not have access to this type of technology at home. One way to change this is for the bank to subsidize and/or facilitate its employees' purchase of home PCs. Providing employees with ready and regular access to a PC can dramatically impact their technical literacy and ability to understand and sell PC-based services. It also says a lot about the commitment of the financial institution to its employees.

The bottom line is that if a bank employee feels comfortable and competent speaking about electronic banking with your customers, your customers will feel more comfortable and excited about accessing your institution electronically. If someone comes to your bank and asks an employee about a new Web site, think of the positive impact on the customer when that employee can answer the question immediately without referring the customer to another employee. A confident response is a confidence builder. Employees who stumble when answering customer questions plant a seed of doubt about the institution's ability to deliver quality products and services.

In many cases, customers are willing to participate in electronic banking initiatives but aren't, themselves, up to speed on electronic commerce. Some studies suggest that as few as 7% of any given bank's customers are technophiles, or people who are technologically advanced. However, if the 25% of the customers who provide your institution's profit base are generally open to new and better ways of banking, a little bit of technical education may go a long way.

A GREAT TRAINING TOOL

Put an Internet-connected PC in your lobby and make it available to customers. By doing this you are "training" your customers to feel comfortable with computers and, more importantly, to associate computers and electronic access with your financial institution. Giving your customers a PC to 'experiment' on will make them more comfortable with and interested in the electronic services you offer.

Another opportunity is customer training sessions. The best times for such sessions are immediately after working hours. At these sessions, you can address viable issues in a comfortable, nonthreatening environment. Invite some select customers to speak specifically about their experience with the product or service. Include bank employees who can answer questions. In addition to providing information about electronic banking, you can also use this opportunity to discuss other kinds of issues that may be very valuable to you and your customers from an investment or regulatory standpoint.

You can provide education and training for both your employees and your customers through a local college, university, or tech school. These sessions are extremely valuable and demonstrate to both your employees and your customers that your financial institution is interested in education and is willing to make the extra effort to help.

MARKETING

A financial institution can decide to purchase the equipment, secure a great vendor, and train employees; but without marketing it's "all dressed up with no place to go." Regardless of how good the product is, people won't use it if they don't know about it.

One of the biggest problems with financial institutions today is a lack of enthusiasm for the products and services they roll out. Most products and services today are very generic and difficult to differentiate from the products and services of other financial institutions.

Proper marketing then begins with the attitudes and enthusiasm of your institution's personnel. Internal staff "buy-in" is a crucial and necessary step before a media plan is developed, brochures are printed, and the product or service is rolled out.

When the staff feel good about a product or service, it sends a clear signal to the customer. It says "we're confident you are being served well at this bank." Most financial institutions' lobbies are not customer friendly. They often feel like a library, a place where people feel inhibited from speaking up, much less free to ask questions. Financial institutions cannot afford to create such environments for their customers, particularly when rolling out an electronic banking initiative. The concept is too new, the questions too many. The lobby should be abuzz with activity, excitement, and vigorous Q&A.

If the institution's attitude about electronic banking is "Well, we have to do this because everyone else is," or "We don't really think it's a good idea, but we have to do it," this attitude will permeate every employee's attitude and effectively disable any marketing effort. Internal enthusiasm for any new product or service is essential for its success.

From a traditional marketing standpoint, the institution should evaluate all media opportunities, possibly with the aid of a professional marketing organization if the bank does not have an experienced in-house marketing team. Brochures, signage, advertising, and public relations activities are as important to launching an electronic banking initiative as to launching any other product or service. The difference with marketing electronic banking is that you reach the type of individual who would seek this type of product.

It is crucial that the financial institution market the product through its Web site. One of the most effective marketing tools is an individual's ability to download a product directly from a Web site. While this does create some security concerns, which can be overcome, it constitutes a marketing coupe. Partnering with other area organizations in joint marketing programs is another way to market a new service, especially if the partner has ties to your target market, such as a local Internet Service Provider (ISP). A financial institution and an ISP can join forces so that the ISP offers a low introductory rate for people who are not Internet-ready but who want to be if the price is low enough.

There may also be opportunities with local computer stores who may agree to pre-load the financial institution's software onto PCs before delivering them to customers. This is a common practice with larger companies such as Microsoft. Today's computer comes equipped with a myriad software options. Adding your product to the mix, and marketing the concept on a local basis, can prove very effective. Many of these relationships may be simple to establish if these vendors are already customers of your financial institution. It certainly makes sense to take advantage of any local relationships you already have.

BEYOND THE INITIAL PUSH

Perseverance is key to marketing any electronic banking product or service. No matter how much enthusiasm is mustered initially, no matter how well the bank trains, no matter how engaging the marketing material, if an institution stops the push after the initial roll-out, the product or service will not succeed in the long run.

The marketing plan must be part of the bank's broader long-term strategic plan, not something that is seen as a novelty product that might succeed or fail on its own. There has to be an ongoing marketing program, combined with ongoing education and training. The financial institution will be releasing upgrades of its electronic service offerings, so it must persistently communicate the evolution and improvement of its products and services.

An ongoing marketing program is particularly important for reaching people who are not psychologically and/or technologically ready at the first roll-out. In 1, 2, or even 6 months after the initial push, another cycle of advertising and marketing should take place that will move to action the person who is then ready to purchase the service.

Again, the key is enthusiasm for the program. Enthusiasm cannot be taught, but it can be caught. Senior management's enthusiasm should infect the rank and file. The vendor or vendors that you work with can often be very helpful in this regard.

Communicate that electronic banking is not a passing fad. This whole issue of electronic access to a financial institution is the future, and it is moving faster than we ever imagined. Just 2 years ago, who would have thought we would be conducting the level of e-commerce we are today.

Electronic banking is the future. It does not matter where your financial institution is physically located. Sooner or later, you will have to reckon with electronic banking. In fact, electronic banking makes geography and location even less an issue. Your electronic location will soon become as important, if not more important, than your physical location. Your electronic location is your institution's on-ramp to the information highway, the world of electronic commerce.

Section III

Appendix

No handbook is complete without a list of products and services. This list represents the product sets and services of the many companies who contributed to this book. It makes a handy reference list for products that will be of interest to you.

Products covered include:

Appendix
Selected Product Briefs

ASSET ALLOCATION

Company Name: Portfolio Management Consultants, Inc.
Address: 555 17th Street, 14th Floor, Denver, CO 80202
Phone: 303-292-1177
800-852-1177
Fax: 303-292-0330
Web Site: http://www.pmcdenver.com
Sales Contact Name: Raquel Hinman, Scott Wilkinson

■ Product: Allocation Manager®

Version Number: 4.0

Description Summary. Allocation Manager creates an effective bridge between your customers and their asset allocation, mutual fund selection, ongoing management, and reporting needs. Working from a graphic user interface, Allocation Manager assists the sales representative in taking the customer through an extensive, yet efficient, electronic profiling questionnaire. Based on the customer's specific investment goals, the program assigns a risk profile ranking. A "what if" function allows for a variety of potential scenarios and investment strategy options to be explored. Once the customer profile and investment objectives are finalized, Allocation Manager provides a preliminary asset allocation recommendation, with mutual funds appropriately allocated. A customized proposal can be printed for client presentation and consideration.

Product Feature List

- Built-in help
- Educational tutorials
- In-depth customer profile

0-8493-9991-2/99/$0.00+$.50

- Asset allocation and portfolio modeling
- Fund selection
- Contract preparation and printing
- Investment policy preparation and printing
- Performance reporting

Pricing. Free

Hardware Requirements. IBM-compatible PC with 486 chip or better; 8 MB RAM; 50 MB disk space; Microsoft Windows NT workstation or Microsoft Windows 95 or greater.

Software Requirements. N/A

ATMs AND KIOSKS

Company Name: KAL
Address: John Cotton Building, Sunnyside, Edinburgh, EH7 5RA, United Kingdom
Phone: +44 (0) 131-659-4900
Fax: +44 (0) 131-652-1193
E-Mail: info@kal.com
Web Site: www.kal.com
Sales Contact Name: Philip Basham

■ Product: Kalypso

Description Summary. Kalypso brings Web-enabled applications to self-service devices such as kiosks and ATMs (Automated Teller Machines). It is compliant with Microsoft's DNA FS framework and uses industry standard ActiveX components. It allows applications to run under Windows NT within a browser, such as Microsoft's Internet Explorer, thereby delivering the user-friendly benefits of multimedia browser technology to self service. Kalypso allows hardware-independent kiosk/ATM applications to be written using an open WOSA XFS approach and with web tools, like Front Page, and languages such as C++, Visual Basic, and Java.

Product Feature List. Compliant with WOSA XFS, DNA FS

Pricing. On application

Hardware Requirements. Hardware independent

Software Requirements. Windows NT

BANK MARKETING

Company Name: Medici Technology, Inc.

Address: P.O. Box 8, Hanover, NH 03755
Phone: 603-643-9575
800-479-0495
Fax: 603-298-8560
E-Mail: Info@medici.com
Web Site: www.medici.com
Sales Contact Name: Harry "Brud" Deas

■ Product: Medici Mosaic

Description Summary. Medici Mosaic is an easy-to-use action-oriented strategic marketing product designed for use by the CEO or Marketing Manager of a small bank. Medici processes account records for a bank and creates a customized CD/ROM containing software, processed bank records, household and commercial prospects, digital map files, and help and tutorial facilities. The CD/ROM contains everything the bank needs to take strategic marketing action; no additional purchases are required. Medici Mosaic is organized to look like a Handbook of Strategic Marketing tailored for the bank. Chapters cover subjects including customer retention, prospecting, site analysis, and competitive analysis. Users can buy household and commercial prospects directly off the CD/ROM through a metering system with no delays for order fulfillment. Medici also offers training and consulting service for implementing strategic marketing initiatives.

Pricing. $10,000 to $20,000 depending on size of bank.

Hardware Requirements. Windows 95 or NT

BANKING SYSTEMS

Company Name: Ionic Systems International Limited
Address: P.O. Box 246, Kelly Street, Rhinecliff, NY 12574
Phone: 914-976-3007
Fax: 914-976-7479
E-Mail:bernardlunn@hotmail.com
Web Site: www.ionicbankware.com
Sales Contact Name: Bernard Lunn

■ Product: The Banking Engine

Version Number: 1.1

Description Summary. The Banking Engine is a multicurrency, multibranch core banking system that supports Retail and Trade Finance operations. The Banking Engine uses a three-tier messaging architecture with a thin client Presentation Layer running on Windows 95, an Application Layer running on NT or UNIX, and a Database Layer that can use SQL Server,

Oracle, Sybase or DB2. The layered, messaging architecture is particularly suited to the integration of multiple delivery channels such as Internet, ATM, voice response, and SWIFT.

Product Feature List. Core Financial Accounting, MIS, Retail Banking, Trade Finance.

Pricing. Price on application

Company Name: Wilco Systems Inc.
Address: 17 State Street, New York, NY 10004
Phone: 212-269-3970
Fax: 212-269-3925
E-Mail: info@wilco-int.com
Web Site: www.wilco-int.com
Sales Contact Name: Bob Santangelo

■ Product: STB2

Version Number: 2.40

Description Summary. An integrated, real-time front- and back-office order processing and information system for private banking that can operate for multiple currencies, sites, and languages. STB2 covers cash and securities operations, customer valuations and performance calculations, and general and analytical accounting. It also serves as a data repository for MIS and regulatory reporting.

Pricing. Not disclosed

BUSINESS INTELLIGENCE

Company Name: Kapstone Systems, Inc.
Address: 9201 State Line Road, Kansas City, MO 64114
Phone: 816-760-5000
888-KAPSTONE (888-527-7866)
Fax: 816-760-5060
E-Mail: marketing@kapstone.com
Web Site: http://www.kapstone.com
Sales Contact Name: Dennis Lynch, Director of Sales

■ Product: Thazar™ Business Intelligence Suite

Version Number: n/a

Description Summary. Kapstone Systems, Inc. provides Thazar™, a comprehensive business intelligence suite designed exclusively for the insurance industry. A combination of software and analytical services, Thazar™ includes a robust Insurance Warehouse™, subject-specific datamarts, comprehensive metadata, and a full spectrum of decision support products. Thazar™ provides the insurance industry with the data analysis capacity to monitor overall business performance, develop pricing strategies, locate profitable business segments, reduce claim reserves, improve customer retention, and the facility to see the business in a perspective previously not available.

Product Feature List

- Thazar™ was developed solely for the insurance industry; therefore, Kapstone consultants can discuss and analyze business strategies specific to the competitive pressures in the insurance environment.
- Thazar™ includes an insurance-specific, enterprise-wide data model and templates, reducing the time and cost of bringing a robust business intelligence system online.
- Thazar™ offers an insurance-specific metadata catalog ensuring the data are consistent across the entire organization.
- Thazar™ is completely customizable and works with major policy issuance, administration, claim, and billing systems, as well as in-house developed systems.
- Thazar™ includes datamarts which are tuned to support the decision-making needs of specific business functions. Current datamarts include sales/marketing, claims, experience, and actuarial.
- Thazar's decision support tools allows the end-user to track, monitor, and analyze insurance data from a simplified to a complex analysis level.

Pricing. Tier-based

Hardware Requirements. Intel 486 class or above, Windows 95, Windows NT, memory as required by operating system

Software Requirements.

- IBM RS6000 or compatible
- IBM AS/400
- Microsoft NT Server
- DB2/6000 DBMS
- DB2/400
- Microsoft SQL Server

Company Name: Rule Machines Corporation
Address: 134 Fifth Avenue, Suite 205, Indialantic, FL 32903
Phone: 407-984-4402
Fax: 407-984-3774
E-Mail: Info@RuleMachines.com
Web Site: www.RuleMachines.com
Sales Contact Name: Robert Zimmer

■ Product: Visual Rule Studio

Version Number: 2.0

Description Summary. Visual Rule Studio enables you to efficiently develop Business Rule applications that are truly robust and sophisticated. Visual Rule Studio leverages the capabilities of the two leaders in separate industries by uniting the powerful Inference Engines of Rule Machines Corporation with the proven Rapid Application Development capabilities of Microsoft Visual Basic 5.0. Visual Rule Studio provides the powerful inferencing strategies needed to solve today's complex business issues. The Visual Rule Studio Inference Engines and Production Rule Language (PRL) are internationally recognized as the best in the industry. PRL is devoted to pure Rules, Demons, and knowledge. This purity combined with its clear, English-like syntax enables almost anyone to learn PRL quickly and easily. This proven technology was first developed in 1984. Today, every industrialized country in the world, 91 of the Fortune 100 corporations, and all major U.S. government agencies use Visual Rule Studio technology.

Product Feature List

- Backward Chaining
- Forward Chaining
- Hybrid Chaining
- Fuzzy Logic Reasoning
- Business Rule Isolation
- Business Rule Abstraction
- Business Rule Integration
- Production Rule Language
- COM Interoperability
- Native Visual Basic Installation

Pricing. $995 to $6995

Hardware Requirements.

Computer/Processor: PC with a 486DX/66 or higher (Pentium or higher recommended).

Memory: 12 MB RAM for Windows 95 or NT 4.0 (recommended: 16 MB or more for 95, 32 MB or more for NT).
Hard Disk: 10 MB.
Drive: CD-ROM.
Display: VGA or higher.
Peripherals: Microsoft Mouse or compatible.

Software Requirements

Operating System. Windows 95 or higher, Windows NT 4.0 or higher (Service Pack 2 recommended with NT 4.0) (Intel).

Software. Visual Basic 5.0 Professional or Enterprise (Service Pack 2 recommended).

CALL MONITORING

Company Name: NICE Systems
Address: 180 6651 Fraserwood Place, Richmond, BC, V6W 1J3 Canada
Phone: 604-207-0600
800-663-5601
Fax: 604-207-0607
E-Mail: na_sales@nice.com
Web Site: www.nice.com
Sales Contact Name: Inside Sales

■ Product: NiceLog

Version Number: 7.5

Description Summary. NiceLog is the most advanced and scalable CTI voice logging system on the market, providing continuous, high-quality digital recording and archiving of telephone conversations. Designed with an open system architecture, NiceLog fully integrates with leading ACD, Turret systems, PBX, and CTI components, and can be controlled, accessed, and maintained locally via LAN, or remotely via WAN/modem.

Product Feature List

- Up to 192 recording channels per unit
- ACA,NICE's proprietary Advanced Compression Algorithm, enabling up to 8760 channel hours of recordings online
- DDS-3 6 DAT tape stores up to 21,000 hours of audio; ability to record both analog and digital inputs in a single NiceLog
- Supports up to 20 output channels
- DAT Library for locating archived calls, with multi-Site DAT Library support (centralized DAT library for multisite logging system)

- Optional disk/DAT mirroring; optional hot standby.

■ Product: NiceCLS

Version Number: 4.2

Description Summary. NiceCLS stores all incoming and outgoing call information in a comprehensive database. NiceCLS enables users to conveniently locate, access (and playback), voice recordings based on call details, such as the date, time, and duration of the call, extension number, calling or called number, agent/dealer ID, transaction ID, customer ID, and business data.

Product Feature List

- Easy-to-use GUI
- SQL,ODBC — compliant, multi-user client-server
- LAN: Ethernet, Token Ring
- Protocols: TCP/IP, Novell IPX
- Remote access via modem
- Remote diagnostics
- Access/security control.

■ Product: NiceUniverse

Version Number: 3.1

Description Summary. NiceUniverse is a comprehensive quality measurement solution that automates call center agent monitoring and screen capture. The system provides objective evaluation tools and helps identify training requirements for call center agents. NiceUniverse uses a switch-independent CTI interface that integrates with leading ACDs and PC networks.

Product Feature List

- Flexible scheduling
- Synchronized voice and screen capture and playback
- Acceleration/deceleration of playback
- Quiet period indication
- Annotations
- Custom surveys
- Folder-based searching capabilities (ANI, DNIS)
- Custom report generator
- Security (seven levels)
- Automatic database management
- Import/export data
- Conversion of voice files to .WAV files

CASH MANAGEMENT

Company Name: ARKSYS
Address:17500 Chenal Parkway, Little Rock, AR 72211-9138
Phone: 501-218-7226
Fax: 501-218-7302
E-Mail: mail@arksys.com
Web Site: www.arksys.com
Sales Contact Name: Scott Zust

■ Product: Commercial-ACCESS and Personal-ACCESS

Version Number: 1

Description Summary. Commercial-ACCESS, a cash management system, designed for the Internet, but ready for use as a secure proprietary online system. Commercial-ACCESS can be used as an Intranet product, allowing you full control over all of your cash management requirements. Personal-ACCESS is a PC-based home banking solution that enables financial insitutions to offer either a proprietary or private interface or a nonproprietary or network (Internet) interface. Personal-ACCESS provides financial institutions with the ability to author and brand its own system.

Pricing. Contact vendor

Hardware Requirements. IBM AS/400

Software Requirements. OS/400, Windows NT server

CHAT

Company Name: Acuity Corporation
Address: 11100 Metric Blvd, #725, Austin, TX 78758
Phone: 512-425-2200
888-242-8669
Fax: 512-719-8225
E-Mail: info@acuity.com
Web Site: http://www.acuity.com
Sales Contact Name: Mark Roycroft

■ Product: ichat ROOMS

Version Number: 4.0

Product Feature List

- Event moderation — advanced event moderation features simplify the management of large, live discussions that can involve thousands of simultaneous users.

- Numerous client options — Java, Netscape Plug-in, ActiveX control, and HTML client interfaces provide numerous options for Windows, Macintosh, and Unix users.
- Intuitive user interface — visitors enter a conversation simply by typing.
- Private messaging — support for public and private messages offers users one-to-one and one-to-many communications channels.
- Multimedia support — ROOMS is multimedia-ready, supporting sound, video and VRML.
- File transfer — a convenient client-to-client file transfer capability increases desktop productivity, allowing users to instantly share files.
- HTML embedding — messages may have embedded hyperlinks and HTML formatting. Important notices or comments can appear in bold text, or a URL can be conveniently displayed as a clickable link.
- Collaborative browsing — ichat ROOMS' support for collaborative site navigation enhances customer service and group interaction.
- Robust administration — administrators have easy access to detailed conversation and server status logs and configuration settings, which can be modified remotely via a simple HTML interface.
- API — C++ extensions (servlets) enable administrators to add new and unique features to ROOMS.
- Seamless product integration — with shared authentication functions, ROOMS functions as part of the ichat real-time enterprise architecture.

Pricing. Concurrent user pricing, starting at $595

Hardware Requirements. Depending on your system, approximately 32 MB of available memory and a minimum of 20 MB disk space is required.

Software Requirements. Available for Windows NT 4.0 and Solaris 2.5.1; works with Microsoft IIS and Netscape Enterprise Web Servers.

Product: ichat Message Boards

Version Number: 2.0

Description Summary. Message boards is a client-server software system that allows users to search for information and post questions and answers in a threaded, hierarchical format. Since Message Boards uses standard HTML and users access discussion forums right from their browsers, no additional client software is needed. Server setup and configuration is conducted through an HTML interface, enabling robust forum management and remote administration.

Product Feature List

- Browser based — employees or customers can instantly access online discussion groups from within their favorite Web browser. No additional software is required.
- Highly configurable interface — a configurable HTML interface allows site administrators to easily create unique, branded user experiences. iHTML, ichat's interactive extension to the HTML standard, allows developers to embed ichat Message Boards functionality within their Web site or intranet.
- NNTP client support — NNTP (Network News Transfer Protocol) client support allows network news users to connect and participate in discussion forums.
- Organized discussions — ichat Message Boards discussion groups are displayed hierarchically, allowing users to easily follow conversation "threads."
- Moderated topics — the moderation option allows administrators to effectively organize and lead discussions. Question and answer message areas can be regulated so that only approved responses are visible to regular users. Similarly, a moderated company information area can contain postings that are prescreened by site administrators.
- Versatile administration — message Boards permits administrators to delegate message management to topic owners and forum moderators. An HTML interface enables quick and easy remote administration, with new topics and moderated threads established with the click of a mouse. Content filtering can also be controlled at the topic group level.
- Text searching — message subject and topic key word search support enables ichat Message Boards to serve as a document and information archive. Frequently asked questions can be quickly sorted or all messages referring to a particular project name can easily be found.

Pricing. Message Boards starts at $2995 for 50 concurrent users

Hardware Requirements. Intel-based Windows NT 4.0 or Sun Solaris 2.5.1; 32 MB RAM and 20 MB disk space (minimums)

Software Requirements. Major web server (Netscape Enterprise Server or Microsoft IIS)

■ Product: ichat Paging System

Version Number: 1.1

Description Summary. The ichat Paging System™ delivers critical new real-time communications capabilities to the desktop. Users can instantly send high-priority messages or determine whether a colleague is online. With a clean, professional interface that displays messages on top of open windows, the Paging System enables individuals to exchange information with new levels of immediacy. When phone calls are routed to voice mail and e-mails are lost in heavy traffic, ichat Pager users benefit from real-time, impossible-to-miss desktop communication. Additionally, by adding contacts to their list of associates, users can see when others are available for instant messaging, invitations to Netscape Conferences and Microsoft NetMeetings, or Quick Chat™ text conferencing.

Product Feature List

Server Features.

- Global messaging — connected to the ichat Global Message Router, individuals and groups can send and receive messages from users of remote Paging Systems. Messages sent to off-line users are stored for later delivery.
- Scalability — add multiple Paging Servers to your Web site or intranet to support tens of thousands of simultaneous users.
- Notify your users — with the ichat Paging Server's flexible administrative tools you can easily communicate with your users by sending instant messages, URLs, or links to live audio streams. Tools are provided to send messages to multiple user categories including all online users, users in specific interest groups, or to individual users.
- Display advertising/informational banners — with an external ad server you can insert images into all user messages. Graphic image size is variable — you can include any sized image and the client application will size to accommodate it. Using an intelligent background file caching scheme, client response is not slowed by the addition of banner graphics to instant messages.
- Customizable interface — administrators can customize the Pager client interface to contain customer logos, links to web sites, links to ROOMS chat or Message Board discussions, or lists of other users.
- Server logging and monitoring — monitoring server events, system messages, and server up-time through the HTML interface is straightforward. You can also track user activity, server load and usage, and message delivery systems.

Administrative Controls. The ichat Paging System is easily administered via an HTML interface. Administrative functions include:

- System Security: encrypted passwords, IP restrictions.
- Text filtering: eliminate specified text or regular expression matches from message content.
- User management.

- Client configuration tools.
- Message gateway application.
- Client features.
- Instant messaging — send and receive instant messages from other users.
- Quick Chat™ — easily initiate a real-time chat session with one or more users.
- Privacy — optionally hide your user profile information, receive pages only from certain users, or ignore individual users.
- User status information — indicates when other users are online, idle, or away from their computer.
- Interest categories — sign up for server-defined interest categories to easily find users.

Pricing. The Paging System starts at $1595 for 100 concurrent users

Hardware Requirements. Intel-based Windows NT 4.0 or Sun Solaris 2.5.1; 48 MB RAM and 64 MB disk space (minimums).

CONSULTING

Company Name: Computer Science Innovations (CSI), Inc.
Address: 1235 Evans Road, Melbourne, FL 32904-2314
Phone: 407-676-2923
888-823-2923
Fax: 407-676-2355
E-Mail: poolplus@csihq.com
Web Site: http://www.csihq.com/lookout
Sales Contact Name: Rudy Hallenbeck (extension 218), vice-president, Sales and Marketing

■ Product: Software Engineering Services (Object-Oriented, Web-Based, or Analytical System Development)

Description Summary. CSI has developed numerous application systems that encapsulate the decision-making process of an expert. These systems often rely on a central information repository. CSI has recently developed custom application systems that make the central repository and the decision process available on a network via browser technology, thus both preserving expertise and enhancing the capabilities of junior personnel. CSI engineers are experienced with a variety of architectures, and utilize a broad range of development platforms, languages, and tools to meet the needs of its customer base, including Oracle, Informix, Sybase, and SQL Server. CSI employs its Cognitive Engineering Methodology (CEM) in developing various types of systems including decision support, pattern recognition, simulation, and predictive applications.

Company Name: IMIS Inc.
Address: 712 Sansome Street, Second Floor, San Francisco, CA 94111
Phone: 415-543-2939
Fax: 415-391-4985
E-Mail: imis@imisinc.com
Web Site: www.imisinc.com
Sales Contact Name: James Balbo

Description Summary. IMIS Inc. is a financial services consulting company specializing in the implementation of technology in the securities industry. We offer consulting services on a time and materials basis and provide trust companies, brokerage firms, banks, mutual fund companies, and insurance firms a cost-effective alternative to traditional "Big 6" consulting. Our 100 consultants average more than 13 years of securities industry experience and currently manage technology projects across the country and internationally for more than 40 financial services companies. Unlike "body shops" who merely process resumes, all IMIS employees are fully salaried and are provided significant benefits and incentive packages which enables us to attract and retain the industry's very best professionals. Our RFPDB software application was recently unveiled at the ABA's NFSOC trade conference in March of 1998 and provides IMIS the opportunity to compete effectively against the larger consulting firms in the system search market. Our proprietary database application, RFPDB, comes preloaded with business requirements for each business segment (brokerage, trust, investment management, etc.) and serves to automate electronically the entire Request for Proposal process, from requirements gathering and weighting to vendor response compilation and comparison. By pairing our software application with an IMIS industry expert and project manager, IMIS can compete head-to-head against the much larger consulting firms with a superior product offering and lower prices.

Company Name: Output Technologies
Address: 322 Eighth Ave., Ninth Floor, New York 10001
Phone: 212-243-2570
Fax: 212-243-6907
E-Mail: info@output.net
Web Site: www.output.net
Sales Contact Name: Kathi Naughton

■ **Product: Business Communication Solutions**

Version Number: Solutions are customized to each client/business

Description Summary. Output Technologies is uniquely suited to help insurance organizations "mass customize" communications that are personalized to individual customers and customized to groups. Through value-added communications, Output Technologies helps organizations achieve: increased customer loyalty, improved communication comprehension, increased revenue generation, improved cash flow, improved customer care, and an increased competitive advantage. Output Technologies' system focuses on leveraging two major resources: information and design. Output Technologies refers to its sophisticated and innovative ability to marry communication "form and function." As digital technologies continue to advance, businesses need highly specialized and refined methods to deliver communications; in some instances, they need to employ multiple means to connect with their customer. Today, Output Technologies' primary distribution options include: electronic printing and mailing, telemarketing and fulfillment, lithography, CD-ROM, computer output microfilm (COM) and the Internet. To help ensure the integrity of business communications, Output Technologies employs the highest quality control and quality assurance methodology to communication generation, production and distribution.

Company Name: Sealund & Associates Corporation
Address: 3001 Executive Dr., Suite 200, Clearwater, FL 33762
Phone: 813-572-1800
800-434-8000
Fax: 813-572-9993
E-Mail: info@sealund.com
Web Site: www.sealund.com

Description Summary. Sealund & Associates Corporation provides full-service custom training solutions for Fortune 500 and 1000 companies such as Chase Manhattan, Lehman, Citibank, IBM, and AT&T. S&A is the country's leading training development company utilizing multimedia and Web-based technologies. S&A is currently developing several online banking training applications for large international banks. These applications function using the latest Internet-based technologies such as Java, Javascripts, and Quick Time. S&A has produced award-winning multimedia titles such as *Basic Enforcement Academy Training (BEAT)*. Created in conjunction with the St. Petersburg Junior College and the Florida Department of Law Enforcement, this project won the Technology Research Award by the Tampa Bay Regional Planning Council. As well, this project is featured in *The Ultimate Multimedia Handbook* (Revised, McGraw-Hill 1997). Sealund & Associates has also received an award from IBM for the delivery of "The Americans with Disabilities Act Compliance Training" using OS/2 and CD-ROM. During the mid-1980s, the company began designing and building computer-based training (CBT) for mainframe systems such as Hogan, M+I, and IBA. Working with national companies such as Michigan National Bank and CNA, S&A developed comprehensive training design and development methodologies that are now used in corporations around the world. Sealund & Associates professionals are top instructional designers, software and system engineers, multimedia specialist, and graphic artists. Founded in 1985 by Barbara Sealund, the company recognizes the need for corporations to move toward more technologically based training solutions to better serve their employees and customers worldwide.

Services Offered.

Training

- System conversions
- Application Training
- Sales Training
- Online Help Systems

Multimedia

- Multimedia-Based Training
- Sales Presentations

Internet/Intranet

- Web-based Training
- Documentation Conversions
- Systems Training
- Site Development

Documentation

- User Guides
- Reference Manuals

CONTACT MANAGEMENT

Company: FDP Corp.
Address: 2140 South Dixie Highway, Miami, FL 33133
800 Number: 800-FDP-CORP
Fax: 305-854-6305
E-Mail: todds@fdpcorp.com
Web Site: www.fdpcorp.com
Sales Contact Name: Todd Sears

■ Product: Contact Partner™

Version Number: 2.5

Description Summary. Full-featured client and contact management system designed to help agents increase sales, streamline client service operations, and maximize office efficiency. Functions as an integrated marketing/ management tool to completely automate the tasks of prospecting, lead follow-up, new application tracking through underwriting, and in-force policy servicing.

Product Features List.

Client Service/Information Management

- Individual Information
- Business Information
- Employee Census Data
- Complete Policy Information
- Basic Investment Information
- Advisor Information
- New Business Tracking
- Underwriting Requirement Tracking
- Client/Policy Service Tracking
- Birthday/Anniversary Date Tracking
- Integrated Notepad
- Mass Modify and Delete
- Custom Screen Creation
- Data Import/Export
- Date Compliance with the Year 2000
- Sales Illustration Storage

Sales and Marketing

- Sales Tracking Module
- Call-backs and Follow-ups
- Appointments
- Agent Production Tracking
- Groups and Filters Wizard
- List Views with saved Groups and Filters
- Reports using saved Groups and Filters

Activity/Time Management

- Complete Interactive Calendar
- Monthly/Weekly/Daily Views
- Appointment Scheduling and Tracking for Multiple Agents
- Call Scheduling and Tracking

- To-Do Lists
- Calendar Reports
- Executive Day Planner Report Formats
- Fax Template
- Auto Dialer

Basic Investment Tracking. Tracks the following types of investments:

- CD
- Mutual Fund
- Stock
- Variable Annuity
- GIC
- Limited Partnership
- Bond
- Segregated Fund
- Liability
- Tracks Owners and Beneficiaries
- Tracks Position History
- Investment Product Prices are tracked through Price History Table
- Security Price Update
- Fee Adjustments
- Reconciliation available for both Position and Transaction Amounts
- Stock Dividends and Splits
- Distribution Adjustments

Investment Reports

- Investment Portfolio Summaries including Variable Life and Annuity Packages
- Investment Performance Reports with IRR Calculations
- Daily Blotter Reports
- Bank Balance Sheets

Investment Transaction Downloads

- DST Fanmail

Office Automation and Management

- Report Generator with preformatted reports
- Link with MSWord
- Label and Envelope Printing
- Mass Mailings/Mailing Lists
- Production Reports
- Customizable Field Help

Pricing. Call for quote: available on a site license and individual basis

Hardware Requirements.

Processor: Pentium 150 MHz and above
RAM: 32 MB
Hard Disk Storage: 70 MB
Display Adapter: VGA (color monitor)
Mouse: Windows compatible
Operating System: Windows 3.1, Windows 95, or above, or Windows NT Workstation

DATA VISUALIZATION

Company Name: Computer Science Innovations, Inc.
Address: 1235 Evans Road, Melbourne, FL 32904-2314
Phone: 407-676-2923
800-289-2923
Fax: 407-676-2355
E-Mail: info@csihq.com
Web Site: http://www.csihq.com
Sales Contact Name: Rhonda Delmater (ext. 213), Program Manager

■ Product: Visualizer Workstation

Version Number: 1.1

Description Summary. CSI's Visualizer Workstation enables users to virtually "fly" around and even through their data, viewing it from various perspectives. Analysts can rapidly identify visual trends and correlations within their data, and then apply powerful statistical and knowledge engineering tools to refine their hypotheses. The N-Dimensional viewing capability aids analysts in discovering new insights about prospects, customers, patients, or other populations of interest. Users can view, manipulate, and analyze sets of discrete data points in up to ten-dimensions simultaneously. Nearness, occlusion, and perspective are preserved. Visualizer Workstation provides a user-friendly front-end for a combination of several CSI data mining software functions including Select, Autocluster, Statistics, and Knowledge-Based Trainer. Data are prepared for visualization through enhancement, by applying tools that find and emphasize information-bearing aspects. Data enhancement tools allow users to determine which data items are "most significant," can rank-order data items by predictive power (salience), and can apply transforms which concentrate information into the smallest number of features.

Product Feature List

- Data Preparation Tools: registration, normalization, and feature extraction.

- **SELECT** provides a menu interface to create a subset of the population for analysis.
- The **ACL** tool (Automatic Clusterer) performs unsupervised data clustering.
- **ND GRAPHICS**, the n-dimensional graphics engine, is used to depict feature vectors.
- **DKBT** (Descriptive Knowledge-Based Trainer) collects descriptive statistics about aggregations within a dataset and displays them in sentence form.
- **STATISTICS** shows histograms by feature by aggregate.
- **REPORTS** provide statistical information in tabular format.

Pricing. Starts at $495 per seat for an individual analyst license. Complementary Advisor tools are also available in configurations to meet the requirements of a large enterprise.

Hardware Requirements

200 MHz
64 MB ram
1 GB available disk space
1024 × 768 resolution,
1152 × 864 or higher recommended

Software Requirements. Microsoft Windows NT Workstation (includes Open GL)

DATA WAREHOUSE

Company: Inventure America
Address: 30 Broad Street, New York, NY 10004
Phone: 212-208-0604
Fax: 212-825-1040
E-Mail: jmcgann@inven.com
Web Site: http://www.inven.com; www.rangersoftware.com
Sales Contact Name: Jim McGann

■ Product: Ranger

Description Summary. RANGER is an innovative new solution for the Distributed Integration of data and analytics. Distributed Integration is a new way to integrate global financial data, analytics, and applications for rapid distribution to a large community of users. Unlike most traditional data warehousing solutions, Distributed Integration does not require that all data be co-located in a single corporate database. Instead, the Distributed Integration architecture relies on Internet technologies to create a virtual data warehouse that is optimized for scalability and cost-effective delivery of critical data to large user communities. For more information, contact the Inventure Web site at www.rangersoftware.com.

Company Name: i.d.Centric
Address: 100 Harborview Plaza, La Crosse, WI 54601-4071
Phone: 608-788-9577
800-551-9491
Fax: 608-788-1188
E-Mail: prodinfo@idcentric.com
Web Site: www.idcentric.com
Sales Contact: Product Information Department

■ Product: Address Correction and Encoding (ACE) Library

Version Number: 5.40

Description Summary. Address Correction and Encoding (ACE) Library is a data warehousing product that parses (identifies), corrects, and verifies street and city names, ZIP+4 Codes, delivery-point barcodes, and county codes. The software can parse completely unfielded address data and provide address correction and standardization at the street level. The callable 'C' library can be integrated into a customer's application. ACE is certified for accuracy.

Product Feature List

- Parses (identifies) individual address components
- Standardizes address information
- Corrects and enhances addresses using empirical data sources
- Verifies and corrects addresses online during data entry
- Ensures data integrity for data warehousing and database marketing applications
- Increases the value of addresses
- Callable C library product

Pricing. Call vendor for pricing information

■ Product: Match/Consolidation Library

Version Number: 5.04

Description Summary. Match/Consolidation Library is a data warehousing product that provides data matching and reporting capabilities. It significantly improves accuracy and performance in matching and consolidating customer data, and identifies customer relationships. The software also includes full business-to-business parsing and multi-pass processing. The callable 'C' library can be integrated into a customer's application.

Product Feature List

- Locates matches within and across databases
- Allows multiple sets of business rules
- Ensures data integrity for data warehousing and database marketing applications
- Ideal for online applications
- Callable C library product

Pricing. Call vendor for pricing information.

■ Product: TrueName Library

Version Number: 2.30

Description Summary. TrueName Library improves the integrity of name information in databases. The software identifies name, company name, and title components even when the information has been entered inconsistently. TrueName intelligently parses (identifies) all elements of name data and standardizes them for greater accuracy in matching records. It is an integratable tool that also locates and identifies business and financial data, such as Trustee, ITF, wros, etc. TrueName provides standard representations of individual and business elements to improve matching and provide a more complete base of customer knowledge.

Product Feature List

- Parses (identifies) name, business, and title information, and provides match standards (such as James for Jim)
- Creates name- and gender-appropriate greetings (precise genderization)
- Ensures data integrity for data warehousing and database marketing applications
- Ideal for online applications
- Callable C library product

Pricing. Call vendor for pricing information.

■ Product: Clear ID Library

Version Number: 1.10

Description Summary. Clear ID Library is the next generation in data quality tools to help companies better understand their individual customers by correcting, verifying, and enhancing their customer data. It is the only product of its kind that combines high-performance data quality processing with a data overlay from an industry-leading data provider. Clear ID Library provides advanced data correction and verification as well as extended data enhancement and move updating.

Product Feature List

- Appends customer demographics
- Verifies the accuracy of existing customer information
- Corrects and completes customer addresses, and adds phone numbers
- Updates the addresses and phone numbers of customers who have moved
- Helps identify relationships between customers
- Ensures data integrity for data warehousing and database marketing applications
- Callable C library product

Pricing. Call vendor for pricing information.

■ Product: i.d.Centric Fusion

Version Number: 1.00

Description Summary. Fusion intelligently consolidates the "best" elements from all available data sources to provide users with a complete customer view. It is the only product of its kind with the built-in logic to help users selectively choose fields and build a "best" consolidated record.

Product Feature List

- Supports priorities on a field-by-field basis
- Complete set of tie-breaker logic
- Builds a consolidated or "best" record
- Not restricted to just name and address information
- Ensures data integrity for data warehousing and database marketing applications
- Callable C library product

Pricing. Call vendor for pricing information.

■ Product: Torrent Operators

Version Number: ACE 5.40 Torrent Operator, TrueName 2.30 Torrent Operator, Match/Consolidation 5.04 Torrent Operator, Clear ID 1.10 Torrent Operator, i.d.Centric Fusion 1.00 Torrent Operator.

Description Summary. i.d.Centric customer data quality and matching products are available for Orchestrate — a parallel software environment from Torrent Systems. The Torrent Operators allow users with very large data sets to develop and deploy large-scale data quality applications for parallel computers without becoming experts in parallel programming.

Product Feature List

- Uses Torrent's framework
- Ease of implementation in the Orchestrate environment
- Takes advantage of parallel systems
- Deals with very large databases (10 million + records)
- Ensures data integrity in data warehousing applications

Pricing. Call vendor for pricing information.

Hardware Requirements. Any parallel system supported by Orchestrate (SMP & MPP)

Software Requirements. Requires Orchestrate from Torrent Systems

E-COMMERCE

Company Name: CyberCash, Inc.
Address: 2100 Reston Parkway, Suite 430, Reston, VA 22091
Phone: 703-620-4200
Fax: 703-620-4215
E-Mail: info@cybercash.com
Web Site: www.cybercash.com
Sales Contact Name: Richard K. Crone

■ Product: Electronic Cash Register for Internet Payments: Credit Card, Electronic Check, and Electronic Cash

Version Number: 3.0

Description Summary. CyberCash is introducing a new Internet payment architecture for our CashRegister that will make it easier to integrate store-fronts, operate payment services, and enjoy upgrades to new services, standards, and options as they become available. With the CR3 Series, we lower the technical and financial hurdles to secure Internet payments. The CyberCash CashRegister connects a storefront or Web site to the Cyber-Cash payment services, enabling businesses to accept secure, real-time payments at their Web site.

Product Feature List

- Secure credit card transactions (including both SSL and SET)

- CyberCoin service, for cash payments from $0.25 to $10
- PayNow electronic check service, for interactive billing applications

Hardware Requirements. All platforms.

Software Requirements. All platforms.

Company Name: GlobeSet
Address: 1250 Capital of Texas Hwy. So., Building One, Suite 300, Austin, TX 78746
Phone: 512-427-5100
Fax: 512-427-5101
E-Mail: info@globeset.com
Web Site: www.globeset.com
Sales Contact Name: Michael Prentice

Product: GlobeSet Payment System

Description Summary. Our GlobeSet Payment System™ includes:

- GlobeSet Wallet™, a cardholder application that stores a buyer's account information and communicates with merchants via the SET protocol
- GlobeSet POS™, a software point-of-sale device that connects the merchant to the buyer's electronic wallet and to the financial payment gateways
- GlobeSet Gateway™, a payment gateway application connecting the merchant to the payment processor's legacy systems for payment authorization
- GlobeSet CA™, a digital certificate application that generates and manages the digital identification certificates supporting SET-based, public-key encryption

Product Feature List. Products support SET transactions over the Internet.

Pricing. Sold through OEM channels.

Hardware Requirements. NT or Unix servers, PC.

Software Requirements. NT or Unix operating systems.

Company Name: Acuity Corporation
Address: 11100 Metric Blvd, #725, Austin, TX 78758

Phone: 512-425-2200
888-242-8669
Fax: 512-719-8225
E-Mail: info@acuity.com
Web Site: http://www.acuity.com
Sales Contact Name: Mark Roycroft

■ Product: WebCenter

Version Number: 2.0

Description Summary. Acuity WebCenter™ 2.0 is an enterprise-class, Web-centric solution for e-commerce and online support. Unlike single-purpose customer interaction tools, WebCenter integrates interactive self-service, automated e-mail response, Web-based question queuing and routing, and live interaction through multiple channels, including live text communications, browser screen synchronization, CTI callback, and voice/video conferencing. WebCenter's highly scalable communications capabilities enable major corporations to deploy Internet-based call centers, driving what Forrester Research estimates will be a 43% reduction in cost per contact vs. traditional call centers, and increasing e-commerce margins by 15 to 25%.

Product Feature List. WebCenter consists of three core components: the Web Response Unit, the WebACD, and the Communication Interface Unit. Features include:

Web Response Unit (WRU).

- Authentication Mechanism. The WRU includes an authentication mechanism that allows verified log-in of registered users; anonymous log-in with optional data collection; or verification through external authentication mechanisms such as SQL databases, LDAP directory servers, or third-party customer interaction packages.
- FAQ Database. The WRU maintains a database of frequently asked questions (FAQs) stored in a format that allows easy import/export and full-text searching of all data.
- User Response Function. All search returns (including natural language queries) allow customers to extend their search or get additional off-line help through e-mail, fax, or a telephone call.
- Integration With External Knowledge Bases. The WRU leverages the in-place data infrastructure by aggregating search results from multiple databases — presenting the customer with a user-friendly interface to obtain information from existing data repositories.
- WebLink™ Module. The WRU includes WebLink, a package of NSAPI and ISAPI interfaces to Netscape Enterprise Server and Microsoft In-

ternet Information Server, allowing easy integration with existing Internet infrastructures.

WebACD (Web Automated Call Distribution)

- Agent Queue Management. The WebACD maintains a queue of available agents, with real-time updates on activity.
- Active Task Queue Management. The active queue contains unresolved tasks. The queue reflects information such as waiting time, number in queue, and priority.
- Integration with Existing Systems. WebCenter can integrate existing customer care systems, ACD systems, and ticket tracking systems.
- E-mail Routing and Automated Response. WebCenter incorporates robust e-mail management capabilities, providing automatic responses to common questions and queuing of other e-mail messages for agent review.
- Real-Time and Historical Reports. Managers and supervisors can run detailed, up-to-the-minute reports on agents or groups.

Communications Interface Unit (CIU)

- Data Wake. To provide session context and aid in problem resolution, agents can view the customer's original question, all attempted knowledge base searches, and the URL of the button used to initiate the session.
- Screen Synchronization. With WebCenter's CIU, agents can push URLs directly to the customer's screen, including links to specific FAQ entries contained in the WRU FAQ database.
- Text Conferencing. Text conferencing offers easy-to-integrate and deploy real-time communications for customer/agent interaction. All interactions are logged, and can be maintained over secure (SSL) connections.
- CTI Callback. Computer Telephony Integration provides a mechanism for customer callback queuing in traditional ACD systems, allowing the customer to specify a telephone number and preferred time for a return call. This process integrates with the existing ACD or PBX system.
- H.323 to PBX Telephony Linkage. An H.323 to PBX gateway allows agents to establish voice conferences with a customer who is using an Internet phone (H.323-compatible) interface.

Core Features

- Standards-Based System. WebCenter embraces industry standards wherever relevant, including (but not limited to) RVP, X509v3, SSL, HTTP, HTTPS, and XML.
- Proven Technology Foundation. WebCenter leverages the ichat Real-Time Enterprise platform to provide a proven, stable Web-based infra-

structure that is currently deployed at over 1100 customer sites and has demonstrated real-world scalability of 20,000+ simultaneous users.
- API Interfaces. Components are accessible via API interfaces, allowing customization of system functionality and integration of third-party applications without modifications to the core applications.
- HTML-Based System Management. WebCenter is easily managed via an HTML-based interface. Agents, managers, and administrators have full control of the system from anywhere in the enterprise.
- Web Security. Secure Sockets Layer (SSL) security is provided for all WebCenter communications through the HTTPS protocol.

Pricing. Traffic-based model starting at $125,000.

Hardware Requirements. Varies by deployment.

Software Requirements. Intel Windows NT 4.0, Web server (Microsoft IIS or Netscape Enterprise server supported).

Company Name: ICentral, Inc.
Address: 225 N. University Ave., Provo, UT 84601
Phone: 801-373-4347
888-373-4347
Fax: 801-373-7211
E-Mail: info@icentral.com
Web Site: www.shopsite.com
Sales Contact Name: Jan Johnson, VP Marketing

Product: ShopSite Pro

Version Number: v3.3

Description Summary. ShopSite Pro is a secure, online store creation and management application designed to meet the needs of site developers and merchants who are seeking to build a professional, yet affordable storefront. In addition to its site creation and management tools and secure shopping basket, ShopSite Pro includes real-time credit card authorization, a site search engine and an Associates Tracking program.

Product Feature List

- Ported to several Unix OS and NT
- Client-side, any platform that supports a standard browser
- Foreign language support
- Unlimited simultaneous shoppers
- Online help

- Payment information encryption
- E-mail notification of orders
- Auto shipping and tax calculation
- First Virtual payment system
- Customizable order system
- Easily indexed by search engines
- Sales Stats
- Traffic Stats
- Page Creation/Site Management Tools
- Direct media upload
- Media library manager
- Database upload
- Order database download
- Credit card authorization
- Stats plus
- Associates tracking
- Site search
- Large database handling tools
- Interface to other applications
- SmartTags
- Discount calculation
- Automatic product upsell
- Global database editing

Pricing. $1295 (MSRP).

Hardware/Software Requirements. These system requirements are for the average functional store.

Operating Systems for Web Server

- OpenLinux, Linux, Free BSD, or BSDI on Intel
- Solaris on SPARC shipping; Solaris on Intel coming soon
- NT and IRIX coming soon
- 16 MB RAM
- 10 MB hard drive space (up to 25 MB may be required for install only)

Hardware Platforms Must Be Running. Stronghold, Netscape, or any NCSA-compatible, secure web server software PERL 5.003 or greater Sendmail.

Client-Side (Web Site Developer or Merchant). Requires Netscape browsers or Microsoft Internet Explorer, versions 3.0 or later, running on the user's system of choice (PC, Mac or UNIX).

Client-Side (Shopper). Browser of choice.

■ Product: ShopSite Manager

Version Number: v3.3

Description Summary. ShopSite Manager is for the small- to medium-sized business manager who wants to begin marketing and selling products on the Internet, or who currently has a Web site but wants to take the next step of selling products online. For Web site designers, it reduces the many tedious tasks involved in maintaining a Web site, allowing them to concentrate on pure design. It empowers merchants, allowing them to make day-to-day merchandising changes without impacting the site designer. For the do-it-yourself merchant, this person can use ShopSite Manager and build an entire site without knowing HTML.

Product Feature List

- Ported to several Unix OS and NT
- Client-side, any platform that supports a standard browser
- Foreign language support
- Unlimited simultaneous shoppers
- Online help
- Payment information encryption
- E-mail notification of orders
- Auto shipping and tax calculation
- First Virtual payment system
- Customizable order system
- Easily indexed by search engines
- Sales Stats
- Traffic Stats
- Page Creation/Site Management Tools
- Direct media upload
- Media library manager
- Database upload
- Order database download
- Credit card authorization

Pricing. $495 (MSRP).

Hardware/Software Requirements. These system requirements are for the average functional store.

Operating Systems for Web Server

- OpenLinux, Linux, Free BSD, or BSDI on Intel
- Solaris on SPARC shipping; Solaris on Intel coming soon
- NT and IRIX coming soon
- 16 MB RAM

- 10 MB hard drive space (up to 25 MB may be required for install only)

Hardware Platforms Must Be Running. Stronghold, Netscape, or any NCSA-compatible, secure web server software PERL 5.003 or greater Sendmail.

Client-Side (Web Site Developer or Merchant). Requires Netscape browsers or Microsoft Internet Explorer, versions 3.0 or later, running on the user's system of choice (PC, Mac or UNIX).

Client-Side (Shopper). Browser of choice.

■ Product: ShopSite Express

Version Number: v3.3

Description Summary. ShopSite Express is a shopping basket software application that allows a site developer to build a site using his or her HTML tool of choice, then quickly and easily add "order" and "checkout" buttons to the web site. Shoppers can click on these buttons and place an order in the secure shopping basket. ShopSite Express offers a simple point-and-click, fill-in-the-blanks interface. Enter product information (name, price, ordering options) into ShopSite Express through the browser interface. After configuring tax and shipping (so it will be calculated automatically for shoppers), click on the "Create Links" button and ShopSite will automatically generate "order" and "checkout" buttons for each product in the ShopSite database. These buttons can be drag-and-dropped onto the HTML editing window.

Product Feature List

- 25-Product limit (no real time credit card handling capabilities, but can capture and store credit card information securely in the order's database for manual processing later)
- Ported to several Unix OS and NT
- Client-side, any platform that supports a standard browser
- Foreign language support
- Unlimited simultaneous shoppers
- Online help
- Payment information encryption
- E-mail notification of orders
- Auto shipping and tax calculation
- First Virtual payment system
- Customizable order system
- Easily indexed by search engines
- Basic Sales Stats

Pricing. Sold only through certified hosting partners, no MSRP available.

Hardware/Software Requirements. These system requirements are for the average functional store.

Operating Systems for Web Server

- OpenLinux, Linux, Free BSD, or BSDI on Intel
- Solaris on SPARC shipping; Solaris on Intel coming soon
- NT and IRIX coming soon
- 16 MB RAM
- 10 MB hard drive space (up to 25 MB may be required for install only)

Hardware Platforms Must Be Running. Stronghold, Netscape, or any NCSA-compatible, secure web server software PERL 5.003 or greater Sendmail.

Client-Side (Web Site Developer or Merchant). Requires Netscape browsers or Microsoft Internet Explorer, versions 3.0 or later, running on the user's system of choice (PC, Mac or UNIX).

Client-Side (Shopper). Browser of choice.

FAX MANAGEMENT

Company Name: Teubner & Associates, Inc.
Address: 623 S. Main Street, Stillwater, OK 74074
Phone: 405-624-8000
800-343-7070
E-Mail: faxgate.sales@teubner.com
Web Site: www.teubner.com
Sales Contact Name: Ed Graves

■ Product: Faxgate

Version Number: 4.5

Description Summary. FAXGATE® is an inbound and outbound fax gateway for host and LAN computing environments that offers an integrated hardware/software solution for electronically sending and receiving facsimiles on an enterprise-wide scale. FAXGATE makes your business more profitable and gives you a competitive advantage by delivering documents faster, more efficiently, and for less money. FAXGATE integrates like no other product, delivering true enterprise fax automation in a unique combination of depth of function, breadth of connectivity, and the strength of production fax. Supporting a multitude of applications, including SAP and extensive messaging and e-mail integration, FAXGATE seamlessly enables your day-to-day business operations.

Pricing. Varies based on configuration. Starts at $2500.

Operating Environment. Windows for NT server.

FINANCIAL APPLICATION DEVELOPMENT

Company Name: The MathWorks, Inc.
Address: 24 Prime Park Way, Natick, MA 01760
Phone: 508-647-7000
Fax: 508-647-7012
E-Mail: finance@mathworks.com
Web Site: www.mathworks.com/finprod
Sales Contact Name: Cathy DeYoung

■ Product: MathWorks Financial Engineering Workshop

Description Summary. The MathWorks Financial Engineering Workshop integrates analysis tools, model design, simulation, and code generation into a single, interactive environment. Based on MATLAB, the Workshop provides a common development platform for research, system design, and rapid prototyping of financial applications. The Workshop provides, in a single, integrated and affordable package, all the tools you need to explore, simulate, prototype, and validate financial models and applications. The components of the Financial Engineering Workshop are MATLAB, Excel Link, and the Financial, Otimization, and Statistics Toolboxes. Optional components include the C/C++ Compiler and C/C++ Math Libraries.

Product Feature List

- Over 500 math functions
- Numerical computation and simulation
- Data analysis and visualization
- GUI building tools
- Multidimensional arrays
- Interactive code profiling and debugging
- Fixed income pricing, yield and sensitivity analysis
- Portfolio analysis and optimization
- Derivative pricing and analysis
- Calendar functions
- Linear and quadratic programming tools
- Direct access from all MATLAB functions from Excel spreadsheet
- Probability distributions and random number generators
- Multivariate analysis
- Parameter estimation and fitting

Pricing. Please call

Hardware Requirements. PC, UNIX, Mac compatible. Specific hardware requirements are available on our Web site.

Software Requirements. PC, UNIX, Mac compatible. Specific software requirements are available on our Web site.

GIS

Company Name: Geographic Data Technology, Inc
Address: 11 Lafayette St., Lebanon, NH 03766
Phone: 603-643-0330
800-331-7811
Fax: 603-643-6808
E-Mail: info@gdt1.com
Web Site: www.geographic.com
Sales Contact Name: Steve Morse

■ Product: Dynamap/2000

Description Summary. Dynamap/2000 is the premier street and boundary database for business geographics applications in the U.S. GDT has more than 50 people dedicated to adding new streets and addresses, keeping up with postal changes, and improving quality and accuracy. Dynamap is available in many formats, compatible with all commonly used GIS, desktop mapping, and geocoding packages.

Pricing. Call

Hardware and Software Requirements. The Dynamap database is used on all current platforms and software including mainframes, workstations, and PCs.

INSURANCE RATING SOFTWARE

Company Name: Computer Science Innovations, Inc.
Address: 1235 Evans Road, Melbourne, FL 32904-2314
Phone: 407-676-2923
888-823-2923
Fax: 407-676-2355
E-Mail: poolplus@csihq.com
Web Site: http://www.csihq.com/poolplus/
Sales Contact Name: Judy Kennedy (extension 231), Product Manager

■ Product: PoolPlus for Windows (Insurance Rating Software for Florida)

Version Number: 1.0

Description Summary. PoolPlus is the most complete and accurate rating program for Florida Independent Insurance Agents.

Product Feature List

- Simultaneously rates Wind premiums with Homeowners or Commercial Property

- Imports saved quotes to expedite rating for the Wind and Flood modules
- Generates and prints Customer Copy of quotes
- Generates and prints Rating Worksheets
- Prints Plain Paper Applications

Pricing. \$120 per copy for each Florida rating module or any three modules for \$299, \$30 annual update subscription.

Hardware Requirements

Intel microprocessor
Random access memory (RAM) 8 MB (16 MB under Windows 95)
Hard disk space available 15 MB
Mouse or track ball recommended
VGA or SVGA monitor

Software Requirements. MS Windows® version 3.1 or Windows 95® (recommended).

■ Product: PoolPlus for Windows (National Insurance Rating Software)

Version Number: 1.0

Description Summary. PoolPlus National Flood Rating software provides flood insurance ratings for the entire United States.

Product Feature List

- Provides Ratings for standard, residential, condominium association, preferred risk, mortgage portfolio, and provisional policies
- Minimizes data entry requirements
- Automatically determines Pre or Post FIRM status
- Automatically calculates CRS discounts and community probation surcharges
- Saves quotes, worksheets, and applications
- Generates and prints Customer Copy of quotes
- Generates and prints Rating Worksheets
- Provides ability to fax or e-mail quotes, worksheets and applications

Pricing. \$279 per seat, \$50 annual subscription.

Hardware Requirements

Intel microprocessor
Random access memory (RAM) 16 MB minimum (32 MB recommended)
Hard disk space available 15 MB
Mouse or track ball recommended

VGA or SVGA monitor
CD ROM

Software Requirements. MS Windows® 95 or Windows NT.

INTERNET ACCESS

Company Name: Resonate
Address: 465 Fairchild Drive, Suite 115, Mountain View, CA 94043
Phone: 650-967-6500
Fax: 650-967-6561
E-Mail: info@Resonate.com
Web Site: www.Resonate.com
Sales Contact Name: Cameron Lorentz

■ Product: Global Dispatch, Central Dispatch, and Application Dispatch

Description Summary. The Resonate Dispatch Family of products enables the fastest and most reliable Internet access through a system of integrated products that intelligently select, schedule, and route requests to the optimal network resource or service.

Central Dispatch. Central Dispatch provides superior control and distribution of Web traffic and allows CIOs, network managers, and system administrators to quickly and efficiently implement scalable, reliable, enterprise-wide, multiserver Web sites.

Global Dispatch. Global Dispatch enables excellent performance from your existing resources by intelligently determining the optimal POP locations for maximized resource availability. Global Dispatch seamlessly integrates with server-level scheduling and load-balancing solutions to provide enterprise-wide availability and performance.

Application Dispatch. Application Dispatch provides dependable access to application services by scheduling requests to the least-loaded, most available application server. You can also set service level priorities that allow more critical application requests to be scheduled according to level of importance.

Product Feature List

Global Dispatch.

- Latency-based scheduling
- High availability for mission critical applications
- Reliability
- Simple set-up

Central Dispatch.

- Resource-based scheduling
- High availability
- Scalability
- High performance
- Heterogeneous support

Application Dispatch.

- High availability
- Service level priorities
- Superior application performance
- Many-to-many mapping

Pricing. Introductory pricing at $10,000.

Hardware Requirements. Platforms supported: Sun SPARCservers, Pentium and Pentium Pro, IBM/AIX servers.

Software Requirements. Supports all commercially available Web server software.

INTERNET BANKING

Company Name: Corillian Corporation
Address: 3601 SW Murray Boulevard, Suite 300, Beaverton, OR 97005
Phone: 1-503-627-0729
800-863-6445
Fax: 1-503-641-5575
E-Mail: info@corillian.com, sales@corillian.com
Web Site: www.corillian.com
Sales Contact Name: Peter Ghavami, VP of Sales

■ Products: Voyager Server; MoneyPAD Personal Financial Appliance

Version Number: Voyager v2.0; MoneyPAD v1.5

Description Summary. The Voyager platform is a high-performance middleware server built on the Windows NT operating system that is designed to handle Internet-delivered core banking and bill payment transactions. The Voyager platform provides a link between financial institution legacy host systems and customers using OFX-enabled personal financial management software and browser-based (HTML) financial interfaces. Voyager Server Applications enable financial institutions to provide their consumers and small business clients with access to a variety of services, including banking, bill payment, brokerage, and point-of-sale transaction initiation. Corillian's Client Applications are customizable browser-based user interfaces based on *de facto* standards such as HTML, JAVA, and Active X. The Browser Banker is a customizable HTML-based user interface. MoneyPAD is the Personal Financial Appliance that performs transactions over the Internet, while providing the financial institution's customer a unique, branded service environment.

Product Feature List

Voyager Platform

- Supports secure real-time banking, bill payment, and brokerage
- Supports FULL synchronization and file recovery
- Built on MS Windows NT operating system
- Uses a three-tier architecture to manage transactions without duplicating existing data/processes
- Integrates legacy financial data
- Incorporates JAVA script technologies
- Uses MS communications technology, distributed COM
- Open system, supporting current and anticipated OFX/GOLD specifications
- Scalable using Intel-based servers
- Stringent Internet security

MoneyPAD

- ActiveX-based software client
- MoneyPAD Banker provides real-time banking, bill payment, and brokerage
- MoneyPAD Designer provides tools for designing, branding, and personalizing

Pricing. Varies; based upon number of "user licenses" and professional services requirements.

Hardware Requirements. Fire wall server hardware; HP Server P6200 Model D4346N; Traffic Cop/Auto IP Switch; Cisco Router; 3Com SuperStack; APC; WAN Monitor; Hardware-based disk redundancy.

Software Requirements. Win NT Server 4.0; MS SQL Server 6.5; MS IIS 3.0; NT Service Pack #3; PC Anywhere 8.0; Crystal Reports 6.0; Voyager; Digital Certificate.

Company Name: Goldleaf Technologies, an Equifax Company
Address: 103 Commerce Street, Suite 120, Lake Mary, FL
Phone: 407-829-4445
888-453-5323

Fax: 407-829-4452
E-Mail: sales@goldleaf-tech.com
Web Site: www.goldleaf-tech.com
Sales Contact Name: Christine Bauer, vice-president of Sales and Marketing

■ Product: ACH Origination, Corporate Cash Management, Home Banking, Telephone Banking, and Internet Banking

Description Summary. Goldleaf markets and supports the CustomerLink™ suite of electronic banking software solutions. These state of the art products include ACH Origination and Cash Management for the financial institution's corporate clients and Telephone, Home, and Internet Banking for the retail client. Feature-rich CustomerLink products are unique in their market. CustomerLink solutions allow independent financial institutions the opportunity to offer affordable, technologically advanced services to clients in a continuously evolving marketplace. Goldleaf now serves over 1400 successful financial institutions with more than 8000 products installed. With the help of Goldleaf's products, these customers generate additional revenue, increase/retain market share, and decrease operating expenses. Today's financial marketplace is extremely competitive for independent banks, savings banks, and credit unions, and Goldleaf is committed to strengthening the customers' relationships with their financial institutions.

Product Feature List. Contact for more information

Pricing. Range $10,000 to $ 50,000

Hardware Requirements. Contact for configuration.

Software Requirements. Contact for configuration.

Company Name: nFront, Inc.
Address: 1551 Jennings Mill Road, Suite 800A, Bogart, GA 30622
Phone: 706-369-3779
Fax: 706-369-8611
E-Mail: apowell@banking.com
Web Site: www.banking.com/www.nfront.com
Sales Contact Name: Alan Powell

■ Product: nHome™

Description Summary. nHome™, the company's Microsoft NT-based Internet banking application, enables banking customers to open new accounts, apply for loans, view account balances and histories, pay bills, transfer funds, download images of cleared checks, customize reports, and download active statements into personal financial management packages at any time, from any location, using any secure browser-enabled device such as personal computers and televisions. From the bank's perspective, nHome allows the financial institution to expand its reach to a broader market, primarily composed of the most profitable banking customers, while taking advantage of the least expensive delivery channel available today. Because customers are afforded greater access to and control over their account information, the bank's customer service overhead ultimately can be reduced. And perhaps most importantly, through the collection of data captured online in this fat server solution, the bank can target specific customers for more efficient and effective cross-selling and marketing campaigns.

Product Feature List

- Secure Account and Credit Applications
- Account Summaries and Histories
- DDAs
- Savings
- CDs
- IRAs
- Mortgages
- Loans
- Equity Lines Lines of Credit
- Funds Transfer
- Bill Payment
- Immediate and future transfers
- Immediate and future payments
- One-time and recurring transfers
- One-time and recurring payments
- Custom Reports
- PFM Downloads
- Account type
- Date
- Check number
- Quicken™
- Transaction amount, Transaction type
- Microsoft Money™
- Interactive Calculators
- Personal Information Manager
- Retirement planning, College planning
- PIN management
- Mortgage estimating

- Loan estimating
- Change of address, etc.
- Check Imaging
- Administrative Interface
- Internet branch reporting
- Data Mining/Cross-selling
- Update rates and product information
- Customer-specific reporting
- Download secure online applications
- Automatic sales message delivery
- View audit tables and customer stats
- E-mail Notification System
- Online Help
- Branded Online Demo

Pricing. Based on asset size of institution.

Hardware Requirements

- Pentium 75 Processor or greater PC
- 16 MB RAM or greater
- 28.8 BPS Asynch modem or greater
- CD ROM drive
- Monitor
- Keyboard
- Mouse
- Dedicated analog telephone line for dial-up connectivity
- PC must be housed in a secure area of the bank and be available to receive daily ACH files and transmit nightly balance files (basically, a PC running Windows 95 with 16 MB RAM and an Asynch modem).

Software Requirements

- Microsoft Windows 95 Version 4.00.950 B or greater on CD ROM
- Microsoft Plus!

Company Name: Q-UP Systems
Address: 8140 N. Mopac Bldg 4, Suite 230, Austin, TX
Phone: 512-342-9910
800-500-3002
Fax: 512-342-9921
E-Mail: info@qup.com
Web Site: www.qup.com
Sales Contact Name: Wade Sanders

■ Product: Internet Banking System/Cash Management

Version Number: 3.0

Description Summary. Internet banking gives bank customers secure, 24-hour access to their accounts and other financial services through the bank's Web site. Internet banking offer customers the latest in technology and convenient banking options. As a premier provider of Internet banking technology for community banks, Q-UP Systems help banks harness the Internet to give their customers the ability to conduct their banking online, from the convenience of home or office. With systems for both retail and commercial banking, Q-UP designs, implements, and supports Internet banking products, from the initial Web site design, through the back-office customization, and ongoing system administration. For more info, visit www.qup.com.

Product Feature List

- View Account Balance
- View Account History
- Export History to Quicken and MS Money
- Transfer Funds
- Pay Bills Electronically
- Create Stop Payments
- Open New Accounts
- Re-order Checks and Change Address
- Search History by check number, amount, or date range
- View Transactions in Checkbook or Standard format
- View Account Details (Interest Rate, Available Balance, Average
- Collected Balance, Overdraft Limit & Balance, Up to 5 days of Float
- Balances and Total Holds)

Enhancement Options

- View Statements
- Memo Posting
- Check Imaging
- Cash Management Tools
- Online Forms for Loan Applications or New Accounts

Pricing. Approximately $25,000 to $35,000.

Hardware Requirements. Pentium grade server, communications line (if going in-house such as ISDN), tape drive.

Software Requirements. Windows NT 4.0, Internet Information Server, tape back-up software.

LIFE INSURANCE AND ANNUITY ADMINISTRATION

Company Name: The Leverage Group, Inc.
Address: 68 National Drive, Glastonbury, CT 06033
800-892-3334
Fax: 860-657-1256
E-Mail: market@levgrp.com
Web Site: www.levgrp.com
Sales Contact Name: Sales Department

■ Product: *PolicyLink*

Version: Version 4.0

Description Summary. The Leverage Group is a leading independent software and services company that develops and markets advanced client/server based system solutions to the life insurance and annuity industry. Founded in 1984 and based in Glastonbury, CT, The Leverage Group is one of the largest software vendors in the insurance industry, with over 100 clients. The Leverage Group provides *PolicyLink* — the year 2000 life insurance and annuity administration system that offers many integrated features and major technological achievements for the optimum processing solution: client/server technology, complete policy administration, commission processing and payout processing, 100% graphical user interface design, rapid product development, multiproduct support, complete variable processing, RDBMS query and reporting, icon-controlled integrated functionality, and it's 100% Web enabled. It's the life insurance and annuity administration system you can depend on for the year 2000 and beyond.

Product Features List

- Production-Proven Life Insurance and Annuity Administration System
- Year 2000 Compliant
- Client/Server Technology
- 100% Graphical User Interface
- Windows and UNIX
- Unlimited Life Insurance and Annuity Policy/Product Volume
- 100% Web Enabled
- Complete Legacy Replacement system
- Multi-Product Support
- Advanced, Rapid Product Development Platform
- RDBMS Query and Reporting
- Icon-Controlled, Integrated Functionality

Pricing. Call

MULTICASTING

Company Name: StarBurst Communications Corporation
Address: 150 Baker Avenue, Concord, MA 01742
Phone: 978-287-5560
800-585-3889
Fax: 978-287-5561
E-Mail: info@starburstcom.com
Web Site: www.starburstcom.com
Sales Contact Name: Bill Andrews

■ Product: StarBurst OmniCast

Version Number: 1.0

Description Summary. StarBurst OmniCast offers a revolutionary information delivery system, which couples extensive file management and multicast group management capabilities with StarBurst's industry-leading Multicast File Transfer Protocol (MFTP) file delivery solution. OmniCast provides reliable, efficient, and simultaneous transfer of data "packages" from a single site to many, even thousands, of recipient sites. It is ideal for software distribution, enterprise-wide business data delivery, intranet information "push," multimedia file distribution, Web site content replication, database replication, and other file transfer applications.

Product Feature List

- Intuitive graphical user interface to rapidly define and manage target receiver groups
- Packaging tools for organizing, bundling, and managing files and directory structures
- File and package compression utility for greater network efficiency
- Flexible scheduler for defining future and regular jobs
- Administrator and user modes
- Real-time job monitoring
- Historical transaction and error reporting
- DNS and DHCP support

Platforms. Windows NT and Windows 95. Sun Solaris planned for release in 1998, t 3.x clients

■ Product: StarBurst Multicast

Version Number: 3.04

Description Summary. StarBurst Multicast provides group management and reliable, efficient, and simultaneous transfer of data files from a single site to many, even thousands, of recipient sites. It is an ideal solution for software distribution, enterprise-wide business date delivery, Internet/intranet information "push," multimedia file distribution, Web site content replication, database replication, and other one-to-many file transfer applications. StarBurst Multicast offers significantly faster file delivery, reduced network traffic, and reduced server resource usage when compared to traditional point-to-point file transfer methods such as TCP-based File Transfer Protocol (FTP).

Product Feature List

- Intuitive Graphical User Interface
- Extensible Command Line Interface for scripted operations
- Unattended installation and operation at remote sites
- Real-time transfer status monitoring
- Extensive sender and receiver logging
- Settable transfer rate allows file transfers to occur simultaneously with other network applications
- Powerful "resume" feature allows stoppage of transfer for resumption later
- Interoperable among diverse client/server platforms

Platforms. Server and Client — Sun Solaris, DEC Alpha Unix, Windows NT, Silicon Graphics IRIX, IBM AIX 3.2.5 and 4.2; Client only — Windows 95, OS/2, SCO UnixWare, SCO OpenServer 3.2 & 5.0, IBM 4690, Sun Interactive Unix.

■ Product: StarBurst Multicast Sender for SMS

Version Number: 1.4

Description Summary. StarBurst Multicast Sender for SMS is an SMS Add-on that significantly reduces network and system costs associated with software management of networkedPCs. StarBurst Multicast Sender improves the software distribution capabilities of Microsoft® System Management Server (SMS) by reducing network traffic, decreasing the load on sending servers, and minimizing software transfer times.

Product Feature List

- Brings MFTP benefits to Microsoft SMS.
- Intuitive SMS-consistent GUI minimizes learning curve.
- Unattended installation simplifies deployment.
- Runs as integral Windows NT service.
- Extensive sender logging.
- Detailed receiver logging to the Windows NT Event Log.

Platforms. Microsoft SMS

■ Product: StarBurst Multicast SDK

Version Number: 1.04

Description Summary. StarBurst Multicast SDK is a rich software development environment for authoring custom applications based on StarBurst's Multicast File Transfer Protocol (MFTP™). End-users, systems integrators, and other developers can utilize StarBurst Multicast SDK to dramatically improve the file transfer efficiency and group management of their own applications. StarBurst MFTP supports the reliable, efficient, and simultaneous transfer of data files from a single site to many, even thousands, of recipient sites. Potential applications for MFTP technology include electronic software distribution, database updates, point-of-sale data distribution, and multimedia content delivery. Applications based on MFTP offer faster file delivery, reduced network traffic, and reduced server resource usage when compared to applications based on traditional point-to-point file transfer methods.

Product Feature List

- Extensive API based on Berkeley sockets exposes all MFTP capabilities
- Common API for Windows 95, Windows NT, plus a variety of UNIX platforms simplifies porting
- Cross-platform support allows interoperability between diverse client/server platforms
- Includes software, sample programs, documentation, and telephone support

Platforms. Sun Solaris, DEC Alpha Unix, Windows NT, Silicon Graphics IRIX, IBM AIX 3.2.5 and 4.2, Windows 95, SCO OpenServer 3.2 and 5.0, OS/2, IBM 4690, SCO UnixWare, Sun Interactive Unix.

MULTIMEDIA

See under CONSULTING

NETWORKING

Company Name: Litton Network Access Systems
Address: 3353 Orange Ave., Roanoke, VA 24012
Phone: 540-342-6700
800-537-6801
Fax: 540-342-5961
E-Mail: info@netaccsys.com
Web Site: www.netaccsys.com
Sales Contact Name: Tom Paredes

■ Products: Litton Network Access Systems Family of ATM Access Products

These include CAM 7665 Communications Access Multiplexer, CAM 7640 ATM Multiservice Multiplexer, and the ATM Circuit Emulation (ACE) Card for IBM Nways ATM Workgroup Switches and Hubs

Description Summary. The CAM family of ATM Access products offer network consolidation of circuit-based and constant-bit-rate traffic over an ATM network, including voice over ATM. Designed for any platform density (from 1 up to 80 T1s), the CAM products can deliver leased line savings in less than 12 months. The ACE card provides the same T1/E1 circuit emulation service as the CAM 7665 and 7640, but is designed as an add-in module for IBM Nways ATM Workgroup Switches.

Pricing. Pricing for the CAM 7640/7650 starts at $15,000. The CAM 7665 basic configurations begin at less than $30,000. The ACE card is offered at approximately $11,000 for 4 ports, $15,000 for 8 ports.

For additional features and hardware/software requirements, please visit our web site at www.netaccsys.com.

OPTICAL STORAGE

Company Name: NSM Jukebox
Address: 2405 Commerce Avenue, Building 2000, Duluth, GA 30096
Phone: 800-238-4676
E-Mail: info@nsmjukebox.com
Sales Contact Name: David Ooley, vice-president, Sales and Marketing

■ Products

See under Description Summary.

Description Summary. The Mercury family is designed for the most demanding multi-user networks. All Mercury products hold up to 150 CDs, all are network enabled, and the Mercury 40 has four high-speed, read-only drives for optimal performance. The Mercury 40 NET has an embedded controller to ensure plug-and-play support for Novell networks. The Mercury 31's concurrent read-write capability enables accurate disc mastering while supporting multi-user read access. The Mercury family is capable of managing both RS232 and SCSI implementations. Prices start at $13,000

The CDR 100 family of jukeboxes is an ideal low-cost solution for all kinds of data-management challenges. For users who require read-write capabilities, the CDR 100 Recordable is bundled with mastering software for automatic, unattended production of hundreds of CDs per day. For users who require read-only access to a prerecorded archive of 100 CDs, the CDR

100 XA features compact efficiency and high-speed robotics for information on demand. Prices start at $5,000

The Satellite family offers the most compact and flexible jukeboxes available. Managing 60 to 135 CDs, the Satellite can be custom fit to meet both the capacity and access needs of the most demanding applications. Up to three read-write drives support automated CD production. If user access has top priority, five read-only drives (a 12:1 disc-to-drive ratio) can deliver data at breakthrough speeds. Only the Satellite can change dynamically in accordance with specific application requirements. Prices start at $10,000.

PAGING

Company Name: Absolutely Software Inc.
Address: 1515 North Federal Highway, Suite 300, Boca Raton, FL 33432-1994
Phone: 561-852-0681
888-922-7638 (888-Y-ABSOFT)
Fax: 561-852-2669
E-Mail: kathy.krebs@absoft.net
Web Site: www.absoft.net
Sales Contact: Name: Eric Brill

■ Product: Air Apparent for Windows NT

Version Number: 1.2

Description Summary. Air Apparent for Windows NT is the most popular suite of paging products for the Windows NT operating system. Air Apparent is an end-to-end paging solution, integrating into virtually every legacy application and diverse computing environment. It provides reliability, fault-tolerance and supports environments with high volumes of paging traffic. Best of all, it was built around the Internet (TCP/IP) protocol as an internal networking backbone. The server page-enables e-mail, help desk, monitoring, and network management software into one centralized paging server. Air Apparent works with all major carriers and was built on open-standard protocols only.

Product Feature List

- Benchmarked at 10,000 pages per hour
- Communicate with on-site terminals; local and nationwide wireless carriers
- Compatible with alphanumeric pagers, iDEN and PCS phones
- Delivers multiple messages per dial-up, increasing throughput
- Detailed audit trails for all communications port activities

- Explorer-like interface
- Maintenance of transaction and error logs
- Maintenance of users, groups, services, and port configuration
- Message Log that tracks activity of pages dispatched

Pricing. From $799 to $6125.

Hardware System Requirements. An Intel 486 or Pentium microprocessor, 32 MB of memory minimum, One 3.5" high-density drive, CD-ROM drive, VGA, Super VGA, or higher-resolution video graphics adapter, Network adapter card, Modem(s), TCP/IP stack.

Software System Requirements. Microsoft Windows NT V3.51 or higher operating system.

PORTFOLIO ANALYSIS/MANAGEMENT

Company Name: Portfolio Management Consultants, Inc.
Address: 555 17th Street, 14th Floor, Denver, CO 80202
Phone: 303-292-1177
800-852-1177
Fax: 303-292-0330
Web Site: http://www.pmcdenver.com
Sales Contact Name: Raquel Hinman, Scott Wilkinson

■ Product: ADAM

Version Number: 5.2

Description Summary. ADAM is a comprehensive analytical portfolio analysis program. ADAM offers: portfolio analysis; a portfolio optimizer; investment policy preparation; risk tolerance questionnaire; database with over 10,000 mutual funds and 250 indices and managers; the ability to analyze mutual funds with a factor analyzer; historical performance calculation and presentation; hypothetical spending scenarios and analyses. Adam also permits you to develop customized slide-show presentations detailing the results of your analysis.

Product Feature List

- Built-in help
- Educational tutorials
- In-depth customer profile
- Asset allocation and portfolio modeling
- Fund selection
- Contract preparation and printing
- Investment policy preparation and printing
- Performance reporting

Pricing. Free

Hardware Requirements. IBM-compatible PC with 486 chip or better; 8 MB RAM; 50 MB disk space; Microsoft Windows 95 or greater.

Software Requirements. N/A

Company Name: Rescom, Inc.
Address: 1150 Waverley Street, Winnipeg, Ontario R3T 0P4 Canada
Telephone: 204-284-2100
Fax: 204-284-3838
Sales Contact Name: Doug Mann

■ Product: MarketMate Enterprise

Description Summary. Object-oriented, 3-tiered client service portfolio management system; multilingual; multicurrency; AIMR compliant. Rescom's newest portfolio management offerings utilize leading edge technologies that are designed to evolve as the needs of the user change.

RES is the term used to describe Rescom's Enterprise Solutions. RES is the architecture infrastructure on which application functionality resides. The first application to reside on RES is MME, or MarketMate Enterprise. RES is an Open Systems Architecture that is vendor neutral and supports enterprise-wide systems. RES architecture can be two-tier or three-tier. In a two-tier client/server configuration, the application logic is either buried inside the user interface on the client (workstation) or within the database (the server), or both. In a three-tier client/server system, the application logic resides in the middle tier, separated from the data and the user interface. This provides substantial cost savings, greater scalability, and is more robust and flexible. Data can be distributed to multiple servers, allows dynamic load balancing, and provides dynamic reporting and controls. RES is architecture driven, utilizes Object Oriented Programming and C++, and was implemented using Relational Database Technology. The development of RES has been separated into five encapsulated layers to provide a very flexible system that offers greater portability to different user interfaces (browsers), TP monitors, and RDBMS's. RES is industry independent and can satisfy the needs for thousands of users in one or many locations, or one or two users operating disconnected from the servers.

MME provides comprehensive browse lists for securities, clients, accounts, portfolios, transactions, and memos. Standard reports within MME can be customized easily by the user selecting and arranging the colums and/or headings from a predefined list. MME can prepare valuations in any currency. Book costs are available in up to four currencies. MME maintains book cost using Average Cost, LIFO, FIFO, and Specific Match accounting. MME supports all AIMR performance presentation standards. The flexibility to calculate performance gross or net of fees with or without cash allocation is included. Performance can be calculated at the holding level or the portfolio level and can be presented by Asset Type, Security Type, Industry Category, Currency, and Country.

The MarketMate Enterprise Solution is designed to evolve as the needs or the user change. It should be thoroughly considered before any new portfolio management solutions are implemented.

Product Feature List. MME presents a whole new level of performance and productivity capabilities. The MME extensive data model supports a large number of key functions including:

- Portfolio Management
- Contact Management
- Portfolio Reporting
- AIMR Compliant Performance Reporting
- Accrual Calculations
- Graphics
- Real Time Mark to Market and Portfolio Valuation
- New Account Opening and Maintenance
- Risk Profiling
- Portfolio Asset Allocation and Rebalancing
- Full Multicurrency
- Multilingual
- Financial Planning
- Electronic Order Entry

Hardware Requirements. HP-UX server; Windows NT client

Software Requirements. Tuxedo; Sybase; Oracle; Informix

Company Name: SS&C Technologies, Inc.
Address: 80 Lamberton Road, Windsor, CT 06095
Phone: 860-298-4500
800-234-0556
Fax: 860-298-4900
E-Mail: SOLUTION@sscinc.com
Web Site: http://www.ssctech.com
Sales Contact Name: Julie Donaldson

■ Product: CAMRA 2000

Version Number: Version 2

Description Summary. CAMRA 2000 offers global investment professionals the power and flexibility to manage the entire investment process efficiently and seamlessly. The core inventory manager delivers a single, consolidated "book of record" which is accessible across your entire enterprise — from front and back office. By accessing detailed information in real-time, CAMRA 2000 facilitates decision-making trading, compliance monitoring, and portfolio management. The result: you focus on your core business — managing investments.

Product Feature List

- Online pre- and post-trade compliance
- Online Trading Room
- Automated BLOOMBERG data exchange
- Multicurrency processing
- Four accounting bases supported: GAAP, STAT, Management, and Tax
- U.S. and Canadian regulatory reporting
- Performance Measurement (consistent with AIMR standards)
- Extensive online market analytics database
- Mutual fund accounting including NAV
- Money market processing
- Automated TBA/dollar roll processing
- Optimized MBS pool allocation with EPN E-Z Link
- Custodian, Pricing, Corporate Action, Factor, F/X, G/L, DTC, and NAIC interfaces
- Integrated SQL report writer with ODBC for ready access to all stored data
- 32-Bit operating environment for improved reliability, memory utilization, and performance
- Supports both Windows 95 (and Windows NT) operating systems on the desktop

Pricing. N/A

Network Information. Windows NT, Novell, Banyan

PC Hardware Requirements. Intel X86 based (P90 recommended)

PC Operating System. Windows 95, Windows NT

PC Memory Requirements. 24 MB (minimum Windows 95) 32 MB (minimum Windows NT)

PROPERTY/CASUALTY POLICY ADMINISTRATION

Company Name: Allenbrook, Inc.
Address: 900 Chelmsford Street, Cross Point, Tower 1, Lowell, MA 01851
Phone: 978-937-2980
Fax: 978-937-5464
E-Mail: marketing@allenbrook.iix.com
Web Site: www.allenbrook.com
Sales Contact: Robert Dolan, VP sales and marketing (x 136)

■ Product: Phoenix Enterprise Insurance Solution

Description Summary. Phoenix from Allenbrook, Inc. is a comprehensive Windows-based property and casualty policy administration and management system that can boost insurance company profitability. Phoenix, a client/server solution, combines fully integrated personal and commercial lines policy, accounting, and claims management modules. Phoenix lets insurers manage flexible plans of insurance, and develop new products quickly to reach additional market niches. Year 2000 compliance is included in the design. Allenbrook delivers enterprise-wide automation benefits and provides expert insurance/technology support to some of the most successful insurance companies in North America.

Product Feature List

- Policy Administration
- Rate quote
- Underwriting
- Billing and collections
- Claims Administration
- Bureau Reporting
- Reinsurance Interface
- Conversion Support

Hardware/Software Requirement. Client/Server, PC-based enterprise insurance application using Novell or NT Server, and SQL Base, Oracle, SQL Server or DB2/400; 32 MB RAM; Pentium processor; 400 MB hard drive (minimum for client level Phoenix components); Windows 95/NT.

RE-ENGINEERING

Company Name: Hamilton Technologies, Inc.
Address: 17 Inman Street, Cambridge, MA 02139
Phone: 617-492-0058
Fax: 617-492-1727
E-Mail: sales@htius.com

Web Site: http://world.std.com/~hti
Sales Contact Name: Hannah Gold

■ Product: 001 (Pronounced "Double Oh One")

Version Number: 3.2.8

Description Summary. Hamilton Technologies, Inc. (HTI) was founded in 1986 to provide products and services to modernize the system engineering and software development process in order to maximize reliability, lower cost, and accelerate time to market. HTI's flagship product, 001, is based on HTI's Development Before The Fact (DBTF) formal systems theory used to develop systems in terms of System Oriented Objects (SOOs). This paradigm integrates systems and software engineering disciplines and transforms the software development process away from an inefficient and expensive curative process to a preventative, more productive, reliable process. 001 is a completely integrated systems engineering and software development environment. It can be used to define, analyze, and automatically generate complete, integrated, and fully production-ready code for any kind of software application with a significantly lower error rate and high reusability. Since 001 has an open architecture it can be configured to generate (or interface to) systems at all levels including hardware platforms, software platforms, programming languages, databases, operating systems, Internet systems, embedded systems, communication protocols, GUIs, and legacy code of choice.

Product Feature List

- Always number one when put to the test. No matter how large or complex the system.
- Formal but friendly language. The same language is used for defining any part of a system at any phase of development.
- Integrated seamless design and development environment. All parts of a system throughout all of its phases and views of development are by their very nature formally integrated.
- Inherently reusable, all 001 systems are systems oriented. They can be object oriented, function oriented, or an integration of both.
- With 001, everything is a system; 001 enables design and modeling of any concept that humans can envision. It could be for example a target system, testing system (including the operational or use model), model of the development process, or model of the enterprise. All "systems" are defined (and if software, automatically developed) in 001 as system-oriented objects.
- No interface errors. All interface errors are automatically found with 001, starting with the definition of a system (over 75% of all errors

found in a traditional environment at testing time after implementation are found before implementation, with 001).

- All objects in a 001 system are under control and traceable.
- Executable specification simulation. A definition has information in it for 001's simulator to understand its behavior and dynamically analyze it for things such as risk, timing, and cost; and a higher-layer operating system to execute it. For software that same definition can be used as input to 001's automatic code generator. The result is a rapid prototype for a system designer or a production-ready system for a software developer. That which is simulated by 001's simulator can be integrated with that which is automatically generated by 001's generator to a very fine or loosely grained level.
- Integrated metrics for predictive systems. A 001 definition can have additional information about it and its relationships provided by the user. This information, together with its formal definition, is used for gathering metrics, providing a mechanism to trace from requirements to code and back again, ensuring that the implemented system meets the requirements.
- 100% Automatic code generation; 001 automatically generates complete, integrated, fully production, ready-to-run code for any kind of system whether it be GUI, database, communications, real time, distributed, client server, multi-user, or mathematical algorithms.
- 001's Generator is accessible to a user to tailor it for his own brand of generated code. and can be configured to interface to a system at all layers. Once configured, 001 will automatically regenerate the new system to reside on that environment. Complete flexibility is provided to the user to define his own primitive type interfaces to chosen API's which 001 integrates with 001's formal definitions.
- Maintenance performed at the blueprint level. The user doesn't ever need to change the code, only the specification, and then regenerates only the changed part of the system. A new implementation of the system is automatically generated, compiled, linked, and executed without manual intervention.
- GUI environment tightly integrated with the development of an application; 001 provides GUI support while preserving traceability, interface integrity and control seamlessly between the GUI part of the application and the other parts of the application.
- Automatic testing. Runtime constraint tests that validate correct object manipulation and construction as well as unit test harnesses for testing each object and its relationships are automatically generated by 001.
- 001 also provides an automatic user interface with the object editor for populating and manipulating complex objects, including storage and retrieval for persistent objects. This provides the ability to regres-

sion test the target system at any input output interface with predefined object test data sets.

- Automatic documentation: 001's documentation environment is tightly integrated with the definition of the system. Documentation can be automatically generated from 001, wrapping in the user's own comments and the formal definition itself, if desired, as well as documentation from other model viewpoints. For example, a resulting document could include descriptions of the requirements, the testing, developer's issues, and developer's decisions made about a definition of a system.
- 001 was completely defined and generated with itself.

Pricing. Seat and component based.

Hardware Requirements. UNIX (HP, Sun, RS6000, Alpha), Windows (NT).

Software Requirements. Developer Package for hardware environment of choice, which includes C compiler and GUI environment (Motif or Windows).

Company Name: New Art Technologies, Inc.
Address: 200 West 79 Street, New York, NY 10024
Phone: 212-362-0559
800-276-1118
Fax: 212-873-8231
E-Mail: info@newarttech.com
Web Site: www.newarttech.com
Sales Contact Name: Rebecca Lakser

■ Product: NA2000 SCAN

Version: 5.0

Description Summary. NA2000 SCAN is an easy-to-use, reliable programming language-independent utility that first finds all of your source program files on stand-alone PCs or LAN networks and then scans them for specified references. NA2000 provides a detailed Analysis report that programmers can use to make their changes as well as a Management report that managers can use to estimate job size and cost. NA2000 SCAN cuts your analytical time down from months to mere hours. NA2000 SCAN provides several hundred Y2K "seeds" which you may modify, add to, or exclude from the scanning process. You may also elect to ignore or exclude any text strings from the scanning process. Any programming language source code file may be analyzed including COBOL, C, HTML, JAVA, FORTRAN, BASIC, VISUAL BASIC. Output analyst reports pinpoint matches per program showing actual lines of code and why that line of code was reported upon as well as a cross reference report which is sorted alpha via variable. All output may be exported to your favorite spreadsheet and/or database program.

Product Feature List

- It can process over 500 programs at a time on a Windows PC.
- Over 450 specific "intelligent" selection criteria find date-related variables.
- Optional user input file permits you to enter up to 499 data names specific to your particular company or industry.
- Optional user "exclude" file permits you to enter up to 50 data names that you wish to exclude from the scan. You may exclude from anywhere in the line of code or specify to exclude if variable is at start of line of code only.
- Optional "ignore" file lets you bypass particular words in a line of code to be scanned.
- NAXREF is an included cross reference facility that lets you see exactly where each variable or routine name is used.
- It can process any language as long as the file is in an ASCII format.
- An included file locator finds files on drives you specify — even your network drive.
- It processes file extensions you specify (e.g., .cbl, .cob, .cpy, .for, .bas, C, etc.).
- Scan processing report details specific program and line number of date related "hits."
- Alternate "short report" limits the number of "redundant hits."
- Export results to spreadsheet or database.
- Management report details number of lines of code requiring modifications.
- Management report details number of hours/man-years required to perform this job and total estimated cost of job.
- Excellent tool for auditing the work of consultants and outsourcers.

Hardware/Software Requirements. Windows 3.1, 95, or NT

■ Product: NAIMPACT

Version: 3.0

Description Summary. NAIMPACT is a Windows-based, interactive analytical tool which provides developers the ability to assess the extent of programming change when they are handed a set of requirements from end-users. NAIMPACT provides a complete programming language-independent impact analysis workbench. With the click of a mouse the programmer analyst can select one or more files to scan and then review and edit those results online. He or she can even export the results to a favorite database and/or spreadsheet program right from NAIMPACT. Either NAIMPACT's Y2K seeds can be used or the programmer analyst can edit the list of seeds right online. Boolean operatives such as AND, OR, and NOT can be used to make NAIMPACT's scanning process extremely flexible. Additionally, the programmer analyst can specify that NAIMPACT constrain its search to either match the search term exactly or "fuzzy" in on a match at a specified percentage level (i.e., 25%, 50%, 75%).

Product Feature List

- Windows-based, completely interactive. Developers can iteratively assess the impact of making changes to one or multiple programs at a time.
- Programming language independent. Can process any language including Cobol, Fortran, Assembler, C, etc.
- Default search criteria file contains over 200 Year 2000 date-related criteria. Developers can choose to use or not use this file.
- Developers can enter up to 499 of their own search criteria.
- Boolean search criteria (consisting of AND, OR, NOT) can be utilized (e.g., STAT AND WORKING OR ACCOUNTS).
- Constrained and nonconstrained searches (constrained search means that there must be a 100% match between the search criteria and the code; unconstrained search means that there doesn't have to be a perfect match).
- Fuzzy search capabilities — ability to match at 75%, 50%, and 25% levels between search criteria and code.
- Impact analysis report details number of hours/man-years required to perform this job and total estimated cost of job. Developer has ability to modify default criteria and iteratively run the impact analysis.
- Scan processing report details specific program and line number of related "hits."
- File viewer permits developer to click on "hit" and see associated program code. You can open your code editor from within NAIMPACT. NAIMPACT stores and recalls your favorite editor name/location.
- Cross Reference report provides alpha listing by "hit" in a spreadsheet-type format.
- Export results to favorite database and/or spreadsheet.

Hardware/Software Requirements. Windows 3.1, 95, or NT.

■ Product Name: NATRACE

Description Summary. NATRACE for COBOL and NATRACE for C are Windows-based, interactive analytical tools which provide developers the ability to "explode" the impact of a single variable throughout a given COBOL or C program down to a depth of 1000 nodes. Particularly useful for Year 2000 analysis, NATRACE which contains language parsers for C and COBOL, easily pinpoints nonobvious impacted related variables. For example, in a given COBOL program you might have a variable called WS-DATE which is an obvious date reference. But as we "explode" WS-DATE we find that it impacts some nonobvious date references, as shown below:

```
MOVE WS-DATE TO WS-D-AREA.
COMPUTE WS-D-AREA = 7 * NUMS.
ADD WS-D-AREA TO WS-TOTAL.
ADD WS-DATE TO B-VAR GIVING C-VAR
```

So we find that WS-DATE impacts both WS-D-AREA, WS-TOTAL, and C_VAR, all nonobvious date-related references. NATRACE will trace and report on all impacted variables.

Product Feature List

- Windows-based, completely interactive.
- NATRACE handles C comments even when the comment spans multiple lines. It also understands bitwise, logical, and shorthand operators.
- Because C may or may not be CASE dependent, NATRACE for C permits you to select whether or not the scan is CASE dependent or not.
- NATRACE for C also permits you to decide whether to perform a search where the structure and the member are joined (e.g., rec.name) or not joined (e.g., name).
- NATRACE for C can trace searched for variables within a structure.
- NATRACE for C provides a listing of traced variables found used by functions.
- NATRACE for COBOL handles redefines as well as variables within group levels.
- Handles COBOL and C programs where a command spans multiple lines; preprocessor "collects" all related code and spans it across one single record for analysis purposes. NATRACE will not lose sight of code where the target is separated by multiple lines from the source.
- Explodes a tree structure of affected variables; each, in turn, becoming a branch of the same tree spawning new branches.
- File viewer permits developer to click on "hit" and see associated program code.
- All report results can be printed as well as stored in a text file.

Hardware/Software Requirements. Windows 3.1, 95 or NT

■ Product Name: NAEXCEL FOR SPREADSHEETS

Version: 3.0

Description Summary. NA-Excel, a Windows-based interactive utility, solves the problem of what to do with those millions of spreadsheets written by both programmers and end-users! With NA-Excel even an end-user can quickly spot date-related references and change them on the spot. It's a must-have for all corporations. While organizations are busy assessing the impact of the millennium date change on their stock of programmer-written systems, a much larger threat looms on the horizon. Many of today's decision support analyses are performed by end-users who use computer-based spreadsheets such as Microsoft Excel and Lotus 1-2-3 to make billion dollar decisions.

Product Feature List

- Can be used for Excel, Lotus 1-2-3, and Quattro Pro spreadsheets.
- Uses Microsoft Excel as an automation server.
- Completely visual.
- Processes a complete workbook within seconds.
- Processes worksheets, macros, as well as modules.
- Can process from one to an infinite number of spreadsheets at one time.
- Full reporting capability lets you see an online report as well as print to paper and to a file for later processing.
- Optional "cell highlighting" in interactive mode colors the "found" cells in red for easy spotting and modification.
- Over 100-date related references included as a starter "search table." The search table may be modified to add additional date variables OR to totally change the criteria. For example, NAEXCEL can be used to search for Eurodollar dependencies just by changing the search table. The starter date-related references include all Excel date and time functions such as: NETWORKDAYS, YEARFRAC, TIMEVALUE, etc.
- Wildcard searching capability.
- Runs under Windows 95/NT.

Hardware/Software Requirements. Windows 95 or NT

■ Product Name: NAWORD for Document Search, Replace, and Comparison

Version: 1.0

Description Summary. NA-Word speedily searches your documents to locate, compare, or replace strings of text you specify. Since Microsoft Word is used as an automation server, NA-Word can process other than text and MS-Word formats: WordPerfect, Microsoft Works, HTML, all programming language code, Microsoft Write — essentially anything that Microsoft Word supports. NA-Word can search your entire local/LAN drive finding files that you specify (of course you can use wildcard searches) then it can "find" (wildcard capability) or even "find and replace" strings that you specify. But it can even do more. Programmers often need to compare two files to one another. NA-Word provides a host of comparative options. Compare on a binary basis or on a document basis — highlighting what's different. You can even perform a compare where you specify the starting and ending record and column numbers for the two comparison files.

Product Feature List

- Useful for all documents. Can also be used for programming languages (e.g., Java, C, and HTML).
- Can process from 1 to n files at a time matching up to 1000 variables at a time.
- Has a file finder which can find files anywhere on your local/network drive.
- Capable of wildcard matching; "sounds like" matching; case sensitive/insensitive; whole word matching; all variation matching.
- Option for "coloring" found matches in red. Ability to "uncolor" red highlighting.
- Can save changed document right online.
- Capable of replacing found text automatically with a replacement term.
- Can scan macros/modules within document.
- File comparison function enables binary compare, document compare, and line by line compare.
- Percentage matching shows ratio of matching one document to another. Ability to specify starting/ending line numbers and starting/ending column numbers.
- Runs under Windows 95/NT workstation.

Hardware/Software Requirements. Windows 95 or NT

RELATIONSHIP MANAGEMENT

Company Name: Baker Hill Corporation
Address: 655 West Carmel Drive, Suite 100, Carmel, IN 46032-2500
Phone: 317-571-2000
800-821-8664
Fax: 317-571-5125
E-Mail: marketing@bakerhill.com
Web Site: www.bakerhill.com
Sales Contacts: Laura Kunkel, Patrick Spencer

■ Product: *One*Point®

Version: 6.3

Description Summary. *One*Point is a Windows-based Relationship Management Solution. *One*Point offers seamless integration from the desktop with Fair, Isaac's SBSS-CreditDesk™, and Dun & Bradstreet data. Its four integrated modules include:

- Sales Management/Business Development
- Underwriting/Credit Analysis
- Pricing & Profitability
- Portfolio Management/Exception Tracking

Pricing. Varies depending on your needs; call for more information

Hardware Requirements. Novell Netware or Windows NT Server

Software Requirements. Windows 3.1, 95, or NT

SECURITIES BACK-OFFICE SYSTEMS

Company Name: Comprehensive Software Systems, Ltd.
Address: 25178 Genesee Trail Road, Golden, CO, 80401
Phone: 303-526-5515
Fax: 303-526-9362
E-Mail: outreach@cssltd.com
Web Site: www.sni.net/cssltd
Sales Contact Name: Jon Farinholt

■ Product: Comprehensive Software Systems

Version Number: n/a

Description Summary. CSS is a complete, front- to back-office, modular financial services software solution for the securities industry. CSS has committed to develop browser-based applications, leveraging the burgeoning power of the Internet and placing CSS at the forefront of emerging technologies. The system encompasses several distinct products — including BrokerView™, Order Management System (OMS) and the Message Switch, Business Process Support, back-office modules, and the database — that can be used as a complete system or can be selected individually and implemented with existing systems. A brokerage firm can run its entire business using solely CSS products, or a firm can select particular products that will most benefit the firm and interface them with any custom or third-party applications. CSS is flexible enough that the products and support offered can easily be tailored to suit the needs of a business of any size, even extending beyond the brokerage industry and into other branches of financial services.

BrokerView is the primary tool that a broker or trader would use, giving access to all of the functionality that they would need to place and maintain orders, manage portfolios and clients' assets, and keep abreast of the market. A set of Profile modules forms the basis of the system, storing necessary data on the firm and its subsidiaries, employees, and associated personnel, and all of the firm's products. The CSS Entitlements module regulates, based on the firm's settings, which of the functionalities are available to which employees, based on log-on. OMS and the Message Switch deliver outstanding speed and reliability for processing orders, and a separate Mutual Funds module means firms can place orders of any type. Business Process Support is a set of modules (Imaging, Workflow, Document Production, and Archiving) that automate business processes and eliminate a firm's reliance on and maintenance of paper documents. CSS has also developed a unique database that is powerful and flexible enough to be a separate product, one with potential applications in other areas of financial services.

Product Feature List

- Scalability and extensibility (to fit any size and to grow with the firm)
- Speed, reliability, and accuracy
- Stand-alone or interfaced with legacy system
- Designed for the complete integration of firm needs
- Browser-based, which provides all functionality from remote locations
- Customizable
- Ease of implementation
- Low-cost hardware requirements
- Year 2000 and OATS compliant

Pricing. Custom, based on user requirements.

Hardware Requirements

CSS Client

Pentium 200 MHz w/256 KB Cache
64 MB RAM
1.6 GB Drive
Video Card w/2 MB
10/100 BaseT NIC

Web Server

Pentium II 333 MHz or dual processor w/512 KB Cache
256 MB RAM
2 GB system drive
2 GB drive
100 BaseT NIC

Application Server

Dual processor Pentium Pro

200 MHz or 333 MHz w/512 KB L2 Cache
256 MB RAM
2 GB system drive
4 GB application drive
100 BaseT NIC
Internal CD-ROM drive

Message Switch Server.

Pentium Pro 200 MHz w/512 KB L2 Cache
256 MB RAM
2 GB system drive
2 GB application drive
100 BaseT NIC

Database Server

Dual or Quad processor Pentium Pro
200 MHz w/512 KB L2 Cache
512 MB or 1024 MB RAM
2 GB system drive
Disk space dependent on database size
100 BaseT NIC
Internal CD-ROM drive

Software Requirements

Microsoft Windows 95 or Windows 98
Microsoft Windows NT Workstation and Windows NT Server
Microsoft SQL Server 6.5
Microsoft Office 97
Internet Explorer 4.01
Internet Information Server 4.0 (including Microsoft Transaction Server)

SYSTEM MONITORING

Company Name: Computer Science Innovations, Inc.
Address: 1235 Evans Road, Melbourne, FL 32904-2314
Phone: 407-676-2923
888-823-2923
Fax: 407-676-2355
E-Mail: poolplus@csihq.com
Web Site: http://www.csihq.com/lookout
Sales Contact Name: Rudy Hallenbeck (extension 218), vice-president, Sales and Marketing

■ Product: Lookout

Version Number: 2.0

Description Summary. Lookout is a task management utility for Windows 95™ or Windows NT™ that initiates the execution of application software, tracks active tasks, and notifies the system operator when the task ends or problems occur. Lookout provides invaluable assistance to system administrators by automatically performing several activities that otherwise require manual intervention. *Windows Magazine* rated Lookout Version 1 as Superior Shareware in May 1997. Lookout is a simple, yet very powerful utility that significantly enhances the productivity of system administrators. Lookout eliminates the mundane task of monitoring application software programs and waiting for tasks to complete. For example, an application may require considerable time to finish processing or an application may be executing which is never supposed to stop. Lookout recognizes when a task ends and can notify the system operator via a traditional message box, a sound file or audible beep, electronic mail, event log (Windows NT™ only), voice telephone, pager, or fax. Lookout can even automatically restart the application, if desired.

Product Feature List

- Lookout offers a variety of job scheduling options.
- Applications can be scheduled to start at a specific time, execute until a specific time, execute at specific time intervals, or execute for a specified duration of time.
- Lookout itself can be initiated at system startup and subsequently execute applications in accordance with a predefined schedule of events completely without human intervention.
- Lookout can be set up to monitor task execution via process status, processor utilization, and now in Version 2, the Windows NT™ event log.

Monitored Activities

- Task Startup
- Task Shutdown
- Task CPU Usage
- Windows NT© Event Lo Notification Methods
- E-Mail
- Sound File
- Message Box
- Event Log (NT only)
- Modem/Beeper
- FAX

Pricing. A single license is $89 and can be obtained via the Internet at http://www.csihq.com/lookout. A demonstration copy with a 30-day trial period is also available at the same site.

Hardware Requirements. N/A

Software Requirements. Windows 95 or Windows NT.

TRADING

Company Name: Wilco Systems Inc.
Address: 17 State Street, New York, NY 10004
Phone: 212-269-3970
Fax: 212-269-3925
E-Mail: info@wilco-int.com
Web Site: www.wilco-int.com
Sales Contact Name: Bob Santangelo

■ Product: Gloss

Version Number: 2.6

Description Summary. An integrated system for the trade processing, clearing, settlement, and accounting of a wide range of instruments including international debt, equities, treasury, and repo. Gloss provides a highly efficient STP environment with an extensive range of functionality for international, domestic, and emerging markets. It is a proven product with a large user base that spans the world's major timezones — an impressive list of international clients includes Nomura, Merrill Lynch, Goldman Sachs, Bear Stearns, and others. Many of these have chosen Gloss as an integral part of their global strategy.

Pricing. Not disclosed.

Hardware Requirements. UNIX server with UNIX NT or Windows clients.

Software Requirements. UNIX operating system and Sybase database.

■ Product: GlossTRADER

Version Number: 1.70

Description Summary. A real-time trading and decision support system for fixed income trading, sales, and repo desks. The system integrates the major tasks faced by a modern trading desk, offering deal capture, position keeping, and pricing functionality.

Pricing. Not disclosed.

Hardware Requirements. Pentium PC or NT workstation.

Software Requirements. Windows NT operating system and MS SQL Server database.

■ Product: Gloss STP Explorer

Version Number: 1.3

Description Summary. Gloss STP Explorer is a unique, proactive exception-handling facility that has recently been added to further enhance the Gloss system's ability to reduce operational risk. Both business and systems processing exceptions are now routed dynamically to the relevant users' desktops the instant that the exception occurs. Users can then analyze, repair, and resubmit using an easy-to-use graphical application. This means that exposure to unsettled trades, regulatory reporting delays, and reduced system performance is kept to an absolute minimum.

Pricing. Not disclosed.

Hardware Requirements. UNIX server with UNIX NT or Windows clients.

Software Requirements. UNIX operating system and Sybase database.

■ Product: GlossHUB

Version Number: 2.6

Description Summary. A transaction-oriented middleware product that provides guaranteed end-to-end messaging between two or more separate systems. GlossHUB handles message format transformation, and routing between systems using different formats and different communications protocols. GlossHUB systems can easily be linked to build a network of message routing systems.

Pricing. Not disclosed.

Hardware Requirements. UNIX server with UNIX NT or Windows clients.

Software Requirements. UNIX operating system and Sybase database.

■ Product: GlossLINK

Version Number: 3.4

Description Summary. Comprises a range of software modules which provide links to major international exchanges, clearing centers, global custodians, and other system. These include Euroclear, Cedel, Trax, ISMA price reporting, Bloomberg trade feed, interface to ADP's Brokerage Processing System (U.S.), Crest (London Stock Exchange), SEGA (Zurich Stock Exchange), DTC (U.S.), DWZ (Germany), CGO (Central Gilts Office, U.K.), SEQUAL, telex, and many others.

Pricing. Not disclosed.

Hardware Requirements. UNIX server with UNIX NT or Windows clients.

Software Requirements. UNIX operating system and Sybase database

VIRTUAL PRIVATE NETWORKS (VPN)

Company Name: Aventail Corporation
808 Howell Street, 2nd Floor, Seattle, WA 98101
Phone: 206-215-1111
888-762-5785
Fax: 206-215-1120
E-Mail: tracy@aventail.com
Web Site: www.aventail.com
Sales Contact Name: Chris Kenworthy, VP of Sales

■ Product: Aventail VPN

Version Number: 2.7

Description Summary. Aventail Corporation develops policy-based VPNs for e-business. Aventail VPN is a client/server software solution that enables orgainzations to share information over the Internet with customers, suppliers, strategic partners, and remote employees. While maintaining a level of security, corporations can develop stronger business relationships and forge closer ties with individuals who need access to confidential resources on their network. Aventail VPN eliminates the risks associated with doing business over the Internet.

Product Feature List

- Secure Enterprise Explorer — enhances the security for connecting to Windows networks through a VPN.
- Intelligent SSL Compression — can significantly improve VPN performance over standard dial-up connections.
- The Customizer — allows administrators to easily preconfigure client software for thousands of users at a time with a wizard-based custom configuration tool. Post-deployment changes are easy, too.
- Time-based access control — being able to limit access based on time of day can be important when extending an intranet to a partner or other user on the extranet.
- Logging and Auditing Enhancements — the additional auditing functionality will help administrators make critical decisions about managing security policies.
- RADIUS Caching — a new caching algorithm will improve performance when checking credentials against a RADIUS server. RADIUS is only one of several supported user databases.

Pricing. Bundled pricing starts at $7995.

Hardware Requirements. Product can run on the following:

Server

- Processors: Sparc, ×86, Power 2, PowerPC, hppa, and Alpha
- Operating Systems — Windows NT 3.51 and 4.0, Solaris 2.5, AIX 4.2, BSD/OS 2.x, Linux 2.x, HP-UX 10.x, and Digital UNIX
- Memory Requirements — 32 MB recommended.

Client

- CPU — 486/50 IBM PC or compatible
- Processors — Sparc, ×86, Alpha, and PowerPC
- Operating Systems — Windows 3.x, Windows for Workgroups 3.11,
- Windows 95, Windows NT 3.51 and 4.0, Solaris 2.5, Linux 2.x, AIX 4.2, HP/UX 10.x, and Digital UNIX
- Memory Requirements — 16 MB recommended
- Software Requirements: Aventail VPN client/server software

VIRUS PROTECTION

Company Name: Trend Micro, Inc.
Address: 10101 N. De Anza Blvd. 4th Floor, Cupertino, CA 95014
Phone: 408-257-1500
800-228-5651
Fax: 408-863-6362
E-Mail: sales@trendmicro.com
Web Site: www.antivirus.com
Sales Contact Name: Jim Leonard

■ Product: InterScan VirusWall

Version Number: 2.52

Description Summary. InterScan VirusWall is a high-performance three-in-one product suite that provides comprehensive virus protection at the Internet gateway. Each product component can be installed and managed independently or in concert, allowing great flexibility and scalability for small to large networks. Real-time scanning stops viruses and other malicious code from using the gateway as an access point to internal networks. Detects viruses and blocks Java and ActiveX malicious code hidden in SMTP mail, HTTP, and FTP traffic. Server-based, Internet-enabled management tools give administrators maximum control over virus protection throughout the enterprise. Available for Windows NT (Intel and DEC Alpha), Solaris, and HP-UX.

Product Feature List

- Scans and Cleans inbound and outbound SMTP mail and attachments in real time
- Optionally blocks Java applets, ActiveX objects and unsigned or non-commercial software (NT version only)
- Detects and removes known and unkown macro viruses on the fly
- Sends customizable warnings messages to sender, recipients, and administrator
- Lets you preschedule pattern file updates for automatic download from the Web
- Includes viewing utility for real time performance monitoring
- Tracks infections through detailed activity log
- Includes Windows GUI and ISAPI/CGI Web browser configuration interfaces
- Available for Windows NT, Solaris and HP-UX; DEC Unix and AIX implem- entations coming soon

Pricing. Up to 25 users, $950.

System Requirements

Windows NT Version. Windows NT 3.51 or above, PC with Pentium processor, 16 MB RAM, 12 MB disk space (at installation).

Solaris Version. Solaris 2.5 or above, 32 MB RAM, 150 MB swap space, 15 MB disk space (at installation).

HP-UX Version. HP-UX 10.x, 64 MB RAM, 100 MB swap space, 100 MB disk space (at installation).

■ Product: OfficeScan for Small Business Server

Version Number: 2.0

Description Summary. OfficeScan for Microsoft Small Business Server (SBS) provides round-the-clock real-time protection against viruses from any source to all desktops on SBS networks. Deploys centrally from an internal Web server, using ActiveX components or log-in scripts to deliver client anti-virus software. Desktop configurations, including scanning and cleaning, are centrally controlled through a single management console. OfficeScan for SBS installs directly to the Internet Information Server and integrates automatically as a separate module into the SBS interface. An HTTP agent at the desktop listens for upgrade, update, and configuration messages from the server and downloads the needed components from the server. Virus activity is reported to the server in real time by the client component.

Product Feature List

- Deploys from the server, using ActiveX components
- Centrally controls desktop configuration
- HTTP agent at the desktop listens for update messages from the server
- Reports virus activities in real time
- Includes real-time scanning of Exchange mailboxes
- Detects and removes known and unknown viruses, including macro viruses

Pricing. Up to 50 users, $450.

System Requirements.

Server. Microsoft Small Business Server (Windows NT)

Client. Microsoft Windows 95

Product: ScanMail for Lotus Notes

Version Number:1.4

Description Summary. ScanMail® for Lotus Notes and Domino detects and removes viruses hidden in databases as well as in e-mail attachments, before infections can spread to the desktop. Scans and cleans e-mail attachments in real time at the router; also scans and cleans databases and modified data during replication in real time. Scans existing message attachments in mailboxes to root out old infections. On-demand database scanning cleans existing infections. ScanMail provides frequent automatic Web-based virus pattern updates and maintains a comprehensive activity log. Its configuration interface is fully integrated with the Lotus Notes user interface. Available for Windows NT and Solaris.

Product Feature List

- Scans and cleans mail and attachments in real time at the mail router
- Scans and cleans databases in real time
- On-demand database scanning to clean existing infections
- Scans and cleans all modified data in real time during replication
- Detects and removes known and unknown macro viruses on the fly
- Functions as a native Notes server task
- Scans Web traffic on Domino servers
- Updates virus pattern files automatically
- Sends customizable warning messages to sender, recipient, and administrator
- Remote management from any Notes workstation
- Tracks infections through detailed Notes-format activity log

Pricing. Up to 25 users, $750.

System Requirements. Windows NT 4.0 or above with Lotus Notes Server 4.0 or above or Sun Workstation running Solaris 2.5 and and Lotus Notes Server 4.0 or above.

■ Product: ScanMail for Microsoft Exchange

Version:1.53

Description Summary. ScanMail® for Microsoft Exchange Server detects and removes viruses hidden in e-mail attachments and public folders in real time before infections can spread to the desktop. Scans manually or at prescheduled intervals. Automatic updates can be configured at prescheduled intervals or accessed manually and are distributed to all connected post offices. ScanMail's virus scanning is transparent unless a virus is detected, when customizable warning messages are sent to administrator, sender, and recipients. ScanMail's powerful scanning engine uses rule-based and pattern recognition technology and includes Trend Micro's MacroTrap, which detects and removes known and unknown macro viruses. Available for Windows NT (Intel and DEC Alpha).

Product Feature List

- Scans and cleans files attached to Exchange mail messages in real time
- Scans and cleans shared files in real time
- Scans and cleans public folders in real time
- Detects and removes known and unknown macro viruses on the fly
- Includes custom solutions to new virus problems through Trend's Virtual Virus Hospital
- Sends customizable warning messages to sender, recipients, and administrator
- Enhanced performance mode for large installations
- Installs and updates at the Exchange Server Automatically
- Lets you preschedule update deliveries for automatic download from the web
- Tracks infections through detailed activity log
- Available for Intel and DEC Alpha platforms

Pricing. Up to 25 users, $750.

System Requirements. Windows NT 4.0 or above with Microsoft Exchange Server 4.0 or later

■ Product: ServerProtect

Version: 4.52

Description Summary. ServerProtect efficiently safeguards multiple servers and domains from virus attack with next-generation anti-virus software that can be installed and managed from a single console. All servers within one domain can be automatically configured and installed concurrently, using native NT or NetWare tools for secure remote management. ServerProtect automatically downloads new virus patterns and distributes them to all servers in the same domain. Provides comprehensive logging and reporting capabilities that take in all desktops in every domain on the network and is available for Windows NT and NetWare.

Product Feature List

- Provides centralized multiple domain installation and management
- Offers secure remote management
- Lets you preschedule automatic scans and update deliveries
- Tracks infections through detailed activity log
- Detects and removes known and unknown macro viruses
- Integrates with and manages Trend's desktop protection software
- Updates and distributes virus patterns with a single click and supports proxy server
- Scans for malicious Java and ActiveX code (NT version)
- Available for Windows NT and NetWare

Pricing. Up to 25 users, $600.

System Requirements

Windows NT. NT Server 3.51 or later, Intel PC with Pentium processor or better or DEC Alpha, 32 MB RAM, and 8 MB free disk space.

NetWare. NetWare 3.11 or later, Intel 386 PC or better, 8 MB RAM, and 8 MB free disk space.

Product: ScanMail Lotus for cc:Mail

Version: 1.62

Description Summary. ScanMail® for Lotus cc:Mail scans traffic passing through the cc:Mail server, stopping viruses from using the network as a distribution mechanism. Scans and cleans files attached to e-mail messages in real time, as well as existing message attachments in mailboxes to root out old infections. ScanMail detects and removes known and unknown macro viruses on the fly, using Trend's powerful virus scanning engine. Includes batch scanning capability for multiple remote post offices. Supports multiple users logging into a single PC and scans manually or at prescheduled intervals. Provides frequent automatic Web-based virus pattern updates. Available for all major cc:Mail platforms.

Product Feature List

- Scans and cleans files attached to mail messages in real time
- Detects and removes known and unknown macro viruses on the fly
- Protects both LAN and remote cc:Mail users
- Batch scanning capability for multiple remote post offices
- Supports up to 512 post offices on one LAN
- Sends customizable warning messages to sender, recipients, and administrator
- Installs and updates at the mail server automatically
- Tracks infections through detailed activity log
- Includes automatic deployment of software from server to workstations
- Provides centralized console administration
- Automatic pattern updates via Internet or BBS, with support for proxy server

Pricing. Up to 25 users, $750.

System Requirements

Server. Novell Netware 3.x or above or Windows NT Server 3.51 or above. Banyan, LANtastic and DEC Pathworks networks are also supported: client piece installation cannot be automated in these environments.

Client. Windows 3.x, Windows 95, or Windows NT Workstation 3.51 or above. cc:Mail: Lotus cc:Mail LAN and Remote 2.x through 8.x: DB6 and DB8 databases supported.

■ Product: Microsoft Mail

Version: 1.0

Description Summary. ScanMail® for Microsoft Mail scans and cleans files attached to e-mail messages in real time, before infections can spread to the desktop. Installs and updates at the mail server automatically and deploys software from the server to workstations. Provides frequent automatic Web-based virus pattern updates. ScanMail's virus scanning is transparent unless a virus is detected, when customizable warning messages are sent to administrator, sender, and recipients. ScanMail's powerful scanning engine uses rule-based and pattern recognition technology including Trend Micro's MacroTrap, which detects and removes known and unknown macro viruses. Available for Windows and Windows NT with Microsoft Mail.

Product Feature List

- Scans and cleans files attached to e-mail messages in real time

- Detects and removes known and unknown macro viruses on the fly
- Sends customizable warnings of virus infections to sender, recipients, and administrator
- Installs and updates at the mail server automatically
- Includes automatic deployment of software from server to workstations
- Tracks infections through a detailed activity log
- Includes custom solutions to new virus problems through Trend's Virtual Virus HospitaL
- Provides centralized console administration
- Includes automatic, pre-scheduled virus pattern updates via Internet or BBS

Pricing. Up to 25 users, $750.

System Requirements

Server. Windows NT 3.51 or above, Windows 95 or above, PC with 486 processor, 8 MB of RAM, 4 MB of disk space.

Client. Windows NT 3.51 or above, Windows 3.1 or above, PC with 386 processor or above, 4 MB of RAM, mapped drive for M:\ for post office.

About the Editor

JESSICA KEYES is president of New Art Technologies, Inc., a high-technology software development firm. Prior to New Art Technologies, she was Managing Director of R&D for the New York Stock Exchange and has been an officer with the Swiss Bank Company and Banker's Trust, both in New York City.

Keyes has a Master's Degree from New York University where she did research in the area of artificial intelligence. She has given seminars at universities such as Carnegie Mellon, Boston University, the University of Illinois, James Madison University, and San Francisco State University. She is a frequent keynote speaker on the topics of competitive strategy using information technology and marketing on the information highway, and is an advisor for DataPro, McGraw-Hill's computer research arm, as well as a member of the Sprint Business Council. She is a founding Board of Director member of the New York Software Industry Association and has recently completed a 2-year term on the Mayor of New York City's Small Business Advisory Council.

A noted columnist and correspondent with over 150 articles published, Keyes is a publisher of the *Small Business Journal* and several other computer-related publications. She also has authored and/or edited 10 books.

The New Intelligence: AI in Financial Services, HarperBusiness, 1990
The Handbook of Expert Systems in Manufacturing, McGraw-Hill, 1991
Infotrends: The Competitive Use of Information, McGraw-Hill, 1992
The Software Engineering Productivity Handbook, McGraw-Hill, 1993
The Handbook of Multimedia, McGraw-Hill, 1994
The Productivity Paradox, McGraw-Hill, 1994
Technology Trendlines, Van Nostrand Reinhold, 1995
How to be a Successful Internet Consultant, McGraw-Hill, 1997
Webcasting: Broadcast to your Customers over the Net, McGraw-Hill, 1997
Datacasting, McGraw-Hill, 1997

Infotrends was selected as one of the best business books of 1992 by the Library Journal. *The Software Engineering Productivity Handbook* was the main selection for the Newbridge book club for computer professionals.

ABOUT THE EDITOR

The *McGraw-Hill Multimedia Handbook* is now in its second reprint and was translated into Chinese and Japanese during 1995. *How to be a Successful Internet Consultant, Webcasting*, and *Datacasting* have recently been translated into Japanese.

Index

A

D

F

J

K

L

M

O

P

Q

R

T

U

V

W

Y